BRITISH AND CANADIAN PERSPECTIVES ON INTERNATIONAL LAW

British and Canadian Perspectives on International Law

EDITED BY

CHRISTOPHER P.M. WATERS

Carl,
At least this one's not about
the Caucasus!
with all good wishes,

MARTINUS NIJHOFF PUBLISHERS
LEIDEN / BOSTON

A C.I.P. record for this book is available from the Library of Congress.

Printed on acid-free paper.

ISBN-13: 978-90-04-15381-3
ISBN-10: 90-04-15381-0

@ 2006 Koninklijke Brill NV, Leiden, The Netherlands
Koninklijke Brill NV incorporates the imprints Brill, Hotei Publishers, IDC Publishers,
Martinus Nijhoff Publishers and VSP.

<http://www.brill.nl>

Printed and bound in The Netherlands.

For my grandparents
Frederick Wilfred Waters (1913–1987)
and Gwyneth Emily Waters (Groves) (1914–2005)
who immigrated to Canada from England in 1957

Contents

Part 3: Rights

Part 4: Human Security

Part 5: Courts

Acknowledgements

This project started with a conference held at Canada House, London, in June 2005 under the auspices of the British Association for Canadian Studies (Legal Studies Group). I thank the staff of the High Commission and my colleagues in the Legal Studies Group for their assistance in organizing the conference. My thanks as well to Gillian Abbotts and Jessica Guitard for their assistance. As ever, I am grateful for the support and professionalism of Annebeth Rosenboom and the staff at Martinus Nijhoff/Brill.

Finally, I thank the Waters, Badalians, Snyders and Smits for their general support over the years.

Notes on Contributors

OSMAN ABOUBAKR

Osman Aboubakr holds a B.A. in Business and Environmental Studies from the University of Toronto and an LLB and BCL from McGill University. He is a solicitor with the Canadian firm of Osler, Hoskin & Harcourt LLP, specializing in mergers and acquisitions, corporate finance and corporate governance.

STÉPHANE BEAULAC

Stéphane Beaulac is an associate professor at the Faculty of Law, University of Montreal, where he teaches public international law and statutory interpretation. He started his career at Dalhousie Law School. He has a Ph.D. in international law from the University of Cambridge and was a law clerk at the Supreme Court of Canada with Justice L'Heureux-Dubé. His works include *The Power of Language in the Making of International Law – The Word Sovereignty in Bodin and Vattel and the Myth of Westphalia* (Martinus Nijhoff, 2004) and *International Human Rights Law and the Canadian Charter* (Carswell, 2006), with William A. Schabas.

SUSAN BREAU

Susan Breau is the Dorset Fellow in Public International Law at the British Institute of International and Comparative Law. She was previously a lecturer at the School of Law, Queen's University, Belfast. She is currently a part-time lecturer at the London School of Economics on their LLM programme and a Visiting Adjunct Associate Professor at the Royal Military College of Canada. Her publications include a book entitled: *Humanitarian Intervention: The United Nations and Collective Responsibility* published in 2005 and she is currently completing a book examining the international law aspects of The Responsibility to Protect.

CATHERINE BROWN

Catherine Brown is a law professor at the University of Calgary, where she has been teaching tax, estate and business planning since 1980. She has published extensively in the tax area, appearing in numerous Canadian Tax Foundation publications and U.S. journals, and as co-author of *Taxation and Estate Planning*. Her work includes studies in international trade and business law and in particular the role of tax in global trade. She was appointed as a Canadian representative on the Indicative List to the World Trade Organization and to the Canada Revenue Agency's International Tax Advisory Council. She is a member of the Ontario and Alberta Bars and a Governor of the Canadian Tax Foundation.

MARIE-CLAIRE CORDONIER SEGGER

Marie-Claire Cordonier Segger is a Fellow of the Lauterpacht Research Centre for International Law at Cambridge University and Director of the Centre for International Sustainable Development Law in Montreal. She provides legal advice on the implementation of international sustainable development treaties through the United Nations to governments in Africa, Asia and Latin America. She is an instructor of international law for the International Development Law Organisation, chairs the International Law on Sustainable Development Partnership under the auspices of the UN Commission on Sustainable Development and lectures in sustainable development for several law faculties in the United Kingdom, Canada, and other countries.

HOLLY CULLEN

Holly Cullen is Reader in Law at Durham University and Deputy Director of the Durham European Law Institute. Before becoming an academic, she was a member of the Barreau du Quebec. She researches in the areas of international and European human rights law, particularly the rights of the child. She is also Rapporteur for the Committee on Theory of International Law of the British Branch of the International Law Association.

CHILE EBOE-OSUJI

Chile Eboe-Osuji, of the Bar of Ontario, is a Barrister at Borden Ladner Gervais LLP, Canada. He has held the posts of Senior Legal Officer and Prosecution Counsel at the International Criminal Tribunal for Rwanda, as well as Head Legal Officer in the Appeals Chamber for that Tribunal.

KAREN ELTIS

Karen Eltis is a member of the Faculty of Law at the University of Ottawa (Civil Law Section), specializing in new technologies, transnational law, health law and comparative law. She served as Director of the Human Rights Research and Education Centre in 2005 and is currently the Co-Director of the National Program, the Faculty's bilingual and bijuridical graduate program. Karen holds law degrees from McGill University, the Hebrew University of Jerusalem and Columbia University School of Law (Harlan Fiske Stone Scholar). She was a comparative law clerk for President Barak of the Supreme Court of Israel and has taught at McGill University.

WILLIAM FLANAGAN

William Flanagan is the Dean of Law at Queen's University in Kingston, Ontario. He teaches in the area of Corporate Law, International Trade and Investment, and Property Law. He is the founder of the International Law Spring Program at the International Study Centre operated by Queen's University in the UK. He has worked for a number of years on international research projects in Russia and Brazil, with a particular focus on HIV-related legal issues and international law. Recent publications include W. F. Flanagan and G. Whiteman, "'AIDS is not a Business': A Study in Global Corporate Responsibility" in *Perspectives on International Corporate Responsibility* (Carnegie Mellon University, 2005).

MARKUS W. GEHRING

Markus W. Gehring is Lecturer in International and European Law at the Centre of International Studies and Fellow in Law at Cambridge University (Robinson College). He is Lead Counsel for Sustainable International Trade, Investment and Competition Law with the Centre for International Sustainable Development Law. He holds an LL.M from Yale and a Dr jur from Hamburg. He is a member of the Frankfurt Bar, and a member of the ILA, German Branch, and serves on the ILA Committee on International Law on Sustainable Development. His most recent book, with Marie-Claire Cordonier Segger, is titled *Sustainable Development in World Trade Law* (Kluwer Law International, 2005).

CHRISTOPHER HARLAND

Christopher Harland is a Canadian lawyer specialising in the fields of international human rights law, international humanitarian law and post-conflict judicial reconstruction. He has worked with the United Nations in Rwanda (human rights and judicial system development), Cyprus (legislative drafting and treaty overview in preparation for the 2004 referendum), the Democratic Republic of Congo (human rights investigation), with the Office of the High Representative in Bosnia and Herzegovina (Head of the Human Rights Department and later member of the High Judicial and Prosecutorial Councils), and is currently Legal Adviser with the International Committee of the Red Cross in Geneva.

ANNE HOLLIDAY

Anne Holliday is a legal researcher with particular experience and expertise in refugee law issues and international human rights as relevant to corporate social responsibility. Recent research projects included an Analysis of UK Gender Guidelines, the Treatment of Unaccompanied Minors within the Asylum Process and a project relating to Corporate Social Responsibility and Business supported by the European Social Fund. She has co-authored a number of articles with Rebecca Wallace relating to the above projects.

DAVID JENKINS

David Jenkins is a Lecturer in Law at the University of Aberdeen School of Law. His primary research interests lie in public law, comparative law, and legal history, fields in which he has published articles in American and Canadian law journals. He studied law at Washington and Lee University and received an LL.M. from the McGill University Institute of Comparative Law, where he is presently a doctoral candidate. He is also an attorney at law in West Virginia and Ohio.

HUGH KINDRED

Hugh Kindred is a member of the Bars of England and Nova Scotia and Professor of Law at Dalhousie University, Halifax, where he teaches international law, commercial law and marine transportation. He has also worked for UNCTAD in Geneva and taught at the University of Sydney, Australia. He has published widely; in particular he is co-general editor and co-author of *International Law Chiefly as Interpreted and Applied in Canada*, now in its 7th edition (2006) together with a documentary supplement and supporting website. In 2003 the Canadian Association of Law Teachers presented Professor Kindred with its Award for Academic Excellence.

TROY LAVERS

Troy Lavers is a Lecturer in Law at the University of Leicester. Her teaching interests include International Law, International Courts and Tribunals and International Criminal Law. She researches in the area of extraterritorial measures and jurisdictional assertions by states within the constraints of public international law. Her publications include "Considerations of Extraterritorial Economic Sanctions" in the Royal United Services Institute Journal. She is currently researching in the area of sovereignty and the principle of complementarity within the Statute of Rome 1998.

HENRY LOVAT

Henry Lovat was educated at Manchester and McGill Universities and the College of Law in London. He is an Associate Fellow at the Montreal-based Centre for International Sustainable Development Law. Mr Lovat qualified as a solicitor with Slaughter and May and is currently completing an LL.M. at the University of Toronto specialising in international law. He was previously an Associate Protection Officer with UNHCR in Sarajevo, where his work focused on refugee and IDP return in the context of the Dayton Peace Accords. He has also worked as Public Affairs Officer for the Scottish Council of Jewish Communities. Legal interests include international trade and competition law and human rights and humanitarian law.

MARTHA O'BRIEN

Martha O'Brien is an assistant professor at the Faculty of Law, University of Victoria, Canada. She holds an LL.M. in Law of the European Community from the Université Libre de Bruxelles (1992) and teaches taxation and European Union law. Her research focuses on direct taxation, international trade, federalism and tax subsidies.

KRISTIN PRICE

Kristin Price is a research assistant with the Centre for International Sustainable Development Law in Montreal, focused primarily on international law and international relations aspects of sustainable international trade and sustainable development law. She received her BA in Political Science from Brown University in May 2005 and commences an MPhil in International Relations at Cambridge University in October 2006.

CHARLOTTE SKEET

Charlotte Skeet is a Lecturer in Law at Sussex Law School, University of Sussex, where her courses include Law and Development and an LLM/MA option on the Human Rights of Women. She has researched extensively in the area of gender and constitutionalism and is currently completing a monograph on constitutional change in the United Kingdom.

JAMES SLOAN

James Sloan was educated in Canada, the United States and England. He currently teaches international law at the University of Glasgow, School of Law. Previously he worked as a Political Advisor to the UN Mission in Bougainville and as legal assistant for Antonio Cassese, then President of the International Court of Justice. He has written on peacekeeping issues and issues relating to international criminal justice.

STEPHEN J. TOOPE

Stephen J. Toope is President of the Pierre Elliott Trudeau Foundation which promotes interaction between researchers in the social sciences and humanities, and policymakers in government, the private sector, the arts community, and the voluntary sector. On leave from the Faculty of Law, McGill University, of which he is a former Dean, Professor Toope's scholarly publications cover a wide range of public international law issues. He is Chair of the UN Working Group on Disappearances, and is a former President of the Canadian Council on International Law. Professor Toope was a law clerk to the Rt. Hon. Brian Dickson, Chief Justice of Canada.

HELENA TORROJA

Helena Torroja is an assistant professor at the Faculty of Law, University of Barcelona, where she teaches public international law, international humanitarian law and United Nations law and practice. She has been a visiting professor at the School of Law, University of Puerto Rico. She has a Ph.D. in international law from the University of Barcelona. She has also studied at the Centre for Studies and Research in International Law and International Relations, The Hague Academy of International Law. Her works include the book "La asistencia humanitaria en la ONU. Fundamentos y perspectivas actuales" (Atelier, 2004).

REBECCA M. M. WALLACE

Rebecca M. M. Wallace, Professor of International Human Rights Law, Robert Gordon University, Aberdeen, also teaches on the Masters programme at the University of Glasgow. She previously held appointments at Universities of Hull, Strathclyde and was Head of Law School, Napier University, Edinburgh (1997–2003). In 1994 she was Aerial Sallows Professor at University of Saskatchewan, Canada. She has written extensively on international law and international refugee law and is a member of ILA's Committees on Teaching of International Law and on Sustainable Development. She is a member of the English Bar, a part-time Immigration Judge and a member of the International Association of Refugee Law Judges.

CHRISTOPHER WATERS

Christopher Waters is a Senior Lecturer in Law at the University of Reading. He holds degrees from Toronto, Queen's and McGill Universities and is a member of the Ontario Bar. Dr. Waters has taught international law at universities in the South Caucasus and Balkans, and is a consultant on rule of law reform projects in those regions. He has monitored elections for the OSCE and is a former member of the OSCE mission to Kosovo. He regularly addresses military audiences on international law, including at the UK's Joint Services Command and Staff College. Previous books include the prize-winning *Counsel in the Caucasus: Professionalization and Law in Georgia* (Martinus Nijhoff, 2004).

PART 1

COMPARING PERSPECTIVES

Introduction

This book compares British and Canadian perspectives on public international law. Comparative international law, however, presents conceptual and methodological challenges. Indeed links between comparative law and international law were first met with skepticism by writers such as Lauterpacht and Gutteridge.[1] As Gutteridge put it in his classic essay from 1944, "So far as it exists at all, any relationship or kinship between comparative law and the law of nations must . . . be of a very shadowy nature."[2] International law was by definition universal (and sometimes regional in the case of custom) and so comparative international law was a *non sequiter*. Comparative law did of course play a minor role in international law, in that it could distil generally accepted principles from "civilized nations" as a source of international law. Gutteridge put it even more cautiously: comparative law could be used "as a corrective tendency there might be on the part of international judges . . . to employ concepts or rules which either belong exclusively to a single system or are only to be found in a few of such systems."[3]

The restrictive view of comparative international law held until the 1970s, when the subject was reborn with the aim of accounting for divergent understandings of international law across the globe. The two fundamental cleavages

---

[1] See H. Lauterpacht, "The So-Called Anglo-American and Continental Schools of Thought in International Law", (1931) XII BYIL 31 and H. C. Gutteridge, "Comparative Law and the Law of Nations" (1944) BYIL 1.

[2] Gutteridge, *ibid.*

[3] *Ibid.*

Christopher P.M. Waters (Ed.), *British and Canadian Perspectives on International Law*, pp. 3–11.

were along East-West and North-South axes. Writers described the decline of classical or European international law and the growing need to accommodate socialist and Third World perspectives. The "hypothesis of one world, one (international) law" was no longer a given.[4] At the same time, though without the moniker of comparative international law, new perspectives on international law were being put forward within the Commonwealth. The founding of the Canadian Council on International Law in 1972 was one of the signposts of a new self-confident and self-consciously Canadian voice on international law. It also heralded an intensification in international law teaching and scholarship. When *Canadian Perspectives on International Law and Organization* was published in 1974, the editors noted that the volume "brought together for the first time a comprehensive Canadian conspectus on current issues and developments in international law."[5] Similar developments were taking place in other parts of the "Old Commonwealth" with, for example, the first book of "cases and material" on international law from an Australian perspective published in 1972.[6]

Following a recession in comparative international law in the late 1980s – prompted largely by the undoing of the socialist legal family – the topic has more recently appeared under the transnational legal process rubric. While there are different strands of this paradigm, which have been mapped by Harold Koh, Anne Marie Slaughter, and others,[7] this process involves horizontal dialogue between actors – courts, administrative agencies, civil society and so forth – across state boundaries. As opposed to traditional preoccupations of a) how states deal with each other and b) how domestic courts apply international law, the transnational paradigm addresses norm development, and the internalization of international law, through a transnational – and particularly transjudicial – dialogue. This process is said to be partly a result of globalization, with judges and other legal actors having easy access to comparative and international legal information, as well as face-to-face contact with counterparts in different jurisdictions.

British and Canadian legal actors show an openness to comparative and international law which invites scholarly treatment under a transnational para-

---

[4] E. McWhinney, "Comparative International Law: Regional or Sectorial Inter-Systemic Approaches to Contemporary International Law" in R-J. Dupuy, *The Future of International Law in a Multicultural World* (The Hague: Martinus Nijhoff, 1984) at 224. And see W. E. Butler, ed., *International Law in Comparative Perspective* (Alphen aan den Rijn, NL: Sijthoff & Noordhoff, 1980).

[5] R. St. J. Macdonald, G. L. Morris & D. M. Johnston, *Canadian Perspectives on International Law and International Organization* (Toronto: University of Toronto Press, 1974) at xiv.

[6] W. E. Holder, G. A. Brennan, *The International Legal System: Cases and Materials with emphasis on the Australian Perspective* (Sydney: Butterworths, 1972).

[7] See H. H. Koh, *Transnational Legal Process* (1996) 75 Neb. L. Rev. 181 and A.-M. Slaughter, "A Typology of Transjudicial Communication" (1994) 29 U. Rich. L. Rev. 99.

digm. Indeed some of the writers in this book explicitly work with a transnational or related paradigm and many others implicitly do so. The celebrated rulings from the House of Lords on the detention of foreign terror suspects and on use of intelligence gained by torture of terror suspects cite the decisions of both foreign and international tribunals with apparent ease.[8] In Canada, decisions on deporting individuals where they might face death or torture have drawn on a similar transnational dialogue with international and comparative sources.[9] Judges on both sides of the Atlantic appear to welcome this transjudicial dialogue. As Justice La Forest of the Supreme Court of Canada put it already a decade ago:[10]

> In the field of human rights, and of other laws impinging on the individual, our courts are assisting in developing general and coherent principles that apply in very significant portions of the globe. These principles are applied consistently, with an international vision and on the basis of international experience. Thus our courts – and many other national courts – are truly becoming international courts in many areas involving the rule of law. They will become all the more so as they continue to rely on and benefit from one another's experience.

Similarly both the British and Canadian governments – at least on a theoretical level – hold multilateralism in high regard and are "joiners" and strong supporters of international organizations. While the argument put forward by Philippe Sands and others that "September 11 and its aftermath shattered [Britain's] internationalist credentials" cannot be dismissed, both countries contribute to UN peacekeeping, and are parties to the International Criminal Court (ICC), Kyoto and so on.[11]

Ironically, at the same time as Canada appears active – and principled – on the international law stage, a prevailing view among commentators in Canada seems to be that the country's stature in international affairs is in decline and

---

[8] *A and Others v Secretary of State for the Home Department*, [2004] UKHL 56 & [2005] UKHL 71.

[9] *United States v. Burns*, [2001] 1 S.C.R. 283; *Suresh v. Canada (Minister of Citizenship & Immigration)*, [2002] 1 S.C.R. 3. For a discussion of the Supreme Court of Canada's mix of international, comparative and domestic understandings, see K. Roach, "Constitutional, Remedial, and International Dialogues About Rights: The Canadian Experience" (2005) 40 Tex. Int'l L.J. 537.

[10] G. V. La Forest, "The Expanding Role of the Supreme Court of Canada in International Law Issues" (1996) 34 Can. Y.B. Int'l L. 89 at 100. For a more recent expression of this view from the bench, see L. LeBel & G. Chao, "The Rise of International Law in Canadian Constitutional Litigation: Fugue or Fusion? Recent Developments and Challenges in Internalizing International Law" (2002) 16 Sup. Ct. L. Rev. 23.

[11] P. Sands, *Lawless World: America and the Making and Breaking of Global Rules* (London: Penguin/Allen Lane, 2005) at 231.

has been for some time. Several high profile commentators argue that in aid, trade, diplomacy and, especially, military engagement, Canada has marginalized its own importance in the world and betrayed it's once proud record as a country of influence. In his bestselling book, *While Canada Slept*, journalist Andrew Cohen compares Canada's role in the world today with a "golden age" following the Second World War: "We are no longer as strong a soldier, as generous a donor, and as effective a diplomat, and it is has diminished us as a people."[12] Canada, once a middle power, is said to no longer have a claim to that title while, by contrast, Britain is said to "punch above its weight".[13] An evaluation of these claims is beyond the scope of a book, but it is ironic that in the field of international law, Canada is often seen as a leader from outside its borders.[14] To twist Cohen's phrase, we are at least as strong an international lawyer. And indeed Canada has taken the initiative with respect to the landmines convention, the ICC and the notions of human security and an "international responsibility to protect" vulnerable populations. Canada's refusal to participate in the 2003 Iraq invasion in particular is seen as having been a strong, principled stand for international law. Furthermore – as reflected by the views of several of the authors in this book – Canada is perceived to be a leader in implementing its international human rights obligations.

It should be stressed, however, that Canada's or Britain's internationalism – and transnationalism – cannot be taken for granted as an inevitable process of globalization. Indeed, it has been vigorously resisted in some quarters. While critical voices argue that it opens the door to weaker legal systems being overwhelmed by the forces of globalization and Americanisation, in the United States itself there is disquiet over the extent to which liberal internationalist and European ideas may be diluting focus on the American constitution and on

---

[12] A. Cohen, *While Canada Slept: How We Lost Our Place in the World* (McLelland & Stewart, 2003) at 2.

[13] Indeed the very idea of Canada aspiring to middle power status or identity has been dismissed by some as process-oriented and insufficiently linked to "hard" power. See Chapter 4 of J. Welsh, *At Home in the World: Canada's Global Vision for the 21st Century* (Toronto: HarperCollins, 2004). In its recent statement on foreign policy, the government itself accepts that "the traditional notion of Canada as a middle power is outdated and no longer captures the reality of how power is distributed in the 21st century." Foreign Affairs Canada, *Canada's International Policy Statement* (April 2005): http://www.dfait-maeci.gc.ca/cip-pic/ips/ips-en.asp.

[14] For example, on the campaign to ban anti-personnel landmines Canada is said to have "presented a striking example of middle power leadership". L. Wexler, "The International Deployment of Shame, Second-Best Responses, and Norm Entrepreneurship: The Campaign to Ban Landmines and the Landmine Ban Treaty" (2003) 20 Ariz. J. Int'l & Comp. Law 561 at 587.

American values.[15] We see this concern within the Commonwealth as well. In Australia, "[i]nternational law has become a charged and politicised field . . . There is a fear that international law undermines Australian sovereignty or the capacity to govern ourselves as we choose."[16] It should be added that the use of international or transnational law has not been trouble-free in the UK or Canada either. Courts in both countries have been accused of approaching international law in an untrained and unprincipled way – of treating international law as persuasive rather than binding or worse, "window dressing".[17]

Although Canada has been lauded internationally for staying out of the Iraq conflict, it articulated its legal and policy reasons for doing so in a untimely and disjointed manner. This can be contrasted with Britain's open and explicitly legal justification (even if wrong in the minds of most international lawyers) for its participation in the 2003 invasion.[18] Another level of concern for internationalists – as Stephen Toope points out in his groundbreaking study in Chapter 1 – is that media reporting on international law is poor in both countries, particularly in Canada. This inevitably impacts on public opinion and the shaping of policy options. Furthermore, as a number of chapters in this book highlight, there is cause for concern in both countries in the human rights field (though as suggested above, Canada's record is viewed as the more progressive of the two). Finally, as is obvious, governments change and foreign policies change with them. Canada's Liberal government which since coming to power in 1993 stressed multilateralism, fell in early 2006. The new Tory government is perceived both home and abroad as placing more emphasis on continentalism rather than multilateralism. Indeed, the new Prime Minister has been described in Britain as 'Pro Bush'.[19]

Given mixed records and shifting policy positions – as well as European or federal institutional constraints – is it sensible to attempt to describe with any confidence what a British or Canadian perspective on international law is? Officially, certainly, Canada for some time, and Britain more recently, have placed good international citizenship at the rhetorical centre of their foreign

---

[15] As the robust Scalia-Kennedy debate shows: see J. Toobin, "Swing Shift" *The New Yorker* (12 September 2005) 42.

[16] H. Charlesworth et al., "Deep Anxieties: Australia and the International Legal Order" (2003) 25 Sydney Law Review 423 at 424.

[17] For a good discussion of this view – and a counter-argument that domestic courts' "translation" of international and comparative law norms is healthy – see K. Knop, "Here and There: International Law in Domestic Courts" (2000) 32 NYU. J. Int'l L. & Pol. 501.

[18] Welsh, *supra* note 13 at 16–21.

[19] J. Borger, "Conservatives head towards victory in Canadian election" *The Guardian* (21 January 2006).

policies. In 1947 Canada's first full-time Secretary of State for External Affairs, future Prime Minister Louis St. Laurent, made the "Rule of Law in National and International Affairs" a key foreign policy plank: "We in this country are agreed that the freedom of nations depends upon the rule of law among states."[20] Canada's most recent foreign policy overview similarly places importance on global governance and multilateralism, linking or conflating (depending on perspective) these international goods to Canada's national interest. At least since the election of the Labour government in 1997, Britain's official perspective has been similar, if tempered by a tradition of (and capability for) projecting "hard" power. Within days of the election, a new foreign policy was launched which emphasized an ethical approach, human rights and multilateralism.[21] Currently, "an international system based on the rule of law" and human rights are included in the UK's strategic priorities in foreign policy.[22] But is internationalism or multilateralism by itself an empty concept in terms of describing national approaches to international law?

Karen Knop has posed the question in the Canadian context along these lines: "[I]f there is something distinctive about the field of international law in Canada, in what sense is it 'Canadian'? Is it only that we are more devout internationalists than everyone else – but then what separates our approach from that of the Nordic countries, for example?"[23] Common perspectives for the UK and Canada are apparent and include the belief that sovereignty is less than absolute, that some openness to human rights scrutiny from outside is useful, and that national interest is closely linked to a predictable and fair world order. Intriguingly, while most of these factors do not separate Canada and the UK from the Nordic countries, there is ample scope for comparison here with other Anglo-American countries – notably the US and Australia – with whom we do share legal and political traditions. Beyond some of these basic points, how-

---

[20] L. S. St. Laurent, "The Foundation of Canadian Policy in World Affairs" [address on 13 January 1947], reprinted in J. L. Granatstein, *Canadian Foreign Policy: Historical Readings* (Toronto: Copp Vlark Pitman, 1986) at 28.

[21] N. J. Wheeler & T. Dunne, "Good international citizenship: a third way for Britain" (1998) 74 International Affairs 847.

[22] Foreign and Commonwealth Office, "UK International Priorities: A Strategy for the FCO": http://www.fco.gov.uk/servlet/Front?pagename=OpenMarket/Xcelerate/Show Page&c=Page&cid=1007029393465.

[23] K. Knop, "Canadian Approaches to International Law? Proposal for a Collaborative Teaching and Research Project" (2005) 31(2) Bulletin of the Canadian Council on International Law. I would suggest that while Canada's positions on internationalism do not depart significantly from the Nordic model, there are peculiarly Canadian motives for the positions. These are, primarily, the desire to promote national unity by projecting Canadian values abroad and viewing multilateralism as a counterweight to 'continental drift'.

ever, none of the authors writing in this book seek to essentialise British or Canadian perspectives. Rather the chapters compare positions across a variety of actors (courts, media, governments and corporations) and across several sub-categories of international law (including international criminal law, human rights, and refugee law). The pattern which emerges is a general orientation to international rules and comfort with the transnational legal process – this book is after all part of that process – in both Britain and Canada. There are few fundamental differences of approach.

The book is divided into five parts: comparing perspectives, crime, rights, human security and courts. As will be evident, this division is not one of watertight categories, with several chapters capable of sitting in more than one part of the book. Indeed many chapters of the book – especially those which adopt a transnational perspective – defy categorization into traditional public international law boxes, sitting as they do at the intersection of international law, comparative law and even 'law and globalization'.[24] A case in point is the other chapter in Part 1, Stephen Toope's analysis of international law content in the print media.[25] His findings show that not only is international law infrequently cited by the media, but references to it are superficial, particularly in Canada. International law is given a chimerical gloss and portrayed as a subject with no answers, a dangerous fact given the media's role in shaping public perceptions.

Part 2 of the book, entitled 'Crime', looks at international criminal law, international humanitarian law and extraterritorial jurisdiction. Christopher Harland's careful comparison in Chapter 2 of how Canada and the UK have internalized international humanitarian law, shows that while there are many similarities there are also some surprising differences, especially with regard to implementing the Rome Statute of the ICC. James Sloan picks up on the two countries' relationship with the ICC, suggesting their militaries are not as insulated from the ICC as has been suggested by politicians. This conclusion is lent credence by Helena Torroja's analysis of the past failures of the two countries to prosecute war criminals. She argues that whether current rhetorical and legislative initiatives to end impunity will be made real is a matter of going concern. Troy Lavers in Chapter 5 argues that Canada and the UK ought in fact to take less of a conservative approach to extending jurisdiction over international and transnational crime than they have traditionally, though she urges that any extensions pay due regard to international law and comity. Finally, in Chapter 6, Chile Eboe-Osuji continues with the theme of international criminal

---

[24] On how globalization studies disrupt the public/private distinction and other categories in international law, see P. S. Berman, "From International Law to Law and Globalisation" (2005) 43 Colum. J. Transnat'l L. 485.

[25] This text of Chapter 1 – with few subsequent edits to the text – was delivered as the keynote address to the Annual Conference of the British Association of Canadian Studies (Legal Studies Group) held in London in June 2005.

justice. However, he looks not at how Canada and the UK internalize international norms, but rather considers how Anglo-Canadian legal concepts can be used at the international level, with particular reference to the issue of 'vague' indictments. This is a classic example of how comparative law can inform international understandings of general principles of law.

In Part 3 of the book, on human rights, Holly Cullen begins in Chapter 7 with a comparison of attitudes towards regional and international human rights systems. She notes that Canada has opened its human rights record to international scrutiny through the UN Human Rights Committee and other UN petition mechanisms while the UK has remained reluctant to engage with these mechanisms. On the other hand, she points out that the UK is part of a comprehensive regional rights regime through membership in the Council of Europe. She considers the benefits and drawbacks of both approaches. In Chapter 8 Charlotte Skeet looks at women's rights on both sides of the Atlantic and suggests that there are lessons to be learned from Canada for the UK in what are still early days for UK's Human Rights Act. Rebecca Wallace and Anne Holliday in Chapter 9 similarly argue that the UK should look to the Canadian experience with respect to women's rights, specifically in the context of using gender guidelines in refugee determination cases. Taking a different tack in Chapter 10, David Jenkins considers the impact of public emergency discourse – particularly in the context of the 'war on terror' – on human rights norms. He lauds decisions from the highest courts in Canada and the UK which have resisted the executives' temptation to erode human rights protection regimes.

Although broad, the concept of human security – the theme of Part 4 – is a useful umbrella for several chapters in this book. As pointed out by Susan Breau in Chapter 11, the concept encompasses the notions of freedom from fear and freedom from want and is increasingly taking on concrete public international law aspects, for example with respect to the notion of a 'responsibility to protect' people from genocide or gross human rights violations. Other aspects of human security include environmental security and economic development. In Chapter 12 Marie-Claire Cordonier Segger considers British and Canadian approaches to sustainable development in international trade law. She suggests that both Canada (considered in the context of the North American Free Trade Agreement) and the UK (considered within the context of the European Union (EU)) have prioritized sustainable development in trade rules at the international, regional and bilateral levels, albeit through different strategies. Markus Gehring and Kristin Price continue with the sustainable development theme, focusing on climate change and the implementation of the Kyoto protocol by Canada and the UK. They argue that the economic instruments which have been pioneered by the two countries – such as emission trading schemes – have great potential, though further integration of carbon abatement schemes are needed at the international and bilateral levels (including Canadian agreements with individual states in the US). In Chapter 14, Henry Lovat and Osman Aboubakr consider the notion of corporate social responsibility (CSR) and the interplay between voluntariness and regulation at the national level. They suggest that domestic regulation and public/consumer pressure at the domestic level is more meaningful to date than efforts at the international level to regulate the conduct of corporations, including transnational corporations, at least insofar as Britain and Canada are concerned. Chapter 15 considers corporate conduct as well, with William Flanagan's discussion of access to medicines, particularly HIV medication, in the developing world. He suggests that the reform of global trade rules – and changes to patent laws in Canada and the UK/EU – are only partial solutions as numerous obstacles exist to treatment, especially poverty. In Chapter 16, Catherine Brown and Martha O'Brien also consider international trade rules, focusing on taxation and tax sovereignty. They argue that in its trade agreements, Canada's tax sovereignty remains essentially intact, while membership in the EU has eroded Britain's sovereignty over direct taxation.

Not surprisingly for a law book, judicial decisions figure in the majority of the book's chapters. The chapters in Part 5, however, are grouped together as they explicitly consider the use of international and comparative law by national courts. In Chapter 17 Karen Eltis considers the transnational judicial conversation currently taking place in the context of transnational crime and efforts to combat it (including information gathering by state agencies on dubious legal grounds). She suggests that that comparative constitutionalism and a new associative community of judges *sans frontières* offer promise for a principled, rights-oriented approach to combating transnational crime. The next two chapters address more traditional concerns of how municipal courts receive international law. In Chapter 18, Stéphane Beaulac takes on the notion that customary international law is automatically a part of the common law, proposing a more nuanced approach which, he suggests, is more in keeping with the divergent natures of international and national law. In the final chapter, Hugh Kindred turns from custom to treaty law, considering national judicial treatment of ratified human rights treaties which remain unimplemented in domestic law. He suggests that Canadian courts have taken a more purposive approach to such treaties which offers greater protection for individuals in Canada than those in the UK or Australia.

Chapter 1

Public Commitment to International Law: Canadian and British Media Perspectives on the Use of Force

Stephen J. Toope*

Until the build-up to the Iraq War of 2003 it was received wisdom that international law was destined to be a bit player in the human drama covered by various media. Indeed, when international law made its brief appearances, it portrayed either a silent bystander or, perhaps worse, a figure of farce; a Hollywood extra or Stan Laurel, if you will. Yet, these impressions were largely untested. No systematic evaluation of the image of international law in the Canadian or British media has been undertaken. As part of a joint research project with Professor Jutta Brunnée of the University of Toronto, I offer this modest beginning.

* The views expressed do not necessarily represent those of the Pierre Elliott Trudeau Foundation. I thank Mario Prost and Vincent-Joel Proulx for their research assistance, and the Social Sciences and Humanities Research Council of Canada for supporting a three-year project of which this research is a part. Jutta Brunnée offered helpful observations on an earlier draft.

Christopher P.M. Waters (Ed.), *British and Canadian Perspectives on International Law*, pp. 13–25.

Given the possible breadth of the topic, and the fact that media content analysis is largely uncharted territory for international lawyers,[1] the aspirations of this research are modest. I will assess the international law content of five leading Canadian daily newspapers and four "quality" British dailies over a three-year-and a half year period (2002–June 2005).[2] I will limit my remarks to one issue area, the use of force, and – not surprisingly – I will focus upon the invasion of Iraq in 2003 by a US and UK-led "coalition of the willing".

The study focuses solely upon daily print media. Daily newspapers, although no doubt less influential than was once the case, remain the print media of record. In addition, newspapers allow for the luxury of relatively extended analysis, which would open up the possibility of more in-depth coverage of international law than might be expected in the electronic media. Nonetheless, electronic media are excluded from this study largely for reasons of time and limited financial resources. If the conclusions of this study prove interesting to

---

[1] That is, self conscious media analysis concerning the role of international law as a discrete topic. Some distinguished international lawyers have, however, made extensive use of the popular media in crafting arguments concerning specific legal issues. See e.g., I. Vlasic, "Raison d'État v. Raison de l'Humanité – The United Nations SSOD II and Beyond" (1983) 28 McGill L. J. 455. It should be added that media analysis is inevitably a part of legal analysis pursued by members of the New Haven School, as they seek to trace out processes of "authoritative decision". For the heirs of McDougal and Lasswell, the media are relevant to the construction of global values, and to assessments of when authoritative decisions have hardened into norms. See e.g., M. McDougal & H. Lasswell, "The Identification and Appraisal of Diverse Systems of Public Order" in R. Falk & S. Mendlovitz, eds., *The Strategy of World Order: International Law* (New York: World Law Fund, 1966) 45; M. Reisman, "International Lawmaking: A Process of Communication" (1981) 75 Proc. Am. Soc'y Int'l L. 101; and M. Reisman, "The View from the New Haven School of International Law" (1992) 86 Proc. Am. Soc'y Int'l L. 118 (1992). A recent, non-American contribution to this discourse, with a specific focus on the role of the media in international normative development, is A. Skordas, "Hegemonic Custom?" in M. Byers & G. Nolte, eds., *United States Hegemony and the Foundations of International Law* (Cambridge: CUP, 2003) 317. Although I do not count myself among the New Haven believers, I am convinced that processes of communication, or rather interaction, are essential to the construction of law. See J. Brunnée & S. J. Toope, "International Law and Constructivism: Elements of an Interactional Theory of International Law" (2000) 39 Columbia J. Trans. L. 19 [hereinafter "Interactional Theory"]; and J. Brunnée & S. J. Toope, "Persuasion and Enforcement: Explaining Compliance with International Law" (2002) 13 Finnish Ybk Int'l L. 273 [hereinafter "Explaining Compliance"]. This issue will be explored briefly immediately below.

[2] For technical reasons having to do with database organization and availability, the timeframe was not exactly parallel for each of the UK and Canadian newspapers, so the statistics are not fully commensurable. However, the periods under review were parallel enough to make comparisons reasonable and useful. It is highly unlikely that the statistics would be off by more than 5 or so references over the entire period under review.

other researchers, one might profitably extend the reach into both the electronic media and into Canadian and UK-based internet resources.

In Canada, the choice of which newspapers to investigate was not obvious. I chose two daily newspapers published in Toronto, as Toronto is the media capital of the country, and both The Globe and Mail and the National Post cast themselves as "national" in scope. The Vancouver Sun is a local newspaper, but part of an integrated pan-Canadian chain. I chose it to ensure inclusion of a Western perspective in the study. Of the two French-language newspapers I selected, Le Devoir is self-consciously "national" in Quebec terms, and is historically the most politically and culturally influential French daily. La Presse is the largest circulation daily. The choice of British newspapers was more obvious, and sought to cover the open ideological preferences of quality dailies: I looked at The Guardian, The Telegraph, The Times, and The Independent. I acknowledge that I biased the work to so-called "nationals" and I may be subject to criticism from Scots, Welsh and Northern Irish patriots!

Before sketching out my broad themes, it is worth pausing for a moment to consider an obvious cavil: why does it matter what the media report about international law? We must leave aside professional ego, the mere desire of international lawyers to receive external validation that what we do is relevant. Such an argument should be entirely unconvincing to non-lawyers, and especially to journalists who must choose to be the observers and record keepers of various scenes, of which international law is but one of many. The central reason that it matters what the media report about international law is that international law is increasingly salient in world politics, and is even influential in domestic politics, as the 2005 British election campaign made abundantly clear.

In a deeply flawed, but nonetheless highly instructive special issue of the flagship journal of the US international relations academy – *International Organization* – in 2000, it was demonstrated that in a range of issue-areas, from trade to human rights to the environment, we are experiencing a "legalization" of world politics.[3] Although the description of legalization provided by the authors is but a caricature of international law,[4] the central point remains: international political actors are invoking legal discourse more commonly than ever before, and legal norms are shaping politics in new and sometimes surprising ways.[5]

---

[3] See K. W. Abbott, R. O. Keohane *et al.*, "The Concept of Legalization" (2000) 54 Int'l Org. 401.

[4] See M. Finnemore & S. J. Toope, "Alternatives to 'Legalization': Richer Views of Law and Politics" (2001) 55 Int'l Org. 743; and J. Brunnée, "Review: Legalization and World Politics. Edited by Judith L. Goldstein, Miles Kahler, Robert O. Keohane, and Anne-Marie Slaughter. Cambridge, MA: MIT Press, 2001" (2003) 1/1 Perspectives in Politics (American Political Science Association) 231.

[5] See e.g., J. Brunnée & S. J. Toope, "The Changing Nile Basin Regime: Does Law Matter?" (2002) 43 Harvard Int'l L. J. 105 [hereinafter "Nile Basin"]; and S. R. Ratner,

Jutta Brunnée and I have argued in a series of articles over the last five years that international law is formed in processes of interaction between international and domestic actors, between social norms and facts, and between political and juridical structures, and actors.[6] The interactional theory of international law reveals how international legal norms are influential. Norms feed back into processes of social interaction and they influence the self-constructed identity of states and their self-understanding of "interests". What is more, legal norms are often taken up by "norm entrepreneurs" to promote specific legal and political change.[7] Recent examples of this process of norm entrepreneurship include the creation of the International Criminal Court,[8] and the conclusion of the Ottawa Landmines Convention.[9]

It has never been more important to understand how international law enables and constrains international politics. While scholars are struggling to explain the role of norms in international society, diplomats and politicians argue over the relevance of international law and institutions in times of crisis. Citizens around the globe are torn between a hope that international law can foster order, security and respect for human rights, and frustration over law's weakness. These hopes, fears and tensions reached a climax during the debates over the use of force in Iraq, debates that serve as a metaphor for wider controversies concerning the role of law in international affairs. During the lead-up to the 2003 Iraq War the President of the United States warned that the United Nations was on the brink of irrelevance.[10] International law was viewed by

---

"Does International Law Matter in Preventing Ethnic Conflict?" (2000) 32 NYU J. Int'l L. & Pol. 591.

[6] "Interactional Theory", *supra* note 1; "Explaining Compliance", *supra* note 1; "Nile Basin", *ibid.*; and J. Brunnée & S. J. Toope, "Interactional International Law" (2001) 3 International Law FORUM de droit international 186.

[7] See M. Finnemore & K. Sikkink, "International Norm Dynamics and Political Change" (1998) 52 Int'l Org. 887 at 895; and M. Keck & K. Sikkink, *Activists Beyond Borders* (1998), *passim*.

[8] Rome Statute of the International Criminal Court, July 17, 1998, U.N. Doc. A/CONF. 183/9 (1998), reprinted in (1998) 37 I.L.M. 999. I do not mean to argue that the Court itself is a success, only that norm entrepreneurs played a determinative role in its creation. For a relatively negative assessment of the Court's future, see S. R. Ratner, "The International Criminal Court and the Limits of Global Judicialization" (2003) 38 Texas J. Int'l L. 445.

[9] Convention On The Prohibition Of The Use, Stockpiling, Production And Transfer Of Anti-Personnel Mines And On Their Destruction, 36 ILM 1507 (1997), entered into force 1 March 1999.

[10] George W. Bush, Address to the UN General Assembly, 12 September 2002, http://www.whitehouse.gov/news/releases/2002/09/20020912–1.html ("All the world now faces a test, and the United Nations a difficult and defining moment. Are Security Council resolutions to be honored and enforced, or cast aside without consequence? Will the United Nations serve the purpose of its founding, or will it be irrelevant?").

many people – detractors and supporters alike – as dead or dying. Yet at no time in recent world history has international law, and specifically the role of the UN as a central institution of contemporary international law, been more debated by elites and even by the person in the street. At this moment of crisis, public cynicism was tempered by expressions of hope and expectation. Millions of people around the world took to the streets. Part of their motivation was a sense that the pending war could not be justified under international law. In such circumstances, it is hard to argue that international law is irrelevant, normatively or politically.

The interactional approach to international law also shows that norm building is not the exclusive domain of states and political elites. The creation of "shared understandings" amongst states and other international actors, a precursor to effective law, sometimes relies upon the engagement of a wider citizenry.[11] However, in many important areas of policy there is no basis for shared understandings because even the informed public lacks knowledge of the relevant issues. It is precisely for this reason that the media are important to the creation and sustenance of international law.

For present purposes, a rather complex argument can be summarized as follows: International law matters in world politics. Ordinary citizens have a role to play in the construction of international law. A well informed citizen needs to be able to appreciate at least the broad outlines of international legal arguments in order to shape her opinions on a series of important public policy questions. These include the lawful use of military force, the promotion and protection of human rights, and limits on the so-called "war on terror". For most people, the media are the primary sources of information through which opinions are shaped. International lawyers should pay more attention to the media in our work.

What role can the media play? Here, I must set out another premise of my research, that the UK and Canadian print media have a responsibility not only to be profitable, but also to help shape an informed citizenry. Media is more than entertainment. If this is true, one must conclude that the print media are largely failing when it comes to enlightenment on international law. The UK newspapers would receive merely a marginal failing grade, or perhaps, from time to time, a "gentleman's third," while the Canadian newspapers fail abjectly. Although the words "international law" are by no means absent from leading Canadian and UK newspapers, there is a striking tendency to invoke the words without any explanation, context or precision. Indeed, international law is often referred to by quoted sources with no effort being made by the journalist to probe, to ask what the legal reference means in a specific circumstance. Indeed the image of international law in Canadian newspapers may best

---

[11] "Interactional Theory", *supra* note 1, at 31.

be described as that of a mime: present, but voiceless and vaguely comic. Like a mime, it is nonetheless perceived to help us draw out a moral. In UK quality dailies, international law appears in a variety of guises: often as a quixotic hero, especially in The Independent and The Guardian, sometimes as an evil aristocrat attacking popular sovereignty, especially and ironically in The Telegraph, but mostly as a psychotic with multiple personality disorder: there is no "answer" in international law.

First, let me provide an overview of the treatment of international law in selected Canadian newspapers. Perhaps not surprisingly, the locally oriented Vancouver Sun contains many fewer references to international law than do the Globe and Mail or the National Post. In the period under study, the words "international law" appeared in the text of National Post articles 409 times, but in the text of the Vancouver Sun, only 169 times. The two Quebec newspapers contain roughly the same numbers of textual references to "droit international" as the Vancouver Sun: 197 in Le Devoir, 188 in La Presse, and each contains significantly fewer references than either of the "national" English-language dailies. One interesting distinction is in the linkage of "international law" with the war in Iraq. In the Globe and Mail, the words "international law" appeared in the same article as the words "war" and "Iraq" 147 times. Similarly, in both Le Devoir and La Presse, this linkage occurred relatively often, indeed proportionately more often than in the Globe and Mail. However, in both the National Post and the Vancouver Sun, "international law" made very few appearances in articles that also contained the words "war" and Iraq," 28 times and 9 times respectively. Across the board, international law is reported rarely and superficially.

Now let us consider the UK newspapers. In the period under review, international law made more appearances in the British newspapers than in their Canadian counterparts. The words "international law" appeared in the text of The Guardian some 837 times, and in The Independent on 688 occasions. The Times used the words 628 times. Interestingly, "international law" was mentioned on far fewer occasions in The Telegraph, where it appeared only 261 times. This relative lack of attention may coincide with the newspaper's editorial policy, which not only supported the invasion but asserted, as we shall see, that the essential questions were purely political and not legal. When the words 'international law" are linked to "Iraq" and "war," exactly the same pattern emerges, with the largest number of references in The Guardian (401), followed by The Independent at 284, The Times at 193, with The Telegraph trailing at a mere 109 references.

Obviously one would not wish to draw too much from raw numbers. What is clear is that globally there were many more references to international law in UK papers than in the Canadian dailies. There is also some correlation between those papers that took a strong stance against the Anglo-American invasion of Iraq and higher numbers of references to international law, but the correlation is not perfect. For example, the Globe and Mail supported the war, as did The Times, but both contained a relatively high number of references to international law.

By actually reading the articles in which international law is mentioned, it is possible to trace out more telling insights about the treatment of international law in Canadian and UK daily newspapers. In the Canadian newspapers in which international law is invoked most often, the Globe and Mail, Le Devoir and La Presse, the references are typically brief, and they often arise in quoted sources. For example, in an article by the leading columnist, Jeffrey Simpson, the author merely mentions what he calls the US "slighting" of "multilateralism and international law."[12] In an article published just after the fall of the Saddam Hussein regime, the Swedish Prime Minister is simply quoted without further comment: "We don't need to regret the fall of Saddam Hussein, though we can regret that it occurred in such a way that it violates international law."[13] In La Presse, in a typical reference during the lead-up to war, a journalist merely states that the US appeared to be less sensitive to the requirements of international law than were most European governments.[14] Similarly, in Le Devoir, international law appeared implicitly, but was rarely invoked directly on use of force issues. It was more commonly cited with reference to human rights and international humanitarian law. A typical reference is to Security Council resolutions without further legal analysis.[15]

Superficiality is likewise apparent in the newspapers where international law is referred to even less frequently in relation to Iraq. In the National Post, "international law" is mentioned in quotations from or articles by political scientists, historians or diplomats.[16] International lawyers do not appear. The only exception is Ed Morgan of the University of Toronto, who happened to be one of the very few Canadian international lawyers who believed that the decision

---

[12] J. Simpson, "The difference between them and us" *The Globe and Mail* (19 March 2003) A23.

[13] R. Mickleburgh, "War's critics happy to see fall of Hussein" *The Globe and Mail* (10 April 2003) A7 (quoting Prime Minister Goran Persson).

[14] R. Pelletier, "L'empire américain, l'Europe et l'Irak" *La Presse* (9 February 2003) A8.

[15] See e.g., J.-R. Sansfaçon, "Une guerre précipité" *Le Devoir* (20 March 2003) A8. The only exception was an article by a retired international law professor from the University of Ottawa. See D. Pharand, "Le droit international et l'emploi de la force contre l'Irak" *Le Devoir* (18 March 2003) A8.

[16] See e.g., C. Owen, "America is justified in striking first" *The National Post* (11 March 2003) A18; G. Weigel, "Declaring war would be the moral option" *The National Post* (20 November 2002) A18; and S Alberts & A. Dawson, "Former UN head calls war breach of Charter" *The National Post* (21 March 2003) A13.

of the United States and Britain to go to war against Iraq in 2003 was legally justifiable.[17]

The UK newspapers are somewhat less superficial in their treatment of international law and the use of force in Iraq. In all of the newspapers we see leading UK international lawyers quoted, sometimes at length, on their understanding of the relevant issues. The person quoted most frequently is Professor Christopher Greenwood, but that is mainly because he is said to have been involved in the preparation of the Attorney-General, Lord Goldsmith's, 'second shot' at advice to the Government on the legality of the Iraq invasion. In effect, Christopher Greenwood became part of the news, rather than being a commentator on it.[18] The same may be said for the second most quoted international lawyer, Philippe Sands, whose book *Lawless World*[19] is a principal source for many of the allegations concerning an alleged disparity between two legal opinions offered to the Government by the Attorney-General,[20] a disparity said to result in part from the contributions of Professor Greenwood.[21]

The letter of sixteen eminent international lawyers, including the holders of the Whewell Chair at Cambridge and the Chichele Chair at Oxford, and which challenged the legality of the invasion, was published in The Guardian and reported upon in other dailies.[22] A similar letter in Canada was never published in full, although it was reported.[23] In a detailed piece published in March 2004,

---

[17] It should be noted, however, that Morgan's contributions to the National Post have not been directly on the Iraq War, though the analysis is often relevant to that context. See, e.g., E. Morgan, "A war of words and the law" *The National Post* (7 October 2003) A16.

[18] See e.g., A. Grice, "PM and the Case for War: A controversy that still damages Blair" *The Independent* (9 March 2005) 8 ("Lord Goldsmith has also been criticised for relying on an expert opinion from Christopher Greenwood QC, professor of international law at the London School of Economics. Critics say he was among a minority in his field to endorse the invasion.")

[19] P. Sands, *Lawless World: America and the Making and Breaking of Global Rules* (London: Penguin/Allen Lane, 2005).

[20] *Ibid.*, at 188–201. See also R. Norton-Taylor, "Revealed: the rush to war" *The Guardian* (23 February 2005) 1; and C. Brown, "Goldsmith fights for survival with denial" *The Independent* (26 February 2005) 4.

[21] O. Bowcott, "Legality of Iraq War: Adviser sticks to his guns" *The Guardian* (1 March 2005) 4; and P. Waugh, "UN Spying row: US told Britain to get new legal opinion on Iraq war, book claims" *The Independent* (1 March 2004) 8.

[22] U. Bernitz, N. Espejo-Yaksic, A Hurwitz *et al.*, Letter to the Editor [War would be illegal], *The Guardian* (7 March 2003); M. White & P. Wintour, "No case for Iraq attack say lawyers" *The Guardian* (7 March 2003) 1.

[23] J. Sallott, "Legal experts say attack on Iraq is illegal" *The Globe and Mail* (20 March 2003) A10; E. Oziewicz, "Is Iraq war justified by international agreements?" *The Globe and Mail* (25 March 2003) A11.

a Guardian journalist interviewed and reported upon the views of 7 UK international lawyers and international relations scholars concerning the legality of the Iraq War.[24]

Perhaps more surprisingly, the legal affairs editor of The Telegraph, Joshua Rozenberg, wrote two thoughtful articles in the spring of 2003, one dealing with the lawfulness of the doctrine of preventive war, and the other with international humanitarian law.[25] In my view, these are the most sophisticated articles treating international law that appeared in either Canadian or UK dailies in the period under study. It may be instructive to know that while he was an Oxford undergraduate Rozenberg studied international law with Ian Brownlie.[26] Happily, it shows.

In the UK we also see a tactical use of the letters to the editor columns and op ed pages by various international lawyers who wanted to articulate their understandings of the legality of the Iraq war. Professors Phillip Allott, Chris Greenwood and Vaughan Lowe each wrote separately in The Times.[27] In addition, various members of the wider legal community wrote op ed pieces arguing pro and con, the most prolific being David Pannick, QC and Rabinder Singh QC in The Times.[28] Often these columns coincided with litigation where the legality of the war was being challenged – unsuccessfully – by the Campaign for Nuclear Disarmament, or where relatives of Iraqi civilians killed during the war were seeking to invoke the European Human Rights Convention and the UK Human Rights Act to require full investigation of the circumstances of death. Here, one family was successful at first instance.

Such extended, and sometimes sophisticated, pieces that really engage with international law arguments are nevertheless rare in the UK dailies. Just as in Canada, most references to international law are mere invocations of the idea,

---

[24] O. Bowcott, "Iraq: the legal challenge" *The Guardian* (2 March 2004) 3.

[25] J. Rozenberg, "Why the sword is mightier than the law" *The Telegraph* (13 March 2003) 24 [hereinafter "Why the sword"]; J. Rozenberg, "The perils of perfidy in wartime" (3 April 2003) 17.

[26] "Why the sword", *ibid*. Rozenberg subsequently declared his support for the Iraq War, so my positive evaluation of his analysis is not predicated upon substantive agreement with Rozenberg's conclusions. See J. Rozenberg, "How one word made the Iraq war legal" *The Telegraph* (20 March 2003) 18.

[27] P. Allott & A. Dashwood, Letter to the Editor [Conflict over legality of launching an attack against Iraq], *The Times* (19 March 2003) 23; C. Greenwood, "Britain's war on Saddam had the law on its side" *The Times* (22 October 2003) 22; V. Lowe, Letter to the Editor [Legal queries over actions on Iraq], *The Times* (23 September 2002) 19.

[28] See, e.g., D. Pannick, "Why the judges should have their say on Iraq" *The Times* (11 March 2003) 4; D. Pannick, "Why we must fight with one hand tied behind our backs" *The Times* (8 April 2003) 4; D. Pannick, "Goldsmith's advice on legality of war must be published" *The Times* (4 November 2003) 4; R. Singh, "Why war is illegal" *The Times* (14 March 2003) 18.

often to legitimize political positions on globalization, American hegemony, multilateralism or US exceptionalism. For example, the Guardian columnist, George Monbiot, often refers obliquely to international law, and simply asserts that the Iraq war was "illegal".[29] Similarly, in The Independent, Charles Kennedy, then the leader of the Liberal Democrat Party, baldly stated that Prime Minister Blair "led us into an illegal war."[30]

Perhaps it was these types of articles that prompted Professors Philip Allott and Alan Dashwood of Cambridge to write to The Times that:

> The question of the legality of the use of armed force against Iraq has assumed a surprising prominence . . ., presumably because the political and moral arguments are so complex and so contradictory. Those professional lawyers who suggest that international law provides a simple and unequivocal answer are misrepresenting the nature and function of international law. The UN Charter system for controlling the use of force by states is not a set of rules to be construed and applied like a road traffic Act.[31]

Allott and Dashwood are pleading for nuance and subtlety, as is the wont of academic lawyers. But how does subtlety play itself out in the media? Nuance is most likely to emerge as false "balance". One sees this in both the Canadian and UK coverage of the legality of the Iraq War. Newspapers like to quote "both sides" of an issue, so it was often contended that professional opinion was deeply divided over the lawfulness of the invasion of Iraq.[32] My view is that this was true only in the sense that opinions were strongly held and power-fully expressed; but the vast majority of international lawyers in both Canada and the UK thought and think that the war was illegal.[33] There was no balance to be had. Seeking it out was a political action, not an expression of journalistic

---

[29] See e.g., G. Monbiot, "One rule for them" *The Guardian* (25 March 2003) 21.

[30] C. Kennedy, "The Prime Minister led us into an illegal war" *The Independent* (14 October 2004) 39.

[31] Allott & Dashwood, *supra* note 27.

[32] See e.g., F. Gibb, "Breach of international law feared if war starts" *The Times* (14 March 2003) 18 ("Opinion among international lawyers is split. There are two main schools of thought: those who think the existing UN resolutions give ample legal authority for military action, and those who think a second specific UN resolution is required." She then went on to quote only Christopher Greenwood and Ruth Wedgwood, two of the rare international lawyers who argued the legality of the invasion).

[33] Witness the letters to the editor in both countries signed by leading international lawyers, *supra* notes 22 and 23 as well as a review of the legal literature since the war: J. Brunnée & S.J. Toope, "The Use of Force: International Law After Iraq" (2004) 53 Int'l & Comp. L.Q. 785; T. M. Franck, "What Happens Now? The United Nations After Iraq" (2003) 97 Am. J. Int'l L. 607; V. Lowe, "The Iraq Crisis: What Now?" (2003) 52 Int'l & Comp. L.Q. 859; and S. Murphy, "Assessing the Legality of Invading Iraq" (2004) Georgetown L.J. 16.

fairness. The idea that international legal opinion was deeply divided was promoted by the UK and US governments and by newspapers that supported the war: we see this argument again and again in The Times, The Telegraph, and The National Post.

My warning is that international lawyers should be wary of too much nuance when they agree to engage with the media. A pose of thoughtful reasonableness must be read against the background noise. That noise is shrill, insistent and damaging. Just consider the following comments drawn from columnists and leader writers in Canada and the UK:

> Least of all do I believe that the Anglo-American decision to bypass the UN Security Council before going to war will mean the 'destruction of the postwar order', based on international law and the authority of the UN. This so-called order never existed.[34]

> That is pretty much it for the United Nations – all over, finished, bye-bye. . . . The UN has been revealed to be not a talking shop, as its dismissive critics have always claimed, but a diplomatic souk in which bribery, vanity and manipulation are the currencies. . . . This is the organisation on which peace protesters and dissident Labour MPs rest their credibility: the great fount of moral legitimacy, the institution which holds the factitious entity called 'international law' under its authority.[35]

> . . . [I]nternational law is anything but clear, being no more than an evolving consensus on what the world will or will not tolerate.[36]

> The most striking thing about this debate is its pointlessness. The "legality" or otherwise of the war is a non-subject, for the simple reason that there is no binding body of international law which compels obedience, either morally or in fact, from the sovereign nations of the globe. . . . "International law", in so far as it ventures beyond the law of the sea, is almost entirely bogus.[37]

It is hard to know where to begin in challenging such tendentious misinformation. For readers of this book, it is not necessary even to try. In an era that has seen the emergence of detailed international regulation on matters of trade, the environment, transport, telecommunications – one could go on – the idea that there is no international law is absurd. But my point is that these are views that shape public opinion. So these views, no matter how ignorant or intentionally misleading they may be, do matter.

---

[34] A. Kaletsky, "War could mean the end of the economic world" *The Times* (18 March 2004) 27.

[35] J. Daley, "UN lets tinpot dictators rule the world" *The Telegraph* (12 March 2003) 26.

[36] A. Coyne, "12 arguments against war, rebutted" *The National Post* (7 March 2003) A15.

[37] "A legal fiction" (leading article) *The Sunday Telegraph* (29 February 2004) 24.

My conclusion is that despite the evidence showing that international law is more salient than ever in international politics, and sometimes in domestic politics as well, international law is not well reported in the UK or the Canadian print media. The UK newspapers did a somewhat better job in disentangling the legal debates over the legality of the Iraq War. Of course, the stakes were much higher in the UK than in Canada, where the Government had finally – after much unfortunate equivocation – decided not to participate in the Anglo-American invasion. British citizens were pressed to decide what they thought about the Iraq War in a way that Canadians were not; one could argue the media may simply have reflected that difference.

But such a conclusion may be too generous to the Canadian print media. Until the very last moment, the Chretien Government kept the public and its allies guessing. It is worth recalling that the Minister of Defence publicly suggested that Canada might indeed participate in the invasion.[38] So the international law questions were relevant; they were just superficially treated. No serious attempt was made to connect with a range of international lawyers to canvass opinion. The letter sent by 31 internationalists to various newspapers was never published. The subsequent paroxysms in British politics over the advice of the Attorney General have been reported in Canada only vaguely.

Can the situation be improved? Is international law doomed to play bit parts, to be a figure of fun or an object of derision? I don't think so. I return to the image of the millions of citizens of the UK, of Spain, of Italy who filled the streets of their capitals in the lead-up to the Iraq War. These people seemed to believe that international law had something relevant to speak to power. The wide reporting in the UK on Philippe Sands' *Lawless World*[39] suggests that international legal issues can be made understandable.

So the challenge is for international lawyers to explain our discipline more clearly. International law is not always as uncertain as we pretend; I wonder sometimes if we delight in our own forms of mystification. Subtlety and nuance are important aspects of professional responsibility; obfuscation and deference to power are not. There are plenty of voices in the media who will claim that international law is illegitimate, that it has nothing coherent to say, that it is bogus. But if we believe that citizens matter, that we all deserve something better than a lawless world, and that international law has some helpful guidance, then we must push back against the glib and ignorant commentators. Our fellow citizens should be able to weigh the contributions of international law when they consider major issues of public policy.

---

[38] D. Rudd, "The Fog of (Phoney) War", Commentary, The Canadian Institute of Strategic Studies, http://www.ciss.ca/Comment_PhoneyWar.htm.

[39] *Supra* note 19.

A year-and-a-half ago ago, the lively UK magazine *Prospect* published a poll listing the top 100 "public intellectuals" in the UK.[40] Of course such efforts are easy to criticise; the methodology is inherently suspect. But as snapshots of public perceptions they are interesting. Amongst the scientists, self-styled ethicists, political pundits, international relations gurus, and arts commentators, there was not a single international lawyer. I have no doubt that the same would be true of a comparable exercise in Canada.

International lawyers have to learn to engage more effectively with the media, not because we seek aggrandisement, but because citizens' opinions are largely shaped in media debates, and citizens' opinions matter in our discipline. Law is constructed in the interaction of elites and publics, governors and governed. To promote fidelity to law, and to combat the cynicism of lawlessness, international lawyers need the media, as frightening as that imperative may seem.

---

[40] *Prospect* [Magazine] 100 (July 2004). A subsequent *Prospect* poll to identify the 100 leading public intellectuals in the world – even more open to debate – produced the same result: no international lawyers. See *Prospect* [Magazine] 101 (August 2005).

PART 2

CRIME

Chapter 2

Domestic Reception of International Humanitarian Law: UK and Canadian Implementing Legislation

Christopher Harland

1) INTRODUCTION

The shared legal traditions of the United Kingdom and Canada include methods of domestic incorporation of international legal obligations. In many common law countries, including Canada and the UK,[1] Parliament usually adopts legislation prior to the entry into force of the international obligation for the country, seeking to have the necessary implementing legislation in place prior to, or coterminous with, the beginning of the entry into force of that international obligation.

---

[1] Canada and the UK are classed here as common law countries, even though both have elements of civil law jurisdictions in Québec and Scotland. Other Commonwealth Members also have mixed legal systems, including South Africa, Mauritius, Cameroon, Seychelles, etc. See, for example, M. S. Amos, "The Common Law and the Civil Law in the British Commonwealth of Nations" (1936–1937) 50 Harv. L. Rev. 1249.

Christopher P.M. Waters (Ed.), *British and Canadian Perspectives on International Law*, pp. 29–51.

Many international humanitarian law ("IHL")[2] treaties require the modification of internal legislation, military manuals and other regulations. In this respect, much has been made of the differences between common law and civil law jurisdictions.[3] Typically, common law states are described as dualist, in which international obligations carry no domestic effect in the absence of legislation. In monist states, on the other hand, domestic effect can be enabled, in some circumstances, through publication of parliamentary consent in the official gazette together with the treaty itself. The problem, however, is that many treaties, especially those containing prohibitions, require additional legislation in order to be properly applied in the domestic context. For example, while the Second Protocol to the Hague Cultural Property Convention[4] sets out explicit criminal provisions that Parties should apply, it does not set out possible sentences or fines for a breach of the provisions.[5] Each state must decide that for itself. Both monist and dualist countries therefore often require the undertaking of similar implementing measures.[6]

The work of the Advisory Service on IHL of the International Committee of the Red Cross ("ICRC")[7] includes encouraging IHL treaty ratification, assisting

---

[2] IHL can be defined as "a set of rules which seek, for humanitarian reasons, to limit the effects of armed conflict. It protects persons who are not or are no longer participating in the hostilities and restricts the means and methods of warfare. International humanitarian law is also known as the law of war or the law of armed conflict." See International Committee of the Red Cross: http://www.icrc.org/web/eng/siteeng0.nsf/iwpList2/Humanitarian_law:IHL_in_brief?OpenDocument.

[3] Seemingly a topic of great interest in the earlier part of the twentieth century, see for example R. W. Lee, "The Civil Law and the Common Law – A World Survey" (1915–1916) 14 Mich. L. Rev. 89 and Amos, *supra* note 1.

[4] Second Protocol to the Hague Convention of 1954 for the Protection of Cultural Property in the Event of Armed Conflict, opened for signature Mar. 26 1999. Civil law states are generally believed to legislate more than common law states, which place a greater reliance on jurisprudence. However, in the domain of treaty implementation, the theory is reversed, given that common law states must normally legislate in order for treaty provisions to apply in domestic law, while civil law states, at least in theory, can allow some elements of treaties to apply directly in internal law without the need for additional legislation.

[5] See article 15 of the Second Protocol to the Hague Cultural Property Convention. Among IHL treaties, this provision is unusual in the degree to which it resembles domestic criminal legislation.

[6] Some states enact generalised enabling legislation which create offences and include sanctions for breaches of international treaty obligations. See, for example, article 356 of the Russian Criminal Code, "2. Use of a weapon of mass destruction prohibited by an international treaty of the Russian Federation, shall be punished by imprisonment for a term from ten to twenty years." See ICRC: http://www.icrc.org/ihlnat.nsf/6fa4d35e-5e3025394125673e00508143/3d8ba4c6eac11068432564eb0034fe05?OpenDocument.

[7] More information is available at http://www.icrc.org/web/eng/siteeng0.nsf/iwpList2/Humanitarian_law:National_implementation?Open.

states in the domestication of these international obligations, and promoting the work of inter-ministerial 'National Committees on IHL'. These Committees carry out work such as drafting of legislation, the dissemination of IHL and recommending government action related to international humanitarian law.[8] Of the 26 principal IHL treaties, protocols and declarations[9] with which the ICRC regularly works on seeking national implementation, Canada has acceded to 23 while the UK has acceded to 22.[10] While both countries generally adopt legislation prior to the entry into force of the legal obligation, Canada's Biological Weapons Convention Act[11] had not yet entered into force as at the date of writing. Canada and the UK both have National IHL Committees.

This paper will examine three treaties or sets of treaties to which both Canada and the UK are parties and for which they have adopted implementing legislation. The first involves the implementation of the Four Geneva Conventions and their Additional Protocols.[12] The second is the International Criminal Court ("Rome Statute")[13] and the third is the Anti-personnel

---

[8] An overview of the work of committees may be found at http://www.icrc.org/Web/eng/siteeng0.nsf/htmlall/section_ihl_nat_national_committees.

[9] For more information, see the fact sheets on the work of the Committees: http://www.icrc.org/Web/eng/siteeng0.nsf/htmlall/section_ihl_nat_national_committees.

[9] Including the 1949 Geneva Conventions and their Protocols (with Article 90 of Additional Protocol I), the Hague Cultural Property Convention and its Protocols, the International Criminal Court Statute, the Environmental Modification Convention, the Biological Weapons Convention and the 1925 Geneva Protocol, the Chemical Weapons Convention, the Convention on Certain Conventional Weapons and its Protocols, the Anti-Personnel Landmines Convention, and the Optional Protocol to the Convention on the Rights of the Child.

[10] Neither country, as of late August 2005, was a Party to the First or Second Protocol to the Hague Cultural Property Convention, nor to the Explosive Remnants of War Protocol to the Convention on Certain Conventional Weapons.

[11] Biological and Toxin Weapons Convention Implementation Act [Not in force] 2004, (Canada) c. 15, s. 106.

[12] Convention for the Amelioration of the Condition of the Wounded and Sick in Armed Forces in the Field, Aug. 12, 1949, 75 U.N.T.S. 31; Convention for the Amelioration of the Condition of Wounded, Sick and Shipwrecked Members of Armed Forces at Sea, Aug. 12, 1949, 75 U.N.T.S. 85, Geneva Convention Relative to the Protection of Civilian Persons in Time of War, Aug. 12, 1949; 75 U.N.T.S. 287 Geneva Convention Relative to the Treatment of Prisoners of War, Aug. 12, 1949, 75 U.N.T.S. 135, Protocol Additional to the Geneva Conventions of 12 August 1949, and Relating to the Protection of Victims of International Armed Conflicts (Protocol I), June 8, 1977, 1125 U.N.T.S. 3, Protocol Additional to the Geneva Conventions of 12 August 1949, and Relating to the Protection of Victims of Non-International Armed Conflicts (Protocol II), June 8, 1977, 1125 U.N.T.S. 609; (1987) 26 I.L.M. 568.

[13] Rome Statute of the International Criminal Court, 2187 U.N.T.S. 90, entered into force July 1, 2002 [ICC Statute or Rome Statute].

Landmines ("Ottawa") Treaty.[14] This examination of legislative instruments touching on IHL is by no means exhaustive, and is merely intended to provide a flavour of the differences in the approaches used by the two countries. Some further aspects of the implementation of international criminal law norms in Canada and the UK are detailed in the other chapters in Part 2.

2) GENEVA CONVENTIONS ACTS

The 1949 Geneva Conventions and their 1977 Additional Protocols form the core of international humanitarian law. They "establish a system of legal safeguards that cover the way wars may be fought and the protection of individuals. They specifically protect people who do not take part in the fighting (civilians, medics, chaplains, aid workers) and those who can no longer fight (wounded, sick and shipwrecked troops, prisoners of war). The Conventions and their Protocols call for measures to be taken to prevent (or put an end to) what are known as 'grave breaches'; those responsible for breaches must be punished."[15]

Canada[16] and the UK[17] both have specific legislation aimed at implementing the obligations in the Geneva Conventions and their Protocols. Most common law states enact Geneva Convention Acts which contain at least three elements: incorporation of the grave breaches, protecting powers notification, and emblem protection.[18] At the time of the updating of the UK 1957 Act to reflect obligations under the 1977 Protocols, there was debate as to how much to incorporate.[19] The UK approach generally appears to be the following:

> We will legislate the minimum, the literal minimum, because we find if we go beyond that, we not only stir up a political hornet's nest, but indeed such an opposition that the legislation may be thrown out in its incipient stages. Moreover, we will find that minimum legislation is easier to understand for the people who have got to apply it.[20]

---

[14] Convention on the Prohibition of the Use, Stockpiling, Production and Transfer of Anti-personnel Mines and on their Destruction, 2056 U.N.T.S. 241, I-35597 [Ottawa Treaty].

[15] See http://www.icrc.org/Web/Eng/siteeng0.nsf/html/genevaconventions.

[16] Geneva Conventions Act 1949 (Canada), R.S.C., c. G-3.

[17] Geneva Conventions Amendment Act (U.K.) 1995, c. 27, modifying the Geneva Conventions Act 1957.

[18] See, for example, the Model Geneva Conventions Act of the ICRC at http://www.icrc.org/Web/Eng/siteeng0.nsf/iwpList566/A8563640C6BD90E7C1256CD400519252.

[19] See P. Rowe and M. Meyer, "Ratification by the United Kingdom of the 1977 Protocols Additional to the Geneva Conventions of 1949: Selected Problems of Implementation" (1994) 45 N. Ir. Legal Q. 343.

[20] G.I.A.D. Draper, whose comments were published in M. Bothe et al., eds., *National Implementation of International Humanitarian Law* (The Hague: Martinus Nijhoff,

a) *Grave breach provisions*

Article 49 of the First Geneva Convention reads:

> The High Contracting Parties undertake to enact any legislation necessary to provide effective penal sanctions for persons committing, or ordering to be committed, any of the grave breaches of the present Convention defined in the following Article.

Each of the other Four Geneva Conventions of 1949 have similar provisions.[21] As the grave breaches were introduced in 1949, both Canada and the UK adopted domestic legislation creating these crimes when they acceded to the Conventions. The First Additional Protocol of 1977 included additional grave breaches, which led to amendments to the Geneva Conventions Acts.[22]

Both Canada's and the UK's grave breach legislation is similar in effect even if wording differs:

Canada[23]	United Kingdom[24]
3. (1) Every person who, whether within or outside Canada, commits a grave breach referred to in Article 50 of Schedule I, Article 51 of Schedule II, Article 130 of Schedule III, Article 147 of Schedule IV or Article 11 or 85 of Schedule V is guilty of an indictable offence, and	1. (1) Any person, whatever his nationality, who, whether in or outside the United Kingdom, commits, or aids, abets or procures the commission by any other person of, a grave breach of any of the scheduled conventions or the first protocol shall be guilty of an offence –
(*a*) if the grave breach causes the death of any person, is liable to imprisonment for life; and	(a) in the case of a grave breach involving the wilful killing of a person protected by the convention or protocol in question, shall be sentenced to imprisonment for life;

1990) at 100. For comments on the Canadian law prior to the incorporation of the grave breaches of the Additional Protocols and the Rome Statute, see the comments of Leslie Green in the same work, at 89–94. For general discussion of the steps necessary to implement IHL, including non-legislative steps, see Y. Sandoz, "Implementing International Humanitarian Law" in *International Dimensions of Humanitarian Law* (UNESCO, 1988) at 259.

[21] Geneva Convention II – Article 50, Geneva Convention III – Article 129, Geneva Convention IV – Article 146.

[22] Through the Geneva Convention Amendment Acts of 1996 in the UK, and 1990 and 1995 in Canada.

[23] Geneva Conventions Act 1949 (Canada), R.S.C., c. G-3.

[24] Geneva Conventions Amendment Act (U.K.) 1995, c. 27, modifying the Geneva Conventions Act 1957.

Table (*cont.*)

Canada	United Kingdom
(*b*) in any other case, is liable to imprisonment for a term not exceeding fourteen years.	(b) in the case of any other grave breach shall be liable to imprisonment for a term not exceeding fourteen years.
	(1A) For the purposes of subsection (1) of this section – (a) a grave breach of a scheduled convention is anything referred to as a grave breach of the convention in the relevant Article, that is to say –
	(i) in the case of the convention set out in the First Schedule to this Act, Article 50;
	(. . .)
	(b) a grave breach of the first protocol is anything referred to as a grave breach of the protocol in paragraph 4 of Article 11, or paragraph 2, 3 or 4 of Article 85, of the protocol.

The UK legislation is more specific with respect to the paragraph numbers which contain offences in the Additional Protocol, while the Canadian legislation is more pithy. The terms of imprisonment foreseen are identical (up to 14 years, or life imprisonment in circumstances in which death ensues).

b) *Protecting Power notification*

Both countries include provisions detailing how protected persons (such as prisoners of war) should be tried. This includes providing notification of their intention to try the individual to the protecting power. A "Protecting Power" is a "State instructed by another State (known as the power of origin) to safeguard its interests and those of its nationals in relation to a third State (known as State of Residence).[25] The system dates back to the 16th century and was used in the

---

[25] J. Pictet, ed., *Commentary to the Geneva Conventions of 12 August 1949, Volume I – Geneva Convention for the Amelioration of the Condition of the Wounded and Sick in Armed Forces in the Field* (Geneva: ICRC, 1952) at 96.

First World War.[26] There exist obligations in the Conventions relating to Protecting Powers regarding procedures to be followed in the trial of prisoners of war and civilian internees. The First Protocol foresees the ICRC acting in place of Protecting Powers.[27] In current practice, use is made of the ICRC and rarely of Protecting Powers.[28] The similarities in the two countries' legislation to implement these obligations can be seen from the following example:

Canada[29]	United Kingdom[30]
5. (1) The court before which	2. (1) The court before which –
(*a*) a protected prisoner of war is brought for trial for an offence, or	(a) a protected prisoner of war is brought up for trial for any offence; or
(*b*) a protected internee is brought for trial for an offence for which that court has power to sentence that internee to death or to imprisonment for a term of two years or more,	(b) a protected internee is brought up for trial for an offence for which that court has power to sentence him to death or to imprisonment for a term of two years or more,
shall not proceed with the trial until it is proved to the satisfaction of the court that written notice of the trial containing, where known to the prosecutor, the information mentioned in subsection (2) has been given to the accused and the accused's protecting power, not less than three weeks before the commencement of the trial, and, where the accused is a protected prisoner of war, to his prisoners' representative.	shall not proceed with the trial until it is proved to the satisfaction of the court that a notice containing the particulars mentioned in the next following subsection, so far as they are known to the prosecutor, has been served not less than three weeks previously on the protecting power and, if the accused is a protected prisoner of war, on the accused and the prisoners' representative.

---

[26] Sandoz, *supra* note 20 at 266 and see Pictet, *ibid.*, at 86–93.

[27] Article 5(4) of Additional Protocol I provides "If, despite the foregoing, there is no Protecting Power, the Parties to the conflict shall accept without delay an offer which may be made by the International Committee of the Red Cross . . ." See also the common articles 10/10/10/11 of the four Geneva Conventions of 1949.

[28] For a practical overview of the use of Protecting Powers since the Second World War, see D. Forsythe, "Who Guards the Guardians: Third Parties and the Law of Armed Conflicts" (1976) 70 A.J.I.L. 41 at 46 to 48. He notes the role of the ICRC and the Protecting Powers in conflicts such as the Suez, Goa, and Bangladesh. He concludes infrequent use of Protecting Powers since 1949 and increasing reliance on the ICRC.

[29] Crimes Against Humanity and War Crimes Act 2000, (Canada) c. 24.

[30] International Criminal Court Act 2001, (UK) c. 17.

c) *Protection of the Emblem*

The third element often found in common law Geneva Convention Acts involves the protection of the emblems in the Geneva Conventions as well as other signs and symbols. This is true of the UK Act, while Canada protects the emblem through trademark legislation.

Canada[31]	United Kingdom
9. (1) No person shall adopt in connection with a business, as a trademark or otherwise, any mark consisting of, or so nearly resembling as to be likely to be mistaken for, ... (*f*) the emblem of the Red Cross on a white ground, formed by reversing the federal colours of Switzerland and retained by the Geneva Convention for the Protection of War Victims of 1949 as the emblem and distinctive sign of the Medical Service of armed forces and used by the Canadian Red Cross Society, or the expression "Red Cross" or "Geneva Cross"; . . .	6. (1) Subject to the provisions of this section, it shall not be lawful for any person, without the authority of the Army Council, to use for any purpose whatsoever any of the following emblems or designations, that is to say – (a) the emblem of a red cross with vertical and horizontal arms of the same length on, and completely surrounded by, a white ground, or the designation "Red Cross" or "Geneva Cross"; . . .

In 1996, when updating its Geneva Convention Act, the UK included the signs and signals that appeared in the 1977 First Additional Protocol.[32] Canada, however, does not appear to have included these provisions in the Trade-marks Act when updating its Geneva Conventions Act following its accession to the Additional Protocols. The perfidious use of the emblem, however, is criminalised through the grave breach provisions in each country's respective Geneva Conventions Act.[33]

---

[31] Trade-marks Act (Canada), R.S. 1985, c. T-13.

[32] In section 6(1)(e) of the Geneva Conventions Act 1949 (UK) as amended.

[33] Through incorporation of the grave breaches in Article 85(3) of the First Protocol Additional to the Geneva Conventions.

3) INTERNATIONAL CRIMINAL COURT IMPLEMENTATION

Of the three sets of treaty obligations considered, there is most variation between Canada and the UK in the methods chosen to incorporate the obligations arising from the Rome Statute.[34] Five elements are examined below: the method of incorporation of the crimes in the Statute, command responsibility provisions, universal jurisdiction rules, double jeopardy provisions, and other defences. Common law States wishing to develop implementing legislation relating to the International Criminal Court may refer to two documents, the *Commonwealth Model Law* and the *ICC Manual*.[35]

a) *Crimes*

Canada[36]	United Kingdom[37]
6. (1) Every person who, either before or after the coming into force of this section, commits outside Canada	50. Meaning of "genocide", "crime against humanity" and "war crime"
	(1) In this Part:
(*a*) genocide,	
	"genocide" means an act of genocide as defined in article 6,
(*b*) a crime against humanity, or	
(*c*) a war crime,	"crime against humanity" means a crime against humanity as defined in article 7, and
is guilty of an indictable offence and may be prosecuted for that offence in accordance with section 8.	
	"war crime" means a war crime as defined in article 8.2.
(3) The definitions in this subsection apply in this section.	

---

[34] Rome Statute *supra* note 13.

[35] *Model Law to Implement the Rome Statute of the International Criminal Court*, Commonwealth Secretariat, March 2005 [*Commonwealth Model Law*], which is focussed primarily on States with a common law tradition, and *International Criminal Court, Manual for the Ratification and Implementation of the Rome Statute*, ICCLR, and Rights and Democracy (Vancouver: May 2000) [*ICC Manual*]. For background on the Rome Statute see O. Triffterer, ed., *Commentary on the Rome Statute of the International Criminal Court: Observers Notes, Article By Article*, (Baden-Baden: Nomos Verl., 1999).

[36] *Supra* note 29.

[37] International Criminal Court Act 2001, (UK) c. 17.

Table (*cont.*)

Canada	United Kingdom
(. . .)	(2) In interpreting and applying the provisions of those articles the court shall take into account:
"war crime" means an act or omission committed during an armed conflict that, at the time and in the place of its commission, constitutes a war crime according to customary international law or conventional international law applicable to armed conflicts, whether or not it constitutes a contravention of the law in force at the time and in the place of its commission.	(a) any relevant Elements of Crimes adopted in accordance with article 9, and
(4) For greater certainty, crimes described in articles 6 and 7 and paragraph 2 of article 8 of the Rome Statute are, as of July 17, 1998, crimes according to customary international law, and may be crimes according to customary international law before that date. This does not limit or prejudice in any way the application of existing or developing rules of international law.	(b) until such time as Elements of Crimes are adopted under that article, any relevant Elements of Crimes contained in the report of the Preparatory Commission for the International Criminal Court adopted on 30th June 2000.

The differences are two-fold. First, the UK legislation refers directly to the provisions in the Rome Statute. Canada, on the other hand, establishes the crimes through custom, but defines custom as including those in articles 6, 7 and 8 of the Rome Statute. Secondly, the UK version incorporates, through regulation, the Elements of Crime established adopted by the Assembly of States Parties, while Canada does not make direct reference to them.[38] The *Commonwealth Model Law* makes reference to both formats, but the *ICC Manual* uses the UK approach.[39] The UK approach is the more commonly used.[40] Reference to custom (section 6(3) above) allows Canada to apply the provisions to acts

---

[38] See The International Criminal Court Act 2001 (Elements of Crimes) (No. 2) Regulations 2004 (UK).

[39] *Commonwealth Model Law, supra* note 35 at 2, *ICC Manual, supra* note 35 at 95.

[40] See, for example, the ICC legislation adopted by New Zealand, Australia and Ireland, available at: http://www.icrc.org/ihl-nat. An overview of the Australian legislation appears in G. Triggs, "Implementation of the Rome Statute for the International Criminal Court: A Quiet Revolution in Australian Law" (2003) 25 Sydney L. Rev. 507.

committed prior to the entry into force of the legislation, consistent with section 11(g) of the Canadian Charter of Rights and Freedoms.[41]

b) *Command responsibility*

Both countries incorporate command responsibility directly into their ICC legislation:

Canada	United Kingdom
5. (1) A military commander commits an indictable offence if	(1) This section applies in relation to:
(a) the military commander	(a) offences under this Part, and
	(b) offences ancillary to such offences.
(i) fails to exercise control properly over a person under their effective command and control or effective authority and control, and as a result the person commits an offence under section 4, or	(2) A military commander, or a person effectively acting as a military commander, is responsible for offences committed by forces under his effective command and control, or (as the case may be) his effective authority and control, as a result of his failure to exercise control properly over such forces where:
(ii) fails, after the coming into force of this section, to exercise control properly over a person under their effective command and control or effective authority and control, and as a result the person commits an offence under section 6;	(a) he either knew, or owing to the circumstances at the time, should have known that the forces were committing or about to commit such offences, and
(b) the military commander knows, or is criminally negligent in failing to know, that the person is about to commit or is committing such an offence; and	(b) he failed to take all necessary and reasonable measures within his power to prevent or repress their commission or to submit the
(c) the military commander subsequently	

---

[41] Section 11 of the Canadian Charter of Rights and Freedoms reads "Any person charged with an offence has the right . . . *g*) not to be found guilty on account of any act or omission unless, at the time of the act or omission, it constituted an offence under Canadian or international law or was criminal according to the general principles of law recognized by the community of nations".

Table (*cont.*)

Canada	United Kingdom
(i) fails to take, as soon as practicable, all necessary and reasonable measures within their power to prevent or repress the commission of the offence, or the further commission of offences under section 4 or 6, or	matter to the competent authorities for investigation and prosecution.
(ii) fails to take, as soon as practicable, all necessary and reasonable measures within their power to submit the matter to the competent authorities for investigation and prosecution.	

The effect of these provisions is similar, and reflects the command responsibility provision of Article 28 of the Rome Statute:

> (a) A military commander or person effectively acting as a military commander shall be criminally responsible for crimes within the jurisdiction of the Court committed by forces under his or her effective command and control, or effective authority and control as the case may be, as a result of his or her failure to exercise control properly over such forces, where:
>
> (i)   That military commander or person either knew or, owing to the circumstances at the time, should have known that the forces were committing or about to commit such crimes; and
>
> (ii) That military commander or person failed to take all necessary and reasonable measures within his or her power to prevent or repress their commission or to submit the matter to the competent authorities for investigation and prosecution.

There are additional provisions in both countries' legislation reflecting obligations for those exercising control over forces where they are not their commander. These provisions were necessary as command responsibility is not normally known in common law jurisdictions.[42] Command responsibility has

---

[42] As the *ICC Manual* points out, "few national criminal codes deal with the concept of the responsibility of commanders. It would be prudent for an implementing law to introduce this concept into national law." (*ICC Manual, supra* note 35 at page 101). The *Commonwealth Model Law* contains a provision similar to the UK and Canadian provisions, see *Commonwealth Model Law, supra* note 35 at 9 and see R. Cryer, "Implementation of the International Criminal Court Statute in England and Wales" (2002) 51 I.C.L.Q. 733 at 740.

been confirmed as a rule of custom in the International Criminal Tribunal for the Former Yugoslavia (ICTY) case of *Delalic*,[43] and the ICRC *Customary International Humanitarian Law Study*.[44] Article 86 of First Additional Protocol to the Geneva Conventions includes command responsibility, but this does not appear to have been incorporated into legislation following the updating of Geneva Conventions Acts in Canada and the UK as a result of their accession to the Protocol.[45] However, some commentators point out that this was not necessary, noting that the Geneva Conventions provisions relating to aiding, abetting and procuring could cover the Article 86 command responsibility provision as indeed could the inchoate offences of incitement, conspiracy or attempting to commit the offence.[46] It is not immediately obvious why command responsibility should be included by both countries in the later Rome Statute incorporating legislation, but not in earlier Geneva Convention First Additional Protocol legislation, both Conventions having command responsibility provisions.

c) *Universal jurisdiction*

The provisions read:

Canada	United Kingdom
8. A person who is alleged to have committed an offence under section 6 or 7 may be prosecuted for that offence if	51. (2) This section applies to acts committed:
	(a) in England or Wales, or
(*a*) at the time the offence is alleged to have been committed,	(b) outside the United Kingdom by a United

---

[43] *Prosecutor v. Zejnil Delalic et al.*, Case No. IT-96-21-T, Judgement, 16 November 1998 ("*Celebici* Trial Judgement"), para. 195, "Based on an analysis of World War II jurisprudence, the Trial Chamber also concluded that the principle of superior responsibility reflected in Article 7(3) of the Statute encompasses political leaders and other civilian superiors in positions of authority. The Appeals Chamber finds no reason to disagree with the Trial Chamber's analysis of this jurisprudence. The principle that military and other superiors may be held criminally responsible for the acts of their subordinates is well-established in conventional and customary law."

[44] J. M. Henckaerts and L. Doswald-Beck, *Customary International Humanitarian Law Volume I: Rules* (Cambridge University Press: 2005) Rules 152 and 153 at 556–563.

[45] "Command responsibility is new to domestic law." See Cryer *supra* note 42 at 740.

[46] See Rowe and Meyer, *supra* note 19 at 353–354.

Table (*cont.*)

Canada	United Kingdom
(i) the person was a Canadian citizen or was employed by Canada in a civilian or military capacity,	Kingdom national, a United Kingdom resident or a person subject to UK service jurisdiction.
(ii) the person was a citizen of a state that was engaged in an armed conflict against Canada, or was employed in a civilian or military capacity by such a state,	68 Proceedings against persons becoming resident within the jurisdiction

(1) This section applies in relation to a person who commits acts outside the United Kingdom at a time when he is not |
(iii) the victim of the alleged offence was a Canadian citizen, or	a United Kingdom national, a United Kingdom resident or a person subject to UK service jurisdiction and who
(iv) the victim of the alleged offence was a citizen of a state that was allied with Canada in an armed conflict; or	subsequently becomes resident in the United Kingdom.
(*b*) after the time the offence is alleged to have been committed, the person is present in Canada.	(2) Proceedings may be brought against such a person in England and Wales or Northern Ireland for a substantive offence under this Part if:
	(a) he is resident in the United Kingdom at the time the proceedings are brought, and
	(b) the acts in respect of which the proceedings are brought would have constituted that offence if they had been committed in that part of the United Kingdom.

The Canadian provision is broader in that it allows for jurisdiction in cases in which a victim of the alleged offence was a citizen of Canada or of a state that was allied with Canada in an armed conflict, which is not included in the UK jurisdiction. Additionally, jurisdiction is given in Canada where the person alleged to have committed the offence is present in Canada, while the UK requires residency rather than mere presence. Describing this as universal jurisdiction, one writer has noted "it is difficult to avoid the conclusion that jurisdiction in this instance may rely on a limited universal jurisdictional claim, albeit one which utilises later residency as a limiter."[47] This jurisdiction appears to be more limited than that able to be exercised under the Geneva Convention Acts of the two countries.[48]

d) *Ne bis in idem*

In this case, Canada incorporates this provision directly from the Statute while the UK does not:

Canada	United Kingdom
12. (1) If a person is alleged to have committed an act or omission that is an offence under this Act, and the person has been tried and dealt with outside Canada in respect of the offence in such a manner that, had they been tried and dealt with in Canada, they would be able to plead *autrefois acquit, autrefois convict* or pardon, the person is deemed to have been so tried and dealt with in Canada. (2) Despite subsection (1), a person may not plead *autrefois acquit, autrefois convict* or pardon in respect of an offence under any of sections 4 to 7 if the person was tried in a court of a foreign state or territory and the proceedings in that court (*a*) were for the purpose of shielding the person from criminal responsibility; or (*b*) were not otherwise conducted independently or impartially in accordance with the norms of due process recognized by international law, and were conducted in a manner that, in the circumstances, was inconsistent with an intent to bring the person to justice.	No specific legislation identified

---

[47] Cryer, *supra* note 42 at 740.

[48] See above on the grave breach provisions.

Thus, Canada has included a "shielding purpose" provision to its *ne bis in idem* (or double jeopardy) provision for international crimes, similar to the provision in the ICTY statute.[49] The Rome Statute provides in Article 17.2:

> In order to determine unwillingness in a particular case, the Court shall consider, having regard to the principles of due process recognized by international law, whether one or more of the following exist, as applicable:
>
> > (a) The proceedings were or are being undertaken or the national decision was made for the purpose of shielding the person concerned from criminal responsibility for crimes within the jurisdiction of the Court referred to in article 5[50]

While not seeming a problem for Canada, some civil law countries have raised concerns with respect to the shielding clause in 17.2(a) of the Rome Statute.[51]

e) *Other defences*

Both countries' legislation refers to defences which would be available to persons charged with offences. Canada provides for defences which are available both at international law and domestically at the time of the commission of the offence or at the time of the proceedings. The UK, however, appears to restrict its defences to those available under UK law:

Canada	United Kingdom
11. In proceedings for an offence under any of sections 4 to 7, the accused may, subject to sections 12 to 14 and to subsection 607(6) of the Criminal Code,	56. Saving for general principles of liability, etc. (1) In determining whether an offence

---

[49] See Article 10(2) of the Statute of the International Criminal Tribunal for the Former Yugoslavia as adopted on 25 May 1993. and as amended.

[50] Rome Statute of the International Criminal Court, 2187 U.N.T.S. 90; (1998) 37 *I.L.M.* 1002, article 17(2).

[51] See the cases under the keyword "International Criminal Court" referred to in the ICRC's database on national case-law, including, on jurisdiction generally, at http://www.icrc.org/ihl-nat.nsf/WebKWD?OpenView, and see, for example Chile: Constitutional Court, *Case No. 346*, 8 April 2002; France: Decision 98–408 DC of 22 January 1999 – Treaty on the Statute of the International Criminal Court, in *Journal Officiel*, No. 20, 24 January 1999, at 1317; Ukraine: Opinion of the Constitutional Court on the conformity of the Rome Statute with the Constitution of Ukraine, Case No. 1–35/2001, 11 July 2001; Ecuador: *Consulta preceptiva de consitucionalidad sobre el proyecto de ley de aprobacion del "Estado de Roma de la Corte Penal Intenacional"*, Exp. 00–008325–0007–CO, Res. 2000–09685, 1 November 2000.

Table (*cont.*)

Canada	United Kingdom

rely on any justification, excuse or defence available under the laws of Canada or under international law at the time of the alleged offence or at the time of the proceedings.	under this Part has been committed the court shall apply the principles of the law of England and Wales.
	
	(2) Nothing in this Part shall be read as restricting the operation of any enactment or rule of law relating to:
	
	    (a) the extra-territorial application of offences (including offences under this Part), or
	
	    (b) offences ancillary to offences under this Part (wherever committed).

4) OTTAWA ANTI-PERSONNEL LANDMINES CONVENTION

Both countries adopted specific legislation in order to put in place their obligations under the 1997 Anti-personnel Landmines Treaty. The implementation of this Convention has been fairly consistent throughout the common law world.[52] Some states have chosen not to adopt legislation, although it is important to ensure that states are able to prosecute all violations of the Convention through their pre-existing legislation.[53]

---

[52] Implementing legislation adopted by common law States is often similar to the ICRC Model Law on the Ottawa Convention, see http://www.icrc.org/Web/Eng/ siteeng0.nsf/htmlall/section_ihl_nat_model_laws?OpenDocument. Stuart Maslen has written a commentary to the Convention, *Commentaries on Arms Control Treaties Volume I, The Convention on the Prohibition of the Use, Stockpiling, Production, and Transfer of Anti-Personnel Mines and on their Destruction* (Oxford: University Press, 2004). An issue not covered here is the consequence on the inter-operability of forces where the forces of at least one country are not party to the Convention, see C. W. Jacobs, "Taking the Next Step: An Analysis of the Effects the Ottawa Convention may have on the Interoperability of Unites States Forces with the Armed Forces of Australia, Great Britain, and Canada" (2004) 180 Mil. L. Rev. 49.

[53] Maslen, *ibid.*, at 248. In the implementation of prohibitions in such treaties, most countries require knowing the maximum and minimum fines and sentences applicable, for example.

a) *Definitions*

Canada[54]	United Kingdom[55]
"anti-personnel mine" means a mine that is designed, altered or intended to be exploded by the presence, proximity or contact of a person and that is capable of incapacitating, injuring or killing one or more persons.	(2) An anti-personnel mine is a landmine which – (a) is designed to be detonated by the presence, proximity or contact of an individual; and (b) is capable of incapacitating, injuring or killing an individual.

Both countries' legislation is based on that found in the Convention, and include provisions related to anti-handling devices. The Canadian definition, however, goes beyond the Convention, including "altered" and "intended" as well as designed.[56] This may be important, for example, in reference to remotely detonated mines which might be altered to explode on contact. The Canadian definition is also presumably not limited to *land-based* mines. The definition from the Convention (article 2(1)) is:

> "Anti-personnel mine" means a mine designed to be exploded by the presence, proximity or contact of a person and that will incapacitate, injure or kill one or more persons. Mines designed to be detonated by the presence, proximity or contact of a vehicle as opposed to a person, that are equipped with anti-handling devices, are not considered anti-personnel mines as a result of being so equipped.

b) *Fact-finding missions*

Both countries provide for a fact-finding mission to visit their country. Canada is more specific in referencing article 8 of the Convention and in describing the

---

[54] Anti-Personnel Mines Convention Implementation Act 1997 (Canada), c. 33.

[55] Landmines Act 1998 (U.K.), c. 33.

[56] For a discussion of the debate on the definition in the Ottawa Treaty negotiations, see Maslen, *supra* note 52 at 111–114. This is one instance in which it is possible that the definitions used differ because of a position at the treaty drafting stage, in the discussion of a function-based approach (broader definition, e.g. Norway's approach) or an intention-based approach (such as promoted by the UK). See also the VERTIC *Guide to fact-finding missions under the Ottawa Convention* available at http://www.vertic.org/publications.html.

work of a mission, but the effect appears to be the same. Both Canada and the UK provide for assistance of public authorities in the work of a fact-finding mission and allow them to participate in the on-site inspections.

Canada	United Kingdom
12. (1) If a fact-finding mission to Canada is authorized under Article 8 of the Convention, the Minister shall issue to every member of the fact-finding mission a certificate	15. (1) Members of a fact-finding mission shall enjoy –
(*a*) identifying the member by name and indicating the member's status and authority to conduct a fact-finding mission in Canada;	(a) immunity from suit and legal process in respect of things done or omitted to be done by them in the carrying out of their functions under the Ottawa Convention;
(*b*) stating that the member enjoys the privileges and immunities under Article VI of the Convention on the Privileges and Immunities of the United Nations, adopted on February 13, 1946; and	(b) the like immunity from personal arrest or detention and the like inviolability for all papers and documents as, in accordance with the 1961 Articles, are accorded to a diplomatic agent; and
(*c*) setting out such other information and any conditions applicable to the member's fact-finding activities in Canada as the Minister considers advisable.	(c) the like exemptions and privileges in respect of their personal baggage as, in accordance with Article 36 of the 1961 Articles, are accorded to a diplomatic agent.
	(5) In this section "the 1961 Articles" means the Articles which are set out in Schedule 1 to the Diplomatic Privileges Act 1964 (Articles of Vienna Convention on Diplomatic Relations of 1961 having force of law in the United Kingdom)

c) *Information gathering powers*

Both countries provide for information gathering powers in order to be able to report to the Assembly of States Parties as required by the Convention:

Canada	United Kingdom
11. (1) The Minister may send a notice to any person who the Minister believes on reasonable grounds has information or documents relevant to the administration or enforcement of this Act, or information that Canada is required by Article 7 of the Convention to report to the Secretary-General of the United Nations, requesting the person to provide the information or documents to the Minister, or to such person as may be designated by the Minister, within a reasonable time specified in the notice.	*Information and records* Information and records for Ottawa Convention purposes. 17. (1) The Secretary of State may, by notice served on any person, require him to give, in such form and within such reasonable period as is specified in the notice, such information as – (a) the Secretary of State has reasonable cause to believe is or will be needed in connection with anything to be done for the purposes of the Ottawa Convention, and (b) is described in the notice; and the information required by a notice may relate to a state of affairs subsisting before the coming into force of this Act or of the Ottawa Convention.

Experience has shown that this is a particularly useful clause for the information-gatherer, and assists in the process of reporting to the Assembly of States Parties.[57] The UK provision is potentially slightly broader, allowing the Secretary of State to gather information in connection with "anything to be done for the purposes of the Ottawa Convention" while the Canadian provision provides powers to gather information relevant to "the administration or enforcement" of the Act.

---

[57] See, for example, the ICRC Information Kit on National Implementation of the *Ottawa Treaty* [http://www.icrc.org/web/eng/siteeng0.nsf/html/57JR2C?Open Document]: "States Parties should consider whether implementing legislation should confer information-gathering powers on the minister responsible for filing these reports and require disclosure of information on AP mines. States may need to review national laws to ensure that they do not impede access to, and full disclosure of, information required to fulfil the Article 7 reporting obligation."

d) *Search and seizure provisions*

Both countries have provisions permitting the fact-finding missions to under-take searches in their country. Most common law states which have similar pro-visions allow for judicial applications for searches and then have them backed up by the police where necessary.

Canada	United Kingdom
15. (1) If the place to be inspected is not a dwelling-house, a member of the fact-finding mission or a designated person accompanying the member may not enter the place without the consent of the person who is in control of the place, except under the authority of a warrant issued under subsection (2).	Power to search and obtain evidence. 18. (1) If –
Authority to issue warrant	(a) a justice of the peace is satisfied, on information on oath, that there are grounds for issuing a warrant under this subsection in relation to any premises, or
(2) On *ex parte* application, a justice may issue a warrant authorizing members of the fact-finding mission and the designated persons accompanying them to enter a place for the purposes of the inspection, subject to such conditions as may be specified in the warrant, if the justice is satisfied by information on oath that	(b) in Scotland, a justice (within the meaning of section 307 of the Criminal Procedure (Scotland) Act 1995) is so satisfied by evidence on oath, he may issue a warrant in writing authorising a person acting under the authority of the Secretary of State to enter the premises, if necessary by force, at any time within one month from the time of the issue of the warrant and to search them.
(*a*) there are reasonable grounds to believe that the members may find at that place any information, document or other thing that is relevant to compliance with the Convention;	. (2) There are grounds for issuing a warrant under subsection (1) in relation to any premises if there are reasonable grounds for suspecting –
(*b*) entry to the place is necessary for any purpose relating to the fact-finding mission; and	(a) that an offence under this Act is being, has been or is about to be committed on the premises; or
(*c*) entry to the place has been refused, there are reasonable grounds to believe that entry will be refused or there has been a failure to comply with a direction under section 13 in respect of the place.	(b) that evidence of the commission of such an offence is to be found on the premises.

While the Canadian legislation makes clear that this is on an *ex parte* application, it is presumed that this would also be the case with the UK legislation as giving the party concerned notice of an intention to search may defeat the purpose of a warrant. Although Canada is normally associated with jurisdictional questions arising from federal and provincial competences, interestingly, here such questions do not arise, while the UK makes reference to the different procedure to be followed in Scotland.

5) CONCLUSION

This paper is but an introduction to domestic implementation of IHL obligations in general and for Canada and the UK in particular. It touches on a small number of important implementation elements, and highlights where there are differences. A summary follows:

Subject Matter	**Wording and effects**
GCs – Grave breaches	Similar
GCs – Protected persons	Similar
GCs – Emblem	Different law used and different in substance
ICC – Crimes incorporation	Different approach
ICC – Command responsibility	Similar
ICC – Universal jurisdiction	Differences
ICC – Ne bis in idem	Different
ICC – Defences	Different
Ottawa – Definition	Different
Ottawa – Fact finding missions	Similar
Ottawa – information gathering powers	Similar
Ottawa – Search and seizure powers	Similar

Of the twelve examples examined,

- In no case was the wording used identical in Canada and the UK;
- in six examples, the wording and effect were similar;
- in six examples, the approach taken by the two countries differed; and
- the greatest differences appeared in the ICC implementing legislation.

Further study would need to be undertaken to conclude with certainty as to the reasons for the differences that exist in the two countries' approaches to the incorporation of international norms. It appears, however, that where different approaches are permissible according to the international instrument which is being implemented, the simple fact that the legislation is being drafted independently leads to different approaches. It also appears that the more complex an instrument, such as the Rome Statute, the more likely states are to choose a variety of means to implement the obligations in the treaty. Other factors, such as the internal (e.g. federal structure) and external (e.g. membership in the European Union) constitutional order, as well as policy considerations at the treaty-drafting stage may also affect the choices made in implementation.

Chapter 3

The International Criminal Court and Domestic Enforcement in Canada and the United Kingdom

James Sloan

1) INTRODUCTION

Since the Rome Statute of the International Criminal Court ("Rome Statute")[1] was agreed to in July 1998, the question of the reach of the International Criminal Court (ICC) has frequently arisen. That is to say, when will it exercise jurisdiction over a case, rather than leaving the matter to state courts? A concern that the ICC will pre-empt national justice systems is among those raised by the United States in its staunch refusal to become a member state.[2] Many, however, dismiss this concern as not being realistic given the many checks and

---

[1] Rome Statute of the International Criminal Court (text circulated as document A/CONF.183/9 of 17 July 1998 and corrected by procès-verbaux of 10 November 1998, 12 July 1999, 30 November 1999, 8 May 2000, 17 January 2001 and 16 January 2002). The Statute entered into force on 1 July 2002. ["Rome Statute"]. All references to "Article(s)" in this discussion will be to the Rome Statute.

[2] See, e.g., D. Scheffer, "The United States and the International Criminal Court" 93 (1999) A.J.I.L. 12.

Christopher P.M. Waters (Ed.), *British and Canadian Perspectives on International Law*, pp. 53–68.

balances in place to ensure the ICC only takes up a matter in limited circumstances.[3] More recently the issue is becoming relevant in those states which
have ratified the Rome Statute. At a session of the House of Lords in July 2005,
where members of the House sought assurance that British service personnel
would not be prosecuted by the ICC, the position of the Bristish government
was said to be that it would take "a catastrophic failure of the UK justice system for the ICC to assume jurisdiction."[4] A senior legal advisor went so far as
to invoke the words of the former Foreign Secretary, Robin Cook, in 2001, that
British service personnel will "never" be prosecuted by the International
Criminal Court.[5]

In the following discussion I want to consider the question of when, if ever,
individuals who have been (or are being) dealt with under the British or the
Canadian justice systems might end up before the ICC. I will contest the view
that British service personnel may "never" be prosecuted, and discuss the ways
in which they, or their Canadian counterparts, might be susceptible to the jurisdiction of the ICC. Key to understanding the ICC's reach and predicting how it
is likely to function is an understanding of the concept of complementarity, one
of the Rome Statute's fundamental principles.[6] Therefore, I will begin by considering the complementary relationship between national judicial systems and
the ICC. Next I will consider the legislation in place in Canada and Britain to
ensure that the crimes under the ICC's jurisdiction are prosecuted nationally.
And, finally, I will consider when, if ever, the justice systems in either state
might be found wanting, with the result that the International Criminal Court
would be required to step into the breach.

---

[3] See, e.g., M. Zwanenburg, "The Statute for an International Criminal Court and the
United States: Peacekeepers Under Fire?" (1999) 10 E.J.I.L. 124.

[4] *Official Report*, Lords, 14/7/2005; col. 1262.

[5] At the Second Reading of the International Criminal Court Bill in the House of
Commons, then Foreign Secretary Robin Cook, told the House that "Members on both
sides of the House should have a robust confidence that the British legal system has adequate remedies for crimes against humanity and can satisfactorily demonstrate to the
International Criminal Court that any such allegations have been properly investigated
and, where appropriate, prosecuted. In short, British service personnel will never be
prosecuted by the International Criminal Court because any bona fide allegation will
be pursued by the British authorities." *Official Report*, Commons, 3/4/2001; col. 222.
(http://www.publications.parliament.uk/pa/cm200001/cmhansrd/vo010403/debtext/
10403–17.htm#10403–17_spnew7).

[6] See M. Arsanjani, "The Rome Statue of the International Criminal Court," (1999)
93 A.J.I.L. 22 at 24–25.

2) COMPLEMENTARITY

The word complementarity is not defined in the Rome Statute. According to the Oxford English Dictionary, it describes a relationship between two bodies which work collaboratively, each with its own particular strengths, "mutually complementing or completing each other's deficiencies."[7] In this case, of course, the two bodies are national judicial systems and the ICC. While the term may suggest that the ICC and states are equal players in the prosecution of violations of international criminal law – and, based on the excitement surrounding the establishment of the Court, it would appear that many perceive the ICC as being the *lead* player in this regard – the Rome Statute makes it clear that the ICC is subservient to national systems. It is only to act in very limited circumstances. Before a matter may come before the ICC that Court's jurisdiction must be "triggered" by a state party, the Security Council or the Prosecutor.[8] In addition, other jurisdictional hurdles must be cleared before there may be a prosecution before the ICC. First, and perhaps most obviously, the crimes must correspond to those in the Rome Statue – genocide, war crimes, crimes against humanity and (eventually)[9] aggression. This means that international crimes not dealt with by the Rome Statute, for example drug trafficking, may not be tried by the ICC. Second, the crimes must have occurred after the entry into force of the Statute.[10] Third, the crimes must be of sufficient gravity.[11]

Even where these hurdles are cleared, however, the concept of complementarity will step in to prevent a matter from being admissible before the ICC if the relevant national criminal justice systems are operational and acting in good faith. This reflects a desire on the part of the drafters of the Rome Statue to ensure that national sovereignty was not unduly impinged upon.[12] Where a state

---

[7] Oxford English Dictionary online on "complementary": http://dictionary.oed.com.

[8] See Articles 13–15.

[9] While included in the Rome Statue (at Article 5(1)(d)), aggression is not yet a crime over which the Court may exercise jurisdiction (see Article 5(2)).

[10] Article 11.

[11] Article 17(1)(d). Also Article 1 provides that the ICC shall "exercise its jurisdiction over persons for the most serious crimes of international concern." Note this is referred to by some as a matter of "admissibility" rather than one of "jurisdiction." There is a certain overlap in the concepts. See, e.g., W. Schabas, *An Introduction to the International Criminal Court* (Cambridge: Cambridge University Press, 2001) at 54–56.

[12] J. T. Holmes, "The Principle of Complementarity" in R. S. Lee, ed., *The International Criminal Court: The Making of the Rome Statute Issues, Negotiations, Results* (The Hague: Kluwer Law International, 1999) 41 at 41 ["Holmes in Lee"].

which has jurisdiction is investigating or prosecuting a matter or has decided the matter does not warrant prosecution, the Court must defer to that state unless that state was "unwilling or unable genuinely" to investigate or prosecute the matter.[13] Where a state has already prosecuted, the ICC will not be able to reconsider the matter unless the original prosecution was designed to shield the accused or lacking in independence or impartiality.[14]

In short, it becomes clear that the ICC will take up a matter only in the rarest and most extraordinary circumstances. Indeed the complementarity approach has been criticized by one commentator as "kow-tow[ing] to state sovereignty."[15] However, that is not to say that a matter may *never* be taken up. We will next consider the provisions at the national level in Canada and the United Kingdom for the enforcement of the crimes under the Rome Statute. Armed with an understanding of the Canadian and UK systems, we will then look closely at the Rome Statute's provisions on complementarity in order to attempt to predict when, if ever, a matter which has been (or which is being) dealt with by either state might come before the ICC.

3) IMPLEMENTING LEGISLATION

a) *Canada*

Canada is rightfully proud of the fact that it was the first country in the world to adopt comprehensive national legislation on the implementation of the Rome Statute of the ICC.[16] Canada's Federal Government, which has authority over matters of criminal law and criminal procedure under Section 91(27) of the *Constitution Act*, 1867, passed the Crimes Against Humanity and War Crimes Act, (2000, c. 24) – the "Canadian Act" – on 24 June 2000,[17] some two weeks before it ratified the Rome Statute on 9 July 2000. The Act provides that every person who commits crimes against humanity, war crimes or genocide[18] within Canada,[19] is guilty of an indictable offence and liable to imprisonment for life.[20]

---

[13] Article 17(1)(a)-(b). This test will be explored further *infra* at Sections 4(a) and (b).

[14] Article 20 of the Rome Statute. This test will be explored further *infra* at Section 4(c).

[15] D. Herman, "A Dish Best Not Served at All: How Foreign Military War Crimes Suspects Lack Protection under United States and International Law" (2002) 172 Mil. L. Rev. 40 at 86, quoting Geoffrey Robertson.

[16] See http://www.dfait-maeci.gc.ca/foreign_policy/icc/crimes-en.asp.

[17] It received Royal Assent on 29 June 2000.

[18] Section 4(4).

[19] Section 4(1).

[20] Section 4(2).

Moreover, it makes provision for liability of superiors[21] and for those found guilty of ancillary offences such as conspiracy, attempt, being an accessory after the fact or counselling the commission of any such offence.[22] The Canadian Act also provides for the prosecution of, *inter alia*, Canadian citizens and members of the Canadian military who commit genocide, crimes against humanity or war crimes *outside* Canada.[23]

As it would appear that members of the Canadian military are most likely to be in situations where allegations of such crimes could arise, it is appropriate to consider what rules apply to them.[24] In addition to being subject to the ordinary laws that apply to all citizens, members of the military are subject to additional liabilities under the Canadian military justice system, including the Code of Service Discipline.[25] The need for a distinct system of military justice has been recognised by the Supreme Court of Canada, citing the need to maintain a state of readiness and the possible need to enforce internal discipline more severely than with civilians.[26] Where offences under the Canadian Act are alleged to have been committed by a person subject to the Code of Service Discipline *inside* Canada, they will be dealt with by the normal, civilian criminal courts;[27] where such crimes are alleged to have occurred *outside* Canada they will be dealt with under military law.[28]

It is a fundamental tenant of the Canadian criminal law that the Prosecution has discretion in deciding whether to prosecute a matter.[29] Courts are loath to

---

[21] Section 5(1) and (2).

[22] Section 5(2)(1).

[23] Sections 6–8. Note the Canadian Act does not provide for prosecution for the crime of aggression.

[24] The Government of Canada is granted exclusive jurisdiction over members of the military under the Constitution Act, 1867 at Section 91(7). Canadian military justice is found primarily in the National Defence Act (R.S. 1985, c. N-5) ("NDA") and the Queen's Regulations and Orders for the Canadian Forces. "The NDA authorizes the Governor in Council and the Minister of National Defence to make regulations for the organization, training, discipline, efficiency, administration and good government of the [Canadian Forces] and, generally, for carrying the purposes and provisions of the NDA into effect." (See "Report of the Judge Advocate General to the Minister of National Defence on the Administration of Military Justice in the Canadian Forces," (1 April 2002–31 March 2003) 5. (available to download at http://www.forces.gc.ca/jag/office/publications/annual_reports/2003annualreport_e.pdf)).

[25] The Code of Service Discipline is found at the Second Division of the NDA.

[26] *MacKay v. The Queen*, [1980] 2 S.C.R. 370 and *R. v. Généreux*, [1992] 1 S.C.R. 259. See also the Judge Advocate General's Report, *supra* note 24 at 50-51.

[27] See section 15(2)(a) of the Canadian Act, read in conjunction with section 70 of the NDA.

[28] Section 130(1)(b) of the NDA.

[29] See D. MacNair, "Crown Prosecutors and Conflict of Interest: A Canadian

review decisions of the executive as to whether to prosecute or not and will only do so in narrow circumstances, such as when there is "flagrant impropriety" or bad faith.[30] The prosecution of persons – civilian or military – under the Canadian Act is no exception. It provides that proceedings may only be commenced with the personal consent in writing of the Attorney General or Deputy Attorney General of Canada and that proceedings must be conducted by them or counsel acting on their behalf.[31]

b) *UK*

On 1 September 2001 the International Criminal Court Act 2001, (2001 Chapter 17)[32] (the "UK Act") came into force[33] implementing the provisions of the Rome Statute in England, Wales and Northern Ireland. While many of the provisions of the Act extend to Scotland, a separate Act – the International

---

Perspective" (2002) 7 Can. Crim. L. Rev. 257. In the words of Justice L'Heureux-Dubé: "It is manifest that, as a matter of principle and policy, courts should not interfere with prosecutorial discretion. This appears clearly to stem from the respect of separation of powers and the rule of law. Under the doctrine of separation of powers, criminal law is in the domain of the executive." (*R. v. Power*, [1994] 1 S.C.R. 601 at 621–623). See also *Krieger v. Law Society of Alberta*, [2002] 3 S.C.R. 372, where Justices Iacobucci and Major noted at para. 43: "Prosecutorial discretion refers to the use of those powers that constitute the core of the Attorney General's office and which are protected from the influence of improper political and other vitiating factors by the principle of independence."

[30] See *Krieger, ibid.*, paras 48 and 49 and para. 3 where the Court observed "So long as they are made honestly and in good faith, prosecutorial decisions related to this authority are protected by the doctrine of prosecutorial discretion." Despite a large measure of discretion, the Attorney General is accountable to Parliament and the public and will still be expected to consult before making a decision, including with Cabinet colleagues and possibly the police. Moreover, he or she is expected to consider the position of the individual and what public interest demands and to act with dignity and fairness. See *The Federal Prosecution Service Deskbook*, (para. 8.1, available at http://canada.justice.gc.ca/en/dept/pub/fps/fpd/ch08.html); see also D.C. Morgan, "Controlling Prosecutorial Powers – Judicial Review, Abuse of Process and Section 7 of The Charter" (1986) 29 Crim. L.Q. 15 at 18–19). The Director of Military Prosecution possesses a similar prosecutorial discretion. See Annex A of the Annual Report, *supra* note 24.

[31] Section 9(3). This requirement of the personal involvement of the Attorney General or Deputy is an uncommon feature. Normally such discretion would be delegated to Crown attorneys as agents of the Attorney General. (See, e.g., *Krieger, ibid.*, per Iacobucci and Major, JJ., para. 42.).

[32] Available at http://www.opsi.gov.uk/acts/en2001/01en17–c.htm.

[33] Sections 7(3), 13(3); 49, 50(3), 79(3) and 80(3) came into force on 13 June 2001.

Criminal Court (Scotland) Act (the "Scottish Act") – was passed to deal with matters that fall within the competence of the Scottish Parliament.[34] Both the UK Act and the Scottish Act incorporate the offences in the Rome Statute into domestic law, relying on the definitions set out therein.[35] According to the terms of the two Acts, it is an offence for anyone to commit crimes against humanity, war crimes or genocide[36] (and offences ancillary thereto) in England,[37] Wales,[38] Northern Ireland[39] or Scotland.[40] Where an offence is committed outside the UK it is an offence against the laws of England, Wales, Northern Ireland and Scotland when committed by a UK national or a UK resident and against the laws of England and Wales only[41] when committed by a person subject to UK service jurisdiction.[42]

Insofar as the application of the law to the military, the situation in the UK is similar to that in Canada. Military personnel continue to be subject to the British laws generally applicable to all, but their "civilian status is modified by the superimposition of a military status. On the whole, the result is that certain rights and freedoms are restricted in order to preserve military discipline and readiness."[43] In the UK, military justice derives from the Naval Discipline Act 1957, the Army Act 1955 and the Air Force Act 1955 (collectively the Service Discipline Acts). As with the Canadian system, crimes over which the ICC has jurisdiction which were alleged to have been committed within the country by military personnel would be dealt with by national civil courts; where such offences were alleged to have been committed overseas, they would be dealt with by court martial.[44]

---

[34] The UK Act deals with certain matters reserved to the UK government under the Scotland Act, 1998 as well as certain matters which, though devolved to the Scottish Parliament, were felt by it to be more conveniently dealt with on a UK-wide basis. See Explanatory Notes at http://www.opsi.gov.uk/acts/en2001/01en17–b.htm.

[35] Section 50(1) of the UK Act and section 1(4) of the Scottish Act.

[36] Both the UK Act (at section 1(1) and the Scotland Act (at section 27(1)) specifically exclude the crime of aggression (see *supra* note 9).

[37] Sections 51 and 52 of the UK Act.

[38] *Ibid*.

[39] Sections 58 and 59 of the UK Act.

[40] Sections 1 and 2 of the Scottish Act. Proceedings against commanders and other superiors are provided at section 65 of the UK Act and at section 5 of the Scottish Act.

[41] Section 51(2)(a) of the UK Act. Prosecution of the same persons for ancillary offences is provided at Section 52(4)(b).

[42] See sections 67, 68 and 70 of the UK Act and section 6 of the Scottish Act.

[43] See "The Armed Forces Discipline Bill [HL]: Bill 53 of 1999/2000," Research Paper, 2000: http://www.parliament.uk/commons/lib/research/rp2000/rp00-012.pdf).

[44] See Section 70(3) of the Army Act 1955 (3 & 4 Eliz. 2c. 18), section 70(3) of the Air Force Act 1995 (3 & 4 Eliz. 2c. 19) and section 42(1)(b) of the Naval Discipline Act 1957 (c. 53).

Proceedings under the UK Act may not be instituted except with the consent of the Attorney General (in England and Wales) or the Attorney General for Northern Ireland (in Ireland).[45] This is normally done in consultation with the Crown Prosecution Service. As in Canada, prosecutorial discretion is a fundamental tenet of the system.[46] Typically factors such as the ability to gain a conviction, the nature of the crime, the potential harm to national security, the best interests of the general public or the best interests of the Service will affect the decision as to whether to prosecute.[47]

4) WHEN MIGHT THE ICC PLAY A ROLE IN A MATTER WITHIN THE JURISDICTION OF CANADA OR THE UK?

As we have seen, the ways in which a matter may come before the ICC are limited. However, let us assume that a matter which would normally fall under the jurisdiction of the Canadian or the British courts were taken up by the Prosecutor of the ICC.[48] In order for the matter to go forward under the complementarity rules, it would fall to the Prosecutor to prove that the state in question was unwilling or genuinely unable to investigate or prosecute or, where the state had prosecuted, that it had been a prosecution designed to shield the accused or lacking in independence or impartiality. Proving such matters would appear to be a difficult task, prompting one observer to remark that "the nature of the 'unwillingness' and 'inability' tests will in many cases demand greater resources . . . than proving the guilt of the alleged perpetrator."[49] We will divide the following discussion into three parts, corresponding with the three bases on which the ICC could argue that it was empowered to try a matter notwithstanding the previous involvement of the UK or Canadian justice system:[50] a) where there was an inability to prosecute b) where there was an unwillingness to pros-

---

[45] Sections 53(3) and 60(3).

[46] See A. Ashworth, "Developments in the Public Prosecutor's Office in England and Wales" 8 (2000) Eur. J. Crime, Crim. L. & Crim. Just. 257 at 257.

[47] *The Code for Crown Prosecutors*, issued by the Director of Public Prosecutions under section 10 of the *Prosecution of Offences Act* 1985, gives guidance on the general principles to be applied when making decisions about prosecutions: http://www.cps.gov.uk/publications/docs/code2004english.pdf.

[48] We will assume that there has been an appropriate triggering mechanism and that the requisite jurisdiction exists as discussed in section 2 *supra*. We will assume further that the Prosecutor considers the matter to represent an appropriate exercise of his discretion.

[49] M. Bergsmo "The Jurisdictional Regime of the International Criminal Court (Part II, Articles 11–19)" (1998) 6 Eur. J. of Crime, Crim. L. and Crim. Just. 43.

[50] The reference to the "involvement" of the UK or Canadian legal system includes the scenario where either national system decides not to take any action. This would be

ecute or c) where a prosecution took place which was designed to shield the accused or lacked independence or impartiality.

a) *Inability by Canada or Britain to investigate or prosecute*

Turning first to the question of inability, the following test is set out at Article 17(3) of the Statute:

> In order to determine inability in a particular case, the Court shall consider whether, due to a total or substantial collapse or unavailability of its national judicial system, the State is unable to obtain the accused or the necessary evidence and testimony or otherwise unable to carry out its proceedings.

Before the ICC may find a matter admissible based on a state's inability to investigate or prosecute, two tests must be met. First, the Court must determine that the state is a) unable to obtain the accused, b) unable to obtain the necessary evidence and testimony or c) otherwise unable carry out its proceedings. Second, the Court must find that one of the elements at a), b) or c) *results from* a total or substantial collapse or unavailability of its national judicial system.[51] In order to be admissible based on inability, a state must not only be unable to investigate or prosecute in circumstances that satisfy these two tests, it must be unable *genuinely* to do so.[52] Depending on the ICC's interpretation, this might be considered yet another element of the test for admissibility.[53]

---

tantamount to the state investigating and deciding not to prosecute and the matter would be considered using the "unable or unwilling tests" – unless the state took no action under its own legal system because it intended to refer the matter to the ICC. In such a case, which is beyond the scope of this discussion, the state is effectively waiving complementarity. For more on this concept, see C. Kress, " 'Self-Referrals' and 'Waivers of Complementarity': Some Considerations in Law and Policy" (2004) 2 J. Int'l Crim. Just. 944.

[51] If the phrase "or otherwise unable to carry out its proceedings" were read to represent a separate test which is not linked to the collapse or unavailability of the state's justice system it would open up the scope of the provision considerably. However such a reading seems unlikely given the wording of the provision. Nor would this appear to be what the drafters intended; see J. T. Holmes, "Complementarity: National Courts *versus* the ICC" in A. Cassese, P. Geata and J. R. W. D. Jones, eds., *The Rome Statute of the International Criminal Court: A Commentary* 667 at 678 ["Holmes in Cassese"] and Holmes in Lee, *supra* note 12 at 49 where he notes that both "criteria must be met for the Court to determine admissibility in this regard."

[52] Article 17(1)(a) refers to a State being "unwilling or unable genuinely to carry out the investigation or prosecution"; article 17(1)(b) refers to the "unwillingness or inability of the State genuinely to prosecute."

[53] Alternatively, a Court might consider that, by virtue of the two-part test at Article

Applying the second aspect of the test to the situation in Canada and the UK, it is clear that a finding by the ICC that either state's justice system had totally or substantially collapsed would be unimaginable. In this context, therefore, there is no need to consider whether the elements in the first part of the test might be met. Somewhat less unimaginable, however, would be a determination that the justice system in Canada or the UK was unavailable.[54] This term is not defined; nor is it clear whether the words "total or substantial" qualify "collapse" alone or whether they also qualify "unavailability." If so the test for unavailability would be much higher. The three factors listed – inability to obtain the accused, inability to obtain necessary evidence and testimony or inability to otherwise carry out proceedings – provide some guidance as to what would be relevant in a finding of inability based on unavailability. The first factor is relatively objective; the second less so (people could easily disagree as to whether evidence and testimony is "necessary"); and the third factor is quite subjective and open to broad interpretation.[55]

Although consideration of the drafting history suggests that states favoured a high test for inability – both as it pertained to collapse and unavailability[56] – based on the text alone, there is certainly scope for the Canadian or British system to be considered by the ICC to be unavailable. It would be more difficult to argue that the unavailability of the justice system in either country was "total or

---

17(2) for inability being met, such inability was, *ipso facto*, genuine. Holmes notes that during the drafting process the term "genuinely" was favoured by some as providing a more objective connotation than alternative words such as "effectively." Holmes in Lee, *supra* note 12 at 49–50. (Holmes was referring to the word in the context of the definition of unwillingness, but the word came to be used to modify both unwillingness and inability.) See also M. M. El Zeidy, "The Principle of Complementarity: A New Machinery to Implement International Criminal Law" (2002) 23 Mich. J. Int'l L. 869 at 900.

[54] Note, however, that many commentators appear to consider "collapse or unavailability" as being a single concept, rather than alternatives and focus on the concept of collapse. See, e.g. Holmes in Lee, *supra* note 12 and El Zeidy, *ibid*.

[55] For example, according to Holmes, it was thought by the drafters to include matters such as "the absence of sufficient qualified personnel to effect a genuine prosecution." Holmes in Cassese, *supra* note 51 at 678.

[56] Holmes traces the development of the admissibility test from one of "may not be available or may be ineffective" in the International Law Commission's Draft Statute to the current wording. (See Preamble, Draft Statute for an International Criminal Court Prepared by the International Law Commission in Report of the International Law Commission on the Work of its Forty-sixth Session, United Nations General Assembly Official Records, Forty-ninth Session, Supplement No. 10, A/49/10 (1994), paras. 42–91.) Clearly one of the concerns of many states was that the original test was too vague or too intrusive and their objective was to narrow the concept of inability. Holmes in Lee, *supra* note 12 at 43–56.

substantially." One example might be where a Canadian prosecutor felt she was unable to obtain the necessary evidence to convict and therefore elected not to bring a case against an individual present in Canada and alleged to have committed crimes which would fall under the Canadian Act. Depending on how active the ICC was, it is certainly possible that it could determine that the Canadian judicial system was "unavailable" or even "substantially unavailable" due to it being "otherwise unable to carry out its proceedings." Similarly, it is not beyond the scope of possibility to imagine the ICC making a determination that the British justice system was "unavailable" due to its inability to "obtain the accused" in circumstances where a trial could not proceed due to an individual accused of breaching the UK Act having left the UK and not being subject to extradition.

While not as damning as a finding that the UK or Canadian justice systems were in "total or substantial collapse," a determination that those justice systems were "unavailable" or "totally or substantially unavailable" might well be controversial. The more so if the ICC was to find itself competent to review the exercise of prosecutorial discretion in Canada or the UK, a concept entrenched in both states as a prerogative of the executive and not normally subject to judicial scrutiny.

b) *Unwillingness by Canada or Britain to investigate or prosecute*

The test for when a state may be adjudged "unwilling genuinely" to investigate or prosecute is more elaborate still and caused considerable controversy in the drafting process.[57] Article 17(2) provides:

> In order to determine unwillingness in a particular case, the Court shall consider, having regard to the principles of due process recognized by international law, whether one or more of the following exist, as applicable:
>
> (a) The proceedings were or are being undertaken or the national decision was made for the purpose of shielding the person concerned from criminal responsibility for crimes within the jurisdiction of the Court referred to in article 5;
> (b) There has been an unjustified delay in the proceedings which in the circumstances is inconsistent with an intent to bring the person concerned to justice;
> (c) The proceedings were not or are not being conducted independently or impartially, and they were or are being conducted in a manner which, in the circumstances, is inconsistent with an intent to bring the person concerned to justice.

In short, there are two elements to a determination by the ICC that a matter is admissible based on a state's unwillingness to investigate or prosecute. First, a matter must fall into one of three categories elaborated at 17(2)(a)-(c) and,

---

[57] Holmes in Lee, *supra* note 12 at 49.

second, regard must be had to "the principles of due process recognized by international law." As with inability above, there may also be a requirement for a determination that the unwillingness is genuine.[58]

Turning to the first aspect of the test, we see that each of the three bases has a high threshold. The first basis for a determination that a state was unwilling to prosecute would appear to be aimed at "sham trials."[59] Proving that the proceedings were "for the purpose of shielding the person," would appear to be a difficult task for the ICC Prosecutor.[60] The second basis for a determination that a court is unwilling to investigate or prosecute, i.e., unjustified delay, would also appear difficult to prove. Not only is there an intent element – intent can be a particularly difficult factor to prove[61] – but the *travaux préparatoires* show the word "unjustified" was deliberately chosen (over the less demanding "undue") to ensure states were given the opportunity to explain away most delays.[62] The third basis, a lack of independence or impartially in national proceedings, has an intent requirement as well. As to the need to have regard to "the principles of due process recognized by international law," although this is a recognition of international human rights law, it would appear to have been inserted with a view to limiting the matters which would be admissible before the ICC. The wording was added in response to some delegations which were concerned that, without it, too much discretion would be vested in the Court.[63]

Predicting how the ICC might apply the above limitations to the Canadian or British justice systems is a difficult endeavour. A finding of "shielding" in either state seems unlikely. While it is not inconceivable that an individual judge or prosecutor in either jurisdiction might shield an accused from criminal responsibility or prosecution in either country, it is difficult to imagine that the justice system as a whole would collude with such an intention. Although govern-

---

[58] See *supra* note 52. However, matters are less clear than with inability. Because Article 17(1)(a) refers to "unwilling or unable genuinely," it is uncertain if the word genuinely modifies "unwilling" or just "unable." Similarly, Article 17(1)(b) of the Rome Statute refers to the "unwillingness or inability of the State genuinely to prosecute." Again it is uncertain if the wording is only dealing with a situation where a state is unable genuinely to prosecute or whether it also covers a situation where the state is unwilling genuinely to prosecute.

[59] Holmes in Lee, *supra* note 12 at 50. Note, it would appear that "proceedings" includes investigations and prosecutions. See El Zeidy, *supra* note 53 at 900, note 136).

[60] See Holmes in Lee, *ibid.* at 50.

[61] See El Zeidy, *supra* note 53 at 901 where he discusses the difficulty proving intent.

[62] Holmes in Lee, *supra* note 12 at 54; El Zeidy notes that this might allow a state to "act in bad faith and rely on an invented justification." (El Zeidy, *ibid.* at 901).

[63] Holmes in Lee, *supra* note 12 at 53. However, see El Zeidy, who notes that one commentator has taken the view that since the phrase is not defined, the Prosecutor is be left with a wide margin of discretion to meet the objective admissibility criteria. (El Zeidy, *ibid.* at 902 and note 152).

mental approval of a "sham trial" is not specifically required by the wording of Article 17(2)(a), it would appear that something more than individual malfeasance would be required. After all, if evidence of such malfeasance was available to the ICC, it would seem highly likely that it would have been available nationally and led to the prosecution of the individual who attempted to interfere with justice.[64]

As to unjustified delay or a lack of independence or impartiality, matters appear less clear. Such claims are not unheard of in either country. Indeed the UK system of military discipline has only recently been modified to address findings by the European Court of Human Rights that it lacked the requisite independence[65] and several of the recommendations of the Somalia Inquiry in Canada involved strengthening the independence of the military prosecuting authority.[66] At the same time, however, the high standard set in the wording of the provisions – including the requirement that the delay or lack of independence or impartiality be inconsistent with an intent to bring the accused to justice – must be borne in mind.

One area where there may be scope for arguing that it would be appropriate for the ICC to reconsider a determination made under the Canadian or British system that a matter did not warrant prosecution is related to prosecutorial discretion. If the decision not to prosecute was based on a lack of evidence, for example, it would be unlikely to attract the ICC's attention.[67] However, if the decision not to prosecute was based on a "public interest" factor such as a desire to avoid a complicated investigation or a fear of disclosure of confidential information, the Prosecutor of the ICC may feel an obligation to become involved. Here the Prosecutor could argue that the decision-making process

---

[64] Holmes notes that "while the State may genuinely be endeavoring to prosecute someone (and therefore shielding is not an issue), there may be individuals who manipulate the conduct of the proceedings to ensure that the accused are not found guilty (for example, engineering a mistrial or deliberately violating a defendant's rights [in order] to taint evidence or testimony)." The drafting group dealt with such a concern by adding the third basis, i.e. lack of independent and impartial proceedings. See Holmes in Lee *ibid.*, 50-51.

[65] See S. Rowlinson, "The British System of Military Justice" (2000) 52 Air Force Law Review 17 at 19–20.

[66] See *Report of the Commission of Inquiry into the Deployment of Canadian Forces in Somalia*, Recommendations, Chapter 40, in particular Chapter 40.22 where guidelines are called for "to assist in the exercise of prosecutorial discretion." (see http://www.dnd.ca/somalia/vol0/v0s28e.htm).

[67] Of course, the scenario could exist where the ICC possessed evidence which the national justice system did not. Presumably this would be solved by Canada or Britain "waiving complementarity" and requesting the ICC to prosecute or by the ICC sharing its evidence with the national court, so long as doing so did not violate matters of national security.

showed a lack of independence and set about to show that the requisite intent was present. Moreover, the ICC might even find that such a decision not to prosecute was designed to shield an accused.

c) *Previous prosecution by Canada or Britain*

Where an individual has already been tried nationally, he or she may not be retried by the ICC for the same conduct absent exceptional circumstance. This is the principle of *ne bis in idem* or double jeopardy. Article 20(3) provides:

> No person who has been tried by another court for conduct also proscribed under article 6, 7 or 8 shall be tried by the Court with respect to the same conduct unless the proceedings in the other court:
>
> (a) Were for the purpose of shielding the person concerned from criminal responsibility for crimes within the jurisdiction of the Court; or
> (b) Otherwise were not conducted independently or impartially in accordance with the norms of due process recognized by international law and were conducted in a manner which, in the circumstances, was inconsistent with an intent to bring the person concerned to justice.

The exception provided at Article 20(3)(a) is similar to the "sham trials" basis for inadmissibility based on unwillingness (Article 17(2)(a)) discussed above, except that the Article 20(3) provision lacks the requirement that regard be had for "the principles of due process recognized by international law" or the word "genuinely." At the same time, Article 20(3)(b) is similar to the lacking "independence or impartiality" basis for inadmissibility based on unwillingness (Article 17(2)(c)). Despite slight variations in the wording, the observations made above regarding the potential for a Canadian or British decision to be reviewed by the ICC based on a finding of a sham trial or a lack of independence or impartiality, would also apply here.[68]

As such, where an accused was tried in Canada or the UK, it would seem highly unlikely that the matter could come before the ICC – even where the accused was found not guilty, found guilty but sentenced to a minimal punishment,[69] or where he or she was tried "for a crime under ordinary criminal law

---

[68] Given the fact that with the "shielding" exception under Article 20(3)(a) due regard needn't be had to principles of due process recognised by international law – wording which the drafters inserted to limit the discretion of the Court (see *supra* note 63 and accompanying text) – it could be argued that the chances of a national decision being reviewed under this provision are higher than under Article 17(2)(a).

[69] "Unfortunately, as a result of the omission of earlier draft provisions, it may be difficult for the ICC, once it has deferred to a state, to exercise jurisdiction in the future if the national proceedings turn out not to be genuine." Human Rights Watch, *Summary*

such as murder, rather than for the truly international offences of genocide, crimes against humanity and war crimes."[70] As noted above,[71] proving that national proceedings[72] lacked independence or impartiality or were designed to shield an accused would be difficult.

5) CONCLUSION

The objective of this discussion was to determine when, if ever, individuals who have been (or are being) dealt with under the British or the Canadian justice systems might end up before the ICC. While it is impossible to predict how matters will unfold with any certainty, we can draw some conclusions based on the foregoing discussion. First, it is clear that the complementarity system under the Rome Statute was designed to be deferential to states. Only in the rarest cases will the ICC be empowered to step in. As Louise Arbour has pointed out, "the admissibility regime essentially requires the Prosecutor to put a domestic system of criminal justice on trial."[73]

Second, the provisions on admissibility discussed above do nevertheless leave scope for a matter which has been (or is being considered) under the Canadian or British justice systems to come before the ICC. Much, however, will depend on how they are interpreted. I believe that it would be wrong to suggest, as some commentators have, that the appropriate interpretation would be an extremely narrow one.[74] There may be times when it is appropriate for the

---

Of The Key Provisions Of The ICC Statute, September 1998: http://hrw.org/campaigns/icc/docs/icc-statute.htm.

[70] El Zeidy, *supra* note 53 at 934.

[71] See the discussion of unwillingness at 4 (b) *supra*.

[72] There is an issue as to whether the word "proceedings" in the chapeau of article 20(3) covers only the trial or whether it extends to the investigation or prosecution leading up to the trial. (See El Zeidy, *supra* note 53 at 935–937).

[73] A.M. Danner, "Enhancing the Legitimacy And Accountability of Prosecutorial Discretion at the International Criminal Court" (2003) 97 A.J.I.L. 510 at 517, quoting from Louise Arbour, "The Challenges of Litigation in the 21st Century: From the ad hoc Tribunals to the International Criminal Court" Address to the American Bar Association, Toronto (3 August 1998), 1998 ICTY Y.B. 445, 446, UN Sales No. E.00.III.P.

[74] One commentator notes that "in the absence of a finding that State officials had the specific intent to 'obstruct justice' by conducting a sham investigation or criminal prosecution, the principle of complementarity should require the ICC to grant 'substantial deference' to the national proceeding." J. Gurulé, "United States Opposition to the 1998 Rome Statute Establishing an International Criminal Court: Is the Court's Jurisdiction Truly Complementary to National Criminal Jurisdictions?" (2001–2002) 35 Cornell Int'l L.J. 1 at 28.

ICC to make a finding that the British or Canadian system is "unavailable" or possibly even "unwilling." Whether a matter being dealt with under the Canadian or British system ever ends up before the ICC will depend in large part on the will of the Prosecutor and, ultimately, the decisions of the Judges of the ICC. A number of factors will impact on how the Prosecutor will interpret the above tests, including his interpretation of the tests, his personality, how much political capital he possesses and whether the ICC's workload is such that he could find the time to pursue a case involving a national of a developed state like the UK or Canada. Ultimately, of course, the matter will rest on the Judges. Here it will be relevant how they view the role of the Court and whether they will have the courage or temerity (depending on how you see it), to question national judicial systems. The ICC will have to choose its battles very carefully.

While it may win me no friends among the many activists fighting in favour of American ratification to say it, I certainly hope that the United States has absolutely nothing to fear by ratifying the Rome Statute. Moreover, I hope that Robin Cook was wrong in his view that British service personnel will "never" be prosecuted by the International Criminal Court.[75] If it were the case that a member state of the Rome Statute with a fully functioning justice system – be it the UK, Canada or perhaps even the US one day – was beyond the reach of the ICC, then the Court would effectively be an institution to oversee the implementation of international criminal justice only for dysfunctional states or states which "waive" complementarity and request the ICC's involvement. I believe that in order for the ICC to be successful, it must have a role in overseeing the implementation of criminal justice in all countries – not merely those countries that are developing, transitional or led by tyrants.

---

[75] *Supra* note 5.

Chapter 4

Accountability for Crimes Against International Law in Canada: An overview and a comparison with UK practices

Helena Torroja*

1) INTRODUCTION

This chapter presents a general overview of the principal legal steps taken by Canada in moving from a culture of impunity to a culture of accountability in the field of crimes against international law,[1] and undertakes a comparative study of practices in the United Kingdom. The paper deals primarily with the prosecution in these states of those suspected of war crimes, crimes against

* The author thanks the International Centre for Criminal Law Reform and Criminal Justice Policy of the University of British Columbia, as well as the British Institute of International and Comparative Law, for their help during a research-stay with them in 2003 and 2005, respectively. This study is carried out within the project "La incidencia de la mundialización en los procedimientos de creación y aplicación del Derecho Internacional Público", Ministerio de Ciencia y Tecnología, Spain (BJU2003–04240).

[1] For a detailed study of this field in Spanish, see: H. Torroja, "Tipificación y represión de los crímenes de Derecho Internacional en Canadá" in E. Mitjans, ed., *Derechos y libertades en Canadá* (Barcelona: Atelier, forthcoming).

Christopher P.M. Waters (Ed.), *British and Canadian Perspectives on International Law*, pp. 69–85.

humanity and genocide when the suspects are originally from other countries and commit these crimes in other states.[2] I argue that after a period of impunity, both countries have entered into a new era of accountability, which can be traced to the beginning of the twenty-first century and the implementation of the Rome Statute of 1998.[3] However, given the close link between mounting social and political pressure and the prosecution of suspected war criminals, as both countries' past practices show, the current legal response represents little more than an initial step. In order to see how the two countries are actually dealing with these problems, one needs to examine how the law is enforced, which is heavily dependent upon the judges and the criminal policies of the respective governments. One would expect these governments to be setting an example within their own borders, given that they have taken leading roles in the fight against impunity outside their borders.

The fact is that since the 1990s, both countries have been closely involved in the fight against impunity at the international level. Canada has made this fight one of the pillars of its Human Security Policy and it was largely instrumental in the establishment of the International Criminal Court (ICC),[4] the *ad hoc* International Tribunals for the former Yugoslavia and for Rwanda, and the Special Court for Sierra Leone. The UK has played a similar role.[5] Along the same lines, one can remark on the UK's recent efforts to convince the United States not to veto the Security Council's referral of the situation in Darfur to the ICC.[6]

The first measure adopted by both countries to strengthen the culture of accountability has been to ratify the Rome Statute. In order to do so, both countries introduced statutes to bring their legislation into line with the provisions of the international treaty; these statutes represent the legal instrument by which

---

[2] The study goes beyond the more narrow issue of Canadian or Brtitish soldiers who commit such crimes abroad, as in the cases of Canadian soldiers in Somalia who were charged and prosecuted in Canada and of UK soldiers in Iraq who were charged with war crimes under the ICC Act.

[3] Statute of the International Criminal Court, 17 July 1998, UN Doc. No. A/CONF. 183/9, 37 I.L.M. 999 (entered into force 1 July 2002) [Rome Statute]. Canada signed the agreement on 18 December 1998 and ratified it on 7 July 2000; the UK signed it on 30 November 1998 and ratified it on 4 October 2001.

[4] On the role played by Canada in the Rome Conference, see R. S. Lee, ed., *The International Criminal Court – The Making of the Rome Statute: Issues, Negotiations, Results* (The Hague: Kluwer Law International, 1999) 79; see also D. Robinson, "The International Criminal Court" in R. McRae & D. Hubert, eds., *Human Security and the New Diplomacy – Protecting People, Promoting Peace* (Montreal and Kingston: McGill-Queen's University Press, 2001) 170 at 175–176.

[5] On its contribution to the Rome Conference, see R. S. Lee, *ibid*. The UK has given strong backing to *ad hoc* International Criminal Tribunals and the Special Court for Sierra Leone, as well as to the establishment of the International Criminal Court.

[6] See UN SC Res.1593, 2005, UN Doc. S/RES/1593.

the two common law countries might implement the Rome Statute in their domestic legal systems.[7] At the same time, these statutes have served to strengthen their respective domestic criminal law systems by ensuring that the two countries cannot be used as *safe havens* by war criminals.

To recap from Chapters 2 and 3, Canada was the first country to implement the Rome Statute, introduced through the Crimes Against Humanity Act in 2000.[8] The Act served as an amendment to a number of previous acts,[9] including the Criminal Code.[10] It includes definitions of crimes against international law as well as other offences and establishes the jurisdictional criteria of Canadian courts, the regulation of specific procedural principles, the circumstances that exempt suspects from criminal responsibility, the procedure for parole eligibility, and the definition of offences against the ICC's administration of justice. The Act also provides for a "Crimes Against Humanity" fund. The UK adopted the ICC Act in 2001.[11] The Act implements the Rome Statute into the law of England, Wales and Northern Ireland. The Scottish Parliament, having its own competence over criminal justice, passed a separate statute for the same purpose: the International Criminal Court (Scotland) Act 2001.[12] The UK's ICC Act, in six parts,[13] also served to amend previous statutes.[14]

---

[7] Both countries adhere to a dualist system for the reception of international treaties.

[8] Crimes Against Humanity and War Crimes Act, S.C. 2000, c. 24 [Crimes Against Humanity Act] (the main provisions of the Act entered into force 23 October 2000).

[9] These included: the Extradition Act, S.C. 1999, c. 18; the Mutual Legal Assistance in Criminal Matters Act, R.S.C. 1985 (4th Supp.), c. 30; the Foreign Missions and International Organizations Act, S.C. 1999, c. 41; and the Witness Protection Act, S.C. 1996, c. 15.

[10] Criminal Code, R.S.C., 1985, c. C-46, ss. 7.3.71–7.3.77.

[11] International Criminal Court Act, (U.K.), 2001, c. 17 [ICC Act] ("An Act to give effect to the Statute of the International Criminal Court; to provide for offences under the law of England and Wales and Northern Ireland corresponding to offences within the jurisdiction of that Court; and for connected purposes"); entered into force 1 September 2001.

[12] International Criminal Court (Scotland) Act 2001, A.S.P. 2001, c. 13 (entered into force 17 December 2001). Some areas are nevertheless covered by the British Parliament Act. For more on this, see P. Arnell, "The International Criminal Court in Scotland, First part" (2001) 290 SCOLAG L. J. 216 and "The International Criminal Court in Scotland, Second part" (2002) 291 SCOLAG L. J. 7; Also see S. Christie, *The International Criminal Court* (2002) 70 Scot. L. Gaz. 11.

[13] Parts 2 to 5 concern provisions for arrest and surrender, other forms of co-operation, enforcement of sentences and definitions of international crimes.

[14] These included: the Extradition Act (U.K.), 1989, c. 33; the Backing of Warrants (Republic of Ireland) Act (U.K.), 1965, c. 45; the Army Act (U.K.), 1955, 3 & 4 Eliz. 2 c. 18; the Air Force Act (U.K.), 1955, 3 & 4 Eliz. 2 c. 19; and the Naval Discipline Act (U.K.), 1957, c. 53.

The section below briefly examines the record of each country in the prosecution of war criminals, before analysing various aspects of the new legislation. This enables one to see the evolution in the culture of accountability for crimes against international law in Canada and the UK and to draw tentative conclusions regarding the future direction this might take.

2) BEFORE THE ROME STATUTE:
BETWEEN IMPUNITY AND ACCOUNTABILITY

Before the Rome Statute, the history of the enforcement of international criminal law by Canadian and UK courts can be divided into two stages.

The first stage began immediately after the Second World War, when both countries prosecuted a number of German Nazi war criminals. The Canadians brought their prosecutions in Aurich (Germany), in accordance with the War Crimes Regulations of 1945.[15] In the British occupation zone, trials by British Military Courts were conducted under the Royal Warrant: Regulations for the Trial of War Criminals of 1945.[16] After 1948, following a recommendation from the British Commonwealth Relations Office, no more prosecutions were brought. The priority now shifted to the social, political and economic reconstruction of Germany rather than the punishment of Nazi war criminals.[17] As the Cold War deepened, the threat of communism replaced the concern of bringing World War II criminals to trial. The Canadian government at this time even adopted a permissive policy and allowed former war criminals into the country, some of whom became Canadian nationals.[18] Thus, it may be suggested that Canada became a safe haven for war criminals. The second stage was set in motion at the end of the 1980s and the beginning of the 1990s. A review of the situation suggests that the process was more or less parallel in the two countries and that despite the legal reforms introduced, jurisdictional enforcement was not particularly successful.

---

[15] War Crimes Regulations, P.C. 1945–5831, C. Gaz. 1945.III.10 (later replaced by the War Crimes Act, S.C. 1946, c. 73). See L. C. Green, "Canadian Law, War Crimes and Crimes Against Humanity" (1988) 59 Brit. Y.B. Int'l L. 217; W. J. Fenrick, "The Prosecution of War Criminals in Canada" (1989) 12 Dal. L. J. 256.

[16] S. R. & O. 1945/81. See A. P. V. Rogers, "War Crimes Trials under the Royal Warrant: British Practice 1945–1949" (1990) 39 I.C.L.Q. 780.

[17] C. A. Amerasinghe, "The Canadian Experience" in M.C. Bassiouni, ed., *International Criminal Law*, 2d. ed. (New York: Transnational Publishers, Inc., 1999) 247.

[18] See D. Matas & S. Charendoff, *Justice Delayed : Nazi War Criminals in Canada* (Toronto: Summerhill Press Ltd., 1987) 17; D. Szabo & A. Joffe, "La represión des crimes contre l'humanité et des crimes des guerre au Canada" in M. Colin, ed., *Le crime contre l'humanité* (Erès: Ramonville Saint-Agne, 1996) 57.

In 1987, Canada amended the Criminal Code granting jurisdiction to its national courts over war crimes and crimes against humanity committed outside Canada, by nationals and non-nationals, before and after the introduction of the new act.[19] This general legislation was enacted to allow the prosecution of Nazi war criminals who were then living in Canada. Social pressure to prosecute these criminals had started to mount since the mid-60s, when it emerged that some Nazi war criminals had been granted refugee status in Canada, and, in some cases, had even been naturalized as Canadian citizens. After attempts to adopt an act prosecuting these criminals in Canada had failed, the then Solicitor General sought their extradition. The first case was that of Albert Helmut Rauca, a Canadian of German origin, who was extradited to the Federal Republic of Germany in 1983.[20] In the intervening years, social pressure had ensured the inclusion of a brief reference within article 11(g) of the Canadian Charter of Rights and Freedoms of 1982,[21] making the future prosecution of Nazi war criminals possible.[22] Later, in 1986, the Government established a Commission of Inquiry into the presence of war criminals in Canada, issuing its final report in 1987.[23] According to its findings, the best solution for dealing with the problem was the extradition of suspected criminals. Alternative solutions included prosecution (though for this to be successful new legislation would have to be introduced), and denaturalization and subsequent deportation as the last resort. A Special War Crimes Unit was then established within the Department of Justice.

---

[19] Act to Amend the Criminal Code, the Immigration Act, 1976, and the Citizenship Act, S.C. 1987, c. 37. See Criminal Code, supra note 10. The Crimes Against Humanity Act was to follow almost exactly the definition of the offences and the jurisdictional criteria included in this reform. Its content will be discussed in more detail below.

[20] See S. A. Williams, "Laudable Principles Lacking Application: The Prosecution of War Criminals in Canada" in T. L. H. McCormack & G. J. Simpson, eds., *The Law of War Crimes: National and International Approaches* (The Hague: Kluwer Law International, 1997) 152.

[21] Canadian Charter of Rights and Freedoms, Part I of the Constitution Act, 1982, being schedule B to the Canada Act 1982 (U.K.), 1982, c. 11.

[22] The purpose was to include the exemption of offences considered 'criminal', according to International Law and the general principles of Law recognized by the community of nations, within the principle of legality. This move reflects the influence of the Canadian Jewish Congress and the Jewish Students' North American Association in Canada (see Szabo & Joffe, *supra* note 18 at 59–60; F. Chevrette, & H. Cyr, "La protection en matière de fouilles, perquisitions et saisies, en matière de détention, la non-rétroactivité de l'infraction et la peine la plus douce" in G. A. Beaudoin & E. P. Mendes, *La Charte Canadienne des Droits et Libertés*, 3d ed. (Montréal: Wilson & Lafleur, 1996) 627.

[23] Canada, *Report of the Commission of Inquiry on War Criminals*, vol. 1 (Ottawa: Supply and Services Canada, 1986) [*Deschênes Commission of Inquiry*]. For a summary of the report, see: http://www.parl.gc.ca/information/library/prbpubs/873–e.htm.

Once the Criminal Code reform of 1987 came into force, the War Crimes Unit brought four cases to the courts.[24] Only one, the *Finta* case, was concluded; in 1994 the Supreme Court upheld a decision by the Ontario Court of Appeal, which had upheld a jury acquittal on all accounts of Imre Finta.[25] While there is no space to discuss the details here,[26] the interpretation – or according to some, misinterpretation – by the majority of judges concerning the "mental element" of crimes against humanity and the defences of "superior's orders" and "error of fact", closed the door on future prosecutions. Once *Finta* established a precedent, it became unlikely that other cases would be successful in Canadian courts. This led the Government to pursue a new strategy: denaturalizing and deporting suspected criminals.[27]

In the UK, the shift towards a culture of accountability did not get underway until a later date, although here again it reflected a response to mounting social pressure.[28] In 1991, following the recommendations of the Report of the War Crimes Inquiry,[29] the War Crimes Act[30] was passed "amidst great controversy".[31] The Act was not adopted by the House of Lords, among other reasons,

---

[24] *R. v. Finta*, [1989] O.J. No. 1041; *R. v. Pawlowski*, [1990] O.J. No. 2682; *R. v. Reistetter*, [1990] O.J. No. 2100; *R. v. Grujicic*, [1994] O.J. No. 2280.

[25] *R. v. Finta*, [1994] 1 S.C.R. 701, 112 D.L.R. (4th) 513 [*Finta Case*]. In 1944, Imre Finta, a former captain in the Royal Hungarian Gendarmerie, was accused of war crimes and crimes against humanity towards Jews in Hungary.

[26] For more information, see I. Cotler, "Case Note on Regina v. Finta [1994] 1 S.C.R. 701, Supreme Court of Canada , March 24, 1994" (1996), 90 A.J.I.L. 460 at 462–463; see also Szabo & Joffe, *supra* note 18 at 56–81.

[27] Cotler, *ibid.* at 461; J. H. Sims & J. Rikhof, "War Crimes and Crimes against Humanity: The Canadian Experience" in Canadian Bar Association, *The 11th Commonwealth Law Conference, Conference papers of the Canadian Bar Association's annual meeting held in Vancouver* (Ottawa: Can. Bar Assoc., 1996) at 6.

[28] See Green, *supra* note 15 at 219–220. News about alleged war criminals living in the United Kingdom came from information provided by the Simon Wishenthal Centre (Los Angeles) in 1986. This led the United Kingdom's Home Office to establish the War Crimes Inquiry in 1988, which then published its results in 1989. See U.K., Home Office, *Report of the War Crimes Inquiry* (Cm. 744) (London: Her Majesty's Stationery Office, 1989) (one of its recommendations was to introduce new legislation to allow for the prosecution of alleged criminals living in the country).

[29] U.K., H.C., "Report of the War Crimes Inquiry" Cmnd 744 in Sessional Papers (1989).

[30] *War Crimes Act 1991* (U.K.), 1991, c.13 [War Crimes Act]. The latter Act entered into force on 9 May 1991 and was amended in 1996 by the Criminal Procedure and Investigations Act 1996 (U.K.), 1996, c. 25.

[31] A. T. Richardson, "War Crimes Act 1991" (1992) 55 Mod. L. Rev. 73. For more information on the background and the constitutional issues raised by the enactment of the War Crimes Act, see G. Ganz, "The War Crimes Act 1991: Why No Constitutional Crisis?" (1992) 55 Mod. L. Rev. 87.

because of its retrospective nature. As a result, it became legislation under the authority of the House of Commons, under the provisions of the Parliament Act 1949.[32] In contrast with Canadian practice, the application of the scope of the Act was restricted solely to Nazi war criminals expressly mentioned in the Act. It granted the British courts jurisdiction over the offences of "murder, manslaughter or culpable homicide (. . .) if that offence (a) was committed during the period beginning with 1 September 1939 and ending with 5 June 1945 in a place which at the time was part of Germany or under German occupation; and (b) constituted a violation of the laws and customs of war" (section 1). The alleged criminal had to be a British citizen or a resident of the UK, the Isle of Man or the Channel Islands, on 8 March 1990 or thereafter. The Attorney General's consent was required before any proceedings could be initiated. Due to the peculiar nature of its drafting, the Act gave rise to a number of complex legal problems.[33] Few proceedings were brought to the Courts under this Act,[34] and only one trial was completed, *R. v. Sawoniuk*.[35] Note that these events coincided with the widely reported case of General Pinochet, the former Chilean Head of State whose extradition from the UK was requested by Spain at this time.[36]

To summarize, after a first short period of accountability immediately following the Second World War, Canada and the UK entered in a stage of certain ambiguity concerning the fight against impunity. On one hand, they brought forward important legal reforms in order to achieve the prosecution of war criminals and others in their countries. On the other hand, one can observe that this legislation was not always easy to pass, its application by the courts

---

[32] On this and the validity of the *Parliament Act 1949*, see S. McMurtrie, "A Challenge to the Validity of the Parliament Act 1949: An Opportunity Lost?" (1997) 18:1 Stat. L. Rev. 46 and "The Constitutionality of the War Crimes Act 1991" (1992) 13:2 Stat. L. Rev. 128–149; T. Tayleur, "A Valid Act?" (1995) 145 New L. J. 1328.

[33] See A. J., Cunningham, "'To the uttermost ends of the earth'? The War Crimes Act and International Law" (1991) 11 L. S. 281. See also S. Cornelius, "Fair trials and effective policing" (1995) 145 New L. J. 1232; R. Cottrell, "The War Crimes Act and Procedural Protection" (1992) Mar. The Crim. L. Rev. 173.

[34] Simeon Serafanowicz was the first person charged under the 1991 Act. For a discussion of this case, see J. Nutting, W. Clegg & P. Badge, "The Case of Simeon Serafanowicz" (1998) 38 Med. Sci. Law 187 .

[35] *R. v. Sawoniuk* (2001) 2 Cr. App. R. 220. The accused was found guilty and sentenced to life imprisonment. See D. Hirsch, "The Trial of A. Sawoniuk: Holocaust Testimony under Cross-Examination" (2001) 10 Soc. & Leg. Stud. 531.

[36] For some studies in Spanish, see M. G. Arán & D. L. Garrido, eds., *Crimen internacional y jurisdicción universal. El caso Pinochet* (Valencia: Tirant lo Blanch, 2000); C. C. Fernández, "Pinochet: balance provisional" (2000) 37 Jueces para la Democracia 6; J. A. Remiro Brotons, "El Caso Pinochet: Los límites de la impunidad" (1999) Política Exterior-Biblioteca Nueva 78.

complex, and methods to deal with war criminals shifted from accountability to denaturalization and deportation.

Now, we can turn to the main changes in the fight against criminal impunity in a more contemporary setting.

3) THE FUTURE FOR ACCOUNTABILITY UNDER CURRENT LEGISLATION

Both the Crimes Against Humanity Act in Canada and the ICC Act in the UK include the three core crimes – war crimes, crimes against humanity, and genocide – and recognise the responsibility attributable to military command and the hierarchical superior.[37] In each of these cases, both Acts punish the direct commission of the crimes in addition to crimes ancillary to them (including conspiracy, the attempt to commit a crime and being an accessory after the fact). Offences against the administration of justice of the ICC are also included in both Acts. The penalties provided for by the Acts are also similar, and follow the general guidelines of the Rome Statute: life imprisonment for offences involving murder; and in all other cases, a term of imprisonment not exceeding 30 years in the case of the UK, and a term that can extend to life imprisonment in the case of Canada. However, the Acts differ slightly in the jurisdictional criteria chosen in conferring competence on the courts.

Before examining the definition of these offences and the jurisdictional criteria applied, it should be noted that in Canadian law, current legislation retains sections dedicated to offences committed outside Canada (sections 6, 7 & 8), reflecting perhaps the 1987 reform which only included such cases, and further sections dedicated to offences committed within Canada (sections 4 & 5). The provisions within each of these respective sections are largely similar; however, their intention differs. The definition of crimes committed within Canada fulfills the function of facilitating the hand-over of suspected criminals to the ICC, so that the "double criminality" requirement that the extradition legislation demands is met;[38] this section can only be applied prospectively. The sec-

---

[37] In Canadian law, this is considered as a specific offence and not only a general principle of procedural law; the definition, under sections 5 & 7 of Crimes Against Humanity Act, differs slightly from article 28 of the Rome Statute. See W. A. Schabas, "Canadian implementing legislation for the Rome Statute" (2000) 3 Y.B. Int'l Human. L. 337; V. Oosterveld, "Implementing the Rome Statute of the International Criminal Court: the Canadian Experience" in International Centre for Criminal Law Reform, *Breaking New Ground: A Collection of Papers in the International Centre's Canada-China Cooperation* (Vancouver: ICCLR&CJP, 2002) 241 at 245–246. In UK law, section 65 of the ICC Act follows article 28 of the Rome Statute; for further details see R. May & S. Powles, "Command Responsibility: A new Basis of Criminal Liability in English Law" (2002) May, The Crim. L.Rev. 363.

[38] Schabas, *ibid.* at 338.

tions dedicated to crimes committed outside Canada fulfill the same purpose as the earlier Criminal Code: defining and giving the judge competence over these crimes. Here, however, retroactive application of the law is permitted. Details are provided regarding the interpretation of legal custom in this area, and the criteria according to which jurisdiction is awarded to the Canadian courts are defined.

In the case of the ICC Act, the definitions of offences and jurisdictional criteria are included in Part 5 (Offences under domestic law); the Act does not have a retrospective application. In the definitions of the offences, the Act does not follow the terms of the 1991 Act. In fact, the influence of the Rome Statute in the UK's ICC Act is clearer than in the case of the Canadian Act.

a) *The definition of offences: a different legislative technique*

In Canadian legislation, the definitions attributed to the offences are somewhat unusual. Schabas refers to them as "relatively crisp and succinct definitions".[39] Indeed, they do not adhere exactly with what are on occasion rather long definitions adopted by the Rome Statute, but instead resort to the concepts used in the 1987 reform. These definitions harken back to international law, which was then necessary in order for the non-retroactive principle of penal law to be reconciled with the repression of crimes committed during World War II; in particular, the reference to the general principles of law recognized by the community of nations. Today, while this logic remains valid, the remission to international law could play another important role: to strengthen the jurisdiction of Canadian courts, as will be discussed below.

An examination of the definitions of the three offences shows that they might be divided into two parts. First, they consist of a relatively short phrase: for example, "crime against humanity" is understood as "murder, extermination, enslavement, deportation, imprisonment, torture, sexual violence, persecution or any other inhumane act or omission that is committed against any civilian population or any identifiable group and that . . ."; "genocide" is interpreted to mean "an act or omission committed with intent to destroy, in whole or in part, an identifiable group of persons, as such, that . . ."; and "war crime" is defined as "an act or omission committed during an armed conflict that . . .". Second, each of the definitions is then completed (after "that") by a phrase that links the content of the definition to the international law in force at the time and place of the commission of the offences, regardless of whether or not it was a violation of the domestic law then in force. This international law is specified in conventional law, customary law and the general principles of law in the cases

---

[39] *Ibid.* at 340.

of crimes against humanity and genocide, and only in conventional law and customary law in the case of war crimes.

It would appear that we should seek to interpret the two parts of the definition together. Relying on international law serves an essential function in each definition and it would be nonsensical for the judges to limit themselves solely to the first part of each definition. This means that in line with the specific wording, it is international law that the judges must apply. In fact, articles 6, 7 and 8 of the Rome Statute are included at the end of the Act. This is important because the first parts of some of these definitions are incomplete or differ from those given in the Rome Statute, customary law or elsewhere. For instance, the first part of the definition of "crimes against humanity" omits reference to a "general or systematic attack", and it omits the acts of "forced disappearance" and "apartheid". Or, for instance, it seems clear that a "war crime" is not just any act or omission committed during an armed conflict, as the first part of this definition affirms. By contrast, in some cases, the first parts of the definitions go further than those of the Rome Statute and international law. This is particularly apparent in the definition of "genocide". For example, the inclusion of "omission" could be seen as opening the door to violations such as cultural genocide, which is not included in the Rome Statute. Or, interestingly, the inclusion of the expression "an identifiable group" opens the door to the consideration of common political ideology as a new criterion for defining the group under attack, while political ideology is neither included in the Rome Statute nor in the Convention on Genocide.[40] However, remittal to international law would apparently close this door. On this point, a number of questions arise,[41] though it is the judges who have the last word.

The legislative technique of remitting to international law has a number of advantages. It has been said that "advances in international law resulting in the development of new offences under customary or conventional law will be incorporated automatically into the Canadian definitions",[42] including the international jurisprudence of the *ad hoc* criminal tribunals and the ICC. It is clear that the Act goes further than the Rome Statute in this sense.[43] A further advan-

---

[40] Convention on the Prevention and Punishment of the Crime of Genocide, GA Res. 260(III)A, UN GAOR, 3d Sess., Supp. No. 1, UN Doc. A/810 (1948) [Convention on Genocide]. *Ibid.* at 339–340.

[41] These questions concern the relation between the national and/or international jurisprudence of various courts.

[42] J. McManus, "A new era of accountability through domestic enforcement of International Law" in Canadian Institute for the Administration of Justice, *The Canadian Highway to the International Criminal Court: All Roads Lead to Rome, Presented at the 13th Conference of the Journées Maximilien-Caron held on May 1–2, 2003* (Montreal: Université de Montréal, 2003) 36 at 37.

[43] M. Rosenberg, "Canadian Legislation Against Crimes Against Humanity and War

tage is that the jurisprudence based on the famous *Finta* case would now seem to be repealed, although opinions have been expressed to the contrary.[44] At least, the interpretation of the due obedience defence has been fully revoked as it is now implicitly expressed in article 14 of the Act.[45]

The general advantage of this legislative technique is that it constitutes a clever means by which Canada can enlarge its material jurisdiction over such crimes in comparison with that of the ICC. In other words, underlying the many references to international law could fulfil a further state interest: the protection of Canadian *ius puniendi* in the face of the ICC. It must be borne in mind that the ICC is ruled by the complementarity principle. In this sense, all states share a vested interest in updating their legislation according to the Rome Statute thereby ensuring that they will be able to prosecute war criminals, including potentially their own service people, as highlighted in the previous chapter.[46] This Act ensures that Canada will, in principle, always *be* able to judge war criminals, those perpetrating crimes against humanity and acts of genocide, if the jurisdictional criteria are met. In this sense, the Canadian legislation not only incorporates the Rome Statute definitions of the offences, but it remits to international law, which can go beyond the Rome Statute.[47]

However, alongside these advantages, there are a number of *a priori* disadvantages associated with this technique. One problem concerns the question as to whether reliance on international law might hinder the decision of the judge. It should be remembered that this reliance is based upon the international law that was in force at the time and place of the commission of acts or omissions. Thus, the judge needs to be familiar with the state of international law at that moment, which in the case of offences committed outside of Canada, could be

---

Crimes" in International Centre for Criminal Law Reform, *The Changing Face of International Criminal Law: Selected Papers* (Vancouver: ICCLR&CJP, 2001) 229 at 232. See also Schabas, *supra* note 37 at 340; Oosterveld, *supra* note 37 at 244 (for Oosterveld, this was the intent of the wording in the provisions, bearing in mind that the *Rome Statute* had not included all international war crimes, *e.g.* the use of chemical or biological arms).

[44] Concerning the interpretation given to the mental element, Amerasinghe considers that *Finta* remains valid (C. A. Amerasinghe, "The Domestic Tribunals' Universal Jurisdiction for War Crimes and Crimes against Humanity: from Finta to Today" in Canadian Institute for the Administration of Justice, *supra* note 42 at 7).

[45] See McManus, *supra* note 42 at 37; M. J. Schwarz, "Prosecuting Crimes against Humanity in Canada: What Must be Proved" (2002) 46 Crim. L. Q. 40.

[46] Yet as regards the legislation defining the core crimes, the Rome Statute leaves state parties free to follow the Statute or not.See Oosterveld, *supra* note 37 at 243. *Contra* McManus, *supra* note 42 at 34.

[47] This is expressed in sections 4.4 and 6.4 of the Act, the content of which will be discussed below.

distant in both space and time. Such difficulties could be even greater in the case of unwritten sources of international law: custom and the general principles of law.[48] Judges would face considerable difficulties in this area, including problems of imprecision and vagueness, to which they must provide solutions.

The law does present certain clarifications. With respect to custom, Canadian law affirms that crimes defined in the Rome Statute are done so in accordance with international custom in the case of offences committed inside and outside Canada, from the date of the adoption of the Statute; to safeguard the application of future developments not included in the Rome Statute, it adds that the Act does "not limit or prejudice in any way the application of existing or developing rules of international law" (sections 4.4 & 6.4). In the case of offences committed outside Canada, the law assists the judge in two respects. First, it affirms that the crimes may be crimes that conform to international custom before the date of the adoption of the Statute (section 6.4). Secondly, it complements this idea by affirming that, "for greater certainty", crimes against humanity were recognised by international custom or the general principles of law before the London Agreement of 1945 and the McArthur Proclamation by the Supreme Commander for the Allied Powers of 1946 entered into force (section 6.5).

The technique adopted in UK legislation for defining these offences might be considered clearer than that adopted in Canada: it consists in a direct referral to articles 6, 7 and 8.2 of the Rome Statute.[49] In addition, the UK's ICC Act states that the ICC's "Elements of Crimes"[50] are to be taken into account by the courts. In this sense, two points which are not clearly resolved in Canadian legislation, are expressly dealt with here: the application of ICC jurisprudence by the courts and the interpretation of the mental element of such offences. To this effect, section 50.5 of the ICC Act establishes that in "interpreting and applying the provisions of the articles [concerned] (. . .) the court shall take into account

---

[48] See Green, *supra* note 15 at 231–232. This is particularly true with regards to the General Principles of Law (*ibid.* at 226). Further, problems may arise when attempting to respect the Principle of Legality (see V. Abellán Honrubia, "La responsabilité internationale de l'individu" (1999) 280 Rec. des Cours 364. Although it must be said that "le seul fait qu'une infraction en soit une de *common law* et ne soit pas codifiée ne contravient pas à l'alinéa 11(g)" of the Canadian Charter of Rights and Freedoms (Chevrette & Cyr, *supra* note 22 at 626).

[49] ICC Act, *supra* note 11 at s. 50.1.

[50] The Act's Final Draft text on the Elements of Crimes (Rome Statute, *supra* note 3, Assembly of State Parties, 1st sess., ICC-ASP/1/3 at Part II-B: "Elements of Crime", formerly, PCNICC/2000/1/Add.2) was incorporated into British law under the International Criminal Court Act 2001 (Elements of Crimes) Regulations 2001, S.I. 2001/2505, as rep. by International Criminal Court Act 2001 (Elements of Crimes) Regulations 2004, S.I. 2004/1080, Sch.

any relevant judgment or decision of the ICC". Moreover, the same section establishes that "account may also be taken of any other relevant international jurisprudence". Secondly, and of special interest to English criminal law is section 66 of the Act, which follows article 30 of the Rome Statute: it offers the first statutory definition of intent in English criminal law.[51]

b) *The jurisdiction of the courts*

The criteria used in granting powers to the tribunals for offences committed outside Canada[52] are directly influenced by the 1987 reform. The specific requirements are almost identical with a few exceptions. Article 8 of the Crimes Against Humanity Act distinguishes two cases.

The first (section 8(a)) involve cases in which there is an active or passive personality link: the Canadian courts have jurisdiction over an offence if, at the time of the commission, the perpetrator is Canadian or a civilian or military employee of Canada;[53] or the perpetrator is a citizen or a civilian or military employee of a state that is in armed conflict against Canada;[54] or the victim is a Canadian national;[55] or the victim is a citizen of a state allied with Canada in an armed conflict.[56] Note that the prerequisite of an armed conflict in two of these situations means that crimes against humanity committed during peacetime cannot be brought before the courts, unless another link exists. At the same time, the Act does not give jurisdiction over non-Canadian criminals who participate in armed conflict in which Canada is not a party if there is no other link.

Although not expressly stated in the Act, it can be deduced that, in all these situations, the presence of the presumed criminals in Canada is not a prerequisite to the commencement of proceedings – this follows from a combination of

---

[51] For a discussion, see "Editorial: The International Criminal Court Act 2001" (2001) Oct. The Crim. L. Rev. 767.

[52] With respect to offences committed in Canada, the principle of "territoriality" means that Canadian tribunals have jurisdiction; therefore, the Act needs not make mention of such cases.

[53] This is similar to the provisions contained in the 1987 reform, where the existence of an armed conflict is not required.

[54] This refers only to offences committed during *international* armed conflicts, excluding crimes committed by nationals or employees of allied states during armed conflict, as does the 1987 reform.

[55] Whether the crime occurs during armed conflict or peacetime is irrelevant (similarly to the 1987 reform, which now has its own section).

[56] No mention is made of the citizens of enemy states, although they could meet the second requirement under "active personality" (similarly to the 1987 reform). See Green, *supra* note 15 at 229.

Sections 8(a) and 9.1 of the Act – although it should be recognised that the opposite interpretation is also possible. However, given that *in absentia* trials are prohibited in Canada (a point which Section 9.2 of the Act reiterates) the accused, in such circumstances, would eventually have to be extradited to Canada for the trial to reach its conclusion. Furthermore, initiating proceedings requires the written authorization of the Attorney General or the Deputy Attorney General (the consent requirement).

The second case involves what has come to be known as universal limited jurisdiction.[57] Section 8(b) grants jurisdiction to the courts in cases in which, after the commission of the offence, the person is present in Canada (the presence requirement). Clearly, the presence of the perpetrator is required if there is no active or passive link with Canada, according to section 8(a). When making this assumption, we are faced with a "middle road position on universal jurisdiction".[58] Although some refer to this as "universal jurisdiction",[59] another doctrine, more in accord with the judicial notion, affirms that this is "*limited universal jurisdiction*".[60]

The doubt that may arise in this case is whether the alleged perpetrator must be present in Canada in order to start the investigation. Based on a reading of Section 9.1 of the Act, it would appear that such presence is not required in order to initiate proceedings. However, such an interpretation tends to render the "presence" requirement meaningless. It would seem more appropriate to consider a link with Canada as being necessary[61] and in such cases presence is determinant. It is unlikely that a procedure would be initiated against a war criminal in Zimbabwe, for example, if the alleged perpetrator is not present in Canada. Thus, the controversy concerning the prosecution of Mugabe in Canada[62] is clear from a legal point: Canada does not have universal jurisdiction, although some would disagree with this statement.[63] A recent example of this middle road position on universal jurisdiction is the case of Désiré Munyaneza, who was arrested in Toronto in October 2005, charged with genocide, crimes against humanity and war crimes committed in 1994 in Butare (Rwanda) and brought before a court in Montreal. Moreover, what is also needed in this second situation is the "consent requirement" and the prohibition of judgement *in absentia*.

---

[57] Rosenberg, *supra* note 43 at 233.

[58] McManus, *supra* note 42 at 37–38.

[59] See Oosterveld, *supra* note 37 at 247; Amerasinghe, "The Canadian Experience", *supra* note 17 at 258.

[60] See e.g. the classical position of Green, *supra* note 15 at 229.

[61] McManus, *supra* note 42 at 37–38.

[62] See S. Nolan "Can Ottawa Act Against Mugabe?" *Globe and Mail* (5 November 2004): http://www.globalpolicy.org/intljustice/universal/2004/1105mugabe.htm.

[63] *Ibid*.

In the UK, the ICC Act grants jurisdiction to the English courts for the offences defined above when they are committed in England and Wales, and also when they are committed outside the UK by a UK national, a UK resident or by a person subject to UK service jurisdiction.[64] Moreover, the consent of the Attorney General is required to initiate proceedings (paragraphs 53(3) & 60(3) of the Act). Therefore, the ICC Act does not generally confer universal jurisdiction on British courts, given the "residence" and "consent" requirements.[65]

4) CONCLUDING REMARKS

Based on the preceding overview of the evolution in Canadian and UK practices concerning the prosecution of those suspected of committing crimes against international law, a number of conclusions can be drawn.

In the period between the war trials held after World War II until the signing of the Rome Statute, Canadian and UK practices can be seen as a token of what McManus has called "the pervasive reluctance among States to address the issue of impunity through the application of the law".[66]

This is more than apparent if we consider that Canada was internationally bound to enact legislation enabling the courts "to prosecute or to extradite" such criminals after 1965, when it passed the Geneva Convention Act.[67] Under this Act, Canada agreed to implement the 1949 Geneva Conventions which included this obligation. Despite this, it was not until twenty years later that Canada decided to amend the Criminal Code. It is obvious that Canada did not amend the Criminal Code because it felt it had to fulfill an international obligation. One could say that the eventual amendment was made in response to European and Canadian social pressure, which had first made itself manifest in the mid-60s, when it emerged that a number of Nazi war criminals had been granted refugee status in Canada, and, in some cases, had even been naturalized as Canadian citizens. This led to the introduction of a brief clause in the Canadian Charter of Rights and Freedoms in 1982, opening the door to the future prosecution of Nazi war criminals. The government also set up the Deschênes Commission of Inquiry in 1986 to examine the presence of war

---

[64] ICC Act, *supra* note 11 at ss. 51.2, 52.4, 54.4. Section 67 clarifies the meaning of these terms, sometimes in a general way (see e.g. s. 67.2 where a UK resident means "a person who is resident in the United Kingdom").

[65] Nevertheless, existing universal jurisdiction was preserved for grave breaches of the Geneva Conventions, (*infra* note 68 at s. 1.) and for torture (Criminal Justice Act 1988 (U.K.), 1988, c. 33, s. 134, although the Attorney General's consent for prosecution is required).

[66] McManus, *supra* note 42 at 12.

[67] R.S.C., 1985, c. G-3.

criminals in Canada, and this led to the amendment of the Criminal Code in 1987 and to a number of prosecutions within Canada. However, the lack of success in these trials saw a change of strategy.

An examination of Canadian domestic practices during this period shows that prosecuting war criminals was one of several political options available to them (including, extradition, prosecution, denial or exclusion of refugee status, revocation of citizenship and deportation from Canada) for dealing with the social problem of the presence of war criminals in its territory. Once the prosecution of these criminals was shown to be difficult, Canada attempted to tackle the problem in other ways.

Similar conclusions can be drawn regarding British practices. The UK passed the Geneva Conventions Act[68] in 1957, to implement the 1949 Geneva Conventions ratified the same year. But it was not until 1991 that Parliament decided, not without controversy, to give jurisdiction to its courts to prosecute Nazi war criminals present in the UK. The social and political pressure brought to bear was also a relevant factor in this case. It would seem that these events in Canada and the UK demonstrate one aspect of the close link between international criminal justice and politics.[69]

Today, both countries have entered a period in which their commitment to a culture of accountability must still be proven. Both states possess, at least at the legal level, the instruments to prosecute war criminals at home. Canada has provided itself with a wide-ranging jurisdiction over such offences and its legislation goes, arguably, beyond the definition of the offences of the Rome Statute. UK legislation includes at least the same offences as those provided for by the Rome Statute and its courts have committed themselves to a consideration of the relevant ICC jurisprudence in the application of its law. Canada combines passive and active principles with a limited universal jurisdiction, due to the "presence" and "consent" requirements. The ICC Act is even more restrictive: it requires the "residence" or the submission of the suspected criminal to UK "service jurisdiction" to start proceedings, as well as the "consent" requirement.

It can be argued therefore, that the legislative technique for defining the relevant offences gives broad material jurisdiction to the national courts in both cases. This appears to serve to strengthen the positions of Canada and the UK with respect to the ICC, taking into account the "principle of complementarity": Canada and the UK should therefore, in principle, be able to prosecute in cases when the aforementioned requisites are met. Whether Canada and the UK will choose to do so, however, is another matter. Similarly, this broad material jurisdiction places Canada and the UK in a challenging position, where they

---

[68] Geneva Conventions Act 1957 (U.K.), 1957, c. 52, as am. by Geneva Conventions (Amendment) Act 1995 (U.K.), 1995 c. 27.

[69] See F. Mégret, "The politics of International Criminal Justice" (2002) 13 E.J.I.L. 1261.

have to choose whether to prosecute, extradite, deport any suspected criminals or to hand them over to the ICC. Several factors are involved in this choice. For example: whether or not there is a request from other states or an International Tribunal; whether or not there is sufficient evidence to prosecute a suspected criminal; and also, the judicial standard concerning human rights in the country of origin.[70] However, the choice made will send a clear message to the international community as to how these countries are dealing with the fight against impunity.[71]

Further, there is a need for *coherence* between the internal and external manifestations of the two countries' international criminal justice policy. If we consider the foreign policy of both countries in this field, the question arises as to whether Canada and the UK are not only legally bound to fight against impunity within their borders, but whether they are also under a strong moral obligation towards the international community.

---

[70] In Canada, such decisions are taken in the context of a joint programme (*Canada's War Crimes Program*), comprising of several Departments: the *Department of Justice*; the *Canada Border Services Agency (CBSA)*; and, the *Royal Canadian Mounted Police (RCMP)*. For more details, see Canada, *Canada's War Crimes Program: Seventh Annual Report* (Ottawa, Supply and Services Canada, 2004): http://www.cbsa.gc.ca/general/enforcement/annual/annual7-e.html.

[71] An interesting case in recent Canadian practices is the *Mugesera case*, which illustrates the close links between the legal, social and political elements involved in the fight against impunity. This case was about the deportation of the Rwandan Hutu politician, Leon Mugesera, a permanent resident in Canada, because of his 1992 speech in Rwanda that incited genocide. On 28 June 2005, the Supreme Court of Canada in *Mugesera v. Canada (Minister of Citizenship and Immigration)*, [2005] 2 S.C.R. 100, upheld the deportation order, which has been previously set aside by the Federal Court of Appeal. Now, the problem remains whether Canada can deport Mugesera without the assurance that he will not be subjected to the death penalty. One could ask whether or not it is a question of political choice or of legal constraint to not prosecute him in Canada.

Chapter 5

Jurisdictional Issues in Extraterritorial Criminal Law

Troy Lavers

1) Introduction

Prior to the 20th century the majority of criminal acts were usually tied to one particular country or territory. It was only with the substantial growth in overseas travel, mass mobility, multinational corporations, and technological advancements in communication that transnational criminal activity became a common phenomenon. The law has been slow to keep pace with criminals who have extended their activities to the international plane.

This chapter seeks to explore the practice of courts when presented with extraterritorial criminal acts, with particular emphasis on UK and Canadian standards, statutes and precedents. The purpose of this discussion is to promote the use of a test for jurisdictional claims as outlined in *R v. Libman*[1] in an

---

[1] *R. v. Libman*, [1985] 2 S.C.R. 178. Canada claimed jurisdiction for an international fraud conspiracy, based on a significant portion of the activities taking place in its territory, even though the victims were in the US and the monies were transferred to a third country.

Christopher P.M. Waters (Ed.), *British and Canadian Perspectives on International Law*, pp. 87–103.
© *2006 Koninklijke Brill NV. Printed in the Netherlands.*

attempt to illustrate that extending jurisdiction can be legitimised within reasonable limits. The legitimacy of the substantial connection test is dependant
on its adherence to the fundamental principles of international law. Specifically,
the substantial connection test is a two-stage test that assesses (1) whether there
is a real and substantial link between the offence and the state-claiming jurisdiction and (2) evaluates whether the claim disturbs comity between states.[2]
The test itself places the emphasis on customary international principles as long
as the broader view of comity is utilised. The broader view of comity extends
beyond the basic or one-dimensional definition of respect and courtesy between
states. Instead it is the reinforcement of the true equality of states on the international plane and each state's sovereign rights. In other words comity restricts
interference in the operation of independent sovereign states.

Traditionally, when jurisdiction is tied to the occurrence of an offence within
a territory, it is practically as well as theoretically based on state sovereignty.
Practically because prosecutions are constrained by the trial cost, logistical
problems with evidence and potential witnesses in other, often distant, countries. Bribery, intricate fraud scenarios, sexual tourism, football hooliganism,
murder, terrorism, and even torture are more difficult to bring to trial because of
the limitations of the customary principles of jurisdiction as interpreted and
applied by states. In the UK, certain statutes have extended jurisdiction because
of the nature of the subject matter and the probability of some aspect of their
occurrence having an international scope, such as the Computer Misuse Act
1990, the Sexual Offences (Conspiracy and Incitement) Act 1996[3] and some
sections of other acts.[4] In short, these examples do not cover the ambit of criminal activities that occur and result in a piecemeal attempt to solve particular
problems ignoring the issues of jurisdiction as a whole. Never before has the
need for clarity and accuracy of criminal jurisdiction been as crucial in international law.

The first part of the analysis of extraterritorial jurisdiction focuses on the
need to move beyond the sometimes incoherent and piecemeal statutory-based
approach to extending jurisdiction within a particular area of conduct. Not only
is this approach inhibiting and complex it also ignores a fairly simple common
law test that could be used for various modes of conduct. Most importantly,
such a test can also reaffirm international customary law principles. Instead of

---

[2] On the formalisation of the doctrine of comity, see J. Paul "Comity in International
Law" (1991) 32 Harv.Int'l L.J. 1.

[3] Sections 6 and 7 of the Computer Misuse Act 1990 (UK), c. 18. and sections 1 and
2 of the Sexual Offences Act 1996 (UK), c. 29.

[4] The Immigration Act 1971 (UK), c. 77., sections 25 A and 25 B. The Merchant
Shipping Act 1995 (UK), c. 21., sections 281 and 282, among other sections. Both these
statutes to allow criminal jurisdiction over acts committed by British individuals outside
the UK.

parliamentary reflex reactions to combat transnational or international crime by increasing extraterritorial jurisdiction with statutes, a reflection on the normative framework of jurisdictional competence is preferable.

The analysis concludes with a comparison between the two conflicting examples of jurisdictional assertions, the considerable extensions of jurisdiction in UK anti-terrorism legislation and the conservative approach in the case of *Pinochet*.[5] Again the positivist or codified view of international law dominates the development of jurisdictional competence through these different legislative instruments. While legislation and international treaties are helpful, especially in the case of the International Criminal Court, the peremptory norms of international law tend to be minimised or ignored in domestic courts and legislatures. The premise remains that extraterritorial jurisdiction in any form must have a firm basis in international law in order to be legitimate in its assertion of competence.

2) THE COMMON LAW APPROACH TO TRANSNATIONAL CRIMINAL ACTS

Previously, UK courts have exercised criminal jurisdiction on a territorial basis, the locus of the crime, either where the offence is commenced or completed referring to the established principles known as 'subjective' or 'objective' theories of territorial jurisdiction. Williams had further defined these as 'initiatory' and 'terminatory' theories,[6] where the potential criminal activity began or where it was concluded. The UK case law reflected a preference for the terminatory theory or the 'last constituent element' apparent in a significant body of case law starting with *R. v. Ellis* and *R. v. Harden*[7] and followed much later by *R. v. Manning*.[8] In the first two cases, the court identified what it deemed to be the 'gist and kernel' or 'gravaman' of the offence in the determination of the jurisdiction. In *Harden,* cheques were procured from Jersey, and in *Ellis*, goods were obtained on credit fraudulently. Conventionally, this basis would greatly limit the number of triable cases in a jurisdiction simply because of the 'last act' requirement. However, Williams argued that the initiatory theory should be adopted, which was proposed in preliminary considerations and proposals for legislative provision by the Law Commission in 1970. "It should be enacted

---

[5] *R v. Bow Street Metropolitan Stipendiary Magistrate Ex p. Pinochet Ugarte* (No. 3), [2000] 1 A.C. 147 (H.L.).

[6] G. Williams, "Venue and Ambit of Criminal law" (1965) 81 276 L.Q.R. 518.

[7] *R. v. Ellis*, [1899] 1 Q.B. 230, *R. v. Harden*, [1963] 1 Q.B. 8., *R. v. Governor of Brixton Prison and Another ex parte Rush*, [1969] 1 W.L.R. 165 (QB). All cases involved false pretences.

[8] [1998] 2 Cr. App. R. 461.

that where any act or omission or any event constituting an element of an offence occurs in England and Wales, that offence shall be deemed to have been committed in England and Wales even if other elements of the offence take place outside England and Wales".[9] Thus both Williams and the Law Commission believed the terminatory approach to be insufficient in the fight against transnational crime. However, adopting the initiatory theory was thought to create a multiplicity of jurisdictions and possibly expand or challenge the English common law view that all crime must be territorially linked.

The well-known case of *Treacy v. Director of Public Prosecutions*[10] (or *R. v. Treacy*) allowed Lord Diplock to confirm jurisdiction in England for a charge of blackmail under section 21 of the Theft Act 1968[11] when the accused had mailed a threatening letter from the Isle of Wight to Frankfurt Germany. Three of the Law Lords felt that the offence was not completed until the letter had been received in Germany. Nevertheless, Lords Hodson and Guest stated that the offence was complete when the letter was posted and the subsequent communication was immaterial.[12] Lord Diplock agreed but felt that the court should consider the intention of Parliament in the creation of the Theft Act 1968 and deemed that Parliament did not intend to be limited by geographic locations. There is not "any reason in comity to prevent Parliament from rendering liable to punishment, if they subsequently come to England, persons who have done outside the UK physical acts which have had harmful consequences upon victims in England."[13]

Hirst has interpreted Diplock's comments to be a realist view of the *actus reas* of blackmail itself, as outlined by the Theft Act 1968, where the offence is completed on the making of the monetary demand payment regardless of the target becoming aware of the demand.[14] Thus jurisdiction should be allowed where the act took place, or where the consequences of that act had effect, which is akin to the 'effects doctrine' as a basis for jurisdiction (as seen in

---

[9] Published Working Paper No. 29, Codification of the Criminal Law: Subject 3, *Territorial and Extraterritorial Extent of the Criminal Law* (Abingdon: Professional Books Ltd, 1977) at 51. Also reiterated in the UK Law Com. No. 91, *Report on the Territorial and Extraterritorial Extent of the Criminal Law* (London: Her Majesty's Stationary Office, 1978) at 2. The Law Commission noted recent cases at that time that supported this view, *Markus v. Secretary of State for Trade*, [1976] A.C. 35 (H.L.), 61 per Lord Diplock and *R. v. Treacy*, [1971] A.C. 537 (H.L.).

[10] [1971] A.C. 537 (H.L.).

[11] (UK), c. 60., section 21.

[12] *R. v. Treacy*, [1970] 55 Cr. App. R113 543 (H.L.). Also quoted in *R. v. Manning*, [1998] 2 Cr. App. R. 461.

[13] *R v. Treacy, ibid*. at 562.

[14] M. Hirst, *Jurisdiction and the Ambit of the Criminal Law*. (Oxford: Oxford University Press, 2003) at 115.

antitrust cases from the US).[15] Far from the previous use and potential abuse of this doctrine to penalise foreign companies for financial repercussions in the US, Lord Diplock's view has the potential to move jurisdictional claims beyond the terminatory theory, but just how far can it be applied is a valid question.

Sir Gerald Gordon[16] divided crimes into two categories, conduct crimes and result crimes; 'conduct' crimes are where the behaviour may amount to the offence being committed sometimes even before the contact with the victim. This was the reasoning in *Treacy*, where Lord Diplock stated the offence was completed on mailing the demand.[17] A 'result' crime requires the victim to receive the demand or incur the injury before it can be considered to be completed. The distinction between conduct and result crimes has been noted in several transnational criminal cases mentioned earlier,[18] however it lacks helpfulness in the analysis of basic jurisdictional problems. Courts in several cases have chosen to rely on this distinction of criminal action, as opposed to the subjective/objective territorial theories or the initiatory/terminatory approach to asserting jurisdiction without a sound basis, merely labelling the theories "esoteric".[19] This distinction may be useful as to the identification and classification of what courts do in their analysis of criminal conduct. However, it can create a minefield when determining certain modes of complex scenarios that either are attempted, planned and developed in the UK or are connected to the UK, unless covered by statute.[20] The practice of the courts has been to use the unhelpful 'conduct and result crimes' labels without considering that change to the view of the principle of territoriality could enable them to be more realistic in future prosecutions.

Lord Diplock was alone in his identification of the offence in *Treacy* as a conduct crime. It is easy to observe the preference in evaluating these offences on a jurisdictional principle analysis for two reasons; it brings England in line with other Commonwealth jurisdictions and it creates a line of case law that is clearer to follow in more diverse cases in the future. How courts make decisions on jurisdictional assertions is paramount to the progression of the theoretical analysis of transnational crime and the comprehensible understanding of jurisdiction.

---

[15] One of the earliest case examples is *U.S. v. Aluminium Co. of America* 148 F 2d 416 (1945).

[16] G. Gordon, *The Criminal Law of Scotland*, 2nd ed. (Edinburgh: Scottish Universities Law Institute, 1967.)

[17] *Supra* note 13 at 565.

[18] See *Markus v. Secretary of State for Trade*, supra note 9, and *DPP v. Stonehouse*, [1978] A.C. 55 (H.L.).

[19] *DPP v. Stonehouse, ibid.* at 78.

[20] See Sexual Offences Act 1996 (UK).

Proceeding from the terminatory approach, the most obvious choice is the initiatory theory of when an act begins in the state claiming jurisdiction. Still further is the possibility of the use of the controversial effects doctrine where a state claims jurisdiction based on the harmful effects occurring within the territory of the state.[21] In reality, the courts in England have been historically conservative about claiming jurisdiction when an offence is transnational unless it has been "completed" in England. However if expanding jurisdictional claims are to become more commonplace they must have an understandable and functional basis relying on a theoretical principle as mentioned earlier. As a Council of Europe report puts it, "It goes without saying that a wide application of the ubiquity and effects doctrines may in fact be tantamount to an extraterritorial application of criminal laws under the guise of the principle of territoriality."[22] The inevitable dialogue remains, can a state expand jurisdiction for transnational crimes and avoid assuming illegitimate extraterritorial jurisdiction?

The extension of jurisdiction by statute was the overall point of the majority of the Court of Appeal in *R. v. Manning*.[23] The court dealt with two problems of jurisdiction, those for substantive offences and those for charges of conspiracy, assuming that they should be treated differently because of their separation in Part I of the Criminal Justice Act 1993.[24] The judgment upheld substantive charges but quashed the conspiracy charges.[25] The reason for this can be found in the final page of the judgment where Lord Buxton calls for the defects in the law to be put right by Parliament through the enactment of Part I of the Criminal Justice Act 1993 without delay. Part I of the Act would allow jurisdiction to the courts of England and Wales over cases of international fraud and other property offences that had a connection with this country but which were not necessarily completed in the UK.

This significant development brought about by the Act in the extension of jurisdiction for 'conspiracy' charges regardless of where they occur, had already been outlined in two previous cases where jurisdiction had been extended, *DPP v. Stonehouse*[26] and *Liangsiriprasert v. United States Government*.[27] In *Liangsiriprasert* Lord Griffiths relied on the reasoning in *Libman*,

---

[21] *U.S. v. S. Brodie, D. Brodie, J. Sabzali*, 250 F. Supp. 2d 462 (2002). A Canadian was convicted of violating U.S. economic sanctions for his actions in Canada because the court found effects within the U.S.

[22] Council of Europe, Legal Affairs, *Extraterritorial Criminal Jurisdiction* (Strasbourg: Council of Europe, Publications and Documents Division, 1990) at 24.

[23] *R. v. Manning*, [1998] 2 Cr. App. R. 461.

[24] C. 36. This section came in force after *R. v. Manning, ibid.*, on June 1, 1999.

[25] *Supra* note 23, also see *R. v. Cox*, [1968] 1 W.L.R. 88 (C.A. Crim Div.), and *R. v. Atakpu*, [1994] Q.B. 69.

[26] [1978] A.C. 55 (H.L.).

[27] [1991] 1 A.C. 225 (P.C.).

stating "the English courts have decisively begun to move away from the definition or obsessiveness and technical formulations aimed at finding a single situs of a crime by locating where the gist of the crime occurred or where it was completed."[28] He felt the courts were examining "where a substantial measure of the activities constituting a crime take place,"[29] restricted only by comity and reasonableness if it should be dealt with in another state. The relevance of jurisdictional claims for conspiracy or inchoate charges might have particular bearing in the anti-terrorism legislation proposed by the government.[30]

Striking similarities also exist between the substantial connection test and the process of determining jurisdiction in Part I of the Criminal Justice Act 1993, which requires an offence to have a "relevant event"[31] occur in the UK. The conservative nature of the courts and their tendency to hold onto the terminatory approach may lead to a restrictive interpretation of what constitutes a 'relevant event.' Since *Manning*, Part 1 of the Criminal Justice Act has been brought into force in 1999.[32] This is a tremendous change from the previous requirement of the completion of the act under English law, although there is a certain amount of hesitation due to the interpretation of the 'relevant event' that is required.

Expanding the basis for jurisdiction of an offence should not be confused with a fragile link to a territory in cases where perhaps only one insignificant element of an offence takes place. The Law Commission Report recommended that, ". . . our courts should have jurisdiction to try a charge of one of the listed offences if any event that is required to be proved in order to obtain a conviction takes place in England and Wales".[33] Otherwise the Commission felt that there would be a weak case for jurisdiction if the court considered only a "preparatory or incidental act".[34] Although a single element should be able to constitute jurisdiction, it must be restrained by a functional test that can be applied regardless of state and level of crime. The substantial connection test provides that a state can establish jurisdiction if there is a 'real and substantial

---

[28] *Supra* note 1, para 42.

[29] *Ibid.*

[30] Statement by Prime Minister Tony Blair on 5 August 2005, outlining the potential offence of condoning or glorifying terrorism: www.guardian.co.uk/attackonlondon/0,161,1543386,00.htm.

[31] Part I s. 2(1), pertaining to any Group A offences such as fraud, obtaining a money transfer, false statements, blackmail, handling stolen goods, and forgery; excluding Group B offences such as conspiracy, attempting and incitement to commit a Group A offence.

[32] SI1999 No. 1189 and 1149.

[33] Law Commission No. 180. *Jurisdiction Over Offences of Fraud and Dishonesty With a Foreign Element* (London: Her Majesty's Stationary Offence, 1989) at 2.27.

[34] *Ibid.* at 2.28.

link' between the offence and the state regardless of where the *actus reus* is completed, the level of the offence or whether it is considered to be a conduct or result crime.

3) SUBSTANTIAL CONNECTION TEST

This test is not new in the common law and certain aspects of international law; it has been frequently used when assessing the enforcements of foreign judgments as in the Canadian case of *Beals v. Saldanha*,[35] where the court upheld the award by a jury in Florida for fraud. The substantial connection test was based on three assessments; that the allegations were new and not subject to prior adjudication, the fact that the foreign procedure was coherent with Canada's concept of 'natural justice,' and the judgment did not go against public policy in Canada.

The most relevant case where the substantial connection test was not limited to enforcement of a foreign judgment but used to establish criminal jurisdiction (extraterritorial application of the conspiracy provisions of the Criminal Code subsection 465(3)), was the Canadian case of *Libman*.[36] Murray Libman had been charged with seven counts of fraud and one count of conspiracy to fraud after it was found that he had organised a group of telephone personnel in Canada to contact US residents in order to induce investments in Central America which he would collect there and return to Canada.[37] The jurisdictional dilemma arose when the accused argued that a portion of the activities on which the charges were based occurred outside Canada. Libman relied on *R. v. Brixton Prison Governor, Ex parte Rush*[38] where the 'last constituent element' test was applied in the decision as to whether a crime was committed in England, since the essential element or 'gravaman' of the fraud and deprivation of the victims occurred outside Canadian territory. The accused's response to the conspiracy charge[39] was to rely on *Board of Trade v. Owen*,[40] where a conspiracy in England to commit a wrongful act somewhere else would not result in a conviction in England. He also argued that the section of the Criminal Code dealing with the conspiracy charge was restricted to criminal offences within Canada. However, the prosecution submitted that the location of the

---

[35] *Beals v. Saldanha*, [2003] 3 S.C.R. 416.

[36] *Supra* note 1.

[37] Material misrepresentations were made in order to sell shares in two corporations which were supposed to be mining gold in Costa Rica. *Ibid.* at para 5.

[38] *R. v. Governor of Brixton Prison and Another ex parte Rush*, [1969] 1 W.L.R. 165 (Q.B.) (a case involving false pretences).

[39] Criminal Code R.S.C. 1970, c. 34 s. 423 (1)(d).

[40] [1957] A.C. 602 (H.L.).

planning and organisation meant that the offences were 'substantially' committed in Canada and relied on another Canadian case which allowed jurisdiction
for prosecution because the proceeds were received in Canada.[41] The use of the
substantial connection test to link the offence with the territory was imperative
to overcome the restriction of the Code, which states that no person "shall be
convicted in Canada for an offence committed outside of Canada".[42] Judge La
Forest reasoned that since the wording in the Code did not specifically outline
the necessity that criminal law would be confined to Canadian territory, the
Code was expressing the principle's overall purpose, not its rigid application.[43]
The Supreme Court of Canada found that the offences were triable in Canada
and granted jurisdiction on the grounds that a significant portion of the offences
occurred within the territory.

The second part of the two-stage test developed to evaluate the basis for
jurisdiction was the court's analysis of any potential offence of international
comity, generally defined as respect of one state's jurisdiction and laws by
another.[44] Judge La Forest noted Lord Wilberforce's comment on the evolution
of comity in *DPP v. Doot*[45] as a basis for justification in *Libman*; "the rules of
international comity are not static and I do not believe that in the modern world
nations are nearly as sensitive about exclusive jurisdiction over crime as they
may have been formerly".[46]

Oppenheim specifies comity in terms similar to La Forest; "rules of polite-
ness, convenience and goodwill observed by states in their mutual intercourse
without being legally bound by them".[47] Even though certain theorists have
concluded that comity is essentially indefinable, the often quoted 1895 US case
of *Hilton v. Guyot* laid the foundation of the modern understanding of comity
as ". . . due regard to both international duty and convenience to the rights of its
own citizens or of others who are under the protection of its laws".[48] In the past,
the majority of references and theoretical discussions of comity have been
linked to the recognition of foreign judgments, similar to the popular use of the

[41] *Re Chapman* (1970) 5 C.C.C.46 (Ont. C.A.).

[42] S. 5(2) of the Canadian Criminal Code 1985 as quoted by Judge La Forest in *R. v.
Libman, supra* note 1, at para. 66.

[43] *Supra* note 1, at paras. 65–66.

[44] See *R. v. Treacy, supra* note 12 at 834 and B. A. Garner, *Black's Law Dictionary*
(St.Paul Minn.; West Group Publishing, 1999) at 261. As stated in *R v. Manning, supra*
note 23 at 475, "Each sovereign state should refrain from punishing persons for their
conduct within the territorial of another sovereign state, where the conduct has had no
harmful consequences within the territory which imposes the punishment."

[45] *D.P.P v Doot* [1973] A.C. 807 (H.L.).

[46] *Ibid., per* Lord Salmon, at 834, as quoted in *Libman, supra* note 1 at para. 39.

[47] *Ibid.*

[48] 159 U.S. 113, 163–164.

substantial connection test in this area. If comity is to be used appropriately as part of the substantial connection test for evaluating jurisdiction, its parameters must be clarified.

Extraterritorial examples of the normative link between comity and international law can also be seen in the interaction between the UK Court of Appeal and the US Government authorities concerning the indefinite detention of a UK national, Abbasi,[49] in Guantanamo Bay as an enemy combatant. While acknowledging the right of the US to formulate and apply its own law, this sovereign right does not negate the requirement for such a law not to breach international principles and laws.[50] The court stated that it was "free to express a view in relation to what it conceives to be a clear breach of international law . . . in apparent contravention of fundamental principles recognised by both jurisdictions".[51] Therefore, comity allows laws of other sovereign nations to be discredited in a domestic sense if this requirement is not met. Two fairly dramatic examples were cited by the Court of Appeal in this area are, *Oppenheim v. Cattermole*[52] and *Kuwait Airways Corporation v. Iraq Airways Co.*[53] The first was a refusal to recognise the 1941 German decree removing German citizenship from emigrated Jews, while the other was a refusal to recognise the Iraqi decree making Kuwait Airways part of Iraqi Airways.

Comity as a doctrine must have at its very core two elements; the reinforcement of the sovereign equality of states and adherence to *jus cogens* in international customary law. While the first element may appear to be an obvious part of comity, the second is equally important not only because of the customary origin of comity, but also due to the necessity of its coherence with the normative framework of jurisdiction and inter-state relations. This substantial connection test may be an innovative technique to link crimes back to the territory for courts seeking a functional test. However its potential misuse is grave unless the particular interpretation of comity is in keeping with *jus cogens*.

The evolution of comity has moved beyond the simplistic interpretation of it as practices by states that are solely motivated by courtesy, such as "saluting the flags of foreign warships at sea".[54] The mature view of comity as a non-binding rule relies on the approach of reasonableness applied with assessing the

---

[49] *R. (Abbasi) v. Secretary of State for Foreign and Commonwealth Affairs*, [2002] EWCA Civ 1598.

[50] *Ibid.* at para. 57. Application for judicial review of the mother of Abbasi to order the Foreign Secretary to make representations to the US Government or give reasons why not. As discussed in T. Endicott, "Symposium: Has Law Moral Foundations? The Reason of the Law." (2003) 48 Am. J. Juris. 83 at 101.

[51] *Ibid.*

[52] [1976] A.C. 249 (H.L.).

[53] [2002] 2 W.L.R. 1353 (H.L.).

[54] M. Shaw, *International Law* (Cambridge; Cambridge University Press, 2003) at 2.

jurisdictional assertion. The court must factor into its analysis a reasonable consideration of whether there is anything in the particular principle of jurisdiction to be used that offends respect to another jurisdiction. This reasonable consideration is similar to the Supreme Court of Canada's analysis in *Beals v. Saldanha*[55] as the foreign judgment could be applied in Canada because it was consistent with natural justice and public policy of the state. These are normative value considerations and therefore must be linked with *jus cogens*.

Returning to the first element of the substantial connection test, this part relates to the 'real and substantial' link between the offence and state-claiming jurisdiction. Recent evaluation of *Libman* has stressed the fairly limited standard of the Supreme Court when defining the test, ". . . all that is necessary to make an offence subject to the jurisdiction of our courts is that a significant portion of the activities constituting that offence took place in Canada".[56] Confusion may arise over the evaluation of what constitutes a 'significant portion' of the activities of an offence and whether the test can be used to link an offence to the territory when only one, albeit important, element is present. Brownlie is broader in his specification of when a state can claim jurisdiction over extraterritorial actions by not limiting the connection to a 'significant portion' provided the link is present and substantial.[57]

Parallels can be drawn between the substantial connection test and the effects doctrine promoted by the Restatement (Third) of Foreign Relations Laws, reaffirming the US view that jurisdiction can be asserted if the intended effects of the offence are substantial.[58] The one caveat noted by the Restatement (Third) is that there must be reasonableness in the assertion of jurisdiction in order to avoid conflicts with other states. However, this similarity of language cannot be used to justify either the controversial effects doctrine itself or its previous use in antitrust cases. The substantial connection test is a method of linking criminal offences to the territory best able or most willing to proceed with the prosecution and it is representative of the norms of international customary law. It takes on a different meaning in a public law sense rather than the private law emphasis of a conflict of laws where the consideration may be on the interests of the parties involved. Criminal prosecutions are part of the general aims of the international community. Finally, the purpose of the test, along with the doctrine of comity and the application of reasonableness generate the inherent legitimacy required for any assertion of jurisdiction of an extraterritorial action.

---

[55] *Supra* note 35.

[56] *Supra* note 1 at para. 74.

[57] I. Brownlie, *Principles of Public International Law* (Oxford; Oxford University Press, 2003) at 309.

[58] The Restatement (Third) of the Foreign Relations Law of the US. (Washington: The American Law Institute Publishers, 1987) Volume 1, § 402 and § 403.

Theoretical support for such a test has been argued to be a "holistic and less technical approach" to the problem of extraterritorial crime, according to Arnell, who proposes the use of, what he aptly describes as an "objective methodology . . . allocating jurisdiction to the state most closely and genuinely connected with the alleged crime", as part of the 'proper law approach'.[59] Without a doubt the substantial connection test leans toward an objective methodology, but in order to achieve such a standard and for it to be a coherent alternative to the thematic approach preferred by certain states its appropriate application requires the understanding of and adherence to comity, reasonableness and *jus cogens*.

4) CONTRASTING EXAMPLES OF EXTRATERRITORIAL JURISDICTION

The reliance on statutory extensions of jurisdiction is represented by the House of Lord's decision in *Pinochet*.[60] Spain's request for the extradition of *Pinochet* was limited by the court to only those acts that occurred after the 1984 Torture Convention had been incorporated into domestic law.[61] The decision minimised the view that torture was a crime under international customary law prior to that time, a view Lord Millet did not necessarily agree with. "The systematic use of torture on a large scale and as an instrument of state policy had joined piracy, war crimes and crimes against peace as an international crime of universal jurisdiction well before 1984. I consider that it had done so by 1973".[62]

Thus, according to Lord Millett, the need for statutory implementation of the Torture Convention into domestic law was not necessary because universal jurisdiction already existed.[63] One of the problems highlighted by Robertson[64] is the lack of understanding of international law principles by the Law Lords,

---

[59] P. Arnell, "The Proper Law of the Crime in International Law Revisited" (2000) 9 Nott. L.J. 39 at 41.

[60] *Supra* note 5.

[61] Convention Against Torture and Other Cruel, Inhuman or Degrading Treatment or Punishment. (New York, 10 December 1984) U.N.T.S. vol. 1465, I-24841. Entered into force 26 June 1987 and ratified by the UK 8 December 1988 with the Criminal Justice Act 1998 (UK), c. 33.

[62] *Supra* note 5 at 276.

[63] Note *Siderman de Blake v. Republic of Argentina* (1992), 965 F. 2d 699. That dealt with the private enforcement of international customary law. The Alien Tort Claims Act required the plaintiffs plead a violation of the law of nations for the jurisdictional claim.

[64] D. Robertson, "The House of Lords as the Political and Constitutional Court; Lessons from The Pinochet Case." *The Pinochet Case a Legal and Constitutional Analysis*. D. Woodhouse, (ed.) (Oxford; Hart Publishing, 2000), at 24.

and their subsequent reliance on the domestic court's 'outlook' of how international law applies domestically, though arguably recent decisions show a growing awareness of the fact that international customary principles can apply to cases before them. Sugarman reiterated this, arguing that "the Pinochet case (amongst other things) is evidence of the need for judges, lawyers, law teachers and law students to be better appraised of the basic concepts and role of international law and how they are increasingly imbricated within domestic law".[65] In this case a clearer understanding of international customary law and a move away from the dependence on incorporation into statute would have led to extradition on many more offences.

The conservative approach of the court in *Pinochet* can be contrasted with the rather determined approach of Parliament when passing anti-terrorism legislation. This may be a rather current example of the tension between the judiciary and the executive in this area of civil liberties. An example of such would be the extremely broad definition of terrorism in the Terrorism Act 2000.[66] Section 62 extends jurisdiction for acts that are for "the purposes of terrorism", "(1) If (a) a person does anything outside the United Kingdom as an act of terrorism or for the purposes of terrorism and (b) his action would have constituted the commission of one of the offences listed in subsection (2) if it had been done in the United Kingdom, he shall be guilty of the offence." Besides the jurisdictional considerations, there are concerns that the Act may apply to general protest groups and/or civil libertarian groups who voiced support for resistance movements against repressive regimes in other countries. Since the House of Lord's decision[67] on the detention of foreign nationals by the Home Secretary under the Anti-Terrorism Crime and Security Act (ATCSA) 2001[68] (Part 4 section 23(1)), house arrest is now being considered by the government.[69]

Overall, several other Acts have extended jurisdiction for the specific purpose of prosecuting terrorist action such as the Taking of Hostages Act,[70] and

---

[65] D. Sugarman, "The Pinochet Case; International Criminal Justice in the Gothic Style?" (November 2001) 64 M.L.R. 933 at 937.

[66] C. 13. Section 1, defines terrorism as a threat of serious violence, endangerment of life, or serious damage to property; or actions that create serious risk to health and safety of the public or a section of the public in the UK or elsewhere, or actions designed to seriously interfere with or disrupt electronic systems.

[67] *A (FC) and Others v. Secretary of State for the Home Department, X (FC) and Another v. Secretary of State for the Home Department*, [2004] U.K.H.L. 56.

[68] C. 24.

[69] "Who are the Terror Detainees", BBC News, 11 March 2005: bbc.co.uk/1/hi/uk/4101751.stm.

[70] The Taking of Hostages Act 1982 (UK), c. 28, section 1 extends jurisdiction regardless of nationality.

the Protection of United Nations Personnel Act.[71] Parliament, with increasing regularity, has responded to its international commitments in treaties and conventions with a plethora of Acts and statutory instruments in an attempt to stem the threat of transnational terrorist actions. These Acts contain a variety of overlapping provisions and sections updating previous Acts, each with their own limitations and idiosyncrasies creating a complex and problematic outlook for successful prosecutions and a true understanding of the principles of jurisdiction. Using specific statutory extensions of jurisdiction ignores the customary law commentary on allocating competencies and avoids adherence to a normative system to administer such on an international plane. Instead of reflex reactions to national and international incidents through the legislative instruments, acknowledging the customary test of evaluating a substantial link to the territory that is bound by two doctrinal factors, reasonableness and comity, can potentially help to create a case law that is more in keeping with peremptory norms of international customary law. Is universal jurisdiction appropriate and necessary for certain statutes relating to terrorism in the UK? The conclusion must be not in its present state; as it does not conform to the restriction of reasonableness and comity, and without a limited definition it may criminalise inoffensive acts as acts of terrorism.

In both these judicial and legislative examples the UK would have been aided by adherence to the elements of the substantial connection test. Specifically, with anti-terrorism legislation the doctrine of comity needs to be considered. Whether a state is prescribing a law or assessing a jurisdictional claim as in *Pinochet* there should be a real and substantial link to the territory in order to keep it within the confines of international norms and principles. This would reinforce its legitimacy.

5) CONCLUSION: THE NECESSITY OF A LINK TO THE TERRITORY

Requiring a link to the territory for a jurisdictional claim or assertion is fundamental to the theoretical basis of jurisdiction with one notable exception, crimes that fall under the universal principle or those that are deemed to be 'against the laws of all nations'. However this does not mean that the operation of universal jurisdiction is without certain difficulties. Crimes that are generally thought to be universal in conduct and nature can arguably be prosecuted by

---

[71] United Nations Personnel Act 1997 (UK), c. 13, section 1 states that "if a person does outside the United Kingdom any act to or are in relation to a UN worker which, if he had done it in any part of the United Kingdom, would have made him guilty of any offences mentioned in subsection 2, he shall in that part of United Kingdom be guilty of that offence."

any state. However besides the famous case of *Eichmann*,[72] domestic courts have been correctly hesitant to proceed with prosecutions that are not linked to the territory in some significant manner.

One of the most famous extensions of jurisdiction is the 1993 Belgian statute. This statute has been restricted to that of 'conditional universal jurisdiction', partially due to the decision in *Sharon, Ariel, Yaron, Amos and Others*.[73] Also, the Belgian Senate, which had been under intense diplomatic pressure from the US, has since amended its universal jurisdiction clause to individuals who are connected in some fashion to Belgian territory.[74] This is what Cassese refers to as the narrow notion of universality, only when the state has possession of the individual, can they prosecute or extradite.[75] He distinguishes 'absolute universal jurisdiction' as the power to prosecute persons regardless of nationality and presence of the individual in the state raising concerns over possible trials in *absentia*.

The Canadian Crimes Against Humanity and War Crimes Act,[76] which arguably allows for universal jurisdiction,[77] has been touted by a group of Zimbabweans in exile and representative lawyers as an appropriate tool for Canada's Attorney General to charge President Robert Mugabe[78] with various human rights abuses. Aware of the ruling in *Congo v. Belgium*,[79] giving immunity to a head of state in office, the reality of a possible charge is on hold, leaving the jurisdictional question split between those who, similar to Schabas,[80]

---

[72] *Attorney General of the Government of Israel* v *Adolf Eichmann* (1962) 36 I.L.R. (Israel) at 5.

[73] *Sharon, Ariel, Yaron, Amos and Others*, (Cour de Cassation de Belgique), 12 February 2003, P.02.1139.F/1: www.droit.fundp.ac.be/cours/pen/JC032C1.pdf.

[74] Either at the time of the act the victim was a national or resident of Belgium or at the date of the proceedings the accused is a national or resident. S. Ratner, "Belgium's War Crimes Statute: A Postmortem" (2003) 97 Am. J. Int. Law 888 at 891. Loi du 5 août 2003 relative à la répression des infractions graves au droit international humanitaire. Translated 42 ILM 1258 (2003).

[75] A. Cassese, *International Criminal Law* (Oxford: Oxford University Press, 2003) at 286.

[76] Crimes Against Humanity and War Crimes Act 2000, c.24. Incorporation of the Statute of the International Criminal Court, (Rome, 17 July 1998) U.N.T.S. vol. 2187, I-38544.

[77] *Ibid.* , sections 6 and 8.

[78] S. Nolen, "Can Ottawa Act Against Mugabe?", *The Globe and Mail*. 5 November 2004.

[79] *Arrest Warrant of 11 April 2000 (Democratic Republic of Congo v. Belgium)* ICJ Gen. List No. 121, Judgment of 14 Feb. 2002.

[80] Author of *An Introduction to the International Criminal Court*. (Cambridge; Cambridge University Press, 2001) and many other publications in the area of international criminal law.

propose that the statute does not require any link to the territory and others who propose that a reasonable link must exist.[81] Re-evaluating the wording of the statute it would appear that the intention is for a link with the territory, hence the various descriptors listed in section 8; "the alleged offender or victim was a citizen in Canada or is now present in Canada or is a citizen of a state that was engaged in armed conflict with Canada".[82] The Canadian Criminal Code stipulates that Canada can assert jurisdiction over an individual present in the territory in conformity with international law.[83] This is not universal jurisdiction but territorial jurisdiction over an extraterritorial offence with a substantial link.

In *Lockerbie*, the Scottish courts claimed jurisdiction based on the location of the debris from the exploding plane on Scottish territory and the subsequent death of Scottish residents to try the Libyan defendants.[84] The subsequent extraterritorial sitting of a Scottish court in the Netherlands as a result of a negotiated arrangement was a unique situation. Other situations allow for presence of the alleged offender and only a part of the offending activity in the territory of the state. These scenarios, and many others, can be addressed satisfactorily through the fitting choice of a principled basis for jurisdictional assertions and the application of the substantial connection test as long as the broad interpretation of comity is not disturbed.

Generally, states will refer to their constitutional limitations when evaluating extraterritorial circumstances, which is a normal part of the legal methodology. The other limitation that can sometimes be minimised is the constraint of international law principles. The appropriate use of prescriptive jurisdiction stems from the limitations of these two aspects when exercising extraterritorial jurisdiction. The substantial connection test revisits the essential aspects of the 'constructive presence' terminology from Justice Holmes in 1912: "when a man is said to be constructively present where the consequences of an act done elsewhere are felt, it is meant that for some special purpose he will be treated as

---

[81] *Supra* note 78. Schabas argued that "The Justice Department is wrong if they say that the intention of the act is that there must be a nexus with Canada. The whole point of the Crimes Against Humanity and War Crimes Act is to give Canada universal jurisdiction, which means you can prosecute people when there is no nexus."

[82] *Supra* note 76.

[83] Constitution Act 1982 c.11 stipulates the primacy of the Constitution above all laws in Canada, Section 52.1. Under Part I Section 11 of the Charter of Rights and Freedoms; Proceedings in Criminal and Penal Matters, "(g) a person is not to be found guilty on account of any act or omission unless, at the time of the act or omission, it constituted an offence under Canadian or International law or was criminal according to general principles of law recognised by the community of nations."

[84] *Questions of Interpretation and Application of the 1971 Montreal Convention Arising from the Aerial Incident at Lockerbie* (*Libyan Arab Jamahirya v. United Kingdom*) Preliminary Objections, ICJ Reports, 1998/9.

he would have been treated if he had been present, although he was not".[85] It is fundamental to any assertion of jurisdiction that a link with the territory is not only present but that it is a real and substantial link. The test for jurisdiction, regardless of the level of offence or specific crime requires this essential element as well as an adherence to comity between states; without it the principles of international customary law cannot be maintained.

---

[85] *Hyde v. U.S.* 225 U.S. 347 (1912) at 386.

Chapter 6

'Vague' Indictments and Justice at the International Criminal Tribunals: Learning from the World of Common Law

Chile Eboe-Osuji

1) INTRODUCTION

The judgment of the Appeals Chamber of the International Criminal Tribunal for the former Yugoslavia (ICTY) in *Prosecutor v Kupreškić*[1] is momentous in the jurisprudence of both the ICTY and of the International Criminal Tribunal for Rwanda (ICTR). Owing to it, Defence Counsel now subject every indictment to exacting scrutiny. The scrutiny has engaged two main questions: (a) whether the pleadings have been vitiated in any way for want of sufficient details, thereby warranting the exclusion of the line of evidence led in regard to such pleadings,[2] and (b) whether the Prosecution may be forbidden to lead a

---

[1] *Prosecutor v Kupreskic & Ors (Judgment)* 23 October 2001 (ICTY Appeals Chamber).

[2] See *Prosecutor v Semanza (Judgment)* 15 May 2003 paras. 41–61 (ICTR Trial Chamber III); *Prosecutor v Kamuhanda (Judgment)* 22 January 2004 paras. 46–60 (ICTR Trial Chamber II); *Prosecutor v Ntagerura (Judgment)* 25 February 2004 paras. 28–70 (ICTR Trial Chamber III).

Christopher P.M. Waters (Ed.), *British and Canadian Perspectives on International Law*, pp. 105–128.
© 2006 Koninklijke Brill NV. Printed in the Netherlands.

particular manner of evidence during trial because the evidence is not within the scope of the pleadings. In this essay, the state of jurisprudence of both international Tribunals will be reviewed and compared with case law from common law jurisdictions, with the objective of stimulating international criminal law with relevant general principles of law recognised by modern nations.[3]

Up to a point, it could be said that whether an indictment meets the mark, and how well it does, are considerations liable to vary from critic to critic. The Canadian case of *R v McKenzie*[4] illustrates this proposition. McKenzie was a taxi driver. By his employment terms, he was to account to the owner of the taxi for all fares and to pay the owner 55% of the day's total receipts, less daily operating costs. One night in March 1970, McKenzie carried five passengers to various destinations, but only reported one trip and failed to account for the total fares received. It was then charged that McKenzie "... at the City of Vancouver, on the 31st day of March AD 1970, unlawfully did commit theft of the approximate sum of $16.50 the property of Dominic Louis Christian contrary to the form of the statute in such case made and provided." The majority of the British Columbia Court of Appeal set McKenzie's conviction aside, reasoning that the charge lacked any averment of the essential ingredients of an offence of theft under the Criminal Code. Davey CJBC dissented, finding that the indictment "was a good charge of theft". On further appeal, the Supreme Court of Canada agreed with Davey.

McKenzie shows how perfectly reasonable lawyers may disagree on whether a pleading is bad for vagueness. As Professors LaFave and Israeal note:

> The major issue presented by the notice function [*ie* that the indictment must fairly inform the accused of the charges against him] is not whether it should exist, but rather what scope it should have. Disagreements exist as to both the subjects for which notice is needed, and the degree of particularization that should be required in providing notice to those subjects.[5]

The essence of LaFave and Israel's observation was captured by the ICTR Appeals Chamber when they said in a relevant context that, "[i]t is well established that when the exercise of discretion is involved reasonable minds may differ."[6]

---

[3] I. Brownlie, *Principles of Public International Law*, 6th edn (Oxford: OUP, 2003) p. 15.

[4] [1972] SCR 409, 4 CCC (2d) 296, 21 DLR (3d) 215 (SCC).

[5] W. LaFave and J. Israel, *Criminal Procedure*, 2nd edn (St Paul, Minn.: West Publishing, 1992) p. 814.

[6] *Prosecutor v Bizimungu and Ors (Decision on Prosecution's Interlocutory Appeals against Decisions of the Trial Chamber on Exclusion of Evidence)*, 25 June 2004 para. 20 (ICTR Appeals Chamber). See the opinion of Lord Hailsham LC to the same effect in *Re W (An Infant)*, [1971] AC 682 at 700 (HL).

That such simple indictments as in *McKenzie* have engendered such judicial polarisation largely establishes the proposition that defects in the form of the indictment, much like beauty, lie in the eyes of the beholder. Such division of opinions seen even in cases so simple must surely raise concerns about the plight of justice in such complex trials as the ones typically conducted before the international criminal tribunals.

A significant factor in this anxiety is the structure of an international criminal justice system that permits only two levels of judiciary – a trial chamber and a final appellate chamber. International criminal tribunals operate without the benefit of a second appellate level (as in Canada, England and USA) in which even a simple case, like *McKenzie*, would enjoy a second opportunity to *verify* that justice has been truly done when accused persons are set free or convicted, in view of claims that the charges have been badly drafted.

2) EXCLUSION OF EVIDENCE LED IN REGARD TO VAGUE PLEADINGS

a) *Prosecutor v Kupreškić & Ors*

The judgment of the ICTY Appeals Chamber in *Kupreškić*[7] is the best starting point for a discussion of the jurisprudence of the *ad hoc* tribunals on exclusion of evidence led pursuant to vague pleadings. In this case, the Trial Chamber of the ICTY convicted two brothers, Zoran and Mirjan Kupreškić (the "Accused"), of persecution, as co-perpetrators of a common plan to ethnically cleanse the village of Ahmići of its Bosnian Muslim inhabitants. Their convictions were primarily based on two factors: their involvement, prior to 16 April 1993, with the troops of the Bosnian Military wing known as the HVO, and their role in an attack on Ahmići on the morning of 16 April 1993. The Trial Chamber found that the HVO had made plans to attack Ahmići during the morning of 16 April 1993, and that by 15 April 1993, the Accused knew of these plans and were ready to participate in it. Most importantly, the Trial Chamber found that, on 16 April 1993, the Accused "were in the house of Suhret Ahmić immediately after he and Meho Hrstanović were shot and immediately before the house was set on fire . . . [and] were participants in the attack on the house as part of the group of soldiers who carried it out."[8] In convicting the Accused, the Trial Chamber relied heavily on this evidence, given by Witness H, who was at the house of Ahmić.[9]

---

[7] *Prosecutor v Kupreškić, supra* note 1.
[8] *Ibid.* para. 77.
[9] *Ibid.* para. 78.

Although it was the sole factual basis upon which the Trial Chamber convicted the Accused of persecution, this event was not pleaded in the indictment.
Two weeks into the trial – on 3 September 1998 – the Presiding trial judge
asked questions of the Prosecutor at the end of the Prosecutor's examination-
in-chief of Witness H, indicating that it was unclear as to whether the
Prosecution was alleging that the Accused played a role in killing Ahmić. The
Prosecution counsel admitted that "[i]t is not charged in the indictment";[10] and
explained that the relevant evidence came late, after one amendment already to
the indictment, so the Prosecution decided not to amend once more but to introduce the evidence anyway, hoping to use it.[11] During the closing submissions,
the Presiding Judge, again, indicated that it was unclear to him what to make of
the evidence since the fact it supported was not pleaded. Not only did the
Prosecution fail to enlighten the Presiding Judge on the matter, but even the
Prosecution appeared, still that late in the day, to be unsure of either the role
that the Accused played in those events or the jural significance of the events.[12]

From the foregoing, it seems clear that everyone involved in the trial was
unclear on how to handle the unpleaded event that Witness H recounted. Still,
the Trial Chamber convicted the Accused on the basis of it, notwithstanding
that the Defence had unsuccessfully challenged the form of the indictment in
six motions made by all of the six defendants before the commencement of the
trial[13] and had continued their objections to it during the course of the trial.[14]

b) *The Rationes Decidendi of the Kupreškić Case*

During appeal the Defence reasserted their objection as to the form of the
indictment. The Appeals Chamber then performed the following three-step
analysis:

   (i) whether the Trial Chamber had convicted on the basis of material facts not
      pleaded in the indictment;
  (ii) if the Trial Chamber did rely on such facts, whether the trial was thereby
      rendered unfair;[15] and
 (iii) whether the Defence had been guilty of waiver.[16]

---

[10] *Ibid.* paras. 102 and 103.
[11] *Ibid.* paras. 102 and 103.
[12] *Ibid.* paras. 106–110.
[13] The Trial Chamber had dismissed the Defence challenges to the indictment in its
Decision on Defence Challenges to Form of the Indictment, 15 May 1998: see
Prosecutor v Kupreškić, supra note 1, para. 123 and footnote 185 (ICTY Appeals
Chamber); and the trial commenced on 17 August 1998: *ibid.* para. 102.
[14] See *ibid.* para. 104.
[15] *Ibid.* para. 87.
[16] *Ibid.* para. 123.

On the first point of the inquiry, the Appeals Chamber found in the affirmative. According to the Appeals Chamber, the Prosecution had an obligation to plead the material facts underpinning the charges in the indictment, with enough detail as to inform a defendant clearly of the charges against him, so that he may prepare his defence.[17] However, the Appeals Chamber went to great length to qualify that obligation in those cases in which it would be impracticable for the Prosecution to plead, with specificity, the identity of the victims and the dates for the commission of the crimes[18] due to "the sheer scale of the alleged crimes".[19] But, held the Appeals Chamber, the *Kupreškić* case was no such case. "On the contrary, the nature of the Prosecution case at trial was confined mainly to showing that Zoran and Mirjan Kupreškić were present as HVO members in Ahmići on 16 April 1993 and personally participated in the attack on two different houses resulting, *inter alia*, in the killing of six people."[20]

Notably, the Appeals Chamber had found that the case against the Accused was "dramatically transformed" during the course of the trial, in that "the thrust of the persecution allegation against them somehow changed between the filing of the Amended Indictment and the presentation of the Prosecution case, so that the latter was no longer reflected in the former."[21] According to the Appeals Chamber, the case was one in which "the Prosecution could, and should, have been more specific in setting out the allegations in the Amended Indictment."[22]

On whether the defects in the indictment rendered the trial unfair,[23] the Appeals Chamber considered whether the Defendants had otherwise been given adequate notice of the material facts pleaded vaguely, such as through the disclosed evidence, the information conveyed in the Prosecution Pre-Trial Brief, and knowledge acquired during trial.[24] It is important to note that the Appeals Chamber did not "exclude the possibility that, in some instances, a defective indictment can be cured if the Prosecution provides the accused with timely, clear and consistent information detailing the factual basis underpinning the charges against him or her."[25] Upon a review of the facts, however, the Appeals Chamber found that the Prosecution had not provided such timely, clear and consistent information to the Defence in the *Kupreškić* case.

---

[17] *Ibid*. para. 88.

[18] *Ibid*. para. 91.

[19] *Ibid*. para. 89. Although the Appeals Chamber did not give examples of concrete cases of this type, clearly many of the cases tried in Nürnberg belong in this category.

[20] *Ibid*. para. 91.

[21] *Ibid*. paras. 93 and 121.

[22] *Ibid*. para. 95.

[23] *Ibid*. para. 87.

[24] *Ibid*. paras. 115–124.

[25] *Ibid*. para. 114.

More specifically, the Appeals Chamber found as follows: the information contained in the Prosecution Pre-Trial Brief was so extremely general in nature that it was difficult to see how it could have assisted the accused in the preparation of their defence;[26] the Prosecution opening statement was also deficient in that it made no reference to the pivotal attack on Suhret Ahmić's house or to the involvement of the Kupreškić brothers in that event (to which Witness H had testified at trial);[27] although by the end of Witness H's examination-in-chief on 3 September 1998, it would appear that the Kupreškić brothers had been informed that the allegation pertaining to the attack on Suhret Ahmić's house was relevant to the persecution count. Nonetheless, the Appeals Chamber found that the information provided did not adequately convey the relevance of Witness H's evidence for the persecution count. No certain conclusion could be drawn as to how that evidence was going to be relied upon by the Trial Chamber for the purpose of deciding the issue of the criminal liability of Kupreškić brothers for persecution. Finally, the disclosure of the witness statement of Witness H was not done in a relatively timely manner; it was "disclosed to them only approximately one to one and-a-half weeks prior to trial [that is to say] less than a month prior to Witness H's testimony in court", thereby engaging the question of prejudice to the Kupreškić brothers.[28]

Finally, on whether the Defence had been guilty of waiver,[29] the Appeals Chamber found that there had been no waiver since the Kupreškić brothers had objected to the form of the indictment before the commencement of the trial, on the same basis as their ground of appeal on the point.[30] Indeed, on 15 May 1998, the Trial Chamber had dismissed six motions, from the six defendants attacking the form of the indictment.[31]

c) *The Doctrine of 'Presumptive Prejudice':*
The Perversion of a Most Important Ratio Decidendi

Perhaps the most regrettable passage of the *Kupreškić* appeal judgment is the following:

---

[26] *Ibid.* para. 117.

[27] *Ibid.* para. 118.

[28] *Ibid.* para. 120. Later in the discussion, we will see how this late notice undermined the defence ability to prepare cross-examination of this witness in a manner that would have exposed her lack of credibility in greater detail.

[29] *Ibid.* para. 123.

[30] *Ibid.*

[31] *Prosecutor v Kupreškić & Ors (Decision on Defence Challenges to Form of the Indictment)* 15 May 1998 (ICTY Trial Chamber).

> The Appeals Chamber *emphasises* that the vagueness of the Amended Indictment in the *present case* constitutes neither a minor defect nor a technical imperfection. It goes to the heart of the substantial safeguards that an indictment is intended to furnish to an accused, namely to inform him of the case he has to meet. *If such a fundamental defect can indeed be held to be harmless in any circumstances, it would only be through demonstrating that Zoran and Mirjan Kupreškić's ability to prepare their defence was not materially impaired.* In the absence of such a showing *here*, the conclusion must be that such a fundamental defect in the Amended Indictment did indeed cause injustice, since the Defendants' right to prepare their defence *was seriously infringed.* The trial against Zoran and Mirjan Kupreškić was, thereby, rendered unfair.[32] [Emphasis added.]

This passage introduced the notion of 'presumptive prejudice' into the jurisprudence of defective indictments – *i.e.*, that prejudice is to be presumed whenever the indictment fails to plead material facts.[33] The passage is unfortunate in that the point the Appeals Chamber had in fact set out to "emphasise" in the opening sentence, and by the other italicized phrases, appears submerged in awkward *obiter* verbiage. The long italicised remark in the middle is one such *obiter*, and it leaves the reasoning open to distracting criticism that it is a fictional exercise aimed at insulating the outcome of the judgment against charges of technical legalism. For example, the observation raises the question of burden of proof of prejudice, but does not indicate on whom the burden rests. Instead, the *dictum* leaves the reader to infer that the burden rested on the Prosecution, who must demonstrate that the defect in the indictment did not materially impair the defendant's ability to prepare his or her defence[34] – hence ordaining a new doctrine of 'presumptive prejudice.'

In this author's view, apart from the old platitude of *ei incumbit probatio qui dicit, non qui negat*,[35] it would be strange to place on the Prosecution the reverse burden of showing that a defect in the indictment did not cause prejudice to the Defence. It is typically the Defence that would assert the prejudice; the Defence is in the better position to make a showing of it, and therefore could demand a change in the course of the proceedings.[36] Furthermore, any judgment by which an accused person is set free on a criminal charge without a consideration of the merits of the charge cannot easily shake off the very criticism of technical legalism.

---

[32] *Ibid.,* para. 122.

[33] *Prosecutor v Blaškić (Judgment)*, 29 July 2004 paras. 235–238 (ICTY Appeals Chamber); *Niyitegeka v Prosecutor (Judgment)* 9 July 2004, para. 198 (ICTR Appeals Chamber).

[34] See also *Niyitegeka v Prosecutor, ibid.*

[35] 'The burden of proof is on him who alleges, and not on him who denies'.

[36] See LaFave and Israel, *supra* note 5 at 503–504.

Nevertheless, a special distinguishing feature soundly justifies the outcome in *Kupreškić* which plainly shows the prejudice of the defective pleading. The Appeals Chamber in *Kupreškić* did not acquit the brothers merely because the pleadings were found to be defective; the Appeals Chamber had also found that the conviction of the Kupreškić brothers rested upon the evidence of one witness – Witness H – who lacked the requisite degree of credibility to make the convictions sound.[37] This finding alone should ordinarily justify the brothers' acquittal on appeal – but the Appeals Chamber had also found that the late disclosure of Witness H's statement to the Defence had undermined their ability to prepare a cross-examination of the witness, hence meeting the prejudice quotient of vagueness in the indictment.[38] It is submitted that this is what the Appeals Chamber was alluding to in the passage quoted above when it said, "Defendants' right to prepare their defence was seriously infringed." Hence, the Appeals Chamber's felt the need to stress: "The Appeals Chamber emphasises that the vagueness of the Amended Indictment in the present case constitutes neither a minor defect nor a technical imperfection."

Subsequent judgments of the Appeals Chambers of both the ICTR and the ICTY appear to indicate some unease with this idea of presumptive prejudice. To this end, efforts have since been made to contain the scope of *Kupreškić*. Such efforts include a tendency to distinguish the particular circumstances of *Kupreškić* from those of other cases in which the 'presumptive prejudice' is urged. The ICTY Appeals Chamber in *Blaškić* proceeded to distinguish the circumstances of that case from those of *Kupreškić*.[39] Also, in *Niyitegeka*, the ICTY Appeals Chamber effectively limited the *Kupreškić* doctrine of presumptive prejudice – but from the perspective of waiver considerations.[40]

Two observations need be made here. First, to say, as the Appeals Chamber has so clearly done in *Niyitegeka*, that the Defence will bear the burden of proof of prejudice where they object for the first time on appeal is indeed clearly to limit the scope of any doctrine of presumptive prejudice that may have been suggested in *Kupreškić*. Secondly, even this much is based on a distinguishing factor in *Kupreškić*, in that the objection to the vagueness of the indictment was never raised for the first time on appeal in that case. As has been noted earlier, there were in fact at least six such objections filed even before the commencement of the trial. This and the other distinguishing factors, already identified, most likely explain why the Appeals Chamber in *Kupreškić* raised, in the first place, the presumption that is now being converted into a

---

[37] *Kupreškić, supra* note 1, paras. 222–246.

[38] *Ibid.*, para. 223.

[39] *Ibid.*, paras. 239–241.

[40] Essentially, the Defence has the burden of proof if they raise the objection for the first time on appeal. But the Prosecution bears the burden if the Defence raised the objection at trial: *Niyitegeka, supra* note 33, para. 200.

'presumptive prejudice' doctrine of general application. But the point that the Appeals Chamber intended to make by that statement was required by the particular circumstances of that case and was perfectly justified in those circumstances. Here they are. The objections were filed on time, ahead of the trial. They were overruled. The Prosecution called Witness H whose testimony emerged like a ghost out of the dark pleadings, to "dramatically transform" the case for the Prosecution. But the Prosecution had not disclosed her statement in sufficient time to permit the Defence to prepare adequately for her testimony. The Appeals Chamber found that her evidence was credibility-challenged: and that "serious" prejudice was apparent from this, given the failure of the Prosecution to give adequate notice of her testimony to the Defence, which notice would have put the Defence in a better position to expose her lack of credibility. With these as the circumstances of the case, it becomes clear that the Appeals Chamber was then saying this: in these circumstances, the onus was on the Prosecution to convince the Appeals Chamber that the Defence did not suffer the prejudice which was so apparent to the Appeals Chamber. Unfortunately, the Appeals Chamber did not express itself so clearly, hence leading to the supposition of a doctrine of presumptive prejudice.

d) *Questionable Reliance on the Kupreškić Case*

It seems fairly clear that the vitality of the *Kupreškić* appeal judgment largely turns on its own facts. Its factual and jurisprudential properties remove it from ordinary usage in the average case. Therefore, reliance on the *Kupreškić* Appeal judgment cannot be faithful unless the same three-point inquiry is made. That is to inquire:

(i) whether the Prosecution is urging the Chamber to rely for conviction on material facts not pleaded in the indictment, recognising especially that in some instances the sheer scale of the case may excuse failure for precision in certain details;

(ii) whether such a reliance would render the trial unfair, recognising especially that a defect in the indictment may be cured by subsequent provision of consistent and timely notice of the missing particulars to the accused; and

(iii) whether the Defence had been guilty of waiver.

Unfortunately, many decisions and judgments, supposedly based on *Kupreškić*, did not make this three-point inquiry.[41]

---

[41] Notably, *Prosecutor v Ntagerura & Ors,* 25 February 2004 (ICTR Trial Chamber III).

e) *Niyitegeka v Prosecutor*

That the three-point inquiry must be made has recently been confirmed by both the ICTR and ICTY Appeals Chambers in *Niyitegeka v Prosecutor*[42] and in *Prosecutor v Blaškić*,[43] respectively.

In the *Niyitegeka* judgment, the Appeals Chamber reiterated that although defective pleadings may "in certain circumstances" result in a reversal of convictions, it is clear that such an outcome is not automatic;[44] it is possible for a defective indictment to be cured "if the Prosecution provide[d] the accused with timely, clear and consistent information detailing the factual basis underpinning the charges against him or her."[45] The ability of such alternatively furnished information to cure would, of course, depend on the nature of the information that the Prosecution provided to the Defence and whether the information compensates for the indictment's failure to give notice of the charges asserted against the accused.[46]

f) *Waiver*

On the subject of waiver, the *Niyitegeka* Appeals Chamber recalled the statement of the Appeals Chamber in *Kayishema and Ruzindana* that, in general, "a party should not be permitted to refrain from making an objection to a matter which was apparent during the course of the trial, and to raise it only in the event of an adverse finding against that party."[47]

But, the Appeals Chamber recognised in *Niyitegeka* that there are certain exceptions to this general rule, in view of the "importance of the accused's right to be informed of the charges against him under Article 20(4)(a) of the Statute and the possibility of serious prejudice to the accused if material facts crucial to the Prosecution are communicated for the first time at trial . . .".[48] Hence the requirement for the Defence to bear the burden of proof if the matter was being raised for the first time on appeal.

Three observations are called for here. First, it seems that such an exception will only arise where the "material facts crucial to the Prosecution are commu-

---

[42] *Niyitegeka, supra* note 33.

[43] *Prosecutor v Blaškić, supra* note 33, paras. 222–224 (waiver), paras. 225–229 (defective pleading), paras. 230–245 (fairness of trial).

[44] *Niyitegeka, supra* note 33, para. 195.

[45] *Ibid.,* para 195.

[46] *Ibid.,* para. 197.

[47] *Niyitegeka, supra* note 33, para. 199.

[48] *Ibid.,* para. 200.

nicated [to the accused] for the first time at trial." Second, the exception oper-ates only so far as to permit the Defence to proceed with the late objection and to show that his or her ability to prepare his case was materially impaired by the dilatory notification of the material. This exception to the doctrine of waiver does not, it seems, permit an unrestricted power to disregard the doctrine. Third, the Appeals Chamber indicated that it has an overriding "inherent juris-diction to do justice" in the case, thus requiring the consideration of waiver to be overlooked. This raises the following concerns. (1) As the parameters of the intended idea have been left unmapped, this reservation of an "inherent juris-diction" to disregard the waiver doctrine certainly introduces uncertainty in the law. The power to convict or acquit an accused person must be founded upon clear guiding principles known to all the parties in advance, thus enabling them to organise and present their cases. Both the *Kupreškić* and the *Kayishema and Ruzindana* appeals judgments introduced that clarity in the law in relation to waiver.[49] Should the doctrine now be operated, in view of *Niyitegeka*, like a helicopter being flown high above in the night sky, with no one knowing its flight path or landing spot? (2) It is not readily apparent why the Appeals Chamber preferred to import the difficult concept of "inherent jurisdiction"[50] into the discussion, rather than invoke the Tribunal's express statutory power to "ensure that a trial is fair".[51] To lawyers from the common law jurisdiction,[52] as well as to others on the planes of the international law,[53] it is doubtful that the Trial or Appeals Chambers of the international criminal tribunals have any "inherent jurisdiction" beyond the powers expressly or impliedly indicated in the Statute creating them, since the Tribunals and their Chambers are statutory creations. Consequently, it is doubtful that such jurisdiction may be brought

---

[49] See also *Prosecutor v Furudnžija (Judgment)*, 21 July 2000, para. 174 (ICTY Appeals Chamber); *Prosecutor v Blaškić (Judgment)*, *supra* note 33, paras. 222–224 (ICTY Appeals Chamber).

[50] See generally P. Gaeta, 'Inherent Powers of International Courts and Tribunals' in L. Vohrah et al., *Man's Inhumanity to Man – Essays on International Law in Honour of Antonio Cassese* (The Hague: Kluwer Law International, 2003) at 353.

[51] See article 19(1) of the ICTR Statute, and the corresponding article 20(1) of the ICTY Statute. See also article 20(2) of the ICTR Statute and the corresponding article 21(2) of the ICTY Statute, providing: "In the determination of charges against him or her, the accused shall be entitled to a fair and public hearing, subject to Article 21 of the Statute."

[52] See *R v Collins* (1970) 54 Cr App R 19 at 19–21 (CA) and *Roberts v Canada*, [1989] 1 SCR 322 at 331 (SCC).

[53] *French Company of Venezuelan Railroads Case* (1905), Ralston's Report, p. 367 at 444 (the Franco-Venezuelan Mixed Claims Commission (1902)). See B. Cheng, *General Principles of Law as applied by International Courts and Tribunals* (Cambridge: Grotius Publications/CUP, 1993, reprinted 1994) at 259.

into existence by the mere declaration or description of the concerned Judges themselves.[54]

For exceptions to waiver, the United States' experience may be useful. There, rule 30 of the Federal Rules of Criminal Procedure indicates that failure to raise timely objections before the trial court would ordinarily result in forfeiture of the right involved. But rule 52(b) permits relevant courts, usually the appellate court, to notice "[p]lain errors or defects affecting substantial rights . . . although they were not brought to the attention of the court." Nevertheless, the Supreme Court of the United States has held that this exception is to be used sparingly, solely to arrest obvious miscarriages of justice.[55] The Court has cautioned against any unwarranted expansion of Rule 52(b) because it "would skew the Rule's "careful balancing of our need to encourage all trial participants to seek a fair and accurate trial the first time around against our insistence that obvious injustice be promptly redressed"."[56] Even less appropriate than an unwarranted expansion of the Rule would be "the creation out of whole cloth of an exception to it, an exception which we have no authority to make."[57]

Now, the question arises as to the interest of justice that is served were the Appeals Chamber to profess "to do justice in the case" by disregarding waiver, in the absence of a showing that the defective indictment had "materially impaired" the ability of the accused to prepare his case. In contexts such as those under discussion, it seems that the administration of justice should involve the removal of unfair burdens and material prejudices.[58] Chief Justice Lamer correctly made that point at the Supreme Court of Canada when he expressed the following view:

> In my view, one vital objective of criminal procedure is to ensure that no person exposed to prosecution shall be found guilty otherwise than by the instrumentality of a trial conducted in a manner which will not prejudice him in making his full answer and defence to the charge against him. . . .
>
> . . . I am firmly of the opinion that the importance of departures from the traditional form of procedure from which no prejudice arises should not be so escalated as to result in the invalidity of the proceedings where a Court is satisfied that the result would have been the same had the trial proceeded in the manner in which it is alleged it should have.[59]

---

[54] Cf *Prosecutor v Blaškić (Judgement on the Request of the Republic of Croatia for Review of the Decision of Trial Chamber II of 18 July 1997)* dated 29 October 1997 (ICTY Appeals Chamber), footnote 27.

[55] *US v Young*, 105 S Ct 1038 (1985) at 1046 (USSC).

[56] *Ibid.* and see *Johnson v US*, 117 S Ct 1544 (1997) at 1548 (USSC).

[57] See *Carlisle v United States,* 517 US 416, 425–426, 116 S Ct 1460, 1466, 134 L Ed 2d 613 (1996) (USSC) and *Johnson, ibid.*

[58] See generally *US v Young, supra* note 55.

[59] *R v Clunas* [1992] 1 SCR 595 at 598–599 (SCC).

Given the foregoing, this "inherent jurisdiction to do justice" which the Appeals Chamber speaks of in *Niyitegeka* must be taken to mean no more than the power of the Appeals Chamber to recognise and act upon specific instances of material impairment of the Defence's ability to conduct its case, due to notice given tardily for the first time at trial, though the Defence has failed to address those particular instances of prejudice on its own.

In *Semanza*,[60] the Trial Chamber proceeded neither in the manner indicated in the *Kupreškić* appeal judgment nor in the *Niyitegeka* appeal judgment. Instead, the Trial Chamber simply failed to take waiver into account. It proceeded by noting that the "Defence has not offered any explanation for its delay in raising many of its specific challenges to the Indictment until its Closing Brief";[61] and that "the Defence failed to articulate any particular instance of prejudice."[62] Nevertheless, the Chamber proceeded to give full consideration to the late objection made by the Defence, on grounds of what the Trial Chamber considered "its duty to ensure the integrity of the proceedings and safeguard the rights of the Accused."[63] Finally, the Chamber found that a count of the indictment had been vaguely pleaded, and therefore acquitted the accused of that count.

There are at least two problems with this approach. First, it utterly negates the whole idea of waiver, which ensures the integrity of the proceedings and safeguards the rights of the accused.

It might be appropriate to contrast the *Semanza* Trial Chamber's attitude in this regard with the contrasting opinion of the US Supreme Court in *Cotton*, a recent case involving failure of the Defence to object to the introduction of evidence that enhanced penalty beyond the statutory maximum, notwithstanding the failure of the Prosecution to plead such facts. The Court of Appeal had held that to convict the accused on grounds of those penalty-enhancing facts was an error which "seriously affects the fairness, integrity or public reputation of judicial proceedings." The Supreme Court disagreed and reversed the Court of Appeal.[64] Having noted "the longstanding rule 'that a constitutional right may be forfeited in criminal as well as civil cases by the failure to make timely assertion of the right . . .'", the Supreme Court went on to say:

> The real threat then to the "fairness, integrity, and public reputation of judicial proceedings" would be if respondents, despite the overwhelming and uncontroverted evidence that they were involved in a vast drug conspiracy, were to receive a sentence prescribed for those committing less substantial drug offenses because of an error that was never objected to at trial.[65]

---

[60] A case prosecuted by the present writer.

[61] *Semanza (Judgment), supra* note 1, para. 42.

[62] *Ibid.*, para. 43.

[63] *Ibid.*, para. 42.

[64] *US v Cotton*, 122 S Ct 1781 (2002); 535 US 625 (2002) (USSC).

[65] *Ibid.* at 634.

Also, there is no valid judicial precedent cited in the *Semanza* judgment to support the suggestion that the Trial Chamber's "duty to ensure the integrity of the proceedings and safeguard the rights of the Accused" must override the consideration of waiver. Notably, in footnote 28, reference is made to several authorities. These references are quite curious in that none of them contains any suggestion to diminish the value of the waiver doctrine on grounds of any duty on the part of the Trial Chamber to ensure the integrity of the proceedings and safeguard the rights of the accused. Quite the contrary, the *Kupreškić* appeal judgment specifically raised the question of waiver, notwithstanding that the Prosecution had not raised it. And paragraphs 95 and 97 of the *Kayishema and Ruzindana* appeal judgment dismissed the objection of the Defence on grounds of waiver. It makes it odd then that the *Semanza* judgment refers to these cases to support the suggestion that waiver may be diminished in deference to the duty to ensure the integrity of the proceedings and safeguard the rights of the accused. Similarly, in *Prosecutor v Ntagerura & Ors*, the ICTR Trial Chamber III was silent on the subject of waiver. In the *Krnojelac* case, not only did the ICTY Appeals Chamber keep silent on the subject of waiver in general, it remained silent even in the face of an assertion by the Defence Counsel that "it was not his role to correct his opponent's mistakes."[66] Chiefly militating against this consideration is that the whole idea of waiver is that justice demands that one must remain alert to violations of one's rights and complain promptly at any such violation, so that *bona fide* complaints may be immediately remedied. An idea, as has been noted earlier, expressed by the US Supreme Court as the "[encouragement of] all trial participants to seek a fair and accurate trial the first time around."[67] Specifically in relation to indictments, failure to complain promptly of vagueness may be taken as an indication that the trial had proceeded with a mutual understanding.[68]

3) Municipal Perspectives

In the foregoing discussion, it was useful to discuss contrasting jurisprudence of some municipal jurisdictions side-by-side with the jurisprudence of the international tribunals, the latter being the focus of attention. This part will focus on the jurisprudence of municipal jurisdictions.

---

[66] *Prosecutor v Krnojelac (Judgment)* of 17 September 2003 (ICTY Appeals Chamber), para. 127.

[67] *United States v Young, supra* note 55; *United States v Frady, supra* note 56; *Johnson v US, supra* note 56.

[68] See *R v RIC* (1986), 32 CCC (3d) 399 at p. 404 (Ont. CA) and also LaFave and Israel, *supra* note 5 at 815 and 822.

From the point of view of municipal jurisdictions, the problem of defective indictments, as a litigation problem, appears to be a peculiarity of common law jurisdictions. Given the central role of the impartial magistrate who investigates the cases and draws up committal orders prior to trial, complaints that accused persons have not been made sufficiently aware of the cause or nature of the charges against him, appear largely to be a non-issue in the inquisitorial criminal justice methods of much of the civil law world.[69] It leaves us then to concentrate our discussion on the state of affairs in common law jurisdictions, specifically, Canada, the UK and USA.

In these common law jurisdictions, the modern practice and procedure emerged from a period during which the indictment was required to adhere to exacting technical standards. As Mr Justice Salhany observed:

> At common law, and particularly by the beginning of the 19th century, the indictment had become a document of extreme prolixity and technicality. Proper words of art were required to be used when framing the charges against the accused. All the facts and circumstances of the offence including the intent had to be set out in the indictment in great detail and with meticulous certainty. This requirement of certainty was so stringently adhered to that any omission or slight defect was fatal to the indictment and resulted in complete impunity for the accused.[70]

It appears that this technical rule served salutary purposes during its reign. Up to the early part of the 19th century, many offences were still classified as capital felonies.[71] There were either no statutory definitions of crimes or they were imprecise.[72] It was not until 1836 that a person accused of a felony was entitled to be represented by counsel[73] and to inspect or demand copies of depositions made by prosecution witnesses.[74] And, except in cases of treason,[75] the first

---

[69] See *De Salvador Torres v Spain* (1997) 23 EHRR 601, (1996) ECHR 21525/93, paras. 27–30 (European Court of Human Rights); *Kamasinski v Austria* (1991) 13 EHRR 36, [1989] ECHR 9783/82 at para. 80 (European Court of Human Rights). See also Clayton and Tomlinson, *Fair Trial Rights* (Oxford: OUP, 2001) §11.242, citing *Ofner v Austria* (1960) 3 YB 322.

[70] R. Salhany, *Criminal Trial Handbook* (Toronto: Carswell, 1998), para. 6.800. See also LaFave and Israel, *supra* note 5 at 808–809.

[71] Salhany, *ibid.*, para. 6.810. See also K. Smith, *Lawyers, Legislators and Theorists: Developments in English Criminal Jurisprudence 1800–1957* (Oxford: OUP, 1998) at 42; L. Radzinowicz, *A History of English Criminal Law*, vol 1 (London: Stevens & Sons, 1948) at 97–103.

[72] Salhany, *ibid.*, para. 6.830; Smith, *ibid*; Radzinowicz, *ibid.*

[73] Salhany, *ibid.*, para. 6.820. See also D. Cairns, *Advocacy and the Making of the Adversarial Criminal Trial, 1800–1865* (Oxford: Clarendon Press, 1998), chapters 2 and 3.

[74] *Ibid.* at 37 and 67. Both the right to representation by counsel and the right to inspect and demand copies of prosecution witness depositions were introduced in the Trials for Felonies Act of 1836, usually called the Prisoners' Counsel Act: Cairns, *ibid.*

[75] Cairns, *ibid.* at 37.

time that an accused person was given notice of the charges against him was during the arraignment.[76] Even well after the accused was entitled to representation by counsel and to inspect depositions of witnesses, professional practice and rules of etiquette did not encourage counsel to be briefed by the solicitor in good time to ensure adequate preparation for the trial.[77] Little wonder then that the judges saw fit to hold the indictment to extremely high standards of perfection.[78] On the downside, however, the administration of justice risked perception as little more than a farcical affair in which "guilt or innocence was a matter of arbitrary uncertainty".[79]

The evolution of criminal law to more humane and modern standards brought with it reforms to the law relating to the indictment. Perhaps the most famous instance of this reform effort was the enactment in December 1915 in England of An Act to amend the Law relating to Indictments in Criminal Cases, and matters incidental or similar thereto, more popularly known by its short title, the Indictments Act 1915. The aim of the reform was to do away with the technicalities and to simplify the form of the indictment – to the end that not only must indictments give accused persons reasonable notice of the crimes charged against them, but that criminal trials were to be conducted according to the merits of the case.[80]

The point here is not so much to suggest that the judges of the international criminal tribunals have been guilty of encouraging attacks against the indictment "from the narrow standpoint of petty preciosity, pettifogging, technicality or hair splitting fault finding",[81] as it is to suggest that the decisions dismissing counts in the indictment on grounds of vague pleadings do not reveal on their face that sufficient regard was had to the consideration that "the guilty shall not escape through mere imperfections of pleading," Rather what comes across appears to be a one-sided consideration regarding the need to protect the accused.[82]

Turning to the relevant features of the reform, for purposes of the present discussion, it may be enough to appreciate the thrust of the reform from the fol-

---

[76] Salhany, *supra* note 70, para. 6.820.

[77] See Cairns, *supra* note 73, at pp. 37 to 38.

[78] See Salhany, *supra* note 70, para. 6.810; Smith, *supra* note 71; Radzinowicz, *supra* note 71.

[79] Salhany, *ibid.*, para. 6.830.

[80] *Ibid.*, para. 6.840.

[81] *Parsons v United States*, 189 F 2d 252 at 253 (1951) (US Ct App, 5th Cir).

[82] As observed by Justice Sutherland (on behalf of the Supreme Court of the United States), the US legislation reforming the law indictments "was enacted to the end that, while the accused must be afforded full protection, the guilty shall not escape through mere imperfections of pleading.": *Hagner et al v United States*, 285 US 427 at 432, 52 S Ct 417 (USSC).

lowing general areas: (a) the scope of the notice of the charge that must be given to the accused; (b) the scope permitted the accused to complain about deficiencies in the required notice, and the remedies that may attend a legitimate complaint of defect.

a) *The Scope of the Notice of the Charge that Must Be Given to the Accused*

Under the modern rules of pleading, an indictment is only required to contain sufficient details as to give to the accused "reasonable information" as to the nature of the charge against him. This requirement is typically set out in s 581(3) of the Criminal Code of Canada which provides as follows:

> A count shall contain sufficient detail of the circumstances of the alleged offence to give to the accused reasonable information with respect to the act or omission to be proved against him and to identify the transaction referred to, but otherwise the absence or insufficiency of details does not vitiate the count.[83]

To a similar effect, s 3 of the Indictment Act 1915 of England and Wales provides:

> (1) Every indictment shall contain, and shall be sufficient if it contains, a statement of the specific offence or offences with which the accused person is charged, together with such particulars as may be necessary for giving reasonable information as to the nature of the charge.
>
> (2) Notwithstanding any rule of law or practice, an indictment shall, subject to the provisions of this Act, not be open to objection in respect of its form or contents if it is framed in accordance with the rules under this Act.

In *Hagner*, the United States Supreme Court observed as follows:

> The true test of the sufficiency of an indictment is not whether it could have been made more definite and certain, but whether it contains the elements of the offense intended to be charged, "and sufficiently apprises the defendant of what he must be prepared to meet, and, in case any other proceedings are taken against him for a similar offence, whether the record shows with accuracy to what extent he may plead a former acquittal or conviction."[84]

In an apparent effort to explain what was meant by "sufficiently apprised", the same Court said in *Hamling v United States*:

---

[83] There are certain special cases such as treason where the indictment must strictly plead 'every overt act' to be relied on in the prosecution: see s 581(4).

[84] *Hagner v US, supra* note 82 at 431. See also *R v Côté* (1977), 33 CCC (2d) 353 (SCC).

> Our prior cases indicate that an indictment is sufficient if it, first, contains the elements of the offense charged and fairly informs a defendant of the charge against which he must defend, and, second, enables him to plead an acquittal or conviction in bar of future prosecutions for the same offense.[85]

It seems clear then that the general standards of notice of the material facts required to be stated in an indictment in Canada, UK, and USA, is that it must *reasonably or fairly inform* the accused of the charges against him. While it may be desirable or advantageous to provide other details of the transaction, a failure to do so does not impugn the indictment.[86]

One theme that resonates unrelentingly in the jurisprudence of Canada,[87] England[88] and America[89] is this: whether or not the indictment has given sufficient details to inform the accused of the charges against him will depend on the particular circumstances of each case and the charges involved. What is sufficient in one case may be deficient in another.[90]

It may be noted in this regard that where the standards of notice in the reviewed jurisdictions require only the statement of what must reasonably or fairly inform the accused, the statutory language at the ICTR and ICTY require the accused "[t]o be informed promptly and in detail in a language which he or she understands of the nature and cause of the charge against him or her . . .".[91] Although in *Kupreškić*, the ICTY Appeals Chamber criticized the Prosecution for failing to plead, among other things, the houses allegedly attacked by the appellants, as well as the victims,[92] it is not clear, however, whether the statute will always be interpreted so as to require the pleading of that which is desirable or advantageous but unnecessary for purposes of giving reasonable or fair notice.[93]

---

[85] 418 US 87 at 117; 94 S Ct 2887 at 2907 (1974) (USSC).

[86] See *R v Chuah and anor* [1991] Crim LR 463.

[87] *R v Douglas* (1991), 63 CCC (3d) 29, at para. 24 (SCC); *R v C* (1986), 32 CCC (3d) 399, at para. 5 (Ont. CA).

[88] Speaking generally on the subject of the right to fair trial (including the right of the accused to be informed in detail of the nature and cause of the charge), Lord Bingham said: "What a fair trial requires cannot, however, be the subject of a single, unvarying rule or collection of rules. It is proper to take account of the facts and circumstances of particular cases, as the European court has consistently done": *Brown v Stott (Procurator Fiscal, Dunfermline) and anor* [2003] 1 AC 681 (Privy Council); see also *R v Forbes* [2001] 1 AC 473, para. 24 (HL).

[89] See LaFave and Israel, *supra* note 5 at 820.

[90] *R v Ryan* (1985), 23 CCC (3d) 1, at p 7 (Ont. CA).

[91] Article 20(4)(a) of the ICTR Statute; article 21(4)(a) of the ICTY Statute; article 67(1)(a) of the Statute of the International Criminal Court.

[92] *Kupreškić, supra* note 1, para. 117.

[93] This is more so considering that the ICTY Appeals Chamber had clearly indicated that the pronouncements in *Kupreškić* were ones that turned on the specific facts of that

b) *Complaints About Deficiencies in Notice and Remedies*

Occasionally a complaint is validly made that an indictment has failed to give the accused reasonable or fair notice of the facts underlying the charges against him. It is perhaps in these circumstances that the reform of the law of indictment reveals its essence. The law requires that even such complaints be made in good faith, with the overall purpose of encouraging an inquiry into the merits of the case rather than avoiding that inquiry through technical tactics. So, defendants are not only required to raise *bona fide* complaints promptly, but trial judges are empowered to order the indictment to be amended in order to cure the defect.

In all these respects, the modern Canadian criminal practice affords a useful case study. Section 601(1) of the Canadian Criminal Code provides as follows:

> An objection to an indictment or to a count in an indictment for a defect apparent on the face thereof shall be taken by motion to quash the indictment or count before the accused has pleaded, and thereafter only by leave of the court before which the proceedings take place, and the court before which an objection is taken under this section may, if it considers it necessary, order the indictment or count to be amended to cure the defect.

First, the Defence must make a motion before the arraignment. Thereafter, any attack against the indictment may only be made with leave of court. And appeals courts do not treat with levity a failure to make the motion before arraignment.[94] In the United States, the courts are loathe to permit Defendants to engage in the practice of "sandbagging" or "gamesmanship" whereby they hold back their objections only to make them when all opportunity to remedy the defect has been lost.[95] Good cause must be shown for failure to object on time, taking into account whether the accused has suffered irreparable prejudice by the impugned failings in the indictment.[96]

Even where a meritorious attack has been made against the indictment, the first consideration is not to quash, but to consider whether the indictment may be cured by way of amendment. The leading authority on this matter is *R v Moore*.[97] Speaking for the Majority of the Supreme Court of Canada, Lamer J

---

case – i.e., a case, unlike some others, in which the Prosecution should have pleaded those facts. *Ibid*. para. 91.

[94] *R v RIC*, *supra* note 68, p. 402. The same is true in the USA: see LaFave and Israel, *supra* note 5 at 815 & 822.

[95] See for example, *United States v Crowley*, 236 F 3d 104 at p 108 (US Court of Appeal, 2nd Circuit).

[96] *R v Robinson* (2001), 153 CCC (3d) 398 at para. 25 *et seq* (Ont. CA). See also *R v Coffen* (1998), Docket No C26902, para. 6 (Ont. CA): www.canlii.org/on/cas/onca/1998/1998onca10017.html

[97] 41 CCC (3d) 289 (SCC).

observed that since the enactment of the Criminal Code provisions giving the court the power to amend indictments, "there has been, through case-law and punctual amendments to [s 601] and its predecessor sections, a gradual shift from requiring judges to quash to requiring them to amend in the stead; in fact, there remains little discretion to quash."[98]

In fact, the power of the court to amend the indictment in order to cure a defect, if such can be done without injustice, is so wide as to authorise an amendment at any stage of the proceeding, even after all evidence has been led, in order to conform the indictment to the evidence led in the case.[99] The Criminal Code of Canada empowers even the courts of appeal to amend the indictment in order to conform it to the evidence led at trial.[100] It is unclear whether appellate courts in the UK and USA are empowered to do likewise. This power not only permits amendments as to form or substance, it includes the power to add or substitute counts.[101] Rule 7(e) of the US Federal Rules of Criminal Procedure grants courts the power to "permit an information to be amended at any time before verdict or finding if no additional or different offence is charged and if substantial rights of the defendant are not prejudiced." It is noteworthy at this juncture that the only point at which the procedure in the US departs from that in Canada and England and Wales is regarding the power to add or substitute a new offence. A review of all statutory provisions and the case law in all these jurisdictions shows as a constant the requirement that any amendment must not result in undue prejudice to the accused.

One advantage offered by this large power of amendment is its value to the rule against double jeopardy. It enables an accused to put it beyond question that (s)he was truly tried for all the crimes and facts reasonably within the contemplation of the earlier trial.[102] Were this not so, it will be possible for the Prosecution to attempt, at least, to commence a subsequent trial to account for the crimes and evidence revealed in the first trial but not charged then; mindful, of course, that prescription has not run against the subsequent trial, and due

---

[98]   *Ibid.* p 311.

[99]   See s 601(2) and (3) of the Canadian Criminal Code. In *Wallace v R* (2002), 53 WCB (2d) 353 (NS CA): the Defence attacked the indictment during its closing submissions. In response, the Prosecution made a motion to amend the indictment. The motion was granted and the appellant was convicted on the amended count. The Court of Appeal dismissed the ground of appeal complaining against the amendment. See also s 5(1) of the Indictment Act of England and Wales; *R v Collison* (1980) 71 Cr App R 249 (CA) (amendment made in the course of jury deliberation on the verdict).

[100]   See ss 683(1)(g) and 686(8) of the Criminal Code of Canada. See also *R v Robinson, supra* note 96, para. 68.

[101]   See *R v Irwin* (1998), 123 CCC (3d) 316, paras. 12 & 24–31 (Ont. CA). See also *R v Johal* (1972) 56 Cr App R 348 (CA).

[102]   See *R v Irwin, ibid.*, paras. 10 and 11.

diligence could explain the omission of its subject matter in the indictment of the earlier trial. It will be difficult in the circumstances for the defendant to plead the double jeopardy of the subsequent trial where he or she had success-fully objected to an amendment of the indictment in the earlier trial which would have covered the subject matter of the subsequent trial.[103]

At the ICTR and ICTY, the Rules of Procedure and Evidence grant the Tribunals the power to amend the indictment. After taking the plea on the indictment, upon initial appearance, the Prosecutor may only amend with leave of the Trial Chamber.[104] The texts of the respective Rules are silent on the scope of the powers of the judges regarding amendment of the indictment. In other words, the texts place no time bar beyond which the amendment shall not be made, nor do they forbid an amendment to be made in order to conform the indictment to the evidence led in the case. It appears therefore that amendments may be made at any stage of the proceedings, without limitation as to form or substance. In *Kupreškić*, the ICTY Appeals Chamber recognised that an amend-ment possibly coupled with an adjournment is one of the options available in the event of the evidence turning out differently than expected.[105] Indeed in *Prosecutor v Akayesu*, the Prosecution was permitted to amend the indictment to add three new counts relating to rape, and an adjournment was granted, after much of the evidence for the Prosecution had been led.[106] Before the amend-ment, the indictment contained no charge relating to rape. Although the Prosecution was permitted to call six new witnesses following the amendment, it was clear that the motivations for the new charges included evidence relating to rape already heard in the case.[107] Without a doubt, the amendment in *Akayesu* was perfectly normal, judging by the standards of criminal practice and proce-dure in Canada, UK and USA. A greater, more creative use of the *Akayesu* precedent may greatly reduce the incidence of attacks against the indictment as insufficiently pleading the facts.

---

[103] Notable in this regard is s 609 of the Canadian Criminal Code requiring a judge to discharge an accused, upon a plea of double jeopardy, where it appears: '. . . (*a*) that the matter on which the accused was given in charge on the former trial is the same in whole or in part as that on which it is proposed to give him in charge, and (*b*) that on the former trial, if all proper amendments had been made that might then have been made, he might have been convicted of all the offences of which he may be convicted on the count to which the plea of *autrefois acquit* or *autrefois convict* is pleaded . . .'.

[104] See r 50 of the Rules of Procedure and Evidence of both ICTR and ICTY.

[105] *Prosecutor v Kupreškić, supra* note 1, para. 92. The other option which the Appeals Chamber considered is to exclude the evidence as outside the scope of the indictment.

[106] See *Prosecutor v Akayesu (Judgment)*, 2 September 1998, paras. 23 and 24 (ICTR Trial Chamber I).

[107] *Prosecutor v Akayesu*: transcript of prosecution oral motion of 17 June 1997.

4) Leading Evidence on Matters Not Specifically Pleaded

Another manner in which the deficiency of the indictment comes into focus is by objections taken against admissibility of certain evidence of prosecution witnesses on grounds that such evidence is outside the scope of the pleadings. This manner of objections has become a more frequent occurrence at the ICTR since the *Kupreškić* case. The jurisprudence of ICTR reveals some interesting treatment of these objections.

In *Prosecutor v Bizimungu & Ors*,[108] the Defence objected to the admissibility of certain prosecution witnesses who were poised to testify as to the alleged criminal conducts of the Defendant Bizimungu in the prefecture of Ruhengeri, Rwanda, during the Rwandan Genocide. The Defence argued that neither the indictment pursuant to which the trial was being conducted, nor the supporting material for that indictment, contained any pleading about Bizimungu in Ruhengeri. Trial Chamber II found that there was indeed no pleading on the fact and held that "in the particular circumstances of this case," the prosecution was not to lead the impugned evidence. On an interlocutory appeal of the decision,[109] the ICTR Appeals Chamber found that the Prosecution had failed to show any error in the decision or reasoning of the Trial Chamber. In holding so, the Appeals Chamber, among other things, dismissed as inapposite the Prosecution's argument that a differently constituted Trial Chamber II, sitting in a different trial – the case of *Prosecutor v Nyiramasuhuko & ors*[110] – had overruled similar objections by the Defence. For, according to the Appeals Chamber, on matters of discretion reasonable minds may differ.[111]

Indeed, in *Nyiramasuhuko*, a similar issue did arise as was the case in *Bizimungu*. But the *Nyiramasuhuko* Trial Chamber dismissed the Defence objection on the basis of a two-pronged reasoning: (a) that the indictment was sufficiently pleaded on the fact in issue, and (b) there was no prejudice to the accused in admitting the evidence, as the Defence had already been given the witness statements containing the information at least 18 months prior to the calling of the witnesses, thereby giving them sufficient time to prepare that aspect of the Defence. In the latter regard, the Trial Chamber reasoned as follows:

---

[108] *Prosecutor v Bizimungu & Ors (Decision on Motion from Casimir Bizimungu Opposing the Admissibility of the Testimony of Witnesses GKB, GAP, GKC, GKD and GFA)*, 23 January 2004 (ICTR Trial Chamber II).

[109] *Prosecutor v Bizimungu and Ors (Decision on Prosecution's Interlocutory Appeals against Decisions of the Trial Chamber on Exclusion of Evidence)*, 25 June 2004 (ICTR Appeals Chamber).

[110] *Prosecutor v Nyramasuhuko & Ors (Decision on Defence Urgent Motion to Declare Parts of the Evidence of Witnesses RV and QBZ Inadmissible)*, 16 February 2004 (ICTR Trial Chamber II).

[111] *Supra* note 109, para. 20.

The Trial Chamber agrees with the Appeals Chamber in *Kupreškić et al* that the issue of failure to plead material facts in the Indictment is distinct from the issue of lack of adequate notice infringing the Accused's right to a fair trial. The significance of this distinction lies mainly in the difference between the material which the Trial Chamber may fairly receive in evidence during the trial of an Accused and the use to which the Chamber may put any material so received into evidence.[112]

On an interlocutory appeal, the Appeals Chamber disagreed with the Trial Chamber on the first prong of their reasoning – i.e., that the facts had been pleaded.[113] Nevertheless, the Appeals Chamber held that the failure to plead the particular fact in question does not in itself render the evidence inadmissible.[114] According to the Appeals Chamber:

> Indeed, pursuant to Rule 89(C) of the Rules, the Trial Chamber may admit any relevant evidence which it deems to have probative value. It should be recalled that admissibility of evidence should not be confused with the assessment of the weight to be accorded to that evidence, an issue to be decided by the Trial Chamber after hearing the totality of the evidence. Consequently, although on the basis of the present indictment it is not possible to convict Nyiramasuhuko in respect of her presence at the installation of Ndayambaje, evidence of this meeting can be admitted to the extent that it may be relevant to the proof of any allegation pleaded in the Indictment.[115]

On that note, the appeal was dismissed. In deciding the appeal in this way, the Appeals Chamber has undoubtedly allowed Trial Chambers room to receive relevant evidence which may not have been sufficiently pleaded. There should be little room to criticise this development legitimately. But for jurisprudence such as this, criminal trials, especially complex ones such as the ones typically tried before the international criminal tribunals, will seldom unfold in such a way as may permit a Trial Chamber to have a clear appreciation of what transpired and the contexts surrounding the events.[116]

---

[112] *Supra* note 110, para. 22.

[113] *Prosecutor v Nyramasuhuko & Ors (Decision on the Appeals by Pauline Nyiramasuhuko and Arsène Shalom Ntahobali on the "Decision on Defence Urgent Motion to Declare Parts of the Evidence of Witnesses RV and QBZ Inadmissible"),* 2 July 2004, paras. 12 and 13 (ICTR Appeals Chamber).

[114] *Ibid.* para. 14.

[115] *Ibid.* para. 15.

[116] The import of this development is consistent with another line of jurisprudence which allows the Trial Chambers to admit evidence of events occurring outside the strict temporal framework of the Tribunals' jurisdiction, in order to "provide a context or background and may be a basis on which to draw inferences as to intent or other elements of the crimes alleged to have been committed within the temporal jurisdiction:" *Simba v Prosecutor (Decision on Interlocutory Appeal Regarding Temporal*

It remains to be stressed, however, that the aspect of the Trial Chamber's reasoning which the Appeals Chamber affirmed rests upon the Trial Chamber's satisfaction that the Defence has not been prejudiced by receiving the evidence in question; the evidence had been disclosed in sufficient time to permit the Defence to prepare to meet it. And while not diminishing the Appeals Chamber's reasoning in the *Bizimungu* interlocutory appeal to the effect that reasonable minds may differ on matters of discretion, this question of prejudice remains a distinguishing feature between the Trial Chambers' decisions in the two cases. While that was a central feature in *Nyiramasuhuko*, there is no mention of it in *Bizimungu*.

We have noted that it was observed in the *Kupreskic* appeal judgment that an indictment could be amended where the evidence called at trial turns out differently than originally expected. We have noted also that precisely that was done during the *Akayesu* trial. We also note the significance of the *Nyiramasuhuko* appeal decision discussed above. A blend of all these should result in a practice (at the international tribunals) approximating that found in Canada and England and Wales which regards as proper the amendment of indictments, even at the end of a trial, in order to conform the indictment to the evidence; provided there is no undue prejudice to the accused.

5) CONCLUSION

The ICTR and the ICTY have often found occasion to draw upon general principles of law for sources of law that govern their work, in the absence of help from customary international law, their statutes and their rules of procedure.[117] Indeed, the Rules of Procedure and Evidence of both ICTR and ICTY clearly point them in that direction.[118] And given the adversarial flavour of their proceedings, the Tribunals have often drawn procedural inspiration from common law jurisdictions.[119] Sadly, though, one area in the proceedings of the Tribunals that greatly beckons them to rely more on common law procedures is in the matter of objections to the indictment on grounds of vagueness.

Jurisdiction) of 29 July 2004 (ICTR Appeals Chamber); *Ngeze and Nahimana v Prosecutor (Decision on the Interlocutory Appeals)* 5 September 2000, Separate Opinion of Judge Shahabuddeen at 4–5 (ICTR Appeals Chamber).

[117] See for instance, *Prosecutor v Rutaganda (Judgment)* 26 May 2003 (ICTR Appeals Chamber), para. 366; *Prosecutor v Furundžija (Judgment)* 10 December 1998 (ICTY Trial Chamber), para. 117; and, *Prosecutor v Kunarac & Ors (Judgment)* 22 February 2001 (ICTY Trial Chamber) paras. 439 and 558.

[118] See r 89(b) in both the Rules of Procedure and Evidence of the ICTR and of the ICTY.

[119] The author was a participant in that process in virtue of his position as a prosecutor and a senior legal officer in the Chambers of the ICTR.

PART 3

RIGHTS

Chapter 7

Comparing Attitudes to International Human Rights Petition Systems

Holly Cullen[1]

1) INTRODUCTION

The potential for international human rights petition procedures to improve the human rights situation within a state depends both on the procedures themselves and on the extent of states' willingness to change their law and practice in light of the determinations of international human rights bodies. Therefore, in evaluating the situations in Canada and the United Kingdom, we need to look both at the main procedures to which they adhere and at the degree of compliance of each state with the resulting determinations. At present, Canada accepts the right of individual petition under the First Optional Protocol[2] to the International Covenant on Civil and Political Rights (ICCPR),[3] the main civil

---

[1] Thanks go to my colleague, Sonia Harris-Short, for helpful comments on an earlier draft of this paper.

[2] First Optional Protocol to the International Covenant on Civil and Political Rights, Signed 1966; in force 1976, Annex to G.A. Res. 2200A, 21 U.N. GAOR, Supp. (No. 16), U.N. Doc. A/6316, (1966).

[3] International Covenant on Civil and Political Rights, Signed 1966; in force 1976, Annex to G.A. Res. 2200A, 21 U.N. GAOR, Supp. (No. 16), U.N. Doc. A/6316, (1966).

Christopher P.M. Waters (Ed.), *British and Canadian Perspectives on International Law*, pp. 131–148.
© 2006 Koninklijke Brill NV. Printed in the Netherlands.

and political rights treaty under the auspices of the United Nations, and some similar rights of petition under other United Nations human rights treaties.[4] The United Kingdom does not accept any rights of individual petition under United Nations human rights treaties except that under the Optional Protocol to the Convention on the Elimination of All Forms of Discrimination against Women (CEDAW). However, it is party to the European Convention on Human Rights (ECHR),[5] the civil and political rights treaty of the Council of Europe, which provides for a compulsory acceptance of the right of individual petition to the European Court of Human Rights. On the question of procedures, therefore, each of these civil and political rights individual petition systems has its advantages and disadvantages in terms of procedure and follow-up. On the question of state compliance, I will argue that there is not much to choose from between the attitudes of Canada and the United Kingdom, both of which demonstrate examples of partial, delayed or reluctant compliance. There is, therefore, despite the acceptance of a wider range of individual petition systems by Canada, substantial room for criticism of both states' approaches to international human rights obligations.

2) POSITION ON THE RIGHT OF INDIVIDUAL PETITION TO UN HUMAN RIGHTS TREATY BODIES

As noted above, Canada adheres to a few of the United Nations individual petition systems, but not its relevant regional convention, the American Convention on Human Rights. The United Kingdom accepts the regional system, the ECHR, but until recently no United Nations systems. In 2004, the Department for Constitutional Affairs published a review of the United Kingdom's position in respect of international human rights treaties, both at UN and regional levels. In deciding to maintain, in the vast majority of cases, its stance of non-acceptance of individual petition systems other than that under the European Convention on Human Rights (ECHR), the review states:

---

[4] Canada also accepts the right of individual petition under the Convention against Torture, signed 1984; in force 1987, (1984) 23 I.L.M., and the Optional Protocol to the Convention on the Elimination of All Forms of Discrimination against Women, signed 1999; in force 2000, (2000) I.H.R.R. 294. It has not accepted the right of individual petition arising under Article 14 of International Convention on the Elimination of All Forms of Racial Discrimination, signed 1965; in force 1969; 660 U.N.T.S 195, nor is it a party to the American Convention on Human Rights of the Organisation of American States, signed 1969; in force 1978, OASTS No. 36.

[5] Convention for the Protection of Human Rights and Fundamental Freedoms, 4 November 1950; in force 1952, 213 U.N.T.S. 221.

The UN monitoring committees which would receive individual petitions from citizens are not courts and cannot award damages, or produce a legal ruling on the meaning of the law. However, they may give their opinion on the compliance or otherwise of a signatory with the provisions of the Convention.[6]

The practical value to the individual citizen is unclear and there is also to be considered the cost to public funds of preparing submissions of the government's opinion on the subject matter of the petition.[7]

This position is, however, not as dogmatic as these paragraphs would indicate. In the same report, the United Kingdom announces that it will ratify the Optional Protocol to CEDAW, in order to evaluate the merits of the UN individual petition systems, with a review to be held after two years as a party to the Protocol.[8] The United Kingdom's adherence to the Optional Protocol is discussed in more detail in the next chapter.

It is undeniable that international petition systems do not involve courts in the way that they are understood in national legal systems, and that individual petitions are not appeals.[9] Not least of the differences between international petition systems and most national courts is the fact that the Human Rights Committee and all of its UN treaty body counterparts operate a purely written procedure in reviewing individual petitions, although the European Court of Human Rights does have an oral hearing stage. Furthermore, they do not engage in findings of fact or the evaluation of the credibility of evidence.

On costs, while there would undeniably be costs for the government in dealing with these individual petitions, the Canadian experience suggests that the number of petitions would be nothing like that under the ECHR. Up to 2002, just over 100 petitions had been filed against Canada, which ranked number two in the number of petitions filed against it.[10]

---

[6] Department of Constitutional Affairs, *International Human Rights Instruments: The UK's Position: Report on the Outcome of an Inter-Departmental Review Conducted by the Department of Constitutional Affairs*, Appendix 5: Rights of Individual Petition to the UN under Various Treaties: http://www.humanrights.gov.uk/ngo/reviews/appendix5.pdf.

[7] *Ibid.*

[8] *Ibid.* The United Kingdom acceded to the Optional Protocol on 17 December 2004: see United Nations, Division for the Advancement of Women, Signatures to and Ratifications of the Optional Protocol, http://www.un.org/womenwatch/daw/cedaw/protocol/sigop.htm.

[9] H. J. Steiner, "Individual Claims in a World of Massive Violations: What Role for the Human Rights Committee?" in P. Alston and J. Crawford, eds., *The Future of UN Human Rights Treaty Monitoring* (Cambridge: Cambridge University Press, 2000) 15 at 27–29.

[10] J. Harrington, "Punting Terrorists, Assassins and Other Undesirables: Canada, the Human Rights Committee and Requests for Interim Measures of Protection" (2003) 48 McGill L. J. 55 at 64.

The United Kingdom government also raises the issue of legal status of views of international human rights bodies. In relation to the Human Rights Committee, most accept that views are not regarded as legally binding.[11] Evatt, a former member of the Human Rights Committee, argues nonetheless that the legal status of the Committee's views cannot be regarded as a simple matter:

> The ICCPR is legally binding as a matter of international law but it is often said that the views of the Committee under the Optional Protocol are not legally binding. Though literally true, this statement should be approached with caution. The Committee is not a court but its views are not without legal consequences. In ratifying the Optional Protocol, the State has recognised the competence of the Committee to receive and consider communications from individuals and to express its views as to whether there has been a violation of the rights set forth in the ICCPR. This alone suggests that the State must co-operate with the Committee and respond to the Committee's views. In addition, there are the obligations of the State under Article 2 of the ICCPR to respect and to ensure rights, to give effect to rights through legislative or other measures and to ensure that any person whose rights or freedoms are violated shall have an effective remedy.[12]

The Committee now routinely makes reference to states' obligations under Article 2 ICCPR when it decides, in the context of an individual petition, that a state has not fully respected the author's rights. Following this approach, the issue of the legal status of the Committee's views cannot be easily separated from that of the nature of the state's obligations under the Covenant in general.[13]

The general position on the binding nature of judgments under the ECHR is that a finding of violation places the state under an obligation to change its law to prevent further breaches of the same nature.[14] There are also examples of controversial policy changes in the United Kingdom following decisions of the European Court of Human Rights. The ban on persons who are gay or lesbian being members of the armed forces was removed after the Court's decisions in *Smith and Grady v. United Kingdom*,[15] and *Lustig-Prean v. United Kingdom*.[16]

---

[11] P. R. Ghandi, *The Human Rights Committee and the right of individual communication: law and practice* (Aldershot: Ashgate/Dartmouth, 1998) at 331.

[12] E. Evatt, 'Reflecting on the role of international communications in the implementing human rights' (1999) Australian Journal of Human Rights 20 (footnotes omitted). Harrington, *supra* note 10 at 65, also subscribes to this approach.

[13] Steiner, *supra* note 9 at 30.

[14] C. Ovey & R. C. A. White, *Jacobs & White: European Convention on Human Rights*, 3rd ed., (Oxford: Oxford University Press, 2002) 419. The authors state that this is derived from Article 46(1) ECHR.

[15] Resolution Res DH(2002) 35 concerning the judgments of the European Court of Human Rights of 27 September 1999 and of 25 July 2000 in the case of Smith and Grady against the United Kingdom, Adopted by the Committee of Ministers on 30 April 2002 at the 792nd meeting of the Ministers' Deputies.

[16] Resolution Res DH(2002) 34 concerning the judgments of the European Court of Human Rights of 27 September 1999 and of 25 July 2000 in the case of Lustig-Prean

However, in some cases, it relies on the United Kingdom courts to reinterpret existing law in light of the decision of the Court. This has been the case in relation to the immunity of the police from civil suit, for example.[17]

3) IMPERFECT ACCEPTANCE OF INTERNATIONAL HUMAN RIGHTS OBLIGATIONS BY BOTH CANADA AND THE UNITED KINGDOM

While examples of significant legal changes as a result of the findings of international human rights bodies can be found in relation to both Canada and the United Kingdom, there are also important examples of resistance. In the case of Canada, these are sometimes the result of an imperfect fit between the constitutional division of powers between the federal and provincial governments and the nature of international legal obligations. However, both countries also have examples of significant delay in complying and of partial compliance.

a) *Examples of acceptance of obligations*

Determinations of international human rights bodies, even if they do not directly have the force of law, may, in conjunction with other factors, have an effect.[18] They therefore can have an indirect impact on the law, prompting changes in the law, which otherwise would not have happened or would not have happened as quickly. The Human Rights Committee's views have in practice sometimes had this result. One notable example is *Ballantyne et al. v. Canada*,[19] on Quebec's language laws in relation to public commercial signs.[20] The Committee found that the law, which required the use of French only in commercial signs, violated freedom of expression, as choice of language is an aspect of expression.[21] The law was disproportionate to the legitimate aim of

---

and Beckett against the United Kingdom, Adopted by the Committee of Ministers on 30 April 2002 at the 792nd meeting of the Ministers' Deputies.

[17] Resolution Res DH(99) 720 concerning the judgment of the European Court of Human Rights of 28 October 1998 in the case of Osman against the United Kingdom, Adopted by the Committee of Ministers on 3 December 1999 at the 688th meeting of the Ministers' Deputies.

[18] H. J. Steiner, "International Protection of Human Rights" in M. D. Evans, ed., *International Law* (Oxford: Oxford University Press, 2003) 757 at 785.

[19] 359, 385/89, decided 31 March 1993.

[20] On the background to this case, see J. Woehrling, "Convergences et divergences entre fédéralisme et protection des droits et libertés: L'exemple des États-Unis et du Canada" (2000–2001) 46 McGill L. J. 21 at 35, and H. Cullen, 'Nation and its Shadow: Quebec's non-French Speakers and the Courts' (1992) 3 *Law and Critique* 220.

[21] Note that the Human Rights Committee accepted that commercial expression, such

protecting the French language in North America – while requiring French to be present could be justified, banning other languages could not. The law was subsequently changed to allow languages other than French on commercial signs, but French must be predominant.[22] While this was considered by the Quebec government as sufficient to meet the requirements of the ICCPR and of the Canadian and Quebec Charters of Rights,[23] Joseph et al. suggest that the requirement of French predominance might still be contrary to Article 19 ICCPR.[24]

Another example of change in the law following a case before the Human Rights Committee is *Lovelace v. Canada*.[25] Ms. Lovelace lost her status as an Indian under the federal *Indian Act* upon marriage to a non-Indian. She successfully argued before the Human Rights Committee that this had the effect of infringing her rights under Article 27 ICCPR which provides that members of minority groups should have the right to enjoy their culture in community with their group. By removing her status as an Indian, and imposing the consequences of that, particularly losing the right to reside on reserve lands, she was denied the right to enjoy her culture as a member of the Maliseet band. The Indian Act was subsequently amended to remove the infringement and to allow women, and their children, who had lost their status to re-register as members of their bands.[26]

On the contentious issue of extradition or deportation of persons who might be subject to the death penalty in the destination state, both the Committee and Canadian law have moved progressively towards a more protective view. In *Kindler v. Canada*,[27] the Committee took the view that extradition from a country which has abolished the death penalty (the sending state) to a jurisdiction which retains it (the requesting state) is not necessarily a violation of the right to life under Article 6 ICCPR. While the sending state is obliged to keep its ICCPR obligations in mind when considering a request to extradite where the

---

as advertising, was protected by Article 19 ICCPR on freedom of expression. The European Court of Human Rights in the *Markt Intern Verlag GmbH v. Germany* (1990) 12 EHRR 161 decided that commercial expression was not to be protected at as high a standard as political or artistic expression, although by a narrow margin (10–9).

[22] Loi modifiant la Charte de la langue française, L.Q. 1993, c. 40.

[23] Woehrling, *supra* note 20 at 35–36.

[24] S. Joseph et al., *The International Covenant on Civil and Political Rights: Cases, Materials and Commentary*, 2nd ed. (Oxford: Oxford University Press, 2004) 543.

[25] 24/77, decided 30 July 1981.

[26] Indian Act, R. S. C. 1985, c. 1–5, ss. 6, 7 and 11. The Human Rights Committee, in its review of Canada's state report in 1999, however, was concerned that this amendment didn't go far enough to redress the original violation as it did not cover subsequent generations: (1999) UN doc. CCPR/C/79/Add.105.

[27] 470/1990, 18 November 1993.

death penalty is a possible outcome, it is not obliged to refuse extradition nor even to seek assurances that the death penalty will not be applied in that case.[28] However, a decade later, when *Judge v. Canada* was decided, the Committee took a stricter view of what was required, particularly in light of the decision of the Supreme Court of Canada in *United States v. Burns*,[29] which stated that Canada must seek assurances that the death penalty will not be imposed before allowing extradition.[30] The Committee explicitly took the view that where a state party has abolished the death penalty, 'there is an obligation not to expose a person to the real risk of its application.'[31]

Immigration and extradition have, not surprisingly, raised particular problems in the United Kingdom as well, although the general attitude until recently has been broadly accommodating to ECHR rulings. The United Kingdom has accepted the view of the European Court of Human Rights that it is contrary to Article 3 ECHR to extradite or deport individuals to states where they will be subject to torture or to inhumane and degrading treatment,[32] but it had few options in this matter. Unlike the situation with detention policy, where the United Kingdom entered derogations to Article 5 ECHR under Article 15 ECHR,[33] it is not possible to derogate from the obligations under Article 3.[34] Instead it has introduced measures first allowing for indefinite detention of persons without a right of abode in the United Kingdom who were suspected of terrorist activities under the Anti-terrorism, Crime and Security Act 2001, and later, after these were declared incompatible with Article 5 of the ECHR under section 4 of the Human Rights Act 1998, allowing for control orders against any individual suspected of terrorist activities under the Prevention of Terrorism Act 2005. Most recently, following the bombings and attempted bombings in London of July 2005, the Prime Minister indicated that the United Kingdom would try to avoid the problems of the Article 3 case law by signing Memorandums of Understanding with countries to which suspected terrorists are deported, with undertakings that they would not be tortured.[35] If this was insufficient, an amendment to the Human Rights Act 1998 in respect of this interpretation would be sought.[36]

---

[28] *Ibid.*, paras. 14.5–14.6.

[29] 2001 SCC 7.

[30] *Judge v. Canada*, 829/1998, 20 October 2003, para. 10.3.

[31] *Ibid.*, para. 10.4.

[32] Notably, *Soering v. United Kingdom*, (1989) 11 EHRR 439; *Chahal v. United Kingdom*, (1997) 23 EHRR 413.

[33] The most recent of these was withdrawn on 16 March 2005, after the adoption of Prevention of Terrorism Act 2005.

[34] Article 15(2) ECHR.

[35] PM's Press Conference, 5 August 2005: http://www.number-10.gov.uk/output/Page8041.asp.

[36] *Ibid.*

b) *Examples of imperfect acceptance by Canada*

The most recent, and probably the most politically-charged example of limited
acceptance – even outright rejection – of obligations under the ICCPR was in
the case of *Ahani v. Canada*,[37] concerning the Committee's request for interim
measures. Interim measures requests have arisen primarily in cases involving
potential deportation or extradition, and in *Ahani*, the conflict between the
Committee's conception of the legal nature of interim measures and that of the
Canadian government was stark. Ahani is an Iranian national against whom a
deportation order was made on the grounds of national security, declaring him
to be a terrorist. After exhausting his potential remedies before the federal court
system in Canada, he filed an individual petition before the Human Rights
Committee. He also requested and obtained interim measures: a request from
the Committee that he not be deported pending consideration of the petition.

The Canadian government proceeded with deportation procedures. Attempts
to obtain an injunction from Ontario courts failed on the ground that the
Committee's requests for interim measures were not binding, either in international law or national law.[38] This decision was strongly criticised within
Canada, notably by Harrington, who argues that recent developments suggest
that the position that interim measures are not legally binding cannot be maintained. She bases this in part on developments within the Committee itself,
whereby it has declared that a failure to respect such requests is now regarded
as a violation of the ICCPR itself,[39] and on developments such as the ICJ's declaration in *LeGrand (Germany v. United States)*[40] that interim measures ordered
by it are binding on states.[41] When the Human Rights Committee issued its
views on Ahani's application it found a separate violation in Canada's refusal to
respect the request for interim measures, asserting that such behaviour 'undermines the protection of Covenant rights through the Optional Protocol.'[42]

---

[37] *Ahani v. Canada*, 1051/2002, 15 June 2004.

[38] *Ahani v. Canada (Attorney General)*, (2002) 208 D.L.R. (4th) 66 (Ont. C.A.),
paras. 31–44, per Laskin, J. A. Although Laskin, J. A, is concerned with the binding
nature of the Committee's views (or rather the lack thereof), his wording in some places
suggests that he sees no binding obligations in the ICCPR itself – see for example, paragraph 37. Rosenberg, J. A., dissenting, at paragraphs 91–104, makes a distinction
between the legal nature of the Committee's final views, which he agrees cannot be
automatically binding in domestic law, and the obligation of the state not to render the
right of petition nugatory by its acts. For a discussion of this decision in depth, see
Harrington, *supra* note 10. The final decision was made by the Ontario Court of Appeal,
the Supreme Court of Canada dismissing an application for leave to appeal.

[39] Harrington, *ibid.*, at 69–72.

[40] (2001) 40 I.L.M. 1069.

[41] Harrington, *supra* note 10 at 72–76.

[42] *Ahani v. Canada, op. cit.*, para. 8.2.

Constitutional arrangements within Canada mean that it is sometimes difficult for the federal government to ensure that a law which violates the ICCPR, but is within provincial competence, is amended following the Committee's views. An example of this can be seen in the case of *Waldman v. Canada*,[43] which also demonstrates the extent of the Committee's follow-up procedures. The Human Rights Committee requests information from states concerning compliance, primarily but not exclusively through the state reporting process, and appoints from within its membership a Special Rapporteur for compliance.[44] This follow-up procedure can provide additional pressure on a state to ensure compliance with the Committee's views.[45]

In *Waldman*, the Committee decided that Ontario's policy of providing publicly-funded Roman Catholic schools, but not schools for other faith groups, was contrary to Article 26 ICCPR, which provides for a general right of non-discrimination. The differential position on funding was based on section 93 of the Constitution Act 1867, which protected rights to religious minority education (specifically Roman Catholics in Ontario and Protestants in Quebec). As a result, the Supreme Court of Canada had declared that the policy could not be reviewed under section 15 of the Canadian Charter of Rights and Freedoms.[46] Only at the level of international human rights law, therefore, could the policy be legally challenged. However, because of the potential costs of compliance, and because of reluctance to unpick the Confederation-era settlement,[47] the Ontario government refused to comply with the Committee's views, leading to public disagreement with the federal government which urged compliance.[48] The Committee engaged its follow-up procedures, including a very rare instance of Canada's ambassador being summoned to explain Canada's non-compliance.[49] The Special Rapporteur for follow-up subsequently met with representatives of the Canadian government.[50] Eventually, the Conservative government in Ontario complied partly with the Committee's views in *Waldman*, by means of tax credits introduced to reduce cost to parents of

---

[43] 694/96, 3 November 1999.

[44] Evatt, *supra* note 12.

[45] T. G. Furrow, "Canada Challenged as a Human Rights Leader: The Human Rights Committee's Decision in *Wald*man" (2001) 11 Transnational Law and Contemporary Problems 225 at 243, notes that the follow-up procedures have had the effect of improving levels of at least partial compliance with Committee views.

[46] *Reference Re: Bill 30* (1987), 40 DLR (4th) 18, and *Adler v. Ontario* (1996), 140 DLR (4th) 385.

[47] Although, as Furrow, *supra* note 45 at 246 notes, this had been done in Quebec and Newfoundland.

[48] *Ibid.*, 244.

[49] *Ibid.*

[50] *Ibid.*, 245.

sending children to private religious schools by 50%.[51] The extent to which this is the result of the Committee's follow-up is difficult to determine, but the follow-up probably helped to keep the issue in the public eye.[52]

The views given by the Committee are not, therefore, valueless in improving the human rights situation in a state, but constitutional arrangements are an important determinant of compliance in controversial cases. The approaches of international legal bodies to particular questions may differ from those existing under national law, particularly constitutional law. This is particularly the case with regard to federal bodies, and will apply to a lesser extent to devolved bodies such as those in the United Kingdom. From an international law point of view, a state is a single entity, and internal constitutional arrangements are no excuse for non-compliance with international obligations. Under Canadian constitutional law, as interpreted by the Judicial Committee of the Privy Council before the development of international human rights law as it is currently understood, the federal government cannot take responsibility for implementing international obligations if a matter is normally within the competence of a province.[53] This was behind the delayed and only partial compliance with the Committee's views in *Waldman*.[54] It is unlikely that such a problem would arise in the United Kingdom. If it were to decide to accept the right of individual petition under the ICCPR Optional Protocol, a minor amendment could be made to the Scotland Act 1998, which already provides that the Scottish Executive has no power to act in a way which is incompatible with the ECHR.[55] A more subtle problem is revealed by the Committee's reasoning in *Ballantyne*. As Woehrling notes, the Canadian constitution tends to define minorities in the context of provinces, notably in the area of minority linguistic or religious education rights (as in *Waldman*).[56] However, in *Ballantyne*, the

---

[51] *Ibid.*, 227. However, these tax credits applied to *all* private education, not just private education for minority religious education not provided within the state school system, and were withdrawn by the new Liberal government in 2003: see The Honourable Greg Sorbara, Minister of Finance, Ontario Economic Outlook and fiscal Review (Toronto: Queen's Printer for Ontario, 2003), at 43.

[52] See Furrow, *ibid.*, for discussion of the media coverage of the Committee's views, the reaction of the federal and provincial governments, and the Committee's follow-up.

[53] Labour Conventions Case: *Attorney-General for Canada v. Attorney-General for Ontario*, [1937] A.C. 326.

[54] See Furrow, *supra* note 45 at 245, where the Special Rapporteur on follow-up of the Committee's views rejected the legitimacy of the argument that the Canadian government could do nothing in light of the matter being one of provincial competence.

[55] Section 57. In fact, it is somewhat surprising that the Act was not amended in such a way in anticipation of accepting the right of petition under the CEDAW Optional Protocol.

[56] Woehrling, *supra* note 20 at 36.

Committee rejected the authors' claim that their rights under Article 27 ICCPR were violated. Article 27 guarantees the members of minorities, including linguistic minorities, to enjoy their culture, including use of their language. The Committee rejected the claim in *Ballantyne* on the ground that Article 27 states that 'In those States in which . . . minorities exist' meant that only groups which could be defined as minorities in relation to the state as a whole were protected by Article 27. Since Anglophones are the majority in Canada as a whole, they are not a minority for the purposes of Article 27, despite the fact that they are a minority in Quebec and the legislation which was contested was provincial legislation. This approach has been criticised,[57] and there was a strong dissent in the case, signed by four members of the Committee, but the Committee does not appear to have had the opportunity to revisit this issue since deciding *Ballantyne*. *Waldman* was decided as a discrimination issue, although it could also have been argued under Article 27, and in any event, members of the Jewish faith would be considered as members of a minority whether at federal or provincial level. The result is that there is a stark inconsistency in the way minorities are defined under the ICCPR and under Canadian constitutional law.

c) *Examples of imperfect acceptance by the United Kingdom*

International human rights bodies cannot be understood as ordering, as opposed to recommending, particular remedies. They have no enforcement mechanisms, only the type of follow-up mechanisms discussed above in the context of *Waldman*. This often leaves states as the arbiters of how they respond to decisions that they have not lived up to their international human rights law obligations. In the case of the ECHR, the follow-up is generally weaker than that engaged in by the Human Rights Committee, as it is the responsibility of a political body, the Committee of Ministers.[58]

An example of the state being, for the most part, the judge of what is required in order to comply with a determination under international human rights law can be seen in the reaction of the United Kingdom government to the decision of the European Court of Human Rights in *T. and V. v. United Kingdom*.[59] The Court ruled that the applicants had not received a fair trial

---

[57] Notably by N. Rodley, "Conceptual problems in the Protection of Minorities: International Legal Developments" (1995) 17 HRQ 48, 70–71. Rodley is now himself a member of the Human Rights Committee.

[58] Article 46 ECHR. For a discussion of the Committee's role, see Ovey and White, *supra* note 14 at 423–436.

[59] *T. v. United Kingdom*, (2000) 30 EHRR 121; *V. v. United Kingdom*, (2000) 30 EHRR 121.

within the meaning of Article 6(1) ECHR, as they had been tried as adults despite being ten years old. The form of trial, while adapted in light of their youth, still left them confused and unable to participate meaningfully in the procedure. After the ruling, Jack Straw, then the Home Secretary, in a statement to the House of Commons, stated that nothing in the decision indicated that the conviction of the two applicants was unsafe:[60]

> In summary, therefore, the court has found . . . against the United Kingdom on issues relating to the trial process, to the way in which the tariff linked to their sentence was set, and to the failure subsequently to review the tariff.
> The judgment does not overturn the verdict of murder in this case, nor does it in any way exonerate the two youths for their part in this terrible crime. The judgment does not direct their release from custody. The parole board remains responsible for deciding release in these cases.

This statement was indeed questioned by a backbench MP, Kevin McNamara, who understandably asked, 'If the European Court has accepted that a fair trial was denied, under article 6(1), how does the verdict stand?'.[61]

The United Kingdom amended certain of its procedures in relation to the trial of young offenders, but it is arguable that these changes do not go far enough. The changes were achieved by means of a Practice Direction from the Lord Chief Justice on 16 February 2000, the basic principles of which were: "The trial process should not itself expose the young defendant to avoidable intimidation, humiliation or distress. All possible steps should be taken to assist the young defendant to understand and participate in the proceedings. The ordinary trial process should so far as necessary be adapted to meet those ends."[62] In *S. C. v. United Kingdom*,[63] the applicant was again very young, 11 at the time of his arrest for attempted robbery. He was tried in an adult court. Although the Practice Direction adopted in response to the judgment in *T. and V.* was not yet in force, the Court of Appeal ruled that the trial judge had kept the European Court of Human Rights' decision in mind when making rulings on the applicant.[64] The European Court of Human Rights found a violation because the trial judge had not taken sufficient account of the evidence that the applicant's ability to understand proceedings was less than average for his age, a point on

---

[60] House of Commons, Hansard Debates for 16 December 1999 (pt. 4), columns 397–399.

[61] *Ibid.*, (pt. 5), column 400. Mr. Straw replied that in English law it was possible for an error to be made in a trial but not such that a guilty verdict need be overturned.

[62] The full text is set out at paragraph 22 of *S. C. v. United Kingdom*, (2005) 40 EHRR 10. The Practice Direction goes on to set out detailed guidelines on how the trial should be adapted.

[63] *Ibid.*

[64] *Ibid.*, para. 31.

which the 2000 Practice Direction says little. In this case, the Court of Human Rights found, trial in an adult court was entirely unsuitable:[65]

> The Court considers that, when the decision is taken to deal with a child, such as the applicant, who risks not being able to participate effectively because of his young age and limited intellectual capacity, by way of criminal proceedings rather than some other form of disposal directed primarily at determining the child's best interests and those of the community, it is essential that he be tried in a specialist tribunal which is able to give full consideration to and make proper allowance for the handicaps under which he labours, and adapt its procedure accordingly.

Arguably the trial judge, who was seen to be attempting to follow the guidance of the European Court of Human Rights in *T. and V.*, would have made the decision to allow the trial in adult court even if the Practice Direction had been in force. The contents of the Practice Direction, therefore, probably do not fully meet the requirements of ensuring a fair trial for young accused. In addition, given the importance of the rights involved, the form of the amendments could also be criticised: perhaps they should have been made in primary legislation rather than a Practice Direction.

Another case of children's rights, *A v. United Kingdom*,[66] also demonstrates delayed and partial compliance with judgments of the European Court of Human Rights. This case involved the acquittal of a stepfather on a charge of assault occasioning actual bodily harm to his nine year-old stepson. The stepfather had hit the child on several occasions using a stick or garden cane, causing visible bruising. The acquittal was on the basis that the hitting constituted reasonable punishment of a child by its parent. The European Court of Human Rights found that the acquittal amounted to a failure by the United Kingdom to live up to its positive obligations under Article 3 ECHR by failing to have effectively deterrent criminal law.[67] In particular, the law on reasonable punishment required the prosecution to prove that the parent had acted unreasonably. Such laws provided insufficient protection to vulnerable children against treatment or punishment contrary to Article 3.

In the proceedings in *A.*, the United Kingdom government accepted that its law was in contravention of the ECHR and should be amended.[68] However, the

---

[65] *Ibid.*, para. 35: "The Court considers that, when the decision is taken to deal with a child, such as the applicant, who risks not being able to participate effectively because of his young age and limited intellectual capacity, by way of criminal proceedings rather than some other form of disposal directed primarily at determining the child's best interests and those of the community, it is essential that he be tried in a specialist tribunal which is able to give full consideration to and make proper allowance for the handicaps under which he labours, and adapt its procedure accordingly."

[66] (1999) 27 EHRR 611.

[67] *Ibid.*, para. 22.

[68] *Ibid.*, para. 24.

delay between the judgment and legislative amendment was over six years. Initially, the United Kingdom argued before the Committee of Ministers that there was no need to amend the legislation concerning reasonable punishment of children by their parents because the Human Rights Act 1998 allowed the United Kingdom courts to apply Article 3 ECHR, and required them to take account of the European Court of Human Rights' interpretations of Convention rights.[69] The Committee concluded that it was not possible to determine on the basis of the information then supplied by the United Kingdom whether its law complied with the judgment of the European Court of Human Rights, but took no further measures. The United Kingdom only amended its law in late 2004, reflecting the fact that the measure was seen as highly controversial, particularly by parents.[70] The Children Act 2004, s. 58, restricts but does not entirely remove the immunity from prosecution of parents who smack their children, in that it abolishes the defence of reasonable punishment clearly only in the case of battery or aggravated assault, not common assault. The reversed burden of proof is gone, as is most of the scope of the immunity, but some campaigners see the judgment in *A.* as requiring the elimination of any legal permission to strike children.[71]

Most individual petitions seek a change in the law. As a result, the lack of a remedy in the conventional sense may be less important than a declaratory judgment that a legal measure or executive act is inconsistent with international human rights obligations. Many individual petitions are part of a wider campaign of litigation and political pressure for a change in the law. Mobilising shame at the international level, with its resulting pressure on national authorities, may well be the desired outcome of such a case, rather than a specific remedy. However, the ability of states to delay and to limit compliance without penalty is a general weakness of the system, as the examples above demonstrate.

---

[69] Committee of Ministers, Interim Resolution DH(2004) 39, concerning the judgment of the European Court of Human Rights of 23 September 1998, in the case of *A. v. United Kingdom*, adopted by the Committee of Ministers on 2 June 2004 at the 885th meeting of the Ministers' Deputies. The Committee concluded that it was not possible to determine on the basis of the information then supplied by the United Kingdom whether its law complied with the judgment of the European Court of Human Rights.

[70] See, for example, research discussed by F. Wheen, 'English see smacking as moral duty', *Guardian Unlimited*, 13 December 2000: http://society.guardian.co.uk/social-care/comment/0,7894,410808,00.html. However, by 2004, public opinion had shifted somewhat: Press Association, '71% support parental smacking ban, survey finds', *Guardian Unlimited*, 19 May 2004: http://society.guardian.co.uk/children/story/0,,1220203,00.html.

[71] Notably, the "Children Are Unbeatable!" Alliance: http://www.childrenareunbeatable.org.uk/.

4) WOULD UNITED KINGDOM CITIZENS BENEFIT FROM ACCEPTANCE OF UN INDIVIDUAL PETITION SYSTEMS?

The United Kingdom's approach to international human rights petition systems seems to argue that the ECHR system is more protective of human rights than are United Nations treaty systems. However, as argued above, there are two elements to the question: the system and the state's attitude to the system. Assuming that the United Kingdom's approach to the ICCPR would be similar to its approach under the ECHR, which is not unlike that of Canada towards the ICCPR, then it may well be asked whether there would be any advantage to the United Kingdom accepting United Nations petition systems. Undeniably, some of the main lines of case law in relation to Canada under the ICCPR Optional Protocol find co-relations with cases under the ECHR, such as cases involving extradition to states which practice the death penalty. In the *Kindler* case, the Committee explicitly took account of the decision on the European Court of Human Rights in *Soering v. United Kingdom*,[72] on the question of whether 'death row phenomenon' could amount to cruel and inhuman treatment contrary to Article 7 ICCPR.[73]

The main area where the ICCPR Optional Protocol would open up new remedies is in the area of discrimination. The ECHR's main non-discrimination provision, Article 14, requires that the applicant claim that there has been discrimination in the enjoyment of another right.[74] It is equivalent, therefore, to Article 26 ICCPR. Article 26 is an entirely free-standing right of non-discrimination. In an early case before the Human Rights Committee, the Netherlands attempted to argue that the scope of Article 26 was limited to civil and political rights, and therefore that it could not be applied to a claim of sex discrimination in relation to social security payments.[75] Such matters, in its view, fell to be considered only under the International Covenant on Economic, Social and Cultural Rights (ICESCR). The Human Rights Committee rejected this approach, finding that the ordinary meaning of Article 26 was clearly that all discrimination in legislation or its application was prohibited by that Article.[76] The Committee distinguished between the obligation in the ICESCR progressively to implement the right to social security and the obligation under Article 26 ICCPR to avoid discrimination in any legislation, which would include social security legislation.[77] The scope of Article 26 is therefore very broad.

---

[72] *Supra* note 32.
[73] *Kindler, supra* note 27, para. 15.3.
[74] *Belgian Linguistic Case*, (1979–1980) 1 EHRR 241 and 252.
[75] 182/1984, *Zwaan-de Vries v. Netherlands*, 9 April 1987, para. 8.3.
[76] *Ibid.*, para. 12.3.
[77] *Ibid.*, para. 12.5.

The equivalent to the ICCPR's Article 26, which prohibits discrimination without a link to another right being necessary, is contained in ECHR Protocol 12, which the United Kingdom has refused to ratify on the basis that it is over-broad, although accepting in principle the need for a free-standing non-discrimination right.[78] However, the consequences of allowing individual petitions under the ICCPR, including Article 26 ICCPR are less drastic than those of ratifying Protocol 12, as the latter would become part of national law by means of the Human Rights Act (unless the Act were amended) whereas the former could only be the subject of individual petitions.

Nonetheless, it may well be that in focussing on benefits to individual citizens in its rejection of most UN individual petition systems, cited above, the United Kingdom government is missing the point. Steiner argues that the main benefit of individual petitions lies on a more macro scale. He notes that the Committee has received comparatively few petitions, and already suffers from a backlog of cases. As a result, the prospect for the individual petition system to develop into a large-scale remedy for individual wrongs is minimal.[79] Instead, he suggests that the value of the Committee's views should lie in the development of our understanding of the Covenant and the dissemination of ideas about human rights as part of an international dialogue of actors, including courts.[80]

Since the ICCPR is the main international petition system for Canada, whereas the ECHR would probably continue to be the preferred route for UK residents, given its fit with national law, it seems unlikely that the ICCPR Optional Protocol would have a great deal of impact. The one caveat to this point is that when ECHR Protocol 14 comes into force, some cases will cease to be admissible under the ECHR, but could be admissible under the ICCPR Optional Protocol. Protocol 14, which attempts to alleviate the pressure on the European Court of Human Rights arising from an increasing number of applications, amends Article 35(3) to allow the European Court of Human Rights to declare inadmissible an application where "the applicant has not suffered a significant disadvantage, unless respect for human rights . . . requires an examination of the application." This creates a new ground of inadmissibility which has nothing to do with the merits of the claim. If applied with the same enthusiasm as the manifestly ill-founded criterion is already applied,[81] a significant

---

[78] Department of Constitutional Affairs, *supra*, Appendix 6: http://www.human-rights.gov.uk/ngo/reviews/appendix6.pdf.

[79] Steiner, *supra* note 9 at 34.

[80] *Ibid.*, 41. However, at present he is somewhat sceptical of the Committee's capacity to contribute to such a dialogue due to the thin reasoning in its views (39).

[81] On the controversial nature of the application of this rule, see D. J. Harris, M. O'Boyle and C. Warbrick, *Law of the European Convention on Human Rights* (London: Butterworths, 1995) at 627–628.

number of cases may be excluded from the ECHR system which might easily pass the admissibility criteria of the ICCPR Optional Protocol. As a result, when evaluating the role of each system, it becomes evident that there is a separate value to the ICCPR Optional Protocol.

5) CONCLUSION

When comparing the practice of the United Kingdom and Canada in respect of international human rights petition systems, it is necessary to examine two dimensions: the role of the state's attitude and the role of the system itself. The limitations of each dimension must be considered.

On first glance, it appears that Canada has a greater engagement with international human rights law than does the United Kingdom, based on its acceptance of more of the United Nations' individual petition systems. However, a deeper analysis reveals that Canada's commitment to changing its policies in the face of criticism by international human rights bodies is not uniformly strong. While some controversial laws have been changed in the face of negative views by the Human Rights Committee, this is not always the case. Political resistance, incompatible constitutional structures and judicial reluctance to grant legal status to the Committee's views have all, at one time or another, acted as barriers to full compliance with the Canada's obligations under the ICCPR.

The experience of the United Kingdom with international petition procedures is at present confined to that under the ECHR. Like Canada, it has mostly complied with rulings against it, but there are significant examples of less than full compliance. Arguably, the United Kingdom's instances of resistance to international human rights law have been higher profile as they have sometimes involved explicit derogations from the ECHR. However, with the *Ahani* case, Canada has moved into the same level of defiance of international human rights rulings. Furthermore, with Canada it has been a matter of ignoring the Human Rights Committee rather than entering a derogation or reservation to the ICCPR. It is right to question whether this behaviour demonstrates any greater acceptance of international human rights law obligations than that of United Kingdom.

With respect to the systems themselves, there are advantages to both systems. The Human Rights Committee has developed a more extensive, non-political, follow-up system,[82] but the judgments of the European Court of Human Rights are more thoroughly reasoned and therefore more likely to influence domestic jurisprudence.

---

[82] See Evatt, *supra* note 12.

As a result, it is legitimate to suggest that the United Kingdom should reconsider its position on the Optional Protocol to the ICCPR. However, the same could likely be said in respect of Canada with regard to the American Convention on Human Rights (which has a Court similar in many ways to the European Court of Human Rights), and which Canada has not ratified. Regional and United Nations systems each have their strengths, and therefore each can contribute to improving state attitudes towards international human rights.

Chapter 8

Strengthening Women's International Human Rights Norms in the UK after the Human Rights Act 1998: Lessons from Canada

Charlotte Skeet

1) INTRODUCTION

International law is gaining greater currency in the constitutional life of the United Kingdom. The Human Rights Act 1998 (HRA) gave effect to the European Convention on Human Rights and Fundamental Freedoms (ECHR) in domestic law but beyond this there has been an expansion in the reference to and uses of international law. This is evident in the courts in a variety of areas: tort, criminal, commercial and human rights,[1] and also through greater awareness and debate on international law in other areas. This has happened to such an extent in the area of human rights that it is possible to say that greater

---

[1] F. Shaheed, *Using International Law in Domestic Disputes* (Oxford: Hart, 2005). The British Institute of International and Comparative Law also recently launched a year-long research initiative to focus on this phenomenon.

Christopher P.M. Waters (Ed.), *British and Canadian Perspectives on International Law*, pp. 149–168.

domestic reception of international human rights law is forming part of an emergent human rights culture in the UK.[2]

What is meant here by an emerging rights culture?[3] Whilst this term can be used in a negative sense by both the right [4]and the left[5] it is used here to refer to a culture where people hold an awareness and respect for the rights of others and in this context can operate as an engine of transformation for equality in society.[6]

Feminist discussion recognises that domestic human rights systems operate in a gendered way and impact differently on men and women. Similar gender analyses relate to international law.[7] Therefore this paper asks what the recourse to international law within the UK means for the human rights of women? Are women's international rights norms being received into UK law, and if so how?

The next section discusses the approach taken by this paper; subsequent sections examine illustrations from the different constitutional branches. The post-Charter Canadian experience is used to read and interpret change and in conclusion the paper focuses on how women's rights might develop further in this context.

2) APPROACH

There is a long-standing debate around the utility of both domestic and international rights instruments as a positive force for women.[8] Debate in the UK con-

---

[2] This paper looks at initiatives which either have a UK wide impact or just impact on the law in England and Wales. There is divergence in terms of rights culture and protection of women's rights emerging between the different constituent parts of the UK but this is beyond the scope of this paper. C. Skeet, *Difference and Constitutionalism: Women and the 1997 Constitutional Reform Programme in the United Kingdom*, Doctoral Thesis accepted at University of Sussex, 2005.

[3] There is a question about whether there really is an emerging rights culture. L. Clements, "Winners and Losers" (2005) 32 Journal of Law and Society 34, suggests there is not. The Joint Parliamentary Committee on Human Rights (JCHR) also said they believed a culture had started to emerge between the passage of the HRA and it coming into force 1998–2000 but had gone into retreat since then. JCHR, *The Case for A Human Rights Commission* Sixth Report of Session 2002–2003 HL 67–1 HC 489–I, para. 94.

[4] See Melanie Phillips' vociferous writings on this area. For instance, "The Coercive Culture of Human Rights," *The Daily Mail (*12 May 2004).

[5] E. Kingdom, *What's Wrong With Rights?: Problems For a Feminist Politics of Law* (Edinburgh: Edinburgh University Press, 1991).

[6] JCHR, *supra* note 3, at paras. 1–35.

[7] H. Charlesworth and C. Chinkin, *The Boundaries of International Law: A Feminist Analysis* (Manchester: Manchester University Press, 2000).

[8] U. O'Hare, "Realising Human Rights For Women" (1999) 21 Human Rights

cerning the impact of the HRA on women's rights continues apace. Yet the UK has less than five years of experience with the HRA so it is important to examine evidence with the benefit of concrete experiences from comparators. The form that the United Kingdom HRA takes is based to some extent on the Canadian Charter of Rights and Freedoms 1982 (Charter): when the HRA was introduced into the House of Lords the enforcement and entrenchment mechanisms within it were described as a hybrid of those used in Canada and New Zealand.[9] Like the UK, Canada has a dualist legal system which means that international rights conventions and treaties do not take direct effect in domestic law. Despite the Canadian federal system and codified constitution there are similarities in political and legal culture within the UK and Canada.[10] Moreover Canada has a full jurisprudence on women's rights and has been praised for international standard setting in this area.[11] There is also a well-developed literature relating to the continuing debate around the Charter's impact on women's rights and equality.[12] For these reasons Canada makes a very useful comparator for the UK in this area. In fact Canada has already been used as a comparator by the courts and other institutions in the UK making it also in some instances a source in itself of rights norms, through transjudicialism.[13]

Quarterly 364. Though Charlesworth and Chinkiŋ, *ibid.,* suggest this is less so in the context of international discourses on human rights.

[9] The Canadian Charter of Rights and Freedoms 1982, Schedule B Constitution Act 1982 (UK) Chapter 11. Discussed by Lord Kingsland, Hansard, House of Lords, 03 November 1997 vol. 582 Col 11235. See also Lord Irvine of Lairg, Lord Chancellor, "The Development of Human Rights in Britain Under an Incorporated Convention on Human Rights" (1998) Public Law 221. It should also be noted that the 1990 New Zealand Bill of Rights based some of its rights content on the Canadian Charter, especially the wording of clauses relating to sex equality.

[10] This is especially true in relation to human rights and the criminal law. The UK and Canada share an adversarial system rather than the inquisitorial system on which so much of the ECHR jurisprudence is predicated.

[11] Concluding Comments of the Committee (CEDAW) Twenty-eighth session, Canada's Fifth Periodic Report CEDAW/C/2003/I/CRP.3/Add.5/Rev.1 at para. 16. Concluding Comments of the Committee (CEDAW) Sixteenth session, Canada's Third and Fourth Periodic Reports CEDAW/C/SR.329 and 330 at para. 323. See also M. Waring, *Three Masquerades: Essays on Equality, Work and Human Rights* (Auckland: Auckland University Press, 1996) Chapter 3.

[12] G. Anderson, ed., *Rights and Democracy-Essays in UK and Canadian Constitutionalism* (London: Blackstone, 1999).

[13] Transjudicialism is the use by judges in one jurisdiction of jurisprudence from other or another jurisdiction. Lord Steyn suggests that in the UK "Charter jurisprudence is of the greatest importance," Lord Steyn, "Deference A Tangled Story," 2004 *Judicial Studies Board Lecture*: Belfast 25 November 2004.

In the UK many women's groups and academics are sceptical about the extent of benefit to women of the HRA given its scope and content.[14] A recent workshop on Gender and the Human Rights Act held at Kent University concluded that research "yields a picture which is at best equivocal in terms of the ability of rights to address the particular concerns of feminist activists in Britain."[15] Favourable accounts are still acutely aware of the shortfalls of the HRA;[16] incorporating as it does rights framed over 60 years ago in the cautious political climate of post-war Europe. Moreover, the prohibition of discrimination in Article 14 of the ECHR is not a freestanding equality clause. Even where discrimination under Article 14 has been argued in relation to other ECHR rights the jurisprudence is wilfully underdeveloped.[17] In contrast the Canadian Charter was framed after the drafting of the International Convention on Civil and Political Rights (ICCPR) and the Convention on the Elimination of All Forms of Discrimination Against Women (CEDAW) and has a carefully worded s. 15 equality clause, protected by s. 28, a "notwithstanding clause."[18] From this Canada has developed world leading equality jurisprudence.[19] The UN Committee on the Elimination of All Forms of Discrimination Against Women (CEDAW Committee) has noted the limitations of rights content under the ECHR for women.[20] Despite this, in 1999 it hailed the enactment of the HRA as a positive step by the UK government in creating "an environment in which women's human rights can be fully developed to comply fully with the

---

[14] Academics who take a sceptical view include E. Kingdom, "What's Wrong with Rights, Reconsidered," *Equality and Rights: Making Constitutional Change Work for Women,* Cunliffe Centre Seminar 19 January 2001; S. Millns and N. Whitty, *Feminist Perspectives on Public Law* (London: Cavendish, 1999); A. McCoglan, *Women Under the Law, The False Promise of Human Rights* (Harlow: Longman, 2000); S. Millns, "Women's Rights After the Human Rights Act 1998," in A. Dobrowolsky & V. Hart, *Women Making Constitutions: New Politics and Comparative Perspectives* (Basingstoke: Palgrave, 2003).

[15] J. Conaghan and S. Milns, Introduction to Special Issue: Gender, Sexuality and Human Rights, (2005) 13 Feminist Legal Studies 1, at p. 2.

[16] *Supra* note 2.

[17] G. Moon, "The Draft Discrimination Protocol To The European Convention on Human Rights: A Progress Report" (2000) 1 European Human Rights Law Review 49.

[18] This ensures that women's equality rights cannot be abrogated by reference to other rights in the Charter.

[19] Charter provisions relating to women and minorities have been copied by many jurisdictions including New Zealand and most recently South Africa. Though it should be noted that while Canada has an excellent record in relation to civil and political rights the same is not true for social and economic rights.

[20] Report of the Committee on the Elimination of All Forms of Discrimination Against Women 20/21st session General Assembly Official Records UN/New York/1999, para. 293.

convention (CEDAW)."[21] The purpose of the paper is not to go over the general debate on the impact of the HRA on women's rights, but to look at whether the HRA can act as a conduit for international women's human rights norms beyond the content of those rights brought into effect by the HRA.[22]

There are different ways of understanding women's rights and women's international human rights norms. In relation to the term "women's international human rights," Hilary Charlesworth suggests that it can be understood at one level quite narrowly as only those rights instruments which deal specifically with women, and tend to be focussed on "elaborations of the norm of non-discrimination."[23] Conversely it may be viewed more generally as concern with how women can be "taken seriously across the entire spectrum of human rights?"[24] She argues for the latter and this is also the position that this paper adopts.

Yet agreement on the definition of women's rights does not guarantee consensus on how best to achieve them. In Canada a range of different perspectives has been used both to analyse the position of women and to promote their rights. LEAF, the Women's Legal Education and Action Fund, has varied its strategy through experience. At first LEAF focussed on a court-based strategy at the expense of other political and participatory strategies. Despite driving the groundbreaking *Andrews v The Law Society of British Columbia*[25] litigation, which moved away from a sameness or "similarly situated" analysis of equality, LEAF initially failed to tackle rights breaches against women of colour and poor women. Women's groups criticised them for this and argued that their approach tended to essentialise women and had narrowed the discourse around women's equality.[26] In the 1990's, LEAF moved to a more participatory organisational form and combined political lobbying[27] with a court-based approach. LEAF also adopted an intersectional[28] approach to discrimination and stopped

[21] *Ibid.* para. 300.

[22] Schedule 1 of the HRA 1998.

[23] H. Charlesworth, "What are 'Women's International Human Rights'?" in R. Cook, ed., *Human Rights of Women: National and International Perspectives* (Philadelphia: University of Pennsylvania Press, 1994) at 59.

[24] *Ibid.*

[25] [1989] 1 S.C.R. 143.

[26] R. Jhappan, "The Equality Pit or the Rehabilitation of Justice?" (1998) 10 2 Canadian Journal of Women and the Law; S. Razack, *Canadian Feminism and the Law* (Toronto: Second Story Press, 1991); L. Gotell, "Litigating Feminist 'Truth': An Antifoundational Critique" (1995) 4 Social and Legal Studies 99.

[27] M. Seydegart, LEAF activist, quoted by Razack *ibid.* at 50.

[28] Intersectionality is a discrimination theory developed by black feminists. This approach argues that where a person holds more than one social positionality, female gender, member of a racial, ethnic, or religious group or are affected by poverty or class, instead of conceiving quantitively of a double or triple burden of discrimination it is

"editing out" any discrimination other than gender from their cases.[29] They also promoted other successful structural changes such as gender representation in the judiciary and social context awareness in judicial training.[30] Canadian experience suggests that broadening strategies beyond the courts and adopting an intersectional approach is most successful in relation to promoting women's rights.

The following sections consider illustrations where, respectively, the UK courts, government and Parliament have supplemented the HRA by reference to other international norms relevant to women's rights.

3) COURTS

Ruth Rubio-Marin and Martha I. Morgan suggest that there are three main ways that international law is received into domestic courts: assimilation, supplementation and interpretive adaptation.[31]

With respect to assimilation Canada's Charter and the United Kingdom's HRA are perfect examples of the introduction of international law through assimilation by constitutional amendment.[32] Though the UK has no codified constitution and the HRA was passed in the same way as any other legislation, its status as a constitutional document is not in doubt.[33]

With the assimilation of ECHR rights through the HRA also comes supplementation. Section 2 of the HRA states that the courts must give consideration to jurisprudence and decisions from the ECHR system so these decisions provide a non-binding supplement to UK jurisprudence. However the ECHR

---

more accurate to see their discrimination as a qualitatively different lived experience affected by the way that their different positions or identities intersects. See K. W. Crenshaw, "Mapping the Margins: Intersectionality, Identity Politics and Violence Against Women of Colour" in M. Albertson & F. Mykitiuk, eds., *The Public Nature of Private Violence* (New York: Routledge, 1994).

[29] *Supra* note 26 at 72.

[30] These successful initiatives have now sparked a backlash. C. Backhouse, "The Chilly Climate for Women Judges: Reflections on the Backlash from the *Ewanchuk* Case" (2003) 15 Canadian Journal of Women and the Law 167.

[31] R. Rubio-Marin & M. I. Morgan, "Constitutional Domestication of International Gender Norms: Categorisations, Illustrations and Reflections from the Nearside of the Bridge," in K. Knop, ed., *Gender and Human Rights* (Oxford: OUP, 2004) at 113.

[32] *Ibid.* at 121–122.

[33] Lord Steyn suggests that the coming into force of the HRA was a landmark in the UK's transition to a constitutional state. "2002–2005: Laying the Foundations of Human Rights Law in the United Kingdom," Address to the British Institute of International and Comparative Law, 10 June 2005: http://wwww.biicl.org.index.

system is not noted for innovative jurisprudence in relation to women.[34] The European Court of Human Rights (ECt.HR) has often inexplicably refused to discuss how Article 14 might be engaged with other rights, even where discrimination is argued and substantive rights breaches have been rejected.[35] But two recent cases seem to show a willingness by the ECt.HR to develop the scope of the ECHR by reading in other instruments, which have stronger concern for women's rights.

In *Christine Goodwin v The United Kingdom*[36] the Court, encouraged by NGO intervention, considered the legal position of Commonwealth states as well as ECHR state parties[37] and took note of Article 9 of the European Charter of Fundamental Rights of the European Union. Unlike Article 12 of the ECHR, Article 9 of the EU Charter omits the reference to 'men' and 'women'[38] when setting out rights to marry. Although the case principally concerned the rights of transsexuals, the decision has a resonance for all women. It relates to who defines 'woman' and how women are defined. Post-Charter Canadian law has "challenged the notion that sex and gender are binary,"[39] thereby expanding the legal discourse around women. Where gender is presented as binary, difference is perceived as a feminine exception to a "supposedly unproblematic male standard."[40] If instead we can find a paradigm, which exposes gender as a multifaceted and not binary relationship, then this expands the scope for finding strategies to positively change discriminatory conceptions of identity.[41] The *Goodwin* case ultimately does reaffirm gender as binary, but both the case and

---

[34] M. Dembour, *Who Believes in Human Rights? The European Convention in Question* [Chapter 7 "The Convention in a Feminist Light"] (Cambridge: CUP, forthcoming).

[35] For instance the ECHR chamber judgment *Leyla Sahin v Turkey* 44774/98 (2004), and Grand Chamber judgment (2005).

[36] (Application no 28957/95) 11 July 2002, 35 EHRR 447.

[37] *Ibid.* at para. 56. It is usual to consider other ECHR member states to decide whether the states in question have gone beyond a "margin of appreciation" in how ECHR rights should be implemented and interpreted.

[38] The court believed that this was deliberate, *ibid.*, at paras. 58 and 100.

[39] S. Cowan, "'Gender is no Substitute for Sex': A Comparative Human Rights Analysis of the Legal Regulation of Sexual Identity" (2005) 13 Feminist Legal Studies 67 at 92; and see J. Roughgarden, *Evolution's Rainbow: Diversity, Gender and Sexuality in Nature and People* (London, University of California Press, 2004) for why we need to look at this again.

[40] J. Habermas, "Paradigms of Law," in M. Rosenfeld and A. Arato, eds., *Habermas on Law and Democracy: Critical Exchanges by Jurgen Habermas* (Berekley, University of California Press, 1998) at 23.

[41] R. Sandland, "Between 'Truth' and 'Difference': Post-structuralism, Law and the Power of Feminism" (1995) 1 Feminist Legal Studies 3.

the subsequent UK Gender Recognition Act 2004 also clearly treat gender as socially constructed, and recognise its fluidity.[42]

Another ECt.HR case, *MC v Bulgaria*,[43] took account of women's rights under international instruments and committees in addition to information on rape trials from a range of countries outside the ECHR system, and from the International criminal tribunals for Rwanda and the former Yugoslavia.[44] In the course of a "strong articulation of the values at stake . . . sexual autonomy and gender equality . . ."[45] the court asserted the positive duties incumbent on all states to enact provisions, and ensure they are used in practice, to investigate, prosecute and punish rape.[46] This further assertion is particularly pertinent to the UK. In the UK the level of reported rapes has risen but the number of prosecutions has fallen and some feminists are blaming the HRA for undermining efforts to improve the situation.[47]

UK appeal courts have also shown a willingness to engage in interpretive adaptation both through transjudicialism and also through the direct consideration of international instruments as an aid to interpretation. In *R v A*[48] the House of Lords drew heavily on the Canadian experience in order to consider whether statutory rape shield provisions could be balanced with defendants' rights.

Canadian women's experience in the immediate years following the Charter was that the courts tended only to balance the rights of defendants in sexual violence trials against those of an all powerful state. The Canadian Charter allows the courts to strike down offending legislative provisions and this is what they did. It was suggested that it was in the area of criminal law that women were most vulnerable.[49] However through study of case reasoning, fem-

---

[42] R. Sandland, "Feminism and the Gender Recognition Act 2004" (2005) 13 Feminist Legal Studies 43 at 59.

[43] *MC v Bulgaria* 39272/98 ECHR [2003] 646.

[44] This material was presented through an intervention by Interights human rights NGO. *MC, supra* note 43 paras. 148 – 166.

[45] J. Conaghan, " Extending the Reach of Human Rights to Encompass the Victims of Rape: MC v. Bulgaria," (2005) 13 Feminist Legal Studies 145 at 155.

[46] *Ibid.* at para. 153.

[47] See for example, S. Millns, "Women's Rights After The Human Rights Act 1998." in A. Dobrowolsky and V. Hart, eds., *Women Making Constitutions*: N*ew Politics and Comparative Perspectives* (Basingstoke: Palgrave, 2003).

[48] [2001] UKHL 25.

[49] C. Dauvergne, "A Reassessment of the Effects of a Constitutional Charter of Rights on the Discourse of Sexual Violence in Canada" (1994) 22 International Journal of the Sociology of Law 291–308 at 305; J. Fudge, "The Effects of Entrenching a Bill of Rights upon Political Discourse: Feminists' Demands and Sexual Violence in Canada" (1989) 17 International Journal of the Sociology of Law 445 at 463. M. Mandel, *The Charter of Rights and The Legalisation of Politics in Canada* (Toronto, Thompson Educational Publishing, 1994) at 389.

inists lobbied for careful re-drafting of legislation to achieve both stronger protection for women as victims and compatibility with protection for defendants. Judicial training in gender context awareness supported these initiatives. More recent cases like *R v Darrach*,[50] *R v Ewanchuk*[51] and *R v Mills*[52] provide positive and innovative jurisprudence for women in common law jurisdictions. In *R v A* the House of Lords took on board the judicial approach found in *Darrach* of recognising the right of the victim to dignity and freedom from damaging rape myths.[53] *Darrach* was cited with approval but, because of the way the English provision was drafted, the court followed the earlier *Seaboyer*[54] in finding the rape shield provision incompatible with the HRA. But instead of issuing a declaration of incompatibility, the court "read down" the legislative clause to reintroduce the judicial discretion, which Parliament had expressly sought to exclude.[55]

A (FC) and Others (FC) (Appellants) v Secretary of State (the *Belmarsh* case),[56] which concerned the detention of non-UK nationals without trial, and *R v Immigration Officer at Prague Airport and another (Respondents) ex parte. European Roma Rights Centre and Others (Appellants)* (Prague Airport case),[57] concerning discrimination against Roma women seeking to enter the UK, are seen as both the high watermark to date of interpretive adaptation and an indication of further things to come in the UK courts.[58] Both delivered strong admonishments to government that they could not discriminate, respectively, on grounds of nationality and race. In each case the nature of the duty to comply with the Article 14 equality provisions under the ECHR was explored through a wealth of references to domestic, transgovernmental, EU and international case law instruments and academic sources. What can feminists draw from these two cases?

---

[50] [2000] 2 SCR 443.

[51] [1999] 1 SCR 330.

[52] [1999] 3 SCR 668.

[53] But in terms of discourse generated, the judgements of the majority of their Lordships show that there is a gap between the rhetoric of women's rights in relation to the relevance of past sexual activity and consent, and what is referred to as "common sense" in this matter. For a discussion of the gendered nature of "common sense" see J. Conaghan and W. Mansell, *The Wrongs of Tort* (London: Pluto Press, 1999).

[54] *R v Seaboyer and Gayme* [1991] 2 SCR 577.

[55] Danny Nicol refers to this type of amendment as a "delete-all-and-replace-amendment." See "Are Convention Rights a No-Go Area for Parliament?" (2002) Public Law 438 at 443; Professor Jenny Temkin argues that judges regularly exercise their discretion to allow in inappropriate evidence. Research (in progress) into the operation of ss. 41–3 of the Youth Justice and Criminal Evidence Act 1999 on behalf of the Home Office with Professor Liz Kelly CBE.

[56] [2004] UKHL 56.

[57] [2004] UKHL 55.

[58] Lord Steyn, *supra* note 33.

The depth of discussion and wide use of international materials plus the strength of commitment to equality in each case is striking. In *Belmarsh* their lordships began by restating a "sameness" view of equality,[59] then rather than allowing the "discriminator to choose the comparator"[60] they moved to a close examination of whom the respondents should be compared to and rejected the government's argument that discrimination was justifiable. This case is also interesting because their Lordships stated that Article 14 was a non-derogable duty. So that even though the UK government had derogated from Article 5, they could not be allowed to discriminate in relation to this article.

The *Prague Airport* case also centres on equality issues. It is not generally raised as a women's rights case because, although the applicants were women, it was not alleged that the applicants were discriminated against in relation to men. But if we take an intersectional rather than a binary view of discrimination against women, then we should not edit out the applicants' sex as unimportant and the case does have specific resonance.[61]

In addition *R v A, Belmarsh* and the *Prague Airport* cases all illustrate the acceptance of third party interventions in human rights cases. These interventions developed in the US Supreme court moved into the international arena and became accepted in the ECt.HR.[62] They were not specifically provided for in the HRA but it was expected that the courts would allow them. While third party interventions can not make up for other forms of representation of women within the legal process and can not replace gender awareness training for legal personnel, they do provide an expansion of discourse and the provision of experience and information, which would not otherwise be there.[63]

Examination of UK cases showing assimilation and interpretative adaptation of international rights norms might and should encourage women to use arguments and interventions based on international law to pursue their rights. But, despite this apparent willingness of the House of Lords to draw on international law and strengthen equality principles in their judgements, research from

---

[59] *Supra* note 56 at para. 46.

[60] Lady Justice Hale in *Pearce* v *Mayfield* [2001] EWCA civ 1347.

[61] Roma women are discriminated against as "Roma" women. Their gender and race are inseparable. The European Roma Rights Centre chose six women for the case. Their website www.errc.org/ details gender specific discrimination against Roma women, which includes forced sterilisation and rape. It also presents comment by CEDAW on state parties treatment of Roma women. If we ignore the gender of people suffering discrimination on racial grounds and it is not conceived of as an issue for women's rights then it both renders gender specific racial discrimination invisible and makes it more difficult for women to raise rights issues within a racial grouping.

[62] C. Harlow, "Public Law and Popular Justice" (2002) 65 Modern Law Review 1.

[63] H. Samuels, "Feminist Activism, Third Party Interventions and the Courts" (2005) 13 Feminist Legal Studies 15.

Canada suggests we should not rely on the courts either to develop a rights culture for women or to guarantee equality outcomes. Evidence shows that domestic courts use international law for a range of reasons and do not feel bound to be consistent in their use.[64] Moreover where the courts have recourse to international law it may not always be to the benefit of women in human rights cases.[65] For this reason its also important to look to the other constitutional branches to develop rights norms.

4) GOVERNMENT[66]

The UK's current Labour government came into office with strong rhetoric around women's rights. But real commitment within government to gender issues has been patchy and is often driven by particular personalities. In 1997, under Robin Cook and Clare Short, the Foreign Office and the Department for Foreign and International Development set up an annual reporting system on human rights in UK policy. The first annual report in 1998 maintained that international women's rights were at the heart of foreign policy, and that UK domestic policy would also reflect this.[67] Successive human rights reports maintain that the principal method of developing women's rights in the UK is through gender mainstreaming,[68] an internationally agreed mode of securing women's equality and rights.[69] Yet submissions to the fifth CEDAW report from the Women's National Commission argued that there had been no substantive

---

[64] R. Bhadi, "Globalisation of Judgement: Transjudicialism and the Five Faces of International Law in Domestic Courts" (2002) George Washington International Law Review 555; K. Knop, "Here And There: International Law in Domestic Courts" (2000) 32 New York University School of Law Journal of International Law and Politics 501.

[65] See especially A. F. Bayefsky, "General Approaches to Domestic Application of Women's International Human Rights Law," in Cook, *supra* note 23; R. Bhadi, "Litigating Social and Economic Rights in Canada in Light of International Human Rights Law: What Difference can it make?" (2002) 14 Canadian Journal of Women and the Law 158.

[66] There is overlap between governmental and parliamentary activity because of the peculiar relationship between the two in the UK. For instance the setting up of the JCHR was a government initiative but subsequent activities of that committee are parliamentary.

[67] FCO, "Getting our Own House in Order": http:/www.fco.gov.uk/files/kfile/HRPD_98.

[68] For instance see the 2004 Human Rights Report p231 http://www.fco.gov.uk/files/kfile/HRPD_2004.

[69] S.M. Rai, ed., *Mainstreaming Gender, Democratising the State? Institutional Mechanisms for the Advancement of Women* (Manchester: Manchester University Press, 2003).

evaluation of mainstreaming by the government and at best there were only pockets of good practice.[70]

Though it cannot yet be said that there is cohesive policy, a number of policy and legislative initiatives from the government have drawn on international rights norms and "transgovernmental" perspectives. A few illustrative examples are presented below followed by consideration of the parliamentary review of international instruments and the passage of the Equality Bill, which are likely to have deeper impact.

Women's right to participation in governance has gained wide international recognition and is expressly recognised in Article 7 of CEDAW. Moreover women's representation, as a facet of participation, can be argued to be a right in itself and is also crucial in achieving other rights gains for women.[71] The CEDAW Committee particularly noted a problem with women's enjoyment of this right in the UK and asked the UK to take action.[72] The Sex Discrimination (Parliamentary Candidates) Act 2002 draws on CEDAW's Article 7[73] and Article 4[74] to render positive discrimination within political parties lawful when choosing electoral candidates. It is likely that the committee expected the UK to use special measures to require rather than allow increased representation. Nevertheless this is a positive initiative that gained cross-party consensus precisely because of its non-mandatory nature. In other areas of government the commitment to women's representation has waxed and waned.[75]

As noted in *MC v Bulgaria* international law has developed in its recognition of the significance of rape as a breach of women's rights. The UK government has drawn on Canadian case law in order to develop reforms to rape trials but has not taken full advantage of the Canadian experience.[76] The change to wit-

---

[70] DTI and Women and Equality Unit, "Changing World Changing Lives: Women in the UK since 1999." Summary of the UK's fifth report to the CEDAW Committee, p. 23.

[71] *Supra* note 2.

[72] *Supra* note 20, para. 302.

[73] Equality in political and public life.

[74] Temporary special measures to accelerate de facto equality between men and women.

[75] See M. Russell, "Women in Elected Office in the UK, 1992–2002: Struggles, Achievements and Possible Sea Change" in Dobrowolsky and Hart (eds.) *supra* note 47; and M. Russell, "Women and Lords Reform," paper for *Women and Westminster*, London, Institute of Commonwealth Studies, 28 November 2003.

[76] This was one area that initially dismayed feminists in Canada. Legislation designed to protect women as victims and witnesses was struck down. See for example J. Fudge, "The Effect of Entrenching a Bill of Rights upon Legal Discourse: Feminist Demands and Sexual Violence in Canada" (1989) 17 International Journal of Sociology of Law 445. However resulting legislation proved to be both more advantageous to women and compatible with other Charter rights. See *R v Park* [1995] 2 SCR 836 and *Ewanchuk* and *Darrach supra* notes 50 and 51.

ness questioning in rape trials, brought in by s. 41 of the Youth and Criminal Justice Act 1999, was supposedly based on the Canadian model. In effect the drafters ignored many of the representations from women's groups to this end[77] and misunderstood the relevant Charter cases and subsequent legislation from Canada.[78] The result was that even this relatively weak provision was successfully challenged under s 6 of the HRA.[79] In contrast, changes to the rules on consent in the Sexual Offences Bill 2002 were based closely on Canadian legislation but unfortunately were killed off at the second reading[80] resulting in an emasculated Sexual Offences Act 2003. These experiences show the importance both of ensuring that transgovernmental models are properly applied and of disseminating transgovernmental / transjudicial experience more widely to "sell" changes.

The Canadian example has also been influential in raising awareness of the gendered nature of international law relating to asylum and refuge, a topic further developed in the next chapter. After the UNHCR released guidelines, Canada became the first country to develop and adopt its own.[81] It was only when the HRA came into force that the Immigration Appeals Authority (now IAT) launched its own draft gender guidelines.[82] It still took a concerted campaign by women's groups and condemnation in the Women's National Commission (WNC) shadow report to CEDAW,[83] before similar guidelines were formally introduced into government asylum policy in March 2004.[84]

Most surprising has been the recent government ratification of the CEDAW optional protocol,[85] which amongst other things allows women to directly petition the CEDAW Committee.[86] Surprising because the government response to

---

[77] Julia Drown MP, *Hansard* 16th July 2002 col. 174.

[78] Per Lord Steyn *supra* note 48.

[79] *Ibid.*

[80] See *Hansard* 19 July 2000.

[81] C. Harvey, (1999) "Engendering Asylum Law: Feminism, Process and Practice" in Millns and Whitty, eds., *supra* note 14. Lord Steyn also drew on the Canadian case of *Attorney-General of Canada v Ward* (1993) 103 DLR when determining that gender could be a ground of persecution in *Islam v Secretary of State for the Home Department; R v Immigration Appeal Tribunal and another ex parte Shah,* [1999] 2 AC 629.

[82] The HRA came into full force in October 2000 and guidelines were drawn up in December 2000 based on those developed by the Refugee Women's Legal Group in 1998.

[83] P. Sen, C. Humphrys and L. Kelly with Womankind Worldwide, Thematic CEDAW Shadow Report 2003: Violence Against Women in the UK, p 36. See www.rwlg.org.uk.

[84] Training was only begun in January 2005.

[85] A/RES/54/4 15 Oct 1999.

[86] Ratified 17 December 2004.

earlier lobbying was that this was out of the question. Groups lobbying the government were referred to the HRA and told that it obviated the need to implement CEDAW'S petition mechanism.[87] When the same issue was raised in parliamentary debate, the government argued both that it was unnecessary to adopt the protocol and that they needed to concentrate on the impact of the HRA before they instituted any other rights change.[88] Despite this, an inter-departmental review of the UK position on international human rights instruments[89] recommended the UK ratify the protocol. Twenty government agencies including the Women's Equality Unit and a further twenty non-governmental organisations (NGOs) including the Equal Opportunities Commission contributed to the review.[90] The report with the government's decisions was released on 20th of July 2004.[91]

Although the decision to adopt the CEDAW protocol is welcomed it is not clear why this is the only instrument that they have acted on; the review also considered petitioning rights under Convention on Racial Discrimination, CERD, the Convention on Torture, UNCAT and the International Convention on Civil and Political Rights, ICCPR. The government stated that this is an experiment and could open the way for the other rights to petition.[92] The Joint Parliamentary Committee on Human Rights and the Ministerial/NGO Forum on Human Rights have both questioned this.[93] They point out that since the protocol is new there are as yet few cases to learn from.[94] Sceptics also suggest that

---

[87] Survey of women's groups – attitudes to and knowledge of the HRA and CEDAW carried out by the author 2000. Respondent 7.

[88] House of Lords, *Hansard,* 31 January 2002 col. 347. Baroness Scotland argued that the UK already had extensive legislation which covered CEDAW. She also believed that the government's priority was to the HRA.

[89] This review was established in 2002 to consider "in the light of the experience of the operation of the Human Rights Act, the availability of existing remedies within the UK, and law and practice in other EU member states . . ." Inter-departmental Review of UK Position on International Human Rights Instruments 2002: http://www.human-rights.gov.uk/ngo/lcdpaper1.htm.

[90] Appendix 2.

[91] Department for Constitutional Affairs, Report on the UK Government's Inter-Departmental Review of the UK's Position Under Various International Human Rights Instruments, July 2004.

[92] *International Human Rights Instruments: The UK Position*, Appendix 5. See also Hansard House of Lords, 16 September 2004 col. WA201.

[93] See JCHR 17th report session 2004–2005 Review of International Rights Instruments HL 99/ HC 264, and Ministerial /NGO Human Rights Forum, 16 September 2004, at point 7.

[94] There are currently two: *a/59/38 communication, 1/2003 Ms B.J. v Germany,* deemed inadmissible, and *2/2003 Ma A.T. v Hungary* – concerning the state's positive duty to protect against domestic violence.

this CEDAW petitioning mechanism was chosen because it is the weakest. The CEDAW committee is overburdened and under resourced; it has not yet been able to consider the UK fifth report submitted in 2003. However Lord Lester suggests the government had no intention of signing up even to the CEDAW protocol, until Patricia Hewitt, then minister for women, applied pressure and insisted that they accede to a trial run.[95]

There are likely to be benefits from ratification of the optional protocol. Ratification will lead to greater awareness of CEDAW within government departments, make government more receptive to being lobbied on CEDAW principles and contribute to discourse around women's rights. Because all remedies must be exhausted before a petition is accepted, argument will have to be presented on CEDAW points in the UK courts first. But courts may adopt an interpretive adaptive stance and construe HRA rights so as to give effect to CEDAW. Christine Chinkin also suggests that the very fact that only the CEDAW protocol has been ratified might mean a raised interest and awareness of women's rights by groups who would not normally consider themselves 'women's groups' but might want to use the provisions to raise intersectional claims in relation to say race or disability.[96]

But it would have been of greater benefit to women had the ICCPR,[97] CERD and UNCAT mechanisms also been accepted and some of the reservations to these instruments dropped.[98] Canadian strategy suggests that for best effect CEDAW needs to be combined with other rights provisions.[99] Moreover the declarations of equality in CEDAW[100] are not as strong as Article 26 of the

---

[95] Lord Lester made this point at a *Human Rights Lawyers Association* (HRLA) meeting 31st January 2005, London.

[96] Comments made at the HRLA meeting, *ibid*.

[97] It was not until the ICCPR heard *Sandra Lovelace v Canada* communication r.6/24 (29 Dec 1977) UN.Doc.Supp.No 40 (A/36/40) at166 (1981) that Canada took action to change provisions of the Indian Act 1876 which discriminated against women. Also CEDAW itself has been held not to be introducing new international rights but providing the detail for the rights already contained in the ICCPR. See *Broeks v The Netherlands* (Communication No. 172/1984) a case brought under the First Optional Protocol to the ICCPR.

[98] For instance the government has reservations to Article 10 of the ICCPR and to article 37(c) of the Convention of the Rights of the Child, requiring juveniles to be detained separately. The JCHR, *supra* note 94 at para. 50, notes that this has gendered consequences and disadvantages young women.

[99] S. Day, *CEDAW: Strategies For Implementation*, Commissioned by the International Women's Rights Project, with financial assistance from the Social Sciences and Humanities Research Council, for the Canadian CEDAW Strategies Meeting in November, 1998, York University.

[100] With the exception of Article 6 which provides for the prohibition of women in absolute terms. See Charlesworth and Chinkin, *supra* note 7 at p. 229.

ICCPR, because they use a sameness approach and therefore do not challenge rights which are applied equally but are gendered in their construction.[101] Although Article 5 of CERD does not reflect the gendered nature of racial discrimination neither does CEDAW specifically seek to protect against racial discrimination. Women's groups, amongst others, also campaigned hard for the government to sign up to Protocol 12 of the ECHR and incorporate it into the HRA; the government's refusal was a bitter if predictable disappointment.

An initiative likely to have wide reach is the Equality Bill. This contains provisions for setting up a Equality and Human Rights Commission (EHRC).[102] The commission is to consider all human rights not just those under the ECHR when carrying out its duties.[103] Further, the Bill sets out a duty for all public authorities to promote gender equality.[104] This latter provision is similar to the duty under the Northern Ireland Act 1998, which the CEDAW committee has praised highly.[105] This suggests a serious government commitment to gender mainstreaming on the mainland. The new Equality and Human Rights Commission meets the Paris Principles[106] but will not be able to adjudicate its own cases. It will replace the Equal Opportunities Commission, Disability Discrimination Commission, and Commission for Racial Equality. Some women's groups are concerned that gender issues would receive less attention than say race or disability, because of the statutory duties imposed to prevent discrimination on those grounds.[107] Nevertheless taken with the new Part III duty to promote gender equality the EHRC also presents an opportunity for promoting women's rights through an intersectional lens.[108]

Canada shows us that the ability of courts to respond to women's rights arguments is greatly developed by judicial training. It was anticipated that the advent of the HRA would stimulate policy in relation to greater training of judges and further representation of women within the judiciary.[109] Both these

---

[101] *Ibid.*

[102] Part III, s. 82. The government only looked into a commission once the Scottish Parliament had announced that they were to set one up.

[103] *Ibid.* Part I, s. 9.

[104] Equality Bill HC 897, Part I.

[105] *Supra* note 20 at para. 297.

[106] Paris Principles Relating to the Status of National Human Rights Institutions 1993, UN Commission on Human Rights Resolution 1992/54 and UN General Assembly Resolution A/ RES/48/134.

[107] WNC Shadow Report to the CEDAW Committee 2005, paras. 9 and 14.

[108] *Ibid.* para. 11.

[109] Mr Justice Brooke "The Administration of Justice in a Multi-Cultural Society" Address to the "Grotius Colloquium on the Fight Against Racism in the Administration of Justice," London, March 27, 2000. http://www.lcd.gov.uk/judicial/speeches/ 27–3–2000.htm.

initiatives have been mooted but not adopted as government policy so far.[110] Professor Peter Duff argues that for instance rape shield provisions will never be successful until judicial training is given and there is a real will to implement whatever provisions are set down. Scottish Women's Aid recommended training not only for the judiciary, but also for all legal professionals and Crown and fiscal officers.[111]

5) Parliament

There has been relatively little debate on women's human rights norms within the two Houses of the United Kingdom Parliament.[112] But there has still been an increase in references to international human rights since the introduction of the HRA.[113] These have included questions to the government on compliance with CEDAW and when or whether the optional protocol to CEDAW would be signed.

It seems that transgovernmental and transjudicial arguments could be used to greater effect in parliamentary debate. As noted above parliamentary debate on legislation has sometimes proved negative in terms of the passage of specific legislation to promote women's rights. But the provisions of the Sexual Offences Act 2003 might have been more severely damaged in the House of Lords were it not for a speech from Lord Cooke of Thorndon explaining how and why the law had been similarly changed in New Zealand.[114] Despite the

---

[110] In 1999, the Equal Treatment Bench Book was re-issued and for the first time included advice on gender, sexual orientation, disability, children and litigants in person. Yet Lord Justice Brooke rightly believes that this is insufficient to achieve positive change, *ibid.*

[111] Evidence given to Scottish Parliament on the Sex Offences (Procedures and Evidence) Scotland Bill on 15 August 2001: www.scottish.parliament.uk/officialreport/cttee/just-2–01/j2r01–13–03.htm. Professor Peter Duff at para. 3 and Women's Aid at para. 1.

[112] The debate surrounded the passage of the Female Genital Mutilation Bill (now an Act) attracted discussion from both sexes in the House of Commons but there were no male speakers in the House of Lords. In the House of Lords debate there was carried out by a "band of sisters" (as described by Baroness Rendell): *Hansard* 12 September 2003 col. 652.

[113] Based on *Hansard* searches of both the House of Lords and House of Commons before and after the HRA. Much greater evidence of rights deliberation can be found in the Scottish, Northern Irish and Welsh context, In Scotland and Wales this is driven by the greater numbers of women in the assemblies and in Northern Ireland by the Good Friday Agreement, Bill of Rights development and Human Rights Commission. See *supra* note 2.

[114] Which had developed its legislation along Canadian lines.

fact that the government's provisions before the house were based on Canadian legislation, there was no attempt to explain the Canadian position and how it has worked in the courts and other areas of practice.[115] Yet Lord Cooke's intervention shows that transjudicialism or transgovernmentalism can be persuasive in parliamentary contexts as well as courts.[116]

One of the most important parliamentary developments to advance discourse around human rights is the Joint Parliamentary Committee on Human Rights (JCHR). This was established in January 2001. It is described as a "unique and unprecedented select committee"[117] in that it combines both investigation and scrutiny. The committee contextualises HRA issues within a transjudicial and international legal framework. Canada is frequently used as a comparator, especially in relation to women's rights.

The JCHR examines draft legislation and can instigate and conduct enquiries into human rights issues. Moreover they can provide accountability in relation to the follow up from international reporting procedures.[118] Previously, only NGOs raised government accountability in this area. JCHR reports have dealt with gender reassignment,[119] the Sex Discrimination (Election Candidates) Bill,[120] Equality Commissions,[121] and have raised other gender equality issues across a range of other reports. Because the JCHR takes evidence from a wide variety of sources and groups it also provides for further interaction on human rights between Parliament and the people.

6) Conclusion

The ECHR has been criticised for its age and limited rights provisions, especially in relation to women. But this paper argues that by domesticating these provisions the HRA has opened up the UK to absorption of international rights norms that go beyond the content and jurisprudence of the ECHR. Canada can be seen in this context as a source of "other" norms and discourses in the UK through both transgovernmentalism and transjudicialism. Canada also serves as

---

[115] Though Lord Alexander of Weedon made brief mention of it: *Hansard* House Of Lords 2 June 2003 col. 1058.

[116] *Ibid.* col. 1049 Lord Alloway's amendment, col. 1058 Lord Cooke of Thorndon's speech, col.1061 Lord Campbell of Alloway withdraws his amendment.

[117] F. Klug, "The Human Rights Act: Can You Spot the Difference?" Lecture given to British Institute of Human Rights, 6 December 2001: http://www.bihr.org/events/klug.htm.

[118] Fourteenth Report session 2004/2005 HL 88/HC 471.

[119] Nineteenth Report of session 2003/2004 HL Paper 188/HC 1276–1.

[120] Fourth Report of session 2001/2002 HL 44/HC 406.

[121] Sixth Report of session 2002–03 HL Paper 67–I, HC 489–I.

a pertinent reminder that an integrated approach is needed to secure women's rights.

The UK courts, especially with the development of third party interventions, provide a useful forum for developing rights discourse on both international and domestic rights norms. But, Canadian experience suggests, courts are not a reliable way in themselves of strengthening women's human rights. Where international norms have permeated government, damage to innovative policy initiatives through the parliamentary process and interpretation in court also argue for an integrated approach to women's rights in the UK.

Problems for the absorption of women's rights norms within the discrete constitutional locations do not disappear when placed together, but taken together they may support and strengthen each other and mitigate difficulties raised in individual locations. As well as discourses generated within given political and social places, discourses are also generated between those different sites.[122] A recent example of this is the influence the JCHR report had on the House of Lords' *Belmarsh* decision.[123] In order to embed legal rights discourse it is not just important that women's perspectives are represented in the courts themselves, but it also makes a difference whether women's perspectives are represented through government and articulated in Parliament and wider civil society.[124]

This paper focuses on the reception of international women's rights norms into the different constitutional institutions in the UK. Missing from this is a separate discussion of the role of civil society. Evidence suggests that while human rights act as a catalyst and mobiliser for civil movements both internationally and in the domestic sphere, so discourse and activism by disadvantaged groups around rights are important to ensure that rights operate as an emancipatory force.[125] Social movements operate in a variety of ways to provide a socialising force in relation to human rights norms,[126] and this operation is particularly important in relation to women's rights.[127] The "women's movement" may

---

[122] E. Laclau and C. Mouffe, *Hegemony and Socialist Strategy: Towards a Radical Democratic Politics* (London: Verso, 2001) at 140.

[123] *Supra* note 60, particularly Lord Bingham at para. 22.

[124] For example in the pre-HRA case of *R. v. R.* [1992] 1 AC 599, which overturned the marital rape exemption, the House of Lords was influenced amongst other things by the fact that, after considerable lobbying by women's groups, Parliament had turned its attention to the problems of marital rape.

[125] N. Stammers, "Social Movements and the Social Construction of Human Rights" (1999) 21 Human Rights Quarterly 980 at 980.

[126] T. Risse, S. Ropp & K. Sikkink, *The Power of Human Rights: International Norms and Domestic Change* (Cambridge: CUP, 1999).

[127] I. M. Young, *Inclusion and Democracy* (Oxford: OUP, 2000); K. Knop,"Why Rethinking The Sovereign State Is Important for Women's International Rights Law" in Cook, *supra* note 23.

make up for an under-representation of women in other areas of public life and a strong movement will also work to strengthen the hand of elected representatives and elite groups working for women's rights.[128] Since the HRA was passed there has been an increase in interest and knowledge about CEDAW by groups supporting women's rights.[129] Ratification of CEDAW's optional protocol will further stimulate awareness and act as a mobilising force for women's rights.[130]

The extent to which international women's human rights norms are permeating should not be overstated. However these developments do indicate a start and a positive opportunity to develop women's rights in the UK.

---

[128] P. Kome, *The Taking of Twenty Eight: Women Challenge the Constitution,* (Toronto: Women's Press, 1983).

[129] Compare survey of women's groups by Charlotte Skeet in 2000, *supra* note 2, with the 45% of respondents polled by the WNC who knew the UK government was scheduled to submit a report to CEDAW in 2003 and the 76% who knew of and supported ratification of the CEDAW Optional Protocol [cited by the CEDAW Shadow Report *supra* note 83].

[130] The organisation Rights of Women (ROW) believes that CEDAW could be raised more often in legal argument but that a lack of knowledge holds back members of the public and lawyers: Comments made at ROW Conference, London, 1 October 2000.

Chapter 9

Application of Gender Guidelines within the Asylum Determination Process: From Reflections on the UK and Canadian Experience

R. M. M. Wallace and Anne Holliday*

1) Introduction

Gender guidelines are designed to facilitate a gender sensitive interpretation of the 1951 Refugee Convention[1] definition. Guidelines seek to ensure claims are handled and analysed both procedurally and substantively within a gender sensitive framework and that determination processes do not marginalise or exclude gender-related experiences of persecution. Canada introduced guidelines in 1993, the United Kingdom (UK) in 2000 and this article reflects on how these guidelines have impacted the Canadian and UK refugee determination processes respectively.

Biological sex is not synonymous with gender; gender embraces the socially and culturally constructed experience of being a woman or a man and a

---

* The views expressed are those of the authors and do no reflect those of the Immigration Appellate Authority (IAA).
[1] Convention relating to the Status of Refugees, 28 July 1951, 189 U.N.T.S. 150 [Refugee Convention].

Christopher P.M. Waters (Ed.), *British and Canadian Perspectives on International Law*, pp. 169–186.

relationship between them in society. "It affects both women and men's social identity, status, roles and responsibilities".[2] What it means to be a woman or a man will vary according to time and place, as well as other factors such as race, age, class and marital status. Persecution in the conventional sense does not always correspond with the experiences of women asylum applicants. This has been to the disadvantage of women, as they have been denied the protection such persecution warrants. In seeking to address this problem, an increasing number of states have introduced guidelines specifically designed to give cognisance to the gender dimension of refugee claims. Gender sensitivity is something required in claims brought either by men or women. Although male claims may also demand a gender perspective, such a perspective is more commonly relevant in claims brought by women. What has prompted the guidelines is the need to overcome barriers confronting women applicants in the asylum determination process.

How may gender manifest itself in an asylum claim of a woman applicant? An asylum seeker may be persecuted in a gender specific manner for reasons *unrelated* to gender, for instance, raped because of her membership to a political party. A woman may be persecuted in a non-gender specific manner on *grounds* of her gender, for instance, flogged for refusing to conform to social norms. A woman may be persecuted in a gender specific manner *because* of her gender, for instance, female genital mutilation (FGM) or honour killing.[3]

2) INTERNATIONAL BACKCLOTH

Acknowledgement of the human rights violations perpetrated against women is reflected in a plethora of international instruments. Certain violations may be characterised as gender-specific forms of harm with women being targeted primarily if not exclusively because of their sex. The veil, which precluded state interference in what was traditionally regarded as 'private', has been pierced. International law now seeks to extend protection to women and children. The Vienna Declaration and Programme of Action[4] provides that:

---

[2] U.K., Home Office, Immigration Appellate Authority (IAA) Asylum Gender Guidelines by N. Berkowitz & C. Jarvis (London: Her Majesty Stationery Office, 2000) at s. 1.12 [IAA Gender Guidelines]. Mrs. Jarvis is now a Senior Immigration Judge and Vice President of the Asylum and Immigration Tribunal.

[3] Other examples are sexual violence, societal and legal discrimination, forced prostitution, trafficking, being refused contraception, forced marriage, forced sterilisation, forced abortion and sexual humiliation. It is acknowledged that sexual orientation has a gender dimension; however, guidelines were designed primarily to deal with the obstacles encountered by women by virtue of the 'traditional' roles attributed to them in society. Therefore sexual orientation is not dealt with in this article.

[4] UN Doc. A/CONF 157/23 (25 June 1993), adopted following the United Nations World Conference on Human Rights.

the human rights of women and of the girl child are inalienable, integral and indivisible part of universal human rights – gender based violence and all forms of sexual harassment and exploitation, including those resulting from cultural prejudice and international trafficking, are incompatible with the dignity and worth of the human person, and must be eliminated.[5]

Whereas the Declaration on the Elimination of Violence against Women[6] explicitly acknowledged that women experience violence attributable to gender, which most notably encompasses:

> any act of gender based violence that results in or is likely to result in, physical or psychological harm or suffering to women, including threats of such acts of coercion or arbitrary deprivation of liberty whether occurring in public or private life.[7]

The Declaration represented advancement on the Convention on the Elimination of All Forms of Discrimination against Women (CEDAW), which had not addressed the issue of violence against women.[8] The Declaration also prompted the appointment of a Special Rapporteur on Violence against Women in 1994.[9]

A woman's vulnerability to rape[10] during hostilities is recognized in, for example, the Statute of the International Criminal Tribunal for the Former

---

[5] *Ibid.* at Part I.18.

[6] GA Res. 48/104, UN GAOR, 48th Sess., Supp. No. 49, UN Doc. A/48/49 (1993) [The Declaration].

[7] *Ibid.* at art. 2. Article 2 defines violence against women by reference to examples of physical, sexual and psychological violence occurring in the family, the general community and that perpetrated or condoned by the forum state. Prior to The Declaration, two General Recommendations on the Issue of Violence against Women were adopted by the Committee on the Elimination of all Forms of Discrimination against Women, namely Recommendation Numbers 12 and 19, whereas Recommendation 14 addressed specifically the issue of female genital mutilation.

[8] Article 6 of CEDAW only made reference to the adoption of appropriate measures including legislation to suppress all forms of traffic in women and exploitation, but it did not define 'traffic' nor did it specify whether states were to suppress exploitation of prostitution or to suppress prostitution itself.

[9] Ms. Radhika Coomaraswamy (Sri Lanka) was Special Rapporteur between 1994–2003 and Dr. Yakin Erturk (Turkey) has been Special Rapporteur since August 2003.

[10] As stated in article 27 of the Geneva Convention Relative to the Protection of Civilian Persons in Time of War (12 August 1949) 75 U.N.T.S. 287, "women shall be specially protected against any attack on their honour, in particular against rape, enforced prostitution, or any form of indecent assault", as endorsed in Protocol Additional to the Geneva Conventions of 12 August 1949, and Relating to the Protection of Victims of International Armed Conflicts (Protocol I) (8 June 1977) 3 U.N.T.S. 1125 at art. 76 (entered into force 7 December 1978).

Yugoslavia,[11] the Statute of the International Criminal Tribunal of Rwanda[12] (articles 5(g) & 3(g) respectively[13]) and their jurisprudence,[14] as well as the Statute of the International Criminal Court.[15] The 1951 Refugee Convention and the 1967 New York Protocol's definition of a 'refugee' is gender neutral and neither recognize gender as an independent enumerated ground for a well-founded fear of persecution.[16] Gender neutrality *per se* is not the cause of the barriers which women applicants have encountered within the asylum determination process. The barriers confronting women are a consequence of the way in which the Refugee Convention definition has been interpreted, primarily from a male perspective.[17] This male bias is reflected in the failure of decision-makers to establish a nexus between the alleged persecution and one of the Convention grounds, as well as a reluctance to characterise certain behaviour perpetrated against women as persecution. Frequently such conduct has been accepted as the 'cultural norm': a characterization made easier given the perpetrators of such conduct are often non-state actors.

However, the United Nations High Commissioner for Refugees (UNHCR) throughout the 1990s adopted a number of initiatives calling for greater gender

---

[11] SC Res. 827, 3217th Mtg., UN Doc. S/RES/827 (1993).

[12] SC Res. 955, 3453d Mtg., UN Doc. S/RES/955 (1994).

[13] Rape is designated as a crime against humanity. For a regional instrument see Inter-American Convention on the Prevention, Punishment and Eradication of Violence against Women (9 June 1994) 33 I.L.M. 1534.

[14] See e.g. *Prosecutor v. Delalic et al.* (1998), Case No. IT-96-21-T (International Criminal Tribunal for the Former Yugoslavia, Trial Chamber); *Prosecutor v. Furundzija* (1998), Case No. IT-95-17/1-T (International Criminal Tribunal for the Former Yugoslavia, Trial Chamber); *Prosecutor v. Kunarac, Kovac and Vukovic* (2001), Case Nos. IT-96-23-T, IT-96-23/1-T (International Criminal Tribunal for the Former Yugoslavia, Trial Chamber); *Prosecutor v. Akayesu* (1998), Case No. ICTR-96-4-T (International Criminal Tribunal for Rwanda, Trial Chamber). See also UN's Fourth World Conference on Women, *Programme of Action* (Beijing: 4–15 September 1995) at Strategic Objective D1–D3.

[15] 17 July 1998, UN Doc. No. A/CONF.183/9, 37 I.L.M. 999 (entered into force 1 July 2002).

[16] A person who falls within the Refugee Convention and the 1967 Protocol, who may be characterised as warranting refugee status, is one who; "owing to a well-founded fear of being persecuted for reasons of race, religion, nationality, membership of a particular social group, or political opinion, is outside the country of his nationality and is unable, or owing to such fear, is unwilling to avail himself of the protection of that country; or who, not having a nationality, and being outside the country of his former habitual residence as a result of such events, is unable, or owing to such fear, is unwilling to return to it", cited in Refugee Convention, *supra* note 1 at art. 1A(2), as am. by the Protocol to that Convention signed at New York City on January 31, 1967 at art. 1.2.

[17] Although women and children make up the majority of the world's refugee population, the 'typical' refugee is a young, single, readily mobile male.

sensitivity and a heightened awareness to the plight of refugee women. Examples of such initiatives include UNHCR Executive Committee (ExCom) Conclusions No. 39 (XXXVI) on Refugee Women and International Protection 1985; No. 54 (XXXV1) 1988; No. 60(XL) 1989; No. 64 (XL1) 1990;[18] and, No. 73 (XLIV) 1993 on Refugee Protection and Sexual Violence. Of these, two are most noteworthy. The first is ExCom. No. 39, which endorses that States:

> are free to adopt the interpretation according to which women asylum seekers, who are the object of inhuman or degrading treatment because they have transgressed social rules of the society in which they live, can be seen as constituting a particular social group in the sense of Article 1A(2) of the 1951 Convention.[19]

The secondly is ExCom No. 73, which specifically addresses sexual violence and emphasised the need to, *inter alia*: ensure the equal access of women and men to refugee status determination procedures; recognize as refugees persons whose claim to refugee status is based upon a well-founded fear of persecution, through sexual violence, for reasons of race, religion, nationality, membership of a particular social group or political opinion; development by appropriate guidelines on women asylum-seekers at the state level in recognition of the fact that women refugees often experience persecution differently from refugee men; and, give particularly sensitive treatment to asylum seekers who may have suffered sexual violence.

These initiatives were reinforced by the 1991 Guidelines on the Protection of Refugee Women (1991 Guidelines), which had as their comprehensive goal that of identifying specific protection issues, problems and risks facing refugee women. The 1991 Guidelines addressed and called for an improved understanding of the various bases upon which women can and should be granted refugee status.

The UNHCR Guidelines on Gender-related Persecution (2002 Guidelines)[20] highlight that gender persecution is *not* a legal term *per se*, but is rather a term

---

[18] ExCom Conclusion No. 54 identified the vulnerability of refugee women and in particular the specific problems with regard to physical security. ExCom Conclusion No. 60 drew attention to the need for further action with regard to personnel training on gender issues and ExCom No. 64 called for the development of comprehensive guidelines on protection of refugee women as a matter of urgency.

[19] See below for consideration on the role of gender in the formation of "particular social group".

[20] These 2002 Guidelines complement the UNHCR Handbook (*infra* note 32) and are the result of the 2nd Track of the Global Consultations on International Protection Process, which examined this subject at its expert meeting in San Remo (Italy) in 2001. Drawing on the results of the Global Consultation, the UNHCR prepared an Agenda for Protection identifying six principal goals, including that of the protection needs of women and children.

employed to encompass the range of different claims in which gender is a relevant consideration in the determination of refugee status. The 2002 Guidelines seek to heighten the decision-maker's awareness of the possible relevance of the gender dimension to a refugee claim. There will of course be instances when the claimant's gender will not be salient to the outcome of the claim. However, notwithstanding cognisance of gender, all claimants are still required to establish a nexus between the alleged persecution and any one or a combination of the grounds enumerated in the Refugee Convention.[21]

3) GENDER GUIDELINES

Canada was the first country to respond to the UNHCR's clarion call; the 1993 Canadian Guidelines[22] are noteworthy as the first instance of a state comprehensively addressing the possible gender dimension of a refugee claim. Guidelines[23] were introduced in the UK[24] in 2000. Both the Canadian and UK

---

[21] This is in line with the inference contained in ExCom No. 73 (XLIV) calling for "recognition as refugees of persons whose claims are based upon a well-founded fear of persecution, through sexual violence, for reason of race, religion, nationality, membership of a particular social group or political opinion".

[22] Canada, Immigration and Refugee Board, Guidelines on Women Refugee Claimants Fearing Gender-related Persecution (Ottawa: IRB, 1993) [Canadian Guidelines]. These were issued 9 March 1993 by the Chairperson pursuant to section 65(3) of the Immigration Act, R.S.C. 1985, c. I-2, as am. by S.C. 1992, c. 49, and were subsequently updated in 1996. The 1993 Guidelines were the first to be issued by the Chairperson; a subsequent six Guidelines have been issued (e.g. Civilian Non-Combatants Fearing Persecution in Civil War Situations and Child Refugee Claimants: Procedural and Evidentiary Issues). The general purpose of Guidelines issued by the Chairperson whose statutory authority is now provided for by paragraphs 159 (1)(h) of the Immigration and Refugee Protection Act, S.C. 2001, c. 27 is to promote consistency, coherence and fairness. See also R. M. M. Wallace, "Making the Refugee Convention Gender Sensitive: the Canadian Guidelines" (1996) 45 I.C.L.Q. 702.

[23] Other states, which have followed suit, include the United States (Immigration and Nationality Service, Consideration for Asylum Officers Adjudicating Asylum Claims from Women (1995); Australia (Australian Department for Immigration and Multi-Cultural Affairs, Guidelines on Gender Issues for Decision-makers (1996)); and, Sweden (The Swedish Migration Board, Guidelines for the Investigation and Evaluation of the Needs of Women for Protection (2001)).

[24] U.K., Immigration Appellate Authority, Asylum Gender Guidelines (London: IAA, 2000) [UK Guidelines]. These guidelines drew upon preparatory work undertaken by the Refugee Women's Legal Group (RWLG), which in turn had also looked at the practice of the Canadian Guidelines and those of other countries. It is acknowledged that the UK Home Office has introduced Asylum Policy Instructions (APIs) in relation to gender. However, consideration of the Gender API falls outside the remit of this article.

Guidelines share the goal of addressing the problems facing women refugee applicants.[25] The Canadian Guidelines, in a 1996 Update, identified four critical issues raised in the context of gender-related refugee claims. First, to what extent can women making a gender-related claim of fear of persecution successfully rely on any one, or a combination, of the five enumerated grounds of the Convention refugee definition? Second, under what circumstances does sexual violence, or a threat thereof, or any prejudicial treatment of women 'constitute persecution', as that term is jurisprudentially understood? Third, what are the key evidentiary elements which decision-makers have to look at when considering a gender-related claim? Finally, what special problems do women face when called upon to state their claim at refugee determination hearings, particularly when they have had experiences that are difficult and often humiliating to speak about?[26]

The UK Guidelines address the same issues and have been recognized as the most comprehensive official guidelines in Europe, referring to legislation, case law and academic sources, to address gender sensitive interpretations of persecution (including that by non-state agents), Convention grounds and procedural issues, including equal access to procedures, sensitive interviewing techniques and assessment of credibility.[27] Both Guidelines provide a framework of analysis and are designed as an instrument to provide decision-makers with the tools to enable a full and effective consideration of the role of gender in asylum claims. The depth of the UK Guidelines reflects the jurisprudence and doctrinal debates of contemporary refugee law. For instance, Professor James Hathaway's approach to the meaning of persecution and his scheme of three levels of human rights is spelt out.[28] Obviously, the UK Guidelines have benefited from the wealth of literature, case law and debate generated in the previous ten years. Whilst the UK Guidelines flag salient factors, they do not provide the schematic framework of analysis clearly presented in the Canadian

---

[25] *Supra* note 22 (Canadian Guidelines) and 24 (UK Guidelines).

[26] *Supra* note 21 at 2.

[27] UNHCR, Evaluation and Policy Analysis Unit (EPAU): Department of International Protection and Regional Bureau for Europe, Comparative Analysis of Gender-related Persecution in National Asylum Legislation and Practice in Europe by H. Crawley & T. Lester (Geneva, EPAU, 2004) at para. 120.

[28] *Supra* note 2 at ss. 2A.3–2A.4. Level 1 Rights are identified as those stated in the Universal Declaration of Human Rights 1948 (UDHR) and the International Covenant on Civil and Political Rights 1966 (ICCPR) to which countries may not derogate even in times of compelling national emergency. Level 2 Rights are those stated in the same two documents but for which states may derogate during an officially proclaimed state of emergency. Level 3 Rights are those contained in the UDHR and developed in the International Covenant on Economic, Social and Cultural Rights 1966 (ICESCR). A state will be in breach a level 3 Rights if it realises the rights in a discriminatory manner or where it takes no steps to realise the rights despite having adequate finances.

Guidelines. This may be a contributing factor as to why the UK Guidelines have not permeated mainstream asylum decision-making.

This failure to infiltrate is endorsed by the authors' conclusions in a recently completed pilot research project.[29] On the basis of visits to a selection of hearing centres and the gathering of information, admittedly much of which was anecdotal, it was evident that the UK Guidelines are only specifically referred to on occasion. One explanation advanced is the view of many decision-makers that the Guidelines are common sense and accordingly are applied subconsciously and regularly, and that specific mention is only demanded when the case is 'exceptional' or 'special'. Another contributing factor to the *ad hoc* employment of the UK Guidelines may be the absence of any requirement for decision-makers to make reference to the UK Guidelines. This is in sharp contrast to the position of Canadian decision-makers who are required to refer to the Canadian Guidelines and a failure to address the issue of gender-related persecution is deemed an error of law. The Canadian Guidelines are not law, but nevertheless, decision-makers are expected to follow them, unless compelling or exceptional reasons exist to depart from the guidelines. A decision maker must explain in his or her reasoning why he or she is not following a set of guidelines when, based on the facts or circumstances of the case, they would otherwise be expected to follow them.[30]

The UK Guidelines have had a chequered application. The seminal case of *Terbas*[31] in the UK led to an acknowledgement by the Immigration Appeals Tribunal (IAT)[32] that an Adjudicator could rely upon the UK Guidelines and

---

[29] The grant awarded by the Nuffield Foundation was primarily devoted to meeting the salary costs of a research assistant employed for two days per week for a period of 24 weeks. The decentralised structure of the U.K., Home Office Immigration Appellate Authority, the financial resources available and the limited number of cases which could be observed, dictated to a large extent the methodology which could be legitimately executed (both empirical and desk-based).

[30] Immigration and Refugee Board, Policy on the Use of the Chairperson's Guidelines, IRB Policy no. 2003–07 (Ottawa: IRB, 2003). See also *Fouchong v. Canada (Secretary of State)*, [1994] F.C.J. no. 1727 at para. 10, in which the Federal Court stated: "The Canadian Guidelines are not law, but they are authorized under s. 65(3) of the Act. They are not binding but they are intended to be considered by members of the tribunal in appropriate cases". See also *Narvaez v. Canada (Minister of Citizenship and Immigration)*, [1995] 2 F.C. 55 (T.D.) [*Narvaez*]. Note that in the case of *Mohamed v. Canada (Secretary of State)*, [1994] F.C.J. 185, an application for judicial review was allowed on the grounds that the Immigration and Refugee Board had erred in law by failing to address in its reasoning the issue of gender-related persecution.

[31] [2002] U.K.I.A.T. 03713 [*Terbas*].

[32] The restructuring of the asylum determination process involved inter alia the establishment of a single-tier Tribunal. The Asylum and Immigration Tribunal (AIT) was created under the Asylum and Immigration (Treatment of Claimants, etc.) Act 2004 (U.K.), 2004, c.19, s. 81.

make reference to them without prior disclosure to the parties involved in the appeal. The IAT held that the use of the UK Guidelines was not inappropriate as they are in the public domain in the same way as the UNHCR Handbook[33] and Country Assessment Reports. The importance of the decision in *Terbas* lies in the recognition accorded to the UK Guidelines by acknowledging that they are readily available and should be consulted as appropriate, and that gender sensitivity should not be regarded as the exception but rather the norm. Initially, the UK judiciary appeared to be receptive to the UK Guidelines.[34] The IAT's determination is encouraging in creating awareness of the possible impact of gender and the need for a just determination to take cognisance of gender. Notwithstanding this positive tone, the use of the word "benefit" for the applicant in regard to the Guidelines' safeguards, although probably inadvertent, was nevertheless somewhat unfortunate, as it suggests the applicant would be advantaged by the employment of the Guidelines. This is contrary to the desired objective of any gender guidelines, which is simply to ensure that applicants are not disadvantaged by a failure to consider the possible gender dimension and gender 'effect' arising in a claim.

This encouraging trend in jurisprudence came to a somewhat abrupt halt with the decision in *M (Sierra Leone)*.[35] Here the applicant's representative maintained that the Adjudicator had failed to follow the UK Guidelines and had erred in not granting a request for an all-female court. In response, the IAT took the opportunity as 'appropriate' to set out its views on requests for 'all female' courts and stated:

> There is nothing in the procedure rules or elsewhere, which requires the IAA to accede to requests for an "all female" court simply on the basis of such a request. Nor is there anything in the Gender Guidelines to require the IAA to grant such a request.[36]

And furthermore it was necessary to:

> ... point out that it is important to consider the practical difficulties involved in acceding to such requests – it can present considerable organisational and administrative difficulties to ensure that the adjudicator, the court usher, and Home Office Presenting Officer are all female ... In most cases we would expect that even if a female Applicant were to be embarrassed about giving evidence regarding a sexual

---

[33] UNHCR, Handbook on Procedures and Criteria for Determining Refugee Status under the 1951 Convention and the 1967 Protocol relating to the Status of Refugees, as re-edited in 1992 (Geneva, UNHCR, 1992).

[34] See the case of *Nawaz*, [2002] U.K.I.A.T. 00230, where remittal was granted, "as the Applicant wishes to benefit from the IAA Gender Guidelines and so be heard by a female Adjudicator and examined by a female presenting officer".

[35] [2003] U.K.I.A.T. 0012.

[36] *Ibid.* at para. 7 of determination.

assault in the presence . . . it would usually be possible for such evidence to be given in written form . . . If however a Presenting Officer insists upon oral cross-examination . . . and it can be shown that his/her case would be prejudiced to a material extent without it, he/she would be entitled to do so unless there is credible evidence from a person suitably qualified to give an opinion that the Applicant concerned would be likely to suffer some significant adverse effect to her health or well being . . . An Adjudicator may in such circumstances continue without cross-examination of the witness although the lack of such cross-examination would be a matter to take into account when considering the weight to be attached to that evidence.[37]

Such a dismissal of the Guidelines, particularly in favour of administrative considerations, is regrettable. In *Kyalisiima*,[38] the IAT recognised[39] that the applicant's allegation of rape had not been fully examined or appreciated under the terms of the UK Guidelines and required to be properly considered in light of the applicant's evidence as a whole. However in *Dijouadi*,[40] the IAT upheld an Adjudicator's determination and found that consideration had been given to whether the applicant's timidity had adversely affected her ability to provide evidence.[41] Canadian jurisprudence also reflects that taking into account Guidelines does not necessarily result in a final decision in the applicant's favour. For instance, in the case of an elderly Georgian woman, although there was documentary evidence to the effect of discrimination against women in employment and spousal abuse being a problem, "elderly women alone in Georgia are not subject to serious harm that would amount to persecution". This was the Immigration Review Board (IRB)'s finding following consideration of the applicant's claim (the applicant was single and retired) in light of the Canadian Guidelines. Accordingly, the applicant was not found to be at risk.[42] Such decisions highlight the *raison d'etre* of guidelines *viz* that every applicant's claim, irrespective of the final decision, should be seen as having been justly decided and the applicant confident in the knowledge that their claim has been dealt with fairly.

---

[37] *Ibid.* The applicant's case was dismissed on the basis of a lack of credibility.

[38] [2002] U.K.I.A.T. 05279.

[39] The case was remitted to be heard *de nova*.

[40] [2002] U.K.I.A.T. 08253.

[41] It is acknowledged that other decisions may have made reference to the UK Guidelines, but this research had a limited time frame.

[42] CRDD T98-00732 (16 March 1999) (Convention Refugee Determination Division, now the IRB Refugee Protection Division). For cases relating to Gender Guidelines, see Immigration and Refugee Board, Compendium of Decisions, Guideline 4, Women Refugee Claimants Fearing Gender-Related Persecution [Compendium of Decisions]: Update (Ottawa: IRB, 2003): <http://www.irb-cisr.gc.ca/en/about/tribunals/rpd/compendium/index_e.htm>.

The lack of acknowledged use of the UK Guidelines is also seen at the level of those representing claimants. Of the cases observed (some fifty), no representative referred to or applied the UK Guidelines as a matter of course and few were familiar with as to how and when they would be relevant. Although a few representatives indicated that they would recommend a female representative for a female applicant, the prevailing view regarding the request of an all female court was that it was possibly more expedient to leave it 'well alone', because of the perception that female decision-makers are 'harsher' than their male counterparts on female applicants.

As previously indicated, the goal of gender guidelines is not to import a gender dimension into every claim, thereby artificially exaggerating the role of gender in asylum claims. Both sets of guidelines illustrate how the existing grounds may have a gender dimension which, once acknowledged, should afford protection to women. The Refugee Convention is intended to provide protection to both men and women and, accordingly, its interpretation should reflect the experiences of both. Women may be persecuted on the grounds of race but their reproductive role as propagating a race or ethnic group may put them at greater risk.[43] Nationality, which should be interpreted in its broadest sense (as opposed to simply citizenship) to include ethnic, religious and cultural and linguistic communities,[44] may, for a woman, be aligned or perceived with that of other members of her family or community, including the family or community she has entered through marriage. Imputed or attributed nationality may therefore be an important reason for persecution of a woman.[45] With respect to religion, a woman may be assigned a particular role or behavioural code and if she refuses, or fails to fulfil what is expected of her, she may face a

---

[43] Acknowledged in the IAA Gender Guidelines, *supra* n. 2 at s. 3.6.

[44] *Ibid.*, at s. 3.8 cited in G. S. Goodwin-Gill, *The Refugee in International Law* (Oxford: Clarendon Press, 1996) at 45.

[45] *Ibid.*, at s. 3.10. For a case in which Gender Guidelines were considered within a claim based on nationality, see CRDD T98-05792 (29 November 1999) (Convention Refugee Determination Division), in which the claimant, a citizen of Ethiopia, claimed to be an ethnic Eritrean through her mother's family and asserted a fear of persecution against both Ethiopia and Eritrea based on her nationality. The panel despite alleged misgivings and because it placed great emphasis on the claimant's gender and youth accepted the claimant was of Eritrean ethnicity and she had a well founded fear of persecution in Ethiopia by reason of her ethnicity and because she did not have a birth certificate and because it was not clear whether her mother had been born in Eritrea or Ethiopia the Refugee Division could not make a finding that Eritrean citizenship would be automatic or a mere formality in the claimant's case. Even if the claimant could obtain Eritrean citizenship she would be in a precarious situation as a young woman alone and would face a serious possibility of persecution because she would be perceived as someone from Ethiopia.

well-founded fear of persecution on the grounds of religion.[46] Given a woman's role in society, it is necessary to ensure that political opinion is interpreted to include women's political activities.[47] Such political activities vary and may include provision of food, clothing, medical care and shelter, as well as the passing of messages. Cooking, for instance, is not in itself a political activity, nevertheless, it may very well be perceived as such if it is part of or supportive of, for example, trade union activities. An imputed political opinion may be attributed to a woman on the basis that the political opinion is aligned with those of the dominant community or family members, including her own birth family and that into which she has married.[48] These activities may put women at risk on the basis of an actual or imputed political opinion, whereas there are other very obvious political activities, such as involvement in efforts to improve the position of women within society.[49] Gender sensitivity acknowledges that women claimants may express political and religious opinions in ways different to that of men.[50] There are occasions when a woman may not see herself making a political statement. The responsibility incumbent on those charged with investigating the facts or determining a case is endorsed by the UNHCR handbook.[51] A woman may be harmed not simply because of her own political views, or indeed those attributed or imputed to her, but with a view of harming an entire family or community for its political views or affiliations.[52]

---

[46] See e.g. CRDD T99-09129 (March 13, 2001) (Convention Refugee Determination Division), where it was found the claimant's fear of persecution based on her being a Christian was well founded on the objective evidence. The claim was also considered against the Gender Guidelines and it was found that women alone in Pakistan are at a considerable disadvantage. Rape was common; the police rarely respond and sometimes are involved. Documentary evidence indicated the most discriminated minority in Pakistan was 'Christian women'.

[47] *Supra* note 2 at s. 3.22.

[48] *Supra* note 2 at s. 3.32.

[49] A case in which the political opinion was relevant concerned the daughter of a former official of the MDN, a right wing party, which allegedly had links with the former military governments in Haiti. The claimant was a close associate of her father and worked within the MDN. In examining her claim it, was found that it was more than a mere possibility that she would be at risk of persecution in Haiti by government agents because of her political opinion and her membership in 'a particular social group', namely her family (CRDD A99-00401 (October 10, 1999) (Convention Refugee Determination Division).

[50] For a case involving a claimant not adhering to cultural or social norms, see *Fathi and Ahmady v. SSHD* (1 December 1996), U.K., 14264 (U.K., Immigration Appeals Tribunal).

[51] *Supra* note 32 at para. 67. It is for the examiner, when investigating the facts of the case, to ascertain the reason or reasons for the persecution feared, as well as to decide whether the definition in the Refugee Convention is met with in this respect.

[52] *Supra* note 2 at s. 3.33.

Of the five Refugee Convention grounds, gender based claims are however most commonly argued under the particular social group (PSG) ground of the Convention. There is a view, at least in the UK since the decision in *Shah and Islam*,[53] that advisers and decision-makers when confronted with a gender based claim attempt to construct a PSG around the claimant without fully considering how the claim may fit into other categories.[54] Construction of PSG has been adopted as the most favoured means of establishing the necessary nexus between the alleged persecutory harm and a Convention ground. It is accepted that 'social group' may be defined by reference to gender. Both the Canadian Guidelines and the UK Guidelines address membership of a 'particular social group'. What is important in the use of gender in the creation of a PSG is that the group suffers, or fears to suffer, severe discrimination or harsh and inhuman treatment distinguished from the situation of the general population, or from other women. A sub-group of women can be identified by reference to their exposure or vulnerability – for physical or other reasons – to violence including domestic violence in an environment that denies them protection. These women face violence amounting to persecution because of their particular vulnerability as women in their societies and because they are so unprotected. It is irrelevant that the PSG consists of large numbers of the female population in the country. There is ample evidence in Canadian jurisprudence of a widening of the interpretation of persecution and PSG, as well as recognition that the perpetrator of the alleged persecution may be a private person (i.e. non-state actor).

The Canadian Supreme Court, in the same year that the Canadian Guidelines were introduced, articulated the meaning assigned to PSG to take into account "general underlying themes of the defence of human rights and anti-discrimination that form the basis for the international refugee protection initiative."[55] The Court also identified the three possible categories of PSG of which the first is a group formed by an innate or unchangeable characteristic such as gender.[56]

---

[53] *Islam v. SSHD; R v. IAT ex parte Shah*, [1999] I.N.L.R. 144 (HL), [1999] Imm. A.R. 283.

[54] Asylum Aid Refugee Women Research Project (RWRP), "Gender Persecution Project Background Paper" Asylum Aid (June 2005): http://www.asylumaid.org.uk/New%20RWRP/RWRP_gender_persecution_ .

[55] *Ward v. Canada (Attorney General)*, [1993] 2.S.C.R. 689 at para. 77.

[56] The other two possible categories were groups formed by voluntary association of members on the basis of reasons so fundamental to their human dignity that they should not be forced to forsake the association by virtue of former voluntary status which is unalterable due to its historical performance. See also K. Musalo, "Revisiting Social Group and Nexus in Gender Asylum Claims: A Unifying Rationale for Evolving Jurisprudence" (2003) 52 DePaul Law Review at 777.

The decision in *Ward*[57] recognised and gave legal endorsement to private persons as perpetrators of persecutory harm. Canadian jurisprudence serves to highlight that 'wife abuse', 'forced sterilisation', 'female genital mutilation' and 'forced prostitution' have been defined as persecution with the corresponding PSG being defined as "unprotected Ecuadorian women subject to wife abuse";[58] "women in China who have one child and are faced with forced sterilization";[59] "women";[60] and, "new citizens of Israel who are women recently arrived from elements of the previous Soviet Union and who are not integrated into Israeli society, despite the generous support offered by the Israeli government, who are lured into prostitution and threatened and exploited by individuals not connected to the government, and who can demonstrate indifference to their plight by front-line authorities to whom they would normally be expected to turn for protection."[61]

The UK Guidelines highlight how discrimination against the group in question may have a definitive role in determining whether the group is a particular group under the Refugee Convention. This reference is a reflection of the House of Lords decision in *Islam and Shah*.[62] It is interesting to note that both the Canadian and UK Guidelines were introduced following an authoritative statement from the highest judicial body of their respective countries. It is not suggested that there is a nexus between the two (i.e. the judgments and the introduction of the guidelines), nevertheless it may be that the judicial climate was such in both countries at the time that the judiciary were perceived as being receptive to such guidelines. However, whereas the Canadian jurisprudence reflects reception of PSG, the UK refugee judiciary has been somewhat more reticent and, at least *prima facie*, less willing to recognize a gender-defined social group. The UK cases where gender is considered as possibly defining PSG do not however refer directly to the UK Guidelines,[63] although a notable exception is the AIT's decision in *NS (Social Group-Women – forced Marriage) Afghanistan Country Guidance Case*.[64] Here, explicit reference was

---

[57] *Supra* note 55.

[58] *Narvaez, supra* note 29.

[59] *Cheung v. Canada (Ministry of Employment and Immigration)*, [1993] 2 F.C. 314 (C.A.).

[60] *Ramirez, McCaffrey* CRDD T93-12198 (May 10, 1994) (Convention Refugee Determination Division).

[61] *Litvinov, Svetlana v. S.S.C. (Minister of Employment and Immigration)* (30 June 1994), IMM-7488-93 (F.C.T.D.).

[62] *Supra* note 2 at s. 3.34 et seq.

[63] See *Fornah v. Secretary of State for the Home Department* (CA), [2205] EWCA Civ. 680; and *'P'and 'M', v. Secretary of State for the Home Department*, [2004] EWCA Civ. 1640.

[64] [2004] U.K.I.A.T. 00328 [NS]. Country Guidance (CG) cases are those in which the decision is regarded as representative and useful as a guide to country conditions.

made to the UK Guidelines.[65] There is a recognised risk that considering gender based claims only under PSG marginalises claims of women and fails to take into account that a woman's claim may fall into one or other of the Refugee Convention categories. If gender persecution is only categorised by reference to PSG, this will stifle the development of a gender sensitive interpretation of Refugee Convention grounds and marginalise gender-related claims by ignoring the social and political contexts of women's experiences.[66] There is need for greater legal analysis of gender in the formation of PSG. This is particularly imperative given the adoption of the European Council Directive on Minimum Standards for the Qualification and Status of Third Country Nationals or Stateless Persons as Refugees or as Persons who otherwise need International Protection and the Content of Protection Granted.[67] The Directive envisages a uniform interpretation of PSG, which will have European wide application. However, before this can be attained, there is a need for identification of best practice as reflected in contemporary refugee jurisprudence.[68]

It is also necessary to remember that notwithstanding Guidelines, there is still a need for the harm alleged and feared to be sufficiently serious to constitute persecution; there must be a likely risk of persecution occurring if the claimant is returned to the country of origin; and, importantly, there must be no reasonable expectation of adequate or sufficient national protection.[69]

The requirement regarding the application of CG cases is that they should be applied, except where they do not apply to the particular facts with which an Adjudicator faces, and can properly be held inapplicable for legally adequate reasons. There may be evidence that circumstances have changed in a material way which requires a different decision again on the basis that proper reasons for that view are given. In NS at para. 140, the Tribunal characterised the system of CG cases as "not having the rigidity of the legally binding precedent but has instead the flexibility to accommodate individual cases, changes, fresh evidence . . .".

[65] *Ibid.* at para. 76.

[66] *Supra* note 54. See also *supra* note 50.

[67] EC, Council Directive 2004/83/EC of 29 April 2004 on minimum standards for the qualification and status of third country nationals or stateless persons as refugees or as persons who otherwise need international protection and the content of the protection granted [2004] O.J.L. 304/12 [the Directive].

[68] The Asylum Aid's Refugee Women's Resource Project is calling for the adoption of European Union wide Gender Guidelines for assessing asylum claims.

[69] See CRDD T92-08429 (May 10, 1994) concerning a Muslim citizen of Iraq who had married an Iranian Jew and resided in Israel from 1980 until leaving for Canada in 1992. She was the victim of spousal abuse and had separated from her husband. The claimant feared that if returned to Israel she would lose her status and be deported to Iran. The IRB found the claimant would not be at risk of such removal and in respect of her fear at the hands of her husband it was found that effective state protection would be available. Accordingly the claimant's application for asylum was dismissed.

Both guidelines address not only substantive aspects of a claim, but also evidential and procedural matters and recognise that women applicants may encounter problems not experienced by male applicants. A woman who is interviewed in the presence of family members may not discuss or disclose certain factors relevant to her claim. This may deny a woman the opportunity to give evidence as to sexual violence, harassment by police precipitated by her own or her family's political opinions, and it may preclude evidence being elicited as to the woman's persecution within the family itself. Both guidelines highlight the need for a non-confrontational exploratory interview and call for an appreciation of cross-cultural nuances as the latter may be reflected in demeanour (i.e. how a woman presents herself physically, such as whether she maintains eye contact or shifts her posture or hesitates in responding).[70] Stereotyping can reinforce prejudices to the detriment of the applicant and should be avoided by those handling women's asylum claims.

The proposal to introduce guidelines frequently precipitated foreboding predictions by opponents of guidelines, *viz* the 'floodgates' would be opened and the number of women applicants would soar. However, as highlighted, the employment of gender guidelines in no way dilutes the burden of proof to be satisfied and guidelines operate within the existing legal framework. The statistics issued by the IRB in 1994, the first year following the introduction of the Canadian Guidelines, identified 328 gender-related claims of which 210 (64%) were decided in the affirmative. In the UK, the Home Office in 2001 produced gender-differentiated statistics on asylum applications and initial decisions.[71] However there has been no quantitative analysis of the number of claims by women in which gender is invoked as a reason for their claim. Furthermore neither the Home Office nor the IAA produced gender-differentiated statistics on appealed decisions.[72] The UK statistics available are such to preclude any meaningful comparison with the Canadian system.

4) CONCLUSION

Gender guidelines have to be seen in the overall context of making the Refugee Convention definition gender inclusive. Guidelines introduced, if complimentary to the existing law, can change attitudes and provide a framework of analy-

---

[70] *Supra* note 2 at s. 5.24.

[71] Of the 71,030 asylum applications that were made, a total of 17,090 (24%) were done so by women and unaccompanied minors.

[72] Crawley & Lester (*supra* note 26) observed that statistics provide quantitative as opposed to qualitative information about asylum outcomes and do not provide evidence about the process by which these outcomes are reached. For further discussion on gender statistics on asylum applications and decisions see, *supra* note 26 at 11–19.

sis for decision-makers. This is borne out in particular by the Canadian Guidelines, which provide evidence that Guidelines can be a useful tool in the hands of decision-makers. Guidelines provide flexibility and allow a gender-sensitive interpretation, whilst still remaining within the parameters of the Refugee Convention. The introduction of Guidelines informs decision-makers who are then in a position to take account, as appropriate, of the gender specific circumstances and requirements of an applicant. Guidelines provide an essential reference point for decision-makers as well as legal representatives and they represent an important policy mechanism for ensuring that gender-specific and gender-related aspects of asylum claims are properly assessed and taken into account in refugee determination procedures.

Crawley and Lester[73] in their summary of recommendations propose that states should produce clear guidance on procedural and substantive issues relevant to gender-related persecution, and this guidance should draw upon and reflect the principles and standards in the UNHCR Guidelines. Such guidance should be applicable to decision-makers at all stages and be non-discretionary. It is also recommended that implementation of such guidance should be monitored and evaluated by states on a regular basis and a report forwarded to the UNHCR.

The findings regarding the use of the UK Guidelines during their first three years are somewhat disappointing especially when compared to the use of the Canadian Guidelines which, within a relatively short time-frame, became an established, required point of reference for decision-makers. It is unfortunate the UK Guidelines have not been widely disseminated and the IAA does not *require* their use. The UK Guidelines are seen as being something specific, rather than being an integral part of the mainstream asylum decision-making process. Nevertheless, the UK Guidelines do represent a step in the right direction and have considerable potential for assisting in redressing the male bias which is still a characteristic of current refugee jurisprudence. These Guidelines should serve as a catalyst for encouraging a more comprehensive and holistic approach to gender based claims. The consideration of gender, even where it is not *the* central issue, should be done as a matter of course so as to provide an understanding and thereby the appropriate outcome of the claim. It is important that the UK Guidelines are not relegated to gather dust at the back of drawers, particularly as the UK is one of the few countries' which has introduced official guidance. The favoured approach to date has been that of adopting gender-related points within general refugee status determination policy or guidelines. The UK Guidelines, when being prepared, recognised the value of the Canadian Guidelines.[74] It could be expedient to follow the

---

[73] *Supra* note 26.
[74] *Supra* note 2 at s.1.3.

Canadian example and make reference to the UK Guidelines a mandatory requirement for decision-makers. This would have much to commend it, at least in making the UK Guidelines an integral part of the asylum determination process and thereby ensuring not only a gender sensitive interpretation, but also a gender sensitive determination procedure.[75]

---

[75] Emphasized by the San Remo expert Round Table in 2001 as necessary for the protection of refugee women.

Chapter 10

Human Rights and Public Emergency Discourse in the UK and Canada

David Jenkins

1) Introduction[1]

In the UK and Canada, recent years have seen the public, politicians, and courts preoccupied with questions of national security; the attacks on New York and Washington D.C. in September 2001, and the bombings of London in July 2005, have charged politics with a fear of terrorism and anti-terrorism legislation continues to raise controversy.[2] In January 2005, for example, the British

---

[1] I would like to thank Michael Plaxton (Lecturer, University of Aberdeen School of Law) and James Rodehaver (Deputy Director, Human Rights Department, OSCE Mission to Bosnia-Herzegovina) for their helpful comments.

[2] See Canada's Anti-Terrorism Act (Can.), S.C. 2001, c. 41, and the UK's Terrorism Act 2000 (U.K.), 2000, c. 11, Anti-terrorism, Crime and Security Act 2001 (U.K.), 2001, c. 24, and the Prevention of Terrorism Act 2005 (U.K.), 2005, c. 2. In October 2005, the U.K. Government introduced into the House of Commons the Terrorism Bill, Bill 55 (2005), that would, among other things, create a criminal offense of glorifying terrorism and permit detention of terrorist suspects for up to ninety days without charge. The Commons rejected the ninety day limit in a vote on 9 November 2005, instead favoring a time period of twenty-eight days.

Christopher P.M. Waters (Ed.), *British and Canadian Perspectives on International Law*, pp. 187–201.

Home Secretary, Charles Clarke, stated: "There are serious people and serious organisations trying to destroy our society. We are in a state of emergency . . . The question is in resisting [the threat] do we have to take steps which we would prefer in a different kind of world not to take? Yes, because my first responsibility is to protect people."[3] In response to the London tube bombings, Prime Minister Blair himself asserted: "Let no-one be in any doubt, the rules of the game are changing."[4] Statements like this, by Government ministers, are not merely rhetorical, but impact upon legal protections for human rights. This paper argues that, within an emerging security culture, the British and Canadian executives can manipulate political discourse about the existence and extent of public emergency, in order to shape the way their respective national legal systems both maintain the rule of law and implement international human rights norms.

Having the primary constitutional and political role in protecting the national security in both countries, the executive can use emergency discourse to alter the legal paradigm in which courts resolve the tensions between public safety needs and individual rights, prioritizing the former. Emergency discourse and a resulting paradigm shift also highlight the relative institutional competencies of the Crown and courts to protect public safety and human rights. In the UK and Canada, the executive and judicial branches are constitutionally counterpoised for achieving these two goals. However, emergency discourse and the paradigm shift allow the executive to upset the rule of law and disestablish human rights as prevailing constitutional principles, at the same time that they elevate the executive branch to institutional predominance over the judiciary. The problems of implementing human rights during emergencies, then, are ones of British and Canadian constitutional structures, as well as normative frameworks. Rights and the rule of law therefore depend upon the judiciary asserting an opposing human rights discourse to preserve as far as possible their constitutional value, and the structural mechanisms for their enforcement.

2) Emergency Discourse and Shifting of the Legal Paradigm

In many western countries, including the UK and Canada, public concerns over terrorism or other security threats have lingered, if not grown, over the last few years. These concerns have led not only to passage of national anti-terrorism

---

[3] R. Sylvester, "Suspects' families will also face tight controls," *The Daily Telegraph* (28 Jan. 2005): http://www.telegraph.co.uk/news/main.jhtml?xml=/news/2005/01/28/nterr28.xml&sSheet=/news/2005/0/28/ixnewstop.html.

[4] 10 Downing Street, Prime Minister's Press Conference (5 Aug. 2005): http://www.number-10.gov.uk/output/Page8041.asp.

laws. The emergence of a "security culture," in which public opinion and political actors are preoccupied with preserving public safety at increasing costs, has impacted other issues, such as whether the invasion of Iraq was necessary to "preempt" its acquisition or use of chemical weapons, or whether extra-judicial and indefinite detention, perhaps even torture, might not in some instances have public safety justifications.[5] Such a security culture presents itself (to borrow language from Stephen Toope) as one of many possible "frameworks of social organization", that gives security issues a unique "discursive power" over the operation of political and legal systems.[6]

In the UK and Canada, past national experiences with terrorism have involved serious violence aimed at destroying the territorial integrity of the state. For Britain, decades of republican and loyalist violence associated with Northern Ireland resulted in much loss of life and a regime of emergency legislation that seriously curtailed individual rights of suspected terrorists.[7] Canada, too, experienced a period of separatist violence in Quebec, at the height of which the Government invoked the War Measures Act[8] to enable executive arrest and detention of hundreds of suspected militant Quebec nationalists.[9]

---

[5] See A. M. Dershowitz, "Should the Ticking Time Bomb Terrorist Be Tortured? A Case Study in How a Democracy Should Make Tragic Choices" in *Why Terrorism Works: Understanding the Threat, Responding to the Challenge* (New Haven, Conn.: Yale Univ. Press, 2002), ch. 4.

[6] S. J. Toope, "Fallout from '9–11': Will a Security Culture Undermine Human Rights?" (2002) 65 Sask. L. Rev. 281 at 282–83.

[7] See H. Barnett, *Constitutional and Administrative Law*, 4th ed. (London: Cavendish, 2002) at 53–58, 823, for a brief review of the Northern Ireland troubles and the resulting British anti-terrorism legislation. See also the European Court of Human Rights' decision in *Brogan* v. *United Kingdom* (1988) 11 EHRR 117 (detention for four days without judicial appearance violated art. 5(3) of the European Convention on Human Rights) and *Brannigan and McBride* v. *United Kingdom* (1993) 17 EHRR 539 (a subsequent British derogation, made in response to the *Brogan* decision, was justified in light of the security situation in Northern Ireland).

[8] War Measures Act, *1914* (Can.), S.C. 1914, c. 2.

[9] For a brief review of the crisis in the larger context of Canada's response to both the Cold War and recent fears of terrorism, see R. Whitaker, "Keeping up with the Neighbours? Canadian Responses to 9/11 in Historical and Comparative Context" (2003) 41 Osgoode Hall L.J. 241 at 249–52. Prime Minister Trudeau invoked the War Measures Act on 16 October, 1970, after the Front de libération du Québec kidnapped British Trade Commissioner James Cross and Québec Labour Minister Pierre Laporte. The day after, authorities discovered the body of Laporte, whom the FLQ had executed. The *Act*, enacted at the outset of the First World War, gave the Governor in Council sweeping authority to make orders and regulations in response to real or apprehended war, invasion, or insurrection. Parliament replaced the War Measures Act with the Emergencies Act (Can.), R.S. 1985, c. 22 (4th Supp.), which among other things attempts more clearly to define the circumstances under which the Governor in Council

These incidents – especially in light of the September eleventh attacks and "the war against terror" – suggest that terrorist violence and national anti-terrorism measures can blur conceptual distinctions between terrorism as criminal activity and acts of war.

Conceptual confusion between terrorism and war can consequently lead to increased exercises of executive power that infringe individual rights and undermine the rule of law, on the basis of public emergency exigencies.[10] When a British or Canadian minister, for instance, warns of a terrorist threat, he or she identifies a national security issue potentially rising to that of a public emergency. Just such a public emergency challenges the normative value of human rights as the fundamental, organizing principles of law and political behavior, by prioritizing public security over rights concerns. Should a security culture take root more deeply within society, the British and Canadian executives might more likely emphasize potential threats, and in turn stoke public fears even higher through the discourse of an existing public emergency. The executive can thereby shift – suddenly or by degrees – the very paradigm in which the rule of law operates. This paradigm shift is one from the operation of law during a period of "normality" or "peacetime," to one of an "exceptionalism" arising from an emergency.[11] The shift might indeed only be temporary for the duration of the emergency, but there remains a risk that exceptional measures might become "normalized," leading to a permanent state of emergency.[12] In

---

may declare a state of emergency and make orders for it. For a brief review of these two acts, see L. E. Weinrib, "Terrorism's Challenge to the Constitutional Order," in *The Security of Freedom: Essays on Canada's Anti-Terrorism Bill*, eds. R. J. Daniels, P. K. Macklem, and K. Roach (Toronto: Univ. of Toronto Press, 2001), 93 at 99–104 [hereinafter *Security of Freedom*].

[10] For a strong criticism of Canada's Anti-Terrorism Act on these grounds, see generally W. Pue, "The War on Terror: Constitutional Governance in a State of Permanent Warfare?" (2003) 41 Osgoode Hall L.J. 267.

[11] O. Gross, "'Once More unto the Breach': The Systematic Failure of Applying the European Convention on Human Rights to Entrenched Emergencies" (1998) 23 Yale J. Int'l. L. 437 at 438–40. The epitome of a public emergency would be total war, such as the two World Wars. What war risks to public security and human rights in terms of military failure, drain on national resources, and unbridled executive power, it offers in clarity of the security threat, the nature of the enemy, and the duration of the conflict. This situation contrasts to "the war against terror", having an unconventional nature, opponents hard to identify, and an indefinite duration. Pue, *ibid.* at 271. For criticism of the war against terror, see M. Kettle, "Are we at war? The answer is beyond doubt: we are not" *The Guardian* (29 Jan. 2005): http://www.guardian.co.uk/comment/story/0,3604,1401324,00.html.

[12] See J. Lobel, "Emergency Power and the Decline of Liberalism" (1989) 98 Yale L.J. 1385 and J. Lobel, "The War on Terrorism and Civil Liberties" (2002) 63 U. Pitt. L. Rev. 767, as well as D. Dyzenhaus, "The Permanence of the Temporary: Can Emergency Powers be Normalized?" in *The Security of Freedom*, *supra* note 9, 21.

the latter case, the paradigm shift might become irreversible, with detrimental results to the rule of law and human rights.[13]

The shift in legal paradigm impacts the British and Canadian constitutions in three ways, all potentially inimical to the rule of law and human rights. First, the dispatch and efficiency of executive action in dealing with public emergencies, as well as the Government's command of parliamentary majority, gives executive action an advantage over slower, independent legislative deliberation or adjudication in the courts. The short debate in the Canadian House of Commons on the Anti-Terrorism Act illustrated how the executive can claim the need for action and manage the legislative process, so as to push through a desired bill and avoid protracted or careful deliberation by legislators.[14] The accepting posture of the UK House of Commons in face of the Government's introduction of the Terrorism Act 2000, the Anti-Terrorism, Crime and Security Act 2001, and the Prevention of Terrorism Act 2005 also illustrate how legislative deference can lead up the proverbial "slippery-slope."[15] That is, the executive, by taking advantage of its parliamentary support, over time can incrementally increase its powers and slowly erode individual rights.[16] In addition to controlling the legislative agenda, the executive can attempt to use the

---

[13] See D. Dyzenhaus, *Hard Cases in Wicked Legal Systems: South African Law in the Perspective of Legal Philosophy* (Oxford: Clarendon Press, 1991).

[14] For an account of the rather brief, but sometimes sharp, debate on Canada's Anti-Terrorism Act, see K. Roach, *September 11: Consequences for Canada* (Montreal & Kingston: McGill-Queen's Univ. Press, 2003) at 56–68 [hereinafter *September 11*].

[15] H. Fenwick, "The Anti-Terrorism, Crime and Security Act 2001: A Proportionate Response to 11 September?" [2002] 65 MLR 724 at 729–30, for example, describes the cursory parliamentary scrutiny of the *Anti-terrorism, Crime and Security Act 2001*. This is not to suggest that either the Canadian or UK House of Commons will always be supine before a Government's legislative agenda, as seen by the UK Commons' rejection of the ninety day detention period in the 2005 Terrorism Bill, *supra* note 2.

[16] Of course, the ability of the Government to control Parliament in actual political practice, rather than the other way around, presents a problem for the constitutional principle of ministerial responsibility. Nevertheless, as Lorne M. Sossin, *Boundaries of Judicial Review: The Law of Justiciability in Canada* (Toronto: Carswell, 1999) at 11, points out, the Supreme Court of Canada has found that, in Canada, the executive's control of the legislature is not "constitutionally cognizable by the judiciary" (quoting *Canada (Auditor General)* v. *Canada (Minister of Energy, Mines and* Resources*)*, [1989] 2 S.C.R. 49 at 103, *per* Dickson C.J.). British courts also will look only to see that a law appears on the rolls, presuming it to have passed both houses of Parliament and received the Royal Assent. Failure to take into account the influence of the executive in the legislative process, however – especially when considering legislation that delegates exceptional powers – risks that the executive will continue to gather power onto itself without any effective check from Parliament, while at the same time legitimizing such authority with a false democratic mandate.

discourse of emergency to stigmatize and chill political opposition, either within Parliament or amongst the public, to the exceptional powers that it seeks for itself.[17]

Second, the discourse of public emergency prioritizes public security and order over individual rights, and in so doing makes the dictates of majoritarian democracy a political imperative. The result is that the British and Canadian executives can democratically legitimize infringements of human rights, especially on account of parliamentary delegation.[18] Interestingly, with the UK's Prevention of Terrorism Act, for example, it was the electorally unaccountable House of Lords that forced the most significant modifications and safeguards to the bill's provisions for executive control orders against terrorist suspects. With its weak democratic mandate, however, Britain's upper house rightly can only delay and revise bills passed by the Commons.[19] Nevertheless, as the legislative "ping-pong" over the Prevention of Terrorism bill highlighted, the Lords' electoral isolation also allowed that house strongly to resist the executive's emergency discourse, and draw political attention to the human rights impact of the proposed bill. The same democratic deficit that enabled the Lords' opposition to the Government, however, ultimately doomed it to succumb to the Government's insistence on the bill. British and Canadian courts, too, enjoy an institutional independence from the electorate that can insulate them from political pressures, but which also bring into question their democratic legitimacy.

The majoritarian imperative of a public emergency reaches beyond legislative and judicial processes into substantive matters, as well. Theoretically, there exists a symbiosis between public security and individual rights, in that no-one can safely enjoy individual rights in an unstable and insecure environment,

---

[17] Roach, *September 11*, *supra* note 14 at 131–32. For an interesting article demonstrating how emergency discourse can shape the political landscape on many levels see D. Leppard, "Poll booths to be put on alert" *Sunday Times* (13 March 2005): http://www.timesonline.co.uk/article/0,,2087–1523646,00.html. In December 2001, US Attorney General John Ashcroft defended the Administration's anti-terrorism measures and confronted the Senate Judiciary Committee with these words: ". . . to those who scare peace-loving people with phantoms of lost liberty; my message is this: Your tactics only aid terrorists – for they erode our national unity and diminish our resolve. They give ammunition to America's enemies, and pause to America's friends." U.S. Senate, Hearing testimony of Attorney General John Ashcroft, United States Senate Committee on the Judiciary, 6 December 2001: http://judiciary.senate.gov/testimony.cfm?id =121&wit_id=42.

[18] See Fenwick, *supra* note 15 at 724, 727–29, suggesting that a Government can also pass off security measures as actually protecting rights, based upon democratic processes and the Government's own assessment of rights impact.

[19] See Parliament Act 1911 (1 & 2 Geo. 5, c. 13), Parliament Act 1949 (12, 13, 14 Geo. 6, c. 103), and House of Lords Act 1999 (c. 34).

while the public as a whole is not truly secure where its constituent individuals have no rights against arbitrary government. Where the executive boasts popular mandate for its security measures, this symbiosis threatens to break down into competing aspirations. The British and Canadian executives, by claiming democratic mandates, can promote a fractured security/rights dichotomy not only to subdue political opposition, but to re-situate the rule of law itself within a public emergency context.

Third, as part of the paradigm shift, British and Canadian courts will increasingly define civil liberties within the emergency context.[20] Just how far courts are willing to go down this jurisprudential path, then, is critical for the maintenance of the rule of law and the implementation of human rights. The response of courts will likely vary depending upon the emergency context, as well as the existence of constitutional rights guarantees that act as reminders of the normative value of rights and regulate the decision-making parameters of government actors. Examples of such guarantees are Canada's Charter of Rights or Britain's incorporation of the European Convention of Human Rights through the Human Rights Act. Both instruments qualify the rights protections therein under proportionality principles that require justification for executive action, and attempt to limit the scope and affect of exceptional executive powers.[21]

---

[20] Although British and Canadian courts at one time extended almost complete deference to executive national security decisions to the detriment of individual rights, they will now scrutinize such actions closely under judicial review principles, as well as, respectively, the European Convention on Human Rights, 4 November 1950, 213 U.N.T.S. 221, Eur. T.S. 5 [hereinafter European Convention], as incorporated under the Human Rights Act 1998 (U.K.), 1998, c. 42, and the Charter of Rights and Freedoms, Part I of the Constitution Act, 1982 being Schedule B to the Canada Act 1982 (U.K.), 1982, c. 11 [hereinafter Charter of Rights or Charter]. Nevertheless, the fundamental premise of earlier cases survives: certain national security decisions are nonjusticiable by courts and might permissibly infringe individual rights. See, for example, *R.* v. *Secretary of State for the Home Department, ex p. Cheblak*, [1991] 2 All ER 319 (CA) and *Operation Dismantle* v. *The Queen*, [1985] 1 S.C.R. 441.

[21] Section 1 of the Canadian Charter provides: "The Canadian Charter of Rights and Freedoms guarantees the rights and freedoms set out in it subject only to such reasonable limits prescribed by law as can be demonstrably justified in a free and democratic society." The Supreme Court of Canada in *R.* v. *Oakes* [1986] 1 S.C.R. 103, *per* Dickson C. J., has interpreted s. 1 to mean that any government action infringing a protected right must be sufficiently important, and reasonably and demonstrably justified under a proportionality analysis. Similarly, the European Court of Human Rights has explained that government actions infringing upon *Convention* rights must be proportional to a legitimate end, although in cases of national security states enjoy a considerable margin of appreciation. See, for example, *Brogan* v. *United Kingdom* (1988) 11 EHRR 117 and *Smith and Grady* v. *United Kingdom* (1999), 29 EHRR 493. Some rights, like freedom from torture, are absolute and resist being balanced away under a proportionality test.

Although the Charter and the European Convention are important bulwarks against arbitrary executive action, considerable infringements of rights might occur under the proportionality principle when a security culture and emergency discourse exaggerate national security risks to the public safety.[22] Any proportionality test remains dependent upon judicial perceptions. In the UK, moreover, the most a domestic court can do when the executive clearly acts under statutory authority is to issue a non-binding declaration of incompatibility under s. 4 of the Human Rights Act. If possessing enough political capital, the British executive could simply ignore such a declaration, at least for a time.[23]

The Charter and European Convention also allow the Canadian and British Governments explicitly to avoid many of their guarantees altogether, and so radically re-situate rights discourse within an emergency context. Section 33 of the Charter allows the Canadian Parliament or a provincial legislature to enact a measure "notwithstanding" guaranteed rights, while art. 15 of the Convention permits states-party to derogate from most of their obligations during times of emergency.[24] Section 33 of the Charter does not limit the circumstances under which Parliament might legislate notwithstanding its guarantees. However,

---

See *Chahal* v. *U.K.* (1997) 23 EHRR 413 (ECtHR) and *Suresh* v. *Canada (Minister of Citizenship and Immigration)*, [2002] 1 S.C.R. 3.

[22] The UK's Prevention of Terrorism Act 2005 allowing the Home Secretary to seek control orders against individuals, presents just such an attempt to maximize the impairment of individual rights under the proportionality test. The Council of Europe's Commissioner for Human Rights, Alvaro Gil-Robles, has criticized control orders as potentially violating the *Convention's* art. 5 right to liberty and security, and art. 6 right to a fair trial. "Report on Visit to the United Kingdom, 4th–12th November 2004," Office of the Commissioner for Human Rights, Council of Europe, Strasbourg (8 June 2005): http://www.coe.int/T/E/Commissioner_H.R/Communication_Unit/CommDH%28200%296_E.doc.

[23] Indeed, the House of Lords, in *A and Others v. Secretary of State for the Home Department*, [2005] 2 AC 68 (HL), declared the indefinite detention of aliens under s. 23 of the Anti-terrorism, Crime and Security Act 2001 to be disproportionate and discriminatory, and thus incompatible with arts. 5 and 14 of the Convention. Nevertheless, the Government continued to hold the appellants in violation of their rights until Parliament had passed the Prevention of Terrorism Act 2005 three months later, enabling the issuance of control orders, just before s. 23 was due to expire under the Anti-Terrorism, Crime and Security Act 2001 (Continuance in Force of sections 21 to 23) Order 2004, SI 2004/751.

[24] The Canadian Parliament has never invoked the notwithstanding clause since adoption of the Charter in 1982. In the past, the United Kingdom has derogated from its art. 5 obligations under the *Convention* to permit detention of terrorist suspects, though it currently has no derogations in force. See, for example, the Human Rights Act 1998, sch. 3, pt. I, as enacted and the Human Rights Act 1998 (Designated Designation) Order 2001, SI 2001/3644, since withdrawn.

art. 15 of the Convention permits derogation only "[i]n time of war or other public emergency threatening the life of the nation," and as "strictly required." The European Court of Human Rights, and now UK courts under the Human Rights Act, will accordingly scrutinize state derogations to ensure that they comply with these emergency and proportionality criteria, thus ensuring some judicial supervision to prevent executive abuse of the derogation provision. However, the European Court of Human Rights has made clear that states enjoy a considerably wide margin of appreciation in determining whether a public emergency exists, and is therefore reluctant to second-guess a derogation decision.[25]

Other international human rights treaties provide no domestic legal protection against government infringement of their guarantees, as neither the British nor Canadian legal system directly incorporates international law.[26] In any case, some conventions allow states to derogate from or restrict the rights guaranteed therein. Article 4 of the International Covenant on Civil and Political Rights,[27] for example, allows derogation under criteria very similar to art. 15 of the European Convention. The Universal Declaration of Human Rights, while not having a derogation provision, accounts for public emergencies by allowing limitations necessary for public order.[28] Section 33 of the Charter and art. 15 of the Convention, along with the domestically unincorporated ICCPR and the Universal Declaration, thus allow the Canadian and British Governments to infringe guaranteed rights to a substantial degree by having the last word over the judiciary as to the existence and nature of a public emergency. The more

---

[25] See *Lawless* v. *Ireland* (1961) 1 EHRR 15 (ECtHR) and *Brannigan and McBride* v. *United Kingdom, supra* note 7.

[26] International law is an interpretive tool for courts in determining rights and statutory meaning in both the United Kingdom and Canada. Treaty rights are not incorporated without parliamentary enactment, although – as highlighted in Stéphane Beaulac's chapter – there is some question as to whether the common law incorporates customary international law. In any event, the domestic application of customary international law remains subject to abrogation by both the UK and Canadian Parliaments. See generally A. W. La Forest, "Domestic Application of International Law in Charter Cases: Are We There Yet?" (2004) 37 U.B.C. L. Rev. 157 and D. Fottrell, "Reinforcing the Human Rights Act – the Role of the International Covenant on Civil and Political Rights" [2002 Autumn] PL 485.

[27] International Covenant on Civil and Political Rights, 19 December 1966, 999 U.N.T.S. 171, Can. T.S. 1976 No. 47, 6 I.L.M. 368 (entered into force 23 March 1976) [hereinafter ICCPR].

[28] Universal Declaration of Human Rights, GA Res. 217 (III), UN GAOR, 3d Sess., Supp. No. 13, UN Doc. A/810 (1948), art. 29 [hereinafter Universal Declaration]. The Universal Declaration, art. 30, would also allow limitations in times of war or political violence as it does not give to "any State, group or person any right to engage in any activity or to perform any act aimed at the destruction of any of the rights and freedoms set forth herein."

that courts succumb to the executive's emergency discourse and so shrink constitutional civil liberties, international human rights norms will likely appear to exist external to, apart from, and possibly even intruding upon the domestic legal system. Government actors and the public might then begin to see international human rights, now appearing to resist the executive's emergency discourse, as impractical and unaffordable luxuries. At the extreme, they might even regard human rights as obstacles that the Government and legal system must overcome for the sake of public security, whatever the costs.[29]

3) HUMAN RIGHTS IMPLEMENTATION AS A PROBLEM OF CONSTITUTIONAL STRUCTURE

The executive's institutional advantages, the majoritarian justification for prioritizing security issues, and the situation of the rule of law within an emergency context, give the British and Canadian executives considerable political power to shape their respective constitution's framework for the implementation of human rights. Rights guarantees can effectively regulate and moderate the resulting paradigm shift, but cannot prevent it; they are only breakwaters rather than impenetrable barriers to more extreme political developments and manifestations of a security culture. The discursive power of emergency is such that it can potentially alter the very perceptions about the relative values of security and rights upon which the judicial enforcement of rights guarantees depends. Emergency discourse and the resulting paradigm shift consequently have structural, as well as normative, implications for the British and Canadian constitutions.[30] The discursive power of emergency, coupled with the rise of a security culture, can enhance the executive's institutional status as Parliament and the courts defer to it and broaden the scope of its legal authority. Such changes in

---

[29] The severance of international human rights norms from national law is consequently traumatic for the domestic legal system not only because it weakens human rights awareness, but because the two sources of law "are closely linked in a symbiotic relationship in which one sphere influences and shapes the evolution of the other." Gross, *supra* note 11 at 444; V. Iyer, "States of Emergency – Moderating their Effects on Human Rights" (1999) 22 Dalhousie L.J. 125 at 162.

[30] "Exigencies tend to provoke 'rally "round" the flag' phenomenon, in which governmental actions perceived as necessary to fight off the crisis garner almost unqualified popular support (at least in the short run). A crisis mentality can seize a whole nation and transform an otherwise peaceful community into a 'nation in arms.' In the process, constitutional structures may be ignored in the name of national security. Governmental efficiency (not to say expediency) becomes paramount, and fundamental constitutional principles may come tumbling down when the trumpets of emergency blow." Gross, *supra* note 11 at 490.

legal and political processes directly affect domestic civil liberties by severing international human rights norms from the now "securitized" constitution and giving executive power centre place. The result, to one degree or another, can be a constitutional pathology, as the devaluation of rights grows with the institutional predominance of the executive.

The first structural problem for human rights is that their implementation ultimately depends upon political, rather than legal, factors. In the United Kingdom and Canada, the executive's authority to protect national security is both legal and political in nature, represented by the Crown's traditionally absolute discretion under the prerogative for the defence of the realm, as well as the institutional initiative which emergency legislation presumes it to have.[31] Furthermore, the scope of executive authority in emergency situations is circumstantially dependent, as it tends to increase along with the seriousness of the emergency. However, the executive can employ emergency discourse to define whether conditions present such an emergency, and just how serious it is. The executive, by defining the security risk through its emergency discourse, can gather unto itself new legislative delegations of power, as well as increase its scope of discretion to circumscribe rights, should it alter the legal paradigm. Likewise, the executive's exercise of greater legal authority in response to emergency needs focuses greater attention upon security issues and can increase the executive's political influence in shaping attitudes and responses to the perceived emergency. In so far as the executive can use emergency discourse to influence the scope of its own legal powers, it destabilizes the rule of law and human rights as constitutional principles in the UK and Canada, subordinating them to the political influence of the executive.

A second structural problem for human rights is closely related to the first. The executive, through emergency discourse, can overshadow the legislature and judiciary, which might oppose its expansion of power in favor of protecting rights. Inadequately checked executive power might continue to grow at the center of the securitized constitution. The devaluation of human rights norms thus accompanies an unbalance in the constitution's structural mechanisms for promoting them against competing security claims. The executive's influence on political attitudes and the security/rights dichotomy allows it to undermine the normative force of international human rights, at the same time that it enhances its constitutional authority at the expense of the legislature and judiciary.[32] This means that domestic rights guarantees, like the Charter or the Convention, risk losing effectiveness, not only because the discursive power of emergency challenges their normative value, but because in both the UK and Canada the judiciary's institutional status declines *vis-à-vis* that of the

---

[31] See *supra* note 20.
[32] Iyer, *supra* note 29 at 130, 186–87.

executive and so undermines structural mechanisms for rights protection. Derogation from rights guarantees, under s. 33 of the Charter or art. 15 of the Convention, best exemplifies the relationship between the legal paradigm shift and structural imbalance, as the courts are thereby disengaged from reviewing certain executive actions.[33] Rights weaken as the judiciary defers to the executive, leaving international human rights as external and domestically unenforceable obligations left to the executive's discretionary compliance.

In considering how best to implement international human rights standards in the United Kingdom and Canada, one must recognize, as one writer has put it, that "their true worth can only be guaged by the effectiveness of the mechanisms for their enforcement."[34] Human rights and the rule of law rely upon courts to resist the security culture and emergency discourse that promote public safety at all costs and risk exaggerating national security threats. However, for reasons already explained, it is the very discursive power of emergency that both the British and Canadian executives can use simultaneously to shift the legal paradigm and undermine judicial independence. Consequently, the implementation of international human rights norms and the protection of public security are inter-dependent with the British and Canadian constitutions' structural mechanisms for realizing these goals. Moreover, this risk is perhaps an unavoidable one, as there can be circumstances where courts appropriately should accommodate security interests and the measures taken on their behalf. Just how courts, and thus human rights, can withstand the discursive power of emergency is constitutionally problematic, since the British and Canadian constitutions necessarily rely upon the executive as the institution most efficient for responding to security needs.

4) Conclusion: Judicial Consciousness and Human Rights Discourse

This rise of a security culture and the discourse of emergency can undermine the value of the rule of law and human rights, and the structural mechanisms

---

[33] Canadian courts have never been faced with a federal act made under the notwithstanding clause. However, the House of Lords has made clear in *A and Others, supra* note 23, that it will review whether a derogation is valid under the requirements of art. 15, thereby requiring both a factual inquiry and proportionality analysis. Again, this review is a brake on but not a guarantee against the executive's excessive interference with rights, should the courts themselves succumb to a security culture and the discursive power of emergency. Furthermore, executive actions falling under a valid derogation would no longer be reviewed against most Convention rights. Gross, *supra* note 11 at 491.

[34] Iyer, *supra* note 29 at 136 and 185–88.

for protecting them, in the British and Canadian constitutions. Even rights guarantees, such as Canada's Charter and the UK's incorporation of the European Convention, cannot conclusively foreclose such a risk in times of public emergencies, either real or wrongly perceived. Nevertheless, courts can consciously promote an opposing discourse of rights that maintains tension between individual rights and public security, and therefore hopefully prevents the permanent "securitization" of the constitution.

Two cases, one from the British House of Lords and the other from the Supreme Court of Canada, demonstrate how courts can employ the discursive power of rights to blunt the executive's emergency discourse. In *A and Others v. Secretary of State for the Home Department*,[35] the House of Lords examined the indefinite detentions of alien terrorist suspects who the Government could not deport under the *Convention* for fear of torture in their home country.[36] It found that a UK derogation from art. 5 to permit such detentions should be quashed, as the measures taken were not "strictly required" under art. 15.[37] The House of Lords accordingly issued "a declaration under section 4 of the Human Rights Act 1998 that section 23 of the Anti-terrorism, Crime and Security Act 2001 is incompatible with articles 5 and 14 of the European Convention insofar as it is disproportionate and permits detention of suspected international terrorists in a way that discriminates on the ground of nationality or immigration status."[38] Although the Lords deferred to the executive's determination that a public emergency existed, they grudgingly did so and with skepticism. The Lords, however, also made an independent assessment of the emergency in determining whether the detention provisions, and the derogation made for them, were proportional. The declaration of incompatibility was not binding in the face of parliamentary sovereignty, but the decision nevertheless placed a high burden on the political branches to comply or openly defy the highest court in the land. The decision did eventually lead to repeal of the offending statutory provision, although Parliament replaced it with onerous control orders applicable to British citizens, as well as foreigners.[39] *A and Others* nonetheless illustrates how a court can rely upon international human rights norms, domestic rights guarantees, and the concepts of proportionality to inject human rights discourse back into open political debate.[40]

---

[35] *Supra* note 23.

[36] See *Chahal, supra* note 21.

[37] Lord Hoffman, concurring, went even further and found that there was no emergency threatening the life of the nation, thus not even reaching the proportionality argument.

[38] *Supra* note 23 at para. 73, *per* Lord Bingham.

[39] Prevention of Terrorism Act 2005, ss. 1–4.

[40] For a defense of the proportionality principle as a brake on executive emergency measures, see E. P. Mendes, "Between Crime and War: Terrorism, Democracy, and the

In Canada, the Supreme Court has also demonstrated the judiciary's ability to employ a discursive power of rights when confronting executive security measures. In *Application under s. 83.28 of the Criminal Code (Re)*,[41] the Court reviewed the constitutionality of a provision, introduced by the *Anti-Terrorism Act*, which allowed compelled testimony of a witness in a terrorism investigation. The Court found the provision to be compatible with the Charter of Rights, but not without contextualizing the Anti-Terrorism Act in a way to prevent it from altering the legal paradigm. Writing the lead opinion, Justices Iacobucci and Arbour recognized a threat from terrorism, but qualified the security concerns by declaring that "[a]lthough terrorism necessarily changes the context in which the rule of law must operate, it does not call for the abdication of law."[42] Rather, the challenge lies in "a balancing of what is required for an effective response to terrorism in a way that appropriately recognizes the fundamental values of the rule of law," with the "cherished liberties that are essential to democracy."[43] The Court thus asserted the normative place of rights within Canada's constitution, which the discourse of emergency could not easily dislodge. In interpreting the Anti-Terrorism Act, it presumed that the statute itself attempted to manage, rather than supplant, a constructive tension between national security and individual rights.[44] Such an assumption, the Court believed, "acknowledges the centrality of constitutional values in the legislative process, and more broadly, in the political and legal culture of Canada."[45]

The Supreme Court, in a paragraph worth quoting in full, then parried the executive's attempt to leverage the legal paradigm through emergency discourse:

> It was suggested in submission that the purpose of the Act should be regarded broadly as the protection of "national security". However, we believe that this characterization has the potential to go too far and would have implications that far outstrip legislative intent. The discussions surrounding the legislation, and the legislative language itself clearly demonstrate that the Act purports to provide means by which terrorism may be prosecuted and prevented. As we cautioned above, courts must not fall prey to the rhetorical urgency of a perceived emergency or an altered security paradigm. While the threat posed by terrorism is certainly more tangible in the aftermath of global events such as those perpetuated in the United States, and since then elsewhere, including very recently in Spain, we must not lose sight of the particular aims of the legislation. Notably, the Canadian government opted to enact specific criminal law and procedure legislation and did not

---

Constitution" in *Special Issue: Between Crime and War: Terrorism, Democracy and the Constitution*, eds. E. P. Mendes and D. M. McAllister (2002) 14 Nat. J. Const. L. 71.

[41] [2004] 2 S.C.R. 248.
[42] *Ibid.* at para. 6.
[43] *Ibid.* at para. 7.
[44] *Ibid.* at para. 28.
[45] *Ibid.* at para. 35.

make use of exceptional powers, for example, under the *Emergencies Act* [citation omitted], or invoke the notwithstanding clause at s. 33 of the *Charter*.[46]

The Supreme Court might have upheld the particular anti-terrorism provision in question, but did so in a way that resisted a shifting of the legal paradigm. It sought to make the Government justify security measures within the normal operation of the rule of law or, if truly necessary, resort to more comprehensive and politically controversial emergency legislation or even the notwithstanding clause. The Supreme Court of Canada made clear, however, that it would not passively give way to the executive's use of emergency discourse. The Court's position helps to maintain a healthy tension between security and individual rights, and resist a security culture that might challenge the constitutional value of the rule of law and human rights.

As these decisions by the House of Lords and the Supreme Court of Canada suggest, the judiciary must remain conscious of the power of emergency discourse and the precarious dependence of international human rights norms on constitutional structures for their domestic implementation. Courts must, in the end, possess *political will* to assert their unique constitutional role as defenders of rights and the rule of law. Of course, courts might not be able to resist an overwhelming security culture in which the executive, the legislature, and public opinion combine to assault an isolated judiciary and dispense with rights and the rule of law as organizing constitutional principles. However, as US Supreme Court Justice Jackson once warned, "[s]uch institutions may be destined to pass away. But it is the duty of the Court to be last, not first, to give them up."[47]

---

[46] *Ibid.* at para. 39.

[47] *Youngstown Sheet and Tube Co. v. Sawyer*, 343 U.S. 579 at 655 (1952), Jackson J. concurring (finding that President Truman had no constitutional authority to seize the nation's steel mills to avert a strike during the Korean War, absent clear authorization by Congress).

PART 4

HUMAN SECURITY

Chapter 11

A Comparison of the United Kingdom and Canadian Approaches to Human Security

Susan Breau

1) Introduction

The notion of human security has been embraced by Canada and cautiously approached by the United Kingdom. Foreign Affairs Canada has a human security web site devoted to its dedicated human security program and Canada is a member of the Human Security Network. The United Kingdom is not a member of the Human Security Network and its stated foreign policy priorities do not include the concept.

This chapter will argue that although human security is not a doctrine of public international law, the resulting obligations from the concept do have international law content, including the main duty arising from this human centred approach to security; the responsiblity to protect. The responsiblity to protect has three main elements, the responsibility to prevent, the responsibility to react and the responsiblity to rebuild. This chapter will primarily focus on the second element, the responsiblity to react within an international law framework.

The Canadian position supporting both human security and the ensuing responsibility to protect reflects an effort to develop public international law

Christopher P.M. Waters (Ed.), *British and Canadian Perspectives on International Law*, pp. 205–223.

and foreign affairs from a state centric to human being centred focus that does not yet reflect current state practice. However, this chapter will also argue that although there may not be a specific policy supporting the concept, the United Kingdom's positions in many areas of international law and foreign policy are embracing the notion of human security. In order to support this position this chapter will, firstly, examine the development of the doctrine of human security, secondly, examine international law elements of the responsibility to protect, and thirdly, place both the British and Canadian positions within current international law practice.

2) THE DEVELOPMENT OF THE NOTION OF HUMAN SECURITY

a) *United Nations Human Development Report 1994*

Chapter Two of the Human Development Report of 1994 published by the United Nations Development Programme introduced the concept of human security. The notion was based on a concern for human life and dignity and was said to have two components: "first, safety from such chronic threats as hunger, disease and repression. And second, it means protection from sudden and hurtful disruptions in the patterns of daily life . . ."[1] Four essential characteristics were that human security was a universal concern, the concepts were interdependent, it was easier to ensure through early prevention rather than later intervention and it was people-centred.[2] The report contained a prediction that I share, that the idea of human security was likely to revolutionize society in the 21st century.[3] The report indicated that freedom from fear and freedom from want were recognized right from the beginning of the United Nations. In fact, these were two of the original four freedoms introduced by President Roosevelt in his speech to Congress prior to the United States' entry into World War II.[4] The notion of human security would bring together these fundamental freedoms into a coherent notion that would change the focus from territorial security to people's security.[5]

The concept emerged as a full priority of foreign policy in the emegence of the Human Security Network in 1999 established by Canada and Norway and

---

[1] United Nations Development Programme, *Human Development Report 1994* (New York: Oxford University Press, 1994) at 23.

[2] *Ibid.* at 22–23.

[3] *Ibid.* at 22.

[4] Franklin D. Roosevelt, Address to Congress, 6 January 1941 in *Cong. Rec.*, vol. 87, I (1941).

[5] *Supra* note 1 at 24.

the UN Trust Fund for Human Security sponsored by Japan. The Human Security Network had its genesis as the 1998 "Lysøen" partnership between Canada and Norway which, building on the success of the landmines campaign,[6] was to encourage cooperation among like-minded governments on a range of other threats to people's safety.[7] The Network is now an informal grouping of states including Canada, Norway, Switzerland, Chile, Jordan, Austria, Mali, Greece, Thailand, the Netherlands, Slovenia and South Africa (as an observer).[8] This group meets annually in ministerial conferences.

b) *The Responsibility to Protect – ICISS*

The Canadian position was empitomised in the report of the International Commission on Intervention and State Sovereignty (ICISS) entitled the *Responsibility to Protect* which was released just after 11 September 2001. Although this was an independent commission, it was funded largely by the Government of Canada and was presented to Kofi Annan by Canada's Ambassador to the United Nations. The report discussed the notion of human security and the resulting obligation of the responsibility to protect. It was defined in the report as:

> Human security means the security of people – their physical safety, their economic and social well-being, respect for their dignity and worth as human beings, and the protection of their human rights and fundamental freedoms . . . One of the virtues of expressing the key issue in this debate as "the responsibility to protect" is that it focuses attention where it should be most concentrated, on the human needs of those seeking protection or assistance. The emphasis in the security debate shifts, with this focus, from territorial security, and security through armaments, to security through human development with access to food and employment, and to environmental security.[9]

The report set out the research question – "the question of when, if ever, it is appropriate for states to take coercive – and in particular military – action, against another state for the purpose of protecting people at risk in that other state".[10] The answer contained a formula for action by the international community.

---

[6] K. Anderson, "The Ottawa Convention Banning Landmines, the Role of International Non-Governmental Organizations and the Idea of International Civil Society" (2000) 11 E.J.I.L. 91.

[7] See Foreign Affairs Canada: http://www.humansecurity.gc.ca/canada_chairmanship-en.asp.

[8] See Foreign Affairs Canada: http://www.humansecurity.gc.ca/hsi_hsn-en.asp.

[9] *Ibid.* at 15

[10] ICISS, *The Responsibility to Protect* (Ottawa: International Development Research Centre, 2001) at XI.

Where a population is suffering serious harm, as a result of internal war, insurgency, repression or state failure, and the state in question is unwilling or unable to halt or avert it, the principle of non-intervention yields to the international responsibility to protect.[11]

The Responsibility to Protect had three interconnected responsibilities: the responsibility to prevent, the responsibility to react and the responsibility to rebuild. The report emphasized that military intervention would only be considered as a last resort when preventive options had been exhausted. The report stated a strong preference for action by the UN Security Council in all three areas of the responsibility. The revolutionary aspect of this concept was the transition from a (disputed) legal *right* of intervention when massive abuses of human rights were being perpetrated, to an *obligation* to act in these situations.

This report has become a key component of Canada's foreign policy. Canada has played a strong leadership role in promoting *The Responsibility to Protect* through high level bilateral and multilateral diplomatic efforts, research initiatives and outreach activities including conferences and roundtables. One of the key elements in Canada's human security agenda with an important international law element is the support for the International Criminal Court. In the words of Darryl Robinson, Legal Officer at DFAIT, the ICC "will be an indispensable mechanism to help replace a culture of impunity with a culture of accountability".[12]

c) *Human Security Now – Independent Commission on Human Security*

The Human Security Network and the Canadian government emphasised the aspect of freedom from fear in human security, which focusses on violent conflict and humanitarian issues. In contrast, the Japanese government focused on the development issues and the aspect of freedom from want, and as a result has been critical of the Canadian approach.[13] In March of 1999, the Government of Japan and the United Nations Secretariat launched the United Nations Trust Fund for Human Security. At the UN Millennium Summit, Kofi Annan called upon the world to advance the twin goals of freedom from want and freedom from fear. The Independent Commission on Human Security was

---

[11] *Ibid.*

[12] D. Robinson, "The Canadian Perspective on the International Criminal Court" (1999) 8 J. Int'l. L. & Prac. 9 at 9.

[13] A. Mack, "The Concept of Human Security" in M. Brzoska & P. J. Croll, eds., brief 30, *Promoting Security: But How and For Whom?* (Bonn: Bonn International Center for Conversion, 2004).

established with the sponsorship of the government of Japan and was chaired by Sadako Ogata, the former UN High Commissioner for Refugees and Nobel Prize economist Amartya Sen. Accorrding to Ogato the purpose of the report from the Commission was to "develop the concept of human security as an operational tool for policy formulation and implementation."[14] The Commission produced their report, *Human Security Now*, in 2003.[15]

Human Security Now did not emphasise intervention to protect human rights but the report did endorse a responsibility to protect by advocating a limitation on "unrestricted national sovereignty" and asserting that there was a need "to develop institutions that allow us to meet our responsibilities to others in today's interdependent world".[16] The report recommended adopting a human security approach to protect people in violent conflict by: placing human security on the security agenda; strengthening humanitarian action; respecting human rights and humanitarian law; disarming people and fighting crime; and preventing conflict and respecting citizenship.[17]

The report was critical of armed intervention stating that "military action is often masked by humanitarian intervention" and advocated a broader and intertwined humanitarian action including political, military and development dimensions.[18]

However, reading this report together with the report of the International Commission on Intervention and State Sovereignty reveals remarkable similarities in the comprehensive approach to human security in terms of the responsibilities to prevent and to rebuild along with protection. In the context of international law, both reports advocated multilateralism and a pivotal role for the United Nations. However, the ICISS report placed more emphasis on actual armed intervention, whereas the Human Security Commission report placed emphasis on empowerment measures including community-building, eliminating poverty, advancing education and improving health.[19]

d) *United Nations Reports – We the Peoples, A more secure world, In larger freedom*

These themes have also been strongly promoted by the United Nations. Indeed, UN Secretary-General Kofi Annan assumed a leadership role in the development

---

[14] S. Ogata, "From State Security to Human Security" (Lecture presented at the Brown University Ogden Lecture, 26 May 2002).

[15] Commission on Human Security, *Human Security Now* (Commission on Human Security: New York, 2003).

[16] *Ibid.* at 12.

[17] *Ibid.* at 24.

[18] *Ibid.* at 26–27.

[19] *Supra* note 14 at 5; *Human Security Now, ibid.* at c. 5–7.

of the notion of human security, addressing this topic soon after the Kosovo conflict. In a statement to the 54th session of the General Assembly, he stated that he intended to "address the prospects for human security and intervention in the next century."[20] For the Millenium Assembly, Annan released a report entitled *We the Peoples; The Role of the United Nations in the 21st Century*. In this report he stated: "Two of the founding aims of the United Nations whose achievement eludes us still: freedom from want and freedom from fear."[21] And in discussing the internal armed conflicts of the 1990s, Annan introduced the new notion of security:

> In the wake of these conflicts, a new understanding of the concept of security is evolving. Once synonymous with the defence of territory from external attack, the requirements of security today have come to embrace the protection of communities and individuals from internal violence. The need for a more human-centred approach to security is reinforced by the continuing dangers that weapons of mass destruction, most notably nuclear weapons, pose to humanity: their very name reveals their scope and their intended objective, if they were ever used.[22]

Annan argued that reducing poverty and achieving economic growth would be steps in conflict prevention. His formula for conflict prevention also prescribed the protection of human rights, protection of minority rights, instituting political arrangements in which all groups were represented, assuring transparency in governance, asserting the centrality of international humanitarian and human rights law and, supporting the creation of an International Criminal Court.[23] He indicated that prevention was the "core feature in our efforts to promote human security".[24]

Annan also discussed the issue of humanitarian intervention and argued that armed intervention remained "the option of last resort, but in the face of mass murder it is an option that cannot be relinquished."[25] Other elements Annan discussed in his section on "Freedom from Fear" were a commission to study peacekeeping, targeting sanctions and nuclear and small arms reductions.[26]

In addition to his support of the Human Security Commission and the ICISS, Annan commissioned his own report in the wake of the Iraq conflict. He appointed his High-Level Panel on Threats, Challenges and Change, interestingly with Gareth Evans, who had been in a similar role in the ICISS, as co-chair. Sir David Hannay was the British member of the Commission. There

---

[20] K. Annan, "Statement to United Nations General Assembly 54th session" (1999).
[21] K. Annan, *We the Peoples; The Role of the United Nations in the 21st Century* (New York: United Nations, 2000) at 17.
[22] *Ibid.* at 43.
[23] *Ibid.* at 45–46.
[24] *Ibid.* at 46.
[25] *Ibid.* at 48.
[26] *Ibid.* at 48–53.

were no Canadians. The panel reported to the Secretary-General in December 2004 in their report entitled: *A more secure world: Our shared responsibility.*[27] The report endorsed the responsibility to protect, and argued for an international responsibility to prevent massive threats to human life whether they be from armed conflict, civil strife, disease or natural disaster. It is within this document that the legal content clearly emerges from the notion of human security. As with the original ICISS report, a formula of five criteria was introduced in *A more secure world* for the use of force in situations of human catastrophe. These were:

i) *Seriousness of threat* – genocide and other large-scale killing, ethnic cleansing or serious violations of international humanitarian law, actual or imminently apprehended.

ii) *Proper purpose* – primary (not sole) purpose to halt or avert the threat in question

iii) *Last resort* – every non-military option for meeting the threat been explored with reasonable grounds for believing other measures will not succeed.

iv) *Proportional means* – scale, duration and intensity the minimum necessary to meet the threat.

v) *Balance of consequences* – reasonable chance of military action being successful with the consequences not likely to be worse than consequences of inaction.

These were virtually the same criteria set out in *The Responsibility to Protect* and it was recommended that these guidelines be embodied in a declaratory resolution of the Security Council and the General Assembly.[28]

Finally the Secretary-General issued his own report, *In larger freedom*[29] which was presented to the General Assembly in March 2005. One key proposal that endorsed the recommendation in *A more secure world,* was the creation of an intergovernmental Peacebuilding Commission to report to the Security Council and to act in the immediate aftermath of war to help countries in the transition from war to lasting peace.[30] Annan also endorsed and recommended to the Security Council that they adopt a resolution setting out the five principles concerning seriousness of threat, proper purpose of the proposed military action, whether means short of force might succeed, whether the force

---

[27] Secretary-General's Panel on Threats, Challenges and Change, *A more secure world: Our shared responsibility* (New York: United Nations Department of Public Information, 2004).

[28] *Ibid.* at 67.

[29] K. Annan, *In larger freedom: towards development, security and human rights for all*, UN Doc. A/59/2005 (31 March 2005).

[30] *Ibid.* at 31.

is proportional and whether there is a reasonable chance of success.[31] He also specifically supported the ICISS and High-Level Panel endorsement of an emerging norm of the responsibility to protect and stated "I believe that we must embrace the responsibility to protect, and, when necessary, we must act on it."[32] This support came under his section entitled "Rule of law". Within this section he supported the International Criminal Court. He also put forward the idea of a Rule of Law Assistance Unit within the proposed Peacebuilding Support office.[33]

The Secretary-General's efforts from the Millennium Summit through to his report in 2005, marry the Japanese and Canadian efforts as his reports and the High-Level Panel reports take a comprehensive approach to human security. The twin tracks of freedom from want and freedom from fear are incorporated into all of the proposed United Nations activities. What is clear is the emergence of a notion of security that is far from the traditional sovereignty approach.

The United Nations, in its 60th session of the UN General Assembly in September 2005, conducted a comprehensive review of the progress of the Millennium Declaration and reviewed the proposals contained in both the High Level Panel report and the Secretary-General's report. Although the Outcome Statement of the summit was not nearly as detailed as the reports there was a critical statement endorsing the idea of a responsibility to protect:

> The international community, through the United Nations, also has the responsibility to use appropriate diplomatic, humanitarian and other peaceful means, in accordance with Chapter VI and VIII of the Charter, to help protect populations from genocide, war crimes, ethnic cleansing and crimes against humanity. In this context, we are prepared to take collective action, in a timely and decisive manner, through the Security Council, in accordance with the UN Charter, including Chapter VII, on a case by case basis and in cooperation with relevant regional organizations as appropriate, should peaceful means be inadequate and national authorities manifestly failing to protect their populations from genocide, war crimes, ethnic cleansing and crimes against humanity. We stress the need for the General Assembly to continue consideration of the responsibility to protect populations from genocide, war crimes, ethnic cleansing, and crimes against humanity and its implications, bearing in mind the principles of the Charter of the United Nations and international law. We also intend to commit ourselves, as necessary and appropriate, to help states build capacity to protect their populations from genocide, war crimes, ethnic cleansing and crimes against humanity and to assist those which are under stress before crises and conflicts break out.'[34]

---

[31] *Ibid.* at 33.

[32] *Ibid.* at 35.

[33] *Ibid.* at 36.

[34] UN GA, *Outcome Document of the 60th Anniversary Summit* (13 September 2005) at para. 139.

In addition to these ideas being introduced in a series of influential reports, there are developments in several areas of international law that support the concept of human security. There is a need for extensive study of various areas of international law for the true development of these ideas, but there are key areas such as the law of state responsibility, international criminal law, international humanitarian law and the international protection of human rights that emerge as likely candidates.

3) INTERNATIONAL LAW AND THE NOTION OF HUMAN SECURITY

a) *The law of state responsibility*

Although human security might have contested meanings, the resulting obligation of the responsibility to protect has serious international law implications as it impinges on one of the principal areas of international law; the law of state responsibility. This law sets out that when one state commits "an intentionally wrongful act" it engages the international responsibility of that state.[35] The traditional law of state responsibility developed from the notion of right of diplomatic protection, where one state would potentially be required to make reparations to another state for damages to citizens or property of that other state.[36] However, it must be stressed that this concept of diplomatic protection had always been considered a right not an obligation. States had the absolute discretion to choose whether or not to act in situations where their citizens were subject to injury or property loss in other nations.

The law of state responsibility has been subject to a tremendous expansion in scope. In tandem with the reports outlined in Part 2 of this chapter was the completion of the work of the International Law Commission on state responsibility. The members of the Commission were finally able to agree on Articles of State Responsibility which were adopted in a General Assembly Resolution in 2002.[37] This resolution was a result of over forty years work by the International Law Commission (the first report on State Responsibility went to the International Law Commission in 1956) and finalizing the draft articles which had their first reading in 1996.[38] Within these articles is the notion that

---

[35] ILC Articles on Responsibility of States for Internationally Wrongful Acts, annexed to GA Res. 86/83, 12 December 2001 at art. 1 [Articles of State Responsibility].

[36] M. Shaw, *International Law* (Cambridge: Cambridge University Press, 2003) at 698–699.

[37] *Responsibility of States for Internationally Wrongful Acts*, GA Res. 56/83, UN GAOR, 56th Sess., UN Doc. A/RES/56/83 (2002).

[38] J. Crawford, *The International Law Commission's Articles on State Responsibility:*

ties human security and traditional international law together; aggravated state responsibility.

Chapter III entitled "Serious Breaches of Obligations under Peremptory Norms of General International Law" introduced this second tier of obligations identified as Aggravated State Responsibility.[39] Article 40 stated:

1. This chapter applies to the international responsibility which is entailed by a serious breach by a State of an obligation arising under a peremptory norm of general international law.
2. A breach of such an obligation is serious if it involves a gross or systematic failure by the responsible State to fulfil its obligation.

It must be made clear that the committee that drafted these articles did not contemplate that these articles would be taken to imply a responsibility to act in the sense meant by the responsibility to protect. It should also be noted that these articles are secondary and do not specify the primary rules of state conduct.

The first controversial element in Article 40 was the definition of what is a peremptory norm of general international law. It has been defined as a fundamental value such as peace, human rights, self-determination, or protection of the environment. All of these types of obligations were owed to all other members of the international community and, therefore, that these were community rights belonging to any other state. A community right could be exercised by any other state, whether or not damaged by the breach. However, this right was to be exercised on behalf of the international community, not just on the part of the claimant state.[40] Article 40 (2) specified that the breach must be gross or systematic, serious or large scale, and examples could be aggression, genocide, or grave atrocities against one's own nationals or all persons belonging to an ethnic group (apartheid as one example).[41]

Chapter III of the Articles of State Responsibility could constitute an important advance towards clarifying how obligations to the international community trigger the secondary rules of state responsibility. At the core of Article 40 was the notion of obligations *erga omnes* as set out in the *Barcelona Traction* case and elsewhere.[42] These breaches would "shock the conscience of mankind" and as such should attract serious consequences.[43] Articles 53 and 64 of the Vienna

---

Introduction, Text and Commentaries (Cambridge: Cambridge University Press, 2002). See Introduction at 1–60 for a history of the Articles on State Responsibility.

[39] See A. Cassese, *International Law* (Oxford: Oxford University Press, 2005) at 262–277 on Aggravated State Responsibility.

[40] *Ibid.* at 262.

[41] *Ibid.*

[42] *Barcelona Traction, Light and Power Co. Case (Belgium v. Spain)* [1970] I.C.J. Reports 3.

[43] *Supra* note 38 at 18–19.

Convention on the Law of Treaties were cited by the drafters as support for these notions as the Vienna Convention recognised the existence of substantive norms of a fundamental character from which no derogation is permitted.[44]

However, it was the consequences of serious breach of obligations under peremptory norms that were a radical change from the traditional notion of state responsibility and close to the idea of a responsibility to protect. Article 41 stated:

1. States shall cooperate to bring to an end through lawful means any serious breach within the meaning of article 40.
2. No State shall recognize as lawful a situation created by a serious breach within the meaning of article 40, nor render aid or assistance in maintaining the situation.
3. This article is without prejudice to the other consequences referred to in this part and to such further consequences that a breach to which this chapter applies may entail under international law.

The first important factor was that *all* other States could take action. All other States were entitled to: (a) invoke the aggravated responsibility by bringing their claim to the notice of the state; (b) demand cessation of the wrong; (c) claim reparation on behalf of the victims; (d) bring the matter to competent international bodies such as the UN or regional organisations; (e) if that international organisation took no action then states could take *peaceful* counter-measures on an individual basis; and, (f) to resort to collective self-defence in the case of aggression.[45]

Under this article, States were placed under a positive duty to cooperate in order to bring an end to serious breaches of obligations owed under a peremptory norm of international law. Article 41 did not specify the form this cooperation should take: it could be organized under the auspices of the United Nations but it also could be "non-institutionalized cooperation".[46]

These articles did not contemplate the idea of a responsibility to protect. The first reason was that these articles were only to cover secondary rules of state responsibility. It could be argued that the responsibility to protect is also a secondary rule as it could be a consequence for the states that have violated peremptory norms of international law. However, it is clear that the notion is far more expansive than a secondary rule. The second and more compelling reason was that even the drafters of the articles acknowledged that aggravated state responsibility was not a doctrine in customary international law. In his commentaries, Crawford recognized that paragraph 1 may not be part of

---

[44] *Ibid.* at 243.
[45] *Supra* note 39 at 274–275.
[46] *Supra* note 38 at 249.

general international law but could constitute a progressive development of the law.[47] There may be future development of "a more elaborate regime of consequences entailed by such breaches."[48] The movement in international law had been from 'sovereignty to obligation' and from 'immunity to accountability'.[49] However, both the reports on the responsibility to protect and the Articles of State Responsibility called for another approach to serious human rights breaches. The focus again was on norms that impacted on human beings, not on the state.

There are indeed common elements in the approach of the committees considering the responsibility to protect and that of the ILC committee. It was obvious that the Articles on State Responsibility as passed by the General Assembly did not contain specific provisions outlining a responsibility to protect or a duty by other states to intervene when this responsibility was ignored. However, the articles on serious breaches of obligations, specifically Article 41, did prescribe positive duties of cooperation and response to violations of peremptory norms of international law. The reports from the United Nations and the ICISS argued similar notions of international responsibility. They were also examining the most serious and sustained violations of peremptory norms of international law. These reports were attempting to push forward a development of a customary doctrine in favour of a responsibility to act. Although neither the reports nor the draft articles reflected the current situation of the international law of state responsibility, the reports on the responsibility to protect did introduce what is perhaps the logical conclusion of the notion of aggravated state responsibility. This was that the international community had an obligation to intervene in some fashion to stop serious abuses of human rights which violated *jus cogens* norms.

However, it should be noted that Crawford in a lecture on State Responsibility on Articles 40 and 41 dismissed their use in armed intervention. Objecting to states taking military action to assist victims, he said:

> Presently we have the spectre of certain States galloping to the aid of victims who are clear that they do not want such aid. As the Court said in the Nicaragua case, if a State purports to act in collective self-defence of another, it must act with the consent of the State which is said to be the victim of the attack. The same principle should apply to State responsibility, especially so far as reparation is concerned.[50]

There is some support for the notion of community responsibility within international jurisprudence. In the decision of the International Court of Justice on

---

[47] *Ibid.* at 249.

[48] *Ibid.* at 253.

[49] J. Crawford, "The Earl A. Snyder Lecture in International Law: Responsibility to the International Community as a Whole" (2001) 8 Ind. J. Global Legal Stud. 303 at 307 & 309.

[50] *Ibid.* at 305.

universal jurisdiction, the *Case Concerning the Arrest Warrant of 11 April 2000 (Democratic Republic of the Congo v. Belgium)*, in the separate opinion of Judges Higgins, Kooijmans and Buergenthal, there was discussion of the evolution of international law. In paragraph 51 the opinion stated:

> The series of multilateral treaties with their special jurisdictional provisions reflect a determination by the international community that those engaged in war crimes, hijacking, hostage taking, torture should not go unpunished . . . And those States and academic writers who claim the right to act unilaterally to assert a universal criminal jurisdiction over persons committing such acts, invoke the concept of acting as "agents for the international community".[51]

In the *Furundzija* Trial Chamber decision in the International Criminal Tribunal for Yugoslavia there was a reference to what amounted to aggravated state responsibility. The Judgment stated:

> Under current international humanitarian law, in addition to individual criminal liability, State responsibility may ensue as a result of a State official engaging in torture or failing to prevent torture or to punish torturers. If carried out as an extensive practice of State officials, torture amounts to a serious breach on a widespread scale of an international obligation of essential importance for safeguarding the human being, thus constituting a grave wrongful act generating State responsibility.[52]

These cases illustrate that the principle of the essential importance of safeguarding human beings has been extensively developed in international criminal law.

b) *International Criminal Law*

The second international law development supporting notions of human security and the responsibility to protect was the jurisprudence of the *ad hoc* International Criminal Tribunals and the establishment of the International Criminal Court. The jurisprudence of the *ad hoc* tribunals reflected this trend of responsibility towards the international community for crimes which are part and parcel of those items that constituted serious breaches of international obligations. International criminal law could fall into the third pillar of the responsibility to protect, as a part of a responsibility to rebuild. Bringing those who perpetrate international crimes to justice can be part of the peacebuilding and reconciliation process.

---

[51] General List No. 121 [2002] ICJ 1 (14 February 2002), Joint Separate Opinion of Judges Higgins, Kooijmans & Buergenthal at para. 51.

[52] *Prosecutor v. Furundzija* (1998), Case No. IT-95-17/1-T (International Criminal Tribunal for the Former Yugoslavia, Trial Chamber) at para. 142 [*Furundzija*].

It is only recently that non-state actors have become a major focus of international law, principally in the fields of human rights and international criminal law. It should also be noted that the responsibility to protect would be triggered in the event of a breach of a primary rule of international law, a *jus cogens* norm, protecting individuals. *Jus cogens* norms have developed primarily in the field of human rights and in international criminal law.

International criminal justice has certainly become an important factor in the development of public international law and the notion that an individual can become the subject of international justice and not just domestic court action. Certainly, the concept of complementarity in the statute of the International Criminal Court still attached supremacy to domestic justice but the international court can act with consent or with an unwillingness or inability on the part of states.[53] The Security Council, with the United States abstaining, recently referred the situation in Darfur to the International Criminal Court.[54] The proliferation of international courts and tribunals dealing with human rights abuses and the notion of justiciability again contribute to the notion of a responsibility to the international community as a whole.

c) *Human Rights Law and International Humanitarian Law*

The third element in this emerging notion of human security is the development of the corpus of human rights and humanitarian law instruments. Major examples are the Universal Declaration of Human Rights (argued now to be part of customary international law), the Genocide Convention, the four Geneva Conventions and their protocols and the two International Covenants of Human Rights. These have been joined by a myriad of international and regional human rights instruments, commissions and courts and by important declarations on indivisibility and enforceability in the 1993 Vienna Conference on Human Rights. The jurisprudence of these commissions and courts develop the content of the responsibility that governments have towards their citizens and those of other nations (for example, in cases of refusal to deport citizens to countries that might subject the person to torture).

Human rights norms will fall into the responsibility to prevent category of the responsibility to protect, as adherence to human rights instruments will ensure compliance with the notion of human security and prevent a responsibility to react. Standard setting in human rights is just the type of activity that promotes human security.

---

[53] Statute of the International Criminal Court, 17 July 1998, UN Doc. No. A/CONF.183/9, 37 I.L.M. 999 (entered into force 1 July 2002) [Rome Statute] at art. 17.
[54] UN SC Res. 1593 (31 March 2005), UN Doc. S/RES/1593.

A field of human rights law yet to be explored in terms of the human security debate is the movement towards justiciability in economic, social and cultural rights. Although only a few nations have dealt with this issue in their courts, most notably South Africa and India, the legal content of these rights is becoming accepted. No longer are economic, social and cultural rights seen as wish lists, but as rights with a defined scope of obligation.[55] These rights are arguably indicative of community responsibility as there is an element of responsibility for richer nations to help poorer nations realize these rights. This could mean an element of international legal obligation in international aid and development policy. This strategy is supportive of the freedom from want portion of human security.

d) *Practice of the United Nations*

The final important element of the development of human security in international law is the practice of the United Nations. The Security Council has traditionally been seen as the most political of bodies, especially during the Cold War when the veto was used liberally to support political alliances.[56] However, examination of the debates of the Security Council since the end of the Cold War reveals a change in discourse towards discussion of legal norms, culminating in the lengthy debates on the Iraqi conflict.[57] This practice of the Security Council can also constitute a source of public international law, as declarations of what constitutes threats to international peace and security may constitute state practice interpretive of either a treaty provision (Article 39) or a doctrine of customary international law (content of human rights obligations, self-defence, *jus cogens*).

Bertrand Ramcharan in an article for the United Nations Chronicle in 2001 analyzed the recent practice of the Security Council. He pointed out several situations of United Nations discussion of human rights catastrophes in the context of international peace and security. These including the situations in Zaire, Georgia, Cyprus, Liberia, Burundi, Croatia, Afghanistan, Sierra Leone, Albania, Guinea Bissau, Somalia East Timor, Bosnia and Herzegovina, Lebanon, and Angola. He also pointed out general debates on civilians in

---

[55] UN Doc. 14/12/90, CESCR General Comment 3 on the nature of States parties obligations.

[56] One of the most stark examples is the debate over the Vietnamese invasion of Pol Pot's Cambodia where the western alliance blocked United Nations cooperation with the new regime, preferring to support Khmer Rouge representatives.

[57] See I. Johnstone, "Security Council Deliberations: The Power of the Better Argument" (2003) 14 E.J.I.L. 437. Johnstone uses the Kosovo conflict as his example of legal discourse.

armed conflict and women's rights.[58] All of these examples reveal a change in focus in Security Council activity from traditional territorial sovereignty to human security concerns.

There are clearly compelling arguments that neither human security nor the responsibility to protect are accepted doctrines within international law or international relations. Countless examples can be given of the continued supremacy of state sovereignty within treaty negotiations, the development of customary international law and in the practice of international justice (the consent based jurisdiction of the ICJ being one such example). Nevertheless, it is clear from the above examples that there is a developing doctrine that might change the focus of international law from the relationship between states to a global community which owes obligations to all of its citizens.[59]

4) THE CANADIAN AND UNITED KINGDOM PERSPECTIVES WITHIN CURRENT INTERNATIONAL LAW PRACTICE

If these doctrines are in their infancy, the question remains as to how the Canadian and British views on human security impact on their current practice. It is clear from a review of both sets of foreign policy priorities that human security plays an integral role in policy formation in the UK, if not in name.

In a Command Paper presented to Parliament in October 2004, the Foreign and Commonwealth Office predicted that the UK through Europe could expect to "influence the development of UN policy".[60] This paper and other declarations have been silent on the concept of human security and the responsibility to protect but a careful examination reveals remarkable support for a twin track approach. The report on UN reform presented to Parliament before the release of the High-Level panel report contained a section on the Secretary-General's Action Plan for the Prevention of Genocide. It contained discussion of the guidelines for identifying extreme cases for military intervention as outlined in the ICISS report. The report expected that the High-Level Panel would make recommendations for achieving consensus on these guidelines and stated that this was an area of work "strongly supported by the UK".[61]

UK priorities in foreign policy include several issues which are in the realm of human security: terrorism and security; drugs and crime; conflict prevention;

---

[58] B.G. Ramcharan, "Thinking Aloud: The Security Council, Human Rights and Humanitarian Issues", *United Nations Chronicle*, Issue 4 (New York: United Nations, 2001) at 23.

[59] *Supra* note 57 at 458–459.

[60] Foreign and Commonwealth Office, *The United Kingdom in the United Nations*, (London: The Stationery office, 2004) at 2.

[61] *Ibid.* at 27.

global economy; human rights; sustainable development; energy security and climate change; and science and innovation. The Labour Government has also led efforts to reduce crippling foreign debt for developing countries and prevention efforts in the sense of governance and capacity building which including the linking of human rights, democracy and good governance in promoting sustainable development. Many of these priorities fit within a human security strategy. The United Kingdom is also a strong supporter of international justice including the International Criminal Court. The hesitation to embrace the notion of human security might be some reticence about the content of the notion of human security most particularly in its legal content.

The clearest indication of support for these developments was a speech given by Foreign Secretary Jack Straw at Chatham House on 2 September 2004 entitled "Shaping a Stronger United Nations".[62] In this speech he addressed new threats to our security linked to "breakdown of order, poverty, disease, crippling injustice, environmental degradation and climate change". He argued these issues had to be tackled for long-term, sustainable global security. He also addressed collective security and stated that although States had the right to non-interference in their internal affairs; they also had "responsibilities towards their own people, but also towards the international community and their international engagements." If these responsibilities were ignored the international community would have to intervene and in extreme cases use military intervention. Finally, he indicated that the UK would have an important role to play in reviewing progress towards the Millennium Development Goals and in following up the work of the High-Level Panel.[63]

Furthermore, following the 60th anniversary Summit at the UN, Jack Straw announced on 28 September 2005:

> At the Millennium Summit two weeks ago, with the UK in the vanguard, major reforms were agreed. New development aid targets; a peace-building commission; a new and more effective human rights council; and, most important of all, a new recognition that sovereign states themselves and the nations of the world as a whole, have a clear "responsibility to protect" all citizens from genocide, from ethnic cleansing and crimes against humanity.
>
> And if this new responsibility had been in place a decade ago, thousands in Srebrenica and Rwanda would have been saved. We would not have had to take action in Kosovo without an explicit UN mandate; and the later divisions over Iraq might (just) have been avoided.
>
> And my pledge to you is to ensure that the fine words on responsibility to protect are translated into collective action.[64]

---

[62] J. Straw, "Shaping a Stronger United Nations" (speech delivered at Chatham House, 2 September 2004).

[63] *Ibid.*

[64] Address delivered by Jack Straw at the Labour Party conference, Brighton, 28 September 2005.

Furthermore, the Canadian and United Kingdom governments are both taking the lead in promoting ratification of the statute of the International Criminal Court. Recently the role of the United Kingdom was pivotal in persuading the United States not to veto the referral of the situation in Darfur to the International Criminal Court. The United Kingdom has identified one of its priorities as promoting an international system based on the rule of law. This rule of law includes as a fundamental element protection of the individual from massive abuses of human rights. Human security is a critical element in an international system based on the rule of law.

With regard to freedom from fear, the United Kingdom has been the leading country promoting the notion of humanitarian intervention. Although they may not have specifically embraced the concept of the responsibility to protect, their public statements surrounding the intervention in Kosovo reflect acceptance of a duty towards nationals of other countries. Canada equally supports humanitarian intervention but with a clearer preference for Security Council endorsement of the action.

In terms of freedom from want, the United Kingdom might be more enlightened than Canada with respect to debt relief and aid. The United Kingdom promotes human rights, democracy and good governance as part and parcel of its development strategy. The UK is taking the lead in the debate over aid and development in Africa. The legal operation of human security is also enhanced through outside scrutiny by human rights bodies – the European Court of Human Rights for the UK and the Human Rights Committee for Canada – the effectiveness of which is explored in other chapters of this book.

These two countries part company in that the UK is more hesitant to embrace new standards and concepts in international law and would prefer notions such as human security to remain tools of foreign policy rather than binding international obligations. Guidelines on the use of force would remain principles rather than legal concepts. The Canadians promoted the responsibility to protect as a binding obligation and the five criteria as essential in considerations of using force.

The Canadian position on human security may not reflect the current situation in international law but it anticipates the gradual but inevitable evolution of international law from a state-centred to a people-centred approach. It might sadly take another 100 years for this to emerge as part and parcel of customary international law but it will do so. The Canadian government in taking such a prominent role in promoting human security and the responsibility to protect may well reflect the global community of the future.

5) CONCLUSION

Human security is argued to be part of a new understanding of sovereignty, where state sovereignty yields to the sovereignty of the peoples.[65] The title of the Annan millennium report, *We the Peoples* implies that the obligation to protect persons supersedes notions of state sovereignty.

This Chapter has discussed possible future developments within public international law that do not reflect the current situation. The Security Council has not yet endorsed the responsibility to protect, nor the five criteria for the use of force. It is clear that these concepts are not fully in the repertoire of current international law practice. There may be strong objections from many nations to codify such criteria and a compromise, regrettably, will be the establishment of a Peacebuilding Commission with a tinkering of institutional reform rather than any substantive developments on criteria for the use of force.

However, it is evident that there are major developments in international law slowly but inexorably changing the nature of the international community. Indeed, the other chapters in this part of *British and Canadian Perspectives on International Law* highlight international law's growing engagement with issues such as environmental and economic security. Furthermore, developments that attract much attention are the growth of international criminal law institutions and jurisprudence, and the expanding corpus of international human rights standards and decisions, topics discussed in Parts 2 and 3 of the book. Lesser known but equally important are the development of international legal standards that limit state sovereignty including the doctrines of state responsibility and the restricted doctrine of state immunity. Detailed examination of these areas of state responsibility, international criminal law, the international protection of human rights, and the practice of the United Nations will reveal the trend towards the obligation to promote and protect human security.

---

[65] S. Mohamad, "From Keeping Peace to Building Peace: A Proposal for a Revitalized United Nations Trusteeship Council" (2005) 105 Colum. L. Rev. 809 at 837.

Chapter 12

Canadian and U.K. Approaches to Sustainable Development in International Trade Law

Marie-Claire Cordonier Segger[1]

1) SUSTAINABLE DEVELOPMENT IN WORLD TRADE LAW

In March 2004, Canada and the European Union (EU), of which of course the United Kingdom is a member, agreed on the scope and framework for "a new

---

[1] This work builds on the author's chapters in L. Bartels and F. Ortino, eds., *Regional Trade Agreements in the WTO Legal System* (Oxford: Oxford University Press, 2006) and in M. Gehring & M. C. Cordonier Segger, eds., *Sustainable Development in World Trade Law* (The Hague: Kluwer Law International, 2005), drawing on M. C. Cordonier Segger & M. Leichner Reynal, eds., *Beyond the Barricades: The Americas Trade and Sustainability Agenda* (Aldershot: Ashgate, 2005) and M. C. Cordonier Segger, "Sustainable Development in the Negotiation of the FTAA – The Free Trade Area of the Americas: Issues and Visions for the Future Interamerican Perspectives" (2004) 27 Fordham Intl. L.J. 1118. She wishes to thank Kristin Price, CISDL Researcher, based at Cambridge University, for her significant substantive contributions, exemplary research and thorough editing skills. She also acknowledges Foreign Affairs Canada, the International Development Research Centre, the Social Sciences and Humanities

225

Christopher P.M. Waters (Ed.), *British and Canadian Perspectives on International Law*, pp. 225–253.
© 2006 *Koninklijke Brill NV. Printed in the Netherlands.*

type of forward-looking, wide-ranging bilateral trade and investment enhance-ment agreement (TIEA)." The mandate for negotiation includes the reinforce-ment of "common objectives, notably [their] shared commitment to promote sustainable development . . ."[2] which has "environmental, social and economic aspects." As "active players on sustainable development issues," they empha-sise "the important contribution that trade and investment policy can play in the development of those objectives."[3] What are current Canadian and UK/EU approaches to sustainable development in international trade law, and what innovations might be included in a new free trade agreement? It is useful to begin by considering the general meaning and status of sustainable develop-ment in international policy and law.

Development can be defined as the process of expanding people's choices, enabling improvements in collective and individual quality of life, and the exercise of full freedoms and rights.[4] These freedoms include the opportunities for individuals to utilize economic resources for the purposes of consumption, production or exchange,[5] and though development means much more than mere economic growth, the expansion of such economic opportunities are an impor-tant component of the development process.

The concept of sustainable development has gained great currency in recent years. While its underlying ideas may have governed the practices of many ancient cultures and traditions for millennia,[6] the term itself likely originated in laws and policies governing forest industry management practices.[7] According to these rules, only as much of the forest should be harvested as could re-grow each year, in order to maintain the forest as a whole (the natural capital). As

Research Council of Canada (SSHRC) and the British Chevening Award, also Prof. Armand de Mestral at the McGill University Faculty of Law and other colleagues in the SSHRC Research Group on Regional Integration Agreements, for their support and encouragement.

    [2] Europa, Canada-European Union Trade and Investment Enhancement Agreement: Framework for the Agreement: http://europa.eu.int/comm/trade/issues/bilateral/coun-tries/canada/tiea.htm.

    [3] *Ibid.* at Title 11.

    [4] See A. Sen, *Development as Freedom* (Oxford: Oxford University Press, 1999) at 35. See also United Nations Development Programme, *Human Development Reports*, available online at: http://hdr.undp.org/. Also refer to United Nations Development Programme, *Making Global Trade Work for People* (London: Earthscan Publications, 2003) at xi.

    [5] A. Sen, *ibid.* at 39.

    [6] As observed by H. E. Judge C. G. Weeramantry in his extraordinary Separate Opinion for the International Court of Justice, Advisory Opinion, *Case Concerning the Gabcikovo-Nagymaros Dam (Hungary v. Slovakia)*, I.C.J. Reports 37 I.L.M. (1998) 162.

    [7] See H. C. von Carlowitz, *Sylvicultura Oeconomica* (Leipzig: Braun, 1713).

such, the sustainable development concept, from inception, did not involve pre-venting economic activity but rather re-directing such activity, in order to ensure the potential for long-term, sustained yields from development activi-ties. The most accepted definition today, from the 1987 *Brundtland Report*, describes sustainable development as ". . . development that meets the needs of the present without compromising the ability of future generations to meet their own needs."[8] This definition may be useful for policy-making, as it is vague enough to have meaning in many diverse contexts and cultures, but it lacks pre-cision for an international legal rule. Indeed, scholarly debates continue as to whether sustainable development can be considered a principle of customary international law, and if so, what its normative effect would be.[9] This chapter does not seek to resolve these questions.[10] Rather, it starts from the recognition that the promotion of sustainable development is the explicit object and pur-pose of many binding treaties negotiated by Canada, and by the UK in its capacity as a member of the European Union, and considers how these jurisdic-tions have approached the matter in international law.

Both Canada and the UK played leading roles in the 1992 United Nations Conference on Environment and Development (UNCED) in Rio de Janeiro,[11] which attracted over 140 heads of state. In Agenda 21, one of the UNCED out-comes, states jointly called for "[t]he further development of international law

---

[8] World Commission on Environment and Development, *Our Common Future* (Oxford: Oxford University Press, 1987) at 43.

[9] As noted by V. Lowe, "the argument that sustainable development is a norm of customary international law, binding on and directing the conduct of states, and which can be applied by tribunals, is not sustainable." See V. Lowe, "Sustainable Developments and Unsustainable Arguments", in A. Boyle & D. Freestone, eds., *International Law and Sustainable Development: Past Achievements and Future Challenges* (Oxford: Oxford University Press, 1999) at 26.

[10] For further discussion, however, see M. C. Cordonier Segger & A. Khalfan, *Sustainable Development Law: Principles, Practices and Prospects* (Oxford: Oxford University Press, 2004) at 45–50 & 95–98. See also generally, D. French, *International Law and Policy of Sustainable Development* (Manchester: Manchester University Press, 2005); M. C. Cordonier Segger & Judge C. G. Weeramantry, eds., *Sustainable Justice: Reconciling Social, Economic and Environmental Law* (Leiden: Martinus Nijhoff, 2004); and A. Boyle and D. Freestone, eds., *International Law and Sustainable Development: Past Achievements and Future Challenges* (Oxford: Oxford University Press, 1999).

[11] Among the outcomes of the UNCED were several international instruments that recognise both environmental and sustainable development objectives, as well as the non-binding 1992 Rio Declaration and Agenda 21 that were adopted by governments. See *Rio Declaration on Environment and Development*, 14 June 1992, U.N.Doc.A/CONF.151/26/Rev.1 (Vol. I) at 3–8 [Rio Declaration]; reprinted in 31 I.L.M. 874 and *Report of the United Nations Conference on Environment and Development* [Agenda 21], in Rio de Janeiro, 13 August 1992, U.N. Doc. A/Conf.151/26 (Vol. II).

on sustainable development, giving special attention to the delicate balance between environmental and developmental concerns."[12] This policy resonates with an often-cited 1997 decision of the International Court of Justice which notes that the "need to reconcile economic development with protection of the environment is aptly expressed in the concept of sustainable development."[13] In 2002, in the Johannesburg Declaration on Sustainable Development, and the Johannesburg Plan of Implementation, Canada and the UK re-affirmed a collective commitment by countries to "advance and strengthen the interdependent and mutually reinforcing pillars of sustainable development – economic development, social development and environmental protection – at the local, national, regional and global levels."[14] And in the 2005 *Iron Rhine* decision, arbitrators in the Permanent Court of Arbitration[15] recognised a duty to prevent

---

[12] Agenda 21, *ibid.* at 39.1 (a).

[13] In rendering a decision in the International Court of Justice, Advisory Opinion, *Case Concerning the Gabcikovo-Nagymaros Dam (Hungary v. Slovakia)* (*supra* note 6) it was found that: "Throughout the ages, mankind has, for economic and other reasons, constantly interfered with nature. In the past, this was often done without consideration of the effects upon the environment. Owing to new scientific insights and to a growing awareness of the risks for mankind – for present and future generations of pursuit of such interventions at an unconsidered and unabated pace, new norms and standards have been developed, set forth in a great number of instruments during the last two decades. Such new norms have to be taken into consideration, and such new standards given proper weight, not only when States contemplate new activities but also when continuing with activities begun in the past. This need to reconcile economic development with protection of the environment is aptly expressed in the concept of sustainable development." For discussion, see V. Lowe, "Sustainable Development and Unsustainable Arguments", in A. Boyle & D. Freestone, *International Law and Sustainable Development: Past Achievements and Future Challenges* (Oxford: Oxford University Press, 1999) at 36. See also A. Boyle & D. Freestone, *International Law and Sustainable Development: Past Achievements and Future Challenges* (Oxford: Oxford University Press, 1999) at 16–18.

[14] 2002 Johannesburg Declaration, in Report of the World Summit on Sustainable Development, 26 August–4 September 2002, UN Doc. A/AC.257/32 at 5.

[15] The Permanent Court of Arbitration reaffirmed the imperative of balancing socio-economic development with environmental protection in its Arbitral Award for the *Arbitration Regarding the Iron Rhine ("IJzeren Rijn") Railway (Belgium v. Netherlands)*, 24 May 2005 at 59, 114 referring to the "notion . . . of sustainable development", stating that: "[e]nvironmental law and the law on development stand not as alternatives but as mutually reinforcing, integral concepts, which require that where development may cause significant harm to the environment, there is a duty to prevent, or at least mitigate such harm. . . . This duty, in the opinion of the Tribunal, has now become a principle of general international law. This principle applies not only in autonomous activities but also in activities undertaken in implementation of specific treaties between the Parties."

or mitigate harm to the environment in international law, and suggested that in accordance with the notion of sustainable development, parties must take this duty into account when implementing economic development treaties.

In spite of this guidance in international policy and law, it is still not always clear what states mean when they commit to sustainable development in a treaty or other legal instrument. Two countries which have made progress on this issue in the past decade, particularly with regard to the role of trade agreements in supporting sustainable development, are the UK and Canada. Both have accepted the objective of sustainable development in different trade and economic integration agreements over the years, including the 1994 North American Free Trade Agreement, the 1994 Agreement Establishing the World Trade Organization and the 2002 Treaty Establishing the European Communities, as well as several bilateral Free Trade Agreements (FTAs). To understand how this objective might be argued or implemented in trade law, it is useful to look to the FTAs which Canada and the UK have agreed to since the 1992 Earth Summit. The rest of this chapter briefly discusses the negotiation processes and texts of Canadian and UK trade treaties that explicitly recognise sustainable development as an objective, and considers how these treaties can contribute to "development that is sustainable",[16] by "integrating economic and social development and environmental protection."[17]

2) Canadian and British Positions on Sustainable Development in Trade Treaties

Both Canada and the UK have committed to addressing sustainable development in their trade policies and practices. This policy is reflected in their statements of principles for trade and economic development, and by the inclusion of trade and investment sections in their sustainable development strategies.

a) *Canadian Policies on Sustainable Development and Trade*

The Canadian position on the role of trade law in sustainable development was explained in a recent policy publication, the *Sustainable Development Strategy*

---

[16] WTO, Report of the Panel on: *United States – Import Prohibition of Certain Shrimp and Shrimp Products Recourse to Article 21.5 of the DSU by Malaysia*, adopted on 21 November 2001, WT/DS58/RW, 6481 as upheld by the Appellate Body Report, WT/DS58/AB/RW, DSR 2001:XIII, 6529 at footnote 202 [*US-Shrimp (Article 21.5)*]. See discussion below.

[17] WTO, Appellate Body Report, *United States – Import Prohibition of Certain Shrimp and Shrimp Products*, adopted on 6 November 1998, WT/DS58/AB/R, DSR 1998:VII, 2755 at footnote 107 [*US-Shrimp*]. See discussion below.

2004–2006.[18] At Goal 2, Canada specifically commits to endorse and strengthen sustainable development objectives, as "both an international priority and a value to which Canadians are committed."[19]

The *Sustainable Development Strategy* declares that Canada is an active player in the World Trade Organization (WTO) and that international trade "provides each country with an opportunity to better utilize its resources through engaging in specialization and maximizing its comparative advantage."[20] Closely following Canada's commitment to Agenda 21,[21] the Canadian policy reaffirms the imperative of "working towards more open [and] predictable, rules-based markets."[22] The policy statement explains that in Canada's view, trade enhances economic efficiency, which in turn contributes to economic growth, greater productivity and higher incomes – and these contribute to sustainable development.[23] The proliferation of goods, services, technologies and ideas is seen as a route to both prosperity and development. The policy statement envisages a "global system of interdependence that helps promote peace and stability worldwide,"[24] suggesting that a global trading system can advance sustainable development by supporting environmental standards, improving labour standards and respect for human rights, and generating additional resources for social policies.[25] It also asserts that in Canada's view, trade and environmental rules and objectives should be mutually supportive.[26] International Trade Canada and Foreign Affairs Canada are tasked with "identify[ing] ways to integrate sustainable development into the policies and ongoing work programs of the international organizations to which [Canada] belong[s] and also into [Canada's] international initiatives."[27] It states directly that International Trade Canada has "a unique role to play in promoting all three pillars of sustainable development in [Canadian] bilateral, regional and multilateral relations."[28]

---

[18] Canada, Department of Foreign Affairs, *Sustainable Development Strategy 2004–2006: Agenda 2006* (Ottawa: DFAIT, 2005): http://www.dfait-maeci.gc.ca/sustain/sd-dd/menu-en.asp.

[19] *Ibid.* at Goal 2.

[20] *Ibid.*

[21] Agenda 21, *supra* note 11.

[22] *Supra note* 18 at Goal 2.

[23] *Ibid.*

[24] *Ibid.*

[25] *Ibid.*

[26] *Ibid.*

[27] *Ibid.*

[28] *Ibid.*

b) *UK and EU Policies on Sustainable Development and Trade*

The UK considers sustainable development to be a fundamental principle underpinning policy initiatives, and is clear that the concept implies encouraging cooperation between social, economic and environmental policy initiatives. According to *Securing the Future*, the UK's 2005 policy statement on sustainable development, "sustainable development is about wealth creation, environmental protection and social justice going hand in hand."[29] Two particular elements of sustainable development – poverty eradication and intra/inter-generational equity – figure prominently in the statement.[30] The UK advocates a truly integrated vision of sustainable development encompassed in five principles: "living within environmental limits; ensuring a strong, healthy and just society; achieving a sustainable economy; promoting good governance; and using sound science responsibly."[31] With regards to economic liberalization, the statement notes the need to foster linkages between trade and sustainable development: "internationally we need to promote the mutual supportiveness of trade liberalisation, environmental protection and sustainable development to help developing countries."[32]

The commitment is reaffirmed in trade policy. After public input and extensive stakeholder consultation, the Department of International Trade published a *Sustainable Development Strategy* in 2000. Though it is mainly focused on domestic initiatives, the strategy commits to *inter alia*: "extend an open and rules based multilateral trading system; improve market access for developing countries; promote mutual supportiveness of trade liberalisation, environmental protection and sustainable development; minimise any negative impacts of trade liberalisation for developing countries; and to reduce level of trade distorting subsidies, particularly in agriculture and fisheries."[33]

The UK is a member of the European Community and hosted an EU Sustainable Development Network Meeting in July 2005 as a part of its recent Presidency. The UK supports the EU Sustainable Development Strategy, while also seeking to strengthen and more effectively operationalize it.[34] The EU

---

[29] U.K., Department of International Trade, *UK Policy Statement on Trade and Environment*: http://www.dti.gov.uk/sustainability/sus/sd.htm.

[30] U.K., Department of International Trade, *Securing the Future: Delivering UK Sustainable Development Strategy* (London: DTI, 2005): http://www.sustainable-development.gov.uk/documents/publications/strategy/SecFut_complete.pdf.

[31] *Ibid.*

[32] *Ibid.*

[33] U.K., Department of International Trade, *Sustainable Development: The Government's Approach – Delivering UK Sustainable Development Together*: http://www.sustainable-development.gov.uk/delivery/international/index.htm.

[34] U.K., Department of International Trade, *Review of the EU Sustainable*

engages in many capacity-building activities specifically related to trade and designed to "make trade an integral part of national development policies, programmes, and poverty reduction strategies."[35] With the philosophy that "accompanied by the proper flanking policies and if used correctly, trade policies can provide opportunities for promoting economic development and tackling poverty reduction,"[36] the EU takes a multifaceted approach to embedding sustainable development measures in trade agreements and forums. Moreover, the EU works to link trade and social development by advocating the (voluntary) inclusion of the issue in the Trade Policy Review Mechanism (TPRM) for WTO members and by supporting further co-operation between international organizations involved in sustainable development activities.[37]

3) Operationalizing Canadian and UK Policies on Sustainable Development in Trade Treaties

There are several ways that Canadian and UK/EU sustainable development strategies have made their way into the negotiation procedures and the texts of actual trade treaties agreed by Canada and the European Communities (for the UK). In particular, the Canada – Chile Free Trade Agreement,[38] the Canada – Costa Rica Free Trade Agreement,[39] the EU – Mexico Association Agreement,[40] and the EU – Chile Association Agreement[41] incorporate sustainable develop-

---

Development Strategy – UK Conclusions and Recommendations: http://www.sustainable-development.gov.uk/international/eu/documents/eu-sds-review-uk-response-final.pdf.

[35] EC, *External Trade: Trade and Development*: http://europa.eu.int/comm/trade/issues/global/development/index_en.htm December 2005.

[36] *Ibid.*

[37] EC, *External Trade: Trade and Social Conditions*: http://europa.eu.int/comm/trade/issues/global/social/index_en.htm January 2006.

[38] Canada-Chile Free Trade Agreement, 5 December 1996, 36 I.L.M. 1067: http://www.sice.oas.org/tradee.asp#canchi.

[39] Canada-Costa Rica Free Trade Agreement, implemented by means of the *Canada-Costa Rica Free Trade Agreement Implementation Act*, S.C. 2001, c.28 (in force 1 November 2002): http://www.sice.oas.org/Trade/cancr/English/cancrin.asp.

[40] EC, *Economic Partnership, Political Coordination and Cooperation Agreement between the European Community and its Member States, of the one part, and the United Mexican States, of the other part*, [2000] O.J.L. 276/45 (adopted on 8 October 1997): http://europa.eu.int/comm/external_relations/mexico/doc/a3_acuerdo_en.pdf 1 March 2006.

[41] EC, *Council Decision of 18 November 2002 on the signature and provisional application of certain provisions of an Agreement establishing an association between the European Community and its Member States, of the one part, and the Republic of*

ment as either an objective, or a principle, and can be compared. The processes and provisions used by these countries in these accords can shed light on the approaches of these two countries to this objective in trade law.

a) *Environmental and Sustainability Impact Assessments of Trade Agreements*

Sustainable development is factored into Canadian and UK / EU approaches to trade agreements before trade agreements are finalised, through the use of new procedures to take environmental, social and economic sustainability issues into account in trade negotiations. One particularly important procedural tool is *ex-ante* impact assessment of trade rules. Critics of trade agreements have warned that the economic growth stimulated by a trade agreement may have significant negative impacts on social and environmental sustainability.[42] Partly in response to this pressure, Canada and the UK/EU have developed national and regional environmental impact assessments to identify potential impacts and either mitigate or prevent them.[43] Social development or human rights impact assessments can also be conducted.[44] Further, social and environmental impacts can be considered together in an assessment, using integrated or 'sustainability impact assessments' that are usually applied to specific chapters of a trade agreement, sector by sector.[45] While not all sustainability impact assessments include a strong social dimension, it is becoming increasingly accepted to do so.[46]

Chile, of the other part – Final Act, [2002] O.J.L. L352/1 (adopted on 30 December 2002): http://europa.eu.int/eur-lex/pri/en/oj/dat/2002/l_352/l_35220021230en00010002.pdf.

[42] See *e.g.*, The Public Citizen, *Global Trade Watch: Promoting Democracy by Challenging Corporate Globalization*: http://www.citizen.org/trade/nafta/; Stop CAFTA: http://www.stopcafta.org/ 23 February 2006; Anti-GATT: http://www.gatt.org/.

[43] UN, Environment Programme, *Reference Manual for the Integrated Assessment of Trade-Related Policies* (Geneva: UNEP, 2001).

[44] S. Walker, "Human Rights Impact Assessments of Trade-Related Policies" in M. Gehring & M. C. Cordonier Segger, eds., *Sustainable Development in World Trade Law* (The Hague: Kluwer Law International, 2005) at 217–256.

[45] C. Kirkpatrick, N. Lee & O. Morrissey, *WTO New Round: Sustainability Impact Assessment Study (Phase Two Report): Sustainability Impact Assessment – Executive Summary* (University of Manchester, Institute for Development Policy and Management and Environmental Impact Assessment Centre, 18 November 1999) (financed by the EC): http://fs2.idpm.man.ac.uk/sia/Phase2/EXSUMFINAL.

[46] H. Blanco, "Evaluacion de la sustentabilidad de los acuerdos comerciales y su aplicacion en el contexto latinoamericano y del ALCA", in H. Blanco, M. Araya &

The UK, as part of the EU, benefits from a fairly sophisticated approach to the assessment of trade agreements' impacts on sustainable development. The 2004 *European Union Sustainability Impact Assessment* states that: "Trade is one of the many policy areas that where decisions can have potentially wide-ranging impacts on the economy, social development and environment that can be both positive and negative for sustainability."[47] The EC's Sustainability Impact Assessment (SIA) Programme, was launched in 1999 to identify sustainability impacts of its current and future trade negotiations. The SIA Programme integrates economic, environmental and social sustainability concerns into the development of trade policy. To carry out these SIAs, the EC has developed methodologies to assess environmental impacts of trade agreements, to identify and enhance projected economic, social and environmental gains, and to mitigate or avoid any negative impacts. SIAs are transboundary in scope: experts analyze environmental and social impacts of trade domestically and on their trading partners.

Each SIA typically involves screening and scoping of economic, social and environmental indicators, impact assessment in all three areas, and recommendations on possible flanking measures. There are two scenarios assessed: the 'base scenario' represents full implementation of existing agreements, in contrast to the 'further liberalization scenario' which encompasses the strongest probable implementation of trade liberalization measures.[48] In the EU-Chile Association Agreement, the SIA sought to identify the long-term social, economic and environmental repercussions of the new Agreement. It sought to optimise outcomes "through the definition of measures aimed at mitigating any negative impacts and enhancing any positive ramifications of trade".[49] It found impacts and benefits in all three areas of sustainable development policy-making. In terms of economic sustainability, the analysis indicated that the Agreement would likely reinforce existing growth trends in Chile, but would not precipitate growth in excess of a normal year's prosperity.[50] It found that Chile's areas of comparative advantage (i.e. processed foods, agriculture, wood, pulp and paper and chemicals) would likely experience increased demand, along with

C. Murillo, *ALCA y medio ambiente: Ideas desde Latinoamerica* (Santiago de Chile: CIPMA/GETS/CINPE, 2003).

[47] EC, *Trade Issues: Sustainability Impact Assessment*: http://europa.eu.int/comm/trade/issues/global/sia/index_en.htm 2 March 2006.

[48] *Ibid.*

[49] Plantistat Luxembourg, *Sustainable Impact Assessment (SIA) of the trade aspects of negotiations for an Association Agreement between the European Communities and Chile (Specific agreement No. 11)*, October 2002 (financed by the EC): http://www.siagcc.org/gcc/download/_sa_nbr1_final_dec_2002.pdf.

[50] *Ibid.* at 12.

the service sector,[51] while steel, motor vehicles and other machinery sectors might be hurt by the accord.[52] In terms of social sustainability, the SIA noted that the combination of increases in total employment and a reduction in prices relative to wages in Chile would help to enhance the standard of living and reduce poverty among the majority of the urban population.[53] However, Chile's "dual economy" and stratified social structure meant that the plight of women and those involved in traditional economic activities (i.e. artisanal fishermen) may not improve.[54] Health and education indicators would likely remain static while agriculture sector workers quality of life might be affected.[55] In terms of environmental sustainability, impacts would depend on the effects of new industrialization technologies, but in general, the SIA suggested that impacts would outweigh benefits for air, water and land quality (e.g. agricultural intensification and mining).[56] Forest sector impacts could be slightly positive (due to new investment), and the Agreement's effects on fishing are largely predicated on domestic regulation.[57] The prospective impacts on biodiversity would be contingent on how energy infrastructure is expanded, in addition to tourism practices.[58] The SIA recommended a strong role for the EU in mitigation and enhancement, and that the EU needed to act "as a source of support where new resources are required for research; and as a partner in a two-way EU-Chile mutual education dialogue in those situations where a consensus is still to be built within Chile."[59]

The Canadians also undertake impact assessments of trade, though their programmes focus only on environmental impacts to date, and only environmental impacts in Canada are assessed. In 1999, Canada introduced the strategic environmental assessment of plans and policies (SEA). The 1999 Cabinet Directive on the Environmental Assessment of Policy, Plan and Program Proposals[60] mandated that every governmental policy should be assessed as to its environmental impact. Trade policy was listed (Annex 1 of the Cabinet Directive)

---

[51] *Ibid.*

[52] *Ibid.*

[53] *Ibid.*

[54] *Ibid.*

[55] *Ibid.*

[56] *Ibid.*

[57] *Ibid.* at 14.

[58] *Ibid.*

[59] *Ibid.* at 15.

[60] Canada, Canadian Environmental Assessment Agency, *Strategic Environmental Assessment – The 1999 Cabinet Directive on the Environmental Assessment of Policy, Plan and Program Proposals; Guidelines for Implementing the Cabinet Directive (Evaluation environnementale stratégique)* (Ottawa: CEAA, 1999): http://www.ceaa. gc.ca/016/directive_e.htm.

because the Canadian Environmental Assessment Act (CEAA) is not applicable to this area.[61] Building on early binding guidelines,[62] a Cabinet Decision on Environmental Assessment of Trade Negotiations was adopted in February 2001.[63] Foreign Affairs Canada has also developed methodologies to conduct EAs of its Foreign Investment Protection Agreements (FIPAs).[64] As the terminology suggests, the Canadian EAs focus almost exclusively on environmental issues. It is considered an important decision-making tool for promoting sustainable development, as EAs seek "to assist Canadian negotiators integrate environmental considerations into the negotiating process by providing information on the environmental impacts of the proposed trade agreement; and to address public concerns by documenting how environmental factors are being considered in the course of trade negotiations."[65] In recognition of the goal that "the public needs to be well informed, properly consulted and engaged on trade issues,"[66] it contributes to "more open decision-making within the federal government by engaging representatives from other levels of government, the public, the private sector and non-governmental organizations in this process."[67]

Canada is part of the NAFTA, and its commitment to undertake such assessments is reflected in one of the NAFTA Side Agreements, the North American Agreement about Environmental Cooperation, which contains the obligation to assess environmental effects of the NAFTA. The Commission on Environmental Cooperation is institutionally separate from the NAFTA Commission. However, according to Art.10.6 d) of the NAAEC, the Council of Ministers of the CEC is responsible for "considering on an ongoing basis the environmental effects of the NAFTA" in cooperation with the NAFTA Commission.[68] While

---

[61] To get a sense of the history, see Canadian Environmental Assessment Agency, *The Canadian Environmental Assessment Act – Introduction*: http://www.ceaa.gc.ca/013/intro_e.htm; complete text at: http://www.ceaa.gc.ca/013/ceaa-2003.pdf.

[62] Canada, Department of International Trade, *Framework for Conducting Environmental Assessments of Trade Negotiations*: http://www.dfait-maeci.gc.ca/tna-nac/EAF_Sep2000–en.asp 25 Aug 2005.

[63] *Ibid.*

[64] Canadian Environmental Assessments consist of three phases. In an initial Environmental Assessment, the assessment team analyses the scope of the negotiations and potential environmental effects. If these are found to be minimal, no formal assessment is undertaken. If potential effects are found, a draft EA is prepared, followed by a final EA. All stages contain extensive public participation requirements. The draft EA is intended to assist the Canadian trade negotiators. The final EA assesses the result of the trade negotiations and how the EAs have influenced it. Ex-post monitoring and assessment might be recommended but are not mandatory.

[65] *Supra note* 62 at 4.

[66] *Ibid.* at Goal 2.

[67] *Ibid.* at 3.

[68] J. Barr, "Final Analytical Framework to Assess the Environmental effects of

seeking broad public participation,[69] the CEC studied methodological approaches[70] and tested them in case studies,[71] leading the CEC Ministerial Council to adopt an Analytic Framework for Assessing the Environmental Effects of NAFTA.[72] The Analytical Framework has since been applied in three case studies, examining Mexican corn, beef production in the United States and in Canada and the electricity market in all three countries.[73] While environmental assessments were not done for either the Canada-Chile Free Trade Agreement, or the Canada-Costa Rica Free Trade Agreement, an Initial Environmental Assessment was carried out for the Canada-Chile Government Procurement Chapter to be added to the Canada-Chile Free Trade Agreement.[74] The ministry concluded that there were no significant environmental impacts in Canada to be expected from the addition of a public procurement chapter to the FTA and thus refrained from conducting a draft EA.

The impact assessments, as well as other reasons, led Canada and the EC to set sustainable development as either objectives, or principles, for various trade agreements. They may also have led to the inclusion of innovative substantive provisions in the accords.[75] In this chapter, only a few of the most common provisions are briefly surveyed, drawing on examples from the NAFTA,[76] the Canada-Chile Free Trade Agreement,[77] the Canada-Costa Rica Free Trade

---

NAFTA", in WWF & Fundación Futuro Latinoamericano, *The International Experts' Meeting on Sustainability Assessments of Trade Liberalisation – Quito, Ecuador 6–8 March 2000, Full Meeting Report* (Gland: WWF, 2000) at 100.

[69] *Ibid.* at iii.

[70] Commission for Environmental Cooperation, *Building a Framework for Assessing NAFTA Environmental Effects – Report of a Workshop held in La Jolla, California, on April 29 and 30, 1996* (Montreal: CEC, 1996).

[71] Commission for Environmental Cooperation, *Analytic Framework for Assessing the Environmental Effects of the North American Free Trade Agreement* (Montreal: CEC, 1999): www.cec.org/files/pdf/ECONOMY/Frmwrk-e_EN.pdf.

[72] *Ibid.*

[73] *Ibid.* at 65.

[74] Canada, Department of International Trade, *Initial Environmental Assessment of the Canada-Chile Government Procurement Chapter to be added to the Canada-Chile Free Trade Agreement*: http://www.dfait-maeci.gc.ca/tna-nac/RB/report_chile-en.asp October 2005.

[75] See M. C. Cordonier Segger, "The WTO, RTAs and Sustainable Development" in L. Bartels & F. Ortino, *supra* note 1. See also Gehring & Cordonier Segger, *supra* note 1 and Cordonier Segger & Leichner Reynal, *supra* note 1.

[76] North American Free Trade Agreement (11, 17 December 1993), (1993) 32 I.L.M. 289 (parts 1–2 of agreement), (1993) 32 I.L.M. 605 (parts 4–8 of agreement) [NAFTA]: http://www.sice.oas.org/trade/nafta.asp.

[77] *Supra* note 38.

Agreement,[78] the EU-Mexico Association Agreement,[79] and the EU-Chile Association Agreement.[80]

b) *Sustainable Development Objectives Recognized in Trade Treaty Preambles*

The Preamble of the Canada-Chile Free Trade Agreement states "The Government of Canada and the Government of the Republic of Chile (Chile), resolved to . . . promote sustainable development . . . have agreed as follows . . ."[81] The Canada-Costa Rica Free Trade Agreement similarly recognises this joint objective. In the EU-Chile Association Agreement, and the EU-Mexico Association Agreement, the Parties agreed on "the need to promote economic and social progress for their peoples, taking into account the principle of sustainable development and environmental protection requirements."[82] Article 1 on Principles also states that the "promotion of sustainable economic and social development and the equitable distribution of the benefits of the Association are guiding principles for the implementation of this Agreement."[83] These explicit resolutions set the promotion of sustainable development as an objective of these FTAs, among other priorities (such as to create new employment opportunities and improve working conditions and living standards; to strengthen the development and enforcement of environmental laws and regulations; to preserve their flexibility to safeguard the public welfare, etc.). But how can this objective be rendered operational? What kinds of provisions, in a regional or bi-lateral trade agreement, can be included to promote sustainable development?

c) *Exceptions for Social Development and Environmental Measures*

As mentioned above, sustainable development involves seeking 'mutual supportiveness' between economic, environmental and social regimes. At a minimum, for a trade regime to 'promote sustainable development', it seems obvious that it should not directly conflict with the rules of other multilateral regimes that seek to achieve sustainable development, or unduly constrain the

---

[78] *Supra* note 39.
[79] *Supra* note 40.
[80] *Supra* note 41.
[81] *Supra* note 38 at Preamble.
[82] *Supra* note 38 at Preamble; *supra* note 40 at Preamble.
[83] *Ibid.* at art. 1.

adoption of legitimate measures to achieve the goals of these regimes. An 'exceptions' provision, modelled on the GATT Article XX,[84] is commonly included in trade treaties to provide space for certain types of legitimate government measures which trade policies might otherwise limit or constrain. If an otherwise inconsistent measure can be shown (by the party claiming the exception) to fall under certain limited exceptions, and also to comply with a 'chapeau' which requires that it does not result in arbitrary or unjustifiable discrimination and does not constitute disguised protectionism, it will be permitted by the FTA. In the section on trade, Article 91 of the EU-Chile Association Agreement contains an exception similar to the one found in GATT, Article XX. As part of the EU-Mexico Association Agreement process, a Decision establishing free trade in goods contains the same exception at Article 22.[85] The Canadian FTAs contain an expanded version of this exception. For example, the Canada-Chile FTA at Article 22.1(1) demonstrates the approach chosen by the Parties:

> Article XXXX: General Exceptions 1. For purposes of Chapters Two through Seven … Article XX of the GATT 1994 and its interpretive notes are incorporated into and made part of this Agreement, *mutatis mutandis*. The Parties understand that the measures referred to in Article XX(b) of the GATT 1994 *include environmental measures* necessary to protect human, animal, or plant life or health, and that Article XX(g) of the GATT 1994 applies to measures relating to the conservation of *living and non-living* exhaustible natural resources [emphasis added].

As such, in the Canadian FTAs, there is an exception for measures that would otherwise violate the terms of the FTA which incorporates Article XX of GATT 1994 and its interpretive notes, with certain specific refinements that 'broaden' the scope of the article to cover, specifically, environmental measures, and living and non-living natural resources.

---

[84] General Agreement on Tariffs and Trade 1994, adopted 15 April 1994, Marrakesh Agreement Establishing the World Trade Organization, Annex 1A, 1867 U.N.T.S. 187, 33 I.L.M. 1153 (1994) at art. XX, which reads: "Subject to the requirement that such measures are not applied in a manner which would constitute a means of arbitrary or unjustifiable discrimination between countries where the same conditions prevail, or a disguised restriction on international trade, nothing in this Agreement shall be construed to prevent the adoption or enforcement by any contracting party of measures: . . . *(b)* necessary to protect human, animal or plant life or health; . . . *(g)* relating to the conservation of exhaustible natural resources if such measures are made effective in conjunction with restrictions on domestic production or consumption . . ."

[85] EC, Decision No. 2/2000 of the EC-Mexico Joint Council of 23 March 2000 [2000] O.J.L. 2000/415: http://europa.eu.int/comm/external_relations/mexico/doc/a4_dec_02–2000_en.pdf.

d) *Parallel cooperation agreements on environmental and social matters*

A second approach to ensure that an FTA contributes to sustainable development was pioneered with the NAFTA, and has continued to be developed in other Canadian trade treaties. This approach involves developing 'value-added' cooperative agreements during trade treaty negotiations, typically addressing labour and environment issues. The Canadian Policy Statement commits that "work will continue with regional and bilateral partners to address sustainable development issues of mutual concern.[86] It explains that "[o]ne practical way to do this is to negotiate environmental and labour agreements at the same time as bilateral and regional trade agreements are negotiated."[87] Indeed, in Canadian negotiations with various countries in recent years, this 'practical way' has yielded clear results. Each of Canada's trade agreements has led to the negotiation of parallel accords on labour and environmental issues.

With regards to social development and labour rights, the first side agreement was the North American Agreement on Labour Cooperation (NAALC), which commits to "improve working conditions and living standards" in all parties, to "protect, enhance and enforce basic workers' rights", through eleven core labour principles.[88] A similar model is used by the 1997 Canada-Chile Labour Cooperation Agreement (CCLCA). Under the CCLCA, Parties commit to maintain and improve labour standards, to effectively enforce their labour law and other guarantees,[89] and create a Commission for Labour Cooperation structured similar to the one in the NAALC.[90] The CCLCA has two main components: a Cooperative Work Program and a procedure for handling issues of concern. Similar to the NAALC, if differences arise, the CCLCA provides for cooperative consultations, independent evaluations, and ultimately, a dispute resolution process. An assessed contribution, which goes into a fund to improve matters, can be levied if a party loses a dispute.[91] While the Canada-Costa Rica

---

[86] Canada, Department of Foreign Affairs, *Sustainable Development Strategy 2004–2006: Agenda 2006*: http://www.dfait-maeci.gc.ca/sustain/sd-dd/menu-en.asp February 2004.

[87] *Ibid.* at Goal 2.

[88] Refer to Article 1 of NAFTA, *supra* note 76: http://www.nafta.org.

[89] See Canada, Department of Human Resources Development, *First Annual Report: Canada-Chile Agreement On Labour Cooperation* (July 1997–June 1998): http://www. labour-travail.hrdc-drhc.gc.ca/doc/ialc-cidt/eng/e/backen.htm#background.

[90] *Ibid.*

[91] See Canada, Department of Human Resources Development, Ministerial Council, *Report on the Three-Year Review of the Canada-Chile Agreement on Labour Cooperation* (Ottawa: HRDC, 2002): http://www.labour-travail.hrdc-rhc.gc.ca/psait_spila/aicdt_ialc/2003_2004/report_english.htm.

Labour Cooperation Agreement (CCRLCA) is structured in a way that parallels the NAALC and CCLCA, there are certain areas where differences are obvious. Administratively, the CCRLCA is much simpler, and does not include provisions for national secretariats, evaluation committees of experts or panel rosters, in order to be simpler to implement for a Party with less administrative capacity. In terms of scope and coverage, all three agreements cover eleven principles and rights. However, the CCRLCA obligations, in Annex 1, are directly related to the 1998 ILO Declaration on Fundamental Principles and Rights at Work, which came into effect after the Canada-Chile LCA and the NAALC. Review procedures also apply to all of Annex 1, so the difference in the area of consultations relates to the scope as well. In the NAALC and the CCLCA, the complaints processes apply to only three areas of enforcement. There are also differences with regard to the issues covered by general and ministerial consultations and, with regard to arbitral panels, the CCRLCA does not provide for monetary fines.[92] Finally, in terms of cooperative activities, the developmental component of the CCRLCA seems stronger than in the CCLCA or the NAALC.

Environmental agreements/chapters seek to facilitate cooperation on environmental protection objectives, including the strengthening of environmental laws and regulations. An early model is the North American Agreement on Environmental Cooperation between Canada, Mexico and the United States, which has been well documented in academic literature.[93] Similarly, the Canada-Chile Agreement on Environmental Cooperation (CCAEC) also provides a framework for bilateral cooperation on environmental issues, committing the parties to effectively enforce their environmental laws and work

---

[92] Communication with Dale Whiteside (Deputy Director, Strategic Trade Policy, Department of Foreign Affairs and International Trade Canada) 26 June 2003, on file with author.

[93] This accord makes environmental integrity a priority, recognizing as objectives the need to "foster the protection and improvement of the environment in the territories of the Parties for the well-being of present and future generations" as well as to "increase cooperation between the Parties to better conserve, protect, and enhance the environment, including wild flora and fauna." Refer to the *North American Agreement for Environmental Cooperation*, adopted 1 January 1994, 32 I.L.M. 1480 [NAAEC]: http://www.cec.org; see M. C. Cordonier Segger "Enhancing Social and Environmental Cooperation in the Americas" in M. C. Cordonier Segger & M. Leichner Reynal, *supra* note 1 at 183–222, as well as C. Deere & D. Esty, eds., *Greening the Americas: NAFTA's Lessons for Hemispheric Trade* (Cambridge, MA: MIT Press, 2002). See also A. de Mestral, "The NAFTA Commission on Environmental Cooperation – Voice for the North American Environment?" in A. Kiss, D. Shelton & K. Ishibashi, eds., *Economic Globalization and Compliance with International Environmental Agreements*, Int'l Environmental Law and Policy Series 63 (The Hague: Kluwer Law International, 2003).

cooperatively to protect and enhance the environment and promote sustainable development.[94] The CCAEC provides a commission for environmental cooperation, the provision of environmental information and a joint public advisory council process.[95] It obliges parties to consider implementing limits to specific pollutants, to the export of domestically prohibited substances, to notify each other of domestic limits or restrictions, ensure transparency through publication and access to justice and finally to include procedural guarantees. It contains provisions for private access to remedies, establishes national secretariats to implement its mandate and recognises any prior commitments under other environmental agreements. The annexes, which phase in the application of the Agreement to Chilean environmental law, led to a comprehensive and valuable revision of environmental law in Chile.[96] The Canada-Costa Rica Environmental Cooperation Agreement focuses more on environmental information exchange and capacity building in the area of environmental enforcement and monitoring.[97] This Agreement contains similar provisions to the CCCAE, but has a stronger focus on access to environmental information and capacity-building for environmental policy and law-makers.[98] Rather than an enforcement process, it includes provisions granting rights to any citizen or non-governmental organisation (NGO) to request information from any party on the effective implementation of environmental law in its territory and the duty to respond to this request (including making summaries of the question and response publicly available), the appointment of focal points for the communication between any party and the public on matters related to the implementation of the cooperation agreement,[99] and the development of mechanisms to inform and involve, when appropriate, the public in the activities carried out under the Agreement.[100]

---

[94] Series of interviews with A. Bowcott (Manager, Environment Canada, International Relations Canada, and Canada's Chief Negotiator for the Canada – Chile, Canada – Costa Rica, Canada – Central America Environmental Side Agreements) January – April, 2003, on file with author.

[95] W. Durbin, *A Comparison of the Environmental Provisions of the NAFTA, the Canada-Chile Trade Agreement and the Mexican-European Community Trade Agreement* (New Haven: Yale Centre for Environmental Law and Policy, 2000).

[96] The Agreement on Environmental Cooperation between the Governments of Canada and the Republic of Chile, adopted 6 February 1997, 36 I.L.M. 1196, at art. 2,10, ss.1–2: http://www.sice.oas.org/trade/chican_e/chcatoc.asp#environ.

[97] E. Gitli & C. Murillo, "A Latin American Agenda for a Trade and Environment Link in the FTAA", in C. Deere & D. Esty, *supra* note 93.

[98] See the Agreement on Environmental Cooperation between the Government of Canada and the Government of the Republic of Costa Rica, adopted 23 April 2001: http://www.sice.oas.org/Trade/cancr/English/enve.asp.

[99] *Ibid.* at art. 10.

[100] *Ibid.* at art. 11.

The EU-Mexico Association Agreement uses a different, more integrated model. It is premised on "respect for democratic principles and fundamental human rights"[101] through cooperation and political dialogue.[102] The Agreement reaffirms the need to preserve the environmental and ecological balances, and commits to:

> Promote the conservation and sustainable management of natural resources; develop, spread and exchange information and experience on environmental legislation; stimulate the use of economic incentives to promote compliance; strengthen environmental management at all levels of government; and develop channels for social participation.[103]

It commits to collaborate to fight poverty and advance social justice by harmonizing economic and social development targeted at vulnerable groups and regions (specifically indigenous populations, the rural poor and women subsisting on low incomes).[104] It also considers refugees, human rights and democracy as priorities. Assisting the development of civil society through education, training and public awareness programs; strengthening the rule of law and institutional efficacy; and advocating human rights and democratic principles are all endeavours laid out in the text.[105] Health measures evident in the Agreement include administrative amelioration and promoting projects to improve the health conditions and social welfare in both rural and urban areas.[106] The EU-Chile Association Agreement is similar in scope. The Agreement addresses human rights and democratic principles,[107] promoting the rule of law and good governance, and achieving environmental protection and social progress within the sustainable development paradigm.[108] As in the EU-Mexico Agreement, strengthening reciprocal dialogue and cooperative projects is at the core of the accord. Article 24 lists steps to be taken to enhance cooperation on issues related to agriculture and rural sectors, rather than simply Sanitary and Phytosanitary ("SPS") measures. It affirms the need to support sustainable agriculture practices and foster rural development, through capacity building, and infrastructure and technology transfer.[109] Moreover, on a related topic, the EU and Chile plan to pool their expertise and resources in the following areas related to environmental protection and poverty eradication:

---

[101] *Supra* note 40.
[102] *Ibid.* at art. 1–3.
[103] *Ibid.* at art. 34.
[104] *Ibid.* at art. 36.
[105] *Ibid.* at art. 39.
[106] *Ibid.* at art. 42.
[107] *Supra* note 41 at art. 2.
[108] *Ibid.* at Preamble.
[109] *Ibid.* at art. 24.

Studies to assess environmental impact of economic activities (especially land use management); projects to reinforce Chile's environmental structures and policies; exchanges of information, technology and experience in areas including environmental standards and models, training and education; environmental education and training to involve citizens more; and technical assistance and joint regional research programs.[110]

The Agreement stresses the importance of supporting educational opportunities at all levels with special attention paid to vulnerable population segments.[111] The preservation, optimal management and promotion of traditional culture is deemed to be essential as is advancing the role of women; modernizing labour relations; improving the formulation and management of social policies; developing an efficient and equitable health system; improving land management policies; and developing mechanisms for civic participation.[112] Both accords clearly address cooperation on sustainable development, among other social and political objectives, in the broadest possible way.

In these FTAs, there is the potential for such parallel environmental and social cooperation accords to be part of the overall agenda-setting process, but also the need for further analysis on what kind of cooperation agendas and instruments are possible and necessary, their mandates, financing and coordination with existing institutions.[113]

e) *Specific operational provisions*

Beyond the exceptions and the parallel side agreement/chapter approach, a more strategic method is beginning to evolve in order to address instances where specific provisions related to the same subject-matter in the FTA/AAs and other treaties related to sustainable development might overlap, constraining policy choices and affecting the potential for effective implementation of social and environmental commitments. When trade, environment and social development regimes overlap, there is seldom a direct conflict of positive obligations, though some parties may see rights gained in one regime limited by commitments in the *lex posteriori*. However, trade rules may work formally or informally to constrain the use of social or environmental measures, affecting

---

[110] *Ibid.* at art. 28.

[111] *Ibid.* at art. 38.

[112] *Ibid.* at art. 44.

[113] See M. C. Cordonier Segger et al., *Ecological Rules and Sustainability in the Americas* (Winnipeg: IISD/UNEP, 2002). See also Cordonier Segger & Leichner Reynal, *supra* note 1 and A. Barcena et al., *Financing for Sustainable Development in Latin America and the Caribbean: From Monterrey to Johannesburg* (Santiago: ECLAC and UNDP, 2002).

parties' ability to implement other important social or environmental commitments and frustrating the sustainable development objectives of all. Measures to support emissions reductions and the use of market-based instruments (carbon taxes) to implement the 1997 Kyoto Protocol to the 1992 UN Framework Convention on Climate Change might be constrained by commitments to reduce subsidies, or to avoid certain types of border adjustments and non-tariff barriers to trade. Measures to develop a multilateral system of access and benefit sharing in the 2004 International Treaty on Plant Genetic Resources for Food and Agriculture (FAO Seed Treaty) might conceivably be limited by commitments to liberalize agriculture. Regional measures to reduce air or water pollution might be found to infringe on the rights of investors, and be subject to compensation claims in closed arbitral processes. Other regional or national measures to meet human rights commitments regarding access to water, health care or education might be blocked as a result of services liberalization.

However, it is also possible, in the context of FTAs, to agree on operational provisions which provide a balanced 'sustainable' solution to such policy and legal overlaps. One example can be provided. The 2001 Cartagena Protocol[114] to the 1992 UN Convention on Biological Diversity[115] procedures on Advance Informed Agreement and Living Modified Organisms (LMOs) for Food, Feed and Processing require both risk assessment and risk management, and expressly permit parties to apply the precautionary principle in their reasoning.[116] Problems may arise from intersections between the right of Parties under the Cartagena Protocol to use precaution in making decisions concerning LMOs, and WTO SPS obligations only to maintain SPS measures that can be justified by scientific methods.[117] The WTO Appellate Body has recognised the challenge of applying the precautionary principle in the context of members' obligations in the SPS Agreement.[118] Under the WTO SPS Agreement, a party

---

[114] See the Cartagena Protocol on Biological Diversity, adopted 29 January 2000, 11 I.L.M. 1416: http://www.biodiv.org/default.shtml.

[115] UN, United Nations Convention on Biological Diversity, adopted 5 June 1992, 31 I.L.M. 822 at 15.

[116] *Supra* note 114 at 15–16.

[117] See *e.g.*, H. Trudeau & C. Nègre, "Precaution in Multilateral Environmental Agreements and Its Impact on the World Trading System" in M. Gehring & M. C. Cordonier Segger, *supra* note 1 at 593–630. See also C. Button, *The Power to Protect: Trade, Health and Uncertainty in the WTO* (Oxford: Hart, 2004).

[118] WTO, Appellate Body Report, *EC Measures Concerning Meat and Meat Products (Hormones) ("EC-Hormones")*, WT/DS26/AB/R, WT/DS48/AB/R, adopted 13 February 1998, DSR 1998: I, 135 at para. 124, stated: "First, the principle has not been written into the *SPS Agreement* as a ground for justifying SPS measures that are otherwise inconsistent with the obligations of Members set out in particular provisions of that Agreement. . . . the precautionary principle does not, by itself, and without a clear textual directive to that effect, relieve a panel from the duty of applying the normal (i.e.

enacting a measure to restrict trade must bear a burden of proof to defend its measure by demonstrating that it is transparent, science-based and strictly necessary for the protection of human, animal and plant health. As such, SPS obligations could be used to restrict measures aimed at controlling trade in LMOs, affecting both health and environmental priorities. However, a different approach is adopted in the Canada – Chile FTA and the Canada – Costa Rica FTA, which establish cooperation mechanisms on SPS measures in the context of the environmental side agreements.[119] These provisions are included even though neither Canada nor Chile has ratified the Cartagena Protocol on Biosafety to the UN CBD. In the EU-Chile Agreement, the reference to SPS measures is made in conjunction with the desire to reform agricultural practices and rural settings, thereby making them more sustainable.[120] Similarly, Article 5 ('Trade in Goods') of the EU-Mexico Agreement mentions the applicability of "regulations and standards, sanitary and phytosanitary legislation" when discussing the process of goods liberalization and the sensitive nature of certain products.[121]

Finally, beyond the provisions which seek to establish cooperation in areas where otherwise, the trade rules might constrain the use of social or environmental measures, a proactive agenda may also be possible. For instance, opportunities may arise when investments arranged under the Clean Development Mechanism (CDM) of the Kyoto Protocol can be protected under investment chapters in FTAs. Similarly, opportunities for more sustainable trade may be encouraged by specific initiatives undertaken to liberalize trade in biofuels, organic shade-grown coffee, and other environmentally and socially sound goods or services. And opportunities might also arise to promote corporate social responsibility (a topic addressed in Chapter 14), socially responsible investment, and harmonise (upwards) social and environmental certification and labelling programmes.

---

customary international law) principles of treaty interpretation in reading the provisions of the *SPS Agreement*".

[119] For instance, in order to apply the WTO SPS Agreement, Canada and Costa Rica, at Art. IX.5, inaugurated a Committee for consultation and cooperation purposes, which may consider the following: "the design, implementation and review of technical and institutional co-operation programs; the development of operational guidelines to facilitate implementation of, inter alia, mutual recognition and equivalence agreements, and product control, inspection and approval procedures; the promotion of enhanced transparency of SPS measures; the identification and resolution of SPS-related problems; the recognition of pest- or disease-free areas; and the promotion of bilateral consultation on sanitary and phytosanitary [SPS] issues under discussion in multilateral and international fora". *Agreement on Environmental Cooperation between the Government of Canada and the Government of the Republic of Costa Rica*, adopted 23 April 2001: http:// www.sice.oas.org/Trade/cancr/English/enve.asp.

[120] *Supra* note 41 at art. 24.

[121] *Supra note* 40 at art. 5.

It can be seen that several models for innovative provisions have been recently included in Canadian and UK / EC trade agreements, in the interest of sustainable development and other related environmental and social development objectives. It is not yet clear which strategies or instruments will have the most success in helping to integrate social and economic development and environmental protection. It is likely that no one single type of provision has an answer to this problem. Rather, many different provisions and instruments are being developed and tested in the regional context.

4) Sustainable Development in World Trade Law

Both Canada and the UK are also part of the WTO, a global trade liberalization process which has shed some light on the meaning of sustainable development in international trade law. A brief review of further negotiations in the WTO, and decisions of the WTO Appellate Body help illustrate the intentions of the Parties and the legal effect of this objective in the WTO. [122]

The Preamble to the 1994 WTO Agreement was likely influenced by the outcomes of the 1992 UNCED. It states:

> Recognizing that their relations in the field of trade and economic endeavour should be conducted with a view to . . . *allowing for the optimal use of the world's resources in accordance with the objective of sustainable development*, seeking both to protect and preserve the environment and to enhance the means for doing so in a manner consistent with their respective needs and concerns at different levels of economic development, . . ."[123] [emphasis added]

While preambular statements do not have the same normative effect that operational provisions do, they play a role in interpretation of a treaty, particularly in the identification of the treaty's object and purpose.[124] In the Preamble of the WTO Agreements, sustainable development is specifically referred to as an objective, and the Parties appear to agree that by conducting their trade in a way that allows for the optimal use of the world's resources,[125] they seek to

---

[122] See also Gehring & Cordonier Segger, *supra* note 1 at 1–24, 129–186; see also Cordonier Segger, *supra* note 75.

[123] Marrakesh Agreement Establishing the World Trade Organization, 1 January 1995 at Preamble. For a deeper discussion of this process, see Gehring & Cordonier Segger, *supra* note 1 at 1–24.

[124] In general international law, the preamble is part of the context in which the international treaty has to be interpreted. See Vienna Convention on the Law of Treaties, 23 May 1969, 1155 U.N.T.S. 331 at art. 31 [Vienna Convention].

[125] This may build on the Preamble of the earlier 1947 General Agreement on Tariffs and Trade, 61 Stat. A-11, T.I.A.S. 1700, 55 U.N.T.S. 194 [GATT 1947], in Geneva, 1 January 1948, which referred to the need for ". . . developing the full use of the resources of the world . . ."

contribute to sustainable development. As is discussed below, the WTO Appellate Body has used this preambular commitment to help interpret the GATT and resolve cases involving sustainable development issues.

In the 1998 Geneva Ministerial Conference, WTO Members stated: "[w]e shall also continue to improve our efforts towards the objectives of sustained economic growth and sustainable development."[126] As such, they formally recognised that sustainable development is not only related to natural resources, or an automatic result of the liberalization process, but is actually one of the goals of the WTO itself. During the 1998–1999 negotiations leading toward the Seattle Ministerial Conference, several countries sought to strengthen the WTO's sustainable development mandate. The European Communities conceived sustainable development to be an integrated concept (encompassing socio-economic as well as environmental concerns).[127] The Canadians saw it more as a reason to ensure that trade and environment policies were mutually supportive.[128] Developing country Members were unconvinced that the addition of further 'non-trade' issues (addressing social or environmental objectives within the WTO) was either warranted or would meaningfully support their development interests.[129] A compromise was found in the 2001 Doha Declaration launching the Doha Round of trade negotiations, which stated, at para. 6:

> *We strongly reaffirm our commitment to the objective of sustainable development, as stated in the Preamble to the Marrakesh Agreement.* We are convinced that the aims of upholding and safeguarding an open and non-discriminatory multilateral trading system, and acting for the protection of the environment *and the promotion of sustainable development* can and must be mutually supportive . . . We encourage efforts to promote cooperation between the WTO and relevant international environmental *and developmental organizations*, especially in the lead-up to the World

---

[126] Geneva Ministerial Declaration, WT/MIN(98)/DEC, adopted on 1 and 25 May 1998.

[127] See Preparations for the 1999 Ministerial Conference – EC Approach to Trade and Environment in the New WTO Round, Communication from the European Communities, WT/GC/W/194, 1 June 1999 at para. 4.

[128] Preparations for the 1999 Ministerial Conference: Canadian Approach to Trade and Environment in the New WTO Round, WT/GC/W/358, October 1999.

[129] See *e.g.*, Preparations for the 1999 Ministerial Conference – Trade, Environment and Sustainable Development, Paragraph 9(d) of the Geneva Ministerial Declaration, Communication from Cuba, WT/GC/W/387, 15 November 1999. See also the statements from Kenya: WT/GC/W/233; Bangladesh: WT/GC/W/251; Pakistan: WT/GC/W/126; Dominican Republic-Honduras-Pakistan: WT/GC/W/255 and Cuba-Dominican Republic-Honduras-Pakistan: WT/GC/W/163, as referenced in *Bridges Weekly Trade News Digest,* Vol. 3, No. 46 (1999).

Summit on Sustainable Development to be held in Johannesburg, South Africa, in September 2002."[130] [emphasis added].

As is clear from this passage, the intent is to conduct the Doha Round in the context of sustainable development objectives. Ministers recognized sustainable development as a goal of the WTO, and placed it into a strengthened context, referring to practical measures such as the need for cooperation with other international environment organizations in the lead-up to the World Summit on Sustainable Development. Furthermore, the social development aspect of the sustainable development concept was emphasized in these practical measures – members explicitly refer to 'development' organizations. Indeed, members went further in concretizing their commitments, taking the unprecedented initiative of operationalizing the objective in the WTO itself. Para 51 specified that:

> [t]he Committee on Trade and Development and the Committee on Trade and Environment shall, within their respective mandates, each act as a forum to identify and debate developmental and environmental aspects of the negotiations, in order to help achieve the objective of having sustainable development appropriately reflected.[131]

Questions remain as to whether these two Committees will be able to fulfill their mandates to identify and debate environmental and developmental aspects of the negotiations, and help to ensure that sustainable development can be appropriately reflected in the trade negotiations.

Negotiations within the WTO policy forum are only part of the global attempts to reach a common understanding of the sustainable development objectives of trade and trade rules.[132] The decisions of the WTO dispute settlement body, particularly its Appellate Body, while not formally binding on further panels, can also shed a great deal of light on how trade law has evolved in recognising and implementing this objective. The WTO Appellate Body has actually been called upon to interpret the concept of sustainable development in

---

[130] Doha Ministerial Declaration, Ministerial Conference, WT/MIN(01)/DEC/, 4th Sess., adopted on 4 November 2001.

[131] *Ibid.* at 1.

[132] Indeed, as suggested by the Panel Report in *US-Shrimp (Article 21.5)*, *supra* note 16, when referring to one such declaration by WTO members: "Insofar as this report can be deemed to embody the opinion of the WTO Members, it could be argued that it records evidence of 'subsequent practice in the application of the treaty which establishes the agreement of the parties regarding its interpretation' (Article 31.3(b) of the Vienna Convention) and as such should be taken into account in the interpretation of the provisions concerned. However, even if it is not to be considered as evidence of a subsequent practice, it remains the expression of a common opinion of Members and is therefore relevant in assessing the scope of the chapeau of Article XX.".

trade law. Two cases, *US – Shrimp*[133] and *EC – Tariff Preferences*[134] are particularly relevant in highlighting the concept of sustainable development in world trade law, as it currently stands. In this chapter, a few brief comments must suffice.[135]

In *US – Shrimp*, the Panel concluded that "the best way for the parties to this dispute to contribute effectively to the protection of sea turtles in a manner consistent with WTO objectives, including sustainable development, would be to reach cooperative agreements on integrated conservation strategies."[136] On appeal, this finding was not overturned. The Appellate Body decision found that the WTO Agreement:

> ... must be read by a treaty interpreter in the light of contemporary concerns of the community of nations about the protection and conservation of the environment ... The preamble of the WTO Agreement – which informs not only the GATT 1994, but also the other covered agreements – explicitly acknowledges 'the objective of sustainable development'.[137]

Footnote 107 of this finding deserves particular attention in understanding the concept from the WTO Appellate Body's perspective. The note explained that "[t]his concept has been generally accepted *as integrating economic and social development and environmental protection.*"[138] (Emphasis added). The note is remarkable for two reasons. First, the WTO Appellate Body expresses itself on the nature of sustainable development, recognising that it is an objective of the WTO Agreements, and that this objective then informs interpretation of these Agreements. Second, the Appellate Body specifically emphasizes the need to integrate all three elements or 'pillars' of sustainable development – social development, economic development and environmental protection. This recognises the important social dimension of the concept. This reasoning was

---

[133] See Panel Report, *United States – Import Prohibition of Certain Shrimp and Shrimp Products,* WT/DS58/R and Corr. 1, adopted 6 November 1998, as modified by the Appellate Body Report, WT/DS58/AB/R, DSR 1998:VII, 2821 [*US – Shrimp*]. See also Appellate Body Report, *US-Shrimp, supra* note 17.

[134] See Appellate Body Report, *European Communities – Conditions for the Granting of Tariff Preferences to Developing Countries,* WT/DS246/AB/R, adopted 20 April 2004 [*EC – Tariff Preferences*].

[135] This section is based on a discussion that is further developed in Gehring & Cordonier Segger, *supra* note 1.

[136] Panel Report, *US – Shrimp, supra* note 133 at para. 9.1.

[137] Appellate Body Report, *US – Shrimp, supra* note 17 at para. 129.

[138] *Ibid.* at footnote 107 reads "This concept has been generally accepted as integrating economic and social development and environmental protection." See *e.g.,* G. Handl, "Sustainable Development: General Rules versus Specific Obligations", in W. Lang, ed., *Sustainable Development and International Law* (London: Graham & Trotman, 1995) at 35.

adopted and applied in *US-Shrimp (Article 21.5)*,[139] when Malaysia argued that the measures taken by the United States did not comply with the recommendations and rulings of the DSB. In particular, the Panel at 5.54 stated that:

> In that framework, assessing first the object and purpose of the WTO Agreement, we note that the WTO preamble refers to the notion of "sustainable development".[140] This means that in interpreting the terms of the chapeau, we must keep in mind that sustainable development is one of the objectives of the WTO Agreement.[141]

In defining this objective, the Panel at note 202 cites the Rio Declaration and the Agenda 21, which refer to balancing environmental protection with the social and economic development needs of developing countries. On appeal, this interpretation was not overturned by the WTO Appellate Body.[142]

In the *EC – Tariff Preferences Case*,[143] the WTO Appellate Body, citing its report in *US-Shrimp*, noted that the objectives of the WTO could be fulfilled through "General Exceptions", observing that 'the optimal use of the world's resources in accordance with the objective of sustainable development' could be achieved through application of the WTO exceptions, such as Article XX (g) GATT.

The reasoning of the WTO Appellate Body and Panel with regard to the "explicit recognition by WTO Members of the objective of sustainable development in the preamble of the WTO Agreement"[144] in these cases, taken together with recent negotiations among Members on this particular issue, suggests that the sustainable development commitment in the Preamble has legal relevance, and can be used to interpret trade obligations, shedding light, in particular, on the meaning of exceptions and other aspects of the WTO Agreements.[145]

---

[139] *Supra note* 16.

[140] *Ibid.* at footnote 202, which reads: "See the final texts of the agreements negotiated by Governments at the United Nation Conference on Environment and Development (UNCED), Rio de Janeiro, Brazil, 3–14 June, 1992, specifically the Rio Declaration on Environment and Development (hereafter the "Rio Declaration") and Agenda 21 at www.unep.org; the concept is elaborated in detailed action plans in Agenda 21 so as to put in place development that is sustainable – i.e. that "meets the needs of the present generation without compromising the ability of future generations to meet their own needs".

[141] Panel Report, *US-Shrimp (Article 21.5), supra* note 16.

[142] Appellate Body Report, *US-Shrimp (Article 21.5), supra* note 16 at para. 131.

[143] *Supra note* 134.

[144] *Supra* note 16 at para. 131.

[145] See Gehring & Cordonier Segger, *supra* note 1 at 1–24, 129–186.

5) CONCLUDING OBSERVATIONS

Sustainable development is clearly an important commitment for both Canada and the United Kingdom, incrementally playing a vital role in framing their respective international trade policies. Sustainable development is reflected as an objective in several international trade agreements and diverse mechanisms have been employed to implement it. However, Canada and the EU/UK approach sustainable development in slightly different ways, with different practical results. The EU/UK appears to view sustainable development as a guiding principle which requires Parties to integrate social and economic development with environmental protection, and as such, they conduct sustainability impact assessments that consider potential social, environmental and economic impacts that could lead to mitigation and enhancement measures in both the EU or developing countries; integrate social development, health, environment and cultural issues all the way through the texts of their free trade agreements; and set in place institutions and structures for dialogue to resolve any pressing issues that might arise. The Canadian approach remains similar to the one taken in NAFTA, conducting simple environmental impact assessments of trade agreements which only consider the impacts in Canada; focusing on ensuring mutual supportiveness between trade and environment measures, and negotiating separate parallel agreements on environmental cooperation.

In addition, Canada and the UK are both WTO Members. The approach taken in the WTO demonstrates that the objective of sustainable development has become an integral part of the world trading system and in particular, can be used to interpret the exceptions provided in the GATT. Legal arguments encompassing an integrated developmental and environmental approach have been made by the parties and accepted by the relevant dispute settlement organs. While sustainable development is clearly not considered a 'trump card' in trade law, the commitment in the preamble has legal relevance, and can be used to interpret trade laws, shedding light on the meaning of exceptions and other aspects of the WTO Agreements.

Understanding these nuances can contribute to a better analysis of how sustainable development plays out in different trade treaties and can also explain some of the divergent innovations and approaches that have developed in negotiations for regimes as diverse as the Free Trade Area of the Americas and the EU-ACP Cotonou Agreement.

Finally, as mentioned above, Canada and the EU have agreed to design a new type of wide-ranging bilateral trade and investment enhancement agreement (TIEA). Their agreement includes a commitment to "reinforce the Canada-EU partnership in the pursuit of common objectives, notably our shared commitment to promote sustainable development . . ."[146] Title 11, on

---

[146] Europa, External Trade, Bilateral Relations, *Canada-European Union Trade and*

Sustainable Development, recognises that both the EU and Canada are "active players on sustainable development issues" recognises that this involves environmental, social and economic aspects, and emphasises "the important contribution that trade and investment policy can play in the development of those objectives." In particular, it states that the TIEA will establish "a comprehensive EU-Canada dialogue on sustainable trade. This dialogue would offer a valuable opportunity to learn from each other's experiences on ways to ensure that trade and investment policies contribute to the objective of sustainable development."[147] Negotiations started on 17–18 May 2005 in Brussels, and as they proceed, it will be interesting to note whether transatlantic convergence develops on the meaning of sustainable development in trade law, and innovative ways to reflect a commitment to promote sustainable development in a trade and investment agreement.

Investment Enhancement Agreement: Framework for the Agreement: http://europa. eu.int/comm/trade/issues/bilateral/countries/canada/tiea.htm.

[147] The proposed EU-Canada dialogue should consist of exchanges of views and information on existing or future initiatives to further promote international sustainable trade, the identification of opportunities for bilateral co-operation on sustainable trade and investment initiatives; and a dialogue aimed at supporting multilateral initiatives and developing new ones (WTO, follow up to World Summit on Sustainable Development (WSSD), the OECD, the International Labour Organisation (ILO), etc.).

Chapter 13

Implementing the Kyoto Protocol in Canada and the UK: A Discussion of the Economic Instruments Employed

Markus W. Gehring and Kristin Price

1) INTRODUCTION

The Kyoto Protocol is a unique international law instrument. The scale and comprehensiveness of the accord is largely unprecedented for international environmental law treaties. The stringent, legally binding targets for reduction of emissions of greenhouse gases (GHGs) are unprecedented in an environmental agreement of this scope and necessitate substantial financial commitment and innovation by so called Annex I countries (mainly industrialized countries). It is the first international agreement to include innovative economic instruments designed to assist Parties in meeting their obligations. Known as the "Kyoto Mechanisms", the Clean Development Mechanism ("CDM") and Joint Implementation ("JI") exude attributes complementary to the market-driven ethos of the treaty. The rationale behind these tools is to facilitate maximum flexibility and cost effectiveness, facilitating compliance with treaty provisions to mitigate climate change.

Given that the climate system is global, the benefits gleaned from abatement in GHG emissions are universally shared. The Kyoto Protocol is formulated

255

Christopher P.M. Waters (Ed.), *British and Canadian Perspectives on International Law*, pp. 255–274.
© 2006 Koninklijke Brill NV. Printed in the Netherlands.

around the sustainable development principle of "common but differentiated responsibilities". Even though Annex I countries[1] bear the responsibility for making meaningful changes to their GHG emissions, the mechanisms devised have great potential for channeling investment and technical assistance in clean technology to developing countries and countries with economies in transition. Projects financed in this way promote sustainable development through positive feedback loops: technology transfer and financing of clean energy projects increase capacity for development through providing reliable energy, thereby fomenting a foundation for poverty eradication.

Leading up to 2008 – the beginning of Kyoto's first emissions reduction period – Canada and the UK have spearheaded the development of flexible mechanisms in general and emission trading in particular. The UK has traded emission allowances since March 2002 and Canada has overseen the voluntary early trading projects, Greenhouse Gas Emissions Reduction ("GERT") and Pilot Emissions Reduction Trading ("PERT"), since the mid 1990s. In light of the innovative aspects of Kyoto, an analysis of these early experiences can be invaluable in assisting the methodological approaches chosen by states that have not yet taken concrete steps to meet their treaty obligations. Furthermore, although Annex I states are given tremendous leeway to devise emissions reduction policies attuned to their economic situation, the successes and obstacles faced by Canada and the UK may be emblematic of those faced by federal and unitary industrialized states in a general sense. This chapter examines the commonalities and disparities between Canada and the UK's early experiences as well as the current issues pertaining to the implementation of the Kyoto Protocol in both countries. Further, the chapter explores the role of fund and covenant mechanisms, highlighting how these tools can become stepping-stones for full Kyoto implementation based on prior UK and Canadian experiences.

Part 1 of the chapter gives a cursory overview of the Kyoto Protocol and provides pertinent definitions and terminology; Part 2 gives a sense of the pivotal role played by Canada and the UK in shaping the Kyoto Mechanisms, in addition to their early experiences, as they work towards achievement of their obligations; Part 3 addresses issues emanating from current implementation in both states, incorporating the role of the European Community Emissions Trading Scheme ("EC ETS") and the Foreign Legal Entities ("FLE") scheme;

---

[1] Kyoto Protocol to the United Nations Framework Convention on Climate Change, opened for signature 16 March 1998, 37 I.L.M. 22 (entered into force 16 February 2005) [Kyoto Protocol]; Framework Convention on Climate Change, opened for signature 20 June 1992, 31 I.L.M. 848 (entered into force 21 March 1994) [Framework Convention]. Annex 1 Parties to the Protocol are the developed states allocated extensive obligations outlined in the Treaty. Articles 4(2)(a) and (b) establishes the quantified emission limitation and reduction commitments of the Annex 1 Parties while Article 2 elucidates various policy, research and promotional measures (in sector-specific terms) related to sustainable development and climate change.

Part 4 is dedicated to the international sustainable development law principles embedded in the Protocol and how minor modifications to policies adopted by the UK and Canada can buttress sustainable development initiatives; and Part 5 addresses prospects for international linking and the potential predicaments arising from prior free trade commitments.

2) OVERVIEW OF THE KYOTO PROTOCOL

Given the gravity of ecological harm expected to be caused by climate change and the international media attention that global warming captures, it is surprising to note that the first steps towards curbing anthropomorphic emissions were only undertaken in the 1980s. The growing concern, and better scientific understanding of climate change processes led to the negotiation and ratification of the 1992 United Nations Framework Convention on Climate Change (UNFCCC).[2] The influence of the 1992 Rio Declaration promoted the Intergovernmental Negotiating Committee of the UNFCCC to integrate principles of sustainable development into the treaty: the precautionary principle;[3] intergenerational equity[4] and common but differentiated responsibilities,[5]

---

[2] See D. Freestone, "The UN Framework Convention on Climate Change, the Kyoto Protocol, and the Kyoto Mechanisms" in D. Freestone & C. Streck, eds., *Legal Aspects of Implementing the Kyoto Protocol Mechanisms* (Oxford: Oxford University Press, 2005) at 3. It is crucial to note that concerns regarding the effects of climate change were not relegated to the environment. The Intergovernmental Panel on Climate Change that preceded the ratification of the UNFCCC recognized that the environmental deterioration caused by climate change was interconnected with socioeconomic implications, thus requiring pragmatic, multifaceted GHG abatement strategies.

[3] The 'precautionary principle' is at the intersection of three areas of law (economic, social and environmental) within the broad rubric of international sustainable development law. The precautionary approach to risk management commits states, international organizations and civil society (particularly the scientific and business communities) to avoid human activity which may cause significant harm to human health, natural resources or ecosystems including in the face of scientific uncertainty. See M. C. Cordonier Segger & A. Khalfan, *Sustainable Development Law* (Oxford: Oxford University Press, 2004) at 100.

[4] *Ibid.* The principle of equity is intimately tied to poverty eradication. This principle of international law relating to sustainable development encompasses both "intra-generational equity (the rights of all peoples within the current generation are allotted fair access to the current generation's entitlement to the earth's natural resources) and intergenerational equity (the rights of future generations to enjoy a fair level of the common patrimony)". The sharing of benefits accrued from the global environment is understood in a broad manifestation, "*inter alia*, economic, environmental, social and intrinsic benefit".

[5] *Ibid.* The principle of 'common but differentiated responsibilities' is principally

among others. The UNFCCC seeks to stabilize the trend of escalating GHG emissions. The timeframe of GHG stabilization was calculated to allow ecosystem adaptation, ensure food production is not threatened and enable economic development to proceed in a sustainable manner.[6] To put the general principles of the UNFCCC into practice, the Kyoto Protocol to the UNFCCC, drafted by 1997 and ratified in 2004,[7] sought *inter alia* to "utilize 'market mechanisms' to assist with massive reductions of [GHG] emissions necessary to arrest the processes of climate change".[8]

The Kyoto Protocol essentially establishes a global economic instrument to address an indivisible environmental and social problem. The Protocol strengthens the commitments of the UNFCCC by enumerating specific reduction targets for GHGs with a view to reducing overall emissions by at least 5% below 1990 levels between 2008 and 2012.[9] Although steps to diminish GHG emissions are only binding on Annex I parties (industrialized states), developing States reaffirmed the imperative of a proactive response to climate change within a sustainable development framework. The market mechanisms embodied in the Protocol allow commitments to be achieved individually or jointly.

a) *Clean Development Mechanisms, Joint Implementation and Emission Trading*

Three flexibility mechanisms are set in place by the Kyoto Protocol. First, taking full advantage of marginal abatement costs associated with investing in clean energy projects in developing states, Articles 6 and 12 outline the mechanisms that allow emissions reductions financed in other countries to be offset against the financier's GHG reduction targets.[10] Joint Implementation (JI), as described in Article 6, allows any Annex I country or authorized stakeholders in the private sector (i.e. International Financial Institutions like the World Bank) to "transfer to, or acquire from, another Annex I country, reductions of

---

based on the contribution that a state has made to the emergence of environmental problems as well as the economic and developmental situation of said state. Developed countries are levied with a "special burden of responsibility in reducing and eliminating unsustainable patterns of production and consumption, *inter alia* by providing financial assistance and access to environmentally sound technology".

  [6] Kyoto Protocol, *supra* note 1 at art. 2.
  [7] Ratification of the Kyoto Protocol took place on 16 February 2005. The conditions for the Protocol to come into force involved the assent of 55 Parties to the UNFCCC, including endorsement by the Annex 1 states that accounted for at least 55% of the total CO_2 emissions in 1990 out of the total of the Parties listed in Annex 1.
  [8] D. Freestone, *supra* note 2 at 3.
  [9] Kyoto Protocol, *supra* note 1 at art. 3.1.
  [10] D. Freestone, *supra* note 2 at 11.

GHG emissions, described as Emission Reduction Units ("ERU"), achieved by project activities".[11] Necessarily supplemental to domestic policies aimed at meaningful restraint of GHG emissions, JI projects require express approval, strict monitoring and verification standards. Parties carrying out the transaction must be in good standing with the UNFCCC and any risk of non-compliance falls entirely on the buyer of ERUs. Second, the modalities of the CDM are apparent in the text of Article 12. The objective of the CDM is to encourage investment in non-Annex I parties, promoting clean energy sources, technology transfer and sustainable development more broadly. Certified Emission Reductions ("CERs"), obtained from a registered and validated CDM are verified though an independent Designated Operational Entity ("DOE").

Participation in CDM projects must be voluntary; "projects must manifest real, measurable and long-term benefits relating to mitigation and climate change; and climate project generating CERs must be additional to that which would have occurred in its absence".[12] Finally, the third flexible mechanism – Emission Trading – is identified in Article 17. Regulated emission trading occurs among Annex I states and is defined as "the trading of parts of Assigned Amounts ("AAUs"),[13] CERs, ERU and removal units ("RMUs")".[14] The Treaty strictly stipulates that emissions trading must be "supplemental to any domestic actions" for the purpose of meeting abatement quotas.[15]

3) EARLY EXPERIENCES WITH EMISSION TRADING BY CANADA AND THE UK

a) *Canada*

On 17 December 2002, Canada became the ninety-ninth country to ratify the Kyoto Protocol. Abiding by the emission reductions outlined in the Protocol, Canada must decrease emissions to 94% of 1990 levels during the first commitment period (2008–2012). Such a commitment poses an extremely difficult challenge, representing a 20 percent to 30 percent reduction from the "business as usual" case.[16] Given Canada's reliance on natural resource exploitation for a

---

[11] *Ibid.* at 11.

[12] Kyoto Protocol, *supra* note 1 at art. 6.

[13] 'Assigned Amounts' refers to the quantity of GHGs a Party to the Protocol is allowed to release in the global atmosphere as calculated in a yearly basis in Annex B.

[14] Kyoto Protocol, *supra* note 1 at art. 17.

[15] *Ibid.*

[16] See W. Thomas et al., "Creating a Favorable Climate for Climate CDM in North America" (2001) 15 WTR NATRE 3.

significant proportion of its prosperity, the need to find innovative, cost-effective solutions is particularly pressing. Indeed, the backdrop to Canadian ratification included fervent regional dissonance about the viability of the treaty itself as well as the likelihood that burdens would be born symmetrically nation-wide. In spite of these reservations, the federal government outlined plans to concentrate on emission trading in the near term, potentially laying the foundation for a future comprehensive legislative framework and implementation program.[17] At this point, the emission trading pilot projects have been superseded by the emerging Kyoto Protocol regime. Yet at the time, their approaches were welcomed to respond to the pressure within the Kyoto negotiations to develop real-life projects, and build a body of expertise with respect to issues of verification, 'additionality' and ownership of reductions.

i) *GERT & PERT*

Since the 1990s, Canadian companies and provincial entities have engaged in voluntary certification and the trading of carbon emission reductions.[18] The majority of the voluntary trading (units traded did not exude the strict Kyoto attributes) took place in commercial deals concerning emission rights, in the context of two pilot programs: Greenhouse Gas Emissions Reduction ("GERT") and Pilot Emissions Reduction Trading ("PERT").[19] Both programs are public-private partnerships set up by memorandums of understanding ("MOU") between the Federal Government, the Ontario Government and private enterprises and are designed to build a body of expertise regarding the issues of verification, 'additionality' and ownership of reductions. The MOU contained the obligations for government partners to credit, to the extent possible, verifiable emission reductions from trades registered under GERT against future emission obligations.

The lifespan of GERT[20] was from 1 January 1997 to 31 December 2002. Attempting to maximize involvement of the private sector, GERT was oriented

---

[17] See M. W. Gehring & B. Chambers, "Canada's Experience in Emissions Trading and Participating in the Kyoto Mechanism" in D. Freestone and C. Streck, eds., *Legal Aspects of Implementing the Kyoto Protocol Mechanisms* (Oxford: Oxford University Press, 2005) at 493.

[18] R. Rosenweig & M. Varilek, *Greenhouse Gas Trading in Canada, Greenhouse Gas Markets 2003* (Geneva: International Emission Trading Association, 2003) at 31.

[19] Gehring & Chambers, *supra* note 17 at 494.

[20] GERT governmental members include: Environment Canada, Natural Resources Canada, British Columbia Ministry of Water, Lands and Air Protection, British Columbia Ministry of Energy and Mines, Alberta Environment, Alberta Department of Resource Development, Saskatchewan Energy & Mines, Manitoba Department of Energy and Mines, Quebec Ministry of Natural Resources, Nova Scotia Department of Natural Resources, Greater Vancouver Regional District, and non-governmental

to accumulate practical experience, explore the costs and benefits (both environmental and economic), and test technical, legal and administrative elements of such a scheme.[21] The precepts of the programs amounted to "an agreement by the participating government to award carbon credits for verifiable emissions reductions by the participants and a registry where the transactions could be recorded".[22] The intention to reward early action by the private sector is apparent. Under program auspices, credits could be traded or sold by the organizations that achieved emissions reduction. Regarding credit ownership,[23] GERT took a novel approach: there were no legal rules, case law or government policy in this realm. In the final assessment, this lack of legal certainty was criticized as impeding incentives to trade and stifled the potential volume of transactions. Only five projects underwent GERT review and there was hardly any trading.[24] Consequently, the need to create legally coherent definitions, thereby minimizing ownership risk figured prominently in the project review. Further, elements of contract negotiations such as ambiguity surrounding the status of surpluses, *force majeure*, vintage, and international requirements were targeted as weaker elements of the pilot project in need of rectification.[25]

The PERT Project, formed in 1996, was conceived to be an industry-led, multi-stakeholder group tasked with standard setting for the development and implementation of a robust emission reduction trading system.[26] Originally, PERT was focused on ameliorating reductions of emissions contributing to smog and acid rain (nitrous oxide (NOx) and sulphur dioxide (SO_2)), but was further expanded to CO_2 abatement. A Letter of Understanding[27] was negotiated in order to provide an industry incentive for early action, with rules about credit

---

members: Canada's Climate Change, Voluntary Challenge and Registry Inc., Canadian Association of Petroleum Producers, Canadian Electricity Association, Canadian Energy Pipeline Association, Canadian Gas Association, Canadian Pulp and Paper Association, Canadian Wind Energy Association, Greenhouse Gas Emissions Management Consortium, Pembina Institute for Appropriate Development, West Coast Environmental Law Association.

[21] Gehring & Chambers, *supra* note 17 at 495.

[22] *Ibid.* at 494.

[23] For the international debates around the ownership problem see M. W. Gehring & C. Streck, "Emission Trading: Lessons from SO2 and NOx Emission Allowance and Credit Systems – Legal Nature, Title, Transfer and Taxation of Emission Allowances and Credits" (2005) 35 Environmental Law Reporter at 10220.

[24] Refer to GERT: http://www.gert.org/projects/index.htm (last modified 10 March 2003).

[25] Gehring & Chambers, *supra* note 17 at 496.

[26] *Ibid.*

[27] CleanAir Canada is a new not-for-profit, federally incorporated organization. For further details, refer to http://www.cleanaircanada.org/notes/letterofunderstanding.pdf.

recognition closely emulating the GERT project. CleanAir Canada,[28] into which PERT eventually morphed, is currently seeking to renew the letter of understanding to safeguard early carbon reductions for the future Canadian ETS. The emission reduction goal, or GHG emission cap, in the PERT system turned out to be key for the functioning of the trading. Retrospective analysis indicated that the cap was at the crux of project-derived incentives and market stimulation.[29] Since the federal government announced that future GHG emissions reduction credit and emission right trading in Canada will be part of a legal regime, efforts to create more voluntary programs have ceased, and there are doubts as to whether voluntary efforts can be integrated into the future trading system.[30]

ii) *Canada's Regulatory Framework for Emission Trading*

Emissions trading officially began on 31 December 2001. Ontario's Emissions Trading Scheme (ETS) is the first provincial air emissions trading program in Canada and it is anticipated to provide valuable points of reference for future Canadian ETS. Legal regulation includes the Emissions Trading Code, which introduces the use of market-based instruments for reducing emissions of NO_x and SO_2 in the province.[31] The Code is intended to supplement Ontario Regulation 397/01, which governs emissions trading under the Ontario Environmental Protection Act.[32] The Ontario system is designed as a 'cap, credit and trade' variety, which combines 'cap-and-trade' features with those of a 'baseline-and-credit' system.[33]

During the first phase of the program, the Ontario Ministry of the Environment was responsible for allocating NO_x and SO_2 emission allowances to Ontario Power Generation, which then distributed these allowances among their stations, free of charge. Beginning in 2004 for SO_2, and in 2008 for NOx,

---

[28] *Ibid.*

[29] G. E. Taylor, *Role of Emissions Trading in Canada's Kyoto Climate Change Plan*, *Greenhouse Gas Market 2003* (Geneva: International Emission Trading Association, 2003) at 36.

[30] *Ibid.* at 37.

[31] Future considerations include adding GHGs such as CO_2 to the list, as well as toxic and carcinogenic compounds such as mercury, cadmium, and arsenic.

[32] The Government of Canada's "Emissions Trading Code" can be found at: http://www.ene.gov.on.ca/envision/env_reg/er/documents/2001/RA01E0020–A.pdf; technical descriptions of NOx/SO_2 emission reductions at:
   http://www.ene.gov.on.ca/envision/env_reg/er/documents/2001/RA01E0020–C.pdf; and, the Province of Ontario's "Emissions Trading Code" at:
   http://www.ene.gov.on.ca/envision/env_reg/er/documents/2003/XA03E0001.pdf.

[33] The UK Carbon Trading Scheme also includes a baseline-and credit system, which complements the cap-and-trade system.

all electricity generators in the province will apply individually for allowance allocations based on their production estimates for the coming year. With a cap on the total number of emissions, allowances will be allocated by the Ontario government to these additional generators at the end of the year based on each station's electricity production during the year.[34] One of the principal lessons from the Ontario example is that the registry can become an essential tool for emissions trading if it has a clear statutory basis and the registry is conceptually integrated into the emissions trading regime.[35]

b) *UK*

Given the UK's geographical location and topographical attributes, the UK's Climate Impacts Program projects myriad disrupting weather patterns caused by climate change.[36] Acknowledging the severity of repercussions has given impetus to policies designed to mitigate GHG production. Indeed, the UK's attempts to combat the deleterious effects of climate change in recent years have been effective: over the last 30 years carbon dioxide emissions per unit of GDP have been halved.[37] Supplementing this positive trend has been an adamant attempt to implement domestic and industrial energy efficiency improvements, in addition to electricity generators switching from coal to natural gas. The UK's legally binding target under the EU's Burden Sharing Agreement is to reduce its emissions by 12.5% compared to 1990 levels. Even though the 12.5% amount was among the most drastic in Europe, the Labour Party won the 1997 elections with a platform promise to reduce CO_2 emissions by 20% from 1990 levels by 2010.

The UK Climate Change Program, a diverse mix of policies and measures, elaborates how the UK will meet both its strenuous domestic and Kyoto targets.

---

[34] Gehring & Streck, *supra* note 23 at 10220.

[35] See M. W. Gehring, "Counting Credits: Emissions Reduction Registries as a First Step Toward Climate Change Regimes in North America" in M. C. Cordonier Segger & Judge C. G. Weeramantry, eds., *Sustainable Justice: Reconciling Economic Social and Environmental Law* (Leiden/Boston: Martinus Nijhoff Publishers, 2005) at 288.

[36] For more detailed information, see U.K., Department for Environment, Food and Rural Affairs, *Scientific and Technical Aspects of Climate Change Including Impacts and Adaptation and Associated Costs* (London: DEFRA, 2004): http://www.defra. gov.uk/environment/climatechange/pubs/pdf/cc-science-0904.pdf.

[37] See C. Dodwell, "UK Emissions Trading Schemes" in D. Freestone & C. Streck, eds., *Legal Aspects of Implementing the Kyoto Protocol Mechanisms* (Oxford: Oxford University Press, 2005) at 445. This effect has been set in particular relief in recent years, as economic growth coincided with carbon intensity reductions of more than 25%.

Published in 2000, it consisted of three main economic instruments: the UK Emission Trading Scheme (UK ETS), the climate change levy and the Climate Change Agreements (CCAs) for energy intensive industries.[38] The Program envelops six general sectors: energy supply, business, transport, domestic, agriculture, forestry and land use and public sector. The fundamental principles underpinning the initiative included endeavoring to take a 'balanced approach' in determining the role of various sectors; enhancing competitiveness (on both domestic and international levels), promoting social cohesion and curtailing harmful health effects; the need for a clear, flexible and stable framework; and focusing on a flexible, cost effective and variegated policy package with a long-term perspective firmly entrenched.[39]

i) *UK Emissions Trading Scheme*

Managed by the Department for Environment, Food and Rural Affairs (DEFRA), the UK ETS was the first emissions trading initiative in the world that facilitated multi-sectoral participation.[40] The UK trading scheme is mainly based on a policy that was not put in the form of a law.[41] Intertwining a 'cap and trade' framework with absolute targets and a baseline-and-credit system in relation to relative or 'unit based' targets, the UK ETS was truly novel in its composition. This framework was designed according to the Government's core focal points:

> to secure a significant quantity of emissions reductions at a reasonable cost; to give organizations early practical experience of emissions trading; to ensure that UK business and finance would be ready to exploit the opportunities available from an international market, allowing the City of London and the UK to become established as a center for emissions trading; and to influence the development of EU action to meet Kyoto targets, by demonstrating the UK's commitment to it.[42]

Situated at the crux of the voluntary 'cap-and-trade' allowance trading scheme are 'direct participants' – companies that have made commitments to reduce

---

[38] See U.K., Department for Environment, Food and Rural Affairs, *Draft Framework for the UK Emissions Trading Scheme* (London: DEFRA, 2001): http://www.defra.gov. uk/environment/climatechange/trading/uk/draft/index.htm (last modified 14 March 2006).

[39] *Ibid.*

[40] *Ibid.*

[41] A consultation document published by the UK Government's Department for Environment, Food and Rural Affairs (DEFRA) provides a review of climate change implementation to date. Available online: http://www.defra.gov.uk/corporate/consult/ukccp-review/index.htm (last modified 31 January 2006).

[42] Dodwell, *supra* note 37 at 447.

their emissions in return for financial incentives from the Government.[43] The reductions levied on the operations of direct participants and the accompanying incentives to be provided were determined in an auction held in March 2002.[44] In terms of coverage of the UK ETS, participation was open to all persons in the UK with emissions of GHGs from 'eligible sources'.[45] Participants were required to choose whether they would participate solely in relation to CO_2 emissions or emissions of all six GHGs. An unusual facet of the coverage of regulated sources, expanding the scope of the Program, is that participants participate in respect of the indirect emission arising from their electricity usage. In order to impede leakage of emissions by the transfer of production to other plants not covered by the scheme, "participants are required to enter all sources operating in any sector and the scheme had detailed rules governing change in operation and source substitution."[46]

Participants were required to agree to overall reductions to be delivered in 2006, with delivery of interim targets, increasing pro-rata on a cumulative basis.[47] Baselines are calculated on the basis of average measured emissions from all sources during the period 1998–2000,[48] unless the participant already has a regulatory limit imposed on emissions from any source. The total cap for the participants is the total of all baselines less the total of all annual targets bid in the auction.[49] Altogether, the emissions reductions bid in the auction represented a 13% reduction in emissions by the end of the scheme.[50]

The Government instituted an Emissions Trading Registry (operating in real time via the internet) in which direct participants opened accounts and managed transactions. Arguably the registry of the UK ETS is indispensable to the scheme's success. Split into the 'absolute sector' and the 'relative sector', the registry enforces a 'gateway' that prohibits a net import of allowances from the relative sector.[51] While banking between years of the scheme is condoned, there

---

[43] *Ibid.* at 449.

[44] *Ibid.*

[45] *Ibid.* at 450. The primary categories of non-eligible sources are: electricity generators (except where electricity is used and generated on-site); land and water transport; domestic households; and facilities covered by CCAs.

[46] *Ibid.* at 451. See Schedule 3 of the Scheme: http://www.defra.gov.uk/environment/climtechange/trading/pdf/trading-rules_rev2.pdf.

[47] Dodwell, *supra* note 37 at 451.

[48] *Ibid.*

[49] *Ibid.*

[50] See U.K., Department for Environment, Food and Rural Affairs, *Framework for the UK Emissions Trading Scheme* (London: DEFRA, 2001): http://www.defra.gov.uk/environment/climatechange/trading/uk/pdf/trading-full.pdf.

[51] See U.K. Department for Environment, Food and Rural Affairs, *The UK Greenhouse Gas Emissions Trading Scheme 2002* (London: DEFRA, 2002): http://www.defra.gov.uk/environment/climatechange/trading/uk/pdf/trading-rules_rev2.pdf.

are no provisions for borrowing during that timeframe.[52] Direct participants are obliged to monitor and report emissions in accordance with approved protocols. Independent accredited verifiers conduct verification of direct participants' compliance with monitoring and reporting standards.[53] Trading is based on seller liability, which is designed to promote liquidity.[54] In 2003, the Government introduced legislation providing for financial penalties of 30 pounds per tonne of excess emissions.[55]

The legal underpinning of the direct participants' involvement in the UK ETS is enshrined in contracts between the Secretary of State and the direct participant, termed Direct Participant Agreements.[56] In particular, under the terms of the Direct Participant Agreement, the Secretary of State agrees to open and maintain accounts at the Registry in the name of the direct participant; allocate allowances; and pay incentive payments and to apply scheme rules in a consistent manner promoting the integrity of the enterprise.[57] Reciprocally, the direct participant agrees to abide by the rules of the scheme including: "limiting its emissions to the agreed levels; monitoring, calculating, reporting and submitting emissions statements and verification opinions in respect of its baseline and its annual emissions; and repaying incentive monies in certain circumstances".[58] The medium of dispute settlement encouraged is mediation.

A pivotal element of the UK ETS is its link with the Climate Change Levy, an energy tax on non-domestic energy users announced by the UK Government in 1999 and in force for all business use of coal, electricity and gas since 2001.[59] An integral element of the Levy is the stipulation that energy-intensive sectors are eligible for an 80% discount if they commit to negotiated reductions in emissions or energy use under Climate Change Agreements (CCAs).[60] Approximately 5000 companies with CCAs are permitted to participate in the UK ETS on a 'baseline-and-credit' basis. In some cases, sector associations

---

[52] *Ibid.*

[53] See U.K., Department for Environment, Food and Rural Affairs, *UK Greenhouse Gas Emissions Trading Scheme 2002: Direct Participant Agreement* (London: DEFRA, 2002): http://www.defra.gov.uk/environment/climatechange/trading/uk/pdf/trading-dp_agreement.pdf. Verifiers certify both the accuracy of the initial baselines and reported annual emissions in each year of the scheme. They are also mandated to oversee the application of special rules regarding the sale of parts of the business or closure.

[54] Dodwell, *supra*, note 37 at 452.

[55] *Ibid.* The statutory authority for these payments derives from the Environmental Protection Act (U.K.), 1990, c. 43, s. 153(4).

[56] *Ibid.* at 453.

[57] *Supra* note 53.

[58] Dodwell, *supra* note 37 at 454.

[59] *Ibid.*

[60] *Ibid.*

trade as a group on behalf of their members that wish to engage in the scheme. Similar registration and verification (i.e. overachievement which is converted to allowances) requirements apply to CCA participants, with the exception that targets are pliable and exist in equilibrium with the quantity of allowances.

4) IMPLEMENTATION ISSUES AND RESULTS TO DATE

Both Canada and the UK have demonstrated that industry can get involved in combating climate change and that economic instruments are feasible. Significant players in myriad Kyoto negotiations, Canada and the UK tapped their respective emissions trading experience to formulate regulations aimed at optimal efficacy. In terms of shaping the Kyoto mechanisms, the CDM benefited from Canada's project-based carbon reduction experience and its adamancy that the framework be developed in simple, certain terms. In this domain, Canada insisted on the inclusion of Land Use, Land Use Change and Forestry ("LULUCFs") projects under the CDM.

a) *Canada's Implementation*

The federal division of environmental responsibilities in the Canadian constitution makes the implementation of a nationwide ETS a complex endeavor. The Federal Government's delegated responsibilities relevant to a carbon trading regime are the ability to sign international treaties on behalf of Canada as well as to devise laws to protect the 'peace, order and good government' of Canada. In contrast, provinces deal with property and civil rights; implement intra-provincial undertakings and regulate forest resources. The express definition of a domestic carbon trading scheme as a 'national concern' would give the Federal Government jurisdictional oversight in theory, but the legitimate extent of encroachment into provincial matters is debatable. Needless to say, plans to attain the Kyoto abatement goals will require significant multi-level cooperation and coordination; if Canada chooses a "cap and trade" system, it could be some time, if ever, before consensus is reached on an initial allocation of permits.[61] Some provinces are advocating internal regulations to achieve Kyoto goals; however, regions that have already made a concerted effort to convert energy production to cleaner sources would prefer the competitive advantage they would receive under a federally mandated initiative.[62]

---

[61] Thomas et al., *supra* note 16.
[62] Gehring & Chambers, *supra* note 17 at 502.

The idea of generating inexpensive GHG emission reduction credits through projects in developing countries appeals to many Canadian constituents.[63] The substantial contribution by Canada to the Prototype Carbon Fund (at $15 million, it is the largest single contribution from any state and 10 percent of the overall investments by all countries),[64] attests to the centrality of CDM among the Kyoto Mechanisms from Canada's perspective. However, it is not clear whether the Canadian Government can devise a domestic emissions trading system that seamlessly meshes with CDM CERs. Part of the enthusiasm for CDM and JI Projects is the anticipation that although regulated industries will have access to credits from international sources, due to the potential for transactions to jeopardize Canada's Kyoto obligations, 90% of the allocations may be held in national credit reserves.[65]

Drafted with broad consultation,[66] the Government of Canada devised a climate change plan in 2005 termed: 'Project Green', *Moving Forward on Climate Change: A Plan for Honouring our Kyoto Commitment*. This plan builds on the *Action Plan 2000* and the *2002 Climate Change Plan for Canada*. It is estimated that the approaches outlined in the Plan, with an associated federal investment in the range of $10 billion through 2012, could reduce GHG emissions by about 270 megatonnes annually in the 2008–2012 period.[67] The main elements of the Plan include: developing competitive and sustainable industries for the 21st century; harnessing market forces; solidifying partner-

---

[63] See Thomas et al., *supra* note 16. Canada is actively seeking bilateral arrangements with a number of developing and Annex 1 countries to facilitate projects in other countries. For example, Canada announced an umbrella agreement with Poland under which Canada and Poland will seek opportunities to implement projects that will qualify under the "activities implemented jointly" provisions of the Framework Convention and which it is hoped will convert into permitted GHG emission trades during the Kyoto Protocol first commitment period when both Canada and Poland will be subject to GHG emission limits.

[64] *Ibid.* at 3.

[65] Gehring & Chambers, *supra* note 17 at 509.

[66] The Canadian government intends to consult the provinces and territories, municipalities, Aboriginal peoples, industry, NGOs and all citizens in the implementation of the plan in order to maximize the conditions of success.

[67] The complete "Project Green" publication can be found online: http://www.climatechange.gc.ca/kyoto_commitments/report_e.pdf. The proposed budget breakdown is as follows: the Climate Fund will receive a minimum funding of $1 billion annually; the Partnership fund will receive an initial $250–300 million with potential incremental increases up to $2–3 billion in the next decade; Renewable energy: the Wind Power Production Incentive will receive $200 million, the Renewable Power Production Incentive will receive $100 million, and there will be $300 million in tax incentives for efficient and renewable energy production; a final $2 billion will be allocated to existing Programs under the Climate Change umbrella.

ships among Canada's governments; engaging citizens; fomenting sustainable agriculture and forest resources and sustainable cities and communities.[68] According to the Executive summary of the document's main themes, the *2005 Climate Change Plan* will "contribute significantly to cleaner air for Canada's cities, enhance biodiversity, help to preserve wild spaces and generally improve the quality of life for Canadians".[69] A long-term focus on the transition to clean energy sources underpins the Plan, but more immediate initiatives include fostering cooperation among governments through the Partnership Fund. Under the Partnership Fund, the Federal government will lead by example (greening its own operations) and will encourage provincial and municipal governments to "identify mutual priorities and share in the undertaking of major investments in technologies and infrastructure development".[70] The Plan anticipates that the Partnership Fund will leverage investment in smaller projects of a local nature, including, for example, the cost-sharing of climate change centres in each province and territory along the lines of Alberta's Climate Change Central. Drafters of the 2005 Plan also made provisions for the Partnership Fund to assist national strategies in areas such as demand-side management, conservation and combined heat and power (cogeneration).[71]

Through the innovative 'Final Emitter System', the government aspires to enable Large Final Emitters (LFEs) to remain competitive whilst contributing tangibly to emissions goals.[72] Companies included under the LFE classification contribute just under 50% of Canada's total GHG emissions and include mining and manufacturing, oil and gas and thermal electricity sectors. Building on accumulated experience, the LFE system will cover about 700 companies operating in Canada; 80–90 of these companies account for an estimated 85% of the LFE GHG emissions.[73] Given that the economic vitality of LFEs is vital to Canada's prosperity, competitiveness is a key concern in adopting a market-based methodology. Building on the *2002 Climate Change Plan for Canada*, the Program will retain flexibility in regards to early action, regional burden and competitiveness, but the overall target has been downgraded from 55 $MtCO_2$ to 45 $MtCO_2$ due to improvements in calculating the business as usual (BAU) quantities. The LFE targets are complied using a distinction between "fixed process" (emissions that cannot be reduced without hampering productivity) and "other" emissions (emissions that can be modified by technological

---

[68] *Ibid.*

[69] *Ibid.*

[70] *Ibid.*

[71] *Ibid.*

[72] For more information on Canada's federal subsidy programs and the regulation of LFEs, refer to A. Lucas, "Implementing the Kyoto Protocol in North America: Canada's Policy and Instrument Choices" (2006) 2 Energy Law and Taxation Review 48.

[73] Project Green, *supra* note 67.

improvements). For the first Kyoto period (2008–2012), fixed process emissions receive a zero percent target and all other emissions have a 15% target.[74]

The cost of compliance to the LFE program will not exceed $15 per tonne of CO_2 equivalent. The system is slated to be implemented through the use of covenants (a system of contractual agreements between government and industry) with a regulatory or financial backstop.[75] There are multiple methods of compliance: investment in in-house reductions; purchase of surplus emission reductions from high performing LFEs; investment in domestic offset credits; and the purchase of international credits that represent verified emission reduction.[76] Further, investment in technology developments, limited to 9 $MtCO_2$, will be counted towards compliance efforts. Rigorous monitoring and reporting standards will ensure a high degree of transparency and public accountability while maintaining the confidentiality of industry competitive practices. The Federal government's preferred route of implementation is through the *1999* Canadian Environmental Protection Act (CEPA), which sets out legislation regarding "Smart Regulations" and is able to facilitate equivalency agreements with provinces, territories and Aboriginal governments.

Another element of the *2005 Climate Change Plan* is the Climate Fund, an allotment set aside to establish a permanent institution for the purchase of emissions reduction and removal credits (both on a domestic level and in international scenarios where "national interest" is perceived) on behalf of the Government of Canada. The government envisions that the Fund will "stimulate innovation; enable Canadians to take action; encourage energy efficiency; deliver cost-effective reductions and sequestration; drive the adoption of the best available technologies and stimulate the development of a domestic trading system".[77]

Even though the Conservative minority government lead by Prime minister Stephen Harper has announced in January 2006 a thorough review of all existing climate policies, it has become clear that the Canadian government will not "pull out" of Kyoto and that the final large emitter program might go ahead with little change, since industry has invested considerably in this area. The allocation of funds however might change considerably.[78]

---

[74] *Ibid.* However, the targeted reductions from these other emissions as a percentage of total emissions cannot exceed 12% of total emissions.

[75] *Ibid.*

[76] *Ibid.*

[77] *Ibid.*

[78] P. Gorrie "Future of Kyoto cash, climate change plan still in doubt" *Toronto Star* (27 January 2006) C1.

b) *UK Implementation*

The *2003 Energy White Paper* explains the UK Government's long-term plans for creating a low carbon economy.[79] The policy paper was written with inter-departmental collaboration, integrated environmental studies and impact assessments and broad consultation. According to the text, three main challenges to the status quo are thought to figure prominently: environmental implications emanating from climate change; diminishing indigenous energy supplies; and the need for modernization of infrastructure.[80] The purported goals of the energy policy are to:

> cut CO_s emissions by 60% by 2050, as recommended by the RCEP with real progress by 2020; to maintain the reliability of energy supplies; to promote competitive markets in the UK and beyond, helping to raise the rate of sustainable economic growth and to improve our productivity; and to ensure that every home is adequately and affordably heated.[81]

The mix of tools proposed to achieve the 15–25 $MtCO_2$ reduction by 2020 includes: energy efficiency in households (4–6 $MtCO_2$); energy efficiency in industry, commerce and the public sector (4–6 $MtCO_2$); transport (2–4 $MtCO_2$); increasing renewables (3–5 $MtCO_2$) and the EU Carbon Trading Scheme (2–4 $MtCO_2$).[82]

As a member of the EU, the UK has become involved in the EC Emission Trading Scheme (EC ETS)[83] in addition to its domestic efforts at emission

---

[79] Refer to the U.K., H.C., "Our Energy Future: Creating a Low Carbon Economy" Cm 5761 in Sessional Papers 2003 (White Paper presented to Parliament by the Secretary of State for Trade and Industry by Command of Her Majesty February 2003): http://www.dti.gov.uk/energy/whitepaper/ourenergyfuture.pdf. For an overview of the UK climate change abatement plan, see A. Hobley, "Emissions Trading in the UK: An Overview" (2001) 9 Environmental Liability 1 at 3–10.

[80] White Paper, *supra* note 79.

[81] *Ibid.*

[82] *Ibid.*

[83] The EU ETS is typified by 'open architecture' established by EC, Council and European Parliament Directive 2003/87/EC of 13 October 2003 amending Council Directive 96/61/EC with regards to establishing a scheme for greenhouse gas emission allowance trading within the Community. Operating at the company level, the EU ETS is a strict 'cap and trade' system operating at the company level. An 'allowance' is defined as the ability to emit one tonne of CO_2 equivalent (tCO_2e) during a specified period. First period (2005–2007): binding caps on CO_2 emissions from installations above certain production capacity or output thresholds. Second period (2008+) EU25 unilaterally include additional installations, sectors and GHGs. National Allocation Plans (NAPs) of EU25 must be approved; largely left to national discretion. Flexibility is achieved through borrowing, banking, buying and selling of allowances. Strict mea-

reductions. The UK formulated a National Allocation Plan (NAP) that was approved by the European Commission after slight revisions.[84] According to the NAP itself, the UK's starting point was to estimate its total projected emissions in 2010 and then to consider the additional savings that the EU ETS sector should deliver.[85] Subsequently, the UK calculated sector allocations by applying the details of the emissions projections in a combination of top-down and bottom-up methodologies and by taking account of the additional EU ETS savings.[86]

The most recent year for which the UK has published emissions data is 2002 when total annual emissions of all greenhouse gases were estimated to be 648.4 $MtCO_2$ equivalent and emissions of CO_2 were estimated to be 551.0 $MtCO_2$. The data show falls of slightly less than 3.5% for all greenhouse gases and slightly more than 3.5% for CO_2 emissions between 2001 and 2002. However, provisional estimates show that emissions probably rose by about 1.5% between 2002 and 2003.[87]

5) CONCLUDING THOUGHTS

It is worthwhile noting that the extensive participation and assessment procedures adopted by legislation in Canada and the UK are unusual from a global perspective. Even the EU – often at the forefront of transforming sustainable development principles into policy implementation – lags behind UK and Canadian climate change legislation in this realm. Promotion of civil society

---

sures regulate monitoring, reporting and verification. The EU permits negotiation of full linking with other national and sub-national systems.

[84] Refer to U.K., Department for Environment, Food and Rural Affairs, *EU ETS: UK National Allocation Plan 2005–2007* (London: DEFRA, 2005): http://www.defra. gov.uk/environment/climatechange/trading/eu/nap/intro.htm. NAPs must be based on objective and transparent criteria including those set out in Annex III of the EU Directive. The criteria include: compatibility with Kyoto Protocol and national Climate Change Programmes; consistency with projected emissions (i.e. no over-allocation); consistency with the potential of activities to reduce emissions and safeguards against discrimination between installations/sectors.

[85] *Ibid.* For the legal background and economic justification of the UK and EU ETS, see S. Blackmore & A. Hobley, "Greenhouse Gas Emissions Trading in the United Kingdom and the EU Compared: Same Destination, Different Routes" (2002) 10 Environmental Liability 2 at 55–66.

[86] *Ibid.* For more information on the revision process undertaken by DEFRA, see "DEFRA Treads Wearily on Expansion of EU Emissions Trading Scheme" (2005) Ends Report 367 at 35–36.

[87] *Ibid.* For a partial explanation of the UK's shortfall, refer to "Oversupply Cripples UK Emissions Market" (2003) Ends Report 340 at 4–5.

participation throughout the process is an important element of sustainable development law, as described in the ILA New Delhi Principles[88] and the Johannesburg Plan of Implementation.[89] Indeed, fostering frictionless coherence amid the balancing of economic, environmental and development considerations requires multifaceted procedural approaches.

As discussed above, resolving the issue of vulnerability has been a central conundrum plaguing incipient emissions trading regimes. Although vulnerability can be addressed by full inclusion of CERs in both systems, Canada's Kyoto Fund provides the preeminent example of an instrument embodying a long-term perspective. Even though at this point in time mitigation has not been allocated a meaningful niche within the emissions trading paradigm, the authors are of the opinion that this does not preclude the concept from becoming a core part of future climate cooperation. Carbon trading fits neatly within the frame of mitigation measures: legal, institutional and policy alterations oriented to slow the myriad effects of climate change. In contrast, adaptation measures are typically more proactive and invasive, responding to inter-sectoral changes stemming from climate change by incorporating a pre-emptive, multifaceted plan with a long-term perspective.[90] Indeed, given the topography of Canada

---

[88] Refer to International Law Association, *New Delhi Declaration On Principles of International Law Related to Sustainable Development* (London: ILA, 2002). Several sustainable development principles espoused by the Declaration are relevant in this context. The 'principle of the precautionary approach to human health, natural resources and ecosystems' necessitates that planning stems from clear criteria, well-defined goals and consideration of all possible options and contingencies in an environmental impact assessment. A precautionary approach to risk management is strongly advised. The 'principle of public participation and access to information and justice' is premised on both the government apparatus and civil society being equally responsive, transparent and accountable in the domains of information access and recourse to justice. Finally, the 'principle of good governance' is replete with references to transparency, accountability and adherence to the rule of law. See M. C. Cordonier Segger & A. Khalfan, *Sustainable Development Law: Principles, Practices and Prospects* (Oxford: Oxford University Press, 2005) at 99–102.

[89] Refer to UN, Department of Economic and Social Affairs, *Johannesburg Plan of Implementation*, Report of the World Summit on Sustainable Development, 4 September 2002, UN Doc. A/CONF.199/20. Document available online: http://www.un.org/esa/sustdev/documents/WSSD_POI_PD/English/POIToc.htm. Chapter X specifies that the means of implementing the sustainable development objectives include risk assessment and risk management as well as education, capacity building and research.

[90] Adaptation policy instruments have several categories: legislative, regulatory and juridical commands (i.e. revision of fishing quotas to meet adaptation goals); financial and market incentives (i.e. water pricing for conservation); educational and informational assistance (i.e. public education to reduce disease exposure) and service delivery (i.e. incorporating climate adaptive capacity into transportation infrastructure).

and the UK (both territories have plenty of vulnerable low-lying coastlines), mitigation, adaptation and prevention should characterize the scope of future climate change policy.

In addition to questions regarding the intrinsic vulnerability of emissions trading and the proper locus of mitigation, facilitating linkages among disparate regimes is another unresolved topic. While the EU permits negotiation of full linking with other national or sub-national systems, the UK and Canada are much more reticent about collaboration. However, in legal terms, expanded direct linking is possible; price cap and "hot air" credits do not obstruct the derivation of a future joint EU-Canadian ETS. Undoubtedly, Canadian businesses can benefit from comprehensive international linkages directed at carbon abatement. Despite the conceivable grounds for NAFTA challenges with regard to trade in services (trading and/or certification services), subsidies (credits from Canadian Kyoto Fund) or investment, adherence to the international "gold standard" classification of credits will largely mitigate litigation. Moreover, galvanizing linking agreements with state-level emissions trading schemes in the US would be a logical progression of Canada's Kyoto project.

In summary, within the international community both Canada and the UK are established leaders in devising innovative climate change legislation and avant-garde economic instruments for implementation. At the multilateral level, both countries actively supported the inclusion of the flexible mechanisms within the Kyoto compact and have shown deference to precepts within the international investment and trade regimes relevant to climate change. Although challenges lie ahead for both Canada and the UK in their attempts to achieve their Kyoto obligations, bilateral and regional implementation efforts will help to assuage the burden. Canada is planning to make extensive use of the Kyoto mechanisms (especially the CDM) and the UK will be manifestly integrated into the EU ETS. However, both countries would benefit from extending and intensifying regime linkages. It makes sense for Canada to take concrete steps to work with the US states embarking on emissions trading. In general terms, bilateral implementation efforts would doubtlessly provide assistance in overcoming some of the domestic challenges associated with getting optimal performance from an emissions trading scheme.

At various junctures throughout this chapter, there have been clarifications regarding the facets of international sustainable development law that resonate with an ideal emissions trading regime. Formulating such a regime requires a variety of inputs from a range of both governmental and civil society stakeholders. Further, procedural transparency and good governance are vital factors in dictating the success of emissions trading. The social, environmental and economic repercussions of climate change make it inherently a sustainable development issue. Proficiently employing economic instruments could make emissions trading a useful prototype for other sustainable development challenges.

Chapter 14

Government Regulation and the Development of Corporate Social Responsibility in the UK and Canada

Henry Lovat and Osman Aboubakr

1) INTRODUCTION

Although Corporate Social Responsibility (CSR) is increasingly discussed in a variety of contexts – in this book in respect of both sustainable development (Chapters 12 and 13) and access to medicines (Chapter 15) – there is no universally accepted or authoritative definition of the concept. Generally speaking, however, CSR may be acceptably defined as the commitment by business "to contribute to sustainable economic development, working with employees, their families, the local community and society at large to improve their quality of life."[1] Accordingly, this will be the meaning given to the term in this paper.

While this definition is certainly open to debate, it fairly accurately reflects two dynamics that are worth noting. The first is that CSR compliance means

---

[1] R. Holme and P. Watts, *Corporate social responsibility: making good business sense* (World Business Council for Sustainable Development, January 2000): http://www.wbcsd.ch/DocRoot/IunSPdIKvmYH5HjbN4XC/csr2000.pdf.

Christopher P.M. Waters (Ed.), *British and Canadian Perspectives on International Law*, pp. 275–289.

going beyond traditional corporate charitable giving. In the stereotypical case, previously a corporation may have exerted itself to maximise its profits within the boundaries of the applicable legal and taxation regimes, and only then might its board of directors have considered what (if any) proportion of its profits it may be able to donate to good causes. CSR compliance would suggest – if not require – that such a corporation take into account the social and other impacts of its behaviour at a much earlier stage – in the course of its revenue-generating activity rather than as a post-dividend afterthought.

The second dynamic is that the span of CSR is broad. It requires, at least to a degree, a corporation to go beyond simple financial measurements of benefit and detriment as far as the impact of its operations is concerned. Thus, proponents of CSR typically refer to CSR as requiring corporations (or at least those corporations that wish to hold themselves out to be CSR-compliant) to take a 'triple bottom line' approach to measuring their behaviour – that is, to measure and to report on corporate performance not solely in terms of financial returns, but with reference also to the social and environmental impact of a corporation's behaviour.[2]

As intimated above, the academic literature on CSR is both extensive and diffuse. A review of the available literature shows that discussions of corporate social responsibility are recorded as long ago as 1969, and in purely legal terms, may arguably extend at least to the circumstances giving rise to the 1919 decision in *Dodge v Ford Motor Co.*[3] It is perhaps indicative of how far this discourse has developed since then that despite Milton Friedman's oft-quoted 1970 dictum that "the social responsibility of business is to increase its profits",[4] more recent authors have stated confidently that "the question is not whether a corporation should be constrained by obligations other than those it owes to its shareholders but instead what social obligations should constrain corporate behaviour."[5] Perhaps unsurprisingly, CSR has also become a multi-disciplinary concern. Aside from the (arguably vested) interest of corporate

---

[2] Making an explicit link between CSR compliance and triple bottom line reporting, Industry Canada has noted that: "while CSR does not have a universal definition, many see it as the private sector's way of integrating the economic, social, and environmental imperatives of their activities. As such, CSR closely resembles the business pursuit of sustainable development and the triple bottom line." See: http://strategis.ic.gc.ca/epic/internet/incsr-rse.nsf/en/Home.

[3] F. de Bakker, P. Groenewegen and F. den Hond, "A Bibliometric Analysis of 30 Years of Research and Theory on Corporate Social Responsibility and Corporate Social Performance" (2005) 44 Business and Society 290. See also *Dodge v. Ford Motor Co.* 204 Mich. 459, 170 N.W. 668 (1919).

[4] M. Friedman, "The Social Responsibility of Business Is To Increase Profits", *New York Times Magazine*, 13 September 1970.

[5] P. Macklem, "Soft Labour Law" at 13. (Draft in progress dated 27/10/2005. Cited with the author's permission.)

lawyers, some commentators have noted that "the field of (CSR) . . . has become firmly embedded in the management sciences."[6] It has also emerged as an area of investigation in International Law, International Relations and International Development literature.[7]

Regardless of the disciplinary approach taken, however, one of the more surprising observations that can be made about CSR compliance to date is that compliance appears to have spread despite such behaviour remaining apparently voluntary.[8] CSR-compliant behaviour by corporations appears to have been driven far more by market and consumer expectations (the promotion of CSR by non-governmental organisations, pressure groups and by corporations themselves) than by inter-governmental or governmental initiatives – whether through regulation or otherwise. However, while government initiatives and regulation may previously have lagged behind both corporate behaviour and market expectations, there are indications that this situation is changing. Moreover, emphasizing the 'voluntariness' of CSR compliance to date may very well run the risk of under-estimating the positive influence legislation and regulation has had and is having on corporate behaviour in relation to CSR.

2) INTERNATIONAL BACKDROP

CSR has long been a topic of concern at the multilateral level, not least since the establishment of the United Nations Commission on Transnational Corporations ('UNCTC') in 1974. The publication in 1976 of the OECD Guidelines for Multinational Enterprises[9] and of the International Labour Organisation's Tripartite Declaration of Principles concerning Multinational Enterprises and Social Policy in 1977[10] further cemented the status of CSR-related issues as being of international concern.

---

[6] *Supra* note 4 at 312.

[7] See e.g. S. Ratner, "Corporations and Human Rights: A Theory of Legal Responsibility" (2001) 111 Yale Law Journal 443; J. Ruggie, "Reconstituting the Global Public Domain – Issues, Actors and Practices" (2004) 104 European Journal of International Relations 499; M. Bryane, "Corporate Social Responsibility in International Development: An Overview And Critique" (2003) 10 Corporate Social Responsibility and Environmental Management 115.

[8] For further information on certain voluntary initiatives relating to CSR, see M. Kerr and M.-C. Cordonier Segger, "Legal Strategies to promote corporate social responsibility and accountability: a prerequisite for sustainable development" (Montreal: CISDL, April 2004).

[9] A revised set of Guidelines was published by the OECD in 2000: http://www.oecd.org/dataoecd/56/36/1922428.pdf.

[10] See http://www.ilo.org/public/english/standards/norm/sources/mne.htm.

While a draft Code of Conduct on Transnational Corporations was produced by the UNCTC in 1982,[11] it was only in the late 1990's that CSR re-emerged onto the multilateral scene in any significant manner. In 1998, the ILO produced a Declaration on Fundamental Principles and Rights at Work,[12] and in 2000 the UN launched the 'Global Compact' in an attempt to: "promote responsible corporate citizenship so that business can be part of the solution to the challenges of globalisation."[13] Most recently, the UN Human Rights Commission's Sub-Commission on the Promotion and Protection of Human Rights adopted a set of 'Norms on the responsibilities of transnational corporations and other business enterprises with regard to human rights.'[14]

Despite the varying levels of commitment shown by states and corporations to these multilateral initiatives, however, states have retained primacy in the area of CSR-related corporate legislation and governance. This is true both legally – indeed the Human Rights Commission's Norms reaffirm the primary responsibility of states to ensure that businesses respect human rights[15] – and practically speaking, especially in states such as Canada and the UK with strong governance capacity.

3) CSR AS AN AREA OF GOVERNMENT POLICY

The UK government's position on CSR is contained primarily in an 'International Strategic Framework' published by the Department of Trade and Industry ('DTI') in March 2005.[16] This document contains what the DTI refers to as the government's "ambitious vision" for CSR: "to see UK businesses taking account of their economic, social and environmental impacts, and acting to address the key sustainable development challenges based on their core competences wherever they operate – locally, regionally and internationally."[17]

---

[11] These were never finalised, and were eventually abandoned altogether.

[12] See www.ilo.org/dyn/declaris/DECLARATIONWEB.static_jump?var_language= EN&var_pagename=DECLARATIONTEXT.

[13] See www.unglobalcompact.org/Portal/.

[14] Adopted by the Sub-Commission in 2003: http://www.unhchr.ch/huridocda/huri-doca.nsf/(Symbol)/E.CN.4.Sub.2.2003.12.Rev.2.En?Opendocument. The norms arguably provide more potential for enforcement of CSR than previous international efforts; see D. Weissbrodt, "Corporate Social Responsibility In The International Context: Business And Human Rights" (2005) 74 U. Cin. L. Rev. 55.

[15] See Weissbrodt, *ibid.*

[16] Department of Trade and Industry, *Corporate Social Responsibility: International Strategic Framework* (Department of Trade and Industry, March 2005): http://www.csr. gov.uk/pdf/dti_csr_finaldoc.pdf.

[17] *Ibid.* at 1.

Somewhat surprisingly, however, the DTI's approach is quite sparing in terms of specific commitments. The UK government commits itself in this document only to "foster[ing] an enabling environment for responsible business practice to maximise the positive contribution that business can make to the UK's objectives on international sustainable development . . . whilst at the same time effectively tackling adverse impacts"[18] through increasing awareness amongst business of the need to take action and through encouraging the continuing "development and application of best practice."[19]

The position in Canada is essentially similar. However, in contrast to the relatively centralised approach taken in the UK, CSR-related issues tend to be addressed as discrete policy areas, and so are dealt with by a variety of government departments and agencies at each of the federal, provincial and municipal levels. The federal departments involved in CSR-related issues have thus included Industry Canada, Environment Canada, Foreign Affairs Canada, Natural Resources Canada and Human Resources and Skills Development Canada.[20]

4) POPULAR CONCERN WITH CSR

Despite the relative paucity of formal governmental commitments in regard to CSR (and certainly the absence of a unified regulatory regime for CSR internationally or domestically) in both Canada and the UK, there seems to be significant public awareness of CSR-related issues. As far as levels of awareness and support for CSR in Canada are concerned, a March 2005 GlobeScan report provides a degree of insight. According to the authors of this report, 92% of Canadians surveyed are more likely to buy the products or services of a company if it acts in a socially and environmentally responsible manner. These preferences extend out to employment and general opinions as to preferred corporate values: 91% of respondents would prefer to work for companies that are socially and environmentally responsible, while 93% believe that CSR "should be as important to companies as profit and shareholder value."[21]

With regard to environmental performance, Canadian views were found to be particularly strong, with 82% of survey respondents reportedly holding companies "completely responsible for not harming the environment."[22] Perhaps

---

[18] *Ibid.* at 2.

[19] *Ibid.*

[20] A relatively comprehensive collection of information on CSR practice and policy is available on the Industry Canada website. See *supra* note 3.

[21] "Expectations for Corporate Social Responsibility Rising With Clear Consequences For Not Measuring Up" (press release): http://www.newswire.ca/en/ releases/ archive/April2005/20/c7666.html.

[22] *Ibid.*

the most interesting statistic, however, relates to investors' concerns – approximately 25% of shareholders surveyed reported that a company's CSR performance was relevant to whether or not they bought or sold shares, while over half of those viewed "socially responsible companies as more profitable than irresponsible ones."[23]

Similar levels of concern have been reported in the UK. According to a February 2004 MORI 'White Paper' report,[24] 84% of those surveyed agreed that a company's degree of social responsibility was at least "fairly important" when considering purchasing a product or service,[25] while 9 out of 10 employees considered it important that their employer act responsibly towards society and the environment.[26]

Also of interest, with respect to the UK particularly, were the views of respondents as regards the behaviour of companies abroad. Thus 71% of the MORI respondents agreed that companies should always ensure good working conditions for their employees in developing countries, above and beyond any minimum requirements in such countries, while 51% of respondents went beyond that, taking the view that "companies should contribute to social issues such as healthcare, housing and education" in these countries.[27]

5) CSR REPORTING

Having reviewed the extent of popular concern with CSR-related issues in Canada and the UK, it is perhaps worth briefly examining the extent to which these views are reflected in corporate behaviour. A recent KPMG/University of Amsterdam survey[28] of corporate responsibility reporting undertaken by the largest 100 companies by revenue in each of 16 countries, including Canada and the UK, allows some observations to be made in this regard.

Specifically, KPMG found that while Japanese companies were most likely to produce stand-alone CSR information, 71% of the top 100 British companies published separate CSR reports, taking them into second place (80% of the top Japanese companies produced such reports). Canada ranked third in the survey, with 41% of the largest 100 Canadian companies publishing separate CSR reports.[29]

---

[23] *Ibid.*

[24] MORI, *The Public's Views of Corporate Responsibility 2003* (MORI, February 2004): http://www.mori.com/pubinfo/jld/publics-views-of-corporate-responsibilty.pdf.

[25] *Ibid.* at 2.

[26] *Ibid.* at 5.

[27] *Ibid.* at 6.

[28] KPMG, *International Survey of Corporate Responsibility Reporting 2005* (KPMG, June 2005): http://www.kpmg.ca/en/news/documents/KPMGCRSurvey2005.pdf.

[29] *Ibid.* at 10.

A previous survey, undertaken by KPMG in 2002 (and referenced in the 2005 survey) may also be useful in enabling time-series comparisons within the UK and Canada. Both the 2002 and 2005 surveys record instances in which companies produced separate CSR reports (as distinct from their annual reports). Using these figures, the increase in the UK between 2002 and 2005 was from 49% to 71% of firms in terms of producing separate CSR reports, while in Canada it was from 19% of firms to a figure just slightly less than 41%.[30] In both countries, therefore, significant increases were identified over time in the proportions of large companies producing CSR information (at least in separate form).

6) CSR REGULATION

Both the UK and Canada have enacted legislation that deals with CSR as a concept in itself (and that attempts to mould corporate behaviour in this sphere generally – as distinct, say, from legislation dealing with corporate behaviour in purely social or environmental contexts). In neither country, however, can a body of 'CSR law' be said to have developed. As will be seen below, the development of CSR compliance, in the absence of comprehensive regulation, can be explained by reference to a number of other factors. However, this should not be taken as understating – again, as will be illustrated later – the centrality of legislation and regulation to corporate behaviour, both generally and in the field of CSR in particular.

a) *The UK*[31]

CSR regulation is relatively well developed in the UK. The UK government has for some time included a Minister responsible for CSR, and under the current Labour government there have been two particularly significant legislative developments on the CSR front: the introduction of an annual Operating and Financial Review ('OFR') for listed companies and the amendment of the 1995 Pensions Act to require pension fund managers to report the extent to which certain non-financial considerations are taken into account in their choice of investments.

The OFR should constitute a review of a company's activities in the relevant reporting year, providing a "balanced and comprehensive analysis"[32] of a com-

---

[30] *Ibid.*

[31] For an overview of CSR regulation in the UK generally, see D. Frank, E. Fife and H. Lovat, "United Kingdom" in D. Frank, ed., *CSR World* (European Lawyer, 2005).

[32] DTI, *Guidance on the OFR and changes to the directors' report* (DTI, April 2005) at 6: <http://www.dti.gov.uk/cld/OFR_Guidance.pdf>.

pany's performance and position, and of "the main trends and factors underlying the development, performance and position of the company . . . and which are likely to affect it in the future."[33] Issues related to the environment and employees, as well as social and community issues, should be considered in the OFR, as far as these are deemed necessary by the directors to satisfy these general requirements. In particular, under new Schedule 7ZA of the Companies Act, the OFR must include information about company policies as regards environmental matters, employees and social and community issues, as well as "information about the extent to which those policies have been successfully implemented."[34] In terms of implementation, UK companies with shares officially listed on the London Stock Exchange or in any other European Economic Area state, or that have been admitted to either the New York Stock Exchange or NASDAQ, will be required to prepare an OFR each financial year for reporting periods commencing 1 April 2005.

As mentioned above, the other particularly significant development in terms of CSR regulation in the UK has been the amendment of the Pensions Act 1995 through the 'OPS Regulations'.[35] Following the coming into force of these regulations, the trustees of many pension schemes are now required to include within their statement of investment principles a statement of their policy as regards "the extent (if at all) to which social, environmental or ethical considerations are taken into account in the selection, retention and realisation of investments."[36]

Aside from the two disclosure-oriented examples cited above, the other main avenue by which CSR compliance has been supported in the UK through legislative means has been through the introduction of Community Investment Tax Relief ('CITR'). This tax relief was introduced in the 2002 Finance Act, and is available to investors (for a minimum of five years) in recognised Community Development Finance Institutions ('CDFI's). CDFIs then "provide finance to business, including social, community and for-profit enterprises that have viable business propositions but are unable to access mainstream sources of finance."[37]

In order to round out this portrayal of the legislative landscape as regards CSR in the UK, the recent publication of a draft Company Law Reform Bill

---

[33] *Ibid.*

[34] The Companies Act 1985 (OFR and Directors' Report) Regulations 2005, SI 2005 No. 1011, para. 9.

[35] The Occupational Pension Schemes (Investment, and Assignment, Forfeiture, Bankruptcy etc) Amendment Regulations 1999, SI 1999/1849.

[36] *Ibid.* at para. 2(4). As Kerr and Cordonier Segger note, certain other jurisdictions "have followed the UK's lead and introduced broadly parallel legislation [*supra* note 8 at 8.]

[37] HM Treasury, *A Guide to Tax Incentives for Corporate Giving*, at 15: http://www.hmrc.gov.uk/charities/guide_tax_incentives.pdf.

should be mentioned.[38] Published in March 2005, the DTI's current proposals go some way beyond the current emphasis on CSR reporting. Specifically, they would require company directors to take into account, in fulfilling their statutory duty to promote the success of the company for the benefit of its members, "any need of the company . . . to have regard to the interests of its employees . . . (and) to consider the impact of its operations on the community and the environment."[39]

As may be evident from the foregoing discussion, the inclusion of such a provision in legislation may well be indicative of a sea change in government attitudes towards CSR. This would certainly represent a significant step forward from the predominantly 'permissive' approach currently taken to CSR reporting.

Lastly, in terms of European influences on CSR legislation in the UK, it is worth noting that the UK seems (in legislative terms at least) to be running ahead of the EU in this area. The European Council has, to date, largely restricted its involvement in the field to calling upon member states to promote CSR at a national level,[40] while a Green Paper on the subject has also been published.[41] The European Commission has also convened a multistakeholder forum on CSR, the membership of which included interested NGOs as well as bodies representing employers and employees.[42] Launched in 2002, this body presented its final report in June 2004. The forum stopped short of specific legislative recommendations, however – perhaps reflecting the definition of CSR adopted by the forum as the basis for its discussions, which emphasised the "voluntary basis" of CSR-compliant behaviour.[43]

---

[38] DTI, *Company Law Reform* (DTI, March 2005): http://www.dti.gov.uk/cld/WhitePaper.pdf.

[39] *Ibid.* at 90.

[40] See EU, *Council Resolution of 6 February 2003 on corporate social responsibility*, O.J.C. [2003] 39/02: http://europa.eu.int/eur-lex/pri/en/oj/dat/2003/c_039/c_03920030218en-00030004.pdf.

[41] See European Commission, *Promoting a European framework for corporate social responsibility* (EC, 2001): http://europa.eu.int/comm/employment_social/soc-dial/csr/greenpaper_en.pdf.

[42] See EU Multistakeholder Forum on CSR: http://forum.europa.eu.int/irc/empl/csr_eu_multi_stakeholder_forum/info/data/en/csr%20ems%20forum.htm.

[43] European Multistakeholder Forum on CSR, *Final Results and Recommendations*, at 3 ("CSR is a concept whereby companies integrate social and environmental concerns in their business operations and in their interactions with their stakeholders on a voluntary basis"): http://forum.europa.eu.int/irc/empl/csr_eu_multi_stakeholder_forum/info/ data/en/CSR%20Forum%20final%20report.pdf.

b) *Canada*[44]

The situation in Canada is similar to that prevailing in the UK.[45] The relevant legislative focus to date has once again been on the areas of corporate reporting and tax credits, although the law relating to directors' duties and liabilities has also developed in a manner that may address certain CSR-related concerns. As in the UK, recent developments indicate an increasingly robust attitude towards CSR compliance on the part of Canadian legislators and courts.

In terms of corporate reporting and disclosure regulations, a significant CSR-related obligation relates to the duty of public corporations[46] to produce an Annual Information Form ('AIF').[47] The AIF is an annual corporate report required by Canadian securities law to contain certain prescribed information and to be made publicly available through the information system SEDAR.[48] It is designed to "disclose material information about a company and its business in the context of its historical and possible future development (and) the information to be disclosed includes a description of the company, its structure and operations as well as its prospects, risks and other external factors that impact the company."[49]

National Instrument 51–102[50] (which came into force in March 2004 and applies to financial years beginning on or after 1 January 2004) requires public corporations to disclose in their AIFs any environmental and health risks relating to them or their business that would be likely to influence an investor's decision to purchase these corporations' securities. The National Instrument also requires that where a "company has implemented social or environmental policies that are fundamental to [its] operations, such as policies regarding [its]

---

[44] For an overview of CSR regulation in Canada generally, see E. J. Waitzer and D. Juricevic, "Canada" in Frank, *supra* note 31.

[45] In Canada, securities regulation falls within the legislative jurisdiction of the Provinces and Territories of Canada and the regulation of business corporations is shared amongst the Federal and Provincial legislative branches. See P. W. Hogg, *Constitutional Law of Canada*, 4th ed. (Scarborough, Ont.: Carswell, 1997).

[46] The term 'public corporation' in this chapter (in the context of Canada) refers to corporations, including financial institutions, whose securities are held by the public and are listed on a securities exchange or have filed a prospectus in connection with the distribution of their securities.

[47] See M. Kerr and O. Aboubakr, "Canadian Securities Regulators Introduce Mandatory Corporate Environmental and Social Disclosure" (Montreal: CISDL, April 2005).

[48] System for Electronic Document Analysis and Retrieval (SEDAR): http://www.sedar.com.

[49] *Supra* note 45 at 2.

[50] National Instrument 51–102 Continuous Disclosure Obligations: http://www.osc.gov.on.ca/Regulation/Rulemaking/Current/Part5/rule_20040402_51–102–cont-disc-ob.pdf.

company's relationship with the environment or with the communities in which it does business, or human rights policies"[51] these should be described in the AIF, along with the steps that the corporation has taken to implement these.

Certain financial institutions are also subject to CSR-related reporting requirements pursuant to the following federal statutes: the Bank Act,[52] the Insurance Companies Act[53] and the Trust and Loan Companies Act.[54] Such institutions, provided they have at least CDN$1billion in equity, are required to publish an annual 'public accountability statement' describing the contribution of the financial institutions and their affiliates to the Canadian economy and society, including descriptions of the institutions' community development, charitable and philanthropic activities.[55]

Another significant development in terms of CSR-related reporting and disclosure in Canada has been the introduction (effective as of June 2005) of new corporate governance rules.[56] The new rules include a recommendation that public corporations should adopt a "written code of business conduct and ethics . . . applicable to directors, officers and employees (and addressing inter alia) . . . fair dealing with the issuer's security holders, customers, suppliers, competitors and employees."[57] If a public corporation has not adopted a written code then it is required to publicly disclose this fact and to describe steps taken to encourage and promote a culture of ethical business conduct. The rules require public corporations that adopt or amend such a code to file a copy of the code and any amendments thereto on SEDAR.

The potential significance for corporations of these CSR-related disclosure requirements is underlined when it is noted that the Province of Ontario has now amended its securities laws to make public corporations and their directors and officers civilly liable to investors who have purchased securities in the

---

[51] *Ibid.*, Form 51–102F2, paragraph 5.1(4).

[52] Bank Act, Section 459.3.

[53] Insurance Companies Act, Section 489.1.

[54] Trust and Loan Companies Act, Section 444.2.

[55] Public Accountability Statements (Banks, Insurance Companies, Trust and Loan Companies) Regulations [SOR/2002–133].

[56] National Instrument 58–101 – Disclosure of Corporate Governance Practices (2005) 28 OSCB 5377, http://www.osc.gov.on.ca/Regulation/Rulemaking/Current/Part5/rule_20050617_58–101_disc-corp-gov-pract.pdf; and National Policy 58–201 – Corporate Governance Guidelines (2005) 28 OSCB 5383: http://www.osc.gov.on.ca/Regulation/Rulemaking/Current/Part5/rule_20050617_58–201_corp-gov-guidelines.pdf. For a broader discussion of these rules see R. Lando et al., "New Canadian Corporate Governance Rules to Come into Effect June 30, 2005" (May 2005): http:// www.osler.com/resources.aspx?id=10211.

[57] National Policy 58–201 – Corporate Governance Guidelines, at para. 3.8: http://www.osc.gov.on.ca/Regulation/Rulemaking/Current/Part5/rule_20050617_58–201_corp-gov-guidelines.pdf.

secondary market "with respect to misleading, insufficient or late corporate disclosure."[58] Under the new statutory liability regime, an investor does not need to establish influence by, or awareness of, the alleged deficient disclosure (at the time of acquiring or disposing of the securities) to advance a claim for damages. The Ontario provisions come into force in December 2005. Given the centrality of Ontario's securities laws to the Canadian securities markets the significance of this provincial development should not be underestimated.

There have also been CSR-related developments in case law in Canada. Most significantly the Supreme Court of Canada, in its 2004 judgment in *Wise*,[59] confirmed that it was not inconsistent with a director's statutory fiduciary duty to act in the best interests of a corporation[60] for a director to "observe a decent respect for other interests lying beyond those of the company's shareholders in the strict sense."[61] The Court went beyond this, however, holding that it accepted "as an accurate statement of law that in determining whether they are acting with a view to the best interests of the corporation it may be legitimate, given all the circumstances of a given case, for the board of directors to consider, *inter alia*, the interests of shareholders, employees, suppliers, creditors, consumers, governments and the environment."[62] It should be noted, however, that the judgment merely states that it *may* be legitimate for directors to consider such interests. The current position of the Supreme Court of Canada thus remains relatively cautious – permitting rather than requiring company directors to take into account such considerations.

In terms of the relationship between company directors and shareholders, one further development that should be noted in the Canadian context is the 2001 amendment of the Canada Business Corporations Act ('CBCA'), which had the effect of enhancing the prospects for shareholder advocacy.[63] Prior to 2001 a shareholder proposal could be rejected if its primary purpose was to promote "general economic, political, racial, religious, social or similar causes."[64] This is no longer the case,[65] and indeed Waitzer and Juricevic have

---

[58] J. M. Fraser et al., "What are you doing to get ready for civil liability in the secondary market?" (Osler, Hoskin & Harcourt, LLP, August 2005): http://www.osler.com/resources.aspx?id=10493&tracklinkSP=SPOTRecentOslerUpdate.

[59] See: *Peoples Department Stores Inc. (Trustee of) v. Wise*, [2004] 3 S.C.R. 461, 2004 SCC 68 [*Wise*].

[60] See Canada Business Corporations Act, Section 122(1)(a).

[61] *Supra* note 59. Major and Deschamps JJ, at para. 42, citing *Teck Corp. v. Millar* (1972), 33 D.L.R. (3d) 288 (B.C.S.C.), [Berger J. at 314].

[62] *Ibid.*

[63] See *supra* note 44 at 36–37 for further details.

[64] *Ibid.* at 36.

[65] Corporations do, however, retain the right to reject a shareholder proposal on the basis that it "clearly appears that the proposal does not relate in a significant way to the business or affairs of the corporation." [*Supra* note 51 at Section 137(5)].

noted that "as a result of the amendments, shareholder resolutions on CSR are becoming more common"[66] – citing resolutions put forward at meetings of steel company IPSCO Inc. and the Bank of Montreal as evidence of the impact of this development.[67]

As in the UK, Canadian governments have also developed tax legislation and tax credits to encourage corporations to behave in a broadly CSR-compliant manner, especially with regard to local communities. To date, these appear to have been initiatives taken predominantly at provincial level, with Waitzer and Juricevic noting that Nova Scotia has introduced a tax credit allowing investors "to receive a non-refundable provincial tax credit of 30 per cent of the amount invested in community development funds."[68] Manitoba has introduced a similar incentive through its Community Enterprise Development Tax Credit.[69]

7) CONCLUSION

As is evident from the foregoing discussion, while distinct bodies of 'CSR Law' have not developed internationally or in either the UK or Canada, there have been significant legal developments in the two countries that have had the effect of encouraging and facilitating CSR compliance by corporations. Arguably the mix of voluntary and mandatory requirements bears out Patrick Macklem's observation that "there exists a spectrum of regulatory options (open to governments) ranging from predominantly voluntary measures to predominantly mandatory measures"[70] as opposed to the either/or approach to voluntary/mandatory regulation that may alternatively be assumed. Corporations also appear to have risen to the challenge posed by high levels of popular support for CSR-related issues, as evidenced in both countries by the increased rates of CSR reporting recorded over the last three years.

The extent to which corporate executives themselves have come to view CSR as a core consideration in decision making is perhaps underlined most emphatically in a recent Economist Intelligence Unit ('EIU') global online survey of and report on the attitudes of senior executives and institutional investors towards CSR.[71] According to the authors of this piece, "eighty-five

---

[66] *Supra* note 44 at 36.

[67] *Ibid.* at 36–37.

[68] *Ibid.* at 33.

[69] See *ibid.* and the Government of Manitoba website for further information: http://www.gov.mb.ca/finance/tao/cedc.html.

[70] *Supra* note 6 at 44.

[71] Economist Intelligence Unit, "The importance of corporate responsibility" (EIU, January 2005): http://graphics.eiu.com/files/ad_pdfs/eiuOracle_CorporateResponsibility_WP.pdf.

percent of executives and investors surveyed said (CSR)[72] was now a "central" or "important" consideration in investment decisions. This figure is almost double the 44% who said (CSR) was "central" or "important" five years ago, demonstrating the growth in (CSR)'s significance."[73]

At least as interesting as these figures, however, are the reasons respondents to the EIU gave for their degrees of concern as to CSR. Notably, over 60% of respondents listed customers and employees as amongst the top three most important sets of stakeholders for their companies.[74] Given this, it is perhaps surprising that there was not a closer match between the concerns of these groups[75] and what those surveyed considered the three most significant factors that have contributed to the increase in importance of CSR. These were "recent corporate scandals,"[76] "greater focus by shareholders on issues of corporate responsibility"[77] and "greater pressure from governments or regulators,"[78] each of which was selected as a "main driver of change" by 29% of all respondents.[79]

While the first of these points to the primacy of reputational factors in enhancing the profile of CSR and its importance to corporate executives, the second and third of these identified 'drivers' point to the importance to corporate executives' thinking of the legal structures that constrain and guide corporate behaviour (including towards shareholders). Given this linkage it is also worth noting that in the same survey 47% of executives surveyed identified a company's "record of compliance with laws and regulation"[80] as their favoured method for judging a company's corporate responsibility.[81]

This last finding underlines the importance of government regulation and of legal frameworks generally in guiding corporate behaviour in relation to CSR. As such, the correlation between legislative developments and corporate behaviour in the UK and Canada in recent years is fairly striking. As we have seen, increases in CSR reporting statistics (as noted in the KPMG/University of Amsterdam study) have been mirrored by legislative and legal developments in both jurisdictions.

---

[72] 'CSR' is substituted for the sake of consistency in place of 'CR' ('Corporate Responsibility') as used by the Economist Intelligence Unit.

[73] *Supra* note 70 at 2.

[74] *Ibid.* at 7.

[75] See MORI and Globescan figures discussed earlier in this paper for the UK and Canada respectively.

[76] *Supra* note 70 at 10.

[77] *Ibid.*

[78] *Ibid.*

[79] *Ibid.*

[80] *Ibid.* at 8.

[81] *Ibid.*

For this reason, despite the apparent determination of many (including international and regional bodies such as the European Commission) to maintain a view of CSR as a primarily 'voluntary' phenomenon, this should not detract from a full appreciation of the role legal and regulatory developments may well have had in the past in facilitating and shaping the extent and manner of CSR compliance in both jurisdictions. Indeed, given the legal initiatives that appear to be underway (including most notably the preparation and publication of the Company Law Reform Bill in the UK) it would be surprising if such legal and regulatory developments did not continue to be relevant in this manner in the future.

Chapter 15

TRIPS and Access to Medicine: Recent Developments in Canada and Europe

William Flanagan

1) INTRODUCTION

As the HIV/AIDS epidemic has continued to grow with devastating effects in the developing world, increasing global attention has been paid to the issue of access to HIV medications. In many parts of the world, most of these medications are under patent protection, a factor that has contributed to the high cost of these medications in the developed world. As a result, much attention has been paid to patent law reform as a means to secure low cost medications for the developing world. This paper examines this process of reform, beginning with reforms at the World Trade Organization (WTO) – namely the 2001 Doha Declaration on TRIPS and Public Health,[1] followed by the TRIPS Council 2003 decision on the Implementation of Paragraph 6 of the Doha Declaration

---

[1] Declaration on the TRIPS Agreement and Public Health (14 November 2001): http://www.wto.org/english/thewto_e/minist_e/min01_e/mindecl_trips_e.htm.

Christopher P.M. Waters (Ed.), *British and Canadian Perspectives on International Law*, pp. 291–315.

on the TRIPS Agreement and Public Health.[2] This WTO reform culminated in Canada's May 2004 reforms to its patent law that will permit in certain circumstances the export of Canadian generic HIV medications to some developing countries.[3] Canada was the first country in the world to enact these reforms following on the WTO initiative. The EU followed suit with similar reform measures in December 2005.[4]

This paper examines these reforms – with a comparative analysis of the Canadian and EU initiatives – and considers the potential they hold to increase access to HIV medications in the developing world. This paper argues that this reform process has made an important contribution to the issue of improved access, particularly for countries such as Brazil that have a strong domestic capacity to produce generics. For developing countries without that capacity, many among the most severely HIV-affected countries in the world, this paper argues that the WTO reform process has been less successful. This paper specifically examines the Canadian and EU patent law reforms and argues that they may not have a large impact on access to HIV medications in the developing world.

The paper concludes that patent law reforms should be understood as only one of a variety of strategies that are necessary in order to secure access to HIV medications in the developing world. Patent law reform is not the only way to reduce prices. Too much focus on patent law reform may risk overlooking other even more important measures to improve access. These other options include market segmentation and differential pricing – sometimes called equity pricing initiatives – where developed and developing country markets are segmented and HIV medications are sold by producers for substantially less in developing countries. Pooled procurement arrangements, where donor agencies increase their bargaining power and purchase drugs for distribution in more than one country, can also reduce prices. On a final note, the paper argues that cost is not the only obstacle to treatment. Numerous other obstacles to treatment exist – the greatest of which is poverty. Without substantial investment in the health care infrastructure in the developing world, HIV treatment will remain inaccessible to most of the people who need it notwithstanding any patent law reforms.

---

[2] Council on TRIPS, Implementation of Paragraph 6 of the Doha Declaration on the TRIPS Agreement and Public Health (August 30, 2003) [hereafter Implementation of Paragraph 6]: http://www.wto.org/english/tratop_e/trips_e/implem_para6_e.htm.

[3] Bill C-9, An Act to Amend the Patent Act and Food and Drugs Act (Royal Assent, 14 May 2004), 37th Parl. 2004.

[4] Commission of the European Communities, Regulation of the European Parliament and of the Council on Compulsory Licensing of Patents relating to the Manufacture of Pharmaceutical Products for Export to Countries with Pubic Health Problems: http://trade-info.cec.eu.int/doclib/html/119802.htm.

a) TRIPS Agreement, Compulsory Licences and Parallel Imports

Knowledge based industries have become increasingly important to the economies in developed countries. These "high tech" industries, producing goods such as computers, software, chemicals, pharmaceuticals and other related research-intensive products, account for an ever increasing share of the economic output of developed countries. Intellectual property rights are rights held in ideas, generally considered to include three major intangible property rights: patents, trademarks and copyright. For example, most governments will generally provide for patents for new "inventions." The patent provides the holder with a temporary government-sanctioned monopoly during which the patent holder will have exclusive rights to work, licence and sell the patented product in exchange for publicly disclosing the "secret" behind the invention, such as the composition of a new medicine. However, once the composition of these goods has been disclosed, they are also easy in most cases to copy and reproduce at a low cost, significantly reducing the benefits that might otherwise flow to the patent holder under the temporary monopoly granted by the patent. Developed countries, particularly the United States, are leaders in the production of these goods and likewise leaders in efforts to promote the temporary exclusive rights of patent holders to profit from the production of these goods.

A variety of international agreements provide for minimum levels of patent protection. During the Uruguay Round negotiations, which concluded in 1994 and resulted in among other things the creation of the World Trade Organization (WTO), the member countries successfully negotiated the creation of the Agreement on Trade-Related Aspects of Intellectual Property Rights (TRIPS).[5] TRIPS has two primary objectives. The first is to improve the minimum levels of intellectual property protections already provided for in existing international agreements. The second is to link these new levels of protection to international trade laws, including access to the effective dispute settlement mechanism of the WTO, a mechanism that could ultimately lead to trade-related sanctions to enforce obligations under TRIPS. During the TRIPS negotiations countries were largely divided along developing and developed country lines. Developed countries wanted to improve the scope and effectiveness of intellectual property regimes. Developing countries were not enthusiastic about these proposals, taking the view that intellectual property is more of a public good than private property. Most developing countries are largely unable

---

[5] The TRIPS Agreement is attached as Annex 1C to the WTO Agreement: http://www.wto.org/english/docs_e/legal_e/legal_e.htm. For a general discussion of TRIPS, see J. S. Thomas and M. A. Meyer, *The New Rules of Global Trade* (Toronto: Carswell, 1997); C. M. Correa, A.A. Yusuf, eds., *Intellectual Property and International Trade: The TRIPS Agreement* (London: Kluwer Law, 1998); and J. Watal, *Intellectual Property Rights in the WTO and Developing Countries* (The Hague: Kluwer Law, 2001).

to take advantage of increased protection for intellectual property because they do not have research intensive industries that would benefit from enhanced intellectual property laws.[6] They argue that any benefits gained by such increased protection for intellectual property would likely be outweighed by the disadvantage of not being able to acquire, adapt or reproduce new foreign technology at little or no cost.[7] What some developed countries might regard as little more than theft, other developing countries tend to regard as a legitimate strategy to promote domestic development and to enable developing countries to catch-up to developed economies.

Although developing countries were unenthusiastic about TRIPS, they were keen to secure other concessions in the Uruguay Round, particularly in the areas where they enjoyed a significant comparative advantage but restricted access to developed countries markets: textiles and agriculture. Largely in exchange for concessions in these areas, developing countries were persuaded to sign on to TRIPS.

TRIPS imposes a number of important obligations in the area of intellectual property. Article 27 of TRIPS requires that patents shall be available for any new inventions in all fields of technology without discrimination as to the place of invention or whether the products are imported or locally produced. Article 28 provides that the patent shall confer on its owner exclusive rights to prevent third parties from making or selling the patented product. The patent period shall be not less than 20 years from the filing date for the patent.[8]

As a result, member states must make 20-year patents available for any new inventions including pharmaceutical chemicals. Prior to TRIPS, in order to reduce prices, many developing countries such as Brazil did not grant patents for pharmaceutical chemicals. TRIPS now requires member countries to grant patents for such treatments. Specifically, HIV medications that constitute an "invention" are subject to the TRIPS provisions. Pursuant to various transitional provisions, these rules did not have immediate effect in the developing world. Most developing nations such as Brazil were permitted to delay the application of these rules until January 1, 2000.[9] Least developed countries originally had until January 1, 2006 to comply with most TRIPS obligations,

---

[6] This is contested by economists and others. Some argue that if developing countries enforce patent laws, this will encourage research and development in developing countries, and in particularly encourage research into problems or diseases that disproportionately affect developing countries and are generally not a subject of intensive research in developed countries, such as malaria or drug-resistant tuberculosis. See e.g. A. O. Sykes, "TRIPS, Pharmaceuticals, Developing Countries and the Doha 'Solution'" (2002) 3 Chi. J. Int'l. L. 47.

[7] M. J. Trebilcock and R. Howse, *The Regulation of International Trade* (London and New York: Routledge, 1999) at 310.

[8] Article 33.

[9] Article 65(2)–(3).

although this period was later extended to January 1, 2016.[10] Developing countries that did not provide patent protection for a particular area of technology, such as pharmaceuticals, prior to the entry into force of TRIPS had until January 1, 2005 to enforce patent rights in that area. This explains the present lack of pharmaceutical patents in India and the significant Indian generic manufacturing of low cost HIV medications.[11]

There are certain exceptions found in Article 27. Members may exclude from patentability inventions which if commercially exploited would have a detrimental effect on public order, morality, human, animal or plant life of health, or seriously prejudice the environment.[12] This is a somewhat confusingly worded provision that might be read as meaning that there is a general "public health" exception to the requirement of patentability, but it has not been so interpreted. Rather is it understood to refer to inventions that might themselves be harmful to public health, such as a new dangerous chemical compound that might injure human health and is banned from commercial exploitation.[13]

Other possible exceptions include Article 30 which provides that members may provide "limited exceptions" to the exclusive rights conferred by patent laws provided "such exceptions do not unreasonably conflict with a normal

---

[10] Article 66(1). This period was later extended under Article 7 of the *Declaration on the TRIPS Agreement and Public Health* (November 14, 2001): http://www.wto.org/english/thewto_e/minist_e/min01_e/mindecl_trips_e.htm.

[11] India is able to produce HIV medications at a much lower cost than in developed countries. A UN study reports that 150 mg of the HIV drug fluconazole costs $55 in India and around $700 to $800 in countries where it is patented, such as Indonesia and the Philippines. Another HIV treatment, AZT, costs $48 a month in India compared to $239 a month in the United States where it is patented: United Nations, Report of the High Commissioner of the Human Rights Commission on Economic, Social and Cultural Rights, The Impact of the Agreement on Trade-Related Aspects of Intellectual Property Rights on Human Rights, UN Doc E/CN.4/Sub.2/2001/13 at 14, para. 44 (2001) ("UNCHR Report"). Combination HIV therapy in the US costs about $10,000 to $15,000 a year. If sourced from the Indian pharmaceutical industry, the same therapy can cost as little as $200–$300 a year. World Bank, *Battling HIV/AIDS: A Decision Maker's Guide to the Procurement of Medicines and Related Supplies* (Washington: World Bank 2004) ["*Battling HIV/AIDS*"] at 80.

[12] Article 27(2): "Members may exclude from patentability inventions, the prevention within their territory of the commercial exploitation of which is necessary to protect *ordre public* or morality, including to protect human, animal or plant life or health or to avoid serious prejudice to the environment, provided that such exclusion is not made merely because the exploitation is prohibited by their law."

[13] The use of the exemption in Article 27(2) is also subject to the requirement that the commercial exploitation of the invention must be prevented and this prevention must be necessary for the protection of the *ordre public* or morality. World Trade Organization, "Overview: The TRIPS Agreement": http://www.wto.org/english/tratop_e/trips_e/ intel2 _e.htm.

exploitation of the patent and do not unreasonably prejudice the legitimate interests of the patent holder, taking account of interests of third parties." Some NGO's have argued that developing countries could simply refuse to issue patents for medications under this Article 30 exception.[14] However, it is unlikely that a blanket refusal to patent pharmaceutical products, or even a limited range of pharmaceutical products such as HIV medications, would be viewed as a "limited" exception.

Instead, most of the focus has been on the exceptions found in Article 31 of TRIPS. Article 31 sets out the obligations relating to other uses of a patent "without the authorization of the patent holder," more commonly known as "compulsory licensing." Unlike other types of intellectual property protected in TRIPS, Article 31 permits the compulsory licensing of patents in certain circumstances. A compulsory licence is permission to produce and sell a patented product without the consent and likely over the objections of the patent holder. A member's patent law may provide for such compulsory licensing and where it does, certain obligations apply. Among other requirements, such use can only be permitted if the proposed user has first made efforts over a "reasonable period of time" to obtain authorization from the patent holder on "reasonable commercial terms."[15] In situations of a "national emergency or other circumstances of extreme urgency or in cases of public non-commercial use" this requirement to negotiate for a reasonable period of time with the patent holder can be waived.[16] The scope and duration of the compulsory licence must be limited to the purpose for which it was authorized and shall be non-exclusive.[17] The use can only be authorized "predominantly for supply of the domestic market."[18] The patent holder is entitled to be paid "adequate remuneration" taking into account the "economic value of the authorization."[19]

Compulsory licences are not a new concept.[20] But they have come under increasing scrutiny in the last few years in light of the impact of the HIV/AIDS

---

[14] See for example, the Consumer Project on Technology: http://www.cptech.org/ip/health/. For a review of the Article 30 proposals, see D. Matthews, "WTO Decision on Implementation of Paragraph 6 of the Doha Declaration on the TRIPS Agreement and Public Health: A Solution to the Access to Essential Medicines Problem?" (2004) 7 Oxford Univ. Press Journal of International Economic Law 73.

[15] Article 31(b) TRIPS.

[16] Article 31(b). "Public non-commercial use" would likely include situations where a government procurement authority is purchasing medications for distribution through public clinics and without seeking to make any commercial profit from such distribution: *Battling HIV/AIDS, supra* note 11 at 121.

[17] Article 31(c) and (d).

[18] Article 31(f).

[19] Article 31(h).

[20] See S. M. Ford, "Compulsory Licensing Provisions Under TRIPS Agreement: Balancing Pills and Patents" (2000) 15 Am. U. Int'l. L. Rev. 941; and A. O. Sykes,

epidemic in developing countries that cannot afford the HIV medications that can slow the progression of HIV/AIDS. A number of developing countries, notably Thailand, South Africa and Brazil have threatened to issue compulsory licenses to local producers in order to produce generic copies of patented HIV medications at much lower costs. These efforts initially met with the opposition of the United States and other developed countries with strong research-based pharmaceutical industries. However, one key feature of Article 31 is that it places no restrictions on the purposes for which a compulsory licence may be issued. In this regard, Article 31 was a significant achievement for developing countries.[21] During the TRIPS negotiations, the US had insisted that there should be only two grounds for the issuance of a compulsory licence: an adjudicated violation of competition laws or a declared national emergency. However, no such restrictions were included in the final draft of Article 31. This suggests that compulsory licences can be issued for any reason including matters as broad as the general public interest.

Article 31(f) contains an important limit on the use of compulsory licences: "any such use shall be authorized predominantly for the supply of the domestic market of the Member authorizing such use."[22] Article 31(f) requires that the compulsory licence be used primarily for domestic consumption and not export. For countries that lack the capacity to produce these medications, Article 31(f) effectively prohibits them from importing medications produced under a compulsory licence in another country. This means that under TRIPS, compulsory licences would only be useful for countries that have the technological capacity to reverse engineer and manufacture a drug.

Another provision that might enable developing countries to obtain lower pharmaceutical prices is the possibility of what are called in WTO parlance "parallel imports" and the issue of the "exhaustion of intellectual property rights."[23] Parallel imports arise in the following circumstance. For example, a pharmaceutical company may produce a patented medication in Country I. The company may sell that drug in Country I at a certain price, say $1 per unit. The same company may sell the same drug for $2 a unit in Country II (where it is

---

"TRIPS, Pharmaceuticals, Developing Countries and the Doha 'Solution'" (2002) 3 Chi. J. Int'l. L. 47; J. Watal, *Intellectual Property Rights in the WTO and Developing Countries* (The Hague: Kluwer Law Inter., 2002) at 318–29; and *Battling HIV/AIDS*, *supra* note 11 at 119–25. For a review of the history of the use of compulsory licences by the US, UK and Canada, see F. M. Scherer and J. Watal, "Post-TRIPS Options for Access to Patented Medications in Developing Nations" (2002) 5 Oxford Univ. Press Journal of International Economic Law 913.

[21] Watal, *Intellectual Property, supra* note 5 at 320.

[22] TRIPS, Article 31(f).

[23] See C. E. Barfield and M. A. Groombridge, "Parallel Trade in the Pharmaceutical Industry: Implications for Innovation, Consumer Welfare, and Health Policy" (1999) 10 Fordham Intell. Prop. Media & Ent. L.J. 185.

also patented), engaging in differential pricing likely because Country II's market is willing or able to pay more for the drug. If the company's patent rights are "exhausted" by the sale to Country I, the purchaser in Country I can turn around and sell the drug to purchasers in Country II for less than $2 a unit, undercutting the price charged by the patent holder. The ability of the patent holder to discriminate across markets (assuming no substantial shipping costs or tariff barriers) will be eliminated. If the patent rights are not "exhausted" by the sale to Country I, the patent holder may retain the power to prevent buyers in Country II from importing the drug from Country I. The purchase by buyers in Country II of the drug sold in Country I is what is called a "parallel import." The exhaustion issue was much debated at the time of the TRIPS negotiations and the parties were unable to come to any agreement, thus Article 6 of TRIPS provides that "nothing in the Agreement shall be used to address the issue of the exhaustion of intellectual property rights." This means that parallel imports may be available to developing countries as another means to obtain lower cost medications.[24]

Although parallel imports might be significant, the most controversial proposals arise under the compulsory licensing provisions because these provisions are the most direct threat to the patent holder's interests. Countries that enjoy a comparative advantage in the area of knowledge based industries have vigorously opposed efforts to read broadly the compulsory licensing of TRIPS. These countries include most prominently the US although this position is largely shared by most developed jurisdictions including Canada and the EU. On the other hand, countries that have less of an interest in protecting knowledge based industries, and instead have a stronger interest in facilitating technology transfer or have a comparative advantage in the production of copied goods, have sought to use the existing international rules such as compulsory licensing or parallel imports to reduce patent protection. This includes most of the world's developing countries, often lead by countries such as India, Brazil or China, that also enjoy a significant comparative advantage in the production of copied goods. Thus the stage is set for a serious conflict between developed and developing countries.

2) WTO Reform: Doha Declaration on Trips and Public Health

A new round of trade negotiations were successfully launched in Doha, a key part of which was the Doha Declaration on the TRIPS Agreement and Public Health.[25] This declaration represented a major success for the developing coun-

---

[24] For more on parallel imports, see *Battling HIV/AIDS, supra* note 11 at 115–7.

[25] *Declaration on the TRIPS Agreement and Public Health* (November 14, 2001): http://www.wto.org/english/thewto_e/minist_e/min01_e/mindecl_trips_e.htm. For com-

tries and their supporting coalition of non-governmental organizations. The Doha Declaration is not a treaty and it is not intended to amend or alter TRIPS; it merely serves as a declaration by WTO members regarding the nature of the TRIPS agreement. The Doha Declaration recognizes the "gravity of public health problems afflicting many developing and least-developed countries, especially those resulting from HIV/AIDS, tuberculosis, malaria and other epidemics."[26] Perhaps the most important provision in the Declaration is the recognition that each WTO member "has the right to grant compulsory licences and the freedom to determine the grounds on which such licences are granted."[27] As noted above, the US had consistently rejected this interpretation of TRIPS in its previous negotiations with Brazil, Thailand, and South Africa, taking the position that compulsory licences could only be issued where there was an adjudicated violation of competition laws or a declared national emergency. However, there is nothing in Article 31 of TRIPS that limits the grounds on which a compulsory licence can be granted, and the Doha Declaration simply states directly what is implicit in TRIPS itself: WTO members can determine for themselves the grounds on which they can issue a compulsory licence. Thus although the Doha Declaration did not alter TRIPS, it nonetheless had the very important result of legitimizing the successful Brazilian strategy by which it negotiated price reductions backed up by the threat of compulsory licensing.

Most developing countries do not have Brazil's technological capacity to reverse engineer and produce HIV medications, thus in these countries the threat of compulsory licensing would not be an effective tool to increase the supply of low cost medications. Article 31(f) of the TRIPS also provides that a compulsory licence may only be "authorized predominately for the supply of the domestic market" which means that medications produced under a compulsory licence cannot be predominately used for export. As a result, countries that cannot produce generics under a compulsory licence are also likely unable to import generics produced elsewhere under a compulsory licence. This was a subject of much discussion at the time of the Doha Declaration and paragraph 6 of the Declaration provides that WTO members "with insufficient or no manufacturing capacities in the pharmaceutical sector could face difficulties in making effective use of compulsory licensing under the TRIPS Agreement."[28] The

---

mentary, see A. Lacayo, "Seeking a Balance: International Pharmaceutical Patent Protection, Public Health Crisis, and the Emerging Threat of Bio-Terrorism" (2002) 33 U. Miami Inter-Am. L. Rev. 295; A. O. Sykes, "TRIPS, Pharmaceuticals, Developing Countries, and the Doha 'Solution'" (2002) 3 Chi. J. Int'l. L. 47; A. Attaran, "The Doha Declaration of the TRIPS Agreement and Public Health, Access to Pharmaceuticals, and Options under WTO Law" (2002) 12 Fordham Intell. Prop. Media and Ent. L.J. 859; and F. M. Abbott, "The Doha Declaration on the TRIPS Agreement and Public Health: Lighting a Dark Corner at the WTO" (2002) 5(2) Journal of Inter. Eco. Law 469.

[26] Para. 1, *Doha Declaration, supra* note 1.

[27] Para. 5(b), *Doha Declaration, supra* note 1.

[28] *Doha Declaration, supra* note 1 at para. 6. See Attaran, *supra* note 25.

Declaration instructs the TRIPS Council to find an "expeditious solution to this problem" before the end of 2002.[29] Following the Declaration were a difficult and long series of negotiations and the 2002 deadline was missed. As the trade ministers prepared to meet in Cancun in September 2003 to continue negations on the Doha Development Round, pressure mounted to reach some agreement. Without an agreement the Cancun talks would almost certainly fail. Negotiations were finally concluded on August 30, 2003 with the decision of the TRIPS Council on the Implementation of Paragraph 6 of the Doha Declaration on the TRIPS Agreement and Public Health.[30]

a) *Paragraph 6*

The August 2003 Decision of the TRIPS Council established a framework whereby certain countries with insufficient or no manufacturing capacities in the pharmaceutical sector can use the compulsory licensing provisions in TRIPS to import less expensive generic versions of patented medications. The Decision provides that the obligations of an exporting Member under Article 31(f) of the TRIPS Agreement, which limits the use of compulsory licences for "predominately for the supply of the domestic market", can be waived in certain circumstances.[31] In other words, in some cases, countries will be permitted to produce less costly generic versions of patented medications predominately for export and not domestic consumption. To take advantage of this waiver, there are a number of conditions on both the importing and exporting countries.

Three requirements apply to the importing country. First, the importing country must provide notification to the TRIPS Council that specifies the names and expected quantities of the products needed. This information will be made publicly available on the WTO web site.[32] The general idea seems to be to provide transparency in the use of the system and to alert patent holders that an importing country intends to make use of the system.

Second, the importing country must provide the TRIPS Council with a notification that confirms that it is an "eligible importing Member" under the

---

[29] *Doha Declaration, supra* note 1 at para. 6.

[30] Council on TRIPS, *Implementation of Paragraph 6 of the Doha Declaration on the TRIPS Agreement and Public Health* (August 30, 2003) [hereafter *Implementation of Paragraph 6*]: http://www.wto.org/english/tratop_e/trips_e/implem_para6_e.htm

[31] *Implementation of Paragraph 6, supra* note 2 at Article 2. Article IX(3) of the Agreement Establishing the World Trade Organization permits waivers of WTO obligations if approved by three fourths of the WTO members: http://www.wto.org/english/docs_e/legal_e/04–wto_e.htm.

[32] *Implementation of Paragraph 6, supra* note 2 at Article 2(a): http://www.wto.org/english/tratop_e/trips_e/public_health_e.htm. No notifications have been made as of June 2004.

Decision. Only certain countries, the "least developed country members" are permitted to import generics under this Decision. This is a UN category that includes 49 countries with a low national income, weak human assets, high economic vulnerability, and a population under 75 million, including Bangladesh, Haiti, Nepal, Uganda, and Zambia.[33] Many of these countries also have severe HIV epidemics, such as Bangladesh, Uganda and Zambia.[34] A number of countries, mostly wealthy, have expressly indicated that they will not use the system set out in the Decision to import generic medications, including Australia, Canada, members of the European Union, Japan and the United States.[35] Other mostly middle income countries have agreed that they will only use the system in "situations of national emergency or other circumstances of extreme urgency", including Hong Kong China, Israel, Korea, Mexico, Taiwan, and Turkey.[36] These countries that have opted out of the system represent by far the largest share of global drug sales.

Other countries fall between these two categories, the first category being the least developed countries who are free to import generics, and the second being those countries that have wholly or partially waived any right to import generics. This in-between category would include some of the countries most affected by the HIV epidemic, such as Brazil, India, China, South Africa, Botswana, Namibia, Kenya and Zimbabwe. As regards this group of countries, the Decision provides these countries can import generics providing they have notified the TRIPS Council that they have insufficient or no manufacturing capacities in the pharmaceutical sector for the product in question.[37] These countries are also limited to importing generics only "in the case of a national emergency or other circumstance of extreme urgency or in cases of public non-commercial use."[38] Some of these countries that fall in this in-between category, such as Brazil, India, China and South Africa, have substantial manufacturing capacities and thus may not be able to make use of this Decision

---

[33] See the UN list of least developed countries (December 2003): http://www.unctad.org/Templates/webflyer.asp?docid=2929&intItemID=1634&lang=1.

[34] UNAIDS, *2004 Report on the Global AIDS Epidemic*, Table of Country Specific HIV/AIDS Estimates and Data as of the end of 2003: http://www.unaids.org/bangkok2004/GAR2004_html/GAR2004_00_en.htm.

[35] *Implementation of Paragraph 6, supra* note 2 at Article 1(b). See *The General Council Chairperson's Statement* (August 30, 2003) which indicates that the new members of the European Union, including the Czech Republic, Cyprus, Estonia, Hungary, Latvia, Lithuania, Poland, Slovak Republic and Slovenia, agree that they will opt out of the system as importers upon their accession to the European Union, which took place in May 2004: http://www.wto.org/english/news_e/news03_e/trips_stat_28aug03_e.htm.

[36] *The General Council Chairperson's Statement* (August 30, 2003), *supra* note 35.

[37] *Implementation of Paragraph 6, supra* note 2 at Article 2(a).

[38] *Ibid.* at Article 1(b).

to import generics.[39] Others, such as Botswana and Zambia, have limited or no manufacturing capacities and would be entitled to import generics.

The third requirement is that the importing country would have to grant a compulsory licence in accordance with Article 31 of TRIPS.[40] Article 31 requires that before issuing a compulsory licence, reasonable efforts must be made over a reasonable period of time to obtain "authorization from the right holder on reasonable commercial terms and conditions."[41] However, this requirement to negotiate can be waived in the event of a "national emergency or other circumstances of extreme urgency or in cases of public non-commercial use."[42] As a result, the importing country might first have to seek a voluntary licence from the patent holder, and failing that, then issue a compulsory licence. Another option would be to declare a national emergency thus waiving any requirement to negotiate with the patent holder. As noted earlier, since TRIPS no countries – including Brazil – have ever issued a compulsory licence for the production of a patented pharmaceutical product, so it remains to be seen if many importing countries will be willing to take this step.[43] The use of a compulsory licence for import, even if TRIPS-consistent, would likely be regarded as a controversial step by the United States and other western countries.

Any WTO member, rich or poor, may use the system to produce and export generic pharmaceutical products.[44] However, to do so, under Article 31(b) of TRIPS, the proposed exporter of the generic medication would first have to make efforts to obtain a voluntary licence from the right holder on reasonable commercial terms. If those negotiations failed, then upon application by the proposed producer, the exporting country could issue a compulsory licence for export, subject to the following five conditions.[45] First, the licence must include only the amount necessary to meet the needs of the eligible importing member.

---

[39] This is a matter of some debate. The *Implementation of Paragraph 6, ibid., Annex*, indicates that "insufficient or no manufacturing capacity" means either (1) "no manufacturing capacity" or (2) some manufacturing capacity but "currently insufficient for the purposes of meeting its needs." Countries like Brazil might be able to argue in some cases that its current manufacturing capacity was insufficient for meeting its needs. It is also important to note that the TRIPS obligations will not apply to India until January 2005, so until that time India is free to continue to produce and export low cost generic HIV medications.

[40] *Implementation of Paragraph 6, ibid.* at Article 2(a)(iii).

[41] TRIPS, *supra* note 5 at Article 31(b).

[42] Article 31(b). See discussion infra note 20. "Public non-commercial use" would likely include situations where a government procurement authority is purchasing medications for distribution through public clinics and without seeking to make any commercial profit from such distribution: *Battling HIV/AIDS, supra* note 11 at 21.

[43] See infra note 52.

[44] *Implementation of Paragraph 6, supra* note 2 at Article 1(c).

[45] *Ibid.* at Article 2(b).

Second, the entire amount produced must be exported to the importing members. Third, the generic product must be clearly identified as produced under this system through specific labelling or marking. Fourth, the generic producer must post on a website information as to the quantity being supplied and the nature of the distinguishing features of the product. Fifth, the exporting country must notify the TRIPS Council of its decision to grant the compulsory licence, including information as to the name of the licensee, the products for which the licence is granted, the quantities to be produced, and countries to which the product will be exported, and the duration of the licence. These various conditions are designed to address the patent-holder's concern that the generic product may be diverted back to one of its major markets primarily in North America, Europe or Japan.

A number of other matters are dealt with in the Decision. "Adequate remuneration" shall be paid in the exporting country, taking into account "the economic value" to the importing country.[46] Given that the importing country would be a developing country, the economic value of the compulsory licence would likely be fixed at a fairly low level. Payment in the exporting country is sufficient to waive any requirement for remuneration to be paid in the importing country. Importing countries must also take "reasonable measures within their means" to prevent re-exportation of the imported product, measures that are "proportionate to their administrative capacities and to the risk of trade diversion."[47] All WTO members are required to make available "effective legal means to prevent the importation" into their territories of products produced under this system.[48] The Decision, which operates only as a waiver to Article 31(f) and (h) of TRIPS, is intended to be replaced by an amendment to TRIPS that would be consistent with the Decision.[49] An accompanying statement by the TRIPS Chairperson states that all WTO members "recognize that the Decision should be used in good faith to protect public health and . . . not be an instrument to pursue industrial or commercial policy objectives."[50] The Chairperson also states that all members recognize the need to take "all reasonable measures" to prevent diversion of the products from the intended markets.

A number of key points emerge from the Decision. First, the United States had lobbied hard to limit the scope of diseases to which the Decision would apply. In earlier negotiations, the United States had attempted to limit the scope

---

[46] *Ibid.* at Article 3. This remuneration is to be paid pursuant to Article 31(h) of TRIPS, which requires that in the event of a compulsory licence, the patent holder shall be paid "adequate remuneration in the circumstances of the case, taking into account the economic value of the authorization."

[47] *Ibid.* at Article 4.

[48] *Ibid.* at Article 5.

[49] *Ibid.* at Article 11. The Decision provides that this amendment is to be negotiated and completed sometime in 2004.

[50] See *The General Council Chairperson's Statement, supra* note 35.

of diseases to HIV/AIDS, malaria, tuberculosis and infectious epidemics of comparable gravity, excluding medications for all other conditions no matter how common or widespread, such as heart disease and diabetes. The United States abandoned this position and the final Decision extends to any pharmaceutical products "needed to address public health problems" as recognized in the Doha Declaration, namely, "the public health problems afflicting many developing and least-developed countries, especially those resulting from HIV/AIDS, tuberculosis, malaria and other epidemics." In short, the Decision includes any pharmaceuticals necessary to address public health problems, a category that could include most if not all patented medications.

Second, the category of countries eligible to import generics is carefully limited. In effect, the category is limited to only least developed country members, such as Bangladesh and Uganda, and a few other developing countries that have insufficient manufacturing capacity, such as Botswana. Depending on their manufacturing capacity, other developing countries may be excluded, such as Brazil, India, China and South Africa. Rather than risk having the uncertain matter of their manufacturing capacity disputed at the WTO, some of these countries may simply forgo any efforts to use this system.

Third, the process is complex. Both the importing and exporting country must issue a compulsory licence. As noted above, since TRIPS no countries have ever issued a compulsory licence for the production of a patented pharmaceutical product. Given the possible negative reaction of the United States and other developed countries, it remains to be seen whether many countries will be willing to do so. There are also other complexities, including the requirement that the patent holder be paid "adequate remuneration" and the requirement to take reasonable measures to prevent diversion, such as labelling and notification requirements. The labelling requirements may raise the cost of production. The system must also not be used "to pursue industrial or commercial policy objectives." If the goal of issuing the compulsory licence is to encourage production and competition leading to lower prices, this might be characterized as an "industrial or commercial policy" objective. Likewise, if an exporting country issues a compulsory licence to encourage growth of a generic industry, this may also run afoul of the requirement that the system not be used for commercial policies.

b) *2005 Amendment to TRIPS*

The August 2003 Decision of the TRIPS Council was later incorporated into an amendment of the TRIPS Agreement, concluded in December 2005.[51] This

---

[51] "Members OK amendment to make health flexibility permanent" World Trade Organization (6 December 2005): http://www.wto.org/english/news_e/pres05_e/pr426_e.htm.

amendment directly transforms the August 2003 "waiver" into a permanent amendment of TRIPS. The amendment will be formally built into the TRIPS Agreement when two thirds of the WTO's members have ratified the change. WTO members have set themselves until 1 December 2007 to ratify this amendment, and the waiver will remain in force until then.

3) CANADA'S AMENDMENTS TO ITS PATENT ACT

In May 2004, Canada became the first country in the world to enact legislation pursuant to the August 2003 TRIPS Council decision.[52] The legislation makes it possible for Canadian generic pharmaceutical producers to obtain compulsory licences to manufacture specified patented medicines for export to certain developing and least-developed countries. In May 2004, Norway also issued regulations that will have a similar effect.[53]

The purpose of the Canadian legislation is to facilitate "access to pharmaceutical products to address public health problems afflicting many developing and least-developed countries, especially those resulting from HIV/AIDS, tuberculosis, malaria and other epidemics."[54] The legislation includes a list of 56 eligible pharmaceutical products, derived primarily from the WHO's model list of essential medicines but also includes all anti-retrovirals currently approved for treating HIV/AIDS in Canada.[55] As noted above, the August 2003 TRIPS Council Decision does not limit the scope of diseases or medications covered under the Decision. However, the Canadian legislation does limit the types of medications eligible for export under a compulsory licence. The federal Cabinet may, upon ministerial recommendation, add other products.[56]

---

[52] Bill C-9, An Act to Amend the Patent Act and Food and Drugs Act (Royal Assent, May 14, 2004). In July 2004, Canada and the US issued a memorandum of understanding that provides the two countries agree to the suspension of Article 1709(10)(f) of NAFTA with respect to compulsory licences issued in accordance with the terms of the August 2003 WTO Decision. Similar to Article 31(f) of TRIPS, Article 1709(10)(f), which deals with similar intellectual property provisions in NAFTA, provides that a compulsory licence shall be "authorized predominately for the supply" of the domestic market only. See: http://www.ustr.gov/Document_Library/Press_Releases/2004/July/U.S._Canada_Agree_to_Assist_Poor_Countries_Access_to_Medicine.html.

[53] Regulations Amending the Patent Regulations (In Accordance with the Decision of the WTO General Council of 30 August 2003, Paragraphs 1(b) and 2(a)), Royal Decree of May 14, 2004, amending the Regulations of December 20, 1996 No. 1162 issued pursuant to the Patents Act. The Norwegian regulations are considerably less complex than the Canadian legislation, however Norway has only a small pharmaceutical industry with few if any producers that have the capacity to undertake the manufacture of generic drugs for export.

[54] Bill C-9, s. 21.01.

[55] Bill C-9, s. 21.03(1)(a) and Schedule 1.

[56] Bill C-9, s. 21.03(1)(a).

Along the lines of the August 2003 Decision, only certain countries are eligible to import generics from Canada, including all countries designated by the UN as least developed countries, whether WTO members or not.[57] Other eligible importing countries include WTO members, mainly developing countries, which have not notified the TRIPS Council that they do not intent to use the system as importers. This includes countries such as Botswana, Brazil, China, India, Kenya, and South Africa.[58] Exports may also be made to that group of WTO members that have indicated that they will import generics only if faced with a national emergency and an insufficient manufacturing capacity, including countries such as Hong Kong China, Israel, Korea, Mexico, Taiwan and Turkey.[59] Finally, export can also be made to non-WTO members who are not least-developed countries, providing they are eligible for assistance according to the OECD, declare a situation of national emergency or other situation of extreme urgency, have insufficient domestic capacity, and specify the name and quantity of the product needed.[60] Countries such as Vietnam might quality under this provision. Other non-WTO members, notably Russia and the Ukraine which both have a severe HIV epidemic, would not qualify because among other things, they are not eligible for assistance under OECD guidelines.[61] They might also be unable to establish that they have insufficient domestic production capacity.

The legislation provides that upon application, the government shall issue a compulsory licence to make, construct and use a patented invention to sell for export to an eligible country.[62] The application must set out the name of the product, the quantity to be produced, the name of the patent holder, the name of the importing country, and the name of the government purchaser (or person or entity permitted by the government to purchase the product).[63] The applicant must also at least thirty days prior to filing the application seek from the patentee "a licence to manufacture and sell the pharmaceutical product for export" to an eligible country, and provide the patentee with a copy of the applicant's written request for a compulsory licence.[64] This requirement was likely inserted to satisfy the requirement of Article 31(b) of TRIPS that requires that before a

---

[57] Bill C-9, s. 21.04(1)(b) and Schedule 2. The Canadian legislation includes all least developed countries, both WTO members and non-members.

[58] Bill C-9, s. 21.03(c) and Schedule 3; see discussion infra note 76.

[59] See discussion infra note 75, and *The General Council Chairperson's Statement*, *supra* note 35.

[60] Bill C-9, s. 21.03(d)(ii).

[61] See the OECD Development Co-operation Committee's (DAC) "*Is it ODA?*" at 157: http://www.oecd.org/dataoecd/21/21/34086975.pdf.

[62] Bill C-9, s. 21.04.

[63] Bill C-9, s. 21.04. This last phrase was included to permit NGO's to purchase imported generics with the permission of the importing country government.

[64] Bill C-9, s. 21.04(3)(c).

compulsory licence can be issued, reasonable efforts must be made to obtain a voluntary licence from the patent holder.[65] The Minister of Health must notify the Commissioner of Patents that the generic product meets the safety and efficacy requirements of the Food and Drugs Act and has been marked and labelled in a manner that distinguishes it from the version of the product sold in Canada.[66] The applicant must also provide the Commissioner with evidence that the importing country is in fact an eligible importing country, as above.[67] For example, in the case of a developing country that is not a least-developed country, such as Botswana or Brazil, the applicant would have to provide a copy of that country's notice to the TRIPS Council specifying the name and quantity of the product to be imported, along with a statement that the importing country has insufficient or no manufacturing capacity for the production of that product and the importing party has granted or intends to grant a compulsory licence for the import of this product.[68]

Before exporting the product, the applicant must establish a website including information about the product being exported, the quantity and its distinguishing features. A royalty must be paid to the patent holder as determined by regulations to the act.[69] The regulations have not yet been released, but it is anticipated that there will be an effective cap of 4% the value of the contract, or less for less developed countries.[70] The compulsory licence is valid for two years.[71] The licence can be terminated for a variety of reasons, including if the product has been "with the knowledge of the holder of authorization, re-exported in a manner that is contrary to the General Council Decision."[72] Finally, the legislation also provides that if the average price of the generic product sold under the compulsory licence is "equal to or greater than 25 per cent of the average price in Canada of the equivalent product sold" by the patentee, the patentee may apply to the Federal Court for, among other things, a termination of the licence on the grounds that the "essence of the agreement under which the product is to be sold is commercial in nature."[73] The Court may not terminate the agreement if the holder of the compulsory licence can establish that "the average price of the product manufactured under the authorization does not exceed an amount equal to the direct supply cost of the

---

[65] See discussion infra note 82.

[66] Bill C-9, s. 21.04(3)(b).

[67] Bill C-9, s. 21.04(3)(d).

[68] Bill C-9, s. 21.04(3)(d)(iii).

[69] Bill C-9, s. 21.08.

[70] R. Elliot, "Canada's New Patent Bill Provides Basis for Improvement", Bridges Between Trade and Sustainable Development (May 2004).

[71] Bill C-9, s. 21.09.

[72] Bill C-9, s. 21.14(f).

[73] Bill C-9, s. 21.17(1).

product plus 15 per cent of that direct supply cost."[74] In other words, there is an effective cap on the profits that can be made by the generic manufacturer.

a) *The Canadian Amendments: To What Effect?*

Although the Canadian legislation has been heralded as an important step in providing low cost medications to countries in need, there is reason to question whether the legislation alone will do much to achieve this objective.

First, the list of eligible medications is limited to 56 products, limiting the potential range of products that could be exported.

Second, Canadian generic manufacturers may not be able to compete with generic manufacturers from countries like India and China that have low cost, reliable and efficient generic industries. India and China could also use the WTO waiver system to export low cost generics in competition with any Canadian firms. In fact, India is currently considering amendments to its patent laws that will permit the export of Indian generics.[75] India is currently the most important world exporter of generic HIV medications.[76] Effective 1 January, 2005, India will be required to provide patent protections for new pharmaceutical inventions patents.[77] After this date, India will only be able to export significant amounts of generic versions of newly patented pharmaceutical inventions pursuant to the August 2003 Decision of the TRIPS Council. India is currently examining patent law reform that will permit these exports. If India enacts such legislation, it will likely remain one of the leading low-cost providers of generic HIV medications and it may be unlikely that the Canadian generic firms could compete with Indian generics. The Canadian generics are also required to demonstrate that their product meets Canada's safety and efficacy requirements, a process that could raise the cost of the Canadian product making it even less competitive.[78]

Third, the range of eligible importing countries is restricted in a manner consistent with the TRIPS Council Decision, effectively limiting the eligible countries to least developed countries and other developing countries with an insufficient manufacturing capacity. For example, this might exclude the largest developed countries that are most affected by the HIV, such as Brazil, India, China and South Africa. If the large markets in these countries are not open to the generic manufacturer, this may operate as a substantial disincentive to invest in the production and sale of these generic medications. It may be

---

[74] Bill C-9, s. 21.17(5).
[75] See discussion *infra* note 96.
[76] See discussion *infra* note 15.
[77] *Ibid.*
[78] See discussion *infra* note 109.

difficult to obtain the economies of scale necessary to provide low cost medications, a problem that may also limit the development of any future Indian generic exports.

Fourth, the Canadian generic firms themselves estimate that it may take at least two years to complete the application process and start exporting generics.[79]

The legislation is also complex. There are a number of reasons why a Canadian generic manufacturer might decide that the risks outweigh the potential benefits. First, after expending the time and cost of developing the generic drug and negotiating a potential sale to an eligible country, the applicant must seek a voluntary licence from the patentee before a compulsory licence can be issued. It is possible that in order to prevent the issuance of a compulsory licence, the patentee may offer to sell its patented medication at the same or lower price than that negotiated by the applicant. The applicant risks losing the deal that it had negotiated. The importing country must also be an eligible importing country under the terms of the TRIPS Council Decision. For example, a country like Brazil might argue that it has insufficient manufacturing capacity to produce a certain medicine. This matter could be contested under the WTO dispute resolution mechanisms and it might be determined that Brazil is not in fact an eligible importing country. This could mean that the applicant would lose a potential sale. The applicant must pay a royalty to the patentee and the legislation places a cap on the applicant's potential profit. Moreover, the applicant risks losing the licence if the product is diverted to another market "with the knowledge of the holder of the authorization." This is a particularly risky prospect. Given the large difference in price between the generic and patented product, it is possible that some of the generic product may be diverted by third parties. If the holder of the compulsory licence simply has "knowledge" of this diversion, the licence may be terminated. The holder would then lose all that the holder had invested in the generic production.

The legislation also does not address the fact that the eligible importing countries are largely very poor countries with a limited or non-existent medical system. Without financial assistance, many of these countries have little capacity to purchase even very low cost medications. With only rudimentary or even non-existent health care systems, these countries also lack the capacity to distribute and monitor the use of HIV medications. The Canadian generic producers may have a reliable and low-cost generic to export, but little in the way of a potential market.

Finally, since the TRIPS agreement was negotiated in 1995, no countries have ever issued a compulsory licence for the production of pharmaceutical products.[80] Although Brazil has threatened to do so on a number of occasions,

---

[79] H. Scoffield, "AIDS Plan could take 2 Years", *Globe and Mail*, 3 October 2003.
[80] See discussion infra note 52.

even Brazil has not yet issued a compulsory licence. For patented products, the TRIPS Council Decision requires both the importing and exporting country to issue compulsory licences. It remains to be seen how many countries will actually be willing to do so.

4) EU PATENT REFORM

Somewhat similar reforms were enacted in the EU in December 2005.[81] The EU regulation is less specific than the Canadian legislation. It is drafted in broad terms and much of the detail has been left to the Member States authorities to create appropriate mechanisms on a country by country basis, something that has not yet been completed. The regulation is designed to ensure that the conditions for granting of compulsory licences for export are the same in all Member States and to avoid any distortion of competition for operators in the single EU market.

There are a number of key differences with the Canadian legislation. While an earlier press release from the European Parliament noted that non-WTO members could use the scheme for import, the EU Regulation provides that "[t]he license shall be strictly limited to the acts of manufacturing the product in question and selling for export to the WTO member or members cited in the application."[82] In addition, the definitions section of the Regulation defines "importing WTO member" but does not contain a definition of importing member that does not reference membership in the WTO. As a result, unlike the Canadian legislation, it would appear that non-WTO countries will not be permitted to make use of this EU legislation.

The Canadian legislation limits the range of eligible products that can be exported, however the EU Regulation defines "pharmaceutical product" broadly in Article 2 as "any product of the pharmaceutical sector." Because the Regulation does not limit the range of medication that can be exported, it is in this respect significantly broader in scope that the Canadian legislation.

---

[81] European parliament, "MEPs back moves to simplify export of generic drugs to poorer countries" (December 12, 2005): http://www.europarl.eu.int/news/expert/infopress_page/066-3029-335-12-48-911-20051128IPR02948-01-12-2005-2005--false/default_en.htm. The draft Regulation of the European Parliament and of the Council on Compulsory Licensing of Patents relating to the Manufacture of Pharmaceutical Products for Export to Countries with Pubic Health Problems (the "Regulation") was adopted at first reading by the European Parliament on December 1, 2005 with 543 votes in favour, 21 against and 35 abstentions.

[82] Article 8(3), Commission of the European Communities, Regulation of the European Parliament and of the Council on Compulsory Licensing of Patents relating to the Manufacture of Pharmaceutical Products for Export to Countries with Public Health Problems online: http://trade-info.cec.eu.int/doclib/html/119802.htm.

Unlike the Canadian legislation, the EU regulation also does not include any reference to the time period in which a compulsory licence shall be issued and the medication exported. This suggests that time delays might be an additional hurdle to the issuance of any compulsory licence under the EU regulations.

Article 5 sets out the procedures whereby "any person" may apply for a compulsory license, suggesting that like the Canadian legislation, NGOs as well as government purchasers could apply for a compulsory license. As under the Canadian legislation, Article 7 requires the applicant to provide evidence that they have attempted to negotiate an authorization from the patent rights holder that have not been successful within a reasonable period of time. As under the Canadian legislation, Article 8 requires that measures must be taken to ensure the medicinal product is properly accounted for and distinctly labelled. Article 11 prohibits the importation into the EU of products subject to a compulsory license under this Regulation.

The Canadian legislation goes much further in determining how payment will be made in s. 21.17 of the Patent Act. The EU Regulation simply provides for payment of "adequate remuneration" in Article 8(9), but leaves greater detail up to the member states.

On the whole, the Canadian legislation is of much greater detail than the EU Regulation. Article 5 of the Regulation provides that competent authorities may prescribe additional formal or administrative requirements for efficient processing of the application.

The UK[83] Patent Office began a consultation process on the proposed EU Regulation in March 2005.[84] This consultation sought comment by interested parties on the following areas:[85]

- Whether the Regulation is a fair reflection of the WTO Decision.
- The Scope of the Regulation in relation to eligible countries who may use the proposed Regulation.
- Determination of the period for negotiation with the rights holder.
- Determination of adequate remuneration levels to the rights holder.

---

[83] While the Regulation will be implemented at the EU level, each EU Member State possesses its own national patent law. An attempt to create a European Community patent failed when a draft law did not receive enough votes from members of the European Parliament. Patents issued through the European Patent Office are filed with a single application but do not lead to a single EU wide patent, rather a bundle of national patents.

[84] See "Consultation on the Proposed Regulation on the compulsory licensing of patented pharmaceutical products for export to countries with public health problems" The Patent Office (September 22, 2005): http://www.patent.gov.uk/about/consultations/compulsorylicensing/responses.htm.

[85] *Ibid.*

- Anti-diversion measures within the proposed Regulation.
- Safety and efficacy of the generic products produced under the proposed Regulation.

Numerous parties responded, including the NGOs Oxfam and Médecins sans Frontières. The UK response to the submissions was that the UK would attempt to see the Regulation apply to non-WTO importing countries. The UK also supported anti-diversion measures. Importantly, the UK also desired a fixed consultation period with the rights holder rather than a flexible 'reasonable time' period as well as the possibility of an EU-wide system for determining adequate remuneration. However, it appears that these UK proposals did not make it into the final Regulation. As noted, the Regulation appears applicable only to WTO importing members, the consultation period was not fixed, and adequate remuneration was left up to Member States.

5) CONCLUSION

This paper has examined the complex trail of developments starting with the 2001 Doha Declaration of TRIPS and Public Health, the subsequent August 2003 TRIPS Council Decision regarding the implementation of paragraph 6 of the Doha Declaration, culminating in the May 2004 amendments to Canada's patent legislation and the similar EU reforms in December 2005.

The August 2003 Decision of the TRIPS Council contains some potential but the process is complex and cumbersome. The most important importing markets in the developing world may be effectively excluded under the Decision, making the development of generic exports of less interest to potential producers. The process is complex, requiring the issuance of two compulsory licences, one by the exporter and another by the importer. Canada's efforts to implement this decision have – at least in Canada – made the process even more restrictive. The Canadian legislation holds many risks for the potential exporter, including the possibility that the licence may be revoked if the product is diverted to another market with the knowledge of the licence holder. There is an effective cap on any rate of return that the potential exporter can realize on its investment. Canada's generic manufacturers may also not be able to complete with generic manufacturers from developing countries such as India and China.

Similar challenges make it also unlikely that many compulsory licences for export will be issued under the EU Regulation. The EU Regulation is even more restrictive in that it does not permit export to non-WTO members and does not include time limits after which a licence shall be issued. It is broader in that it is not limited to only certain medications and it does not include any express cap on the price that can be charged for the generic product.

However under either the Canadian or EU approach, compulsory licensing will remain at best only a partial solution. But patent law reform and the export of generics is fortunately not the only way to reduce prices. Although it is beyond the scope of this chapter to develop these proposals more fully, there are a number of other options.[86] These other options include market segmentation and differential pricing, where developed and developing country markets are segmented and HIV medications are sold for substantially less in developing countries.[87] This is also sometimes called an equity pricing initiative, where pharmaceutical companies unilaterally decide to offer medications in developing markets at reduced prices.[88] Pharmaceutical companies might adopt such policies for a variety of reasons. First, it may make economic sense to reduce prices in low-income markets where the consumer is likely to be more price-sensitive. Rather than forgo all sales in the low-income market, because the price is too high, a producer might be willing to sell the product at a reduced price in the low-income market because this is better for the producer than no sales at all in the low-income market. However, for the price differential to be sustainable, markets have to be segmented to prevent what economists call "physical and informational arbitrage." To prevent physical arbitrage, parallel imports of cheap drugs from the low-income market to developed country markets would have to be prohibited.[89] Likewise to prevent information arbitrage, governments and consumers in developed country markets would have to agree not to demand similar discounts.

Equity pricing initiatives can be obviously risky for pharmaceutical companies if these types of arbitrage cannot be effectively prevented, and this is likely the reason why they were slow to adopt equity pricing initiatives in Brazil and

---

[86] For a review of various options, see *Battling HIV/AIDS, supra* note 11. See also D. Matthews, "WTO Decision on Implementation of Paragraph 6 of the Doha Declaration on the TRIPS Agreement and Public Health: A Solution to the Access to Essential Medicines Problem?" (2004) 7 Oxford Univ. Press Journal of International Economic Law 73.

[87] For a review of this option, see Scherer and Watal, *ibid.* and P.J. Hammer, "Differential Pricing of Essential Aids Drugs: Markets, Politics and Public Health" (2002) 5 Oxford Univ. Press Journal of International Economic Law 883; see also *Battling HIV/AIDS, ibid.*

[88] *Battling HIV/AIDS, ibid.*

[89] To support equity pricing initiatives, in May 2003, the European Union adopted a regulation to help prevent diversion of low-cost generic medications back to the EU. Pharmaceutical manufacturers can put their products on a tiered-price list if the medicine is available at less than 75% of the price in OECD countries or at the cost of production plus 15%. These products will bear a logo which will mean imports of these products from low-income countries into the EU will be prohibited. *Battling HIV/AIDS, ibid.* at 91. Likewise, developing countries can support equity pricing structures by agreeing to prevent the resale of publicly procured drugs.

elsewhere. However, as in Brazil, political pressure can be brought to bear upon pharmaceutical companies, making them more willing to incur these risks. Without demonstrating some flexibility on pricing, there may be increased domestic and international pressure to adopt more radical restrictions on patent protection, a matter of great concern to these companies. Inflexibility may also lead to compulsory licences. This may be one of the most important outcomes of the WTO reform process which legitimized the Brazilian strategy of using threats of compulsory licences to encourage price reductions. This process also opened the door, albeit narrowly, to the use of compulsory licences for the importation of low cost generics in countries with insufficient domestic capacity. These threats have no doubt contributed to the willingness of pharmaceutical companies to adopt equity pricing initiatives and offer steep price discounts to developing country governments, international purchase funds and non-for-profit organizations.[90] Shareholders in these companies can also expect the research-based pharmaceutical companies to be good corporate citizens, in a manner consistent with the corporate social responsibility commitments of these corporations.[91] Failure to meet these expectations may damage the company's reputation and injure its customer relations. Equity pricing initiatives can be even more effective where there are pooled procurement arrangements, where donor agencies such as the World Health Organization increase their bargaining power and purchase drugs for distribution in more than one country.[92]

Although there are a number of options to reduce prices, it cannot be overstated that cost is not the only obstacle to treatment. Numerous other obstacles to treatment exist – the greatest of which is poverty. Even at hugely reduced prices, HIV medications will remain unaffordable to most patients in the developing world, where 3 billion people live on less than $2 a day. HIV treatment is also complex. It must be continued for life and it must be periodically monitored by health care professionals. Many developing countries lack the basic health care infrastructure to deliver and monitor such treatment. Without substantial investment in the health care infrastructure in the developing world,

---

[90] There has been less willingness to offer discounts on wholesale prices to other purchasers. Likely the pharmaceutical companies prefer offering discounts to the public and non-profit sector, as this sector may have more bargaining power and the risk of legal or illegal parallel trade may be lower when sold to the public sector. *Battling HIV/AIDS, ibid.* at 85. For more information about these price discounts, see Medicins Sans Frontières "Untangling the Web of Price Reductions: A Pricing Guide for the Purchase of ARV's for Developing Countries" 6th ed. (April 2004): http://www.accessmed-msf.org/prod/publications.asp?scntid=22420041625454&contenttype=PARA&

[91] See discussion infra note 39–43.

[92] *Battling HIV/AIDS, supra* note 11 at 71–74.

HIV treatment will remain inaccessible to most of the people who need it notwithstanding any patent law reforms. In the end, the financial contributions by Canada and the EU Members States to agencies such as the Global Fund to Fight AIDS, Tuberculosis, and Malaria, may result in a more important contribution to the fight against HIV/AIDS than any amendments to their patent laws.

Chapter 16

Tax Discrimination and the Cross-Border Provision of Services

Catherine Brown and Martha O'Brien[1]

1) OVERVIEW

The importance of cross-border trade in services globally has been recognized both in the agreement governing the largest international trade group, the World Trade Organization Agreement ("WTO Agreement"),[2] and in trade agreements entered into in smaller trade blocks such as the North American Free Trade Agreement ("the NAFTA")[3] and the Treaty establishing the European

---

[1] The authors wish to thank Professor Leigh Hancher for kindly reviewing and commenting on a draft of this paper. Professor Hancher is partner in Kennedy Van der Laan, a law firm, in Amsterdam where she heads the Energy Practice Group, and Professor of European Law at the Catholic University of Brabant, Tilburg.

[2] Final Act Embodying the results of the Uruguay Round of Multilateral Trade Negotiations, April 15, 1994, Legal Instruments – Results of the Uruguay Round, vol. 1 (1994), 33 I.L.M. 1141 (1994) [hereinafter WTO Agreement].

[3] North American Free Trade Agreement, December 17, 1992, 32 I.L.M. 289 (1992) [hereinafter NAFTA] (entered into force January 1, 1994).

Christopher P.M. Waters (Ed.), *British and Canadian Perspectives on International Law*, pp. 317–346.

Community (TEC).[4] These trade agreements demand significant commitments of their signatories with respect to market access and non-discrimination in the cross-border supply of services. However, trade discipline over direct taxation[5] including the taxation of foreign service providers, was either largely carved out of these trade agreements (WTO and NAFTA),[6] or at least not expressly included (TEC). In the WTO agreements and NAFTA, bilateral tax treaties, usually based on OECD Model Tax Conventions, were selected as the appropriate primary mechanism to regulate discrimination in direct taxation.[7] Canada, the United States and Mexico[8] have entered into such bilateral agreements with each other ("NAFTA tax treaties"), and with many of their other WTO trade partners.

---

[4] Consolidated version: O.J. 2002/C 325/01.

[5] For the purposes of this paper, direct taxation refers to corporate and personal income tax.

[6] In the case of the General Agreement on Trade in Services ("the GATS"), this was not without considerable controversy. It was widely recognized throughout the negotiations for the GATS that discrimination in direct taxation could have just as deleterious an affect on the cross-border trade in services as the non-tariff barriers under review. Nonetheless, in hotly disputed negotiations resolved virtually on the eve of the deadline for signing the WTO agreement, direct taxation was almost entirely removed from the GATS agreement and so remains subject to the terms of an applicable bilateral tax treaty. Discipline over direct taxation issues has also been largely carved out of the NAFTA.

[7] See for example the GATS Articles XIV(e) and XXII(3), the NAFTA, Articles 2103(2) and 2103(4) and the OECD Committee on Fiscal Affairs, Model Tax Convention on Income and on Capital (Paris: OECD, 2003) (loose-leaf) [hereinafter OECD Model].

[8] Convention for the Avoidance of Double Taxation and the Prevention of Fiscal Evasion with respect to Taxes on April 8, 1991, Can.Mex. S.C. 1992, c. 3 Part III [hereinafter Mexico-Canada Treaty]; Protocol to the Convention, April 8, 1991, Convention Between Canada and The United States of America with respect to Taxes on Income and on Capital, signed on September 26, 1980, as amended by the Protocols signed on June 14, 1983; March 28, 1984; March 17, 1995 and July 29, 1997; Enacted in Canada by S.C. 1984, c. 20; 1995 Protocol enacted in Canada by S.C. 1995, c. 34, Royal Assent November 8, 1995; 1997 Protocol enacted in Canada by S.C. 1997, c. 38, Royal Assent December 10, 1997 [Canada-U.S. Treaty]. Convention for the Avoidance of Double Taxation and the Prevention of Fiscal Evasion with respect to Taxes on Income, with Protocol, Sept. 18, 1992, U.S.-Mex., S. Treaty Doc. No. 103–07, reprinted in 2 Tax Treaties (CCH) 5903 [hereinafter U.S.-Mexico Treaty]. In 1995, a second protocol came into force expanding the scope of coverage of the exchange of information provision to include all taxes imposed by the contracting states, including state and local taxes. A third protocol was signed in 2002.

The UK has entered into a similar series of bilateral tax treaties with its trading partners, including fellow EC members.[9] However, despite the fact that direct taxation as a restriction on trade is not directly addressed in the TEC, both the UK's domestic direct taxation laws and the provisions of its bilateral tax treaties may be "inapplicable" if they are contrary to the TEC or EC secondary law. The result is that, notwithstanding the commonality of the obligations assumed under tax treaties and the WTO agreement, both the approach to tax discrimination and the remedies available to Canadian recipients and providers of services are very different from those available to their UK counterparts.

This paper compares the interaction of direct taxation and trade in services under the General Agreement on Trade in Services ("GATS"), in the NAFTA block and the EC to demonstrate the significant distinctions between the obligations assumed by Canada and the UK in their regional trade agreements. In addition to differences in direct tax discrimination rules in these three trade agreements, there are important distinctions in the control of tax subsidies to domestic providers and in the dispute resolution processes and remedies available to governments and service providers, the discussion of which are beyond the scope of this paper. And the expansion of the scope of EC law, primarily through rulings of the European Court of Justice ("ECJ"), means that, willingly or not, the UK has relinquished a much greater measure of its sovereignty in direct taxation than has Canada under the NAFTA.

It is perhaps useful at this point to briefly outline the meaning of the term discrimination as well as the principles underlying non-discrimination in tax and trade agreements. Discrimination in the international trade context has been defined as "treating persons unfavourably for reasons that are unreasonable, arbitrary or irrelevant."[10] The principle of non-discrimination is one of the basic tenets of most trade agreements, in particular the principles of most favoured nation (MFN) and national treatment (NT). Under the MFN rule a host country is required to extend to service providers from one foreign country treatment no less favourable than it accords to service providers from any other country. According to the NT principle, the host country is required to treat foreign service providers in the same or comparable way as a domestic service provider. The scope of the MFN and NT provisions in any trade agreement depend on the extent of the exceptions attached to them.

---

[9] The UK has bilateral tax treaties with over 100 other countries, including all 24 of the other EC Member States and the members of the NAFTA block: http://www.hmrc.gov.uk/international/treaties1.htm.

[10] See B. Arnold, "Tax Discrimination Against Aliens, Non-Residents, and Foreign Activities: Canada, Australia, New Zealand the United Kingdom and the United States" (Toronto: Canadian Tax Foundation, 1990).

Tax treaties generally contain a non-discrimination clause that is derived from Article 24 of the OECD Model. From its historic origins, this is generally understood to be a NT clause and not an MFN clause.[11] Its first objective is to prevent a treaty partner from granting to foreign nationals treatment that is "other or more burdensome" than that granted to its own nationals, provided that the former are in the same or substantially similar circumstances as the latter. Its second objective is to ensure that companies are not treated differently based on whether the capital is held by its own nationals rather than those of the other contracting party. There is no implied obligation to provide MFN treatment in the OECD Model, although various tax treaties, including those in the NAFTA block, do contain specific MFN clauses.[12]

2) INTERNATIONAL TRADE AGREEMENTS AFFECTING TRADE IN SERVICES IN THE NAFTA BLOCK: A CANADIAN PERSPECTIVE

Canada's primary obligations with respect to the regulation of trade in services can be found in the NAFTA, which came into effect on January 1, 1994, with respect to Canada, the U.S. and Mexico, and in the GATS, which came into force on January 1, 1995, as part of the agreement establishing the World Trade Organization (WTO agreement). As a signatory to the WTO agreement, Canada agreed to honour all of her obligations under the GATS, but has assumed additional obligations to her NAFTA partners.[13] The immediate discussion focuses on these two trade agreements. A brief examination of the NAFTA tax treaties and the specific provisions that impact the cross-border trade in services follows.

---

[11] Clauses of the kind found in the OECD Model were used in international agreements such as treaties of friendship or commerce to provide protection for nationals long before their appearance in tax treaties. See Commentary to Article 24 of the OECD Model para. 2.

[12] See for example the Canada-US Treaty art. XXV(2). A significant issue underlying the discussion in the case of Canada, will be the scope of the non-discrimination clause in the relevant tax treaty, and in particular to what extent the non-discrimination clause will restrict the right to challenge the NT or MFN obligation other than under a tax treaty.

[13] The NAFTA explicitly provides that in case of inconsistency with other agreements, unless otherwise specified in the NAFTA, the NAFTA will override other agreements that existed at the time the NAFTA became effective (Article 103). The WTO agreement (1994) became effective after the NAFTA. In the final analysis, the choice of forum rules determines which of the WTO or NAFTA rules apply.

a) *General Agreement on Trade in Services (GATS)*

i) *Overview*

The GATS, a multilateral agreement covering trade in the services sectors, applies to all WTO Members and thus applies to both Canada and the UK Its scope and coverage is reliant on basic definitions about who is a service supplier, and what is considered a measure "affecting trade in services".[14] The commitments by Members with respect to such measures may be categorized into two broad groups: first, general obligations, which apply directly and automatically to all Members and services sectors, and second, specific commitments concerning market access and NT in designated sectors. These specific commitments are set out in individual country schedules,[15] the terms of which vary widely.

ii) *Most Favoured Nation*

The general obligations assumed under the GATS include a commitment to MFN treatment to the service suppliers of other Members ("foreign service suppliers"). This obligation requires that each party "accord immediately and unconditionally to services and service suppliers of any other Party, treatment no less favourable than that it accords to like services and service suppliers of any other country."[16] Some deviation from this standard was permitted provided the Member listed such measures in the "Annex on Article II Exemptions" and the conditions for such exemptions were met.[17]

---

[14] Specifically, GATS applies to measures by Members "affecting" trade in services. A measure is broadly defined as "any measure by a Member, whether in the form of a law, regulation, procedure, decision, administrative action, or any other form." Trade in services is defined as the "supply of a service". The *Panel on EC – Bananas III* WT/DS 27/R/USA May 22, 1997 defined the scope of application of this in the following terms: "[N]o measures are excluded *a priori* from the scope of the GATS as defined by its provisions. The scope of the GATS encompasses any measure of a Member to the extent it affects the supply of a service, regardless of whether such a measure directly governs the supply of a service or whether it regulates other matters but nevertheless affects trade in services." *Panel Report on EC – Bananas III*, para. 7.285. The Appellate Body upheld this finding and held that no provision of the Agreement "suggest[s] a limited scope of application for the GATS" Appellate Body report on EC-Bananas para. 220.

[15] GATS Article XX.

[16] The wording "treatment no less favourable" in Article II(1) has been interpreted broadly by the WTO Appellate Body to include both *de facto* as well as *de jure* discrimination. See for example the *Appellate Body Report on European Communities – Regime for the Importation, Sale and Distribution of Bananas*, WT/DS27/ab/R, (September 25, 1997) at para. 234.

[17] Almost all countries claimed some MFN exemptions in areas such as civil and maritime aviation, telecommunications and financial services. All exemptions are subject to review and should in principle not last longer than 10 years. Further, GATS

In addition to the claimed exemptions for tax measures, the GATS further limits the MFN obligation with respect to direct tax matters if the obligation is assumed under a tax treaty. Specifically, Article XIV(e) provides that "subject to the requirement that such measures are not applied in a manner which would constitute a means of arbitrary or unjustifiable discrimination between countries where like conditions prevail (. . .) nothing in this Agreement shall be construed to prevent the adoption or enforcement by any Member of measures inconsistent with the MFN obligation provided that the difference in treatment is the result of an agreement on the avoidance of double taxation."

iii) *National Treatment*

Unlike the MFN obligation, each Member's commitment to provide NT to foreign service suppliers is negotiated under the GATS.[18] A Member may not impose discriminatory measures benefiting domestic services or service suppliers over foreign services or service suppliers that are contrary to the specific commitments it has made in its country schedule. A Member may, however, subject the NT commitments in any particular sector to conditions and qualifications. Each country's NT obligations thus tend to reflect national policy objectives and constraints.

The NT obligation is also subject to a number of general exceptions. In particular, Article XIV(d), provides that any Member may adopt or enforce direct tax measures that are inconsistent with NT, provided that they do not constitute "arbitrary or unjustifiable discrimination" in trade in services and "provided that the difference in treatment is aimed at ensuring the equitable or effective imposition or collection of direct taxes in respect of services or service suppliers of other Member countries." The meaning of the expression "equitable or effective" is defined in a footnote that provides illustrations of taxes and tax policies that may be excluded from NT requirements.[19] These include, for example, the right to impose a withholding tax.[20]

---

allows groups of Members to enter into economic integration agreements (such as the TEC and the NAFTA) or to mutually recognize regulatory standards, certificates and the like if certain conditions are met. See Schedules to the GATS to view a specific country's schedules. For Canada, see GATS/EL/16 date 15/04/94. Canada has claimed exemptions for film, video and television co-production, as well as with respect to fishing, banking, trust and insurance services, air and marine transport, and for certain services related to agriculture.

[18] GATS Article XVII.

[19] The footnote identifies six measures taken by a Member under its taxation system that will meet the criteria including measures that apply to non-resident service suppliers in recognition of the fact that the tax obligation of non-residents is determined with respect to taxable items sourced or located in the Member's territory; or apply to non-residents in order to ensure the imposition or collection of taxes in the Member's territory; or to prevent the avoidance or evasion of taxes, including compliance measures.

[20] GATS Article XIV(d).

Like the MFN requirement, the NT obligation in respect of direct tax matters has also been largely removed from GATS discipline if a bilateral tax treaty is in effect between the Member countries. GATS Article XXII(3) provides that the non-discrimination clause in an international agreement relating to the avoidance of double taxation (a tax treaty) has primacy over the GATS national treatment provisions[21] in resolving disputes involving the taxation of services and service suppliers with respect to measures that fall within the scope of the agreement.[22]

As a result there may be little room to challenge as discriminatory a direct tax measure under the GATS that relates to the NT obligation if a tax treaty is in place between the two countries.[23] At issue will be whether all matters related to NT fall within the scope of a tax treaty's non-discrimination article. In contrast, a direct tax measure that violates the MFN obligation may form the subject matter of a potential complaint under the GATS, if it is not listed as an exemption by the country complained of or justified under a tax treaty. The MFN obligation assumed under the WTO may prove of particular significance in the NAFTA block, as no there is generally no MFN obligation with respect to direct taxation under the NAFTA agreement.[24]

---

[21] GATS Article XXII(3).

[22] This step alone was apparently not considered sufficient to restrict discipline over direct tax matters to a tax treaty. A footnote to Article XXII(3) of GATS further provides that if there is a disagreement about whether the matter falls within the scope of a tax treaty and the tax treaty was in existence at the time the WTO agreement entered into force, one country cannot unilaterally challenge the issue of the treaty's scope under WTO procedures. Both parties to the existing tax treaty must consent if the WTO dispute resolution procedures (rather than tax treaty procedures) are to be used. However, if future tax treaties are silent on the issue, either tax treaty partner may unilaterally bring a tax dispute based on a jurisdictional issue before the Council for Trade in Services, which may then refer the matter to binding arbitration.

[23] Article XXII(3) may preclude one country from challenging the scope of Article XIV(d) (e.g. whether one country's income tax measure applicable to a non-resident is either inequitable or an arbitrary or unjustifiable discrimination), to the extent that the issue falls within the scope of a tax treaty. As a type of NT obligation is imposed under most tax treaties with respect to nationals or Citizens of a Contracting State who are residents of the other Contracting State, there is arguably little scope to challenge a tax that violates the NT obligation, at least under GATS. At issue will be the precise scope of the non-discrimination article in the tax treaty. This issue, according to GATS, is also to be resolved under an established tax treaty unless the Parties consent otherwise.

[24] Some tax treaties include MFN obligations. See Articles XXV(2) and (5) of the Canada-U.S. tax treaty, which respectively require MFN treatment for citizens and companies.

b) *The North American Free Trade Agreement (NAFTA)*

i) *Overview*

Chapter 12 of NAFTA establishes basic rules agreed to by Canada, Mexico and the U.S. for regulating the provision of services across their respective borders. The agreement calls for NT and MFN treatment,[25] and prohibits local presence requirements. It exceeds the GATS both in scope and coverage, bringing all existing and future government measures relating to cross-border, non-financial services within the scope of the Chapter. Thus unlike the GATS, under which no general NT commitments are provided and specific commitments are separately negotiated country by country, NAFTA operates in reverse and requires each party to state explicitly – in various annexes – if it does not intend to conform to the general rules in Chapter 12 with respect to MFN, NT and other NAFTA obligations.[26]

The principal provisions on services are contained in four chapters: cross-border trade in services,[27] telecommunications and financial services,[28] investment[29] and temporary entry for businesspeople.[30] Three annexes complement these: land transportation,[31] professional services[32] and specific reservations and exceptions.[33]

Under the NAFTA, the cross-border provision of a service is defined as providing a service from the territory of one Party into the territory of another Party; in the territory of one Party by a person of that Party to a person of another Party; and by a national of a Party in the territory of another Party.[34] Unlike the GATS, which includes in this definition services provided by a

---

[25] NAFTA Article 1204 requires that Parties accord to service providers of other Parties the better of NT and MFN treatment.

[26] These exceptions are provided in lieu of grandfather provisions. Annex 1 of NAFTA contains the three countries' reservation Schedules for their non-conforming federal measures. Article 1206(a)(i). Laws and regulations that are grandfathered or listed as a reservation in Annex 1 cannot be challenged as long as they do not become more inconsistent with the agreement.

[27] NAFTA Chapter 12.

[28] NAFTA Chapters 13 and 14.

[29] NAFTA Chapter 11.

[30] NAFTA Chapter 16. To facilitate access to other signatory countries, the NAFTA establishes the principle that business persons of one country who fall into any one of four categories (business visitors, traders and investors, intra-company transferees, and professionals) will be granted temporary entry into the territory of the other countries. See Annex 1603.

[31] NAFTA Annex 1212.

[32] NAFTA Annex 1210.5.

[33] NAFTA Annex 2106 (exempting Canadian Cultural Industries).

[34] See the definition of "cross-border provision of a service" in NAFTA Article 1213.

service supplier of one Member through a commercial presence in the other, the NAFTA addresses this mode of supply through the Investment Provisions in Chapter 11. A number of obligations from Chapter 12 (Services) are cross-referenced to the Investment Chapter.

Overall, the NAFTA agreement is designed to significantly liberalize the trade in services by providing for common licensing rules,[35] transparency provisions,[36] dispute resolution procedures[37] and an ongoing commitment to automatically include new services. The agreement, however, does not generally affect the respective income tax laws of each country or affect a country's sovereign right to tax profits earned by non-residents within its borders. Thus, although many non-tariff barriers may be reduced or eliminated under the NAFTA, direct taxation discrimination remains largely undisciplined under this agreement.

ii) *Taxation*

Although it may not generally discipline direct tax matters, the NAFTA, like the GATS, specifically addresses the issue of taxation. The principal provisions that relate to taxation are contained in Article 2103. It begins by stipulating that nothing in the NAFTA will apply to any tax measure except as specifically provided for in Article 2103(1).

NAFTA then clarifies the status of tax treaties entered into by NAFTA signatories. In general, these are to have priority in all cases of inconsistency with the NAFTA agreement.[38] As a result the NAFTA, like the GATS, requires that

---

[35] NAFTA parties also committed to encourage professional bodies to develop mutually acceptable standards for licensing professionals and reciprocal recognition of each other's professional accreditations. This was an important step in eliminating a significant non-tariff barrier to free trade in services. Unfortunately there is no time limit on this process under NAFTA, although some progress has been made with respect to the engineering profession and foreign legal consultants (NAFTA, Annex 1210.5(1)). The NAFTA also requires the parties to fairly review and answer applications by the NAFTA party nationals for professional licensing.

[36] NAFTA Articles 1207 and 1209.

[37] NAFTA Article 2003.

[38] There are two exceptions to the primacy of tax treaties in tax matters specifically listed in the NAFTA. The first is with respect to the national treatment obligation as it relates to the trade in goods. The national treatment obligation, as proscribed in Article III of GATT, will have primacy over lesser obligations assumed under a tax treaty. The second is with respect to export taxes: specifically the provisions of Article 314, which allows Mexico to impose an export tax on basic foodstuffs, and Article 604, which addresses the imposition of export taxes on energy in defined circumstances. These exceptions may be of little practical effect as such matters are not normally addressed in a tax treaty. In addition, Article 2103(6) provides that Article 1110 (Expropriation) shall apply to taxation measures subject to certain procedural rules.

disputes about tax matters covered by a tax treaty be resolved exclusively under the applicable tax treaty provisions.[39]

Limited NT protection is provided in respect of direct taxes affecting the purchase or consumption of cross-border services and financial services.[40] Article 2103(4)(a) provides that, subject to an applicable tax treaty, NT applies to direct taxation measures in respect of the purchase or consumption of particular services.[41] This provision would presumably prevent, for example, a NAFTA country's income tax law from allowing for the deduction of consulting services purchased from a domestic consulting firm but not from firms in other NAFTA countries.[42]

The NAFTA obligations with respect to direct (and indirect) taxation measures are limited by a number of important exceptions. Specifically, the non-discrimination provisions do not apply to any: MFN obligation with respect to an advantage accorded by a party pursuant to a tax convention; taxation measures in existence at the time that NAFTA went into effect (January 1, 1994) or to the renewal or any amendment of a tax measure that does not decrease its conformity; or new tax measure aimed at ensuring the equitable and effective imposition or collection of taxes and that does not arbitrarily discriminate between persons, goods or services of the parties or arbitrarily nullify or impair benefits accorded under those articles.[43]

iii) *Performance Requirements*

Discipline with respect to measures that affect performance requirements are also covered in Article 2100. These will be of interest to service suppliers who establish a commercial presence in a NAFTA country, opening up arguments under Chapter 11 of the NAFTA.

Chapter 11 contains general prohibitions that prevent one NAFTA Party from imposing certain conditions on an investment by an investor from another NAFTA Party in its territory. Article 1106(1) prohibits seven different types of

---

[39] NAFTA, Article 2103(2).

[40] With regard to financial services, para. 4(a) applies only to the cross-border provision of a financial service under para. 1405(3).

[41] Specifically, in relation to direct taxes, subparagraph 4(a) provides that certain direct tax measures listed therein (taxes on income, capital gains or the taxable capital of corporations and the Mexican asset tax) are, but for listed limitations, subject to the NT obligation with respect to the cross-border provision of services, including financial services. However, with regard to financial services subparagraph 4(a) applies only to the cross-border provision of a financial service under para. 1405(3).

[42] See NAFTA Implementation Act, (U.S.) Final Draft September 1993 c. 21.3. Taxation: c) Income & Capital Tax Measures Affecting Cross-Border Services & Financial Services.

[43] NAFTA Article 2103(4) (c–h).

practices, including achieving a given level or percentage of domestic content; and purchasing, using or according a preference to goods produced or services provided in its territory or to purchase goods or services from persons in its territory.

In addition to these general prohibitions, NAFTA prohibits certain performance requirements made in connection with the conferral of benefits by a government. Such benefits would include subsidies, financing assistance and tax concessions. Specifically, NAFTA provides that "no Party may condition the receipt or continued receipt of an advantage, in connection with an investment in its territory of an investor of a Party or of a non-Party, on compliance with" any of the following requirements:

(a) to achieve a given level or percentage of domestic content;
(b) to purchase, use or accord a preference to goods produced in its territory, or to purchase goods from producers in its territory;
(c) to relate in any way the volume or value of imports to the volume or value of exports, or goods and services while Article 1106(3) only applies to goods;
(d) to restrict sales of goods or services in its territory by relating such sales to the volume or value of its exports or foreign exchange earnings.[44]

Article 2103(5) incorporates these performance prohibitions into the NAFTA tax provisions and provides that subject to an applicable tax treaty, the prohibitions shall also apply to tax measures. As a result a government is prohibited from tying a tax advantage, such as a tax holiday, "to the purchase of locally produced goods or the manufacture of goods with a certain level of domestic content."[45]

However, a Party is not prohibited from "conditioning an advantage, in connection with an investment in its territory of an investor, or compliance with a requirement to locate production, provide a service, train or employ workers, construct or expand particular facilities or carry out research and development in its territory."[46] Thus a Party may condition the receipt of a tax advantage on the performance of services in its territory.

In summary, NAFTA generally leaves direct taxation to the domestic law of the three NAFTA Parties and the tax treaties between them. The NT obligation under NAFTA will apply to the purchase or consumption of particular services, but even then is subject to the proviso that nothing in the NAFTA "shall affect the rights and obligations of any Party under any tax convention."

---

[44] NAFTA Article 1106(3).
[45] NAFTA Article 2103(4)(a) requires NT in these circumstances.
[46] NAFTA Article 1106(4).

c) *NAFTA Tax Treaties*

As discussed, Canada's MFN and NT obligations with respect to the direct taxation of non-resident service suppliers have, for the most part, been carved out
of both GATS and NAFTA, and are instead regulated by tax treaties. Canada's
tax treaties, once enacted as Canadian domestic law, take precedence over other
domestic law such as the Income Tax Act. Thus the NAFTA tax treaties assume
considerable importance both in the taxation of service suppliers in the NAFTA
block and in preventing tax discrimination.[47]

Because they are bilateral, each of the three NAFTA tax treaties addresses
the matter of non-discrimination differently, including the determination of
what taxes the treaty covers, and how the non-discrimination article is to be
interpreted and applied. The Canada-U.S. Treaty itself addresses the potential
role of the WTO/GATS in resolving tax matters. Article 29(6) of the Treaty
(added by the Third Protocol, effective in 1996) provides that for the purposes
of the NT obligation (Article XXII(3)) in the GATS, a tax measure will fall
under the tax treaty only if it relates to a tax measure to which Article 25 (non-
discrimination) applies, or if it does not relate to non-discrimination, it falls
within another tax treaty provision, The Canada-U.S. Treaty also clarifies that
any issue as to the interpretation of the scope of a treaty provision, and
specifically whether the tax treaty applies, will be resolved under the Mutual
Agreement procedure of the tax treaty.

In the case of the U.S.-Mexico Treaty, a Third Protocol was signed on
November 26, 2002 to further clarify the primacy of the tax treaty. The
Protocol is very explicit and far-reaching. Paragraph 3(b) provides that no other
agreement to which the U.S. and Mexico are parties shall apply with respect to
taxation measures unless the competent authorities agree that the measure is
not within the scope of the non-discrimination provisions of Article 25 of the
U.S.-Mexico Treaty. Accordingly, if the non-discrimination article in the tax
treaty applies to a taxation measure, no NT or MFN obligations undertaken by
Mexico or the U.S. in any other agreement (including the NAFTA and GATS),
shall apply to that taxation measure.

The Mexico-Canada Treaty was in existence prior to the entry into force of
the GATS, and there has not been a subsequent Protocol agreed. In consequence, although the treaty is silent about the role of the GATS, according to

---

[47] To understand the Canadian position in the NAFTA block it is important to note
that Canada has consistently maintained and negotiated a right to discriminate against
non-residents in its tax treaties and has reserved her position under the non-discrimination article in the OECD Model. As a result, the provisions and the effect of the non-discrimination article in the Canada-Mexico treaty vary considerably from that of the
Canada-U.S. treaty, where the U.S. rigorously pursued a non-discrimination article that
was closer to the OECD Model.

the GATS understanding, the non-discrimination article in that tax treaty will have primacy over the GATS NT obligations. As well, the parties will be subject to the GATS requirement that both parties must consent to have the issue of the treaty's scope settled by the Council for Trade in Services.

In summary, if tax discrimination is alleged, both the questions of whether a tax treaty applies and if not, whether obligations under either the NAFTA or the GATS have been violated, must be addressed before a determination can be made that the tax is discriminatory. An additional question is what will be the appropriate forum for dispute resolution – the NAFTA or the WTO?[48]

3) International Trade Agreements Affecting Trade in Services in the EC: A UK Perspective

a) *Introduction*

Although the UK, like Canada, is a WTO member and bound by the GATS, its most significant trade obligations are owed to its 24 fellow EC Member States under the TEC. The preceding description of how the GATS applies to direct taxation of trade in services shows that provisions governing direct taxation in bilateral tax treaties generally take precedence over MFN and NT obligations in the GATS. As noted, the UK has a very extensive network of bilateral tax treaties with other WTO members, so that most tax discrimination disputes, except in cases involving the UK's EC partners, will be resolved in accordance with the applicable tax treaty rather than under the GATS.

The UK's obligations under the TEC with respect to direct taxation take priority over its obligations in its tax treaties with other EC Member States. Accordingly, EC law will apply where UK tax laws create restrictions on trade in services with its EC partners.

Although procedure and remedies are generally beyond the scope of this article, it is important to note that EC taxpayers have easier access to remedies for tax discrimination. Individuals or corporations can directly enforce, in their national courts, their fundamental EC rights to provide or receive services within the EC without restriction based on nationality or residence. EC taxpayers can thus sue their own and other Member State governments, and are

---

[48] To reach a conclusion about whether a tax is discriminatory, and if so, how it is to be disciplined, a series of questions could be posed. These might include: What is the tax issue being complained about? Does a tax treaty apply? If not, which of the WTO (GATS) or NAFTA applies? If the answer is either, which is the best forum from the complainant's perspective for dispute settlement?

entitled to a refund of any tax collected contrary to EC law.[49] While UK service providers or recipients can request their national government to take action against another WTO Member government if they consider that they are being discriminated against contrary to the GATS, they may not take direct action on their own behalf in any dispute resolution process. This means that when the dispute is between a taxpayer and an EC Member State tax authority, it will normally be resolved under the TEC. A Canadian service provider does not have direct access to a judicial remedy for any infringement of its NAFTA entitlements, unless the restriction on access to a NAFTA partner's market amounts to a violation of Chapter 11. In that case there is a limited exception to the rule that states are the only actors that can launch international legal disputes, which permits a foreign NAFTA national to pursue an investor-state action against a host government under the NAFTA investor-state arbitration rules.

b) *Services and Direct Taxation in the EC*

Free trade in services is one of the fundamental principles of the single market project begun under the Treaty of Rome (now the TEC) in 1958. The four components of the GATS definition of trade in services[50] are governed by two separate chapters in the TEC, the Right of Establishment[51] and Services.[52] Freedom of services protects the right of a person to provide services to a recipient in another Member State without establishing a commercial presence in that other Member State. Once a service provider has set up an establishment in the other

---

[49] The European Commission may also take action directly before the Court of Justice against a Member State for failure to fulfill its Treaty obligations if its laws contravene the Treaty (TEC Article 226). Until recently, the Commission seemed reluctant to take this action. A Member State of the EC may also commence action in the Court against another Member State (TEC Article 227), but this is extremely rare.

[50] Article 2 of the GATS defines trade in services as comprising four types of activity: (1) supply of a service from the territory of one Member to the territory, or (2) to a consumer of, another Member; services supplied through (3) commercial presence in the territory of another Member, and (4) through presence of nature persons in the territory of another Member.

[51] TEC Articles 43–48. The right of establishment requires a Member State to allow a corporation or individual who is a national of another Member State to set up an establishment (for example, an office in the case of an individual offering professional services, or a branch or subsidiary in the case of a corporation) for the purpose of carrying on any type of business (not just providing services) on the host Member State's territory under the same conditions as nationals of the host Member State.

[52] TEC Articles 49–55, which also incorporate the principles of Articles 45–48 in the chapter on the Right of Establishment. The TEC division very roughly corresponds to the NAFTA chapters on Services (Chapter 12) and Investment (Chapter 11).

Member State, the Right of Establishment chapter applies in priority to the Services chapter. In this article, the focus will be on Treaty provisions and cases specifically relating to trade in services, though reference will be made to the right of establishment where necessary.

The TEC chapter on services applies to services of an industrial, commercial, craft or professional character provided for remuneration. Service providers who are individuals, corporations and firms[53] are all entitled to NT (though that phrase is not used) as they may not be subject to restrictions under the law of a Member State which are different than those faced by nationals of that Member State providing the same kind of services. Article 49 expressly protects services providers who are EC nationals, but who are neither nationals of, nor established in, the Member State where the recipient of the services is located. In addition, the freedom to provide services has been held to be infringed where a Member State's laws, regulations or administrative policies or practices are liable to deter its own nationals or residents from seeking to obtain services from suppliers not resident or established in that State.[54]

With respect to direct taxation, the Council of the European Union has a general power to adopt directives for the harmonization of laws, regulations and administrative positions of the Member States in order to establish and ensure the proper functioning of the internal market.[55] In the case of tax harmonization measures, the Council must adopt a legislative proposal of the Commission unanimously.[56] The difficulty of obtaining unanimity of all Member States in the Council means that the number of directives in the field of direct taxation are few (though those that have been adopted are significant in their effects). The result is that Member States retain general competence over direct taxation, but with an important caveat: They must exercise that competence in accordance with Community law. This means that they may not enact or maintain in force any tax measure that is contrary to the TEC or secondary EC legislation.

As with the other fundamental freedoms[57] contained in the TEC, the prohibition against discrimination in services is not limited to "overt discrimination", that is, situations where a provision of a Member State's law differentiates specifically between nationals and non-nationals. Discrimination consists in treating those in comparable situations differently, as well as in treating persons

---

[53] Companies and firms formed under the law of a Member State and which have their registered office, central administration or principal place of business in a Member State of the EC are treated as nationals of that Member State: TEC Article 48.

[54] Case C-118/96 *Safir* [1998] E.C.R. I-1897 at para. 30 and Case C-294/97 *Eurowings* [1999] E.C.R. I-7447 at para. 37.

[55] TEC Articles 94 and 95.

[56] TEC Article 95(2).

[57] In addition to freedom of establishment and services, the TEC provides for free movement of goods, workers and capital.

in different situations the same.[58] Application of distinguishing criteria other than nationality is prohibited where in fact it leads to discrimination on the basis of nationality. Thus, a provision of national law which treats non-residents less favourably than residents is prohibited as "covert discrimination" where non-residents can demonstrate that they are in a comparable situation to residents and where, as a practical matter, the impact of the measure is felt primarily by non-nationals.[59] This is usually the case, as non-residents of a Member State are much more likely than residents of that State to be non-nationals. The issue of whether residents and non-residents are in a comparable situation with respect to direct taxation will be discussed more fully below.

c) *EC Cases on Direct Taxation and Services*

Many of the cases on free movement of services have arisen in the area of insurance and pensions.[60] However, the types of services addressed in the cases range widely, from aircraft leasing,[61] lotteries,[62] research contracting,[63] providing professional training courses[64] to the services of a professional musician.[65] The form of tax discrimination varies, but in each case involves tax rules of a Member State which impose a heavier tax or administrative burden either on the foreign supplier of services, or on the person who obtains such services from a supplier who does not have an establishment (either a subsidiary or a branch) in the Member State in which that person resides or is established. Three cases are briefly outlined here to illustrate the application of the prohibition of direct tax discrimination in trade in services in EC law.

Vestergaard[66] was a case involving deductibility of professional training expenses. Danish administrative policy, upheld in numerous Danish court rulings, was to impose a presumption that professional training courses held at foreign tourist resorts contained such a significant tourism element that

---

[58] Case C-279/93 *Schumacker* [1995] E.C.R. I-225 at paras. 27–30.

[59] Case 152/73 *Sotgiu v. Deutsche Bundespost* [1974] E.C.R. 153 at para. 11.

[60] See among others, Case C-204/90 *Bachmann v. Belgium* [1992] E.C.R. I-249; Case C-300/90 *Commission v. Belgium* [1992] E.C.R. I-305; Case C-118/96 *Safir supra*, note 54; Case C-136/00 *Danner* [2002] E.C.R. I-8147; Case C-42/02 *Skandia and Ramstedt* [2003] E.C.R. I-6817; Case C-334/02 *Commission v. France* [2004] E.C.R. I-2229.

[61] *Eurowings, supra*, note 54.

[62] Case C-42/02 *Lindman* [2003] E.C.R. I-13519.

[63] Case C-39/04 *Laboratoires Fournier SA*, March 10, 2005, not yet reported.

[64] Case C-55/98 *Vestergaard*, [1999] E.C.R. I-7641.

[65] Case C-234/01 *Gerritse*, [2003] E.C.R. I-5933.

[66] *Supra*, note 64.

expenses of attending such courses were deemed not deductible.[67] Further, the practice of the Danish authorities was to require the taxpayer, in order to rebut the presumption, to demonstrate that the foreign location was indispensable to the objective of the training course.[68]

Mr. Vestergaard was a Danish auditor, employed by a company of which he held all the shares, who attended a tax course specifically for Danish auditors in Crete. The Danish authorities allowed the deduction of the expenses of Mr. Vestergaard's attendance at the course by his company, but included them in Mr. Vestergaard's income as additional salary or bonus. The same course held at a Danish tourist resort would not have been subject to the presumption against deductibility of expenses.

The ECJ held that the administrative presumption was contrary to Article 49 in that it subjected the service of providing professional courses to different tax rules depending on whether the services were provided in Denmark or in another EC Member State (Greece). There was unequal treatment, making it more difficult to deduct costs of courses organized abroad than in Denmark, which constituted a restriction on non-Danish service providers' freedom to offer their services to Danish taxpayers.

In another case, *Gerritse v. Finanzamt Neukölln-Nord*,[69] the taxpayer was a Netherlands resident. He provided services as a professional drummer for a radio station in Berlin in 1996 for which he was paid approximately 6000 DEM. He incurred business expenses directly related to the services provided in Germany of DEM 698. German law provided for (and the 1959 tax treaty between Germany and the Netherlands allowed) a deduction at source of 25% of the gross income earned by the taxpayer in Germany as his final German tax liability.

Mr. Gerritse argued that he was subject to discrimination contrary to TEC Article 49 because the flat 25% withholding from his gross earnings did not allow him the basic exemption threshold of approximately DEM 12,100 which German residents, and non-residents who earned greater than 50% of their income in Germany, or who had income of less than DEM 12,000 in other

---

[67] Article 24 of the OECD Model prohibits this discriminatory treatment of business expenses. The tax treaty between Greece and Denmark prohibits (and prohibited at the time) Denmark from disallowing a deduction for a disbursement made to a Greek resident which would be deductible if paid to a Danish resident so that presumably Mr. Vestergaard could have relied on the tax treaty. It may be that Mr. Vestergaard's company paid the amount to a Danish travel agent or other organization, or that the allowance of the deduction to the company meant that the tax treaty did not strictly apply.

[68] The rare example of a successful rebuttal of the presumption given in Advocate General Saggio's opinion was of a professor of classical history who was allowed to deduct expenses of a course held in Greece.

[69] *Supra*, note 65.

countries, were allowed. He also argued that disallowing the deduction of his expenses incurred in providing the services in Germany was discriminatory, since suppliers of services resident or established in Germany were permitted to deduct such expenses in computing their income subject to tax.

Mr. Gerritse was unsuccessful on the first argument. The ECJ ruled that in relation to direct taxation, residents and non-residents are not generally in comparable situations. A Member State may thus apply different rules to residents than to non-residents. It is for the State of residence to make provision for social objectives such as reduced ability to pay related to personal and family circumstances and to ensure progressiveness in the personal income tax system. The Netherlands did this by taking into account the German tax in computing his worldwide income subject to Netherlands tax.[70]

On the second argument Mr. Gerritse was successful. The ECJ ruled that refusal to allow the deduction of expenses incurred in order to earn the income was a clear disadvantage to services providers not resident or established in Germany, and no precise argument had been put forward to justify the discriminatory treatment.

In a very recent case, *Laboratoires Fournier*,[71] the ECJ held that French tax law, which provided a tax credit of 50% of the expenses incurred for research activities carried out in France, but not in other Member States, was contrary to Article 49. Laboratoires Fournier is a pharmaceutical manufacturer that contracted research services to research facilities in various Member States in 1995 and 1996, and claimed the tax credit against its French corporate tax liability in respect of the expenses incurred. Following an audit, the French tax authorities denied the credit because the research had not been carried out in France. The ECJ held that failure to allow the same tax advantage for research expenses incurred in any Member State of the EC infringed the freedom of research services providers in other Member States to offer their services to French purchasers of services, and deterred the latter from obtaining such services from other Member States, and thus constituted a restriction on the freedom to provide services guaranteed by Article 49.[72]

A number of defences have been raised by Member States to justify their direct taxation provisions against allegations that they infringe the freedom to

---

[70] The relationship of EC discrimination law with bilateral tax agreements is discussed in more detail below.

[71] *Supra*, note 63.

[72] Note that the non-discrimination article in the OECD Model would not have prohibited this measure, as the Model only requires that a Contracting State allow a deduction for an expense where the amount is paid to a resident of the other Contracting Party in any case where the expense would be deductible if paid to a resident of the first State. The OECD Model provision does not address tax credits.

provide services (and other fundamental freedoms in the TEC).[73] The argument is frequently made that the impugned tax measure is necessary to maintain the cohesion of the national tax system. In two cases,[74] among the earliest to be decided on direct discrimination, this defence was successful. The Belgian tax measure at issue in both cases allowed a deduction to a resident of Belgium in respect of pension contributions paid to an insurance company resident or established in Belgium, but denied the deduction for such payments to an insurance company not established in Belgium. The ECJ found that the measure constituted a restriction on free movement of workers and services, but was justified because there was no less restrictive way for Belgium to ensure that deductions would only be permitted where the insurance and pension benefits which would later be paid would be subject to tax in Belgium. This was due to the fact that the individual seeking to deduct premiums paid to a non-Belgian insurer was most likely to be a non-Belgian, who would return to his home country to collect his pension. There was a direct link between the deduction of the premiums and the taxation of the benefits in relation to one and the same taxpayer by the same tax authority, so that cohesion could only be maintained by making the deduction contingent on the resulting benefits being taxable.

Another justification for a discriminatory tax measure that has been accepted by the ECJ in principle is ensuring the effectiveness of fiscal supervision (preventing tax evasion or avoidance). However, a discriminatory rule will only be justified if it applies only to purely artificial arrangements intended to evade tax laws and permits a case by case assessment of whether the taxpayer has in fact illegitimately avoided tax. It is not sufficient that the measure have as its purpose the prevention of tax evasion. The ECJ frequently refers to Council Directive 77/799/EEC concerning the mutual assistance by competent authorities of the Member States in the field of direct taxation as ensuring that national tax authorities have the necessary means of obtaining information from other Member States to prevent tax evasion.

The ECJ refuses to allow a tax measure to be justified on the basis that it is necessary to protect government revenues or the tax base, stating that a measure that contravenes a fundamental Treaty freedom cannot be justified on purely economic grounds.[75] Nor may a Member State apply tax rules that seek to equalize the tax burden on a particular form of cross-border income that is lightly taxed in another Member State.[76]

---

[73] TEC Article 46 provides for general exceptions to Article 49 where a Member State can demonstrate that its law is necessary to protect public policy, public health or public security, but these defences have not been put forward in direct tax cases.

[74] *Bachmann v. Belgium* and Case C-300/90 *Commission v. Belgium, supra* note 60.

[75] See for example Case C-315/02 *Lenz* July 15, 2004, O.J. 2004/C 228/10.

[76] *Eurowings, supra* note 54.

See also *Lenz, supra* note 75 and Case C-319/02 *Manninen* September 7, 2004, not yet reported.

d) *The relationship of bilateral tax treaties to EC law*

TEC Article 293 obliges Member States to enter into negotiations with each other to secure for the benefit of their nationals "the abolition of double taxation within the Community", but does not directly refer to the elimination of tax discrimination. The network of bilateral tax treaties among EU Member States is virtually complete, and remains a very important component of direct tax law for the Member States, particularly with respect to individuals.[77]

i) *Case law on bilateral tax treaties and discrimination*

The relationship of tax treaties to EC law has been considered in several ECJ judgments and opinions of Advocates-General. In the earliest direct tax decision, "*Avoir Fiscal*", the ECJ ruled that the rights conferred by the TEC (in that case, the right of establishment) were unconditional, and could not be subordinated to the provisions of a tax treaty concluded with another Member State.[78] This is no more than a statement of the principle of supremacy of EC law over national law, which applies whether the national law is enacted before or after accession to the Community. Since the provisions of tax treaties form part of domestic law, their provisions are subordinate to EC law in the event of a conflict.

Tax treaties normally only apply specifically to trade in services in the case of individual service suppliers temporarily providing services in the Contracting State of which the individual is not a resident. This engages either the provision based on former OECD Model Article 14, governing independent personal services or Article 17, governing the activities of artists and athletes.[79] Corporate service suppliers are governed by Article 7, which, like former Article 14, allows for taxation of services income derived in the Contracting State of which the supplier is not resident only where the supplier has a permanent establishment (or "fixed base" in the case of former Article 14) through which the income is earned in that State. As noted earlier, in the EC system,

---

[77] The various direct taxation directives adopted at the EC level since 1990 eliminate withholding tax on dividends, royalties and interest between subsidiary and parent corporations in different Member States, facilitate cross-border mergers, and provide for mutual assistance in the exchange of information and recovery of tax claims.

[78] Case 270/83 *Commission v. France* [1986] E.C.R. 273 at para. 26.

[79] Article 14 was eliminated from the OECD Model in 2000, so that the distinction previously created by Article 14 between individuals providing "independent personal services" and general business profits in Article 7 no longer exists. In the current Model, the only provision that treats service providers differently from other businesses is Article 17, which deals with "Artistes and Sportsmen". However, most tax treaties still contain a provision equivalent to OECD Model Article 14, even such recent ones as the pending treaty between the UK and France, signed in 2004.

once a services supplier has a tax nexus in another Member State in the form of a permanent establishment or fixed base, the discussion moves from free movement of services to the right of establishment. Thus most of the cases that involve a tax treaty are resolved by reference to freedom of establishment, and the issue is often the unequal treatment of corporations that have a branch as opposed to a subsidiary in another Member State,[80] or unequal tax treatment of permanent establishments of foreign corporations compared to subsidiaries of such corporations.

The *Gerritse* case is an example of the way tax treaties are applied in the case of individuals supplying services to a recipient in another Member State. The ECJ has developed a distinct approach to non-discrimination on the basis of residence or nationality in direct taxation, sometimes referred to as the "*Schumacker* principle"[81] in the case of individuals. The concept of covert discrimination is conditioned, in direct taxation cases, on the taxpayer demonstrating that non-residents and residents are in a comparable situation as regards their liability to direct taxation in the Member State whose tax measure is challenged. The ECJ has frequently recognized in its rulings that residence is the primary criterion used by the international tax system for determining liability to direct taxation, and that in general, residents and non-residents are not in comparable circumstances. Thus not every difference in treatment will amount to discrimination, particularly where the issue is access to deductions or credits based on family or personal circumstances.

In the case of performing artists (such as Mr. Gerritse) and athletes, treaties following the OECD Model allocate primary taxing jurisdiction to the State where the services are performed. The Netherlands-Germany tax treaty followed this model, so that Germany could impose a 25% final tax on Mr. Gerritse's income derived from services performed in Germany. Even though this was different treatment from that which applied to a resident of Germany, it was not found to be contrary to Article 49 of the TEC, because Mr. Gerritse was not in a comparable situation to a German resident, entitled as he was to allowances for his personal and family circumstances in the Netherlands, where he earned most of his income. Further, the Netherlands allowed Mr. Gerritse a tax credit for the German tax paid against his Netherlands tax liability, which fairly compensated him while maintaining progressive taxation, so he could not demonstrate that he was deterred from supplying services in Germany.

On the other hand, the Court ruled that the refusal by Germany to allow deduction of expenses incurred by the service provider in computing the income subject to the withholding tax was discriminatory, as German service

---

[80] See, for example, Case 270/83, *Commission v. France, supra* note 78, Case C-141/99 *AMID* [2000] E.C.R. I-11619 and Case 307/97 *Saint-Gobain* [1999] E.C.R. I-6161.

[81] Case C-279/93 *Schumacker* [1995] E.C.R. I-225 at paras. 31–35.

providers were entitled to deduct their expenses so that tax was imposed on net rather than gross income. Neither the Commission nor the Member State governments who intervened in the *Gerritse* case put forward a convincing argument that residents and non-residents were in objectively different situations regarding deduction of their expenses in computing income subject to tax. The fact that the Netherlands-Germany tax treaty permitted Germany to impose the withholding tax on the gross income of the service provider could not justify the measure if it was contrary to Article 49 TEC.

With respect to discrimination against corporate service suppliers from other Member States, the ECJ has not had occasion to consider the interaction of a tax treaty with Article 49 of the TEC. However, in the numerous cases concerning freedom of establishment and free movement of capital, the same type of approach is followed as in *Gerritse*. After reiterating that in the area of direct taxation, residents and non-residents are not generally in comparable circumstances so that different treatment is not necessarily prohibited discrimination, the ECJ considers whether in the particular circumstances residents and non-residents are in a comparable situation. If a branch establishment of a UK corporation located in France (for example) is otherwise subject to direct taxation on the same basis as French corporations, then the existence of a bilateral treaty between the UK and France that permits France to tax the UK corporation's branch more heavily than a French corporation will be considered contrary to EC law.

ii) *Impact of tax treaties on justifications for discriminatory measures*

Somewhat curiously, when a Member State has made the argument that a matter has been regulated under a bilateral tax treaty which should be respected, the ECJ has used the existence of the tax treaty as a double edged sword to eliminate discriminatory tax provisions. On the one hand, the tax treaty itself is subordinate to EC law so that if it allows a restriction on the exercise of a fundamental freedom, it is inapplicable. On the other hand, the existence of a tax treaty between two Member States has the effect of negating the argument that a measure is necessary to preserve the cohesion of a Member State's tax system.[82] The ECJ regards the bilateral agreement allocating tax jurisdiction as moving cohesion to a different level, involving reciprocity between the two Contracting States, rather than as between a taxpayer and a single Member State. Therefore, the direct link between a tax advantage and a tax obligation with respect to a single taxpayer and a single Member State, necessary to support the cohesion justification, is absent.

---

[82] Case C-80/94 *Wielockx* [1995] E.C.R. I-2493.

iii) *Most Favoured Nation as a principle of EC law*

The TEC contains no provision expressly imposing a MFN principle on Member States. The EC functions as an independent legal system governing Member States and their citizens independent of the concept of reciprocity. The nationals of all Member States are entitled to the same fundamental trade freedoms, even where a person's own State denies to nationals of other Member States the freedom he or she seeks to assert.

The issue of whether EC law requires a Member State to treat nationals and residents of another Member State no less favourably than it treats the nationals and residents of the Member State (or third country to whom is extended the most favourable treatment under a bilateral tax treaty) was resolved by the ECJ in the "D" case on July 5, 2005.[83] The D case concerned free movement of capital,[84] but the same principles would be applicable where free movement of services is at issue. D, an individual resident in Germany and subject to Netherlands wealth tax on his real property situated in the Netherlands, claimed the benefit extended by the Netherlands-Belgium tax treaty to residents of Belgium who have property subject to wealth tax in the Netherlands. The Netherlands-Belgium Treaty provides the same threshold exemption to Belgian residents as is allowed to residents of the Netherlands under Netherlands domestic law. The Netherlands-Germany treaty provides no threshold exemption for residents of Germany.

The argument that MFN applies so that a resident of any Member State is entitled to the most favourable treatment available to a resident of any other Member State was an alternative argument in the D case.[85] The primary argument was that the Netherlands was unjustifiably discriminating against D in denying him the threshold exemption available to Netherlands residents, and was thus imposing a restriction on free movement of capital.

In his Opinion of 26 October 2004, Advocate General Ruiz-Jarabo Colomer concluded that D should succeed on his primary argument. The Advocate General considered the MFN argument, and gave the opinion that the right to equal treatment for all EU nationals cannot be subordinated to the principle of reciprocity that governs bilateral tax treaties. Member States must take the utmost care in negotiating their tax treaties with other Member States to ensure that they do not hinder the establishment of the single market. If obligations undertaken in a bilateral tax treaty run "counter to the fundamental ideas

---

[83] Case C-376/03 *D. v. Inspecteur van de Belastingdienst.*

[84] TEC Article 56.

[85] In Case C-397/98 *Metallgesellschaft* [2001] E.C.R. I-1727 the question was referred to the ECJ as to whether the UK was obliged to grant the same type of tax credit for UK advance corporation tax to German residents as it granted to residents of the Netherlands under its tax treaty with the Netherlands, but neither the Advocate General nor the court responded to this question.

driving the construction of a unified Europe" then, in the Advocate General's opinion, the Member States concerned must find other solutions that do not breach Community law or prejudice citizens of other Member States.

The Advocate General nevertheless concluded that the ECJ should decline to rule on the MFN argument, as an affirmative ruling would "create upheaval in the legal systems of the Member States" and the system of bilateral agreements. The ECJ, sitting in a Grand Chamber of 13 judges, rejected both the advice not to rule, and the principle of MFN where the more favourable treatment is the result of a bilateral tax treaty between two Member States. The Court held that a resident of Belgium, which has a favourable tax treaty with the Netherlands, is not in a comparable position to a person who is resident in Germany, which does not have the same preference in its tax treaty with the Netherlands. Residence in a particular State is a distinguishing criterion which is fundamental to the application of the tax treaty, and the allowance accorded under one treaty to residents of the Contracting States had to be regarded as part of the treaty's overall balance, rather than as a discriminatory provision which was contrary to the free movement of capital in TEC Articles 56 and 58.

The result of the D case on the MFN principle is quite surprising, given the very strong rulings of the ECJ in the past restricting the scope of Member States to justify different treatment of residents and non-residents by relying on a tax treaty. It is less controversial that the ECJ also found that the Netherlands' refusal of the wealth tax allowance to Mr. D was not itself an infringement of TEC Articles 56 and 58, because only 10% of Mr. D's total wealth was situated in the Netherlands. He was not, therefore, in a comparable situation to a Netherlands national or resident who had the greater part of his wealth situated in the Netherlands and subject to Netherlands wealth tax.

With respect to services, the reasoning in the D case would seem to allow Member State X to accord more favourable treatment to service providers from Member State Y than to those from Member State Z, if the provisions of the tax treaty between X and Y provide for the more favourable treatment. However, where the tax treatment by a Member State of non-resident service providers is less favourable than for residents, even though residents and non-residents are in comparable situations with respect to their tax liability, the different treatment may still constitute an infringement of Article 49.

4) TAX DISCRIMINATION: SOME COMPARATIVE EXAMPLES

The following are some hypothetical examples of tax discrimination that, in principle, violate either the MFN and NT obligations under a trade agreement. A discussion of how the matter would be addressed in both Canada and the UK follows to underline the differences in result.

a) *First example*

Assume Canada's income tax law prohibits a deduction for amounts paid to non-residents of Canada that exceed $100,000 per annum. A U.S. engineer, earning more than $100,000 for services performed in Canada in 2005, is denied further work by a Canadian client. The U.S. seeks to challenge the Canadian provision as a violation of the NT obligation under the NAFTA. Is their remedy restricted to the competent authority procedure under the Canada-US Treaty? The answer is yes. Article 25(7) of the tax treaty, provides *inter alia* that in determining the taxable profits of a resident of Canada, disbursements paid to a resident of the US shall be deductible under the same conditions as if they had been made to a resident of Canada. As a result, any dispute about a tax measure that impacts the deductibility of fees paid to a non-resident who is a US resident by a Canadian resident must be resolved under the tax treaty.

The answer changes if the province of Ontario denies the deduction for purposes of computing provincial income tax liability. The Canada-U.S. Treaty applies only to tax levied by the Government of Canada.[86] Thus there is no restriction, based on the argument that the matter is covered by a tax treaty, to prevent a dispute about a discriminatory provincial income tax from being brought by the U.S. against Canada under the NAFTA. Further, the NAFTA imposes a NT obligation as the tax relates to the purchase or consumption of cross border services.[87] There is thus a clear argument that the NT obligation in the NAFTA has been violated.

Can the U.S. Government argue there has been a NT violation in respect of the federal tax prohibition under the GATS, assuming a commitment by Canada in this sector? The answer again appears to be no because Article 26(7) of the Canada-U.S. Treaty addresses the issue of the deductibility of disbursements paid to a non-resident, so the matter must be addressed under the tax treaty.

If the engineer is from Mexico, can the Mexican Government argue there has been a NT violation under the GATS? The answer is "maybe". There is no clause in the Canada-Mexico Treaty similar to that found in the Canada-U.S. Treaty that addresses the deductibility of disbursements paid to non-residents. Whether a claim can be made under the WTO dispute resolution procedures will therefore depend on the commitments and exemptions claimed by Canada

---

[86] Provincial taxes do not fall within the scope of the tax treaty, except for the limited purpose of defining the scope of the obligation of the other Contracting State to provide relief from double taxation. Article 24(7) Canada-U.S. Treaty.

[87] The same is true if the engineer were from Mexico. The Canada-Mexico Treaty applies only to taxes imposed by the Government of Canada under the Income Tax Act and not to income taxes imposed by the provinces. Thus the Mexican government can also challenge the tax as being in violation of Canada's national treatment obligation under the NAFTA.

in its schedule to the GATS[88] and the interaction between Article XXII (3) of the GATS and the Canada-Mexico Treaty. Specifically, the issue is whether the matter falls with the 'scope' of a tax treaty, given the non-discrimination article and interpretive rules in the Canada-Mexico Treaty.[89]

The Canada-Mexico Treaty addresses the rights of a national who is a resident of Canada. Thus it is arguable that all aspects of the NT obligation fall within the scope of the tax treaty and that there is no obligation of non-discrimination in respect of a national who is a non-resident of Canada. Another view is that the NT obligation in respect of payments to a national who is a non-resident does not fall within the scope of a tax treaty and thus access to the WTO dispute resolution procedures is available. If this view is not correct, there is no remedy to prevent this type of discriminatory tax treatment under the WTO or the NAFTA.

If the engineer were British, the UK would face the same issue as Mexico in disputing the denial by Canada of the deduction of the disbursement in excess of $100,000 under the GATS. The Canada-UK Treaty,[90] like the Canada-Mexico Treaty, contains no non-discrimination provision requiring deduction of disbursements incurred to non-residents on the same basis as deduction of disbursements incurred to Canadian residents.

If it were the French government that denied the deduction of expenses for services over €100,000 if paid to a British engineer (but would not if the engineer were French), the discriminatory treatment would infringe Article 26(3) of the pending 2004 UK-France Treaty.[91] In addition, EC law would require France to treat UK service providers according to the same rules as French service providers, and either the British engineer or the French company could successfully obtain a ruling from the French courts that the French law was contrary to Article 49, based on the *Laboratoires Fournier* case.

---

[88] See discussion *supra* note 21.

[89] The OECD commentary to Article 25 at para. 44.5 includes the following discussion of the scope of a tax treaty: ". . . the phrase 'falls within the scope' is inherently ambiguous, as indicated by the inclusion in para. 3 of Article XXII of the GATS both an arbitration procedure and a clause exempting pre-existing conventions from its application in order to deal with disagreements related to its meaning. While it seems clear that a country could not argue in good faith that a measure relating to a tax to which no provision of a tax convention applied fell within the scope of that convention, it is unclear whether the phrase covers all measures that relate to taxes that are covered by all or only some provisions of the tax convention."

[90] Convention for the Avoidance of Double Taxation and the Prevention of Fiscal Evasion with respect to Taxes, CanUK S.C. 1980–81–82–83, c. 44 Part X [hereinafter Canada – UK Treaty]; Protocols to the Convention, April 15, 1980, October 16,1985 and May 7, 2003.

[91] This is the equivalent provision to Article 24(7) of the Canada-U.S. Treaty and Article 24(3) of the OECD Model.

b) *Second example*

UK Conventions Inc. (UK Corp) organizes conventions at its facility at Charing Cross. UK Corp's bid to host the next annual meeting of Cancorp, a large Canadian corporation, was rejected by Cancorp, because the costs of the meeting would not be deductible if it is held at Charing Cross. The problem, Cancorp explains, is a Canadian tax restriction on the deductibility of expenses for conventions held outside the NAFTA block.

Has Canada violated its MFN obligation under the GATS by refusing the deduction of meeting expenses in the UK? The answer is yes. Canada must meet the MFN obligation unless the difference in treatment is the result of a tax treaty or is specifically listed as an exemption in Canada's country annex.[92] Neither condition is met. In contrast, the MFN obligation is not violated if the preference with respect to the deduction of convention expenses were given in respect of conventions held by Cancorp in the U.S. because Article XXV(9) of the Canada-U.S. Treaty provides for the deduction of such expenses.

What is the result if the analysis is performed under the NAFTA (assuming there is no tax treaty exemption from MFN)? Can a complaint be made by Mexico that Canada has violated its MFN obligation under the NAFTA, if a deduction is permitted by Canada for convention expenses incurred in the U.S. but not Mexico? The answer is no.

The NAFTA does not apply to any taxation measure except as specifically provided in Article 2103. There is no requirement to provide MFN treatment with respect to taxes on income and capital gains in these circumstances. As a result, it would appear that there is no MFN obligation in respect of the favourable tax treatment for payments to service providers from one country over another. Further, there is no NT obligation, assuming the relevant tax provision was in effect at the time the NAFTA entered into force.[93]

If it were the UK that denied the deduction for convention expenses of a UK company's meeting held in France, the result would be the same as in the first example: discrimination contrary to TEC Article 49 (*Vestergaard* and *Laboratoires Fournier cases*) and violation of (pending) UK – France Treaty article 26(3).

If the UK tax authorities allow a deduction, in conformity with EC law, for expenses in respect of conventions held on the territory of the EC, must it provide the same treatment for conventions held in Canada under the GATS MFN provision? The answer is no. Article V of the GATS permits Members to enter into economic integration agreements, such as the TEC, and to offer more favourable treatment to its partners in the economic integration agreement than to other WTO/GATS members.

---

[92] GATS Article II(2).
[93] NAFTA Article 2103(4)(c).

c) *Third example*

Canada's Income Tax Regulations require a person paying a fee, commission or other amount, in respect of services rendered in Canada, to a non-resident, to withhold 15% of the gross amount on account of the non-resident's potential Canadian tax liability. While a waiver of the withholding requirement is sometimes available from the Canada Revenue Agency (CRA) if the services income is not attributable to a fixed base or permanent establishment of the non-resident in Canada, the process for obtaining a waiver can be complex and time-consuming, and must be initiated at least 30 days before the services are performed. A non-resident corporation that is not subject to Canadian tax on the income from providing services in Canada because it has no permanent establishment in Canada[94] must file a non-resident tax return to obtain a refund of the amount withheld at source from the Canadian government. Non-residents providing services in Canada are thus treated unfavourably compared to Canadian resident service providers.

Can either the U.S. or Mexico complain that Canada is not according their service providers NT under the GATS or the NAFTA? The answer in both cases is no. The GATS provides an exemption from the NT obligation "provided the difference in treatment is aimed at ensuring the equitable or effective imposition or collection of direct taxes."[95] There is a similar exemption under the NAFTA.[96]

Assume the UK imposes a withholding obligation identical to Canada's in respect of services performed in the UK by non-residents. Could a Portuguese firm (which has no permanent establishment in the UK), which supplies translation services to a UK newspaper through the intermittent presence of a Portuguese translator in the UK, challenge the withholding rules under TEC Article 49? Note that the Portuguese firm will be able to obtain a full refund (some months later) of the tax withheld by filing a UK tax return and relying on its exemption under the UK-Portugal tax treaty. Alternatively, it may obtain a waiver of all or part of the withholding requirement from the UK tax authorities through an administrative process.

The issue is whether the additional administrative burden imposed on either the services recipient (to withhold and remit 15% of the fees paid for the services performed in the UK by the Portuguese firm) or the services provider (to either obtain the waiver or file an income tax return to obtain the refund) is a restriction on the exercise of free movement of services.

---

[94] See Article 7 of Canada's tax treaties, as well as of the OECD Model.

[95] The GATS Article XIV(d). A footnote refers specifically to measures by members to ensure the imposition or collection of taxes in their territory.

[96] NAFTA Article 2103(4).

Alternatively, is the requirement imposed on the translation firm to pay an amount on account of UK tax, at the time the newspaper pays for the services, with no refund for several months, a restriction on the ability to offer services in the UK contrary to TEC Article 49?

In joined cases C-397/98 *Metallgesellschaft Ltd.* and C-410/98 *Hoechst*[97] a disadvantage for UK subsidiaries of EC parent companies (compared with UK subsidiaries of UK parent companies) caused by the availability of an election to the latter but not the former was held to be a violation of freedom of establishment. Subsidiaries of EC parent companies suffered a cash flow disadvantage by not being able to make the election (to defer payment of the now repealed Advance Corporation Tax ("ACT") in respect of dividends paid to their parent companies). The subsidiaries of EC parent companies lost the use of the amount of ACT they had to pay at the time of making a distribution (essentially an advance payment on account of their final corporate tax liability), and could not elect out of the ACT payment as could UK subsidiaries of UK parent companies, effectively permitting the latter to defer payment for several months. Subsidiaries of UK parent companies and EC parent companies were otherwise subject to the same rules regarding final corporate tax liability.

The ECJ held that the eligibility of the subsidiaries of UK parent companies for the election that was denied the subsidiaries of EC parent companies was discriminatory and, contrary to TEC Article 43, constituted a restriction on the freedom of establishment. In addition, it held that EC law entitled the plaintiffs to interest, on the amounts of ACT which they ought to have been allowed to elect to defer, for the period of advance payment.

The requirement that service providers from other EC states pay 15% of gross fees as UK tax by requiring the service recipients to withhold this amount is, by analogy with *Metallgesellschaft*, a restriction on the freedom to provide services, discouraging foreign service providers from offering their services in the UK, and creating a disincentive for UK purchasers of services to obtain them from providers in other Member States.[98] The cash flow disadvantage is real and significant, especially as the withholding applies to gross fees, as was held to be discriminatory in *Gerritse*.

---

[97] [2001] E.C.R. I-1727.

[98] Indeed, the Commission has commenced an infringement action against Belgium (Case C-433/04, O.J. C 300, 04.12.2004, p. 34) claiming that Belgium's requirement to withholding 15% of gross amounts paid to construction industry subcontractors not established in Belgium infringes Article 49.

5) Conclusions

Some 25 years elapsed between 1958, when the TEC came into force, and the filing of the first case alleging that a Member State's direct tax measure infringed a Treaty freedom. However, in the past fifteen years there have been a dozen decisions of the ECJ on direct tax discrimination in trade in services, (some 60 decisions on direct tax discrimination in total) and many more cases are pending. Combined with the positive harmonization of Member States' direct tax laws through secondary legislation, the rulings of the ECJ imply the formation of the first true international taxation regime based on common rules and enforced by an independent international court. As a Member of the EC, the UK is now finding that its trade relationship with its EC partners, with respect to services as well as in other areas, has a significant and growing impact on its supposed sovereignty over direct taxation. While the D case allows different treatment of residents of other Member States if it is the result of a tax treaty and the non-resident is not in a comparable situation to a resident, it remains to be seen how broad an exception to the strict non-discrimination rules this ruling will support.

By contrast, the trade agreements to which Canada is a party expressly exclude application to direct taxation measures in most circumstances, leaving Canada's tax sovereignty legally intact. The NAFTA does not envisage the deeply integrated single market constructed under the TEC, so it is not surprising that the integration of tax and trade has progressed much farther in the EC as compared to the NAFTA block. However, the impact of the trade provisions of the TEC on direct taxation in the EC Member States was not foreseen, and the NAFTA block is just over ten years old. Canadian policy makers will have to study the potential impact of closer trade relations with the United States and Mexico carefully, with a view to the impact, both positive and negative, that membership in the EC has had for the UK and other Member States.

PART 5

COURTS

Chapter 17

The Democratic Legitimacy of the "International Criminal Justice Model":[1] The Unilateral Reach of Foreign Domestic Law and the Promise of Transnational Constitutional Conversation

Karen Eltis

1) INTRODUCTION

United Nations Security Council Resolution 1373 in the matter of counter-terrorism[2] may be said to reflect a new-found accord amongst democratic nations. This fresh consensus regards both the insufficiency of the domestic

---

[1] Canada, Dept. of Justice, "Address by Irwin Cotler, Minister of Justice and Attorney General of Canada (as he then was), to the Canadian Bar Association Annual Meeting, Law Without Borders: Agenda for Justice" (Ottawa: Department of Justice, 2004): http://canada.justice.gc.ca/en/news/sp/2004/doc_31202.html.

[2] SC Res. 1373, UN SCOR, 56th Sess., UN Doc. S/Res/1373 (2001) condemning the terrorist attacks of September 11, 2001.

Christopher P.M. Waters (Ed.), *British and Canadian Perspectives on International Law*, pp. 349–377.

criminal law model in a post 9/11 world, and the need for heightened
international collaboration, if terrorism, said to pose an "existential threat to
the whole human family",[3] is to be effectively repelled.[4] In pursuit of this
objective, transnational intelligence gathering and sharing is critical.[5]

While the ever-increasing inadequacy of exclusively domestically-
based counter-terrorism strategies is categorical,[6] increased state interdependence ensuing from the adoption of what has been called an "International

---

[3] I. Cotler, "Terrorism, Security and Rights: The Dilemma of Democracies" (2002)
14 N.J.C.L. 13 at 18.

[4] *Ibid.* at 19: "For the juridical war on terrorism cannot be fought here – or won – by
one country alone. Rather, one has to 'think outside the box' and invoke an international
criminal justice model having regard to both the nature of the threat and the proportionality of the response. Simply put, combating the trans-national super-terrorist suicide-
bomber will require trans-national investigative and procedural mechanisms that are as
preventative as they are punitive; that are anchored in a justice system underpinned,
inter alia, by the related principle of universal jurisdiction, and which gives the domestic criminal justice system a global jurisdictional reach". See also L. Weinrib,
"Terrorism's Challenge to the Constitutional Order" in R. J. Daniels, ed., *The Security of
Freedom: Essays on Canada's Anti-terrorism Bill* (Toronto: University of Toronto Press,
2001) at 93. See also S. A. Cohen, "Policing Security: The Divide Between Crime and
Terror" (2004) 15 N.J.C.L. 405 at 414, citing R. Mosley, "Preventing Terrorism – Bill
C-36: the Anti-terrorism Act 2001" in D. Daubney, W. Deisman, E. Mendes &
P. Molinari, eds., *Terrorism, Law and Democracy: How is Canada Changing Following
September 11* (Toronto: Université de Montréal, 2002): "The consensus that emerged in
the Security Council and in most nations after September 11th is that the nature of terrorism requires a different approach to disrupt terrorism before it can carry out its
design. See also A. I. Aldesco, "The Demise of Anonymity: A Constitutional Challenge
to the Convention on Cybercrime" (2002) 23 Loy. L.A. Ent. L.R. 81 at 88: "The globalization of crime impedes traditional investigative procedures in several ways. First,
deterring and punishing cyber criminals requires an international legal framework to
investigate and prosecute computer offenses. Because information can be transmitted
through data networks that span the globe, an online offender can operate from a location outside the jurisdiction that proscribes his activities . . .".

[5] In Anne-Marie Slaughter's words: "States can only govern effectively by actively
cooperating with other states and by collectively reserving the power to intervene in
other states' affairs", in "Sovereignty and Power in a Networked World Order" (2004)
40 Stan. J. Int'l. L. 283 at 285.

[6] See A. Etzioni, "Implications of the American Anti-Terrorism Coalition for Global
Architectures" (2002) 1 Journal of Political Theory 9 at 11: "[T]he rise in transnational
problems is *prima facie* evidence that the existing system, which is centered around
nation states, is not sufficiently effective, Indeed, the Nation's capacity to control its own
affairs is declining".

Criminal Justice Model",[7] has, for its part resulted in a disconcertingly intrusive 'law without borders'.[8]

The somewhat inevitable corollary of this borderless approach to counterterrorism and cyber crime (*inter alia*) is an oft-unilateral application of coercive foreign law to citizens residing in their own home state. Therefore, individuals on their own soil may quite simply be subject to sanctions meted out by virtue of legislation promulgated by a distant sovereign not accountable to them, enacted via a process in which they had absolutely no input. Perhaps more importantly, and beyond their impugned procedural defects from a positivist perspective, these laws – often the object of much division in their home states – raise serious human rights concerns and arguably risk running contrary to substantive fundamental values enshrined in both the target state's domestic constitutional documents[9] and their international counterparts.

Fundamental principles such as accountability, transparency and – perhaps most importantly – human rights, shaped by their respective communities and as understood by them, may be reduced to nothing more than the singularity of their absence in a borderless world.

This disquieting invasiveness is perhaps best illustrated by the USA Patriot Act's potent reach in Canada.[10] Indeed, the Patriot Act may permit US authorities to access personal information of Canadians through the outsourcing of

---

[7] A.-M. Slaughter, *A New World Order* (Princeton: Princeton University Press, 2004) at 184: "the state . . . is disaggregating into its separate parts, functionally distinct parts. These parts – courts, regulatory agencies, executives, and even legislatures – are networking with their counterparts abroad, creating a dense web of relations that constitutes a new, trans-governmental order. Today's international problems – terrorism, organized crime, environmental degradation, money laundering, bank failure, and securities fraud – created and sustain these relations". See also A.-M. Slaughter, "A Global Community of Courts" (2003) 44 Harv. Int'l. L.J. 191.

[8] See *Restatement of the Law (Third), Foreign Relations Law of the United States* §402(1)(c) (1987): "we are approaching a global society. Under modern jurisdictional doctrine, prescriptive jurisdiction enables states to make their laws applicable to cases where the conduct has or is intended to have substantial effect within its territory". See also M. Fagin, "Regulating Speech Across Borders: Technology versus Values" (2003) 9 Mich. Telecomm. & Tech. L. Rev. 395 at 395, discussing the "increasing willingness of courts and states to regulate online activities and content across borders".

[9] See British Columbia, Office of the Information and Privacy Commissioner, *Privacy and the USA Patriot Act: Implications for British Columbia Public Sector Outsourcing* (British Columbia: Office of the Information & Privacy Commissioner, 2004) at 63 [Loukidelis Report], discussing FISA's potential violation of Canadians expectation of reasonable protection under the Charter of Rights and Freedoms.

[10] *Ibid.* Particularly section 215 of the *USA Patriot Act*, 2001, Pub. L. No. 107–56, 115 Stat. 252 [Patriot Act].

public services, as in the case of British Columbia.[11] More specifically, section 215 of the Patriot Act allows for secret court orders that enable the FBI to access "any tangible thing" for use in foreign intelligence or to fight terrorism[12] and may be used to compel financial institutions and ISPs (Internet Service Providers) to turn over foreign (in this case Canadian) citizens' personal information.

Another example of this exterritorial application of national law (again in this case, US law to Canadians), which often involves co-opting the private sector with staggering privacy implications,[13] is found in the new provisions in the CIBC (Canadian Imperial Bank of Commerce) cardholder agreement. The agreement subtly allows the US government to obtain disclosure of Canadian cardholders' information under certain circumstances.[14] It therefore stands to reason that, for all intents and purposes, Canadians are effectively – albeit indirectly – subject to and governed by coercive American legislation, which may offend the Canadian Charter of Rights and Freedoms.

In the same vein, the FBI's controversial DSC-1000 program (formerly known as the "Carnivore"), which enables investigators to sort through an Internet Service Provider's (ISP) e-mails, is worthy of mention. As Internet traffic originating in the United States is often routed by ISPs into Canada, DSC-1000 is said to monitor Canadian web traffic and e-mails.[15]

---

[11] *Ibid.* As the BC Ministry of Health Services is attempting to contract out the administration of BC's public health insurance program to US companies, a practice challenged in court.

[12] *Ibid.* See sections 218 and 505 of the Patriot Act.

[13] *Ibid.*

[14] *Ibid.* In a press conference interview, BC's Privacy Commissioner, David Loukidelis, discussed legislative changes – Bill 73 – and privacy issues Canada-wide: "The B.C. government passed a law this month aimed at preventing U.S. authorities from examining information about British Columbians held by private U.S. companies. It included fines ranging from $2,000 for individuals to $500,000 for corporations", Loukidelis said. Nova Scotia employs a U.S.-based company to manage provincial government databases, including social assistance, payroll and motor vehicle registration. Control of the database remains in Canada. Saskatchewan has outsourced some government services to U.S. companies and Ontario has outsourced social assistance operations to a private company. Even Statistics Canada has signed a contract with Lockheed Martin Canada – which has a U.S. parent – to develop the hardware and software to process census forms". See "B.C. report raises alarm about U.S. Patriot Act" *Canadian Press* (30 October 2004): http://www.ctv.ca/servlet/ArticleNews/story/CTVNews/1099091347396_54.

[15] See T. Hamilton "FBI software can take bite out of Canadians' privacy" *Toronto Star* (25 March 2001). See also A. J. Cockfield, "Who Watches the Watchers? A Law and Technology Perspective on Government and Private Sector Surveillance" (2003) 29 Queen's L.J. 364.

Needless to say, the Patriot Act's potential application in Canada is but an example of personal information crossing borders in a legal vacuum, in a world of transnational collaboration.[16] While a "discernible decline in the American deference to foreign sovereignty"[17] is lamented by some, it is worth noting that the US is by no means immune to this law without borders phenomenon, finding itself on the other side of the fence at times, as illustrated by the now infamous Yahoo! decision.[18] The case, in which a French court ruled that US-based Yahoo!, whose servers were located outside French territory, should be held legally liable under a French law prohibiting the exhibition or sale of racist paraphernalia, served to anger American civil libertarians at the "imposition" of French policy respecting hate speech.[19] Significantly, the impugned website targeted American rather than French citizens (themselves catered to explicitly by Yahoo.fr).

---

[16] Loukidelis Report, *supra* note 9 at 43 quotes a *National Post* article citing a KPMG report warning that "banks worldwide are being called upon by regulators and governments" to transmit private information in the fight against terrorism.

[17] H. H. Koh, "Transnational Public Law Litigation" (1991) 100 Yale L.J. 2347 at 2392.

[18] *Yahoo! Inc. v. La Ligue Contre Le Racisme et L'Antisemitisme,* 169 F. Supp. 2d 1181, 1192–1193 (N.D. Cal. 2001) [*Yahoo case*]: http://www.cdt.org/publications/pp_6.20.s.html. See R. S. Whitt, "A Horizontal Leap Forward: Formulating a New Communications Public Policy Framework Based on the Network Layers Model" (2004) 56:3 Fed. Comm. L.J. 587 at 639: "The court held that Yahoo! unlawfully allowed French citizens to access auction sites for World War II Nazi memorabilia". See also Judge Jeremy Fogel, in A. Oberdorfer Nyberg, "Is All Speech Local? Balancing Conflicting Free Speech Principles on the Internet" (2004) 92 Geo. L.J. 663 at 663: "What makes this case uniquely challenging is that the Internet in effect allows one to speak in more than one place at the same time".

[19] See M. Fagin, *supra* note 8 at 396: "The disfavored status within international law of unilateral state-based regulations that target extraterritorial actors arises from the inherent challenges such actions represent to state sovereignty". On the other hand, as Etzioni points out *supra* note 6 at 2: "Nations that object to materials communicated over the Internet (e.g. violent material, pornography, and Nazi propaganda) have great difficulty in upholding policies that ban such material, which they were previously able to enforce". As J. Reidenberg explains: "The French court ruling that ordered Yahoo! to block French users' access to the company's promotion of Nazi memorabilia was necessary to support French public policy. Any other decision would have negated the democratically chosen law in France on hate speech. At the same time, the U.S. court's refusal to recognize the French decision in the United States rested on the court's belief that the French ruling was in conflict with the First Amendment and its fundamental policies for the American democracy". See J.R. Reidenberg, "Lex Informatica: The Formulation of Information Policy Rules Through Technology" (1998) 76 Tex. L. Rev. 553.

Plainly put, the unprecedented reach of foreign laws,[20] affecting individuals residing in their own state with no apparent democratic recourse when rights and interests are not respected, raises several conceptual difficulties specifically pertaining to democratic legitimacy that the literature has thus far overlooked.

Rather, the focus heretofore appears to have been almost exclusively on *sovereignty*,[21] voicing concerns regarding the potential offence to *national* or *state* interests.[22] Dwelling on sovereignty issues is a penchant borrowed from the traditional debate that has haunted international law for decades.[23] This framework lends itself poorly to a proper analysis of the subject at hand – one involving the imposition of *domestic* norms on alien actors at home.

Seen instead from the optic of democratic theory and its imperatives, the unilateral application of the fruit of one political community's coercive laws to the members of another's, invites democratic legitimacy analysis. Wherefrom can foreign-made law, claiming our allegiance whilst violating basic rights – as defined by our own community-derived legitimacy?

Accordingly, the following proposes to highlight the legitimacy difficulties inhering from the independent application of national law on extraterritorial actors in their own state. Accepting the insufficiency of the domestic model in combating borderless phenomena afflicting all humanity, the blight of terrorism and cyber crime in particular, it will subsequently endeavor to underscore the theoretical requirements facilitating the International Criminal Justice model's compliance with substantive democratic requirements.

---

[20] See N. W. Garnett, "Dow Jones & Co. V. Gutnick: Will Australia's Long Arm Jurisdictional Reach Chill Internet Speech Worldwide?" (2004) 13 Pac. Rim L. & Pol'y J. 61 at 61: "In December of 2002, the High Court of Australia issued its decision in Dow Jones & Co. V. Gutnick, holding that Dow Jones could be hauled into court in Australia for the publication of defamatory material on the Internet. This decision was surprising because the material in question was published in the United States on Dow Jones's New Jersey web servers. This decision makes Australia the only country that allows an action against a foreign defendant based solely on an Internet download in that country".

[21] See especially V. D. Dinh, "Nationalism in the Age of Terror" (2004) 56 Fla. L. Rev. 867.

[22] In the Loukidelis Report, *supra* note 9 at 63, the author expresses concern regarding the "unilateral extension of FISA is offensive to Canadian sovereignty" and mentions that it may offend the Charter "contrary to our reasonable expectations that Canadian constitutional protections [. . .] will apply". See also K. Roach, "Did September 11th Change Everything? Struggling to Preserve Canadian Values in the Face of Terrorism" (2002) 47 McGill L.J. 893 at 897: "There are real concerns that Canada hasn't done enough since September 11th to preserve a sovereign foreign policy . . .".

[23] See L. Henkin, "That 'S' Word: Sovereignty, and Globalization, and Human Rights, Et Cetera" (1999) 68 Fordham L. Rev. 1.

In so doing, the chapter will propose an analytical framework, positing that complementary analytical tools pertaining to democratic legitimacy be adopted.[24] It will be submitted that the renaissance of comparative constitutional law houses an alternative source of legitimacy, anchored in shared ideas of human rights. Far from purporting to redress all of the difficulties plaguing the unilateral application of questionable domestic law under the international criminal law model, comparative constitutional law, it is posited, can serve to palliate some of the conceptual hurdles deriving from the absence of an "associative community"[25] as decision maker. In effect, it will be argued that transnational judicial conversations can help foster an imaginative associative community, predicated on shared constitutional values.

The valuable function of comparative constitutional law in bolstering what Irwin Cotler has referred to as a "principled approach" to counterterrorism[26] is perhaps best illustrated by the recent House of Lords decision, impugning the lawfulness of detaining non-U.K. nationals, suspected of terrorist offences.[27] Two of the principles underlying this "principled approach"[28] – proportionality

---

[24] Criteria that better lend themselves to changed circumstances, rather than the ill-suited norms developed with the traditional nation state in mind. Surely, clinging to outdated precepts in an altered juridical reality, as Bruce Ackerman cautions, is unhelpful. Indeed, "If the American reaction is any guide, we urgently require new constitutional concepts to deal with the protection of civil liberties. Otherwise, a downward cycle threatens: After each successful attack, politicians will come up with repressive laws and promise greater security – only to find that a different terrorist band manages to strike a few years later": B. Ackerman, "The Emergency Constitution" (2004) 113 Yale L. J. 1029 at 1029.

[25] See R. Dworkin, *infra* note 49.

[26] I. Cotler, "Raoul Wallenberg Day, International Human Rights Symposium" (Address at Osgoode Hall Law School, January 17th, 2005).

[27] *A.(F.C) and others v. Secretary of State for the Home Department*, [2004] UKHL 56. Lord Bingham's opinion is replete with references to comparative and international law, including the UDHR, the ICCPR and the ECHR. Examples of references to specific shared values relevant for our purposes are the following: paragraph 31 (6) – reference to the fundamental right to personal liberty as protected by the ECHR; paragraph 34 – quotes the European Commissioner on Human Rights on proportionality; paragraph 36 – references article 5 of the ECHR; paragraph 39 – reference to LaForest J. in *RJR-Macdonald Inc. v. Canada (A.G.)*, [1995] 3 S.C.R. 199, regarding judicial review; paragraph 46 – discussion of discrimination including reference to US decisions and the ECHR; paragraph 58 – reference to UDHR principles of equality and non-discrimination; paragraph 63 – reference to the "Paris Minimum Standards of Human Rights Norms in a State of Emergency" regarding proportionality and non-discrimination; paragraph 62 reference to International Convention on the Elimination of All Forms of Racial Discrimination and the committee set up to monitor its implementation re. non-discrimination, equality before the law and equal protection by the law.

[28] *Ibid.*

and judicial oversight – are referenced therein by Lord Bingham, who, as shall be discussed, significantly cites leading Canadian Charter cases, as well as international instruments, in support thereof.[29] The significant use of Canadian precedent in what has been called the House of Lords' "most important constitutional decision"[30] appears to suggest that, as this chapter puts forward, human rights principles – particularly those relevant to counterterrorism – would benefit from harmonization via transjudicial conversation, a conversation alluded to at the start of this book.

2) AN 'ASSOCIATIVE COMMUNITY' FOR EXTRATERRITORIALLY APPLIED LAW? A BRIEF OVERVIEW OF DEMOCRATIC THEORY

Certainly, the extraterritorial application of national laws is longstanding in the realm of international commerce, as transnational transactions are routinely governed by 'borderless law'. Thus, individuals are regularly subject to norms not of their sovereign's making.[31] Notwithstanding, the International Criminal Justice Model is distinct, not by reason of its "indirect extraterritorial regulation per se, but rather the *scope* of indirect extraterritorial influence",[32] in addition to its long term goals.[33] It is further distinctive by reason of its ability to shake a community's most treasured values (privacy, expression . . .) by its very nature, at times without even the possibility of input, transparency or accountability. These difficulties are exacerbated when the cherished values affected unilaterally are those on which respective political communities sharply diverge.[34]

---

[29] *R. v. Oakes*, [1986] 1 SCR 103 at paras. 69–70. They also cite *Libman v. Attorney General of Quebec*, [1997] 3 S.C.R. 569 at para. 38, holding that the means deployed to achieve the legislative objective of guarding against the terrorist menace must respect the proportionality requirement set out therein.

[30] J. Booth, "Analysis: Britain's Guantanamo" *The Sunday Times* (16 December 2004). Said Lord Hoffman: "This is one of the most important cases which the House has had to decide in recent years . . . [I]t calls into question the very existence of an ancient liberty of which this country has until now been very proud: freedom from arbitrary arrest and detention."

[31] The emergence of a global trading system.

[32] J. L. Goldsmith, "The Legitimacy of Remote Cross Border Searches" (2001) U. Chicago Legal F. 103. See also Etzioni, *supra* note 6 at 6, who believes instead that the coalition is "narrowly crafted in scope" but broad in its 'globality' and duration: "The coalition is significantly *more global* than many if not all coalitions that preceded it" although he concedes some room for "mission expansion".

[33] See Etzioni, *supra* note 6.

[34] As best illustrated by the *Yahoo case, supra* note 18, involving the distinct construction of freedom of expression in the United States and France. See also A. Oberdorfer Nyberg, *supra* note 18.

Further disconcerting is not the international aspect of globalized law but its criminal facet. The line between national security intelligence gathering, to which this International Model is best suited, and ordinary criminal investigation, is increasingly blurred.[35] The distinction is highlighted by the Loukidelis Report of the British Columbia Privacy Commissioner.[36] The question of what renders a coercive norm authoritative has, needless to say, long intrigued scholars and policy makers alike. While it is beyond the scope of this endeavor to delve into the matter in any detail, suffice it to note that the difficulty is intensified when the legitimacy of the source of coercion is brought into question, as discussed. This is particularly true in light of dissonant policies in respect to criminal law and constitutional rights, primarily privacy.

Democracy is most often offered as justification for the legitimacy of state coercion.[37] Traditionally, therefore, "the rightfulness of law is tested by the idea of democracy, mainly of democracy as rule by the demos through the democratic process or popular sovereignty".[38] This said, let us now embark on a brief overview of democratic theory and legitimacy prior to turning to the International Criminal Justice Model.

The legitimacy of a particular political order, claiming obedience through its laws, stems from its satisfaction of certain criteria.[39] Conventionally, a participatory democracy, whose laws justify compliance, was said to meet four essential

---

[35] Loukidelis Report, *supra* note 9 at 29, per S. Cohen: "A universal and fundamentally acknowledged principle of privacy protection is that, with only limited exceptions, personal information gathered for one purpose may only be used for that purpose. Where personal information is gathered for national security purposes – often under special relaxed legal standards – its later use for law enforcement or other purposes raises troubling questions."

[36] Loukidelis Report, *supra* note 9 at 32: "Secrecy and opportunism are vital to the success of intelligence gathering".

[37] According to Habermas: "Legitimate law-making itself is generated through a procedure of public opinion and will-formation that produces communicative power". J. Habermas, *Between Facts and Norms*, trans. by W. Rehg (Boston: MIT Press, 1996).

[38] A. M. Bernal, "Constitutionalism and Democracy in the EU: The Case of the Convention on the Future of Europe" (Paper presented to the Contemporary Politics Workshop, Yale University, February 20th 2004).

[39] R. Pildes, "The Constitutionalization of Democratic Politics" (2003) 118 Harv. L. Rev. 28 at 43: "Democratic systems are typically justified by their ability to realize a variety of aims: to secure political stability; to express the equal moral status of all citizens; to ensure that the exercise of coercive political power is accountable through elections that select and reject those who hold power; to enhance (some would say maximize) the welfare of citizens by making policies responsive to their interests; to enable sound decision-making through the generation of necessary information; and to unleash individual energy in other spheres as a result of the sense of efficacy that participation in self-government generates. Conceptions of democracy vary widely. Minimalist theories view democracy as little more than selection of rulers by competitive elections.

elements: accountability, reciprocity, transparency and human rights.[40] Needless to say, "An individual's stake in how laws are promulgated, enforced, ratified, altered, or repealed can be correlated with the level of commitment the individual has in the success of his or her community".[41] Participation and accountability (itself requiring transparency) were of course emphasized by Rousseau, who attributed legitimacy to the collective exercise of popular sovereignty.[42] The legitimacy of laws, Habermas similarly instructs, further requires a dialogue between law makers and law followers.[43] The substantive element, for its part, may be said to trace its origins to the writings of John Locke, who only recognized the legitimacy of political orders in so far as they respected the individual rights and liberties of their members.[44]

Insisting on both procedural and substantive propriety,[45] modern theorists further put forward that legitimacy encompasses both a normative and an

---

Participatory theories conceive democracy as requiring direct engagement of citizens in substantive decision-making. Deliberative theories emphasize the quality of "public reasons" that justify collective choices. Substantive visions build into the very idea of democracy the liberal commitments to individual liberty and nondiscrimination. Some even justify democracy as the unique means of arriving at objectively rational collective outcomes".

[40] A. Etzioni, "Law in Civil Society, Good Society and the Prescriptive State" (2000) 75 Chicago-Kent. L. Rev. 355 at 356: "The values of civil society are those of political participation, state accountability, and publicity of politics . . . . The institutions of civil society are associational and representative forums".

[41] See *e.g.*, F. Michelman, "Democracy and Positive Liberty" (1996) 21 Boston. Rev. 3: http://bostonreview.net/BR21.5/michelman.html.

[42] J.-J. Rousseau, *The Social Contract*, trans. by C. Betts (Oxford: Oxford University Press, 1994): "Laws stem from the collective will of the people."

[43] Habermas, *supra* note 37. Habermas' theory predominantly relies on the ability of individuals to discourse with each other in an effort to co-create legitimate laws that draw their legitimacy from a legislative procedure based for its part on the principle of popular sovereignty. See also M. E. Warren, "Deliberative Democracy and Authority" (1996) 90:1 Am. Pol. Sci. Rev. 46 at 46 (recommending that authority is not coercion in deliberative democracy but rather "a justifiable surrender of judgment by subjects to those who rule on their behalf"). See J. M. Bessette, "Deliberative Democracy: The Majority Principle in Republican Government", in R. A. Goldwin & W. A. Schambra eds., *How Democratic Is the Constitution?* (Washington: AEI, 1980). See also D. M. Estlund, "Who's Afraid of Deliberative Democracy? On the Strategic/Deliberative Dichotomy in Recent Constitutional Jurisprudence" (1993) 71 Tex. L. Rev. 1437. See also J. E. Fleming, "Securing Deliberative Autonomy" (1995) 48 Stan. L. Rev. 1.

[44] J. Locke, *Two Treatises of Government*, ed. by P. Laslett (Cambridge: Cambridge Univ. Press, 1967).

[45] H. L. A. Hart, *The Concept of Law* (Oxford: Clarendon Press, 1994), at v. See also H. L. A. Hart, *Law, Liberty, and Morality* (Stanford: Stanford University Press, 1963). Hart argues that law consists of rules formed by the law-making body recognized by the population. See also H. L. A. Hart, "Positivism and the Separation of Law and Morals"

empirical aspect.[46] Thus, normatively (or formally),[47] legitimacy is contingent upon whether or not the lawmaker is worthy of obedience. It is therefore seen to correspond to legality. Empirically, legitimacy (or social legitimacy) is assessed by law subjects' *perception* of why obedience is warranted or, as Weiler defines it "a broad social acceptance of the system".[48] Dworkin[49] predicates law's moral authority and citizens' duty to obey it, on associative obligations inherent to their membership in an *associative community*.[50] This view is echoed by Raz, who through his identification thesis, acknowledges respect for law, to the extent that it is an aspect of the community. But what of norms without borders, targeting a 'global community'? Can they be said to meet these criteria when they derive from one community's vision, imposed on another, divorced from its making? It would surely stand to reason that some connection to the associative community is necessary if these norms, boasting extra-jurisdictional reach are to legitimately claim allegiance. This is the issue that the following section proposes to examine.

(1958) 71 Harv. L. Rev. 593 at 603: "[N]othing which legislators do makes law unless they comply with fundamental accepted rules specifying the essential lawmaking procedures." See also Habermas, *supra* note 37. For Habermas, only a procedurally proper law can have legitimacy in today's pluralist societies. Habermas ties the legitimacy of laws to its production through a democratic process as people more likely will obey a law when they have participated in its formulation and application.

[46] D. Robertson, *Routledge Dictionary of Politics* (New York: Routledge, 2003) at 278–279.

[47] Joseph Weiler's framework distinguishes between formal and social legitimacy. See J. Weiler, "Bread and Circus: The State of the European Union" (1998) 4 Colum. J. Eur. L. 223.

[48] *Ibid.* See Bellamy & Castiglione in the same vein (in the context of the EU) arguing that legitimacy "possesses an internal and external dimension, one linked to the values of the political actors . . . the other to the principles we employ to evaluate a political system and assess its effects for outsiders as well as insiders." R. Bellamy & D. Castiglione, *Constitutionalism in Transformation: European and Theoretical Perspectives* (Oxford: Blackwell, 2003) at 8.

[49] R. Dworkin, *Law's Empire* (Cambridge, Mass: Belknap Press, 1986). See especially Dworkin's chapter on integrity.

[50] *Ibid.* at 199–201: "An associative community is one: 1. that holds certain attitudes about the responsibilities members of a community owe one another. These responsibilities are special; they are owed not to everyone, but to members in the group 2. Whose members accept the responsibilities they owe another as personal – *i.e.*, each member owes them to every other member 3. Whose members see their community responsibilities as flowing from a general of concern for the well-being of the others in a group 4. whose members suppose that the group's practices show an equal concern for all members In addition to meeting these 4 criteria, the associative community must also be a "bare" community; its members cannot be involuntary, honorary members of the community. Political obligation, including the obligation to obey the law, is a form of associative obligation".

3) Applying Democratic Theory to the New Global Architecture[51]: The Procedural/Formal Requirement of Legality

In discussing what he calls "a new global architecture", Amitai Etzioni acknowledges that such an order may present certain legitimacy problems, noting that "the global state would have to command some of the loyalty and possess some of the political legitimacy and value endorsement now commanded by nation states".[52] But what of laws – such as the Patriot Act, for instance – not promulgated by any supranational institution but by a given political community, capable of binding members of another?

Habermas' proceduralist view, for its part, raises difficult questions regarding the legitimacy of any law that is not formulated and executed through democratic processes. According to this approach, only the state is invested with the power to "act" and can only legitimately do so if the formal decision-making procedures within that state possess a discursive character, capable of preserving the democratic sources of legitimacy. What then does this entail for counterterrorism laws *inter alia*[53] passed by a foreign sovereign state by a process, which while valid in one political community, also applies to non-citizens, outsiders who cannot avail themselves of any of the mechanisms of participation, let alone accountability that the domestic process otherwise provides?

More importantly perhaps, if norms demand obedience by virtue of one's association to a particular political community, how can binding 'outsiders', who can neither identify with nor help shape an alien society's institutions, ever be justified?

From a strictly procedural perspective, and applying a traditional sovereignty-based framework, it stands to reason that the source of legality, if it exists, is to be found in the 'outsider's' own nation state. Thus, for instance, Canada's and Britain's adherence to both treaties and UN Security Council Resolutions mandating a commitment to international cooperation for counterterrorism and related purposes, may be taken to reflect indirect respect for the formal requirements of democratic law making,[54] at the very least.[55] Likewise,

---

[51] Etzioni, *supra* note 6, asks whether the American anti-terrorism coalition formed in 2001 heralds a new "global architecture".

[52] See A. Etzioni, "On the Need for More Transnational Capacity" (2004) 56 Fla. L. Rev. 921.

[53] *Inter alia* but perhaps more pertinently due to their coercive character.

[54] Habermas, *supra* note 37 at 135: "A procedure of lawmaking that begets legitimacy".

[55] R. Howse, "How to Begin to Think About the 'Democratic Deficit' at the WTO" in S. Griller, ed., *International Economic Governance and Non-Economic Concerns: New Challenges for the International Legal Order* (Wien & New York: Springer-Verlag,

security *ententes* between governments or the European Convention on Cyber-Crime,[56] signed by 33 countries including Canada and most G8 countries may similarly be of interest. While plausible to some extent, this sovereignty-based formalist justification, is as indirect as it is far removed, leaving us wanting.

4) SUBSTANTIVE REQUIREMENT: RESPECT FOR BASIC HUMAN RIGHTS AS INDICIA OF LEGITIMACY

Mere legality, of course, does not alone impart legitimacy. Rather, as is now well established,[57] norms legitimately begging our allegiance must equally comport with the basic values we hold most dear. On this point, Israeli Supreme Court President Barak's comments are instructive:

> . . . . real or substantive democracy, as opposed to merely formal democracy, is not satisfied by the presence of these [formal] conditions. Democracy has its own internal morality, based on the dignity and equality of all human beings. Thus, in addition to formal requirements, there must also be substantive requirements.

2003) at 2, discussing the precommittment as justification. See also I. Cotler, *supra* note 3 at 19: "The international criminal justice model of the anti-terrorism legislation finds expression in the domestic implementation of international legal undertakings, in particular, the domestic implementation by Canada of the twelve international conventions that Canada has both signed and ratified which address specific terrorist acts, as well as those undertakings mandated by United Nations Security Council Resolutions: United Nations Convention on the Suppression of Terrorist Bombings (12/97); UN Convention on the Suppression of the Financing of Terrorism (12/99); UN Convention Against the Taking of Hostages (12/79); UN Convention for the Suppression of Unlawful Acts Against the Safety of Civil Aviation (Montreal Convention) (9/71); UN Convention for the Suppression of Unlawful Seizure of Aircraft (Hague Convention) (12/70); UN Convention on the Marking of Plastic Explosives for the Purpose of Identification (3/91); UN Convention on Offences and Other Acts Committed on Board Aircraft (Tokyo Convention) (9/63); UN Convention on the Physical Protection of Nuclear Material (10/79); UN Convention on the Prevention and Punishment of Crimes Against Internationally Protected Persons (12/73); Protocol for the Suppression of Unlawful Acts Against the Safety of Maritime Navigation (3/88); Protocol for the Suppression of Unlawful Acts of Violence at Airports Serving International Civil Aviation (2/88); Protocol for the Suppression of Unlawful Acts Against the Safety of Fixed Platforms Located on the Continental Shelf (3/88)." UN S/Res/1373 (2001); see also S/Res/1368 (2001); S/Res/1363 (2001); S/Res/1269 (1999); S/Res/1189 (1998); and S/Res/731 (1992).

[56] European Convention on Cybercrime, 23 November 2001, *Eur. T.S. No. 185* (note that Canada has signed but not yet ratified the treaty).

[57] A. Barak, "Substantive Human Dignity" (Address at Hebrew University Faculty of Law, Jerusalem, Israel, February 1999).

> These are reflected in the supremacy of certain underlying values and principles
> based on human dignity, equality, and tolerance. There is no (real) democracy
> without recognition of values and principles such as morality and justice. Above
> all, democracy cannot exist without the protection of individual human rights that
> the majority cannot take away by force of its numerical superiority . . .[58]

In consequence, norms said to offend basic human rights cannot legitimately
command our obedience. For our purposes, the domestic legislation implemented by many countries in the wake of 9/11 has been the object of copious
condemnation in their respective states, their respect of basic rights and liberty
seriously impugned.[59] *A fortiori*, when the alleged violations of human rights
are perpetrated not by one's own government – one that purportedly shares and
is held to respect specific values, as understood by a given community – but
instead derive from laws passed by foreign officials, themselves abiding by
altogether distinct constructions of a given value, then what? The best illustration of conflicting perspectives on the construction of a given right in the context of counter-terrorism is of course the conflicting meaning that the US as
opposed to Europe attaches to privacy.[60]

In exploring the legitimacy of norms, Dworkin, like Raz to a certain extent,
posits the following: a community's political practices might, among others,
aim to express the model of political association based on principle. This model
is based on the premise that a political community has to have a shared understanding, and that understanding is based on common principles, by which the
members of the group accept that they are governed. This kind of group would
be an associative community, one with shared attitudes about personal responsibilities that members owe to one another, responsibilities that flow from an
equal and reciprocal concern of members for each others' well being.

If the International Criminal Justice Model's failings lie in its inability to
correspond to an 'associative community', from whence it might derive normative and primarily social legitimacy,[61] than the challenge perhaps, as the next
part proposes to elucidate, is to uncover such a community. As noted, various
routes for law's legitimation offer themselves. Most fitting to this new reality,
the following will argue, is one that allows the object of norms to appropriate it,

---

[58] See A. Barak, "The Role of a Supreme Court in a Democracy and the Fight against
Terrorism" (2003) 58 U. Miami L. Rev. 125 at 127, citing R. Dworkin, *A Bill of Rights
for Britain* (London: Chatto & Windus, 1990) at 35–36.

[59] See *e.g.* the *Anti-terrorism Act*, S.C. 2001, c. 41 in Canada, the Patriot Act, *supra*
note 10, in the U.S.

[60] For an in-depth discussion on the subject see K. Eltis, "The Emerging American
Approach to E-mail Privacy in the Workplace: Its Influence on Developing Caselaw
in Canada and Israel: Should Others Follow Suit?" (2004) 24 Comp. Lab. L. & Pol'y
J. 487.

[61] Both substantive, and to a certain extent procedural.

and make the law their own. That, to borrow Michelman's expression, may be achieved by drawing on "a fund of normative references",[62] a set of narratives that will enable otherwise distinct communities to imagine themselves as a juridical associative community. Comparative Constitutionalism, as the newest incarnation of democratic constitutionalism, it is submitted below, may just provide such discourse.

5) ALLEVIATING THE 'DEMOCRATIC DEFICIT' OF THE INTERNATIONAL CRIMINAL JUSTICE MODEL: DEMOCRATIC CONSTITUTIONALISM'S PROGRESSION

The tragic events of the 20th century effectively revolutionized our understanding of democracy and of the legitimacy of norms. Legality alone or unqualified positivism, once revered as determinant indicators of democratic organization,[63] were rejected as incapable of preventing atrocities or providing any effective guidelines respecting legitimacy in a *post bellum* world.[64] The Second World War therefore served as a catalyst for what Lorraine Weinrib calls "the post-war paradigm",[65] a transformation deemed "the constitutionalization of democratic politics".[66] But the fact that Constitutional law now also "shapes the

---

[62] Michelman, *supra* note 41.

[63] Particularly by German attorneys prior to and during Hitler's rise. See *e.g.* I. Muller, *Hitler's Justice: The Courts of the Third Reich* trans. by D. L. Schneider (Cambridge: Harvard University Press, 1991) and F. Weinschenk, "'The Murderers Among Them' – German Justice and the Nazis" (1999) 3 Hofstra L. & Pol'y Symp. 137.

[64] "War Crimes", College of Wooster, Philosophy department [www.wooster.edu/philosophy/seniors/article02.htm]: "it has been argued that Nazi Germany provided a clear illustration of the inherent unacceptability of legal positivism and provided proof that any legitimate legal system must be grounded in natural law."

[65] L. Weinrib, "The Globalization of Constitutional Analysis: The Post-Second World War Constitutional Model" (Paper presented to the Migration of Constitutional Ideas Conference, Toronto, October 2004). For a description of post-war human rights documents, recognizing human dignity, see L. Henkin et al., *Human Rights* (New York: Foundation Press, 1999).

[66] R. H. Pildes, "The Constitutionalization of Democratic Politics" (2004) 118 Harv. L. Rev. 28 at 31: "Over the last generation, issues concerning the design of democratic institutions and the central processes of democracy have increasingly become questions of constitutional law throughout the world", citing R. Hirschl, "Resituating the Judicialization of Politics: Bush v. Gore as a Global Trend" (2002) 15 Can. J.L. & Jur. 191 at 217: "[I]t would be more accurate to consider the election judgment as symptomatic of a global trend whereby national high courts and supranational tribunals have become crucial political decision makers. As we have seen, Bush v. Gore – a

contours of fair political representation and political equality, as well as the role of group identities in the design of democratic institutions"[67] cannot solely be attributed to the atrocities of this past century. Instead, the transformed nature of direct democracy – first by its representative form, then by Constitutions, as judicially construed – is due to both the impracticability of the former and by a deep disaffect with traditional democratic institutions characterizing the latter.[68]

Constitutionalism for its part, introduced to subdue both the dangers posed by a content-neutral approach and the inefficiencies otherwise engendered by familiar institutions,[69] inevitably imports judicial review. The judiciary, in President Barak's words, is henceforth entrusted with protecting democracy.[70]

To be sure, more than a few scholars have fervently questioned the legitimacy of judicial review, arguing that allowing the unelected and arguably unaccountable to "pass judgment on issues that are more rightly the domain of democratically elected representatives"[71] offends democracy, as traditionally understood. Vituperative voices against the judicial branch by public figures repeatedly invited us to rethink the reconcilability of judicial review and democracy over the past few decades.[72] This critique, however, applies conventional criteria for assessing democracy, arguably in abstraction of contemporary needs.

The legitimacy of judicial review in a democratic society is conventionally justified by either the advancement of traditional counter-majoritarian

---

quintessential example of judicialized politics – illustrates merely one of four emerging areas of judicialization of 'mega' politics worldwide." See also R. Hirschl, *Towards Juristocracy: The Origins and Consequences of the New Constitutionalism* (Cambridge: Harvard University Press, 2004) at 169–211, chronicling emerging constitutional oversight of the design of democratic institutions and processes.

[67] Pildes, *ibid.*

[68] *Ibid.* at 37: "concerns about political accountability and responsiveness have become pronounced in mature democracies. For paradoxically, as the idea and practice of democracy are spreading worldwide, the long-established democracies are experiencing disaffection, distrust, and disillusionment with the institutions of democracy".

[69] See M. A. Glendon, *Rights Talk: The Impoverishment of Political Discourse* (New York: The Free Press, 1991).

[70] A. Barak, "The Role of A Supreme Court in a Democracy and the Fight Against Terrorism", *supra* note 58 at 125: "I do know that one of the lessons of the Holocaust and of the Second World War is the need to have democratic constitutions and ensure that they are put into effect by Supreme Court judges whose main task is to protect democracy. It was this awareness that, in the post-World War II era, helped disseminate the idea of judicial review of legislative action and make human rights central. It led to the recognition of defensive democracy and even militant democracy."

[71] C. P. Manfredi, *Judicial Power and the Charter: Canada and the Paradox of Liberal Constitutionalism* (Toronto: M & S, 1993). See also M. Mandel, *The Charter of Rights and the Legalization of Politics in Canada* (Toronto: Wall & Thompson, 1989).

[72] *Ibid.* Indeed, much ink has been spilled in endless discussions on this very predicament.

arguments[73] or, more recently, by the notion of dialogue.[74] Simply put, when the political branches fall down on the job, the argument goes that judicial review sparks a dialogue between branches. Therefore, rather than being understood as merely advocating minority interests, its defenders submit that judicial review may be labeled an integral part of the democratic process, whose role is not to quash or replace parliamentary decisions, but to complement them by engaging in a dialogue aimed at stimulating debate. Accordingly, present democracy is revitalized by sparking animated discussion between the various sectors of the population and their representatives on often neglected issues of policy, thereby compensating for the shortcomings of the political process.[75]

This more nuanced view of the uses and implications of judicial review, in light of both disillusionment with the inefficacies of representative institutions and the inadequacy of the legality criteria, lends a measure of legitimacy to judicial review in the modern context.[76] More importantly for our purposes, it derives from an implicit recognition that traditional criteria for assessing democratic legitimacy may not always be appropriate, and are best adapted to the needs of the epoch. For this reason, judge-made law arguably legitimately claims to obligate not by virtue of traditional rationales (such as positivist legality) but by responding to modern imperatives of democratic necessity.[77]

Just as direct democracy, in its pure Athenian form, was deemed unfeasible, so to is its unchecked representative form, in a modern heterogeneous polity, where minorities risk oppression and even un-moneyed majorities might easily go unheard. In other words, the shortcomings of the political process, specific to present-day conditions (namely, the difficulty associated with presenting one's case to elected officials, coupled with increasing abdication of politicians

---

[73] See *inter alia* J. H. Ely, *Democracy and Distrust: A Theory of Judicial Review* (Cambridge: Harvard University Press, 1981). As pointed out by former Canadian Justice Minister Kim Campbell, judicial intervention is appropriate "where it serves to strengthen the workings of the democratic process in order to correct the failures of the process, thereby making public institutions more responsive. Thus, courts can properly intervene where Parliament loses its way, either in disregarding fundamental values enshrined in the [basic laws] Charter or in failing to give sufficient regard to minority interests". A. K. Campbell, "The Charter and Good Government" in F. L. Morton, ed., *Law, Politics and the Judicial Process in Canada* (Calgary: University of Calgary Press, 1992) at 425–6.

[74] P. W. Hogg & A. A. Bushell, "The Charter Dialogue between Courts and Legislatures" (1997) 35 Osgoode Hall L. J. 75.

[75] *Ibid.*

[76] See A. Bayefsky, "The Judicial Function under the Canadian Charter of Rights and Freedoms" (1987) 32 McGill L. J. 791 *inter alia*.

[77] See F. Michelman, "Law's Republic" (1988) 97 Yale L. J. 1493 generally, responding to exclusion by proposing an inclusive constitutionalism, rethinking constitutionalism's relation to democracy.

of their traditional role as *initiators* of policy), create a need that the courts must satisfy.[78]

Likewise and by analogy, in a manner similar to the changed imperatives that first mandated constitutionalism as a necessary implement of democratic dialogue, this new reality – the so called "post 9/11" reality – too must cause us to revisit the measures used to evaluate democratic legitimacy and indeed democratic constitutionalism's own progression.

Theories of the state, to paraphrase Claude Klein, cannot be disassociated from their respective era.[79] In illustration of this ever-present need for contextual analysis,[80] Klein, for instance, attributes Hobbes' advocacy of absolute control to his fear of anarchy, living in a fierce and unruly world.[81] The elements generally invoked for the purpose of measuring democratic legitimacy were developed at a time when states could fulfill their primordial duty of protecting their citizens by their own laws.[82]

Today, "the dangers that we face are global in scope".[83] Quite obviously, terrorism and cybercrime, *inter alia*, are transnational and for that very reason cannot easily escape the control of individual nation-states, thus necessitating international cooperation. David Held speaks to this changed reality,[84] describing its noteworthy evolution:

> States today are locked into a world of multilayered authority and multilayered
> governance . . . most of our key political ideas, to do with self-determination,

---

[78] Lorraine Weinrib, for instance, argues that the judiciary does not usurp but rather complements the political function, if democracy is understood substantively, as it should be. See L. E. Weinrib, "Constitutional Conceptions and Constitutional Comparativism" in V. C. Jackson & M. Tushnet, eds., *Defining the Field of Comparative Constitutional Law* (Westport, CT: Praeger Publishers, 2002).

[79] Comments made by C. Klein in a seminar on Law and the State at the Hebrew University of Jerusalem in Winter 2001.

[80] Similarly advocated by Canada's Supreme Court; see Wilson J. in *Edmonton Journal v. Alberta (Attorney General)*, [1989] 2 S.C.R. 1326, 64 D.L.R. (4th) 577, cited by I. Cotler, *supra* note 3 at 16.

[81] See T. Hobbes, *The Elements of Law, Natural and Politic*, ed. by F. Tonnies (London: Frank Cass, 1969), setting forth the law of nature and the obligations and functions of a good sovereign. See also T. Hobbes, *Leviathan*, ed. by A. P. Martinich (Peterborough, Ont.: Broadview Press, 2002), expanding on the rights and obligations of a sovereign as well as citizens.

[82] See Reidenberg, *supra* note 19, discussing the democratic state's obligation to assure security, order and the rule of law.

[83] As David Dyzenhaus warns: "The Permanence of the Temporary: Can Emergency Powers Be Normalized?" in R. J. Daniels, ed., *The Security of Freedom: Essays on Canada's Anti-terrorism Bill* (Toronto: University of Toronto Press, 2001).

[84] D. Held, *Democracy and the Global Order: From the Modern State to Cosmopolitan Governance* (Stanford: Stanford University Press, 1995).

accountable government and so on, were ideas formed in the era in which states were being created and consolidated. The challenge now is somewhat different. Today, some of the most fundamental problems we face, are not issues which can any longer be solved by states or a people acting alone. Most modern political theory presupposes the idea of a self-determining people that can set it's own fate. Today, we're in a world of 'overlapping communities of fate', where the fate of different peoples is interconnected . . . Decisions made by other political communities impinge on one's own, with no obvious democratic recourse when rights and interests are not respected.[85]

While this author cannot support the somewhat utopian solution proposed by Held[86] – to establish a "cosmopolitan democracy"[87] – the *rebus sic stantibus* behooves us to rethink the normative criteria for evaluating the satisfaction of legitimacy, in favour of more "pragmatic viability".[88] In reality, doggedly clinging to dated notions risks undermining the public's confidence in its government and, worse yet, reduce the human rights we've toiled to secure to mere impracticable rhetoric, as governments hand over the uglier tasks of violating liberties to counterparts whose understanding thereof is far narrower.[89]

Indeed, as Bruce Ackerman cautions:

> No democratic government can maintain popular support without acting effectively to calm panic and to prevent a second terrorist strike. If respect for civil liberties requires governmental paralysis, serious politicians will not hesitate before sacrificing rights to the war against terrorism. They will only gain popular applause by brushing civil libertarian objections aside as quixotic.[90]

---

[85] Interview of David Held, Graham Wallas Professor of Political Science, London School of Economics by Montserrat Guibernau, Senior Lecturer in Politics at the Open University, "Globalization, Cosmopolitanism and Democracy: an Interview" (11 March 2001): http://www.polity.co.uk/global/held.htm.

[86] Consider both the 'democratic deficit' experienced by supra-national European institutions and the inefficiency of international ones such as the UN; see critiques by G. Majone, "Europe's Democratic Deficit" (1998) 4:1 Eur. L.J. 5; R. Dahl, "Can International Organizations be Democratic? A Skeptic's View" in I. Shapiro & C. Hacker-Cordon, eds., *Democracy's Edges* (Cambridge: Cambridge University Press, 1999) at 19–36.

[87] *Ibid.*

[88] A. Moravcsik, *"Is there a 'Democratic Deficit' in World Politics? A Framework for Analysis"* (2004) 39:2 Government and Opposition 336. See also A. Moravcsik, *"In Defence of the Democratic Deficit: Reassessing Legitimacy in the European Union"* (2002) 40:4 Journal of Common Market Studies (40th Anniversary Edition) 603.

[89] Hamilton, *supra* note 15: "Jones is convinced it is only a matter of time before Carnivore is used in Canada – if it hasn't been used already. He is concerned the FBI may begin working with the RCMP, providing information on Canadians' online activities that the Mounties could not otherwise get legally".

[90] *Ibid.*

It is therefore imperative that we cast our reflections on those conceptual mechanisms most apt for assuaging and possibly begin redressing[91] the above-described 'democratic deficit'[92] associated with the International Criminal Justice model.

6) THE PROMISE OF GLOBAL COMPARATIVE CONSTITUTIONAL LAW: A DECLINE IN LEGAL PARTICULARITY AND A NEW "ASSOCIATIVE COMMUNITY"?

As noted, representative democracy, in its traditional Westminster form, has arguably been all but supplanted by the constitutionalism of the Post-War world.[93] Far from remaining static, constitutionalism *itself* has evolved, converging and culminating in what has come to be known as globalized law. The perpetuation of this phenomenon has been significantly helped along by heightened "transjudical communication", itself evincing the decline of constitutional idiosyncrasy.

Judges – particularly those hailing from higher or constitutional courts – are increasingly conversing, most notably with regard to their role as guardians of democracy and human rights in regards to counterterrorism.[94] These significant exchanges are best evidenced by international judicial associations and increasingly frequent international judicial conferences, where a harmonized approach is often favoured,[95] as is the more frequent use of comparative law.[96]

---

[91] Indeed to live in security is a *sine qua non* for all other rights.

[92] See Weiler, *supra* note 47.

[93] As Ran Hirshl notes: "Over the past two decades the world has witnessed an astonishingly rapid transition to what may be called juristocracy. Around the globe, in numerous countries and in several supranational entities, fundamental constitutional reform has transferred an unprecedented amount of power from representative institutions to judiciaries. Most of these polities have a recently adopted constitution or constitutional revision that contains a bill of rights and establishes some form of active judicial review". R. Hirshl, "The Political Origins of the New Constitutionalism" (2004) 11 Ind. J. Global Legal Stud. 71 at 71.

[94] Culminating in the 2nd International Conference on the Training of the Judiciary: Judicial Education in a World of Challenge and Change, Ottawa, October-November 2004: www.nji.ca/internationalforum. See A. Barak, "The Role of a Supreme Court in a Democracy and the Fight Against Terrorism" *supra* note 58 at 126: "Judicial protection of democracy in general, and of human rights in particular, characterizes the development of most modern democracies", citing M. Kirby, "Australian Law – After 11 September 2001" (2001) 21 Austl. B. Rev. 21; A. Mason, "A Bill of Rights for Australia?" (1989) 5 Austl. B. Rev. 79; B. McLachlin, "The Role of the Supreme Court in the New Democracy" (2001) [unpublished, archived at the Harvard Law School Library] at 13–15.

[95] *Ibid.*

[96] Israel being one very obvious example, as its Chief Justice, President Barak, notes

As noted above, the best evidence for the increasing recognition of comparative constitutional law's potential contribution to fostering a "principled approach" to counterterrorism[97] is its recent use by the House of Lords in one of the few cases dealing with the post 9/11 legislation. Significantly, in ruling that the UK Government was in breach of the European Convention on Human Rights (ECHR) by holding nine "suspected international terrorists" in indefinite detention without trial,[98] the House of Lords drew on comparative constitutional jurisprudence. The senior Lord, Lord Bingham, cited the Supreme Court of Canada's proportionality test, outlined in *R. v. Oakes*, in support of his finding. Proportionality, the principle set forth in Oakes, is particularly central to the "principled approach",[99] as illustrated by the House of Lord's decision to strike down the detention Order for its "disproportionate interference with liberty and equality and unlawfully discriminated against foreigners".[100]

---

in his article "A Judge on Judging: The Role of a Supreme Court in a Democracy" (2002) 116 Harv L. Rev 16 at 110: With comparative law, the judge "expands the horizon and the interpretive field of vision. Comparative law enriches the options available to us." citing C.A. 295/81, *Estate of Sharon Gavriel v. Gavriel*, 36(4) P.D. 533, 542–43.

[97] See Irwin Cotler's address, *supra* note 26.

[98] The ruling quashed the indefinite detention order with respect to non-U.K. nationals and deemed section 23 of the *Anti-terrorism, Crime and Security Act 2001* (U.K.), 2001, c. 24 [ATCSA] incompatible with articles 5 and 14 of the European Convention insofar "as it is disproportionate and permits detention of suspected international terrorists in a way that discriminates on the ground of nationality or immigration status": *A (F.C.) v. S.S.H.D.*, *supra* note 27 at para. 73. To pass the ATCSA, the UK had to withdraw from part of the ECHR through a special derogation Order. The Convention allows states to derogate from it: "in times of war or public emergency threatening the life of the nation" but only "to the extent strictly required by the exigencies of the situation". Any measures taken must not be "inconsistent with [the contracting party's] obligations under international law." The derogation Order's validity came into question before the House of Lords. By an 8–1 majority, the Law Lords concluded that the UK Government had not acted within the constraints of the derogation right by reason of lack of proportionality to the situation and because the order – applying to non-nationals only – was discriminatory (there were no similar powers to lock up British nationals).

[99] I. Cotler, *supra* note 3 at 19: ". . . one has to 'think outside the box' and invoke an international criminal justice model having regard to both the nature of the threat and the proportionality of the response . . . [I]ndeed, the invocation or application of the principle of proportionality – that the juridical response to terrorism must be proportional to the threat – requires that we have an appreciation of this cluster of dynamics that characterizes the increasingly lethal face of contemporary trans-national terrorism . . . Thus, while we are dealing with extraordinary legislation, responding to an extraordinary threat, the legislation must still comport with the principle of proportionality – of just remedies serving just objectives".

[100] *A (F.C.) v. S.S.H.D.*, [2005] UKHL 71. Because British terror suspects thought to pose a similar risk cannot be locked up without charge or trial. Setting forth the principle that Common Law development should be in harmony with international obligations and that statutes should be interpreted so that they uphold treaty obligations, if possible

However noteworthy, this is not at all surprising. Judicial interaction and constitutional cross-pollination is on the rise, as evidenced by a Judicial Training Conference in Ottawa, organized by the National Judicial Institute's International Cooperation branch, which brought together close to two hundred magistrates from all over the globe, interested in discussing the judicial role and democratization.[101]

Even the United States Supreme Court, a bastion of isolationism,[102] has arguably begun to show signs of openness to this phenomenon in the post 9/11 world. Thus, Justice Stephen Breyer – although in the minority – has forcefully declared that "comparative analysis emphatically is relevant to the task of interpreting constitutions and enforcing human rights".[103] Coming from a Supreme Court judge (rather than a constitutional scholar),[104] such a statement, running counter to the "American anomaly"[105] respecting the worth of comparative law, is undoubtedly quite revolutionary.[106]

(para. 27), the case deals with use of evidence obtained by torture in another jurisdiction being introduced into UK proceedings. It features an extensive discussion of public international law (paras. 27 – 45) and the UK's obligations.

[101] See *supra* note 94.

[102] Sujit Choudhry, who argues that "the legitimacy of universalist modes of comparative constitutional reasoning will constantly be put in question", skillfully summarizes the dialectic between the traditional isolationist model (thus far adopted by the US) and the increasing appeal of comparative constitutional law: "The increased migration of constitutional forms stands at odds with one of the dominant understandings of constitutionalism – that the constitution of a nation emerges from, embodies, and aspires to sustain or respond to a nation's particular national circumstances, most centrally, its history and political culture". S. Choudhry, "The *Lochner* Era and Comparative Constitutionalism" (2004) 2 Int'l. J. Const. L. 1 at 51, 48.

[103] S. Breyer, "Keynote Address"(2003) 97 Am. Soc'y Int'l. L. Proc. 265 at 265, quoting R. Bader Ginsburg & D. Merritt, "Affirmative Action: An International Human Rights Dialogue" (1999) 21 Cardozo L. Rev. 253 at 282. See also R. Alford, "Misusing International Sources to Interpret the Constitution" (2004) 98 Am. J. Int'l. L. 57 and A. Lester, "The Overseas Trade in the American Bill of Rights" (1988) 88 Colum. L. Rev. 537.

[104] In Anne-Marie Slaughter's words: "Justice Breyer's remarks on comparative constitutional law, if they had appeared in a law review article, would have been quite unremarkable. . . . As part of a judicial opinion, they were altogether remarkable. Why should that be? The reason is that if Justice Breyer's insertion into the case of comparative constitutional law materials had gone unchallenged, it would have been a step towards legitimizing their use as points of departure in constitutional argumentation . . ." in "A Global Community of Courts" *supra* note 7 at 202.

[105] Referred to as "The American Anomaly" by the Harvard Law Review in (2001) 114 Harv. L. Rev. 2049 at 2064. See C. L'Heureux-Dubé, "The Importance of Dialogue: Globalization and the International Impact of the Rehnquist Court" (1998) 34 Tulsa L. J. 15 at 24.

[106] Indeed, more than one Justice on the U.S. Supreme Court has suggested that the area of constitutional rights relating to terrorism demands international cooperation and

Law's globalization, therefore, coupled with the augmented interaction of judges engaged in "judicial dialogues"[107] and the entrenchment of universal ideals of human rights,[108] is conducive to fostering conversations between legal traditions and legal cultures. This in turn might allow for a measure of harmonization between systems, at least with regards to matters of transnational concerns, otherwise inadvertently governed by the unilateral application of domestic law, within a legal vacuum.[109]

It therefore stands to reason that harmonizing basic constitutional concepts on the level of principle[110] – while not without obstacles – might nevertheless serve to alleviate some of the above-described 'democratic deficit' by fostering a juridical "associative community",[111] united by shared constitutional values.

---

the study of comparative constitutionalism. See R. G. Teitel, "Comparative Constitutional Law in a Global Age" (2004) 117 Harv. L. Rev. 2570. See also Justice Sandra Day O'Connor, "Keynote Address Before the Ninety-Sixth Annual Meeting of the American Society of International Law" (2002) 96 Am. Soc'y Int'l. L. Proc. 348. See also "Terrorism and Civil Liberties" in P. Gewirtz & J. K. Cogan, eds., *Global Constitutionalism: Privacy, Proportionality, Terrorism and Civil Liberties* (Supp. 2002); "Terrorism: Detention, Judicial Responsibilities" in P. Gewirtz & J. K. Cogan, eds., *Global Constitutionalism: Terrorism, Freedom of Expression, the Proposed European Constitution* (Supp. 2003). "Following the dialogical approach, the potential for comparative constitutional analysis goes beyond its uses in domestic constitutional adjudication. When engaged in by a transnational judiciary, comparativism offers the potential for global solidarity": A.-M. Slaughter, "A Global Community of Courts", *supra* note 7 at 218–19 (opining that transnational adjudication can contribute to a "global community of courts").

[107] Term attributed to Canadian Supreme Court Justice Claire L'Heureux-Dubé (ret.), *supra* note 105. See A.-M. Slaughter, "A Typology of Transjudicial Communication" (1994) 29 U. Rich. L. Rev. 99 for Anne-Marie Slaughter's argument regarding the influence of different courts on one another through their engagement in "judicial dialogues". See also L. R. Helfer & A.-M. Slaughter, "Toward a Theory of Effective Supranational Adjudication" (1997) 107 Yale L. J. 273.

[108] L. Henkin, *Human Rights, supra* note 65: "Insofar as there is contemporary movement toward constitutional convergence, the movement occurs primarily in the area of international human rights, which one might characterize as the 'law of humanity', the most robust of these being transnational human rights law peremptory norms, elucidated in and by comparative law, structure a threshold rule of law across nations that operate as an unwritten constitutional regime for a global order. Substantial agreement among national constitutions and conformity with international conventions (p. 3) demonstrate a consensus on basic human rights". On the "law of humanity", see also R. G. Teitel, "Humanity's Law: Rule of Law for the New Global Politics" (2002) 35 Cornell Int'l. L.J. 355.

[109] As argued above.

[110] Brought to the highest level of abstraction.

[111] Dworkin's expression, *supra* note 49, referring to a measure of normative legitimacy.

Arguably, this process is already underway. We need look no further than an emerging phenomenon, that of a "growing tendency of jurists and human rights activists from different countries to identify themselves as part of a unified international community".[112] Accordingly, speaking to the increasingly border-less character thereof, Ruti Teitel observes that "constitutionalism extends beyond the state, complicating constitutional law's relation to contemporary politics".[113] Significantly, this identification would tend to satisfy another important indicator of legitimacy – what Weiler terms a "broad social accep-tance of the system".[114] This might facilitate reconciling legal traditions, in cer-tain respects pertaining to the issue of the International Criminal Justice model's unruly and oft-unintended unilateral application.[115]

More specifically for our purposes, this penchant, associated with the con-vergence of law generally and the reinvigoration of comparative law particu-larly, may be strategically harnessed in order to offset the pitfalls associated with the extra-jurisdictional reach of transnational law. What is more, doing so may serve to significantly bolster the so called "International Criminal Law Model's" *social legitimacy*, which, as noted[116] is assessed by law subjects' *per-ception* of why obedience is warranted.[117]

The progression from unchecked representative democracy to democratic constitutionalism in the post war era has already been documented, as has the need for constitutionalism's own evolution, in light of recent developments. Although it cannot claim to redress the profound deficiencies highlighted above, the renaissance of comparative constitutional law, and the judicial inter-action it engenders, may help rectify the substantive aspect of the described conundrum. This by creating *a new constitutional associative community*, predicated on a shared understanding of substantive, universal democratic val-ues, not to be transgressed. As Sujit Choudhry notes, "Constitutional interpreta-tion across the globe is taking on an increasingly cosmopolitan character, as

---

[112] See D. Barak Erez, "The International Law of Human Rights and Constitutional Law: A Case Study of an Expanding Dialogue" (2004) 2 Int'l. J. Const. L. 611 at 612. See also A.-M. Slaughter, *A New World Order, supra* note 7.

[113] R. G. Teitel, "Comparative Constitutional Law in a Global Age" *supra* note 106 at 2570.

[114] Referring to the "democratic deficit" of the European Union's supra-national insti-tutions. See also Bellamy & Castiglione in the same vein, *supra* note 48 at 8.

[115] Discussed above. "Reconciling legal traditions" is discussed in greater detail by H. P. Glenn, *Legal Traditions of the World: Sustainable Diversity in Law* (Oxford: Oxford University Press, 2000) at 318–38. See also H. P. Glenn, "Persuasive Authority" (1987) 32 McGill L. J. 261, discussing the "reception" of foreign law.

[116] As Joseph Weiler defines it a broad "social acceptance" of the system. See Weiler, *supra* note 47.

[117] See Bellamy & Castiglione, *supra* note 48.

comparative jurisprudence comes to assume a central place in constitutional adjudication".[118]

Brought to a high level of abstraction, the constitutional concepts underlying the vast majority of contemporary democracies are predicated on shared precepts pertaining to the respect of basic human rights.[119]

Via comparative constitutionalism,[120] the respective judiciaries of each community, guardians of their own democracies,[121] united by similar convictions, might help harmonize norms pertaining to the International Criminal Justice Model, thus ensuring that – at a basic level – these develop universally in accordance with basic rights. This has been referred to as "universalist interpretation", which "asserts that the law is best understood as a body of principles rather than rules, and invites a style of adjudication that is openly normative in character . . . Most controversially, it claims that these moral principles are transcendent – that is, they are shared by more than one legal system".[122]

Plainly put, were our respective judiciaries to form an implicit 'associative community' of sorts – albeit with a circumscribed finality, (to address present-day transnational needs, premised on shared constitutional values), a certain measure of legitimacy may be lent to intrusions related to the International Criminal Justice model.

The increased relevance of comparative constitutionalism, in view of interstate cooperation relating to transnational issues is being recognized, particularly by Anne-Marie Slaughter, who points to the cooperation between national

---

[118] Choudhry, *supra* note 102. See also Choudhry, "Globalization in Search of Justification: Toward a Theory of Comparative Constitutional Interpretation" (1999) 74 Ind. L.J. 819.

[119] See *e.g.* V. C. Jackson, "Holistic Interpretation, Comparative Constitutionalism, and Fiss-ian Freedoms" (2003) 58 U. Miami L. Rev. 265 at 265: "Comparative constitutional law can be helpful, because most Western liberal democracies have written constitutions that made commitments simultaneously to freedom of expression and equality values. The constitutional case law in other Western democracies can illuminate interpretive approaches grounded in simultaneous commitments to freedom of expression and human equality".

[120] As discussed below.

[121] S. Choudhry, "Globalization in Search of Justification: Toward a Theory of Comparative Constitutional Interpretation", *supra* note 118, citing Dworkin's *A Bill of Rights for Britain, supra* note 58 at 13–14, notes: "As Ronald Dworkin – perhaps the most prominent constitutional theorist supportive of the worldwide convergence to constitutionalism – observes, every member of the European Community as well as other 'mature democracies' (in Dworkin's words) subscribe to the view that democracy must protect itself against the tyranny of majority rule through constitutionalization and judicial review".

[122] Choudhry, *ibid.* at 890: "Transcendence is the linchpin of universalist interpretation, because it justifies the use of comparative case law without regard to national boundaries. It is important to reiterate, though, that transcendence".

judiciaries and the emergence of 'globalized jurisprudence', advocating its reinforcement for improved governance and accountability.[123] She speaks of "constitutional cross-fertilization . . . . Increasing cross-fertilization of ideas and precedents among constitutional judges around the world is gradually giving rise to a visible international consensus on various issues – a consensus that, in turn, carries compelling weight".[124]

To be clear, this is not to suggest that the nation be effaced or discrete communities reinvented. Rather, the shared discourse referred to is merely juridical, a province of law, delineated by a common understanding of the universal values.[125] Agreement on what is unacceptable and a strengthened common understanding of human rights is therefore cardinal. To this end, both clear definition[126] and harmonization of norms,[127] which seeks ways to *accommodate* juridical concepts of various systems procedurally would by far be preferable to *unification*, which seeks to neutralize juridical conflicts by adopting uniform rules.[128] The goal here is to find the "common" and mitigate the differences between legal systems via comparative constitutional concepts, while refraining from threatening cultural distinctiveness.[129]

---

[123] A.-M. Slaughter, *A New World Order, supra* note 7. Slaughter argues that governments are increasingly cooperating through transnational networks. This "global governance" is evidenced by judges' activities, among others, in working with foreign counterparts.

[124] What Slaughter refers to as "An Emerging Global Jurisprudence" in "A Global Community of Courts", *supra* note 7 at 202.

[125] A microcosm of this harmonization and a precedent for this type of harmonization is found in, of course, the European Union and the shared principles reflected in their emerging jurisprudence, all while attempting to preserve national distinctiveness. See M. Rosenfeld, "Constitutional Adjudication in Europe and the United States: Paradoxes and Contrasts" (2004) 2 Int'l. J. Const. L. 633. The reference here is not to the supranational institutions but to the shared principles themselves.

[126] See Irwin Cotler's discussion of the importance of properly defining terrorism, *supra* note 3. Perhaps an important first step in this direction was taken by the UN's recent adoption of a definition of terrorism (although this is by no means meant to suggest that the UN – rather than local judiciaries – should be entrusted with defining these terms).

[127] The traditional tool for facilitating cross-border commercial transactions. The best example is Article 100 of the *Treaty Establishing the European Community* (Rome, 25 March 1957) [*Treaty of Rome*].

[128] Enacted by a "supranational" authority and ratified by the participating legislatures.

[129] S. Zamora, "NAFTA and the Harmonization of Domestic Legal Systems: The Side Effects of Free Trade" (1995) 12 Ariz. J. Int'l. & Comp. L. 401 at 405: "To use a musical analogy, an orchestra plays harmoniously when each section of instruments plays different notes and the composer gives range to the distinct characteristics of each instrument. Ideally, a system of separate jurisdictions applying harmonious laws should be able to

Globalized law, therefore – not via the establishment of supra-national bodies – but instead through the harmonization of constitutional concepts,[130] particularly those pertaining to the International Criminal Justice Model – may, to some extent, address some of the listed concerns, particularly with respect to social legitimacy.[131] Ultimately, and as Teitel points out in a different context, "[C]omparative constitutional law's current extension, therefore, offers an alternative conception of legitimacy,[132] grounded in core human rights and aimed at reinforcing the nascent global order".[133] Transposed to the issue at hand, that is to say, the democratic legitimacy of the extraterritorial application of law under the International Criminal Justice model, this assertion rings all the truer.

If the judiciary has effectively become the modern guardian of democracy,[134] and that guardian – in all of its outpost in democracies worldwide – commonly turns to comparative principles as sources of law animating their decision, that

---

simultaneously respect local differences. Again, this is why harmonization should not be confused with unification of laws, or with the imposition of one legal model on all jurisdictions".

[130] This process is described by one of its proponents, Israel's Chief Justice, President A. Barak, *supra* note 96 at 111: ". . . because many of the basic principles of democracy are common to democratic countries, there is good reason to compare them ('macrocomparison'). Indeed, different democratic legal systems often encounter similar problems. Examining a foreign solution may help a judge choose the best local solution. This usefulness applies both to the development of the common law and to the interpretation of legal texts. Naturally, one must approach comparative law cautiously, remaining cognizant of its limitations. Comparative law is not merely the comparison of laws. A useful comparison can exist only if the legal systems have a common ideological basis. The judge must be sensitive to the uniqueness of each legal system. Nonetheless, when the judge is convinced that the relative social, historical, and religious circumstances create a common ideological basis, it is possible to refer to a foreign legal system for a source of comparison and inspiration."

[131] Indeed, as Etzioni points out, rather than cooperating on an international level (i.e. through institutions as is often the case with supranational legislation) states have "made several significant and especially rapid and synchronized changes in domestic laws and policies *in their own countries*, for purposes of counterterrorism". Amitai Etzionni Notes are accessible online: http://www.amitai-notes.com/blog/archives/001010.html.

[132] Her discussion of legitimacy dealt with the legitimacy of the use of comparative law by the judiciary.

[133] Teitel, *supra* note 106.

[134] See Barak, *supra* note 58. See also N. Redlich, "Judges as Instruments of Democracy" in S. Shetreet, ed., *The Role of Courts in Society* (Dordrecht: Nijhoff, 1988) *inter alia*. Of course, as Barak elucidates in "The Role of a Supreme Court in a Democracy and the Fight against Terrorism" *supra* note 58 at 126–127: "The purpose of this modern development is not to increase the power of the court in a democracy. The purpose is the protection of democracy and human rights. An increase in judicial power is a side effect, since judicial power is one of many factors in preserving democratic balance".

may serve as precedent for the elaboration of new constitutional concepts, able
to satisfy the new imperatives of transnational democracy. Potentially, this
'community of courts',[135] adopting a shared legal discourse pertaining to universal human rights,[136] may act to both satisfy democracy's substantive
element[137] and indeed incarnate Dworkin's "associative community" – (albeit
imagined), thereby offering a source of normative legitimacy in uncertain
times.[138]

7) A FINAL WORD: COMPARATIVE CONSTITUTIONAL LAW[139] AND THE "JUDICIAL ROLE IN TImes OF TERROR"[140]

Of course, as Justice Brennan[141] cautioned, "[A]bstract principles announcing
the applicability of civil liberties during times of war and crises are ineffectual
when a war or crisis comes along unless the principles are fleshed out by a

---

[135] See A.-M. Slaughter, *supra* note 7.

[136] As President Barak warns, the use of comparative constitutional law is feasible
only in the face of shared allegiance to common values: "Democratic countries have
several fundamental principles in common. As such, legal institutions often fulfill similar functions across countries. From the purpose that one given democratic legal system
attributes to a constitutional arrangement, one can learn about the purpose of that constitutional arrangement in another legal system. Indeed, comparative constitutional law is a
good source of expanded horizons and cross-fertilization of ideas across legal systems.
Nonetheless, as we have seen, interpretive inspiration is only proper if there is an ideological basis common to the two legal systems and a common allegiance to basic democratic principles" A. Barak, *supra* note 96 at 112.

[137] As discussed above.

[138] There is indeed a strong correlation between the expansion of constitutionalism
and democracy, observed by various scholars: "Most scholars of constitutional politics
agree that there is a strong correlation between the recent worldwide expansion of the
ethos and practice of democracy and the contemporaneous global expansion of judicial
power. . . . The expansion of judicial power has indeed been associated with political
and economic liberalization in post-authoritarian or quasi-democratic polities".
Although he questions its efficacy: "The widespread transition to democracy cannot provide a coherent explanation for the significant variations in judicial power among new
democracies. Likewise, it fails to account for the significant variations in the timing,
scope, and nature of the expansion of judicial power among established democracies".
Hirshl, *supra* note 93 at 73–74. See also B. Friedman & C. Saunders, "Symposium:
Constitutional Borrowing, Editors' Introduction" (2003) 1 Int'l. J. Const. L. 177. See
http://www.nji.ca/internationalForum/ for an example of how the Canadian government
has introduced programs aimed at 'training' judges in fledgling democracies.

[139] M. Tushnet, "The Possibilities of Comparative Constitutional Law" (1999) 108
Yale L.J. 1225.

[140] Barak, *supra* note 96 at 156.

[141] *Ibid.*

detailed jurisprudence explaining how those civil liberties will be sustained against particularized national security concerns". If comparative constitutional law is to develop into an analytical tool of any practical merit, it is imperative that the respective judicial branches of sister democracies first avail themselves of this means, strive to foster inter-judicial communication and attain some consensus on "jettisoning false moral equivalencies",[142] endeavoring to agree on definitions of crucial principles such as 'proportionality',[143] thus decreasing the possibility for distortion or abuse.[144]

Needless to say, comparative constitutional law acting at a global level is raised merely to assuage, not fully resolve, the above-highlighted legitimacy difficulties, deriving from the unilateral external application of domestic law. The utilization of this attribute – an international judiciary's unified voice – must be *complemented* by effective procedural tools, aimed at relieving concerns that the judiciary tends to be deferential to the executive in times of crisis.[145] For that reason, it would be wise to draw on the work of scholars and privacy experts who propose various procedural mechanisms, aimed at satisfying the pillars of democracy.[146]

---

[142] Irwin Cotler discussing the importance of unequivocal definitions pertaining to terrorism, *supra* note 3.

[143] As did the House of Lords in *A (F.C.) v. S.S.H.D.*, *supra* note 27.

[144] The best illustration of the impact of such uncertainty was the Ashcroft-Abu Grahib 'scandal'.

[145] See Ackerman, *supra* note 24.

[146] A set of particularly instructive recommendations is to be found in the Loukidelis Report, *supra* note 9. While the report deals only indirectly with the transnational imposition of domestic norms on alien actors, and focuses primarily on the privacy implications of cross-border information transfer, its suggestions are nonetheless pertinent.

Chapter 18

Customary International Law in Domestic Courts: Imbroglio, Lord Denning, Stare Decisis

Stéphane Beaulac*

1) THE THEORIES: APPARENT SIMPLICITY

René Provost said it well when he recently spoke of the "*apparent* simplicity of the idea of the application in domestic law of international norms."[1] The key word here being "apparent," of course, because this matter is obviously nothing but, in Canada, in the United Kingdom and in many Commonwealth countries.[2]

* The author thanks René Provost (McGill) for his comments and suggestions. Also, the competent assistance of Attieha Rebecca Chamaa, which was supported by the Borden Ladner Gervais Grants, is gratefully acknowledged.

[1] R. Provost, "Le juge mondialisé: légitimité judiciaire et droit international au Canada," in M.-C. Belleau & F. Lacasse, eds., *Claire L'Heureux-Dubé à la Cour suprême du Canada, 1987–2002* (Montreal: Wilson & Lafleur, 2004), 569, at 569 [emphasis added]. The original French version reads: "L'apparente simplicité de l'idée d'appliquer en droit interne les normes internationales".

[2] See, generally, F. G. Jacobs & S. Roberts (eds.), *The Effect of Treaties in Domestic Law* (London: Sweet & Maxwell, 1987); A. Mason, "The Influence of International and Transnational Law on Australian Municipal Law" (1996) 7 Public L. Rev. 20; K. Keith,

Christopher P.M. Waters (Ed.), *British and Canadian Perspectives on International Law*, pp. 379–392.
© 2006 Koninklijke Brill NV. Printed in the Netherlands.

This is also true in the legally isolationist United States, as recently witnessed.[3] The first fundamental problem is the existentialist self-doubt of the discipline of "international law."[4] Although the expression coined in 1789 by Bentham[5] is relatively recent, the substance dates back to Vattel[6] and Grotius,[7] along with the very question of whether the "law of nations" is law at all.[8] The actual sources of international legal norms (codified in the *Statute of the International Court of Justice*[9]) continue to be debated by contemporary scholars,[10] espe-

---

"The Impact of International Law on New Zealand Law" (1998) 6 Waikato L. Rev. 1; B. R. Opeskin "Constitutional Modelling: The Domestic Effect of International Law in Commonwealth Countries – Part I" [2000] Public L. 607; and B. R. Opeskin, "Constitutional Modelling: The Domestic Effect of International Law in Commonwealth Countries – Part II" [2001] Public L. 97.

[3] These issues are also front and centre in that jurisdiction with the Supreme Court cases *Lawrence v. Texas*, 123 S.Ct. 2472 (2003), and *Roper v. Simmons*, 125 S.Ct. 1183 (2005). See also, generally, J. F. Murphy, *The United States and the Rule of Law in International Affairs* (Cambridge: Cambridge University Press, 2004); and, specifically, S. G. Calabresi & S. D. Zimdahl, "The Supreme Court and Foreign Sources of Law: Two Hundred Years of Practice and the Juvenile Death Penalty Decision" (2005): http://ssrn.com/abstract=700176; J. Ku, "Structural Conflicts in the Interpretation of Customary International Law" (2005) 45 Santa Clara L. Rev. 857; R. D. Glensy, "Which Countries Count? Lawrence v. Texas and the Selection of Foreign Persuasive Authority" (2005) 45 Virginia J. Int'l L. 357; and J. Larsen, "Importing Constitutional Norms from a 'Wider Civilization': Lawrence and the Rehnquist Court's Use of Foreign and International Law in Domestic Constitutional Interpretation" (2004) 65 Ohio St. L.J. 1283.

[4] See, generally, S. Beaulac, *The Power of Language in the Making of International Law – The Word Sovereignty in Bodin and Vattel and the Myth of Westphalia* (Leiden & Boston: Martinus Nijhoff, 2004). On international law today, see B. Kingsbury, "The International Legal Order" in P. Cane & M. Tushnet, eds., *The Oxford Handbook of Legal Studies* (Oxford: Oxford University Press, 2003).

[5] This British author introduced it in his influential book *An Introduction to the Principles of Morals and Legislation* (London: Pickering, 1823), first published in 1789.

[6] E. de Vattel, *Le Droit des Gens; ou Principes de la loi naturelle appliqués à la conduite & aux affaires des Nations & des Souverains*, 2 vols. (London: N.p., 1758). See also S. Beaulac, "Emer de Vattel and the Externalization of Sovereignty" (2003) 5 J. History Int'l L. 237.

[7] H. Grotius, *De Iure Belli ac Pacis Libri Tres. In quibus ius naturae & gentium: item iuris publici praecipua explicantur* (Paris: Buon, 1625).

[8] See the classic piece by G. L. Williams, "International Law and the Controversy Concerning the Word 'Law'" (1945) 22 British Y.B. Int'l L. 146. See also A. A. D'Amato, "Is International Law Really 'Law'" (1985) 79 Northwestern U.L. Rev. 1293. *Contra* see T. M. Franck, *Fairness in International Law and Institutions* (New York: Oxford University Press, 1995), who speaks of the post-ontological era of international law.

[9] *Statute of the International Court of Justice*, adopted on 26 June 1945, U.N.T.S. 961, Can. T.S. 1945 No. 7 (entered into force 24 October 1945), at article 38(1).

[10] See D. B. Hollis, "Why State Consent Still Matters – Actors, Treaties, and the Changing Sources of International Law" (2005) 23 Berkeley J. Int'l L. 137. On sources

cially customary international law.[11] It is therefore in a context of lingering theoretical difficulties with the norms on the international plane that the uneasy situation concerning the relation between the international and the domestic legal realities must be considered.[12]

Putting aside this initial problem, let us proceed on the premise that, indeed, international normativity exists. In such a scenario, is the conceptualisation of the international / national interface not straightforward, with the classic heuristic tools that are the "monist" theory for customs and the "dualist" theory for treaties?[13] Simply put, the former postulates a non-*ad hoc* structural link between the international and the national legal spheres which, for customs, would mean that no implementation measure by a state is needed to give them legal effect domestically. From the national point of view, one speaks of the "adoptionist" model – or "incorporationist" model in British terminology – according to which international customary norms would be automatically part of the law of the land. On the other hand, dualism affirms the legal reality division between the international and the national which, for treaties, would mean that incorporation by means of individual state measure is required to allow them any domestic legal effect. From a national perspective, one speaks of the "transformationist" model, to the effect that treaty norms would not be part of the law of the country unless and until formally implemented.

---

theory, generally, see P. Allott, *Eunomia – New Order for a New World* (Oxford & New York: Oxford University Press, 1990); M. Koskenniemi, *From Apology to Utopia* (Helsinki: Lakimiesliiton Kustannus, 1989); and A. Carty, *The Decay of International Law? – A Reappraisal of the Limits of Legal Imagination in International Affairs* (Manchester: Manchester University Press, 1986).

[11] Recent literature includes: A. T. Guzman, "Saving Customary International Law" (2005): http://ssrn.com/*abstract=708721; E. T. Swaine, "Rational Custom" (2002) 52 Duke L. J. 559; A. E. Roberts, "Traditional and Modern Approaches to Customary International Law: A Reconciliation" (2001) 95 American J. Int'l L. 757; J. P. Kelly, "The Twilight of Customary International Law" (2000) 40 Virginia J. Int'l L. 449; M. H. Mendelson, "The Formation of Customary International Law" (1998) 272 Recueil des Cours 155; and D. P. Fidler, "Challenging the Classic Conception of Custom" (1997) German Y.B. Int'l L. 198.

[12] On the influence of the sources theory on the interplay between the international and the national legal spheres, see L. Ferrari-Bravo, "International and Municipal Law: The Complementary of Legal Systems," in R. St. J. Macdonald & D. M. Johnston (eds.), *The Structure and Process of International Law* (Dordrecht: Martinus Nijhoff, 1983).

[13] For some classic contributions on the subject, see H. Triepel, *Droit international et droit interne* (Oxford: Oxford University Press, 1920); G. Fitzmaurice, "The General Principles of International Law: Considered from the Standpoint of the Rule of Law" (1957) 92 Recueil des cours 263, at 389–418; I. Seidl-Hohenveldern, "Transformation or Adoption of International Law into Municipal Law" (1963) 12 Int'l & Comp. L.Q. 88; and G. Sperduti, "Dualism and Monism: A Confrontation to be Overcome?" (1977) 3 Italian Y.B. Int'l L. 31.

2) REAL SITUATION: AN IMBROGLIO

This picture is not simple but simplistic, as monism and dualism have actually come to be seen, rightly so, as hiding more than explaining.[14] Important among many questions unanswered by these two theories are these: What is meant by domestic incorporation pursuant to the dualist logic? Is it still by means of implementing legislation,[15] done either directly by reference in a statute or indirectly by legislative harmonization,[16] or can it be seriously said that there are no less than ten ways to implement treaties,[17] including on the basis of pre-existing domestic legislative norms?[18] Is it intellectually honest to say

---

[14] See, for instance, J. H. Currie, *Public International Law* (Toronto: Irwin Law, 2001) at 197.

[15] The traditional proposition that domestic transformation of treaty norms needs to be done through legislation comes from the *Labour Conventions* case – that is, *Attorney General for Canada v. Attorney General for Ontario*, [1937] A.C. 326, at 347, *per* Lord Atkin: "Within the British Empire there is a well-established rule that the making of a treaty is an executive act, while the performance of its obligations, if they entail alteration of the existing domestic law, requires *legislative action*" [emphasis added]. One author has suggested that implementation could be done by non-legislative means such as government policy measures: E. Brandon, "Does International Law Mean Anything in Canadian Courts?" (2001), 11 J. Environmental L. & Prac. 399, at 407. This proposition is clearly unsupported by case law and actually runs in the face of the three rationales behind the doctrine of transformation, namely separation of powers, federalism and democracy. For more detail on them, see S. Beaulac, "Arrêtons de dire que les tribunaux au Canada sont 'liés' par le droit international" (2004), 38 Rev. jur. Thémis 359, at 378–381.

[16] This is the long-standing position, as recently summarised by R. Sullivan, *Sullivan and Driedger on the Construction of Statutes*, 4th ed. (Markham, Ont. & Vancouver: Butterworths, 2002), at 430. See also, for an analytical scheme of the persuasive force of international treaty norms based on these two techniques of legislative incorporation, S. Beaulac, "National Application of International Law: The Statutory Interpretation Perspective" (2003), 41 Canadian Y.B. Int'l L. 225.

[17] This is what Gibran van Ert has claimed recently, though unconvincingly because the proposition is unsupported by case law and practice: G. van Ert, "What is Treaty Implementation?," in C.C.I.L. (ed.), *Legitimacy and Accountability in International Law – Proceedings of the 33rd Annual Conference of the Canadian Council on International Law* (Ottawa: Canadian Council of International Law, 2005), 165, at 168–169.

[18] Also known as "passive incorporation", this novel proposition really seems to have been suggested out of the blue in the context of international human rights law in Canada by I. Weiser, "Effect in Domestic Law of International Human Rights Treaties Ratified without Implementing Legislation," in C.C.I.L. (ed.), *The Impact of International Law on the Practice of Law in Canada – Proceedings of the 27th Annual Conference of the Canadian Council on International Law* (The Hague: Kluwer Law International, 1999), 132, at 137–139. See also I. Weiser, "Undressing the Window: Treating International Human Rights Law Meaningfully in the Canadian Commonwealth System" (2004), 37 U. British Columbia L. Rev. 113.

that the domestic courts of a sovereign state are indeed "bound"[19] by treaties,[20] or is it more sound to view the role of such norms within the interpretative function constitutionally entrusted to the judiciary,[21] more particularly in terms of the contextual argument of construction.[22]

With respect to customs, if the international and the national are really one pursuant to the monist logic, how can domestic legal actors, such as judges, resort to such international norms domestically? Are legal counsel limited to the customs already discovered internationally or can they make a demonstration of the constituting elements of such norms in a domestic court? How realistic is this scenario in terms of resources and costs?[23] If a custom has yet to be discovered internationally but has been recognised as such by courts of another jurisdiction, say Australia, is relying on this legal norm in Canada an argument of international law or of comparative law? For a custom to enjoy automatic domestic legal effect, must there be evidence of that particular state's implicit consent to it by means of practice and *opinio juris*?[24] What effect, if any, does

[19] On this way of formulating the issue, see S. Beaulac, "On the Saying that 'International Law Binds Canadian Courts'" (2003), 29 C.C.I.L. Bulletin 1.

[20] See, for instance, what was candidly written by J. Brunnée & S. J. Toope, "A Hesitant Embrace: The Application of International Law by Canadian Courts" (2002), 40 Canadian Y.B. Int'l L. 1, at 55.

[21] In Canada, it has been suggested that the so-called "modern principle" of statutory interpretation, from the work of Elmer Driedger, constitutes the most appropriate way to resort to the international law argument. See S. Beaulac, "L'interprétation de la Charte : reconsidération de l'approche téléologique et réévaluation du rôle du droit international" in G.-A. Beaudoin & E. P. Mendes (eds.), *Canadian Charter of Rights and Freedoms*, 4th ed. (Markham, Ont.: LexisNexis Butterworths, 2005), 27; reprinted in (2005), 27 Supreme Court L. Rev. (2d) 1; and S. Beaulac, "International Treaty Norms and Driedger's 'Modern Principle' of Statutory Interpretation", in C.C.I.L. (ed.), *Legitimacy and Accountability in International Law – Proceedings of the 33rd Annual Conference of the Canadian Council on International Law* (Ottawa: Canadian Council of International Law, 2005), 141. A similar view, that international law can only be "influential" or "persuasive" in the interpretation and application of domestic law, is expressed by K. Knop, "Here and There: International Law in Domestic Courts" (2000), 32 New York U.J. Int'l L. & Pol. 501.

[22] On how it is a better strategy to use international treaties as a contextual argument of construction, instead of referring to a presumption of legislative intent, known as the presumption of conformity with international law, see S. Beaulac, "Le droit international comme élément contextuel en interprétation des lois" (2004), Canadian Int'l Lawyer 1; and S. Beaulac, "Recent Developments on the Role of International Law in Canadian Statutory Interpretation" (2004), 25 Statute L. Rev. 19.

[23] On this reality, see A. W. La Forest, "Domestic Application of International Law in *Charter* Cases: Are We There Yet?" (2004), 37 U. British Columbia L. Rev. 157, at 194.

[24] This is an important aspect of the issue discussed by R. Provost, *supra*, note 1, at 575–578, who opined that the difficulty with the state-specific consensual basis of customary international legal norms explains in large part why Canadian courts prefer to

the codification of a custom into a treaty have in relation to the national application of the legal norm? What is the story with *jus cogens*,[25] peremptory customary international law from which there can be no derogation?[26]

This enumeration of queries, which is far from exhaustive, explains the suggestion in the title of the chapter that the situation with respect to the national application of customs is beyond problematic and confusing. It is nothing short of an imbroglio, really. The following discussion attempts to address one major flaw in the reasoning that led to the general belief that customs obey the logic of monism but, ironically, it might very well create more uncertainties and chaos. The argument is quite straightforward, namely that the most allegedly authoritative British case law (relied upon also in some Commonwealth countries) for the proposition that customary international law is automatically part of the law of the land is fundamentally wrong. The proposed analysis must be understood, however, having in mind the traditional basic tenets of our international relations system and of our international law system.

3) THE INTERNATIONAL TENETS: WESTPHALIA

The matrix within which international affairs are conducted and in which international law operates is based on the Westphalian model of international relations, at the centre of which is the "*idée-force*"[27] of state sovereignty.[28] The

resort to treaty-based international law arguments, which raise no question of voluntary acceptance of the norms.

[25] The *Vienna Convention on the Law of Treaties*, adopted 23 May 1969, 8 I.L.M. 679 (1969), Can. T.S. 1980 No. 37 (entered into force 27 January 1980), defines peremptory norms at article 53.

[26] At a symposium organised by the Department of Justice of Canada at McGill University, Montreal, on 15–16 June 2005, on issues relating to the relationship between international and domestic law, Stephen Toope expressed the opinion during the discussion that the *jus cogens* nature of some customary international legal norms should have no influence whatsoever on their use by the courts. The present author finds this position untenable and must strongly object to the suggestion that legal norms which the international community considers of the outmost importance should not be recognised as such when they are considered at the domestic level. In fact, the decision of the Supreme Court of Canada in *Suresh v. Canada (Minister of Citizenship and Immigration)*, [2002] 1 S.C.R. 3, at para. 61–65, is a recent example where the *jus cogens* character of the legal norm at issue (that is, the prohibition against torture) was recognised and given weight in the consideration of the international law argument. On this aspect of the case, see S. Beaulac, "The *Suresh* Case and Unimplemented Treaty Norms" (2002), 15 Rev. québécoise d. int'l 221.

[27] That is, "idea-force." See A. Fouillée, *L'évolutionnisme des idées-forces* (Paris: Félix Alcan, 1890), at XI.

[28] Of course, Westphalia is an "aetiological myth" (that is, a myth of origin), created by international society to explain the whens, wheres and hows of its becoming and

international reality consists of a community of sovereign states, which are independent from one another and have their own wills and *raisons d'être* as corporate-like representatives of the people or peoples living on their territories. This model involves an international realm that is distinct and separate from the internal realm. John Currie explained thus: "Public international law is not so much an area or topic of the law as it is *an entire legal system, quite distinct from the national legal systems* that regulate daily life within states."[29] As far as the relation between international law and domestic law is concerned, there is no inherent link because the two systems are distinct and separate[30] – "public international law exists outside and independent of national legal systems."[31] Dwelling on these issues, Justice LeBel of the Supreme Court of Canada (extra-judicially, with Gloria Chao) pointed out: "At the heart of the debate is the tension between the democratic principle underlying the *internal legal order* and the search for conformity or consistency with a developing and uncertain *external legal order*."[32] Appositely, Karen Knop schematically explained that "domestic law is 'here' and international law is 'there.'"[33]

The continuing distinct and separate reality within which our modern state system is conceptualised, explains two fundamental principles of international law.[34] The first one is that, from an international point of view, a sovereign state cannot invoke its internal law – including its constitutional structure[35] – to

---

its being. This acknowledgement, however, does not diminish in any way the most extraordinary semiotic effects of Westphalia on the consciousness of international society. See S. Beaulac, "The Westphalian Model in Defining International Law: Challenging the Myth" (2004), 8 Australian J. Leg. History 181; and S. Beaulac, "The Westphalian Legal Orthodoxy – Myth or Reality?" (2000), 2 J. History Int'l L. 148.

[29] J. H. Currie, *supra*, note 14, at 1 [emphasis added].

[30] It follows that the suggestion that the legislative power of a sovereign state has the competence to "violate" international law is completely nonsensical because, in addition to being a fundamentally flawed inquiry for countries of the British-type constitutional system based on the supremacy of Parliament, this statement wrongly assumes some kind of inherent connection between the international plane and the national level – see G. van Ert, *Using International Law in Canadian Courts* (The Hague: Kluwer Law International, 2002), at 55 ff.

[31] J. H. Currie, *supra*, note 14, at 1.

[32] L. LeBel & G. Chao, "The Rise of International Law in Canadian Constitutional Litigation: Fugue or Fusion? Recent Developments and Challenges in Internalizing International Law" (2002), 16 Supreme Court L. Rev. (2nd) 23, at 24 [emphasis added].

[33] K. Knop, *supra*, note 21, at 504.

[34] There is absolutely no doubt that the Westphalian model of international relations, governed by the Vattelian legal structure, continues to represent our system's paradigm, in spite of the globalisationist claim of the progressive end of the sovereign state. *Contra*, see P. Allott, *The Health of Nations – Society and Law beyond the State* (Cambridge: Cambridge University Press, 2002).

[35] See R. Jennings & A. Watts, *Oppenheim's International Law*, 9th ed., vol. 1 (London: Longman, 1992), at 254.

justify a breach of its international obligations.[36] Indeed, such an argument is impossible because these norms and duties are part of two distinct and separate legal systems. The second core principle of international law flowing from the international / internal divide relates to the administration of the relationship between the two systems. John Currie referred to this feature as the "international-national law interface" and wrote that the relationship "will depend on legal rules that determine, as a matter of law, how one legal system treats another."[37] Like many other Commonwealth countries,[38] Canada's rules of reception bring into play constitutional norms, which are unwritten;[39] they come from the British parliamentary tradition through the preamble to the *Constitution Act, 1867*,[40] which provides that Canada shall have "a Constitution similar in principle to that of the United Kingdom."

4) LORD DENNING IN *TRENDTEX*: THE REVERENCE

Stephen Toope once wrote that, in Canada, "[w]e know for certain that we *do not* know whether customary international law forms part of the law of Canada."[41] However, this does not represent the majority view in the country where, along with the highly influential piece by Ronald St. John Macdonald,[42]

---

[36] The basic authority for this proposition is the arbitration decision in the *Alabama Claims* case (United States/United Kingdom) (1872), Moore, *Arbitrations*, i. 653. This rule was codified in section 27 of the *Vienna Convention on the Law of Treaties, supra*, note 25.

[37] J. H. Currie, *supra*, note 14, at 193. See also F. G. Jacobs, "Introduction" in F. G. Jacobs & S. Roberts (eds.), *The Effect of Treaties in Domestic Law* (London: Sweet & Maxwell, 1987), xxiii, at xxiv.

[38] See, for instance, the Australian situation with the *Commonwealth of Australia Constitutional Act*, 63 & 64 Victoria, c. 12 (U.K.), and the decision of the Australian High Court in *Minister for Immigration and Ethnic Affairs v. Teoh* (1995), 183 C.L.R. 273, at 286–287.

[39] As Lamer C. J. confirmed in *Re Provincial Court Judges* [1997] 3 S.C.R. 3, at 68, "the general principle [is] that the Constitution embraces unwritten, as well as written rules."

[40] 30 & 31 Victoria, c. 3 (U.K.), reprinted in R.S.C. 1985, Appendix II, No. 5.

[41] S. J. Toope, "The Uses of Metaphor: International Law and the Supreme Court of Canada" (2001), 80 *Can. Bar Rev.* 534, at 536 [emphasis in original]. See also S. J. Toope, "Inside and Out: The Stories of International Law and Domestic Law" (2001), 50 U. New Brunswick L.J. 11, at 16–17.

[42] R. St. J. Macdonald, "The Relationship between International Law and Domestic Law in Canada," in R. St. J. Macdonald, G. L. Morris & D. M. Johnston (eds.), *Canadian Perspectives on International Law and Organization* (Toronto: University of Toronto Press, 1974), 88. For an even earlier statement, see C. Vanek, "Is International Law Part of the Law of Canada?" (1949–1950), 8 U. Toronto L.J. 251.

most international law scholars opine that the adoptionist model (or incorporationist model) applies.⁴³ The Canadian law on the matter was in such a mess,⁴⁴ Toope once scorned, that he felt forced to use British precedents in his public international law course, including what he called the "marvelous contribution"⁴⁵ of Lord Denning in *Trendtex Trading Corp. Ltd. v. The Central Bank of Nigeria*.⁴⁶ "Because we are told that our constitution [Canada's] is modeled in principle on that of the United Kingdom," wrote Toope with a tint of colonialised complex, "I prefer to rely upon Lord Denning's pronouncement that customary law is automatically incorporated within our domestic law."⁴⁷

That Lord Denning in *Trendtex* is revered in such a way by Toope is a bit troubling and, from a Canadian perspective, completely unjustified. Neither the Supreme Court of Canada⁴⁸ nor any lower court in this country⁴⁹ – except in

---

⁴³ For recent examples, see H. M. Kindred, "Canadians as Citizens of the International Community: Asserting Unimplemented Treaty Rights in the Courts," in S. G. Coughlan & D. Russell (eds.), *Citizenship and Citizen Participation in the Administration of Justice* (Montreal: Thémis, 2002), 263; and W. A. Schabas, "Twenty-Five Years of Public International Law at the Supreme Court of Canada" (2000), 79 Can. Bar Rev. 174.

⁴⁴ The Supreme Court of Canada has never properly addressed, let alone settled, the issue of whether or not the national application of international customs follow the monist logic. See *Reference as to Powers to Levy Rates on Foreign Legations and High Commissioners' Residences*, [1943] S.C.R. 208; *Municipality of Saint John v. Fraser-Brace Overseas Corp.*, [1958] S.C.R. 263; *La Republique Democratique du Congo v. Venne*, [1971] S.C.R. 997; *Re Newfoundland Continental Shelf*, [1984] 1 S.C.R. 86; *Reference re Secession of Quebec*, [1998] 2 S.C.R. 217; *114957 Canada Ltée (Spraytech, Société d'arrosage) v. Hudson (City)*, [2001] 2 S.C.R. 241; and *Mugesera v. Canada (Minister of Citizenship and Immigration)*, 2005 SCC 39, 28 June 2005.

⁴⁵ S. J. Toope, "Canada and International Law," in C.C.I.L. (ed.), *The Impact of International Law on the Practice of Law in Canada – Proceedings of the 27th Annual Conference of the Canadian Council on International Law* (The Hague: Kluwer Law International, 1999), 33, at 36.

⁴⁶ [1977] 1 Q.B. 529 [hereinafter "*Trendtex*"].

⁴⁷ S. J. Toope, *supra*, note 45, at 37.

⁴⁸ See the cases in footnote 44, *supra*.

⁴⁹ See *Bouzari v. Iran* (2004), 243 D.L.R. (4th) 406 (Ont. C.A.); *Foxford Entreprises S.A. v. Cuba*, [2003] 4 F.C. 1182 (F.C. T.D.); *Wier v. British Columbia (Environmental Appeal Board)* (2003), 19 B.C.L.R. (4th) 178 (B.C. S.C.); *Mack et al. c. Canada (Attorney General)* (2002), 217 D.L.R. (4th) 583 (Ont. C.A.); *Rahaman v. Canada (Minister of Citizenship and Immigration)*, [2002] 3 F.C. 537 (F.C.A.); *Copello v. Canada (Minister of Foreign Affairs* (2003), [2002] 3 F.C. 24 (F.C. T.D.); *R. v. Rumbaut* (1998), 127 C.C.C. (3d) 138 (N.B. Q.B.); *R. v. Kirchhoff* (1995), 172 N.B.R. (2d) 257 (N.B. Q.B.); *Zolfagharkhani v. Canada (Minister of Employment and Immigration)*, [1993] 3 F.C. 540 (F.C.A.); *Rudolph v. Canada (Minister of Employment and Immigration)*, [1992] 2 F.C. 653 (F.C.A.); *R. v. Palacios* (1984), 7 D.L.R. (4th) 112 (Ont. C.A.); *Reference re Mineral & Other Natural Resources of Continental Shelf*

one somewhat incongruous case,[50] that quoted the key passage but in the context of treaty law – has ever paid any attention whatsoever to this precedent for the issue of the national application of international customary law.[51] Even in Great Britain, it has only been relied upon in a few subsequent cases to justify the adoptionist model for customs.[52] Merely three such references occurred in our Commonwealth counterparts, Australia[53] and New Zealand.[54] The latest instance in Britain is *R. v. Jones and others*,[55] where the Court of Appeal was asked whether the crime of aggression at international law was a crime in domestic law and thus a justiciable issue in courts; this question was answered by the negative, a conclusion that is under appeal at the House of Lords, judgment pending.

5) LORD DENNING IN *TRENDTEX*: THE CHALLENGE

What is viewed as so extraordinary in the reasons Lord Denning gave in *Trendtex* is the detailed analysis of the "two schools of thought" concerning the domestic utilisation of customs, namely the doctrine of incorporation (that is,

---

(1983), 145 D.L.R. (3d) 9 (Nfld. & Lab. C.A.); *Alberta Union of Provincial Employees v. Alberta*, [1980] A.J. No. 531 (Alb. C.Q.B.)

[50] *R. v. Bonadie* (1996), 109 C.C.C. (3d) 356 (Ont. Ct. Prov. Div.), at 370.

[51] This is a material fact that could not be silenced by the unconditional advocates of the adoptionist model for international customary law. See, for example, G. van Ert, *supra*, note 30, at 158.

[52] See *The Uganda Co. (Holdings) Ltd. v. The Government of Uganda*, [1979] 1 Lloyd's Rep. 481 (Q.B.); *I Congreso del Partido*, [1983] 1 A.C. 244 (H.L.); *The Goring*, [1987] Q.B. 687 (C.A.); *J. H. Rayner (Mincing Lane) Ltd. v. Department of Trade and Industry* (1989), [1990] 2 A.C. 418 (H.L.); *Westland Helicopters Ltd. v. Arab Organisation for Industrialisation*, [1995] Q.C. 282 (Q.B.); *Chagos Islanders v. The Attorney General and another*, [2003] E.W.H.C. 2222 (Q.B.).

[53] See *Koowarta v. Bjelke-Petersen and others* (1982), 39 A.L.R. 417 (H.C. Aust.); and *Re Jane* (1988), 85 A.L.R. 409 (Fam. Ct. Aust.). In Australia, however, courts have adopted what is known as the "source view" of customs, to the effect that "international law is not a part, but is one of the sources, of English law" – J. L. Brierly, "International Law in England" (1935), 51 L.Q.R. 24, at 31. See *Chow Hung Ching v. The King* (1948), [1949] A.L.R. 298; *Nulyarimma v. Thompson* (1999), 165 A.L.R. 621; and *Commonwealth of Australia v. Yarmirr and others* (2000), 101 F.C.R. 171. See also G. Brennan, "The Role and Rule of Domestic Law in International Relations" (1999), 10 *Public L. Rev.* 185; and A. Mason, "International Law as a Source of Domestic Law," in B. R. Opeskin & D. R. Rothwell (eds.), *International Law and Australian Federalism* (Melbourne: Melbourne University Press, 1997), 215.

[54] See *Marine Steel Ltd. v. Government of the Marshall Islands*, [1981] 2 N.Z.L.R. 1 (H.C.). See also, on the situation with regard to international customary law in New Zealand, T. Dunworth, "The Rising Tide of Customary International Law: Will New Zealand Sink or Swim?" (2004), 15 Public L. Rev. 36.

[55] [2004] 4 All E.R. 955.

adoption) and the doctrine of transformation. After considering each of them in turn and asking which is the correct one, he held:

> Seeing that the rules of international law have changed – and do change – and that the courts have given effect to the changes without any Act of Parliament, it follows to my mind inexorably that the rules of international law, as existing from time to time, do form part of our English law. It follows, too, that a decision of this court – as to what was the ruling of international law 50 or 60 years ago – is not binding on this court today. International law knows no rule of stare decisis. If this court today is satisfied that the rule of international law on a subject has changed from what it was 50 or 60 years ago, it can give effect to that change – and apply the change in our English law – without waiting for the House of Lords to do it.[56]

Most clearly, therefore, the only reason behind Lord Denning's conclusion that the adoptionist model (or incorporationist model, as called in Britain) should prevail with respect to customary law is the doctrine of *stare decisis*. Indeed international law knows no *stare decisis*, but English law does. Hence the monist logic is warranted for customs because, otherwise, changes in international law would not be reflected in domestic law.

This reasoning based on *stare decisis* is the fundamental flaw in Lord Denning's decision in *Trendtex*. Two criticisms: The first personal; the second substantive. How can his Lordship's statement about *stare decisis* enjoy credibility when his disregard for precedent is commonly known. *Cassell & Co. Ltd. v. Broome*,[57] the *cause célèbre* on punitive damages,[58] drives the point home. In that case, not only did Lord Denning cavalierly disregard the recent precedent by the House of Lords in *Rookes v. Barnard*,[59] but he audaciously invited the lower courts to ignore it.[60] Beyond this credibility problem, however, there is a substantive one that destroys the *stare decisis* argument in *Trendtex*.

---

[56] *Trendtex, supra,* note 46, at 554.

[57] [1972] A.C. 1027 (H.L.).

[58] On this issue and, particularly, the said episode by Lord Denning, see S. Beaulac, "A Comparative Look at Punitive Damages in Canada" (2002), 17 *Supreme Court L. Rev. (2d)* 351, reprinted in S. Beaulac *et al.* (eds.) *The Joy of Torts – Essays in Honour of Mr. Justice Allen M. Linden* (Markham, Ont.: LexisNexis Butterworths, 2003), 351; and S. Beaulac, "Les dommages-intérêts punitifs depuis l'affaire *Whiten* et les leçons à en tirer pour le droit civil québécois" (2002), 36 Rev. jur. Thémis 637.

[59] [1964] A.C. 1129 (H.L.).

[60] See the judgment at the Court of Appeal, *Broome v. Cassell*, [1971] 2 Q.B. 354 (C.A.), at 384, *per* Lord Denning: "This case may, or may not, go on appeal to the House of Lords. I must say a word, however, for the guidance of judges who will be trying cases in the meantime. I think the difficulties presented by *Rookes v. Barnard* are so great that the judges should direct the juries in accordance with the law as it was understood before *Rookes v. Barnard*. Any attempt to follow *Rookes v. Barnard* if bound to lead to confusion."

Simply put, perhaps because of Lord Denning in fact[61] – or maybe in spite of or unrelated to him – the doctrine of *stare decisis* is not at all what it used to be in the common law systems of the UK, Canada and other Commonwealth countries.[62] The old 19th century directive which even bound the House of Lords to its own previous decisions, as stated in *London Street Tramways Co. Ltd. v. London County Council*,[63] is now long gone. It has been replaced by the *Practice Statement (1966)*,[64] where their Lordships proposed "to modify their present practice and, while treating former decisions of this House as normally binding, to depart from a previous decision when it appears right to do so."[65] This new approach to legal precedents at the country's highest instance had an obvious trickling down effect on the lower courts, where the doctrine of *stare decisis* is known perhaps more in its breach than in its adherence.[66] It has also influenced, most certainly, judicial decision-making all over the Commonwealth.[67]

At the Supreme Court of Canada, the strict doctrine of *stare decisis* was also professed in the early 20th century with *Stuart v. Bank of Montreal*[68] but, before the end of the 1950s, started its progressive relaxation.[69] Since *Watkins v.*

---

[61] See H. Carty, "Precedent and the Court of Appeal: Lord Denning's view explored" (1981), 1 Legal St. 68.

[62] On the doctrine of *stare decisis* and on its history in the common law tradition, see R. Cross & J.-W. Harris, *Precedent in English Law*, 4th ed. (Oxford: Clarendon Press, 1991); J. Evans, "Change in the Doctrine of Precedent During the Nineteenth Century," in L. Goldstein (ed.), *Precedent in Law* (Oxford: Clarendon Press, 1987), 35; A. Joanes, "Stare Decisis in the Supreme Court of Canada" (1958), 36 Can. Bar Rev. 175; D. H. Laird, "The Doctrine of Stare Decisis" (1935), 13 Can. Bar Rev. 1; R. von Moschzisker, "Stare Decisis in the Courts of Last Resort" (1923–1924), 37 Harvard L. Rev. 409; and J. A. Salmond, "The Theory of Judicial Precedent" (1990), 17 L.Q. Rev. 375.

[63] [1898] A.C. 375 (H.L.).

[64] [1966] 1 W.L.R. 1234; [1966] 3 All E.R. 77.

[65] *Ibid.*

[66] See G. Slapper & D. Kelly, *The English Legal System*, 7th ed. (London: Cavendish Publishing, 2004), at 81–89.

[67] See H. P. Glenn, "Sur l'impossibilité d'un principe de stare decisis" (1993–1994), 55 Rev. recherche jur. 1073, at 1080–1081.

[68] [1909] 41 S.C.R. 516.

[69] See, for instance, *Re Farm Products Marketings Act*, [1957] S.C.R. 198; *Binus v. The Queen*, [1967] S.C.R. 594; *Peda v. The Queen*, [1969] S.C.R. 905; *Paquette v. The Queen*, [1977] 2 S.C.R. 189; *McNamara Construction (Western) Ltd. v. The Queen*, [1977]; *Rathwell v. Rathwell*, [1978] 2 S.C.R. 436; *Minister of Indian Affairs v. Ranville*, [1982] 2 S.C.R. 518; and *Hunter Engineering Co. Inc. v. Syncrude Canada Ltd.*, [1989] 1 S.C.R. 426. See also R.J. Sharpe, "The Doctrine of *Stare Decisis*," in D. J. Guth (ed.), *Brian Dickson at the Supreme Court of Canada, 1973–1990* (Winnipeg: Canadian Legal History Project, 1998), 193; and G. F. Curtis, "Stare Decisis at Common Law in Canada" (1978), 12 U. British Columbia L. Rev. 1.

Olafson[70] and *R. v. Salituro*[71] at the turn of the 1990s, the issue has ceased to be about bindingness of precedents and is now centred on the framework within which courts can adapt and develop common law rules. In the latter case, Iacobucci J. wrote: "Blackstone's static model of the common law has gradually been supplanted by a more dynamic view. This Court is now willing, where there are compelling reasons for doing so, to overturn its own previous decisions."[72] He offered these edicts: "Judges can and should adapt the common law to reflect the changing social, moral and economic fabric of the country;"[73] but they should limit themselves "to those incremental changes which are necessary to keep the common law in step with the dynamic and evolving fabric of our society."[74] These remarks are apposite to alleviate Lord Denning's concerns that, because of *stare decisis*, domestic legal norms based on international customary law could not change over time.

The new reality of the weaker role for *stare decisis* in common law jurisdictions goes a long way to justify putting aside *Trendtex* as a precedent for the proposition that customs may be used domestically pursuant to the adoptionist (or incorporationist) model and its monist logic. Indeed, it is not true anymore (assuming it once was) that the rigidity of the doctrine means that an old legal precedent will stand in the way of allowing judge-made-law to evolve. Similarly, it is not true nowadays – nor, arguably, was it already when *Trendtex* was decided in 1977 – that customary law at the international level that was nationally applied by means of case law cannot see changes in its legal norms be given domestic effect because of strict precedents. "International law knows no rule of stare decisis,"[75] as Lord Denning put it; national law in common law countries, for its part, knows a considerably watered-down such doctrine. Customary international law evolves over time, no doubt, but so does the national judge-made-law that gives it legal effect domestically, according to the contemporary version of *stare decisis*.

What happens then if Lord Denning's reasoning in *Trendtex*, based on *stare decisis*, is fundamentally wrong? In terms of positive law, it shatters the authority of the case and allows back the traditional, and more accurate, British case law on the national application of international customary law. One such instrumental case is *Chung Chi Cheung v. The King*,[76] where Lord Atkin declared: "It must always be remembered that, so far, at any rate, as the Courts of this country are concerned, international law has no validity save in so far as its

---

[70] [1989] 2 S.C.R. 750.
[71] [1990] 3 S.C.R. 654.
[72] *Ibid.*, at 665.
[73] *Ibid.*, at 670.
[74] *Ibid.*
[75] *Trendtex, supra*, note 46, at 554.
[76] [1939] A.C. 160 (P.C.).

principles are accepted and adopted by our own domestic law."[77] This passage
was read by Lord Denning in *Trendtex*[78] as rejecting the adoptionist (or incorporationist) model for customs and as requiring implementation by means of
legislation. This interpretation is totally unfounded; it is not what Lord Atkin
stated and it is crucial in these concluding remarks to address this point.

The suggestion that, if not applied nationally pursuant to the monist logic,
customs have to be incorporated through legislation is based on a complete
misconception of this international law source, as well as on a fundamental
misunderstanding of the incorporationist model and, with it, the dualist logic.
Customary law is on the international plane, in a way, what common law is in a
domestic jurisdiction, namely unwritten legal norms. Just like conventional law
is internationally, in a way, what statutory law is domestically, namely written
legal norms. Now, bearing in mind that the Westphalian paradigm postulates
two distinct and separate legal realities which need to be bridged somehow, the
following propositions appear logically sound: Common law, and its unwritten
national legal norms, is the proper vehicle to incorporate unwritten international legal norms found in customs. Statutory law, with its written national
legal norms, is the proper vehicle to transform written international legal norms
found in treaties.

In the end, recalling that the dualist theory is essentially about requiring a
state measure to link the international and the national, there is no difficulty in
seeing that customs know a faith similar to treaties. The state measure to transform a treaty is accomplished by the legislator, with an implementing enactment establishing the statutory rule, while the state measure to incorporate a
custom is done by the judicial branch of government, with a decision identifying the common law rule.[79] The remaining question, which will have to wait for
another day, is whether this process ought to be viewed still through the prism
of the adoptionist (or incorporationist) model. Is it not really an application of
the transformationist model, the only difference being the type of state measure
that gives domestic effect to international law? Could this conceptualisation
mean less chaos, less of an imbroglio situation, as regards the national application of customary legal norms? One can only speculate as to what Lord
Denning would answer.

---

[77] *Id.*, at 167.

[78] *Supra*, note 46, at 554.

[79] This point was made by F. Rigaldies & J. Woehrling, "Le juge interne canadien et
le droit international" (1980), 21 C. de D. 293, at 305–306.

Chapter 19

The Challenge of Internalizing International Conventional Law: The Experience of Australia, England and Canada with Ratified Treaties

Hugh M. Kindred

1) INTRODUCTION

This is an account of four hapless migrants whose entanglements with the legal systems in their desired destinations challenged judicial inventiveness. It is unlikely that these four members of visible minorities had any intention, or desire, to disturb the equanimity of the legal systems in three traditionally white, major member countries of the British Commonwealth. Teoh, Ahmed, and Baker and Suresh just wanted to stay in Australia, England and Canada respectively. Yet their legal battles to do so provide a comparative snapshot of recent judicial thinking about the effects of international conventions within the national legal system.

In each of these four cases, the applicant had applied to the courts to overturn a deportation order made against her or him. In order to do so, each urged on the courts a right to benefit from the provisions of a treaty that had been ratified externally by the executive but had not been implemented internally by the legislature. It is commonplace that in parliamentary democracies on the British

Christopher P.M. Waters (Ed.), *British and Canadian Perspectives on International Law*, pp. 393–404.

model, which obtain in Australia, Canada and England, the government of the day may exercise the Crown's prerogative power to conduct foreign relations and thus to commit the country to treaties externally, but it may not be able to apply them internally. Pursuant to the constitutional doctrine of the supremacy of parliament, along with the division of powers in the federal constitutions of Australia and Canada, if the provisions of a treaty affect domestic law they may not be applied until the appropriate legislature has transformed them into local law by an act of legislation.[1]

When faced with requests to respect duly concluded and ratified treaties, courts in the past have often refused even to consider them.[2] Nowadays, as highlighted in the Introduction, an appreciation of the finite limits of the world and the global interdependence of its peoples appears to have infused the minds of the judges with a different view. Thus a measure of internationalised justice,[3] of which these four cases are examples, has taken hold. Adherence by the state to a multilateral treaty, especially one for the protection of human rights, is not a matter to be disregarded lightly. The participation of the people's elected government in treaty making in order to create an operable international regime surely means something. The commitment of the courts to the rule of law presumably does not stop at the state's frontiers. This was the dilemma that faced the courts of Australia, England and then Canada in the 1990s and was addressed in these four cases. But the pursuit of internationalised justice has been different in Australia and England compared to Canada. The courts of Australia and England have employed the administrative law technique of legitimate expectation, while Canadian courts have developed a contextual and interpretive approach. In discussing the four cases chronologically, the merits of the different judicial techniques will be exposed and compared.

---

[1] *Attorney General for Canada v. Attorney General for Ontario (Labour Conventions Case)*, [1937] A.C. 326 (P.C.).

[2] E.g. *Francis v. The Queen*, [1956] S.C.R. 618; *Capital Cities Communications Inc. v. Canadian Radio-Television Commission* (1978), 81 D.L.R. (3d) 609 (S.C.C.); *J.H. Rayner (Mincing Lane) Ltd. v. Department of Trade and Industry (International Tin Council Case)*, [1990] 2 A.C. 418; *R. v. Secretary of State for the Home Department, ex p. Brind*, [1991] 1 A.C. 696.

[3] Or "judicial globalization": see A.-M. Slaughter, "Judicial Globalization" (2000) 40 Va. J. Int'l. L. 1103. See also D. Dyzenhaus, M. Hunt & M. Taggart, "The Principle of Legality in Administrative Law: Internationalisation as Constitutionalisation" (2001) 1 Oxfd. U. Cmwlth. L.J. 5.

2) *TEOH'S* CASE IN AUSTRALIA IN 1995[4]

Ah Hin Teoh was a Malaysian citizen who went to Australia in 1988 on a temporary entry permit. There he shortly married an Australian citizen who had been his deceased brother's common law partner. Subsequently Teoh applied for a permanent entry permit, which would have given him resident status, but, while his application was pending, he was convicted of smuggling heroin and sentenced to six years' imprisonment. Shortly after conviction he was denied resident status. He appealed without success and was ordered deported. Teoh challenged the decision denying him resident status all the way to the way to the Full Federal Court where he succeeded. The Minister for Immigration then appealed to the High Court of Australia. In the intervening seven years Teoh had three children with his wife to add to her existing four.

By a majority of 4–1, the High Court dismissed the Minister's appeal in judgments that addressed "an important question concerning the relationship between international law and Australian law."[5] The question concerned the domestic impact of a treaty that had been concluded and ratified by the Commonwealth Government. Justices Mason and Deane first expressed the view that a ratified but unincorporated convention should be used as an aid in the interpretation of a statute, according to the canon of construction that the legislature does not intend to legislate contrary to international law, and as a guide in the development of common law.[6] They went on to accept Teoh's argument that a ratified treaty also gave rise to a legitimate expectation that the administrative discretion of a government official acting under an enabling statute would also be exercised in conformity with its provisions. Legitimate expectation was already a recognised administrative concept: the significance of the case was the Court's readiness to extend its scope of application to ratified treaties.

In this instance, Teoh successfully asserted that the official had not taken the best interests of his Australian children into account as a primary consideration in her decision as was to be expected in light of Australia's ratification of the UN Convention on the Rights of the Child. As Justices Mason and Deane wrote:

> Moreover, ratification by Australia of an international convention is not to be dismissed as a merely platitudinous or ineffectual act, particularly when the instrument evidences internationally accepted standards to be applied by courts and administrative authorities in dealing with basic human rights affecting the family and children. Rather, ratification of a convention is a positive statement by the

---

[4] *Minister of State for Immigration and Ethnic Affairs v. Teoh* (1995), 128 A.L.R. 353, 183 C.L.R. 273 (H.C.A.) [*Teoh* cited to C.L.R.].

[5] *Ibid.*, per Mason C.J. & Deane J. at 279.

[6] *Ibid.* at 287–288.

executive government of this country to the world and to the Australian people that the executive government and its agencies will act in accordance with the Convention. That positive statement is an adequate foundation for a legitimate expectation, absent statutory or executive indications to the contrary, that administrative decision-makers will act in conformity with Convention, and treat the best interests of the children as "a primary consideration." It is not necessary that a person seeking to set up a legitimate expectation should be aware of the Convention or should personally entertain the expectation; it is enough that the expectation is reasonable in the sense that there are adequate materials to support it. . . .

But, if a decision-maker proposes to make a decision inconsistent with a legitimate expectation, procedural fairness requires that the persons affected should be given notice and an adequate opportunity of presenting a case against the taking of such a course. So, here, if the delegate proposed to give a decision which did not accord with the principle that the best interests of the children were to be a primary consideration, procedural fairness called for the delegate to take the steps just indicated.[7]

On the facts of the case, the two justices concluded that the Minister's delegate had turned her mind to the plight of Teoh's family but had not regarded the children's interests as a primary consideration, and therefore her decision lacked procedural fairness.

The opinion of the Court occasioned a flurry of public attention, which generally divided the legal community according to their professional interests, with administrative lawyers (against) opposing international and human rights lawyers (for).[8] Yet it was a hollow victory for the importation of international law since the ruling itself contained the grounds to overreach it. As Justices Mason and Deane noted, the expectation is only legitimate "absent statutory or executive indications to the contrary." Very quickly the much concerned Australian government issued an executive statement denying all expectations of compliance with any ratified convention, and successive Commonwealth governments of different political persuasion introduced bills in parliament to the same effect.[9] As a result, the expectations legitimately aroused by ratified

---

[7] *Ibid.* at 291 footnotes omitted. See also the judgment of Toohey J. at paras. 300–302.

[8] See e.g. M. Allars, "International Law and Administrative Discretion" in B. R. Opeskin & D. R. Rothwell, eds., *International Law and Australian Federalism* (Melbourne: Melbourne University Press, 1997) at 232; J. McMillan, "*Teoh*, and Invalidity in Administrative Law" (1995) 5 A.I.A.L. Forum 10; S. Roberts, "Minister of State for Immigration and Ethnic Affairs v Ah Hin Teoh: The High Court decision and the Government's reaction to it" (1995) 2 Aust. J. Hum. Rts. 133; M. Taggart," Legitimate Expectation and Treaties in the High Court of Australia" (1996) 112 L.Q.R. 50.

[9] Joint Statement of the Minister of Foreign Affairs and the Attorney-General, *International Treaties and the High Court Decision in Teoh*, 10 May 1995; Administrative Decisions (Effect of International Instruments) Bill 1995 (Cth); Joint Statement of the Minister of Foreign Affairs and the Attorney-General, *The Effect of*

treaties are most unlikely to be fulfilled. Yet one has to wonder what the Australian government has in mind when it signs and ratifies a treaty, thus obligating the whole country with its provisions, but fails to implement it domestically by legislation, as it has the power to do,[10] and denies its people any expectation of conformance.

3) *AHMED'S* CASE IN ENGLAND IN 1998[11]

An approach similar to the Australian High Court's befell Ahmed in the English Court of Appeal. Ahmed had entered the United Kingdom from Bangladesh in 1990 or 1991 by using a false passport. He subsequently married a UK resident and together they had a daughter. Shortly after her birth in 1996, Ahmed applied for leave to remain in the country, but, when he admitted to having arrived on a false passport, he was given notice of illegal entry and was refused permission to remain. In essence, Ahmed's application was denied because he had not been married and living with his wife in the United Kingdom for two years before the decision and his daughter, being well under ten year's of age, could be expected to adapt to life abroad.

The decision was made pursuant to the deportation policies issued by the Secretary of State for the Home Department (the Home Secretary) as guidance to immigration officers in their exercise of discretion when to allow an applicant to enter or remain in the United Kingdom on concessionary grounds. Such non-statutory executive policies are based on Crown prerogative. Exercisable by the Home Secretary on behalf of the Crown, this power in relation to foreigners is expressly maintained by the 1971 Immigration Act.[12] At the time of the decision in Ahmed's case, the European Convention on Human Rights (ECHR) had been ratified by the United Kingdom but had not yet been legislatively imported into English law. The Human Rights Act[13] was only just in the making so Ahmed could not require the Home Secretary, so said the Court of Appeal following the House of Lords' decision in *Brind*,[14] to have to conform

---

Treaties in Administrative Decision-Making, 25 February 1997; Administrative Decisions (Effect of International Instruments) Bill 1997 (Cth).

[10] *Commonwealth of Australia v. Tasmania* (1983), 158 C.L.R. 1 (Aust. H.C.); *Richardson v. The Forestry Commission* (1987), 164 C.L.R. 261 (Aust. H.C.); *Queensland v. The Commonwealth* (1989), 167 C.L.R. 232.

[11] *R. v. Secretary of State for the Home Department, ex p. Ahmed,* [1998] I.N.L.R. 570 (C.A.). See also *R. on application of Lika v. Secretary of State for the Home Department,* [2002] EWCA Civ 1855.

[12] (U.K.) 1971, c. 77, s. 33(5).

[13] (U.K.) 1998, c. 42.

[14] *Ex p. Brind, supra* note 2 at 717–718. See also the *International Tin Council Case, supra* note 2; *R. v. Lyons,* [2003] 1 A.C. 976; *Re McKerr,* [2004] 1 W.L.R. 807 (H.L.).

to the ECHR as that "inevitably would result in incorporation of the Convention into English domestic law by the back door."[15]

In these circumstances, Ahmed sought leave to apply for judicial review of the decision against him by urging the Court that it had been taken without due regard for his legitimate expectations. He argued that the act of entering into the ECHR – itself a prerogative act – gave rise to a legitimate expectation of compliance with its provisions upon which he was entitled to rely. Lord Woolf M.R. responded to this plea in a similar way to the High Court in *Teoh's* case, from which he quoted. He observed:

> I will accept that the entering into a treaty by the Secretary of State could give rise to a legitimate expectation on which the public in general are entitled to rely. Subject to any indication to the contrary, it could be a representation that the Secretary of State would act in accordance with any obligations which he had accepted under the treaty. This legitimate expectation could give rise to a right of relief, as well as additional obligations of fairness, if the Secretary of State, without reason, acted inconsistently with the obligations which this country had undertaken.[16]

In the result, Ahmed was wholly unsuccessful because the Court of Appeal held the Secretary of State's deportation policy guidance had effectively inhibited any legitimate expectation based on the ECHR that was contrary to them. Once again, contrary executive policy statements trumped any legitimate expectation of conformity with the ratified treaty. The English Court of Appeal paid even less attention than the Australian High Court to the inconsistency of Her Majesty's government in agreeing to respect a set of personal rights under a treaty but denying them effect.[17]

The consequences of these two cases in Australia and England are most unsatisfactory. The courts have shown fealty to the supremacy of parliament in refusing to give direct effect to unincorporated treaties but they have also demonstrated imagination in legitimating expectations of compliance. The fault is the executive's. Recall that the UK government has both the power to make treaties internationally, by reason of Crown prerogative, and to implement them internally, on account of its majority position of leadership in Parliament. These principles apply equally in Australia where the constitution has been held also to grant the Commonwealth government powers both to conclude and to implement treaties even though the country is a federal state.[18] What was either government's purpose in concluding the treaty in question – particularly a human rights convention – if it did not intend to implement it, worse indeed, if it proposed to take executive action to contradict any expectations of compliance?

---

[15] Per Lord Ackner in *Brind, ibid.* at 761–762.

[16] *Supra* note 11 at 583. See also Hobhouse L.J.'s judgment at 592.

[17] Possibly the Court was moved by the anticipated enactment of the *Human Rights Act, supra* note 13, and, with it, full implementation of the protections of the ECHR.

[18] *Supra* note 10.

4) *BAKER'S* CASE IN CANADA IN 1999[19]

Slight attention has been given by Canadian courts to legitimate expectations because another, more powerful approach towards ratified but unimplemented treaties has been conceived and pursued. The initial step was taken in *Baker's* case. Ms Baker entered Canada from Jamaica as a visitor in 1981 and remained illegally for eleven years until ordered deported in 1992. During this time she gave birth to four children, all Canadian citizens. Seeking to stay in Canada, Baker requested an exemption from the requirement to apply for permanent residence from outside Canada on the basis of humanitarian and compassionate (H & C) considerations, as permitted by the Canadian Immigration Act.[20] Her request was denied and she appealed successively through the federal courts to the Supreme Court of Canada. Of the three issues of appeal identified in the Court, two are directly relevant to the present discussion:

(2) Were the principles of procedural fairness violated in this case? . . .
(3) Was [the immigration officer's] discretion improperly exercised because of the approach taken to the interests of Ms Baker's children?[21]

Canadian immigration officers are provided with a set of ministerial guidelines in an immigration manual instructing them how to exercise their discretion in making H & C decisions. These guidelines directly address situations involving dependents and take account of the hardship that may result to family members from requiring applicants to leave Canada and apply from abroad. They do not appear to refer specifically to the Convention on the Rights of the Child, which Canada has ratified.

When Justice L'Heureux-Dubé addressed the issue of procedural fairness, she quickly dismissed the existence of any legitimate expectation based on the Convention, which would have rendered the officer's decision unfair. Speaking for the whole court on this point, L'Heureux-Dubé J. expressed the view that the Convention was not the equivalent of a government representation about how H & C applications would be decided. Her opinion is cause for some concern if no legitimate expectation arises in Canada from the Convention in H & C applications, as it would in similar situations in Australia and England, as discussed above. But perhaps that is of little consequence as, following *Teoh* and *Ahmed*, the ministerial guidelines could readily be read as an indication of contrary executive intent, sufficient to override any legitimate expectation.

Justice L'Heureux-Dubé took a more purposive approach to the Convention when she considered whether the officer's discretion had been improperly

---

[19] *Baker v. Canada (Minister for Citizenship and Immigration)*, [1999] 2 S.C.R. 817.
[20] R.S.C. 1985, c. I-2, s. 114(2).
[21] *Supra* note 19 at 832.

exercised on account of Baker's children. Baker argued that administrative law requires that the discretionary power should have been exercised in accordance with the Convention and, consequently, the officer should have applied the best interests of her children as a primary consideration in the decision. L'Heureux-Dubé J. adopted this approach in observing:

> Determining whether the approach taken by the immigration officer was within the boundaries set out by the words of the statute and the values of administrative law requires a contextual approach, as is taken to statutory interpretation generally . . . In my opinion, a reasonable exercise of the power conferred by the section requires close attention to the interests and needs of children. Children's rights, and attention to their interests, are central humanitarian and compassionate values in Canadian society. Indications of children's interests as important considerations governing the manner in which H & C powers should be exercised may be found, for example, in the purposes of the Act, in international instruments, and in the guidelines for making H & C decisions published by the Minister herself.[22]

In her consideration of the relevant international instruments, L'Heureux-Dubé J. directly addressed the Convention on the Rights of the Child, amongst others. While recalling that, since the Convention has not been specifically implemented domestically by legislation, its provisions have no direct application in Canadian law, she emphasized that "the values and principles of the Convention recognize the importance of being attentive to the rights and best interests of children when decisions are made that relate to and affect their future."[23] The justice also found support for due consideration of the interests of children in the objectives of the Act and in the ministerial guidelines. In light of the evidence, she allowed Baker's appeal, saying in conclusion:

> The principles discussed above indicate that, for the exercise of discretion to fall within the standard of reasonableness, the decision-maker should consider children's best interests as an important factor, give them substantial weight, and be alert, alive and sensitive to them. That is not to say that children's best interests must always outweigh other considerations, or that there will not be other reasons for denying an H & C claim even when children's interests are given consideration. However, where the interests of children are minimized, in a manner inconsistent with Canada's humanitarian and compassionate tradition and the Minister's guidelines, the decision will be unreasonable.[24]

The force of this decision lies in the contextual approach to statutory interpretation, referred to by Justice L'Heureux-Dubé. For many years now the Supreme Court of Canada has consistently propounded the contextual approach to

---

[22] *Ibid.* at 860.

[23] *Ibid.* at 861. On this point 2 of the 7 justices dissented; see the judgment of Iacobucci J. at 865.

[24] *Ibid.* at 864.

statutory interpretation in place of the traditional literal rule and its exceptions for ambiguity and uncertainty.[25] *Driedger on the Construction of Statutes* has summed up the Court's practice, with its approval, as follows:

> There is only one rule in modern interpretation, namely, courts are obliged to determine the meaning of legislation in its total context, having regard to the purpose of the legislation, the consequences of proposed interpretations, the presumptions and special rules of interpretation, as well as admissible external aids.[26]

This "modern" approach to interpretation is supported by an older presumption of legislative conformity with international obligations. The presumption was explicitly relied upon by Justice L'Heureux-Dubé when she also quoted from *Driedger*:

> [T]he legislature is presumed to respect the values and principles contained in international law, both customary and conventional. These constitute a part of the legal context in which legislation is enacted and read. In so far as possible, therefore, interpretations that reflect these values and principles are preferred.[27]

Together the modern approach and the presumption combine to produce a powerful technique for the interpretation of statutes and of administrative authority. They demand that Canadian courts respect the values and reflect the principles of international treaty obligations (even when the treaty provisions lack domestic incorporation) in the interpretation of any statutes and statutory powers to which they are relevant. Just how powerful is this judicial technique was demonstrated by the Supreme Court itself in the subsequent case of *Suresh*.

5) *SURESH'S* CASE IN CANADA IN 2002[28]

Manickavasagam Suresh came to Canada from Sri Lanka in 1990 and was recognised as a refugee. He applied for landed immigrant status – the initial step under Canadian law to permanent residency and ultimately naturalization – but was detained on security grounds before a decision was made. The

---

[25] See *Hills v. Canada (Attorney General)*, [1988] 1 S.C.R. 513; 2747–3174; *Quebec Inc. v. Quebec (Régie des permis d'alcool)*, [1996] 3 S.C.R. 919; *Verdun v. Toronto-Dominion Bank*, [1996] 3 S.C.R. 550; *Royal Bank of Canada v. Sparrow Electric Corp.*, [1997] 1 S.C.R. 411; *R. v. Hydro-Québec*, [1997] 3 S.C.R. 213; *Re Rizzo & Rizzo Shoes Ltd.*, [1998] 1 S.C.R. 27; *R. v. Gladue*, [1999] 1 S.C.R. 688; *R. v. Sharpe*, [2001] 1 S.C.R. 45; *Chieu v. Canada (Minister of Citizenship and Immigration)*, [2002] 1 S.C.R. 84.

[26] R. Sullivan, *Driedger on the Construction of Statutes* (Toronto: Butterworths, 1994) at 330.

[27] *Ibid.* at 330, quoted in *Baker, supra* note 19 at 861.

[28] *Suresh v. Canada (Minister of Citizenship and Immigration)*, [2002] 1 S.C.R. 3. See also *Ahani v. Canada (Minister of Citizenship and Immigration)*, [2002] 1 S.C.R. 72.

Canadian Security Intelligence Service (CSIS) certified that Suresh was a member of and fundraiser for the Tamil Tigers, an association regarded by the Canadian government as a terrorist organisation. At the time the Tamil Tigers were engaged in a brutal civil war with the government of Sri Lanka and its forces. Suresh was ordered to be deported regardless of his refugee status. The order was made under the Immigration Act which forbids admission to Canada of anyone who is a member of a terrorist organisation.[29] The Act also incorporates article 33 of the Convention Relating to the Status of Refugees[30] by which Canada has accepted that it will not return (*"refouler"*) a Convention refugee to a country where s/he would be threatened for reasons of race, religion, nationality, membership in a particular social group or political opinion, except when there are reasonable grounds for regarding him or her as a danger to the security of Canada.

Suresh appealed the order against him in part on the ground that removal to Sri Lanka would constitute deportation to torture at the hands of Sri Lankan authorities. He produced evidence of that likelihood and argued that his expulsion in the face of a substantial risk of torture would be contrary to the Canadian Charter of Rights and Freedoms[31] and Canada's international legal obligations. Specifically, he pointed out that section 7 of the Charter guarantees "everyone . . . the right to life, liberty and security of the person and the right not to be deprived thereof except in accordance with the principles of fundamental justice," which, he argued, included prohibition against expulsion to torture on the authority of the Convention Against Torture (CAT) and the International Covenant on Civil and Political Rights (ICCPR).[32]

Canada has ratified both these conventions but, unlike the Refugee Convention, it has not specifically implemented them domestically by legislation. Upon a traditional analysis, the case might have appeared straightforward. The treaties against torture not being part of Canadian law, the Immigration Act alone would have governed the matter and Suresh, regardless of his status as a Convention refugee, would have been liable to be deported as a security risk. In fact, the Supreme Court took a much more broadly informed perspective and gave significant weight to all the relevant treaties. Following the modern approach to statutory interpretation, the Court regarded the CAT and the ICCPR as part of the context for construing the scope of the statutory power to expel a refugee if it would mean returning him or her to torture.[33] The Court

---

[29] R.S.C. 1985, c. I–2, s. 19.

[30] Can T.S. 1969 No. 6 in *ibid.* s.53(1).

[31] *Constitution Act, 1982*, being Schedule B to the *Canada Act* (U.K) 1982, c.11.

[32] Can T.S. 1987 No. 36 and Can. T.S. 1976 No. 47 respectively.

[33] The Supreme Court has deliberately and consistently employed international legal sources as aids to interpret the scope of the rights in the Canadian Charter almost from its establishment in 1982: see *Ref. re Public Service Employee Relations Act (Alta),*

agreed with Suresh that its inquiry into the principles of fundamental justice in the Charter should be informed not only by Canadian experience and jurisprudence but also by international law.[34] The Court consequently explored the provisions of the CAT and the ICCPR and reached the categorical conclusion that "international law rejects deportation to torture, even when national security interests are at stake. This is the norm which best informs the content of the principles of fundamental justice under s.7 of the Charter."[35] The court explained that the Minister for Immigration had to make her discretionary decisions under the Immigration Act consistently with the Charter and therefore she had to balance the relevant factors of personal rights and public security. The balance struck in each individual case has to conform to the principles of fundamental justice under section 7 of the Charter and therefore "insofar as the Immigration Act leaves open the possibility of deportation to torture, the Minister should generally decline to deport refugees where on the evidence there is substantial risk of torture."[36] The Court's judgment laid bare how Canada's ratified but unimplemented international treaty obligations impacted the interpretation of the Immigration Act via the Charter:

Insofar as Canada is unable to deport a person where there are substantial grounds to believe he or she would be tortured on return, this is not because Article 3 of the CAT directly constrains the actions of the Canadian government, but because the fundamental justice balance under s. 7 of the Charter generally precludes deportation to torture when applied on a case-by-case basis.[37]

In essence, the Supreme Court deployed two ratified treaties, the CAT and the ICCPR, via the Charter, to read down the scope of the section of the Immigration Act that implements the exception to *non refoulement* in the Refugee Convention. Although the Refugee Convention had been incorporated by legislation in Canada, the two subsequently ratified treaties, even though they have not been specifically implemented into Canadian law, gave rise to a narrowed interpretation of the existing legislation.[38]

[1987] 1 S.C.R. 313 at 348 per Dickson J. dissenting; *Slaight Communications Inc. v. Davidson*, [1989] 1 S.C.R. 1038 at 1056–1057. In fact, this practice may have been the genesis of the modern approach to statutory interpretation.

[34] *Supra* note 28 at 31.

[35] *Ibid.* at 45.

[36] *Ibid.* at 46.

[37] *Ibid.* at 46–47.

[38] The treaties discussed in *Baker* and *Suresh* have been treated as if they have not been implemented in Canadian law because that is how the Supreme Court spoke of them. Yet, an intriguing alternative analysis suggests they may have been passively implemented. That is to say, the government has not presented incorporating legislation for enactment because the Crown officers advised that Canadian law already fulfills the provisions of the conventions and therefore no legislation is necessary. However, although the courts have always said that implementing legislation is only necessary

6) CONCLUSION

The Canadian courts, in *Baker* and *Suresh*, have accorded a wholly different degree of respect and domestic impact, compared to the Australian and English courts in *Teoh* and *Ahmed*, to ratified treaty obligations. Relatively speaking, application of the administrative law notion of legitimate expectation is a limited and passive approach to the challenge to domestic law of ratified treaty obligations. Government decision-makers are not bound to have regard for the provisions of a ratified treaty at all, though if they do not they must take the small step of so informing the person whose application they are deciding. Even so, the government or the appropriate minister can countermand expectations by orders or policy directives, which may be specifically or generally contradictory. This seems an disingenuous way to treat citizens' interests and raises doubts about the government's integrity in concluding the treaty in question in the first place.[39]

The Canadian approach, by comparison, is positive and potentially unlimited. Building on the presumption that the legislature does not intend to legislate in violation of international law, Canadian courts assume that administrative discretion granted by the legislature should also be informed by Canada's international obligations. It bears repeating that the provisions of ratified treaties may not be applied directly unless they have been legislatively transformed into domestic law. But ratified international conventions are admissible, where relevant, as extrinsic evidence of the context in which the statute in question has to be interpreted. Further, their underlying principles and values may be used to inform an appropriate interpretation. Indeed, the modern approach to statutory interpretation demands that Canadian courts and officials engage in this inclusive technique. In other words, Canadian decision-makers are bound to take affirmative account of relevant international treaties binding on Canada, weighing the impact of their purposes and values to their full intrinsic worth, in balance with all other contextually relevant factors. Such a purposive regard for ratified but unimplemented treaties is a functionally effective solution to the challenge of their internal impact in domestic law.

---

when the obligations of a ratified treaty affect domestic law, they have yet to acknowledge such passive implementation and continue to respect only active transformation.

[39] As the New Zealand Court of Appeal observed in speaking against the freedom of administrative decision-makers to ignore ratified treaties: "That is an unattractive argument, apparently implying that New Zealand's adherence to the international instruments has been at least partly window-dressing." See *Tavita v. Minister for Immigration*, [1994] 2 N.Z.L.R. 257 at 266.

Index